City Art

New York's Percent for Art Program

Joan —
Thanks so much for making this book happen —

Joan,
Thanks for everything.

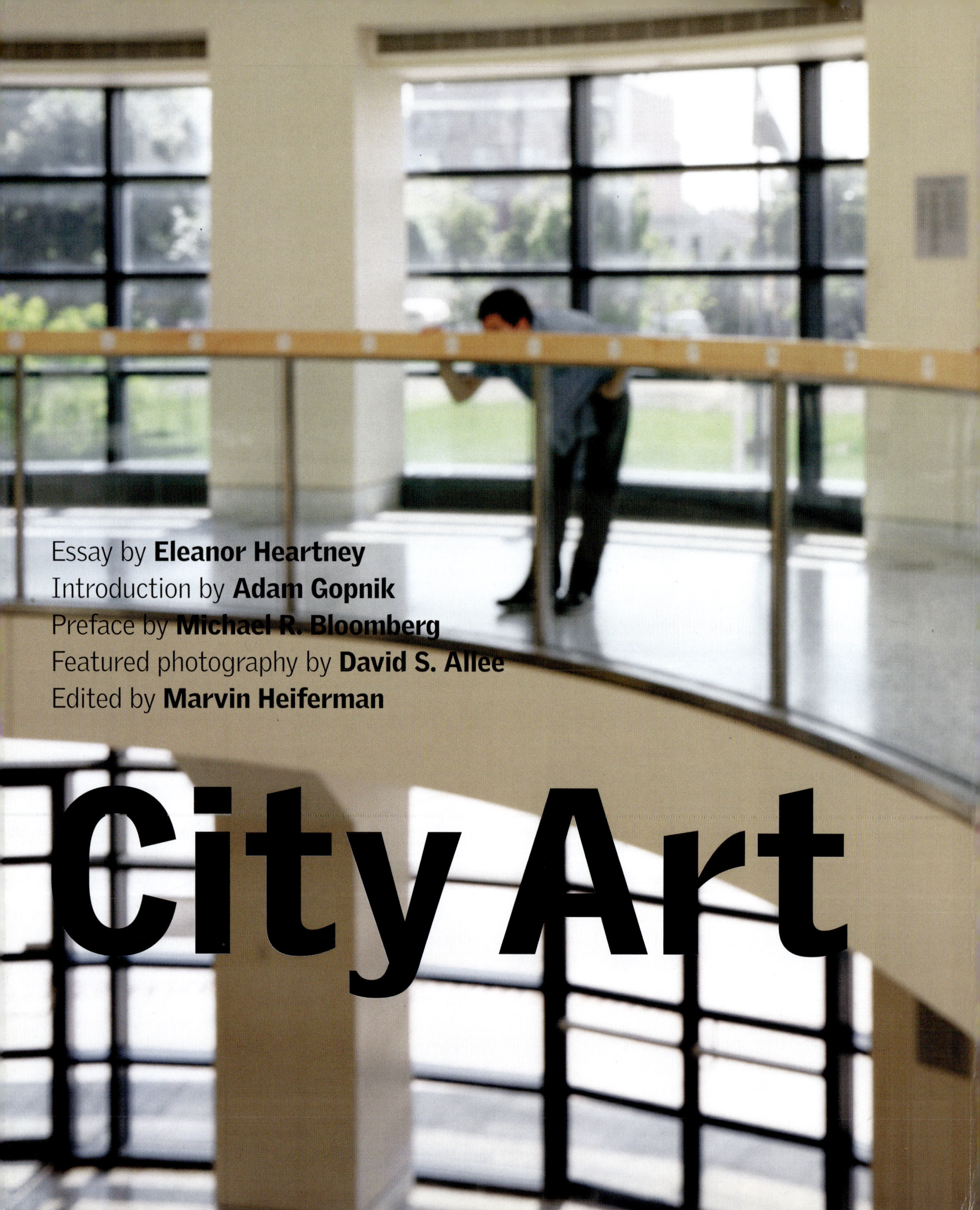

Essay by **Eleanor Heartney**
Introduction by **Adam Gopnik**
Preface by **Michael R. Bloomberg**
Featured photography by **David S. Allee**
Edited by **Marvin Heiferman**

City Art

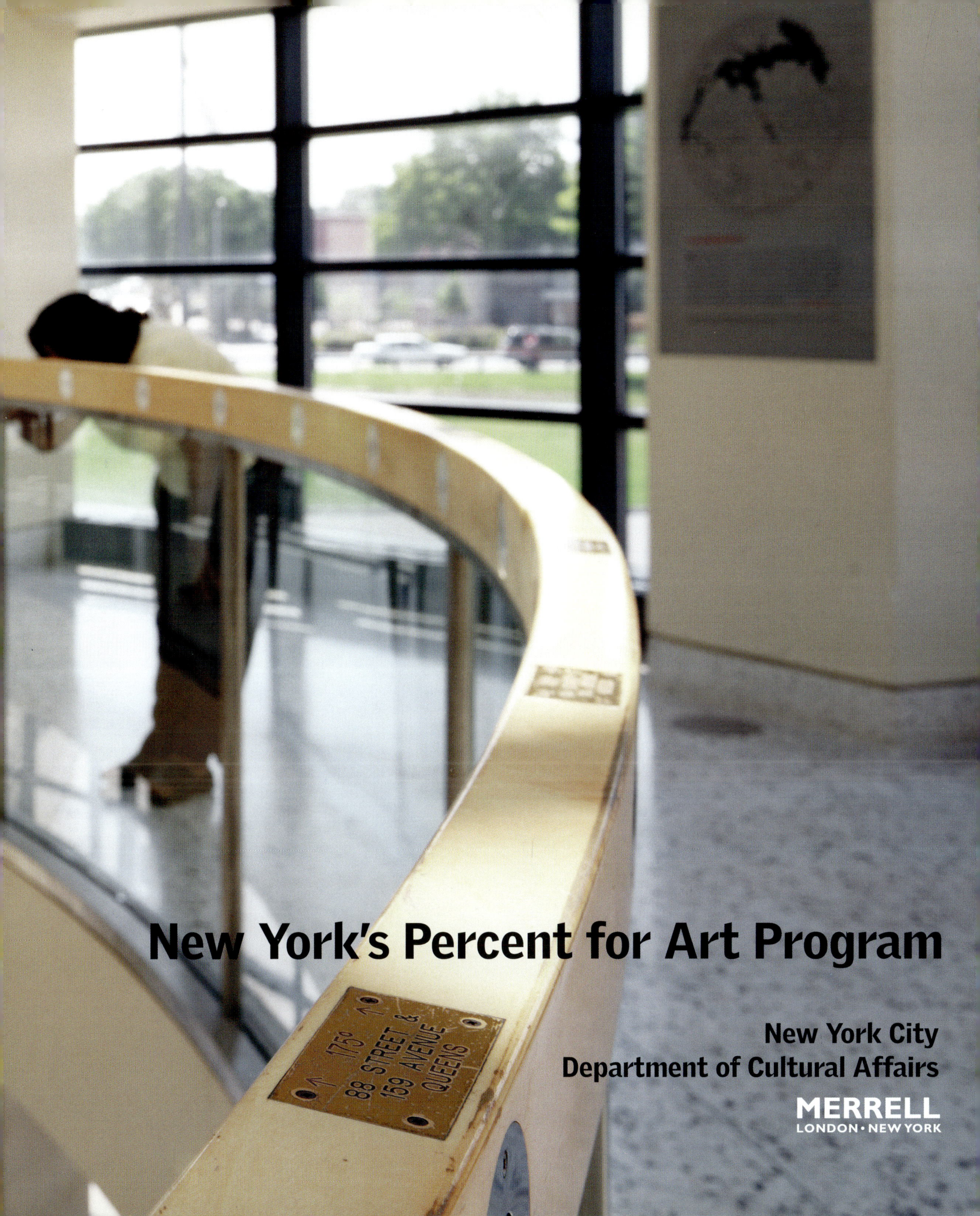

New York's Percent for Art Program

New York City
Department of Cultural Affairs

MERRELL
LONDON • NEW YORK

Contents

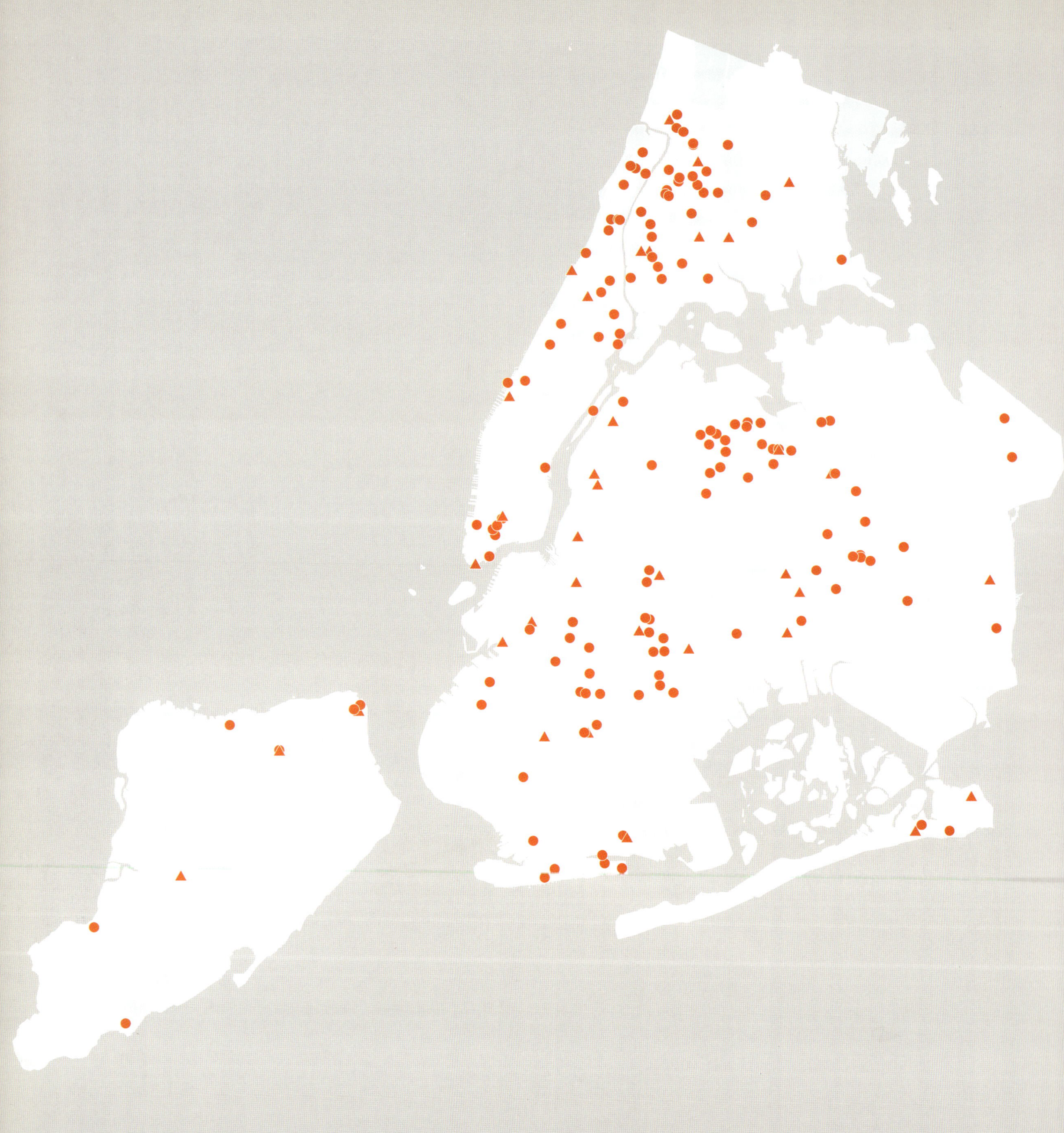

The red symbols on this map indicate the locations of the 189 completed Percent for Art projects (●) as well as the 39 projects currently in progress (▲). These sites reflect various patterns of new public development throughout New York City since the Percent for Art program was implemented in 1983. In many cases, more than one project is located at the same site.

Preface

Michael R. Bloomberg
Mayor of the City of New York

By establishing the Percent for Art program, New York City set a new standard for improving public space. As Mayor, I am very proud that my administration continues this tradition of excellence in urban design, and recognizes the distinctive role that public art plays in humanizing our communities and in changing the way we interact with our surroundings. Government's ability to cultivate artistic achievement while offering New Yorkers a voice in their environment is something to protect for generations to come.

It gives me great pleasure to present readers with the first comprehensive photographic documentation of New York City's Percent for Art program. *City Art* features the nearly two hundred works of public art completed since the program was implemented in 1983, along with an extraordinary portfolio of new photography of the artworks by David S. Allee. Essays by critics Adam Gopnik and Eleanor Heartney, and interviews with the key participants in the program, provide a vivid sense of how the Percent for Art program is stitched into the fabric of neighborhoods across New York City.

City Art also provides a window into the many different points of view that bring these works of public art to life. The outcome of this unique collaboration between artists and communities is a body of artwork that is both approachable and engaging. It tends to be more boisterous than restrained, more experiential than cerebral, more subtle than apparent, and more democratic than exclusive. Above all, it is art for the public, and each piece echoes the philosophy behind the program that every New Yorker deserves an enriching built environment. After all, good design doesn't necessarily cost more; it's just better.

It is no surprise that in a city as richly diverse and artistically dynamic as New York, we lay claim to one of the most extensive and influential public art programs in the world. But the program didn't just happen spontaneously. Making it a reality took the vision and tenacity of so many individuals working in the City's public domain, among them former Mayor, Ed Koch; former Deputy Mayor, Ronay Menschel; former Chief of Staff to the Mayor, Diane Coffey; and the founder of the Public Art Fund, Doris C. Freedman. Collectively, these individuals drafted, advocated for, and, with the approval of the City Council, signed into law the 1982 Percent for Art legislation requiring that one percent of the City's budget for eligible construction projects be directed toward funding public artworks. The program is administered through the City's Department of Cultural Affairs. Commissioner Kate Levin and the Percent for Art staff deserve our thanks for their thoughtful and dedicated work in stewarding this program, which offers City government the rare opportunity to partner with individual artists to animate the public spaces in which our citizens live, work, and learn.

Since its inauguration at City Hall more than two decades ago, Percent for Art has left an indelible mark on the physical and cultural landscape of New York City. *City Art* serves as a fitting tribute to this legacy.

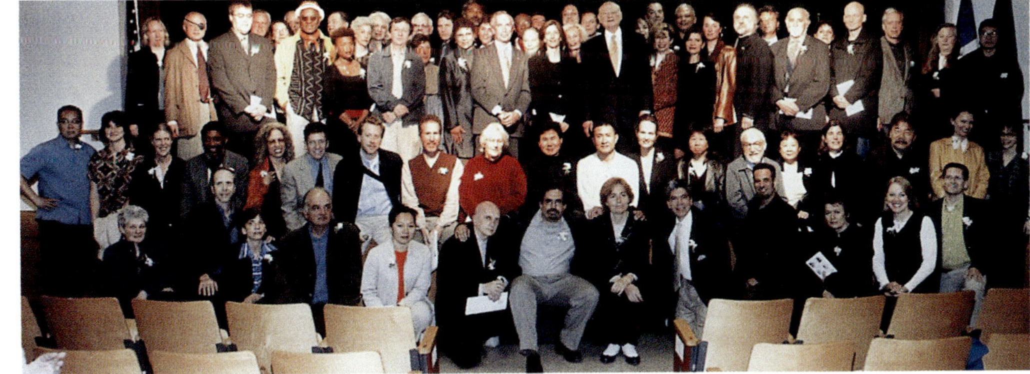

Mayor Michael R. Bloomberg, President of the Public Art Fund Susan Freedman, former Mayor Edward I. Koch, and artists commissioned by the New York City Percent for Art program on the occasion of the Doris C. Freedman Award Ceremony on May 14, 2003. The award was given to Edward I. Koch in honor of the twentieth anniversary of the Percent for Art program.

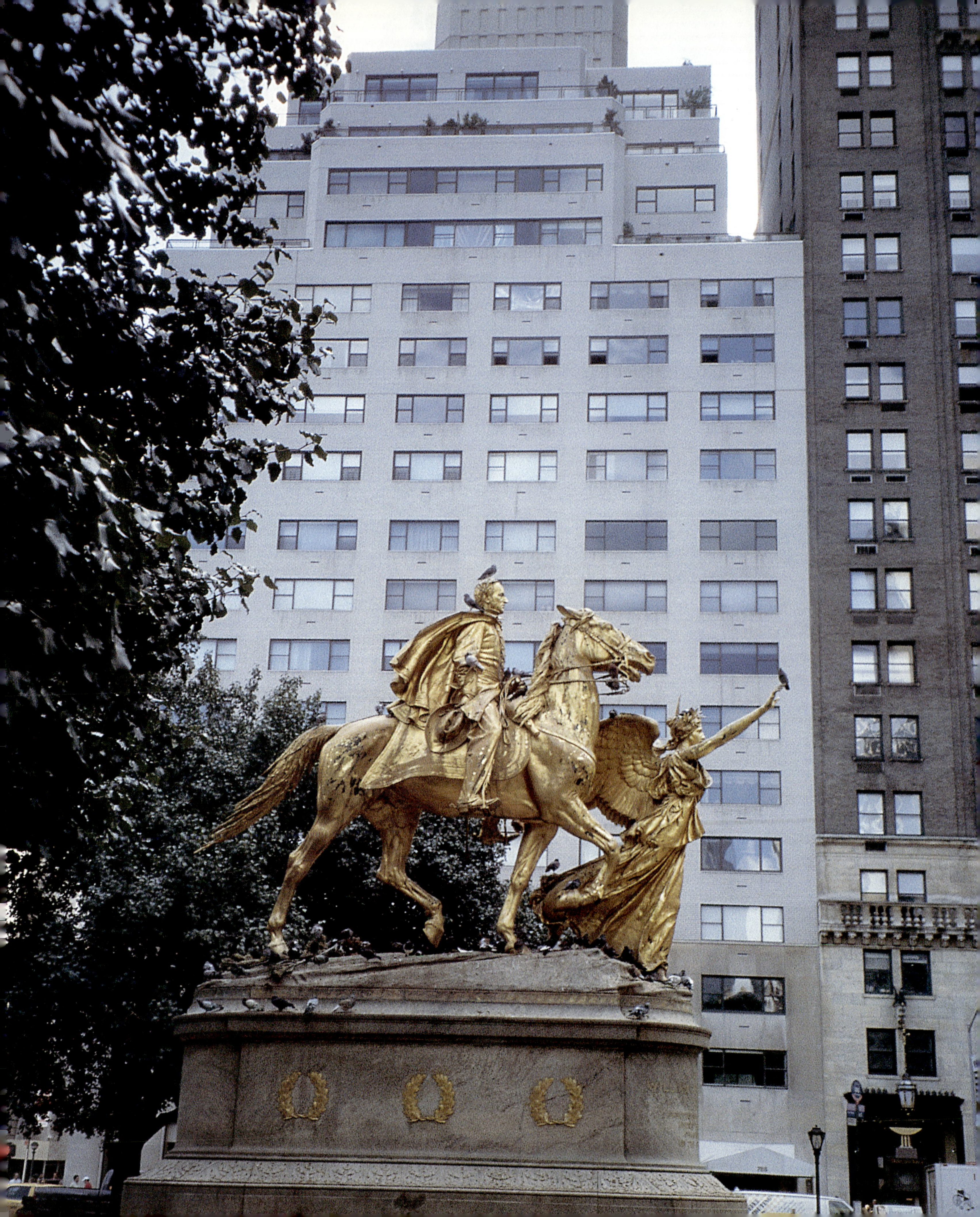

Introduction: Art in the City

Adam Gopnik

The book you hold in your hands is the story of an extraordinary artistic success achieved in the most improbable way: by civic diktat, through a bureaucratic program, and in the strange, discouraging world of public art made for city places. Art ought, of course, to be a city thing. It is certainly a city subject, liable to argument, melodrama, and, truth be told, most often to a failure to connect. Art in the old-fashioned plastic Beaux-Arts sense—still objects that vibrate in open minds—has been made almost entirely in cities, and, New York having been blessed as the world's leading art-making city for so long, one would expect the City to be filled with first-rate public art of all kinds.

But the truth is that the history of public art in New York, made for New York, is largely a history of failures, misunderstandings, and good intentions gone wrong. In all of New York, only Augustus Saint-Gaudens's 1903 statue of the mounted General Sherman on Grand Army Plaza, Manhattan, comes instantly to mind as completely successful monumental art, being both a major work by a major artist and an easy part of the civic landscape. (And even then, it is its glitter and its location as much as its ostensible subject that give it authority. The unintended serenity of its triangulation with Bergdorf's and the Plaza is what gives it its New Yorkishness; when the statue appears on the cover of a Sinatra album, it is not Sherman but East 59th Street that is signified.)

More typical, perhaps, are the countless statues—from that of Daniel Webster to that mounted Polish king with his alarming crossed swords—that fill Central Park, and have now faded into amiable bronze Pop art, pompous in ways that the City and the picnickers around them are not and never will be. Something goes wrong with big outdoor art in a big city, or in this big city anyway. This history of unhappiness reached its apex with the notorious example of the greatest American sculptor since Saint-Gaudens, Richard Serra, and his *Tilted Arc* (1981; page 10)—a story that ended just two decades ago with artist, art-haters, and art-defenders all going down the drain together in a little whirlpool of fury and misunderstanding. And more common even than this high drama are the endless depressing commissioned sculptures conceived as amenities and failing as artwork. The Museum of Modern Art's garden sculpture—the Matisse "Backs" and the Rodin Balzac—are entirely successful, yet their enclosure in a garden works best by not really being in the city, but in something just apart.

Part of the problem has been one of scale, and part one of common meaning. In the past, at least, public art has meant mostly sculpture and, while sculpture achieves much of its effect by being big and heavy, the city and its architecture is bigger and heavier than any art can be. Michelangelo's *David* (1501–04) looks imposing even by the scale of Florence's Palazzo Vecchio (the one on the square is a copy, but the statue was originally meant for that space, though there were arguments about where exactly in the square it ought to go). But nothing looks as imposing as a skyscraper. Claes Oldenburg's projects for colossal monuments, so wonderful as drawings, always fail in their realizations, simply because they can never be big enough, never large enough to make the comic folly as large as the straight men around it.

The problem of common meaning is thornier and more familiar. The artist, for the past hundred years, has been praised, and rewarded, as the man or woman who makes up his own system and his own

Augustus Saint-Gaudens, *The Sherman Monument*, 1892–1903, Grand Army Plaza, Manhattan.

symbols. Patient looking, over a long time, is a necessity for decoding these private languages, and this is not available to a hurried passer-by. The "lyricism" and even "elegance" of *Tilted Arc*, so apparent to those with eyes trained to appreciate Serra's work, might have sounded like mere words to others.

Despite this by now familiar history of good intentions and multiple frustrations, a smaller, unpublicized, and, in conventional art circles, mostly unseen program has been alive in New York for more than twenty years. In 1982, during the Koch administration, and at a time when the City was only just making the turn from Serpico Seventies to Trump-ish Eighties, a law was passed that created the Percent For Art program. The law insists, in effect, that one percent of a new public building's budget (a large sum when tens of millions of dollars are involved) be devoted to art, and the program has, over twenty years and largely in silence, produced nearly two hundred new works of art for the City. It has caused art to be made for firehouses, schools, police precincts, courthouses, hospitals, ferry terminals, juvenile detention centers, parks, sanitation facilities, and sewage treatment plants. Though almost entirely unknown to the conventional art world, save when some well-known artist is commissioned, it is without question the largest, most significant campaign of public art in New York City since the Works Progress Administration (WPA) and the Great Depression.

This book is a visual summary of what has been achieved in that time, and is an occasion to think hard about what city art might be, and what conditions make it work. It is easy to imagine what a skeptic might have said when the program began, or what a skeptic might say even today. Can Modernist or Post-modernist art, the skeptic asks, ever really speak to the condition of large numbers of people on whom it is simply "imposed"? Is the program not possibly a boondoggle for artists who continue to speak their private languages even when working in public spaces? Could the whole thing not, in the end, be seen as a comic instance of what happens when you have an economy of supply with no real demand, more artists than there is the demand for art, and the work piling up like a mountain of subsidized butter in Wisconsin?

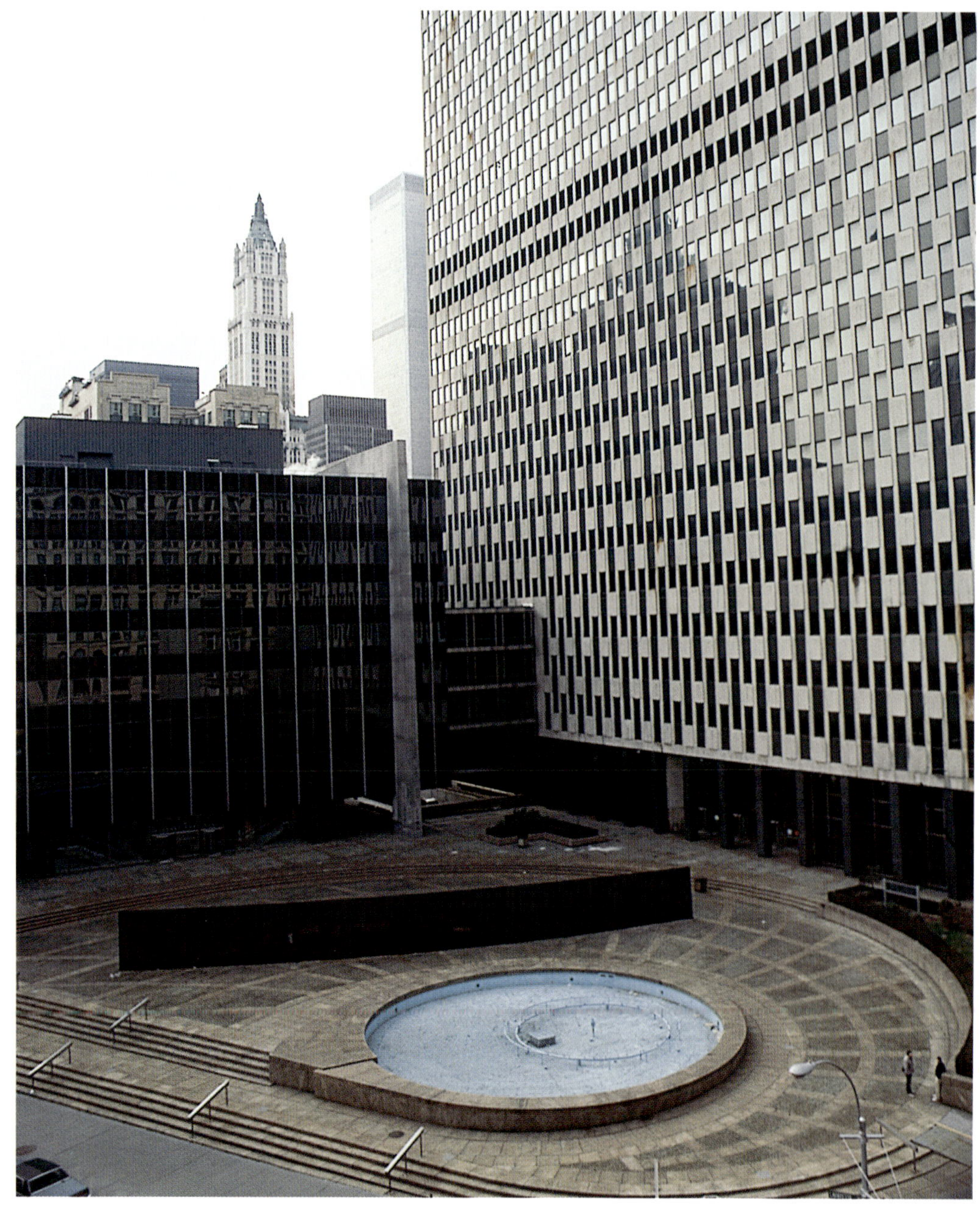

Richard Serra, *Tilted Arc*, 1981, Federal Plaza, Manhattan. Commissioned by the United States General Services Administration; removed in 1989.

And, even if the program works in the narrow sense that work gets made, does it work in the more significant sense that some connection has been made between public and artist?

But, as this survey demonstrates, on the whole the new art defeats any doubts about the program. Much, perhaps most, of what has been commissioned by the City does work, in the only way that art can work—that is, not by leading but by whispering at the right moment in the right ear. Some of the energies of the program have gone into conventional decorative murals—a few of heroic ambitions, and some of those of real force, as in Daniel Galvez's mural of the life of Malcolm X, created for the Audubon Ballroom on Broadway where the civil rights leader was killed (pages 135–37). In other cases, the energy has gone, rightly, into allowing well-known sculptors to continue to express their vision in a new and larger arena. Stephen Antonakos's haunting project for the 59th Street Marine Transfer Station, where his signature red neon lines are used as haloes around window frames, is visible at a distance and is vibrant throughout the night (page 120).

Although the Percent for Art program has sponsored its share of sculptural chunks and bumps and oblique hunks of matter—some lovely-looking, some less so—the best work it has inspired has often been sociable and charming, and has added a decorative richness to the New York cityscape not seen since its Art Deco days, an ornamental layering that is not always merely ornamental. Few people walking by Public School 234 in Tribeca, for instance, could fail to have delighted in Donna Dennis's wrought-iron sculpture of historical boats and ships that enliven its fences (page 133); and just as few have stopped to think that they are there because of an obscure law and an official plan.

The very best work the program has commissioned has created something genuinely new in the public-spirited experience of art. The greatest success of the program lies in its expansion of the meanings of the more esoteric reaches of conceptual art. In retrospect, the real triumphs of the public art of the 1930s tend after all to lie in its achievements in decorative Cubism, in the way it helped turn the private visions of Picasso and Fernand Léger into a common, large-scale civic language (Isamu Noguchi's bas-relief on the old Associated Press building is a particularly endearing instance of this kind). In a way that seems engagingly parallel, the most enduring work of the Percent for Art program seems likely to be its commissioning of what might be called decorative, or intimate, conceptualism. That is, the program has midwifed into existence a kind of artwork that takes the forms of "Conceptual" and "Installation" art as it has evolved since the 1970s—that by-now familiar conglomerate of found objects, borrowed photographs, and obliquely poetic texts—and shaped it into something more modest and discreet. The occasional mystifications of such art becomes arrestingly enigmatic in the new public work, and its weakness for didacticism becomes compellingly poetic.

Dennis Adams's *Tributaries* for Long Island City High School, for instance, takes borrowed photographs of the civil rights movement of the 1960s, and positions them above the school's water fountains—wittily

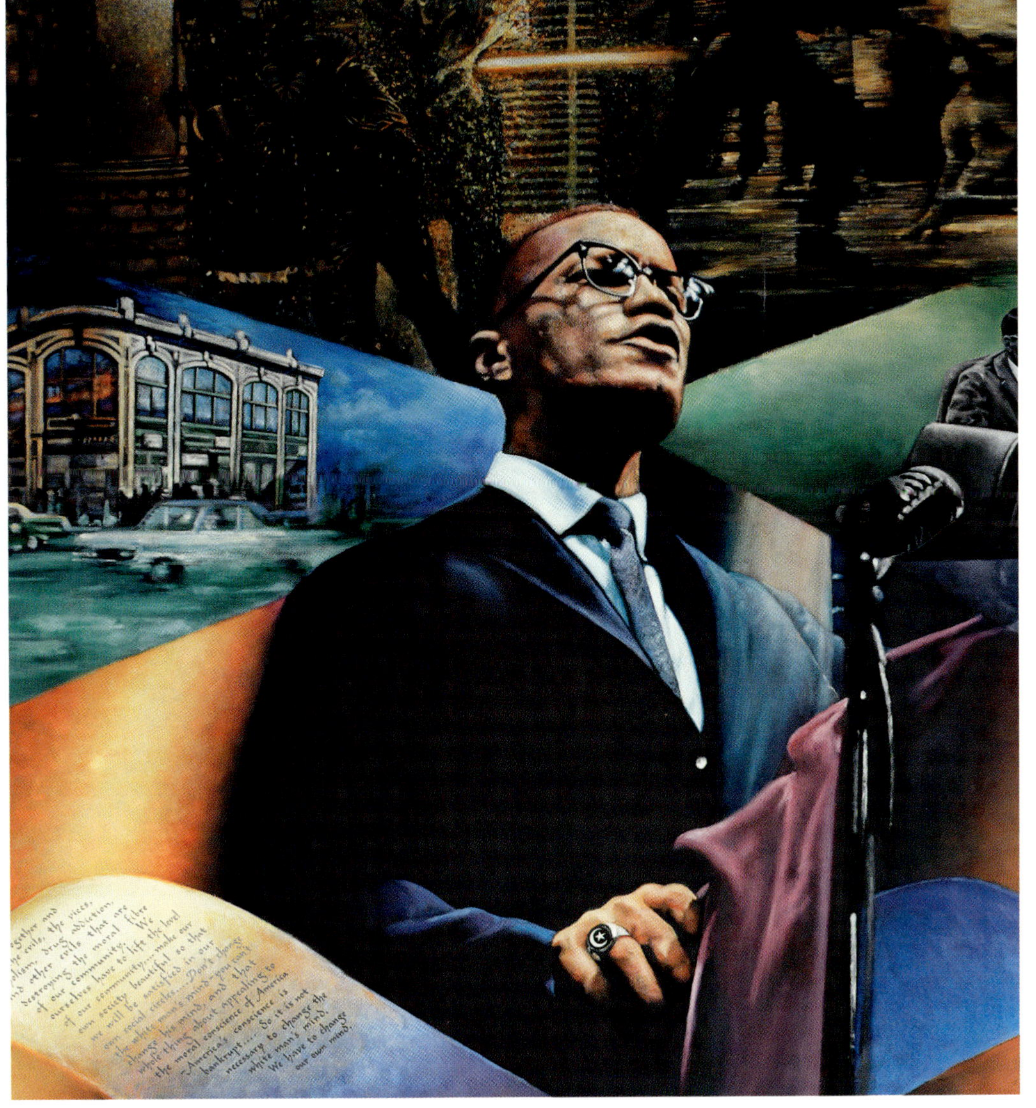

Daniel Galvez, *Homage to Malcolm X* (detail), 1997, Audubon Ballroom, Manhattan (pages 135–37).

used here as markers of what was once a cause worth fighting and dying for but today can seem merely historical (pages 166–67). No high-schooler today can, after all, recall a time when the country tore itself apart about whether white and black people should each have their own water fountains. The photographs are made into high-contrast transparencies and placed in illuminated lightboxes, so that they glow above the water fountains, and are scored with oblique references to events and famous people of the period. Nothing is "explained"; the photographs are not the entrenched, iconic images of heroic protestors and evil segregationists with their dogs, but far more obscure and peripheral images of marches, schools, and faceless people. The effect is not didactic but oddly light, elusively somber. What, the skeptic asks, can the students "learn" from this? Well, they are there to do their learning in the classrooms, and what Adams provides is knowledge, at the most casual moment of the day, of another world and mode of inquiry, in which the explicit is less important than the implied, the overt less necessary than the mysterious. If the image is "manipulated," it is manipulated to engage and to invite, not to insist and instruct. The artist commemorates history by refusing to commemorate it—by asking the students to open their minds in the free time they find between classes. Knowledge is found in the classroom, where you use your mind; art is found in the hallway by the water cooler, where you free it.

Or take another brilliantly successful project. Kristin Jones and Andrew Ginzel have executed, for the venerable Stuyvesant High School in Tribeca, a project of four hundred glass cells filled with esoterica—glass bricks that have been made into Joseph Cornell-like boxes. Eighty-eight of

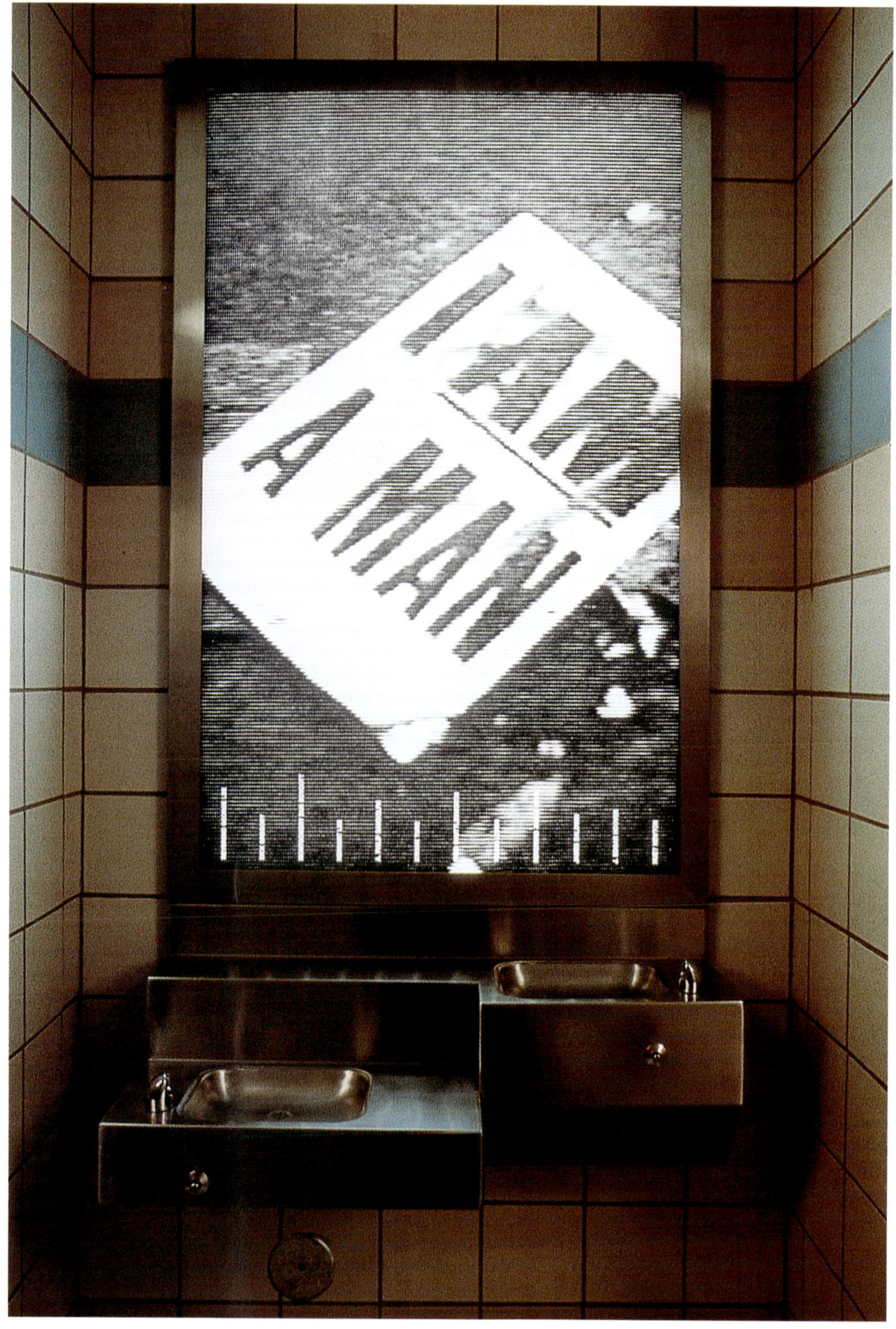

Dennis Adams, *Tributaries* (detail), 1995, Long Island City High School, Queens (pages 166–67).

the boxes commemorate the school's history, and the students can catch, in hurried glimpses, an encapsulated survey of the school's past, from its early Jewish through its current Asian periods. Other boxes seem to have been left over from some early nineteenth-century *wunderkammer*, and are filled with a collection of the world's strange treasures—water from the Nile and the Ganges, melted snow from Mount Fuji, and even a fragment of the Great Wall of China. A symmetrical eighty-eight blocks have been left empty, there for the twenty-first century's graduating classes (pages 144–46).

How do the students at Stuyvesant High see this work? For that matter, how often do they see it? And how do the students at Long Island High really see the work by Dennis Adams? To ask these questions is to move deep into areas of reception—of the "ownership" of art, in the broadest sense—that are tricky to comprehend, and where an experienced reporter knows that what is said in public is not always what is felt in private. Every artist believes that his or her work speaks to the people for whom it is meant, even if the people who are running the place for which it is meant have their doubts. And certainly the testimony one hears from students and lawyers, if not perhaps from prisoners, about their feelings on the new public art in the buildings they spend time in, is encouraging: from all reports, it seems to matter to the people it is supposed to matter to. Yet anyone who has spent time among ordinary people, young and old, to whom fancy or at least elliptical art is addressed, knows that their dutiful acceptance of the art as something that might be good for you, is not always the same as the joyful instant embrace we hope the art experience will be.

Yet perhaps the issue of reception is wrongly presented. Art doesn't need to be examined closely every day to offer a deep experience over time. Its being there at all matters a lot. The sense of a secret history, an encoded past, a surprise, a surplus of meaning—that very sense of "more-than-we-need" that gives a museum, or for that matter a Gothic cathedral, its overcharge of meaning—is, for once, present in an otherwise utilitarian educational environment. It changes and alters the environment of feeling in the place. A language that, in its formal art-world uses, can seem deadeningly pedantic and enclosed, here becomes, instead, secretive and sly: there's more to your world, even to your high school, than quite meets the eye, the art announces, and the students hear even if they do not always listen.

In these projects, the weaknesses of such conceptual schemes when they appear in more conventional art-world circles—their urge for the didactic and the churchy—are almost magically short-circuited. One wonders if, in these projects and many others like them, some part of the mystifying code of public art for the city has, at last, been cracked. Despite its discouraging history, we do like some city art after all, and that which we love is most often not the colossal but the intimate and appliquéd: the forgotten bas-reliefs at the Rockefeller Center, the amateur mural in the Lower East Side playground. For all the scale and even grandeur of the art commemorated in this book, some of the best of it gives us the same emotion as these old small and easily overlooked works: things of capricious beauty and serene craft discovered against the odds in unlikely institutional places.

For one of the secrets of city life, after all, is that though we speak pompously of public space—parks and plazas, atriums and avenues—our experience is largely of private spaces. What makes life and art cityish, if not piously civic, is exactly its atomization, its capacity for anonymous intersection. City life affords, in fact, very few one-on-manys and an infinite number of one-on-ones. In offering us private experience encoded in beguiling form, in insisting on the primacy of the individual imagination even in places of dulled institutional experience, the Percent for Art program has shown that civic art can be big while remaining little. Public art, we now know, need be not only the province of the orator, searching for a soapbox, but also of the poets whispering their secrets on the park bench, at the water fountain, or in the school hall. To get the message, all you have to do is steal a look on your way to life.

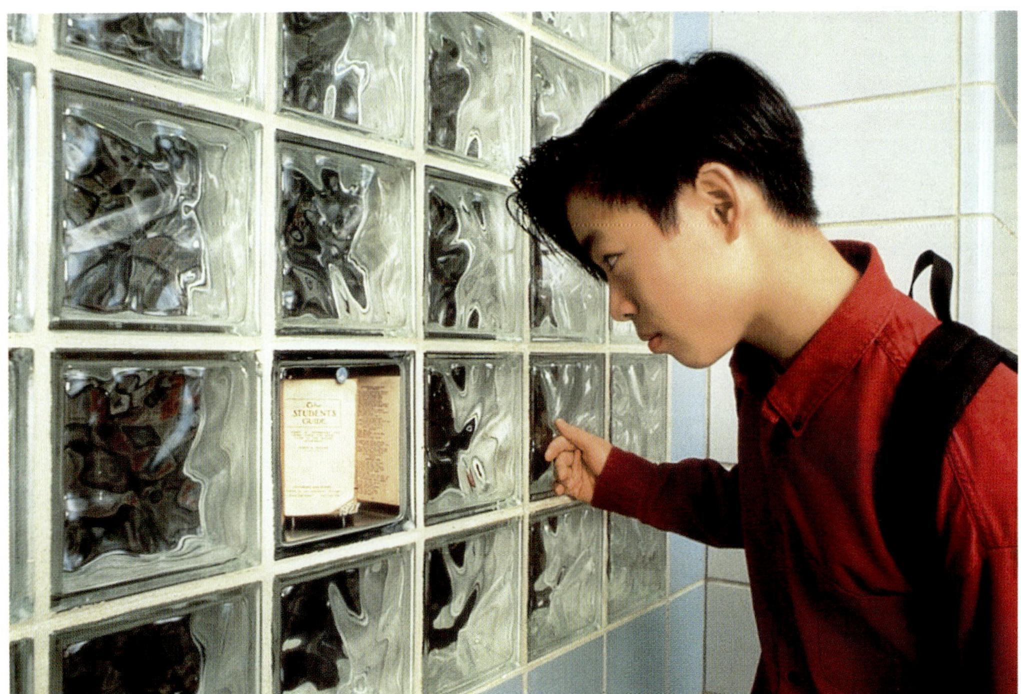

Kristin Jones and Andrew Ginzel, *Mnemonics* (installation detail), 1992, Stuyvesant High School, Manhattan (pages 144–46).

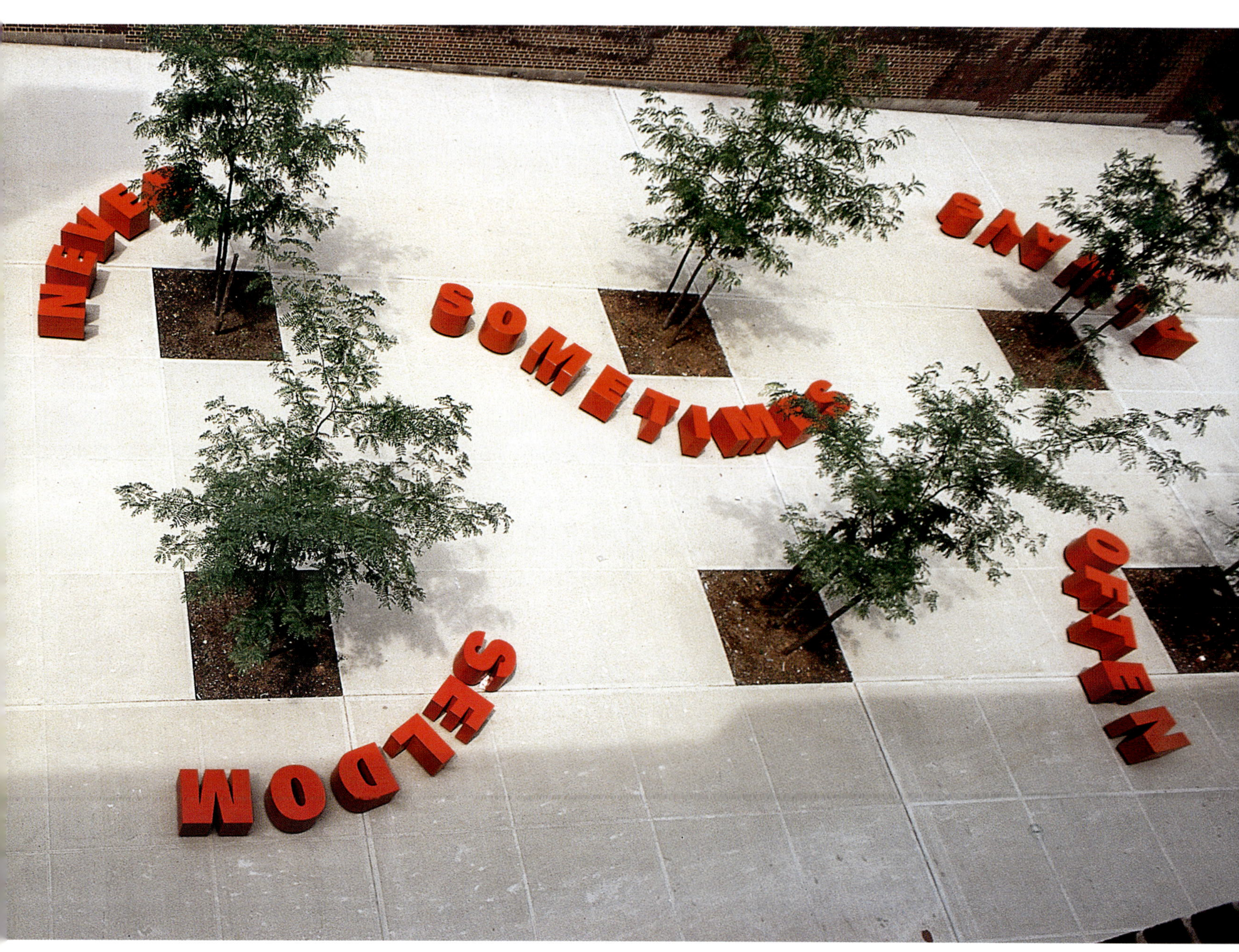

Nancy Dwyer, *Multiple Choice*, 1993, Port Richmond High School, Staten Island (pages 232–33).

The City as Laboratory: Two Decades of New York's Percent for Art Program

Eleanor Heartney

What is public art? Traditionally, it was the equestrian statue in the village square or, more recently, the tangle of metal in front of the city hall. But now public art also encompasses everything from artist-cooked communal meals and artist-led walks in the park to texts printed on milk cartons and choreographed dances of garbage trucks. What's going on here?

In part, this development reflects a change in art itself. Ripped from the frame, knocked off the pedestal, conceptualized, dematerialized, recontextualized, and post-modernized, art is harder than ever to define. And neither is it so clear anymore what we mean by "public." Is it shorthand for "communal"? Is it anything supported by public funds? Is it simply "not private"? Is there even such a thing as a "public"? Is there a difference between public art and art in public places?

Equally up for grabs is any consensus about the purposes of public art. Is its function to provide adornment for government or corporate architecture? Or is it a form of architecture in itself? Does public art promote democracy? Ought it to be educational? Or should it simply insert a bit of pleasure into the busy lives of passers-by?

At times the debate over such questions has nearly come to fisticuffs. One art lover's public sculpture is another's "plop art," that dismissive term for work that is dropped into a city square or plaza with no regard to its context. "City Beautiful" types often stress functionalism, seeing public art as an extension of architecture or landscape design; as a means of more artfully adding amenities like benches, bus shelters, and fountains to the public square. Others maintain that public art should celebrate society's diversity and reflect the lack of consensus over questions of value and social good. For commentators like Rosalyn Deutsche, good public art resists capitulating to the forces of development. Instead, she maintains, "art cannot assume the preexistence of a public but must help produce one . . . ."[1] For critics and artists of her bent, public art has an active role to play in urging people to question the power structures and decision-making processes that determine how public space is used. "Critical" public art of this nature is often temporary, provocative, and designed *not* to blend in with its surroundings.

Public art is and will probably always be contested territory because it reflects the real tensions embedded in our civic life. This may explain why even old-fashioned monuments have become problematic—how do we honor the hero in the square when no one agrees who the heroes are? This is especially the case when the events to be memorialized mean different things to different people. Maya Lin's solution for the Vietnam Veterans Memorial in Washington, D.C. was to deal with this still-controversial war by placing the name of each fallen American soldier on a black granite wall that made no claims about the rightness or wrongness of the conflict itself. Though veterans' groups insisted that a more traditional group of bronze figurative sculptures of soldiers be placed in the vicinity of this memorial, over the years these have come to seem unnecessary and even intrusive. Instead, the Vietnam memorial has ushered in a more abstract visual vocabulary for the construction of memorials that is more in keeping with our diversity of opinions.

The coexistence of multiple agendas for our public spaces also explains why public art occasionally ignites controversy. Public art often serves as the most visible manifestation of the powers that be, and hence becomes a rallying point for those frustrated with their sense of powerlessness. The annals of public art are full of tales of artworks that, though apparently innocuous in themselves, have become tinder for full-scale uproars about the "ownership" of public space.

- - -

Thus it was with a certain amount of bravery that, in 1982, the City of New York passed legislation for what would become one of the nation's largest Percent for Art programs. The program, initiated by Mayor Edward I. Koch, was modeled on similar programs then popping up in other cities around the country, the earliest being that in Philadelphia, established in 1959. Originally, the Percent for Art program was administered by the Public Art Fund, which was founded by Doris C. Freedman, one of the New York's earliest and most energetic supporters of public art. It set aside a percentage of the construction budget of any new municipal building for art. (The title Percent for Art is something of a misnomer, as there is a cap of $400,000 for any single project, unless partnering City agencies elect to spend more.)

Diane Coffey, who was Mayor Koch's Chief of Staff at the time, notes that New York's Percent for Art program was initiated at a particular moment in New York's history:

> With Mayor Koch's first year in office came a balanced budget, ending the quagmire of budget deficits and a long-stalled capital program. During the 1980s the City could then point with pride to an invigorated building program. What better way to celebrate an energized design and construction plan than the Percent for Art program, a welcome enhancement to the City's signature. People debated the kind of face the City was presenting in its various new projects, but they also agreed that a public project was more exciting with the inclusion of a work of art, whatever form it might take.[2]

The program came into being in the midst of a major controversy over Richard Serra's *Tilted Arc* (page 10). An 84 foot (25.6 m) long curtain of steel, Serra's minimalist work cut across Federal Plaza between a pair of office buildings in downtown Manhattan. Commissioned by the General Services Administration, it was installed in 1981 and removed in 1989 after massive community protests.

Jennifer McGregor, who followed Jenny Dixon as Director of New York's Percent for Art program, after the Department of Cultural Affairs took over full responsibility for the program in 1986, recalls that from one perspective the controversy over *Tilted Arc* had a positive impact. "Everyone was very aware that public art is not just guys on horseback," she says. "In fact the controversy became a place to launch discussion. We didn't run into the same problems because from the start our program incorporated a lot more community involvement."

And the *Tilted Arc* controversy coincided with a sea change in thinking about how art should relate to the lives of ordinary people. The charges of elitism cast by Serra's critics were leveled in a climate in which artists and arts institutions were increasingly dedicated to public outreach and interaction. Doris C. Freedman's Public Art Fund took art off the walls and placed it in spaces used by the general public. Creative Time, another not-for-profit organization, inaugurated its Art on the Beach program in 1978 by inviting artists to create temporary artworks on the landfill that would become the site of the World Financial Center. Alternative artist groups such as PAD/D (Political Art Documentation/Distribution) undertook "guerrilla" actions, placing politically provocative artworks in highly visible places around the City. For a brief period in the early 1980s, the whole East Village in Manhattan seemed to become a collective art space, encompassing funky storefront galleries, street art, and raucous exhibitions organized in empty parking lots and abandoned buildings. In this environment, it wasn't hard for the Percent for Art program to make the case that art had a place in the lives of the general public.

The Percent program is administered by the Department for Cultural Affairs and is responsible for commissioning artworks for a hugely diverse set of City-owned buildings throughout New York's five boroughs. These include schools, firehouses, police stations, libraries, courthouses, hospitals, day-care centers, passenger terminals, detention centers, parks, and sanitation facilities. This points to one of its principal distinctions in relation to other public art programs in the City: while other programs place temporary works in high-density and heavily traveled locations and draw on a highly varied cross-section of New York residents and visitors, the Percent for Art program's permanent projects are often in far-flung buildings with specific uses and, hence, must appeal to very particular constituencies.

The Percent program is also distinctive in the way it intersects with different interest groups. Percent for Art artists are required to work closely with a specific building's architect or engineer. Artists must take note of community feedback. They must be aware of the requirements, bureaucracy, and internal politics of the City agencies overseeing the project as a whole. And they must be cognizant of how their project will play to the press and local politicians. Tom Finkelpearl, who was Percent for Art's second director at the Department of Cultural Affairs from 1990 to 1996, suggests that artists become ad hoc diplomats. "They are obliged to be intermediaries between different countries that don't understand each other," he says.

The Percent for Art staff are responsible for managing the project's whole process—from artist selection to contracts, and from design to construction and installation. Over the years, the Percent program has undergone subtle shifts as it evolved from a new and untried idea to a well-established program with a long track record. McGregor reports that in the early years, her most important job was building relationships between artists and architects, and between artists and City agencies. Finkelpearl's tenure coincided with an explosion of school construction projects, requiring a substantial influx of new artists. Charlotte Cohen, who has been director since late 1996, notes that the public has become much more savvy about good design, thanks in part to its awareness of initiatives such as the ongoing development of, and public access to, New York's waterfront, and the restoration of New York's parks and open spaces. The debate over the rebuilding of Lower Manhattan in the wake of the September 11 attacks has also raised the level of consciousness of design issues on the part of ordinary New Yorkers. Meanwhile, Cohen notes that under her watch, Percent for Art has become more involved in infrastructure projects such as bridges and streetscapes, allowing greater opportunities for the program to respond to planning issues at a macro-level. All these developments have created a degree of expectation and awareness of good design that challenges the program to pursue an ever more sophisticated response to the City's needs.

- - -

Artists who become involved in public art find that creating an artwork for a public building involves a different set of skills than that used in working on personal projects, alone in their studios. First, they must pass through a series of selection panels. The initial one convenes after the architect has been chosen for a particular project. Architects are invited to suggest possible sites or approaches for the art, and even specific artists, but these suggestions are not binding. The names of artists are drawn from the program's slide registry or from the suggestions of various art professionals on the panel, and the Percent staff. Percent for Art then convenes a panel comprised of representatives from the Department of Cultural Affairs, the City agencies that are sponsoring the new building, and the architectural or design firm, as well as several art professionals, preferably with ties to the borough or community where the project will be built. Each of the different constituencies that will be affected by the art project is invited to raise questions and express preferences. All kinds of issues surface in such meetings: How will it impact on the neighbors? What kind of visual language is appropriate to the users of the space? Which artists seem most interested in working with different communities? The committee looks at slides, mulls over the list and narrows it down to five or six possible artists who will be interviewed at the next panel meeting.

At a second panel meeting these finalists are then asked to present possible approaches to the project. Various non-voting observers are invited to attend this presentation, among them representatives from the community board, the offices of the Borough President and the City Council, New York City's Art Commission, and other interested parties. This time the chemistry between the artist and the committee members is crucial. As artists present ideas for the project, the various observers and panelists look for flexibility, inventiveness, and a genuine interest in interaction. The artist's previous experience in public art can be an important factor in the decision, but first-time public artists whose ideas are sufficiently compelling have often been awarded commissions. Once artists are selected, their proposals are still subject to change as they work with the architects

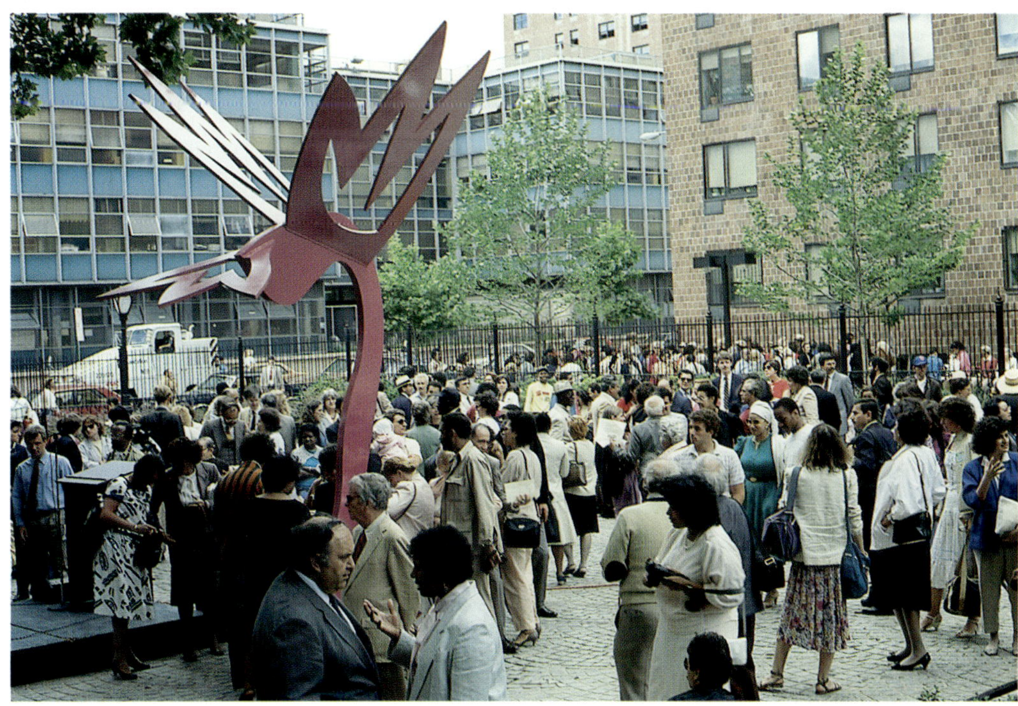

Dedication ceremony for Jorge Luis Rodriguez's *Growth*, East Harlem Artpark, 1985 (page 154).

and design team over the course of the building's construction.

It takes a special kind of artist to run these gauntlets. Finkelpearl points out the importance of adaptability. "The worst artists for this process are those who insist on sticking to their first idea," he says. "The best ones are charismatic and enjoy interaction with others."

This complicated process deters some artists. Yet others thrive on it. Allan and Ellen Wexler are public art veterans and have completed three school-based projects for Percent for Art. Allan Wexler remarks, "It's very different placing work in a gallery and working as a public artist. I was trained as an architect and I like the resistance given to us by the public. It narrows our field. I like to make problems into resources—in the same way that the need to deal with rain and snow makes architecture more interesting. We actually find that it's more difficult to start without any restrictions."

If artists can rise to the challenges, the Percent for Art program offers unique opportunities. One of these has to do with context. Percent for Art projects are incorporated into community sites where people live and work, and often their primary audience consists of people who might never go to museums. Such projects require a different kind of conceptual style and visual language, and a more creative approach to the act of connecting to the viewer. Artists can't assume that art-historical references will be understood, and often they find they have to immerse themselves in the history of the site or the politics of the community in order to create something that will speak to the various constituencies of a particular project.

Finkelpearl notes that while some Percent for Art programs exempt schools altogether, New York's school projects have been particularly rich and varied. This is in part a reflection of the enormous boom in school construction that occurred in New York during the 1990s, when the School Construction Authority built almost one hundred new school buildings. One of the first Percent for Art school projects, completed before this boom, became a kind of touchstone for later projects. This was Donna Dennis's fence for Public School 234 in Lower Manhattan (pages 132–33). This work broke new ground for the young program. McGregor recalls that the architect originally wanted a group of artists to create works for small sites scattered throughout the building. Instead a single artist was commissioned to design the fence, an architectural element that was already in the plan. "When the Board of Education discovered that the fence had been taken from the contractor and given to the artist, they were very nervous," she reports. But the fence was so well received that it became a model for future projects. Finkelpearl notes that when he came on

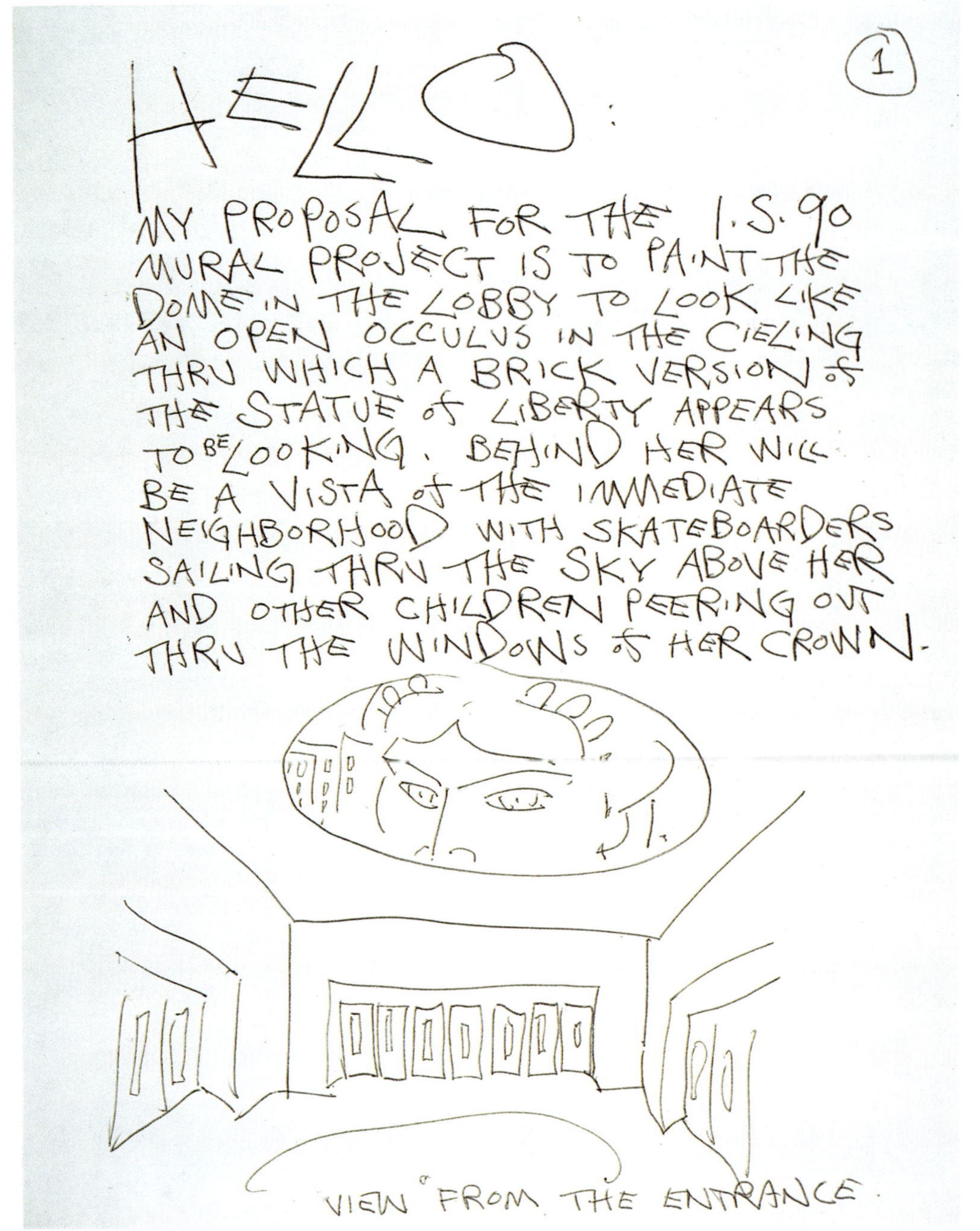

Martin Wong, proposal for *Miss Liberty Face*, ceiling mural at Intermediate School 90, Manhattan; completed 1995 (page 163).

board in 1990, "instead of wanting a bust of a hero, everyone wanted a fence."

In fact, the possibilities explored by Percent for Art artists working on schools have been remarkably diverse. An early school project in 1991 in the Bronx by Justen Ladda (page 48) similarly set a standard for collaboration with the design team. Ladda designed lively color and pattern schemes for the school interior, and created playful sculptures and mosaics for placement throughout the common areas. Other school projects focus on the educational potential of public art. At Long Island City High School in Queens, Dennis Adams placed illuminated lightboxes documenting important moments in the civil rights struggle over the drinking fountains in the hallways (pages 12, 166–67). Yet other school projects were designed with an eye to giving students a larger voice in the life of the school. Janet Zweig's letter-boxes at Walton High School in the Bronx are based on the idea of suggestion boxes, inviting

Nov. 21, 1988
A short story by ~~Amanda~~ Gale
One day a lady was passing by
our school. She stopped and
looked at the fence. "Oh what
a nice fence" she said. she
stood there admiring the
fence. She walked over to
one of the boats. "That boat
looks just like the may flower"
she said. Soon she saw many
kids bursting out the doors,
"it must be recess" she said,
as she looked at her watch.
She was still gazing at the
fence. Soon she saw some
kids climbing the fence, she
looked at them, "stop climbing that
fence!" she said, "this fence is a
piece of art!" She said to them
in amazement. They looked at her
and ran away. "I guess I'd better
go home" she said.

The END

A Short Story **by Amanda Gale, November 21, 1988, written by a student at Public School 234 in response to Donna Dennis's** ***Dreaming of Far Away Places: The Ships Come to Washington Market,*** **1988 (pages 132–33).**

students to deposit notes detailing their wishes, fears, dreams, secrets, and other private thoughts (pages 70–71).

The Wexlers used their three school sites to encourage students to think more deeply about their surroundings. Noting that in each case the students were occupying new school buildings, they designed their projects to inspire the students really to look at the school as architecture (pages 68, 69, 162). At Public School 340 in the Bronx, they created a wall mural featuring blueprints of the school building, complete with information on hidden elements such as plumbing, wiring, and wall construction materials. At Public School 254, also in the Bronx, they placed the surface materials used by the architects in museum-style frames, mingling the notion of art and architecture. And at West Side High School in Manhattan, they created a *faux* natural park, using Day-Glo-colored architectural materials to create a playful landscape of artificial "boulders," "water," and "grass."

One of the most ambitious school projects was created by Kristin Jones and Andrew Ginzel for Stuyvesant High School in Manhattan (pages 13, 144–46). The high school, which was founded in 1904, has a remarkable history, having been attended by famous alumni such as Nobel prize-winning scientists, and cultural figures such as the jazz musician Thelonious Monk and the actors James Cagney and Tim Robbins. The artists wanted to incorporate aspects of the school's history into the new building and to suggest its engagement with, and connections to, the larger world. They inserted over four hundred glass blocks into the walls of the school's public areas. Each was hollow and designed to be filled with evocative objects. Two hundred and thirty blocks contain objects from New York and around the world: some were obtained from individuals and through an extensive mailing campaign to embassies and consulates; other blocks present both man-made and natural elements, such as rare minerals labeled with their place of origin, bits of famous buildings, even samples of water from the Nile and sand from the Sahara Desert. Another eighty-eight blocks were devoted to the graduating classes from each year of the old school's existence. To fill these blocks, the artists scoured the school archives for memorabilia and solicited treasured items from alumni. The final eighty-eight blocks were left open, to be filled by successive graduating classes up to the year 2080, so that eventually the piece will stretch as far into the future as it reaches back in time.

Picking up on its status as an encyclopedia of memories, the work is called *Mnemonics*. As public art, the project is both unique and exemplary. For one thing, this decentralized work is installed throughout the building, and must be experienced over time. Ginzel notes that it operates like a star field or a dust cloud disseminated throughout the entire structure of the building. He says, "Looking at a single block you see 1/400th of the whole. You experience one part of it, but it needs to grow."[3] In this respect, *Mnemonics* relates to larger tendencies in the art world, moving away from artworks as precious objects in favor of the idea of art as experience.

Mnemonics is also exemplary in the way it gives the community a central role in the creation of the artwork. By bringing so many other people into the project, Jones and Ginzel gave away a certain amount of authorship of the work. In doing so, they endorse the idea of viewer as creator, encouraging a more active engagement on the part of the public for whom the work was made.

Many Percent for Art projects respond to their specific architectural settings. At Stuyvesant High School, the glass blocks echo vitrines full of sports trophies or science specimens, while the Wexlers' projects often employ elements of the building fabric itself. Dennis Adams takes advantage of the frequency with which students use the water fountains. Possibilities and solutions are found that are tailored to each context.

- - -

The same is true of the Percent for Art projects in other kinds of City buildings. Matt Mullican's inset granite plaza in Flushing Meadows Corona Park is full of imagery celebrating the World's Fairs of 1939–40 and 1964–65, which took place there (page 210). Colin Chase's glass windows at the Queens Hospital Center draw on imagery of birds and mandalas as metaphors of healing (page 180). A terrazzo cosmogram on the lobby floor of the Schomburg Center for Research in Black Culture in Harlem by Houston Conwill, Estella Conwill Majozo, and Joseph DePace celebrates the poetry of Langston Hughes, whose ashes are actually interred under their floor piece (pages 128–29).

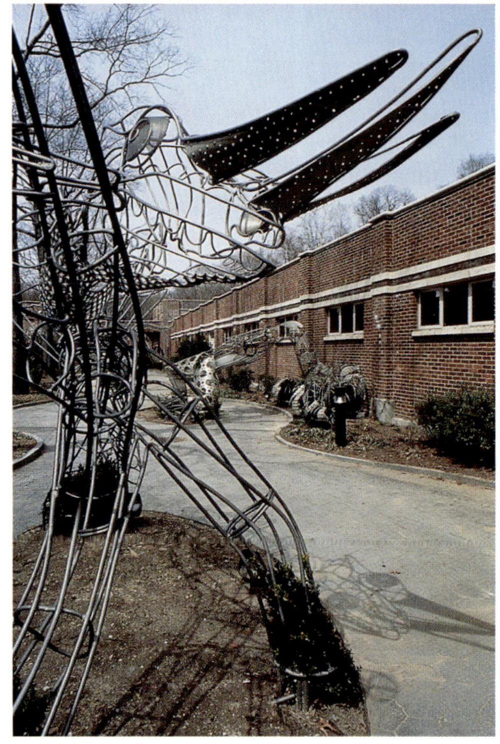

Mags Harries, *Topiary: A Twenty Year Project* (installation view), 1993, Prospect Park Zoo, Brooklyn (pages 94–95).

Percent for Art also allows artists to explore different dimensions of time. Unlike temporary public artworks that exist only for a few weeks or months, the Percent projects are designed to last for decades. Sometimes artists build an awareness of that duration into the work. Stuyvesant High School is an ongoing work that won't be "finished" till the late twenty-first century. At the Prospect Park Zoo, Mags Harries has installed a bestiary composed of playful metal topiary armatures that will be filled out with living plants in twenty years or so (pages 94–95). Fred Tomaselli has created a kind of urban time capsule along the handrail of the rotunda of the New York Hall of Science in Flushing Meadows Corona Park (page 218). Illuminated slide images made in 1993 reveal seventy-two views of the City, each equidistant from the center of the rotunda. There are backyards, industrial sites, busy intersections, and river views. As the cityscape of New York continues to change, the images here will gradually, and inevitably, become historical relics from an ever more distant moment in time.

Meanwhile, the many constituencies involved in any Percent for Art project introduce another set of opportunities. Artists interacting with different communities can sharpen their artworks' focus, or even become its primary focus. A set of sculptures created by Bill and Mary Buchen for the playground of Public School 23 in the Bronx are actually sound machines—bronze tables and seats are drums, a pair of large stainless-steel drums are actually parabolic disks that magnify sounds made between them, and an echo chamber reverberates through a buried storm drain (pages 40–42). The works may look like abstract sculptures, but they come alive when children use them. The project at the Horizon Juvenile Center in the Bronx by Tim Rollins + KOS is interactive in a different way (pages 56–57). Using the collaborative strategy that is this group's trademark, KOS worked with residents of a juvenile detention center to create artworks based on texts from *The Iliad* and *The Odyssey*. Rollins notes that Achilles and Ulysses seemed particularly appropriate as metaphors for the condition and hopes of the young residents of this facility. "Achilles' rage and anger take him to the brink of destruction, while Ulysses enters into war because he is dissatisfied with his boring life, only to spend years struggling to return home," he says. A series of paintings was created by KOS after extensive workshops with facility residents. The group also created a bronze sculpture for the center's inner courtyard. It depicts two identical boys reading a book with inscriptions from Homer's epics that speak to the states of mind of anger and reconciliation.

Interaction with City agencies and the local community is at the heart of Mierle Laderman Ukeles's work at Fresh Kills in Staten Island, the enormous landfill that received New York City's garbage for over fifty years (page 226). As an unsalaried Artist in Residence at the Department of Sanitation since 1977, Ukeles already had a relationship with the City agency in charge of the operation. One of her early Sanitation projects, for example, consisted of shaking the hands of all 8500 New York sanitation workers. More recently, Ukeles has been deeply involved in issues of recycling, transformation, and landfill reclamation.

As the Percent for Art artist chosen to work with the master plan design team of the Fresh Kills Landfill, Ukeles sits in on discussions of technical matters such as closure design, aeration, and gas management. Her particular contribution involves ideas for transforming the site into an urban asset. The landfill has not accepted garbage since March 2001, and only reopened after September 11, 2001, to accept the debris from the World Trade Center site. The official landfill closure will not be completed until 2012, and Ukeles has been pressing for bureaucratic and technological transparency, coming up with ways of revealing the complex systems involved in landfill engineering to the public. Ukeles is in a unique position to influence the direction of this massive infrastructure project because she has spent years building relationships with government officials and experts in the field. Her long years of work with the Department of Sanitation have opened doors normally closed to artists, and created a remarkable situation of trust. As a result, she is now able to interject an artist's thinking into a world usually dominated by engineers, urban planners, and technicians of various sorts. Fresh Kills has the potential to offer an unprecedented model for the kinds of projects that might be possible when artists are made official members of a planning team.

\- - -

The diversity of projects enacted under New York City's Percent for Art program raises provocative questions about the nature of public art. Who, in the end, is the ultimate audience of a public project? What happens when community desires are in conflict with art-world standards of quality? What happens when a work that plays off of conventions about style, subject-matter, and visual vocabulary that are well known within the art world proves to be unreadable to a public not trained in the intricacies of current art debates? Are judgments of an artwork's "quality" absolute, or do they depend on whom the art is for? Does public art answer to a different set of standards than "museum art"? What makes public art good? And what makes it successful?

Interestingly, the last two questions are not necessarily the same. Because public projects like those presented in this book are contingent on so many outside factors, their success cannot always be measured using

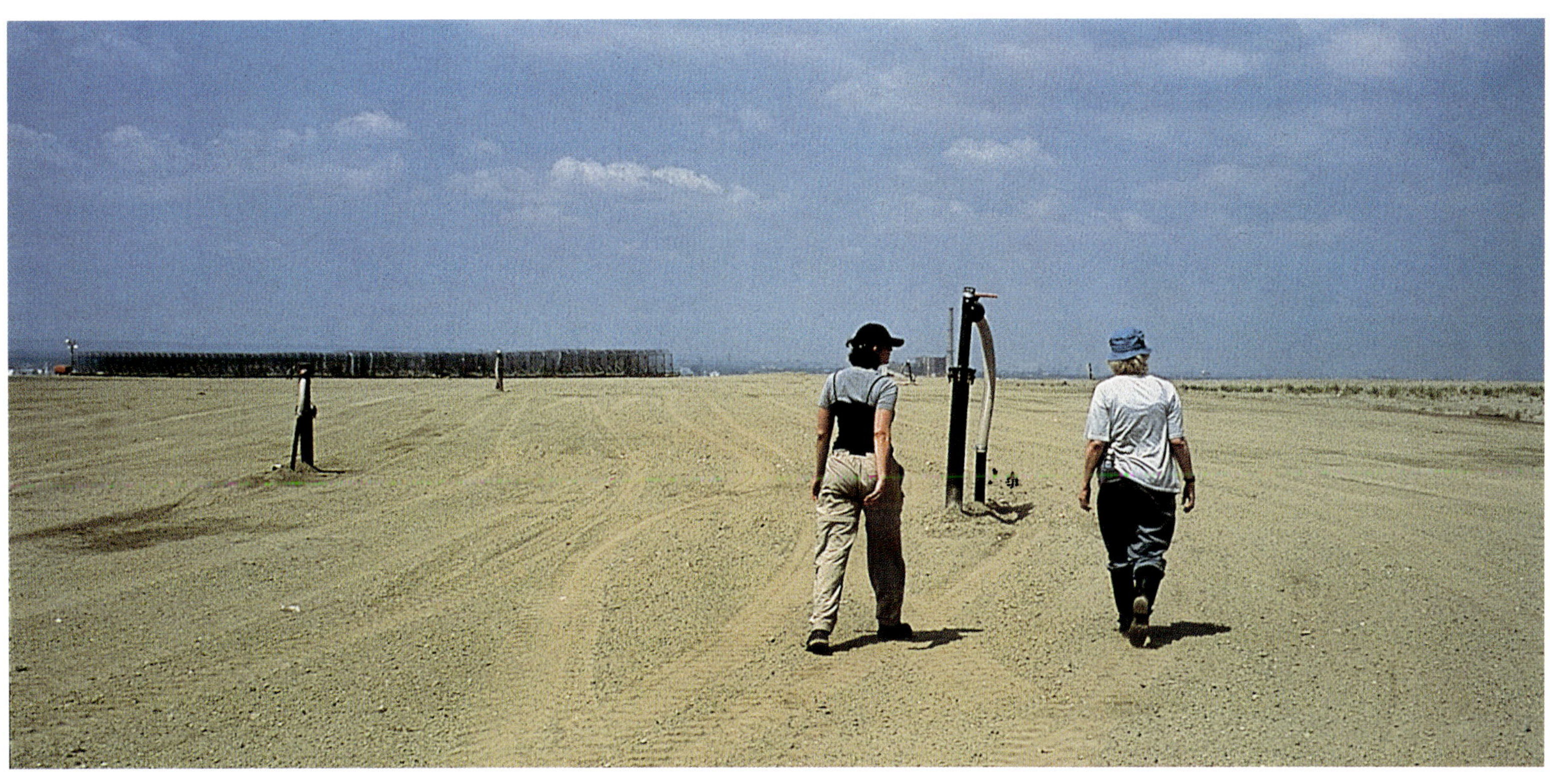

Mierle Laderman Ukeles (right) and landscape architect Michal Paryente at Fresh Kills Landfill, Staten Island, 2001 (page 226).

traditional criteria of conceptual clarity or aesthetic coherence. For instance, by any traditional standard, Carrie Mae Weems's beautifully executed mosaics for Walton High School in the Bronx would be considered highly successful (page 65). Using models drawn from the student body, she created four iconic portraits of young people below words symbolizing the ideal integration of body and mind. Each was depicted in a bathing suit because the work was designed to go above the school's renovated swimming pool. But when this renovation didn't happen, they were placed instead in the gym. Does it matter that the mosaics speak to a context other than the one for which they were created? Does this affect their "success," if we define success as a seamless integration into the site?

A similar issue has arisen in connection with Siah Armajani's lighthouse and pedestrian bridge, which connects the St. George Ferry Terminal with the North Shore Esplanade on Staten Island (page 228–29). It was designed to lead to the Esplanade (which was completed) and to historic coast guard buildings (which are slated for future renovation and use as a lighthouse museum). Thus the bridge has not been used as much as anticipated. Again, does this affect how we judge the work?

The question of success was raised most poignantly by the case of a project for a Bronx police station created in 1991 by John Ahearn (page 38). In keeping with Percent for Art's desire to work with an artist connected to the community, Ahearn was chosen in part because he lived in the Bronx and had received both local and art-world acclaim for his cast sculptures of actual community members. Aware of the frictions between public and police in this area, Ahearn proposed to make bronze sculptures of three Bronx residents and place them on pedestals in front of the police station. In that way, he aimed to reverse the traditional sculptural formula of the great man in the square, by suggesting that ordinary people are our contemporary heroes.

However, when the three sculptures went up, protests ignited a firestorm as certain residents argued that the figures Ahearn had chosen—a young man with a boombox and basketball, another in a hooded sweatsuit kneeling by a pit-bull terrier, and a girl on roller skates, represented negative and racist stereotypes. It did not help that, although Ahearn had lived in the community for twenty years, he was white.

Anguished at this unexpected response to his work, Ahearn asked that it be taken down. Later, he reflected that he had not been able to reconcile art-world standards, which hailed the "edgy" quality of the work, and the standards of local residents looking for "positive imagery." "I believed that answering the needs of the community, answering your own private problems that you are working out, dealing with art-historical problems, that these things could all be made in one piece." Now, in retrospect, he muses, "To say it's possible—that is easy. To say you are doing it is more difficult."[4] Today, the Ahearn sculptures, which were moved from the Bronx police station they were commissioned for, stand in Socrates Sculpture Park in Queens. In this very different context, they are appreciated and accepted by an art public for whom their "edgy" quality is viewed as a positive thing.

One of the great challenges of Percent for Art projects is that they require artists to deal with diverse, and often conflicting, publics. Rollins notes that when he worked on the detention center project, he had to field complaints from community residents that the City was creating a nicer environment for young criminals than for the students going to the school across the street. Ukeles, in a project involving a firehouse in the Bronx, discovered that her desire to address tensions between firefighters and the local community by opening up the firehouse to neighborhood

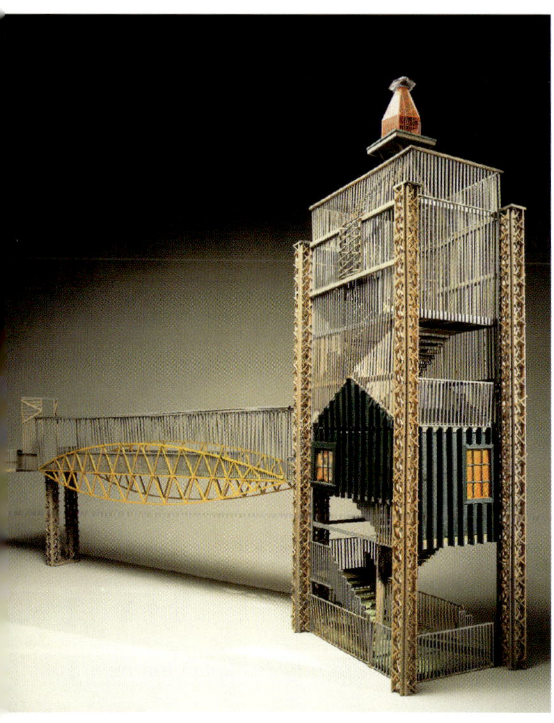

Siah Armajani, model for *Lighthouse and Bridge on Staten Island*, 1996, North Shore Esplanade, Staten Island (pages 228–29).

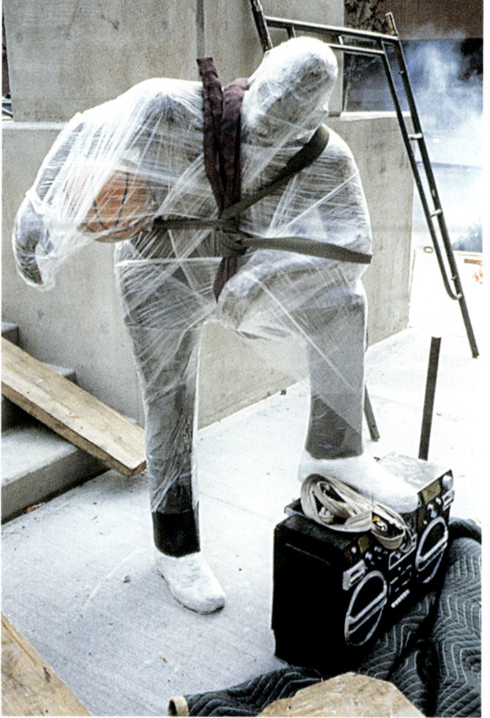

John Ahearn, *Corey*, 1991, for Police Precinct 44, Bronx (page 38); currently displayed at Socrates Sculpture Park, Queens.

residents, was met by fierce resistance from the firefighters themselves (pages 62–64).

Which leads to the last set of questions: What can we expect from public art, and do we expect too much? Public artists sometimes complain that they are brought in as the clean-up squad to fix bad planning and bad architecture. On another level, public art is sometimes presented as a panacea or a distraction from entrenched social ills such as poverty, inequality and racism. However, during the controversy over *Tilted Arc*, Richard Serra remarked, "Art is not supposed to be democratic. It is not for the people."[5] Clearly, thinking about public art has now swung in the other direction as artists talk about participation, empowering local communities, and creating transparency. But how much is really possible?

Perhaps the most useful way to think about public art is to see it as a process or a kind of society-wide experiment that uses the public sphere as its laboratory. On that score, New York City's Percent for Art program fares well. Over two decades, it has presented literally hundreds of different ways to think about art's role in New York's daily life. Simply on the basis of its scale alone, it has provided opportunities unmatched elsewhere. It has also been able to tap into the remarkable creative energy provided by New York's unrivaled concentration of artists. It should be no surprise that projects like Jones and Ginzel's *Mnenonics* and Mierle Ukeles's participation at the Fresh Kills Landfill site are known and lauded worldwide.

New York's Percent for Art program reveals what can happen when the different points of view of artists, City agencies, and the general public come together in a mutual pursuit of a beautiful and functional urban environment. In the years since its inception, the program has been nurtured by an ever-growing cohort of individuals from all corners of the City's civic life. Through its mandate to have faith in the ability of art to enhance the lives of ordinary citizens, New York's Percent for Art program has helped artists discover new ways to address the larger world. And it has helped make New Yorkers more aware of the remarkable experiment that is the City itself.

Overleaf: Milo Mottola, *Totally Kid Carousel*, 1998, Manhattan (page 151).

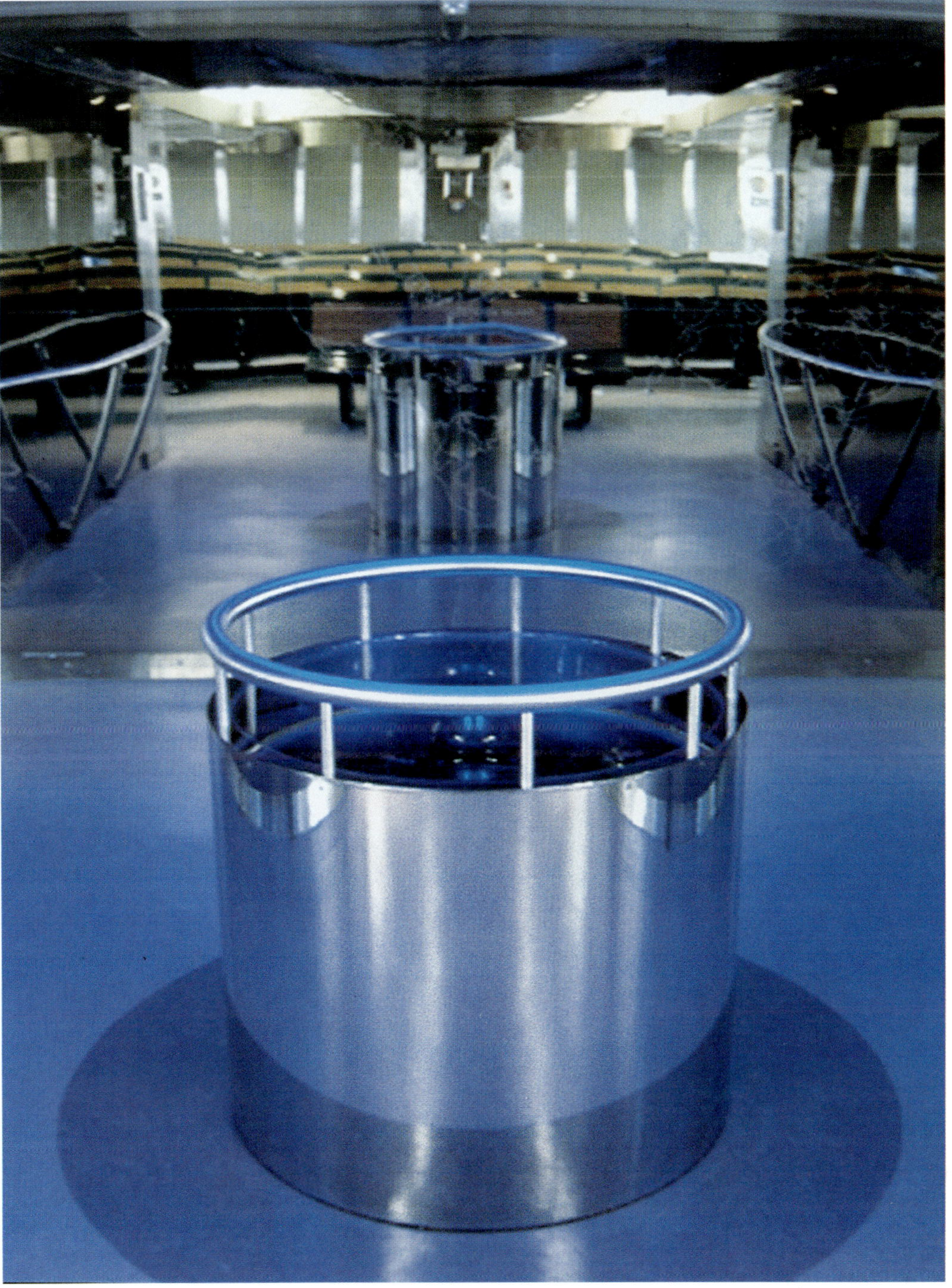

Work in progress on Werner Klotz and John Roloff's's *The Middle of the World*, 2004, Staten Island Ferry Boats.

Notes

1 Rosalyn Deutsche, "Uneven Development: Public Art in New York City," *October* 47, Winter 1988, pp. 3–52.
2 Unless otherwise noted, quotations are from interviews with the author, July 2004.
3 "Interview: Kristin Jones and Andrew Ginzel on Mnemonics," in Tom Finkelpearl, *Dialogues in Public Art*, Cambridge MA (MIT Press) 2000, p. 375.
4 "Interview: John Ahearn on the Bronx Bronzes and Happier Tales," in Finkelpearl 2000, p. 93.
5 Richard Serra, quoted on PBS website accompanying the television series *Culture Shock* (www.pbs.org/wgbh/cultureshock).

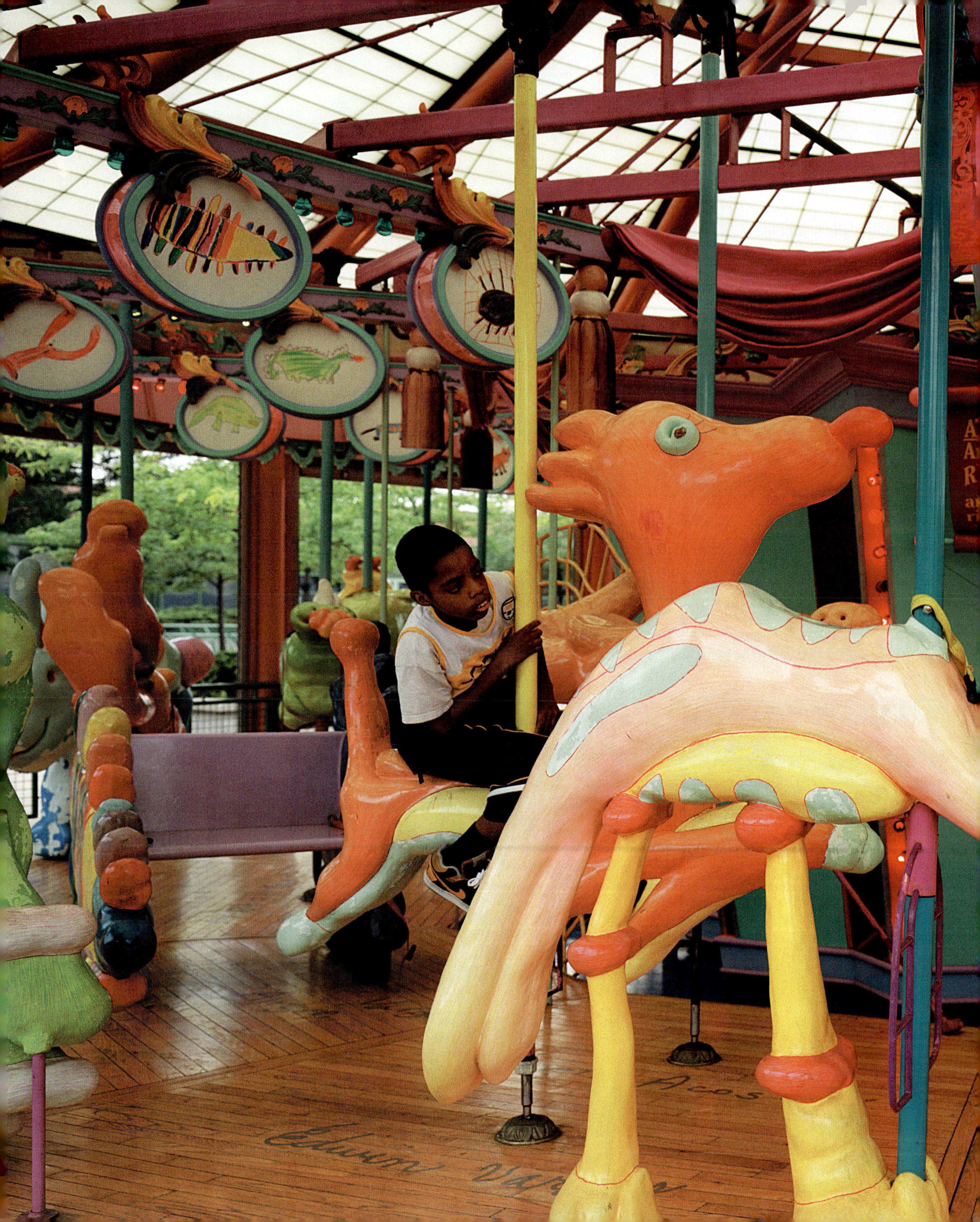

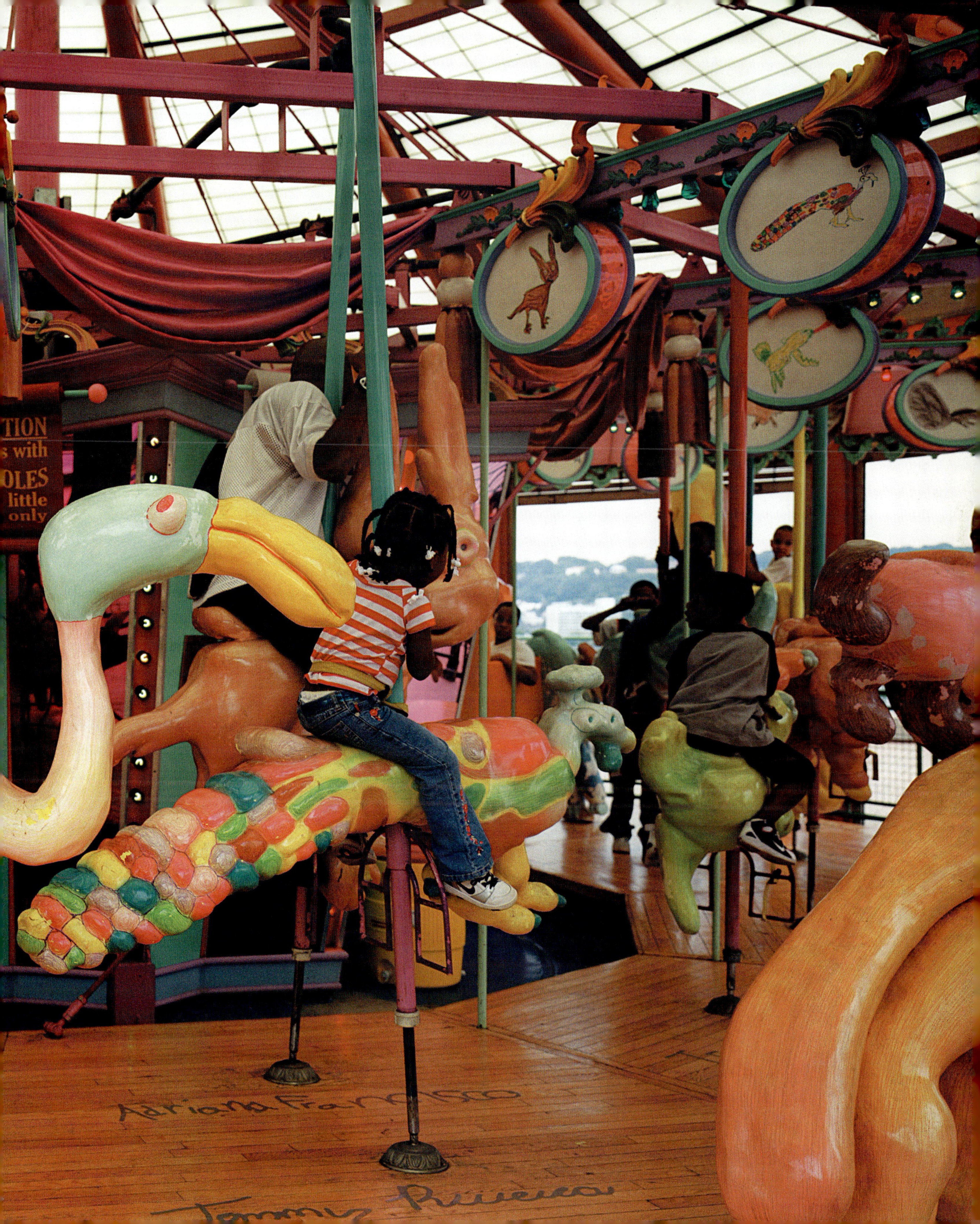
TION
s with
OLES
little
only

Interview

Kate D. Levin

Commissioner of the New York City Department of Cultural Affairs

The Percent for Art program touches on a fissure in civic discourse. On the one hand, people yearn for government to be less faceless and more humane, and on the other, they get nervous about government sanctioning an expression of individual opinion when the product might be something they don't like. The challenge for government is to produce art in a way that is not condescending or elitist but actually combines creative expression with a democratizing process.

Percent for Art really operates at this intersection, and I think it does so very successfully. It gives artists a say in how the public domain is built and, at the same time, it works with communities to deliver something that New Yorkers can embrace.

Naturally, embedding artworks into the design and construction of public buildings is going to produce results that are different from objects displayed on black velvet under a pin spot in a museum. But that doesn't mean the art is not as good. Like all art, public art at its best is both beautiful and engaging.

What makes public art unique is that it is meant to function in a way that is subtle and integrated into the fabric of our daily lives. It is not meant to intimidate or necessarily to awe. In some cases the art is like dessert—something playful and pleasurable that makes you happy when you look at it. In other cases, your interaction with it depends entirely on your frame of mind or awareness of your surroundings. Each work is the product of the individual imagination. But the program as a whole is art generated by and for the City, where the grit of the oyster produces the pearl.

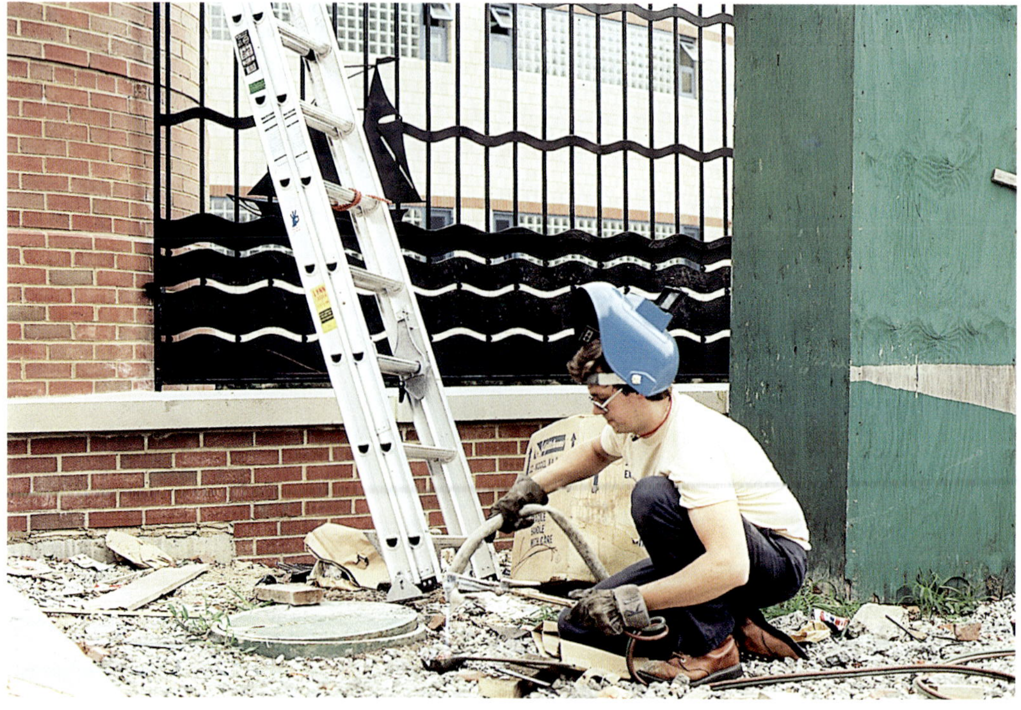

Work in progress on Donna Dennis's *Dreaming of Far Away Places: The Ships Come to Washington Market*, 1998, at Public School 234, Manhattan (pages 132–33)

Interview

Vinnie Medugno

Class of 2004, Port Richmond High School, Staten Island

I noticed *Hallway Highway* [Nancy Dwyer, 1995; pages 232–33] as soon as I started coming to this school. Actually, even before, when my brother was here and I'd come along for parent–teacher conferences and saw this piece. I didn't know what it was then, but I thought it was cool. Elementary and intermediate schools had regular floors in them; this had designs on it.

Most people don't know why or how these words wound up being here. It's just one of those things. But I like them. When we were freshmen, a bunch of us walked up and down the hallways, reading all the words. "Five minutes of freedom" reminds me of period changes. "What's up?" is like when you see your friends; those are the words that always come out of everybody's mouth first. *Hallway Highway* captures the experience of high school life, and it's become a symbol of the school. There's a picture of it in this year's yearbook. And on the page of unanswered questions about the time we spent at school, one of them is: "What do those words in the hallway actually mean?"

I notice it every time when I'm walking; like I'll be right in the middle of it, staring at the perfect line and the words as I go by. Sometimes I feel like I'm driving a car. There's that perfect line, like a highway. And people really do walk on one side of it or on the other; a group on the left side will be coming, and a group on the right side will be going. It's great that they put this in the hallway, something that helps you pay attention to the behavior of kids—the ones you get aggravated with 'cause of the way they walk; the ones who drag their feet; the ones who walk fast, then stop short; the ones who cut in front of you or weave in and out; the ones who are like the mayor, and have to stop and say hello to everybody.

Some people may take this for granted, but sometimes we get into group discussions about it, about how the artist got the idea for this and why she did it in this school. It makes me wonder about other work that she's done, and what people who succeed in life can get to do.

Vinnie Medugno (third from left) and students at Port Richmond High School, Staten Island, with Nancy Dwyer's *Hallway Highways* (1995; pages 232–33).

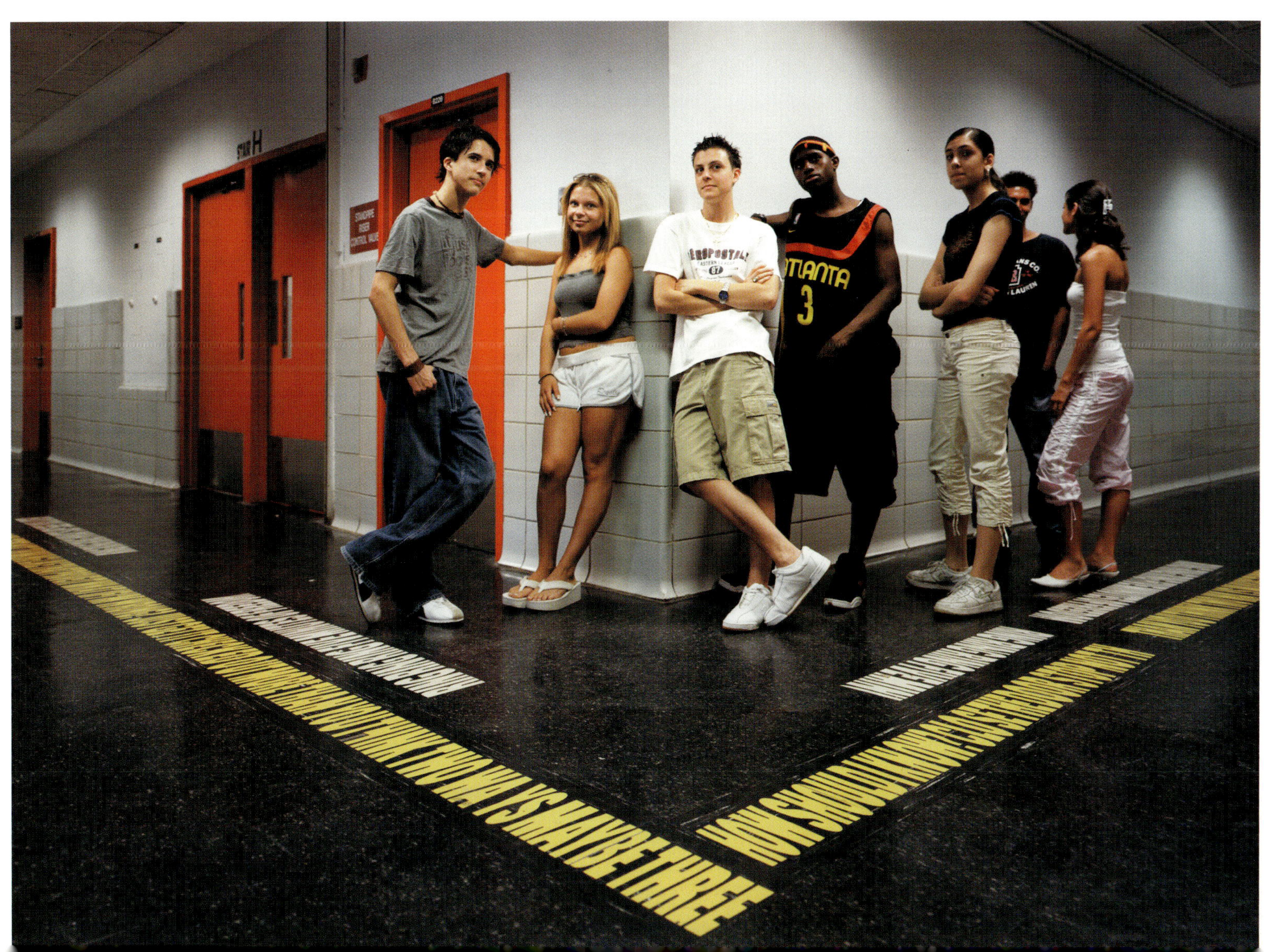

Interview

Edward I. Koch

Mayor of the City of New York, 1978–89

I became aware of the need to have legislation for an arts program like Percent for Art when I was in Congress, where John Brademas sponsored important federal programs for the commissioning of art. As Mayor of New York City, I always remembered that program, and other municipal programs like it. Ronay Menschel—who had been my Chief Administrative Assistant in Congress, and became a Deputy Mayor in New York—was interested in, and kept pressing for, Percent for Art legislation for the City. And so did Doris C. Freedman, who was a major advocate for public art and directed the City's Office of Cultural Affairs in 1968 (the agency did not become the Department of Cultural Affairs until 1976). I initiated the Percent for Art legislation, even though the City had not yet fully recovered from the near bankruptcy that had taken place. New York didn't invent this kind of program; you don't have to reinvent the wheel. But we made it successful, on a local level, in New York.

Why should New York City care about art? Well, art is something that is fundamental to us. It's part of our soul, some would say. And if the buildings the City constructs will last for many, many generations, so will the art that's in them. I believe that government has a responsibility to fill the need for art the same way it has the responsibility to fill the population's other elemental needs. People live in and respond to their environment. And art is an integral part of the environment. It inspires us; it reflects something deep within us that needs to be expressed.

The people of New York understood that. Nobody got up, as they often do, to say that as long as one child didn't have all its needs responded to, the City couldn't engage in this kind of program. This was, after all, making art a part of the total construction program of the City, and part of the capital program in terms of monies allocated. The Percent for Art program is the biggest permanent public art project in New York since the extraordinary programs of the Works Progress Administration (WPA), which I'm sure faced much greater resistance than I did. When people looked at our program, they understood that New Yorkers, aside from worrying about the basics of life, such as eating and housing, could all hold their heads up higher, and look into the future.

In selecting art for the City, it was never up to me, nor was I qualified, to set the limits on what the City should be doing, or what kinds of art the City should be choosing for this program. For that, you look to experts, and in New York there's plenty of them. But what's always been important to the Percent for Art program is that the selection process included the City's communities, and took into account what people would like to see. Percent for Art isn't and shouldn't be an elitist operation. And while art should not be made to please the lowest common denominator, it has to take into consideration what people feel comfortable with.

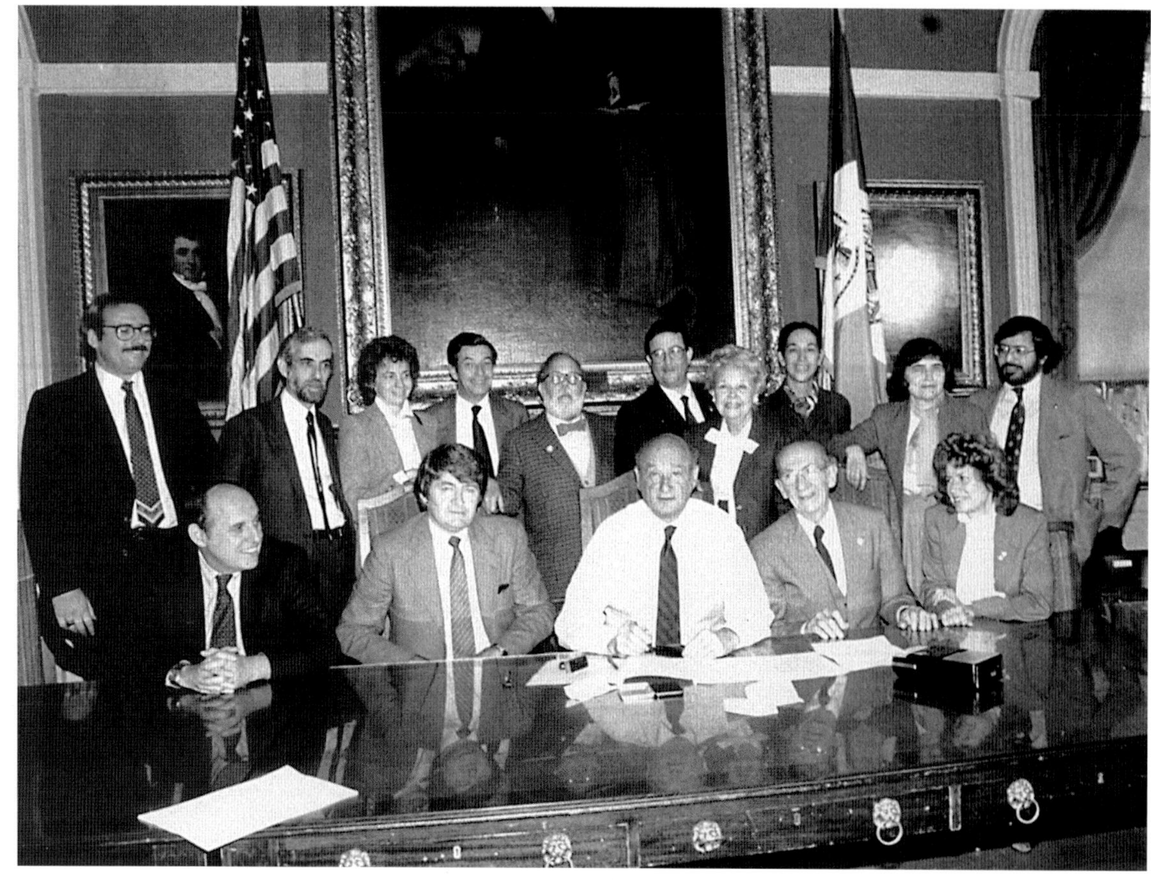

Former Mayor Edward I. Koch signing the Percent for Art Law, October 29, 1982.

Interview

Margarita Hunt-Tejada

District Manager for Community Board 4, Bronx

The community board is the most local form of government in New York. Its members' job is truly to represent the community's concerns. So it's important that every Percent for Art project needs to go through us before it is approved. The community really appreciates that we're asked for our input; it makes everyone feel involved. And now, when new construction projects are presented to us, we ask: "Will a Percent for Art piece be included?" And if the answer is no, we request or recommend one.

The community board gets directly involved when Percent for Art is ready to select an artist for a project. We select a board member who is interested in art to represent us on the panel, and to look at proposed artists and their ideas, from the community's perspective. We generally know more about the entire community than the rest of the panel. Our presence is important, and has led to a successful partnership. The community gets a chance to express itself in the planning for the site and in the selection of an artist. This way, new artworks are not just something brought in from the outside and placed there.

These artworks are distinctive, and become landmarks for the community. They give people the opportunity to view art outside the museum. They turn a bland wall or an underpass into something beautiful. Wherever you go, or if you're just waiting around, you have something interesting to look at, something that makes you look twice.

Most of the time, the community is really pleased with the artworks developed for our neighborhood. And when people aren't, believe me, we hear about it. Years ago, there were some sculptures by John Ahearn that were placed in front of the police precinct that looked like people from the neighborhood—you know, a guy with a boombox, a guy with a pit-bull. And everybody in the community was complaining—mothers, fathers, young people—*everybody*. What they wanted was an "art" piece as opposed to a "reality" piece. In the end, everyone, including the artist, agreed that the piece offended so many people, it was better that it be removed altogether.

For a new project that's going to be installed at the criminal courthouse, the artist Cai Guo-Qiang presented something that looked like a huge, long chain with links that you could sit on. But the community didn't like it. This neighborhood in the Bronx is half African-American and half Hispanic. At the community board meeting, some people said that the artwork brought to mind the old chain gangs. They felt strongly that it wasn't the right kind of image or work for the courthouse. And so we discussed the problems and worked with the artist. We didn't tell him how to change it, but we liked how he did. Now we're waiting for this huge granite sculpture that has interlocking cubes instead of chain links. And everyone is pleased. It's going to be outstanding.

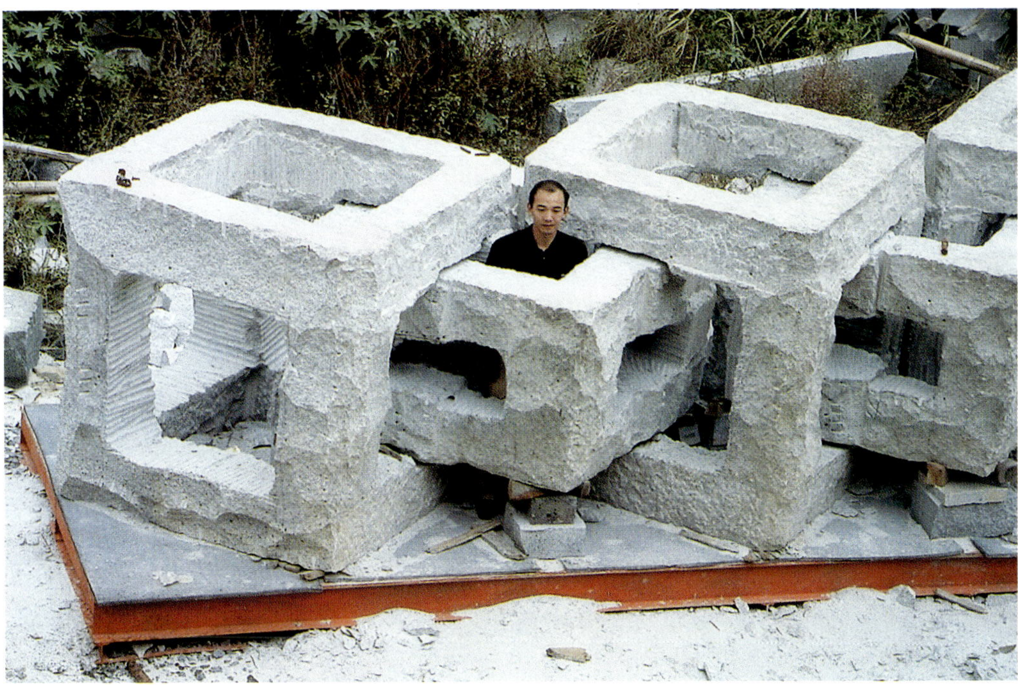

Work in progress on Cai Guo-Qiang's *One Stone*, Bronx Criminal Court Complex, 2004.

Interview

Ronay Menschel

Deputy Mayor and Executive Administrator of New York City, 1978–82; Metropolitan Transit Authority Board Member, 1979–90

New York City's Percent for Art program grew out of the work of Doris C. Freedman who, in addition to her leadership at the Urban Center and the Public Art Fund, passionately advocated the power of art to define and enhance public spaces. Freedman believed that New York City should have a Percent for Art Law. There were predecessor Percent for Art programs in the country. But New York City—the art capital of the world and home to many artists—didn't have a law mandating that art be a part of the design and construction of its buildings.

The Percent for Art legislation was ultimately passed in 1982. Its adoption was timely. New York had just come out of the financial crisis of the 1970s. Capital construction had declined to almost nothing. In addition, most of the buildings that had been constructed in the 1960s and 1970s were spare—in design, materials, and construction quality. By 1982 the City budget had been balanced, and the capital program restored. New York was about to build again. There also was a growing recognition that art adds to the aesthetics and quality of buildings and, further, that the public is entitled to government facilities that offer a quality environment to visit and that contribute to the aesthetics of neighborhoods, not detract from them.

Percent for Art was not hard to sell to the New York City Council. We made the case that engaging artists in the design of new facilities would contribute to City life and its public spaces. The program made sense. The City's Department of Cultural Affairs already had the largest budget of any municipality supporting our cultural institutions and arts programming. The legislation was signed into law with enthusiasm. I am only sorry that Doris C. Freedman did not live to participate in this bill signing or to witness the launch of the program.

Initially, there were concerns about how the artist selection process could produce art high enough in quality to merit permanent installation. And there was a question of how community representatives would respond to proposed artists if they did not have experience in collecting art or working with artists. We quickly found that artists' creative genius was superb in solving design problems and coming up with proposals that were suitable for the particular facility in question. The quality of the artists interested in developing art for public spaces was high. Community representatives were cooperative in bringing to bear their community concerns, but they did not attempt to impose a particular aesthetic. From the start, everyone agreed that artists would be chosen who would express their vision and that the work would *not* be designed by committee.

Percent for Art's successes provided a model for the Metropolitan Transportation Authority (MTA) to follow in the mid-1980s. The MTA's Arts for Transit program has brought art—performing as well as visual—to travelers throughout the metropolitan area. The program has had a positive impact on the design guidelines of the station modernization program. It led to the commissioning of two artists to design all of the new grillwork installed in the subways, and helped improved the design standard of numerous MTA facilities. So today a new bus depot, for instance, is a better neighbor than it otherwise would have been. Most importantly, art has given stations a special identity and improved appearance, and signaled to travelers the respect that the system has for its customers.

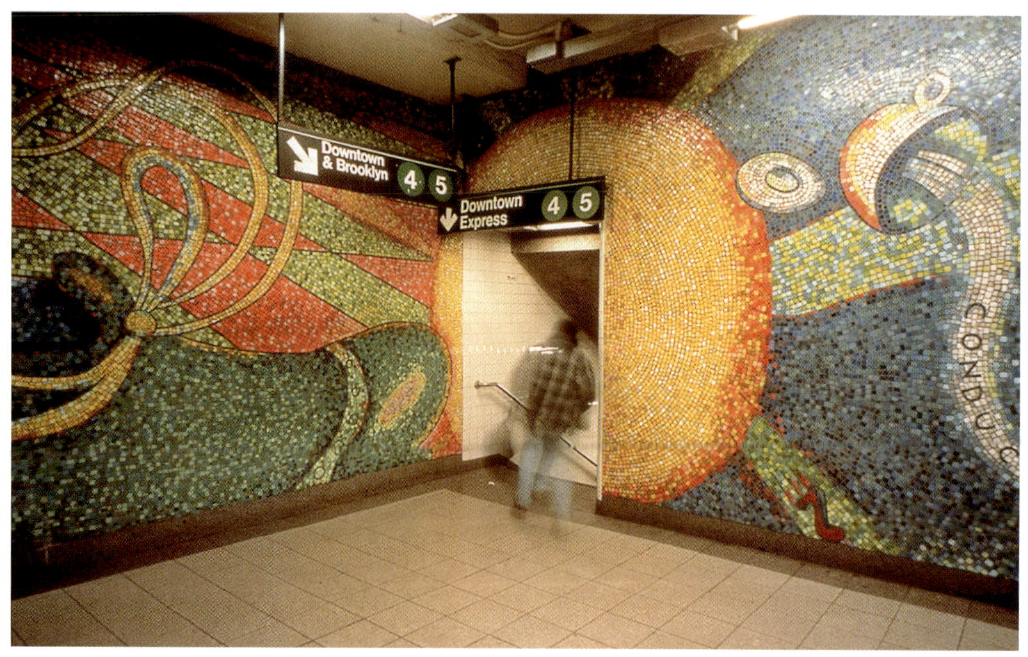

Elizabeth Murray, *Blooming*, 1996, 59th Street and Lexington Avenue subway station. Commissioned and owned by Metropolitan Transportation Authority Arts for Transit.

Interview

Ursula von Rydingsvard

Artist

It's difficult to design a building that will be used as a family court. Henry Cobb and his associate, Ian Bader, went out of their way to humanize the space. And in terms of my role, they both understood what artists try to do, and did whatever was in their power to try to support that. There was a tremendous amount of trust involved. When I started, I did not have a precise idea of what I intended to do. I did have a notion of working in the heart, the core of the building. And the proposal I made was ambitious, ultimately far more ambitious than the budget could support, and in what I thought this project would take in terms of time and energy.

I was thrown into a process and a bureaucracy that were truly the land of the harsh and the tough: a harassing situation, unpleasant because of the rules and parameters of the work site. But I can't speak more highly about the way the architects related to what I wanted to do. Our relationship wasn't collaborative; I had my ideas of what the piece would be like. But many things needed to be facilitated through the layers of bureaucracy, with which Gerry Vasisko at Gruzen Samton Architects was helpful.

I chose the space for my work; the atrium seemed like the most evident, obvious, soulful part of the building, under a 40 × 40 foot (12.2 × 12.2 m) skylight that generously allows daylight to come through. My thinking was to help bring more of that light down into the space, by making structures that would relate, in a rather energetic way, to the two nearby escalators. In thinking about materials for the piece, I thought about the building, full of brick and

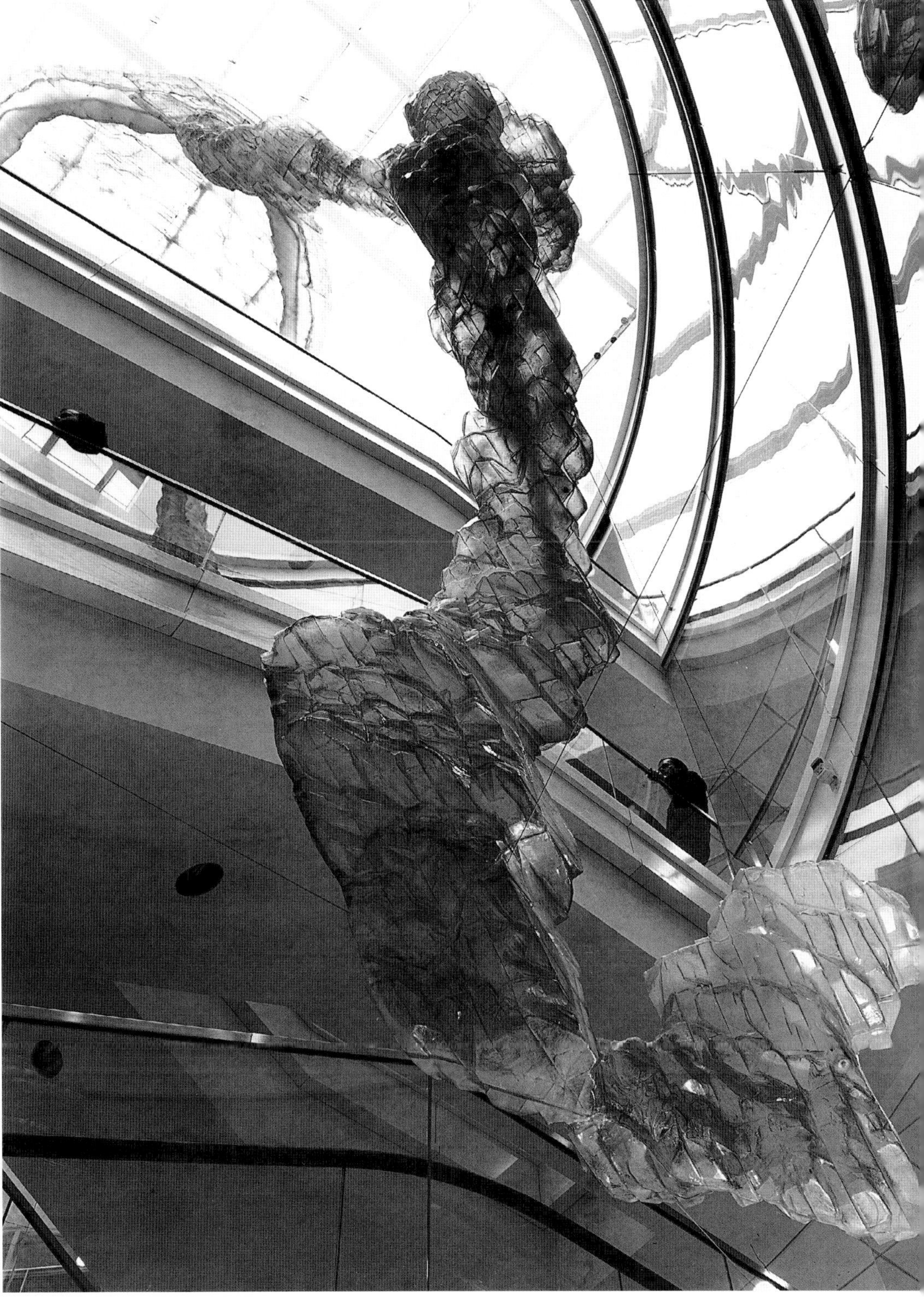

Ursula von Rydingsvard, *katul katul*, 2003, Queens Family Courthouse. Pei Cobb Freed & Partners/Gruzen Samton Architects (page 220).

shiny elements such as glass and stainless steel. Everyone assumed I was going to make the piece out of cedar—there was no way I would; it would block out all the light. I wanted the piece to feel lighter physically and psychologically, more broken up, more muted, hanging there, below the huge skylight. And I wanted it to carry the light at least partially through the five floors, not in a sensational or entertaining way, but in a very gentle and subtle way.

While I did make the full-scale model for the sculpture out of cedar, I cut it apart, and cast it in 220 vacuformed sections of copolyethelene. Then I couldn't leave the plastic shiny as it was too de-humanizing. So I blasted some of the surfaces with a very fine pearl bead and, on top of that, put a gentle no-color like that of water, ice, or a cloud.

It was far and away my most anxiety-ridden project, in part because it was my first hung piece, my first sculpture of plastic (five stories' worth of copolyethelene). I felt that I was treading in places that were not a part of my usual world. There was a tremendous amount of learning involved, a tremendous number of meetings, huge risks. But in the end, I was able to keep control over the visuals of the piece. And I would put everything on the line for that.

Interview

Henry Cobb

Founding Partner, Pei Cobb Freed & Partners, Architects

The single most important challenge of an art-in-architecture program is that the artist and the architect must each make room for the other. The responsibility falls first on the architect, because there's a tendency for contemporary architects to imagine their works as essentially complete, and hence not to welcome any significant intervention by artists or works of art.

A hundred years ago, art was more conventionally imagined as completing the architecture of a building. Today there is less agreement on what constitutes the relationship between art and architecture. If the architect conceives of a building in such a way that it invites the participation of the artist, there's a risk involved; the architect may envision a space for the art, but the artist may not respond to it. The artist has to be willing to take account of the architecture, and some contemporary artists are not much interested in doing that. Nonetheless, on balance, I believe it's a good thing that we no longer have the kind of lock-step relationship between art and architecture that existed in the Beaux-Arts period. We have instead a fundamentally unstable and often fractious, but potentially livelier and more adventurous, affiliation.

My colleagues and I have designed a number of courthouses, but the Queens Family Courthouse is special. It is filled with people, all the time, who are very troubled, very angry, very upset. The challenge was for the art to be in a place, and of a type, that would connect with and help people in some way. It would have been a waste to put a statue outside the building that people would rush past. In this case, the vertical atrium at the heart of the building was clearly the right site for art, but a difficult one because it was encumbered by the escalators essential to its circulatory function. It would be difficult for the art to find its place, and in this situation it was the artist who had to make the larger accommodation.

What Ursula von Rydingsvard did was both intelligent and courageous, an amazing high-risk performance on her part. The work that she produced is engaging to the eye, while its meaning is elusive and invites multiple interpretations. Some may find the work merely strange, and dismiss it. Others, in repeated encounters as they go up and down and through that space, will surely find themselves moved by it.

If this courthouse had been built a hundred years ago, the architect would have set aside surfaces for paintings that would have been expected to be realistic, allegorical, and integral to the architecture. But in this case, as in most contemporary buildings, the art is definitely another voice being introduced as a counterpoint to the inescapably institutional character of the building. A decade or two from now, we will perhaps be better able to assess the enduring value of the dialogue thus engendered between this particular work of architecture and this particular work of art.

Interview

Harriet F. Senie

Director of Museum Studies, Professor of Art History, The City College of The City University of New York

What is public art? It's defined by where it is, a public site that anybody has access to, at no charge. What form it takes depends on the time, the place, the artist, and the parameters of the commission. There have been movements, fashions, and a steady evolution in what public artists seem to be most in need of saying.

Whatever form it takes, we should always be aware of how people may come to a work of public art. If this were Utopia, art education programs in our public school system would include art making, art appreciation, and art history. That would make a real difference in our experience with art. Not that it would mean that everybody would like whatever was out there, but they could have a meaningful experience and conversation about it, about what the artist was thinking when she or he created it—a dialogue that goes beyond shock, a "what is it?" or a kind of "get it out of my face" reaction.

One of the most difficult challenges confronting public art programs is providing an entry point to engage the public in experiencing public art. Communities play an important role in that process, in terms of educating the commissioning agencies and artists about their sites. The more activist they are in presenting information about the kinds of activities that take place in a space, and about the people who live or work there, the more successful the public art is going to be. People who serve on art commissions and panels get critical information from community members, which influences the kinds of artists they will select. Artists listen to community members, and what they hear has an impact on what their project will look like or do. Community involvement is critical. Who is "the community"? It can be people involved with community groups, community boards, religious, social, or cultural organizations. And where does the community end? Five blocks away? Ten blocks out?

And while it's necessary to listen to communities, it's important to remember that communities change and so the meaning of permanent public art changes. In the same way that equestrian statues are important because they remind us of our history, today's public art represents our history, now. Public artworks, then and now, become manifestations and anchors of our lives and history; without them we live in an urbanscape of denial.

Still, the biggest challenge public art faces is to establish a connection between the viewer and the work of art. And it's my sense that the current generation of public artists is aware of that. The divide between the artist and the public was more historically true when public art was envisioned as a civic collection comparable to a museum collection; you'd have your Segal, your Serra, your Oldenburg. But the sense of what's appropriate public art, and the ways artists think about it, have changed. The artists I have been talking to recently are more involved in thinking through how to engage the site, the community, and the public. They are responding to what they think society needs, stepping in to fill a social void, and to effect civic engagement.

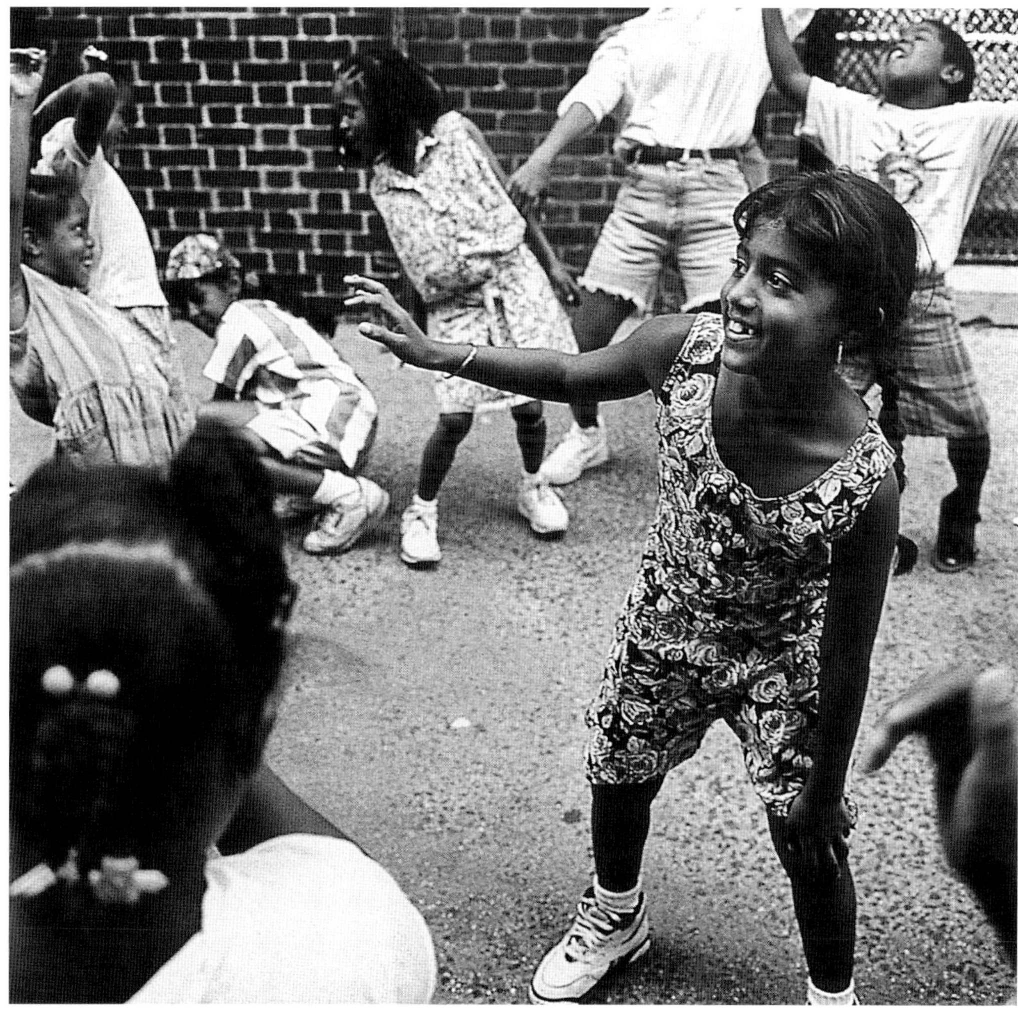

Photograph from Pablo Delano's series *Images of Washington Heights*, 1995, Public School 4, Manhattan (pages 130–31).

Completed projects ● (see map)

1 Vito Acconci
2 John Ahearn
3 Candida Alvarez
4 Andrea Arroyo
5 Monica Banks
6 Bill and Mary Buchen
7 John Fekner
8 Ricky Flores
9 Walton Ford
10 Noah Jemisin
11 Kristin Jones and Andrew Ginzel
12 Vitaly Komar and Alexander Melamid
13 Justen Ladda
14 Justen Ladda
15 Gregg LeFevre
16 Steven Mayo
17 Matt Mullican
18 Tom Nussbaum
19 Bob Rivera
20 Freddy Rodriguez
21 Tim Rollins + KOS
22 Christy Rupp
23 David Saunders
24 Vicki Scuri
25 Alison Sky
26 Alison Sky
27 Therman Statom
28 Jorge Tacla
29 Brinsley Tyrell
30 Mierle Laderman Ukeles
31 Anton Van Dalen
32 Carrie Mae Weems
33 Allan and Ellen Wexler
34 Allan and Ellen Wexler
35 Janet Zweig

Projects in progress ▲ (see map)

36 Willie Cole
Watching Over our Children and our Community
Suspended sculpture
Seabury Day Care Center, East 170th Street and Stebbins Avenue
Architect: BKSF Architects
Design Agency: Department of Design and Construction
Sponsor Agency: Agency for Child Development

37 Michael Davis
Equilibrium
Suspended sculpture
Bronx Criminal Court Complex, 215 East 161st Street
Architect: Rafael Vinoly Architects
Design Agency: Dormitory Authority of the State of New York
Sponsor Agency: Office of Court Administration

38 Cai Guo-Qiang
One Stone
Granite sculpture
Bronx Criminal Court Complex, 215 East 161st Street
Architect: Rafael Vinoly Architects
Design Agency: Dormitory Authority of the State of New York
Sponsor Agency: Office of Court Administration

39 Arlan Huang
Suspended glass installation
Jacobi Medical Center, 1400 Pelham Parkway South
Architect: Cannon Design
Design Agency: Dormitory Authority of the State of New York
Sponsor Agency: Health and Hospitals Corporation

40 Martha Jackson Jarvis
Techno 368
Mosaic
Intermediate School 368, Tibbets Gardens and 230th Street
Architect: STV Group
Design Agency: School Construction Authority
Sponsor Agency: Department of Education

41 Iñigo Manglano-Ovalle
Portrait of a Young Reader
Glass wall installation
Bronx Regional Library Center, 310 East Kingsbridge Road
Architect: Richard Dattner and Partners Architects
Sponsor Agency: New York Public Library

42 Juan Sanchez
Paintings
Bronx Coalition Community High School, 1300 Boynton Avenue
Architect: Kliment & Frances Halsband Architects
Design Agency: School Construction Authority
Sponsor Agency: Department of Education

43 Alison Sky
Portal design
161st Street Underpass
Engineer: URS
Sponsor Agency: Department of Transportation

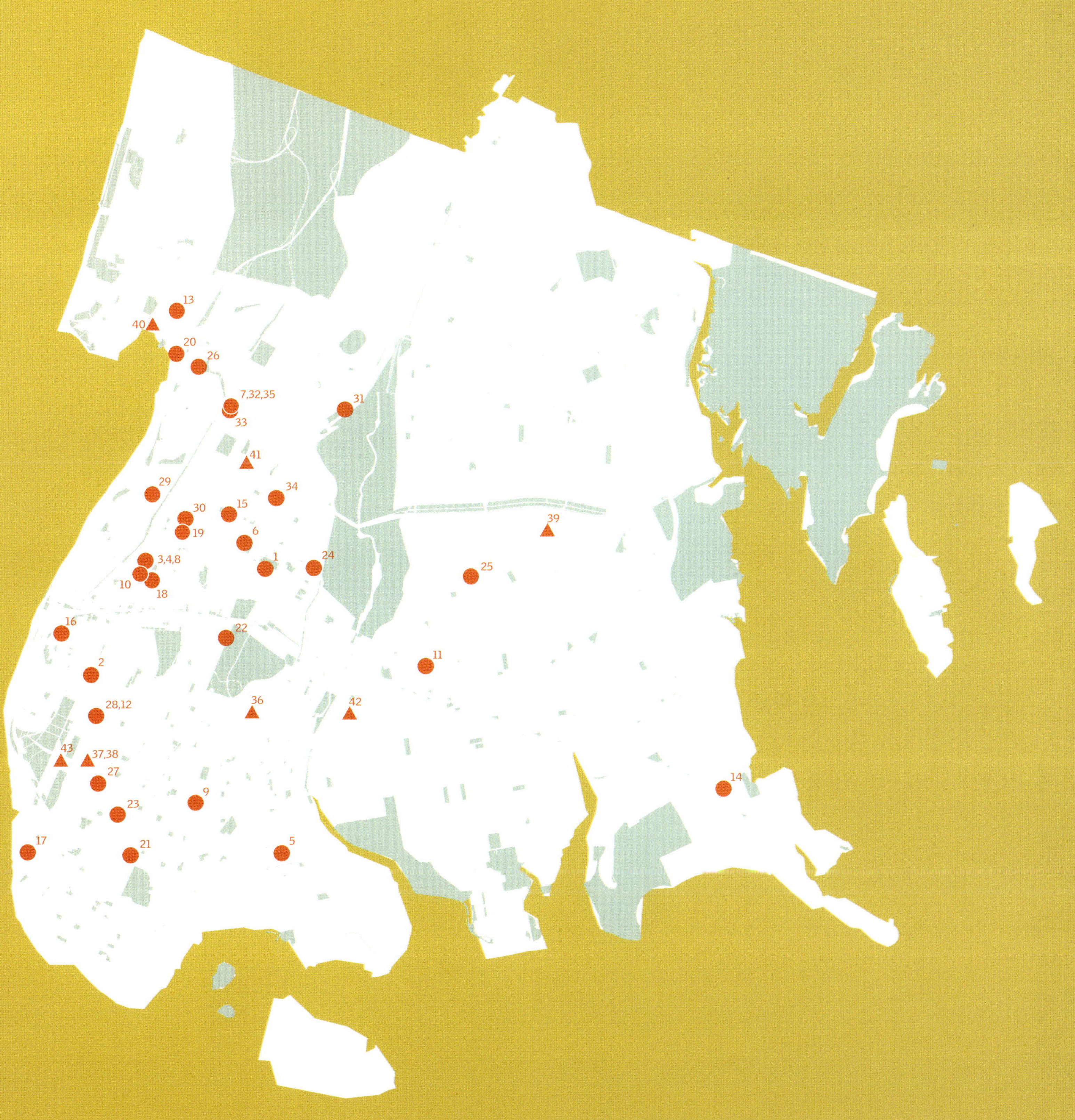
13
40
20
26
7,32,35
33
31
41
29
34
30
15
19
6
39
3,4,8
1
24
10
18
25
16
22
2
11
28,12
36
42
43
37,38
27
14
9
23
17
21
5

Bronx

Interview: Iñigo Manglano-Ovalle

Portrait of a Young Reader is a DNA portrait that will be rendered on a vast scale in the new Bronx Regional Library Center. To create it, I'll work with the library staff and community representatives to select twelve boys and girls who'll participate in workshops and reading sessions on the topic of art portraiture and the effects of DNA on contemporary representation. With their parents' permission, the kids will gently rub the inside of their cheeks with a small, sterile brush, and take small samples of genetic material. From these dozen samples, I will randomly select one, so the actual identity of the person who becomes the subject of the portrait will remain unknown. Then that sample will be sent to a genetics lab for DNA analysis, which produces what looks like an abstract image, of genetic material. That image will provide me with visual information, and will serve as the basis of this large-scale artwork.

In effect, the resulting DNA portrait will be of an unknown young reader, but also a representative portrait of all the young participants and a reminder that all of us were once young readers, too. The huge piece will cover the walls of the library's main staircase and adjacent areas. Cylinders of colored glass, cut in various lengths and mounted on to a perforated metal backing, will present the scientific information from the genetic sample in an accurate, yet abstract, manner. And at the top of the stairs, in a black metal vitrine set into the wall, the original DNA sample of the anonymous young reader will be on display, along with information about the project. As library visitors move down and through this space they will, in a sense, be moving through the portrait, momentarily merging with both the portrait and the architecture.

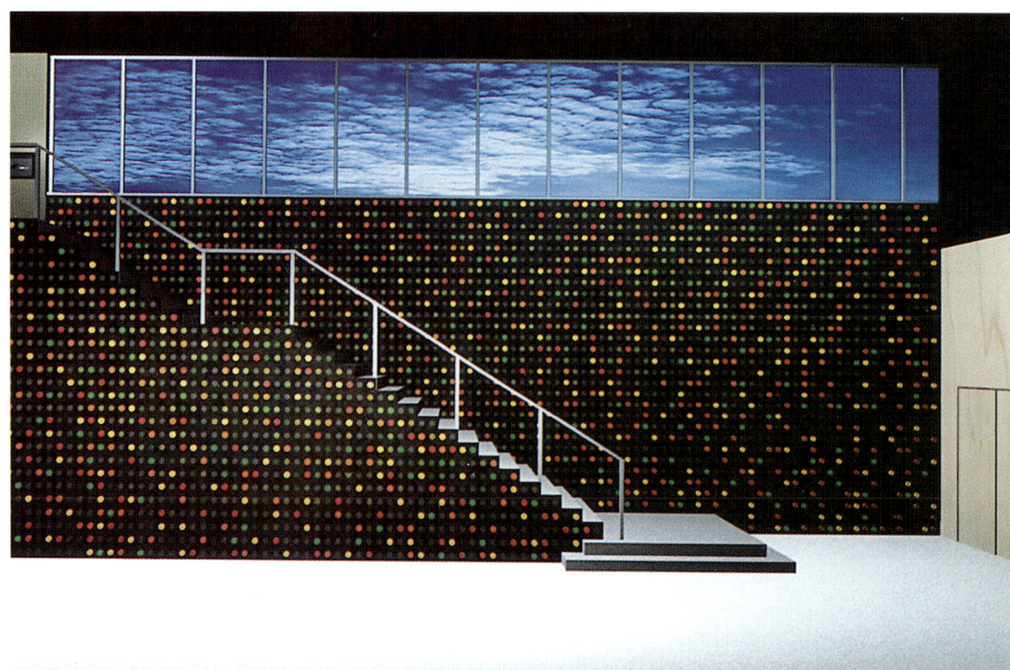

Inigo Manglano-Ovalle, Proposal for *Portrait of a Young Reader*, 2004, Bronx Regional Library Center.

This project is an exploration of DNA as a code, a catalogue, and a library, with volumes of information to be unlocked and stories to be written. The piece, made for a library, is meant to be challenging. When people talk about public art and suggest that there is a different public for art—with different needs and different capabilities—I shudder. I've never taken the position that in order to give something meaningful to "a public" you have to develop a language that they're capable of understanding. That is a really demeaning stance to take.

In this project, I'm doing something that a lot of art has done, and still does—questioning the very notion of existence. I'm interested in the science that's already become part of the larger cultural language. What I'm trying to suggest, in this public space, is a series of questions about the very existence of genetic technology, and about our role in developing and making use of it. But I have failed if a viewer's experience of my piece is dependent on their prior understanding of DNA or genetics. This work has to hit you first as an artwork, something to experience. And if it generates meaning to you, and you want to investigate further the ideas it suggests, that's fine, too.

Courtyard Design
1995
Stamped concrete, steel seating, plantings

Public School 3,
2100 La Fontaine Avenue

ARCHITECT
Perkins & Will
DESIGN AGENCY
School Construction Authority
SPONSOR AGENCY
Board of Education

Vito Acconci redesigned the courtyard of P.S. 3 to reflect the architectural elements of the school building. Benches and planters represent the windows, and designs in the pavement represent other elements of the school's façade. The result is an enhanced architectural environment wherein, as the artist describes, "the walls that enclose the children inside become the ground that children walk over and play on, outside."

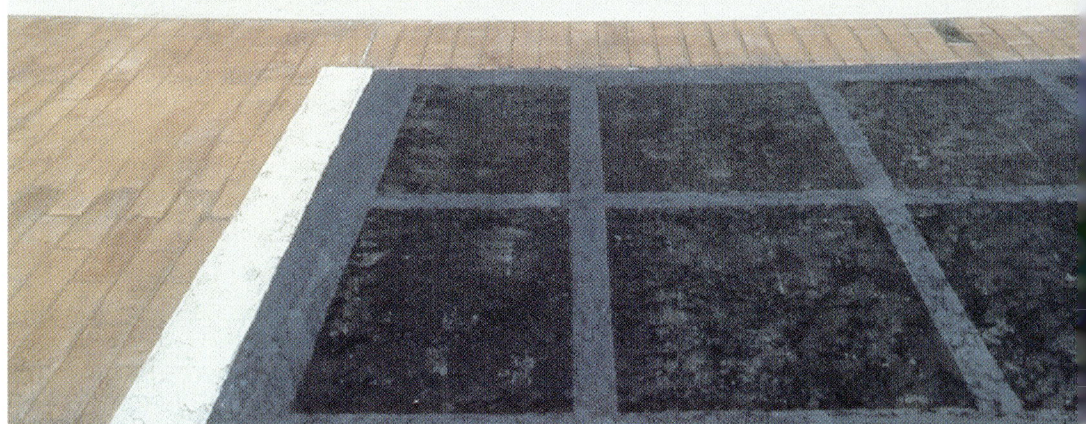

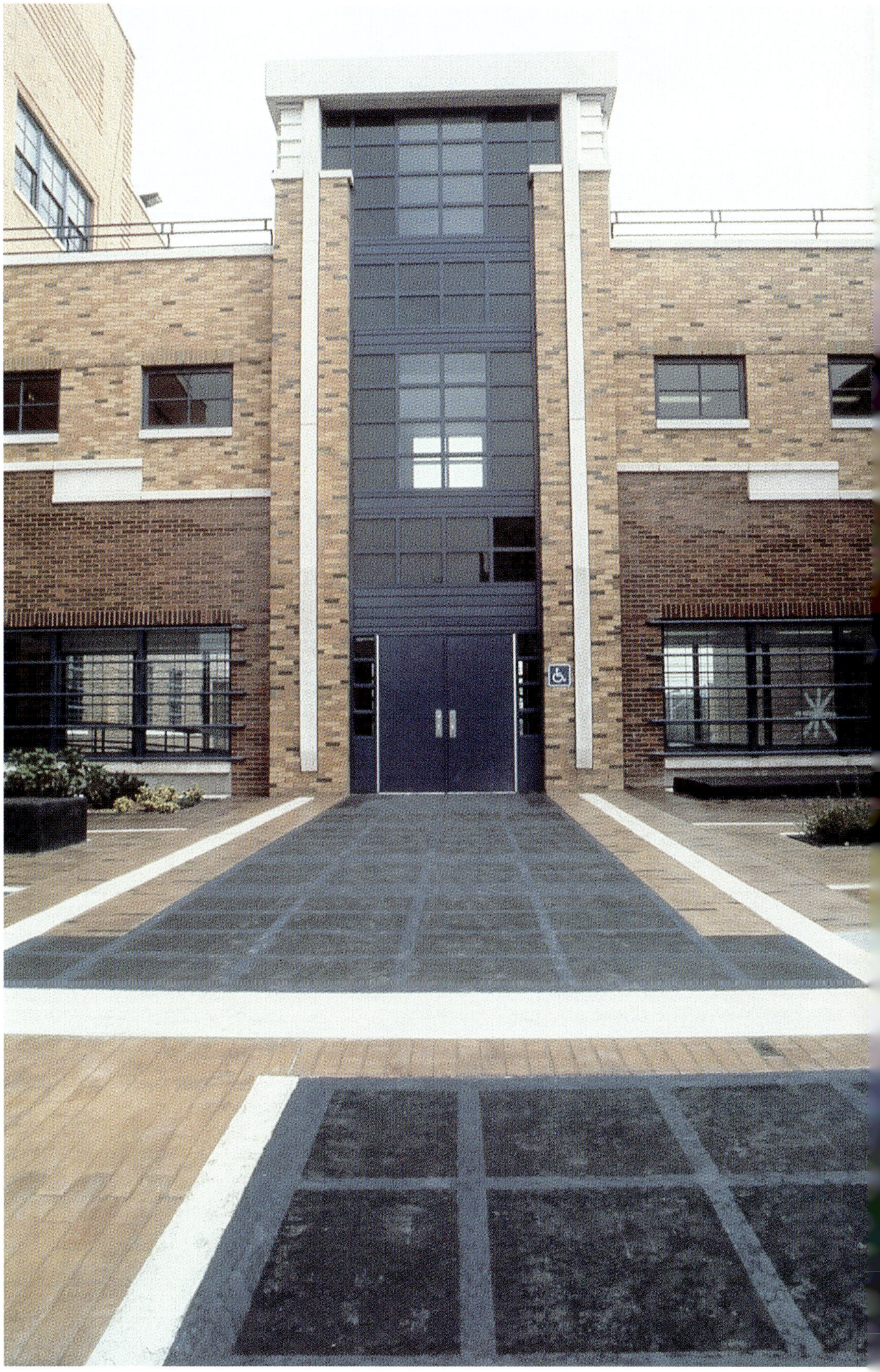

Vito Acconci

Daleesha, Toby and Raymond, and **Corey**
1991
Painted bronze

Commissioned for Police Precinct 44, 169th Street and Jerome Avenue
Currently located at Socrates Sculpture Park, Queens

ARCHITECT/DESIGN AGENCY
Department of General Services
SPONSOR AGENCY
Police Department

Originally commissioned for the 44th Police Precinct, John Ahearn's painted bronze sculptures, *Daleesha, Toby and Raymond,* and *Corey,* were based on actual residents of the precinct's South Bronx neighborhood. The sculptures, which were created from plaster life-casts, were placed on three separate pedestals in front of the precinct, but were removed soon after they were installed because of objections from members of the community. The artwork is currently on display at Socrates Sculpture Park in Queens.

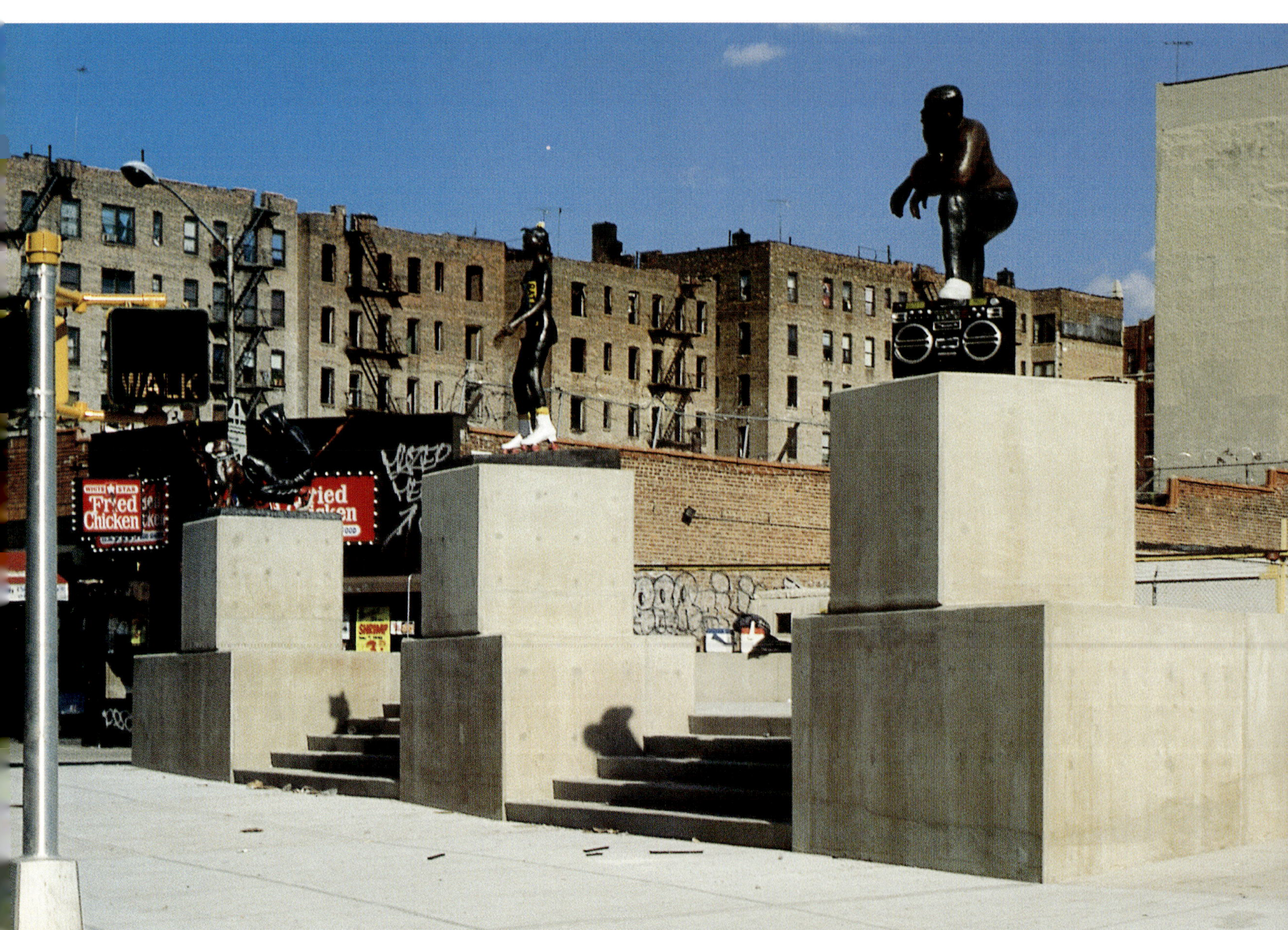

John Ahearn

Candida Alvarez

What Do You See?
1994
Hand-blown antique glass, lead, bronze

Public School 306,
40 West Tremont Avenue

ARCHITECT/DESIGN AGENCY
School Construction Authority
SPONSOR AGENCY
Board of Education

Located on several floors of P.S. 306 (known as P.S. 206 when the piece was commissioned), Candida Alvarez's work consists of six banks of windows containing a total of forty-eight individual glass panels. Alvarez integrated subject matter drawn from the middle-school curriculum into the panels, including imagery taken from life science, earth science, and mathematics classes. For example, the windows on the fourth floor explore mathematical concepts and use geometric shapes to lead students to discover polygons, angles, diagonals, and various units of measure. On the third floor, the windows focus on basic human life systems, with images that suggest the workings of the human body.

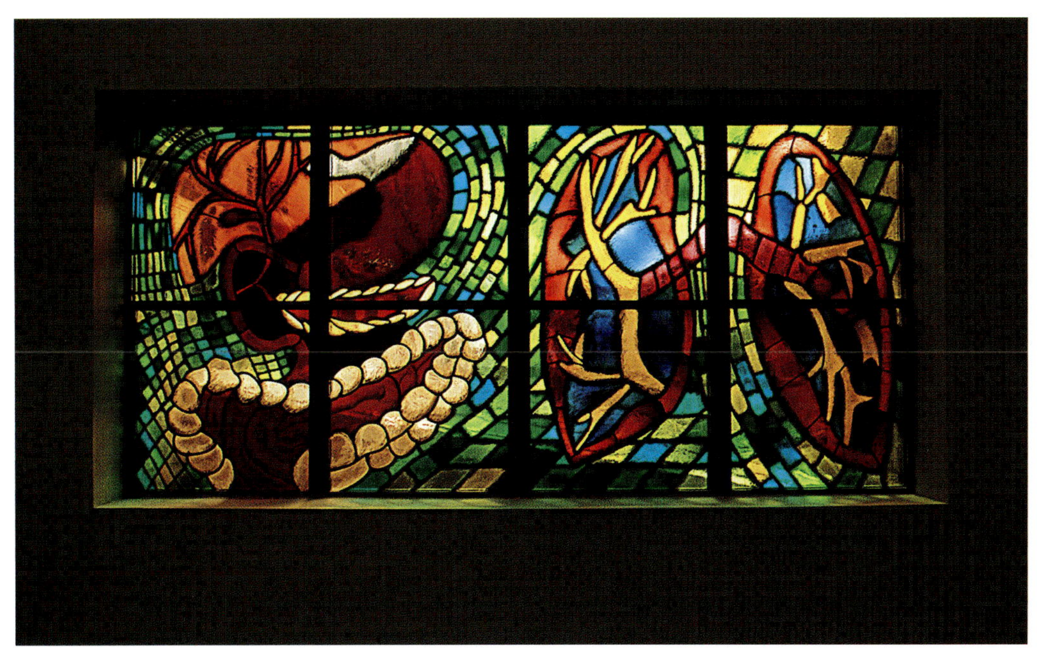

Andrea Arroyo

Harmony I and **Harmony II**
1994
Fiberglass

Public School 306,
40 West Tremont Avenue

ARCHITECT/DESIGN AGENCY
School Construction Authority
SPONSOR AGENCY
Board of Education

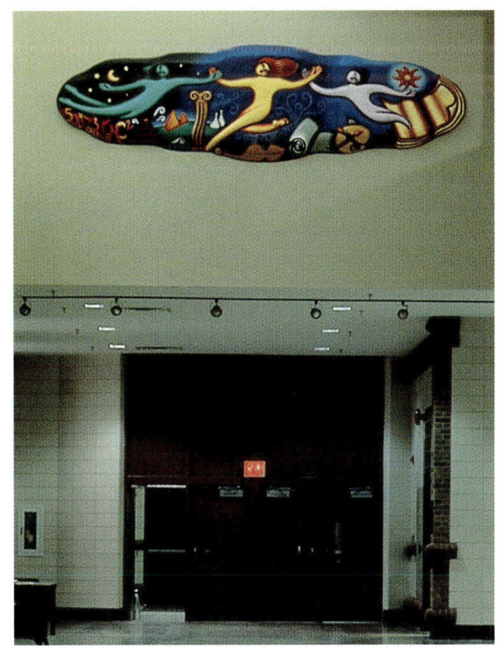

Andrea Arroyo combined painting and sculpture in these two lyrical, vibrantly colored fiberglass reliefs for P.S. 306 (formerly known as P.S. 206). *Harmony I* features two figures, a man and a woman, supporting an image of the Earth flanked by a cityscape on one side and images from nature on the other. *Harmony II* (left) depicts three limber figures floating among symbols of music, art, and science. The theme of Arroyo's work, as the titles suggest, is harmony—between nature and the city, and between different races and cultures.

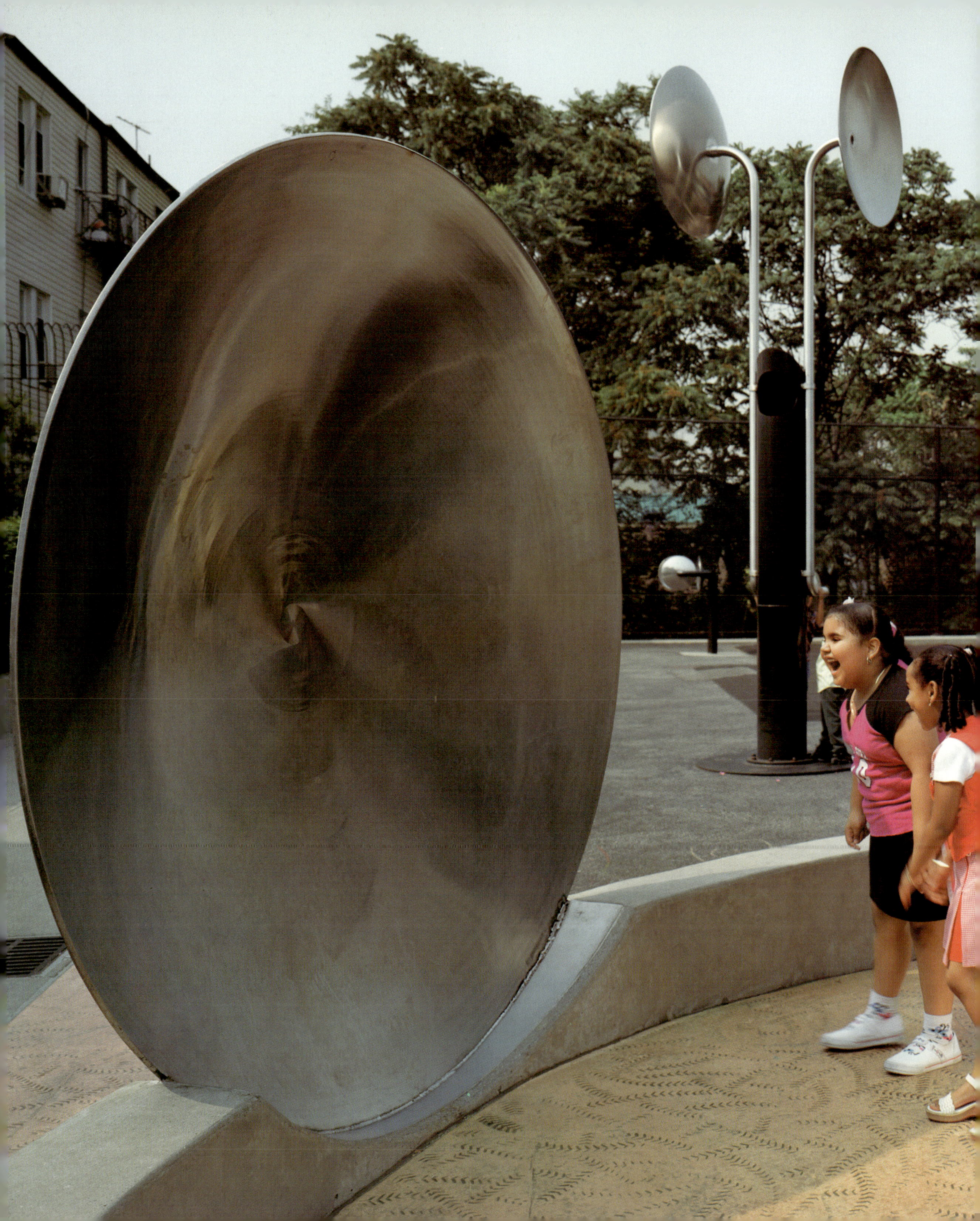

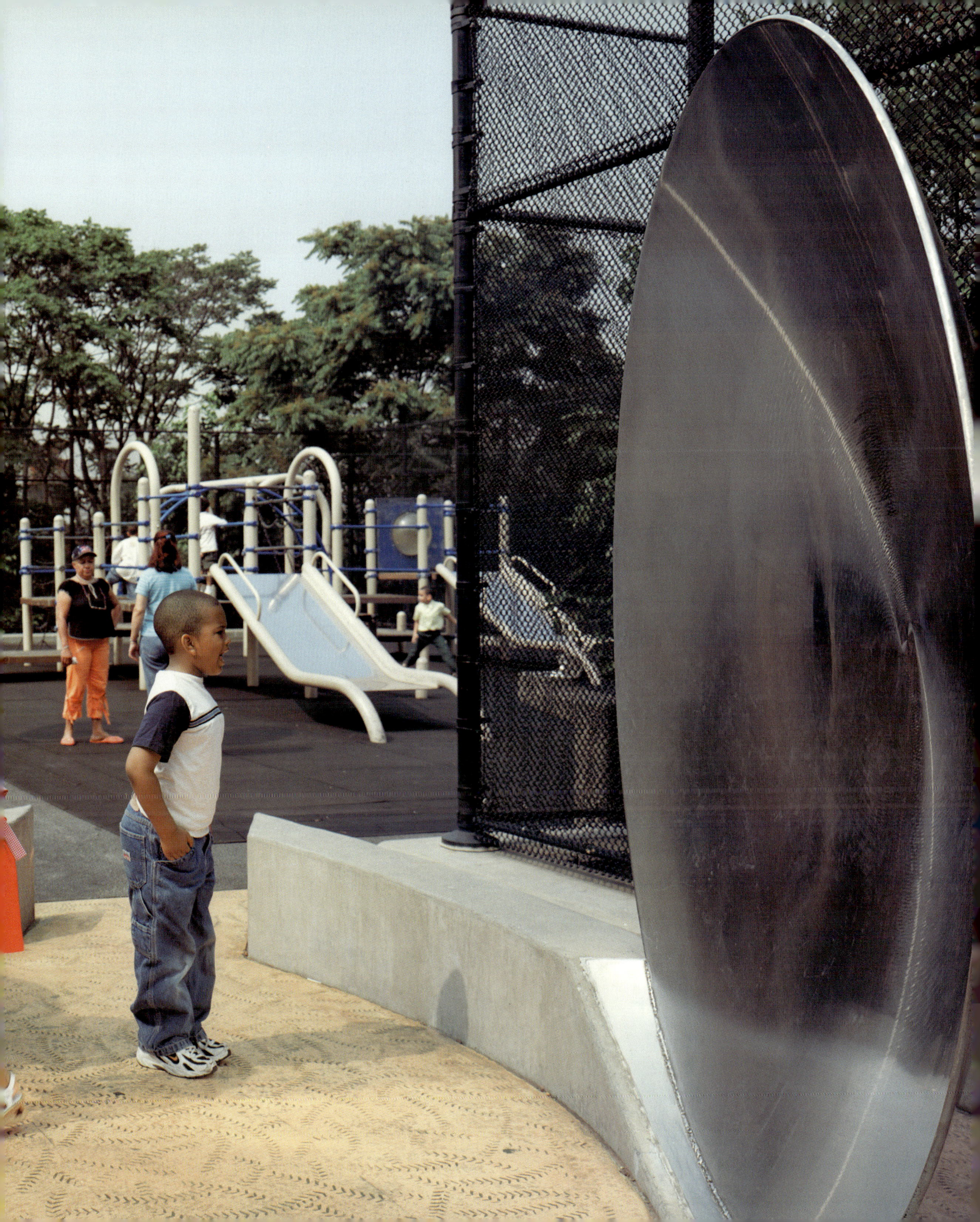

Monica Banks

Louisa and **Rusty**
2002
Steel

Hunts Point Recreation Center,
765 Manida Street

ARCHITECT
Castro-Blanco Piscioneri Associates/Hanrahan and Meyers
DESIGN AGENCY
Department of Design and Construction
SPONSOR AGENCY
Department of Parks and Recreation

Monica Banks created two large steel sculptures for the Hunts Point Recreation Center: *Louisa* (right), a horse located by the indoor basketball court, and *Rusty*, a dog located in the lobby near the front desk. Both sculptures were forged from continuous steel rods, and each resembles a three-dimensional line drawing. The artist has explained that, by installing these "functionless" sculptures at a recreation center, she hoped to inspire children's interest in creating and admiring works of art.

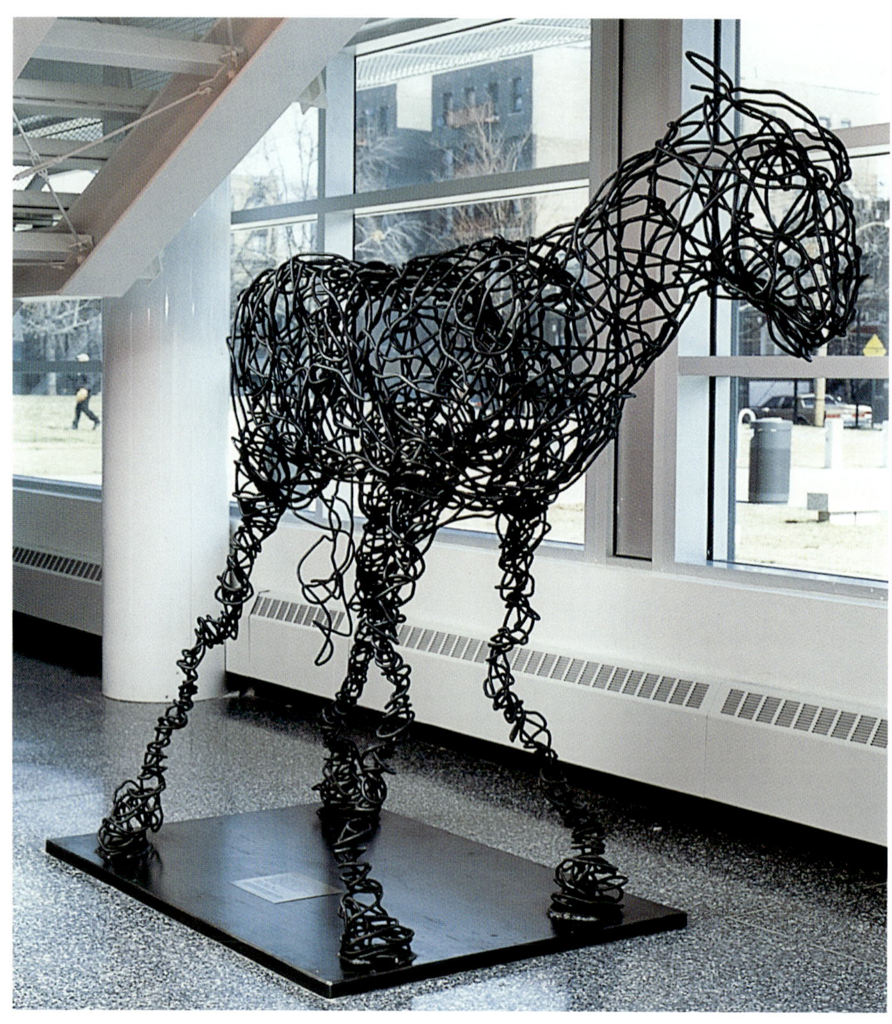

Bill and Mary Buchen

Sound Playground (previous pages)
1992
Bronze, concrete, steel

Public School 23,
2151 Washington Avenue

ARCHITECT
Perkins & Will
DESIGN AGENCY
School Construction Authority
SPONSOR AGENCY
Board of Education

Bill and Mary Buchen designed the landscaping, seating, and textured paving of *Sound Playground* to create several distinct outdoor areas where children can explore acoustic and visual phenomena. The bronze tables and seats double as hollow drums for communal music-making. The *Parabolic Bench* invites children up an inclined walkway toward two large stainless-steel dishes. When they clap their hands or sing, sound waves bounce between the two dishes until they are silenced by a wave of the hand. The sculpture *Big Eyes/Big Ears*, which is 17 feet (5.2 m) tall, transmits sounds as the children peer into a rotating periscope to view an image of the planet Earth 6 feet (1.8 m) above their heads. *Echo Chamber* invites children to speak into an acoustic sculpture and listen to their voices reverberate through an underground acoustic chamber in which rainwater collects. Small wind-bells chime across the top of a chain-link fence, and the large bells on the school roof can be programmed to play songs composed by the students and teachers.

Traces
1999
Lacquered magnesium, aluminum
Melody in 1's and 0's
1999
Glass interlaid with digital prints

Walton High School,
2780 Reservoir Avenue

ARCHITECT
Lev Zetlin Associates
DESIGN AGENCY
School Construction Authority
SPONSOR AGENCY
Board of Education

John Fekner's two multimedia installations are located in the lobby of Walton High School. For *Traces*, Fekner asked Walton students and teachers to nominate individuals they thought had made important artistic and humanistic contributions to society. The artist then created portraits of the nominated individuals on lacquered magnesium plates alongside the students' and teachers' signatures. Featured figures include the Puerto Rican poet Julia de Burgos, Walt Disney, and Rosalyn Yalow, a Walton graduate and the first woman to win a Nobel prize in medicine. Fekner's second installation, *Melody in 1's and 0's* (below), consists of laminated glass panels that depict the inner thoughts of a boy writing a love song. Represented in the panels are a young girl, the boy's local neighborhood, and fragments of classical instruments.

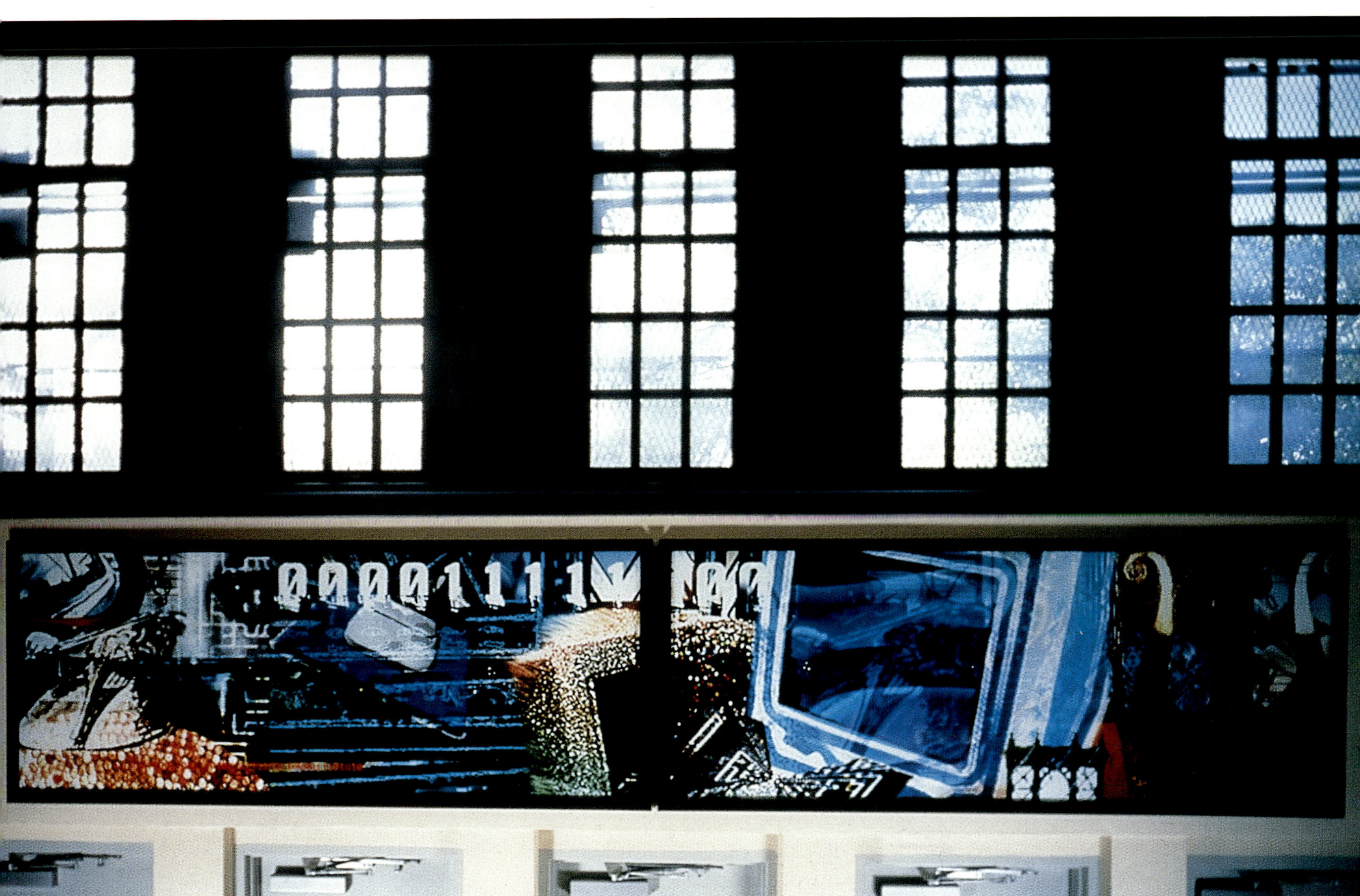

John Fekner

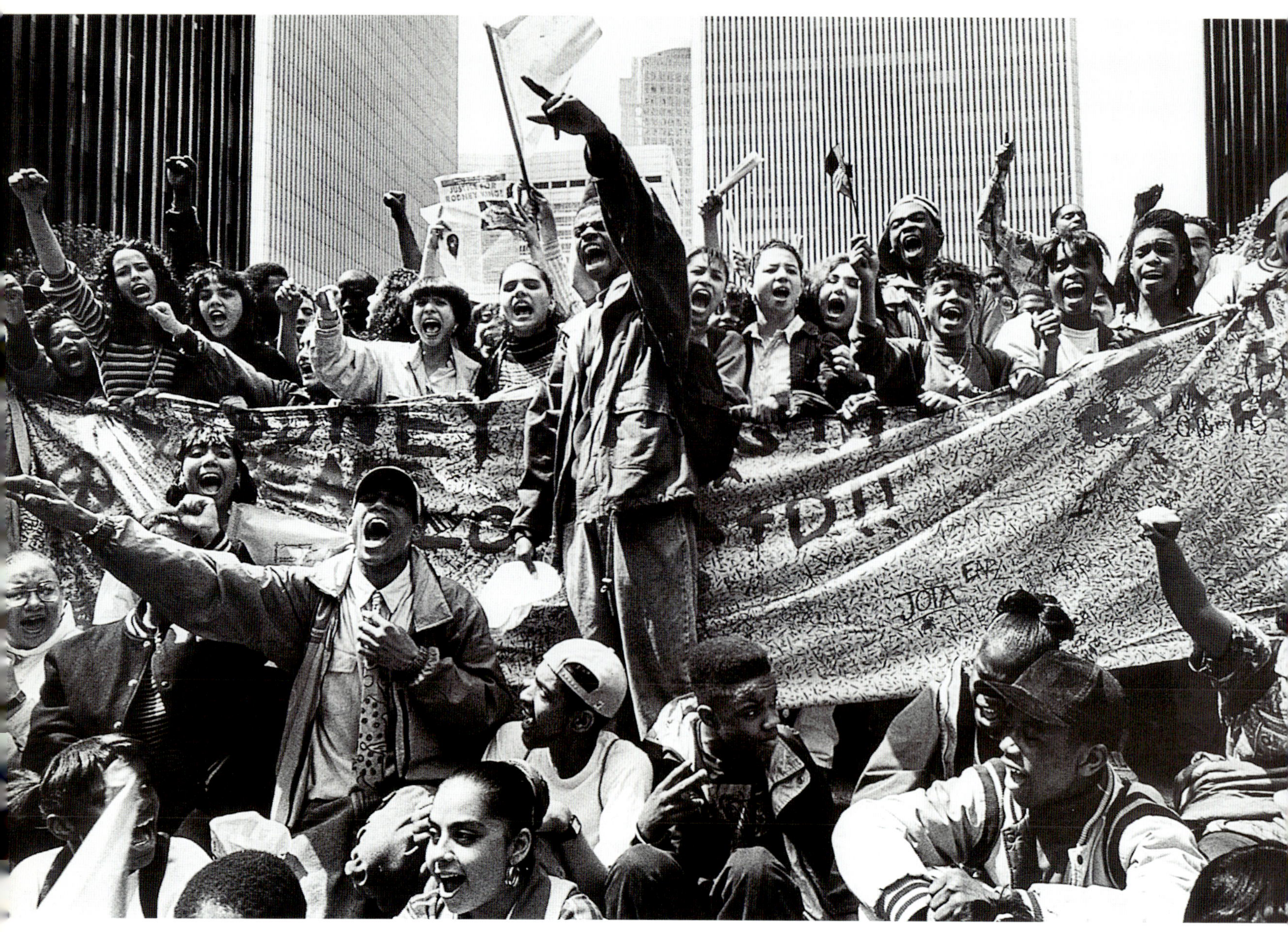

Ricky Flores

License to Dream
1995
Gelatin silver prints

Public School 306,
40 West Tremont Avenue

ARCHITECT/DESIGN AGENCY
School Construction Authority
SPONSOR AGENCY
Board of Education

Twenty-six of Ricky Flores's gelatin silver prints hang in the vestibule of the auditorium at P.S. 306 (formerly P.S. 206); three additional prints are displayed in the school's main office. The photographs depict both scenes from everyday life in New York City and events of political significance, such as a peaceful student demonstration held after the Rodney King verdict in Los Angeles. The installation also features a statement by the artist: "*License to Dream* is the right to build a better tomorrow, to ask questions that will define boundaries and to seek ways to surpass them. It's the right to not be limited by what history and society have imposed upon us, but to challenge those constraints to the best of our abilities, to redefine those limits, to go beyond them."

Walton Ford

The Call and **Inside-Out**
1999
Acrylic on canvas

Jane Addams Vocational High School,
900 Tinton Avenue

ARCHITECT
Paino/Soffres Architects
DESIGN AGENCY
School Construction Authority
SPONSOR AGENCY
Board of Education

Drawing from students' research into the lives of historical figures, Walton Ford painted two murals for the Jane Addams Vocational High School. *The Call* (right), a circular ceiling mural located in the school's lobby, depicts Dr. Charles Drew, the doctor credited with desegregating the Red Cross blood supply; Madame C.J. Walker, an early female entrepreneur in cosmetics; the civil rights activist Rosa Parks; and the Mexican painter Frida Kahlo. The figures appear to be looking down, offering students notes, flowers, and ladders. For the school's auditorium, Ford painted *Inside-Out*, a two-part mural that flanks the stage and features mythical figures, such as Artemis, the Greek goddess of the hunt; Horus, the Sun god of Egypt; and Ixchel, the Mayan spirit of healing.

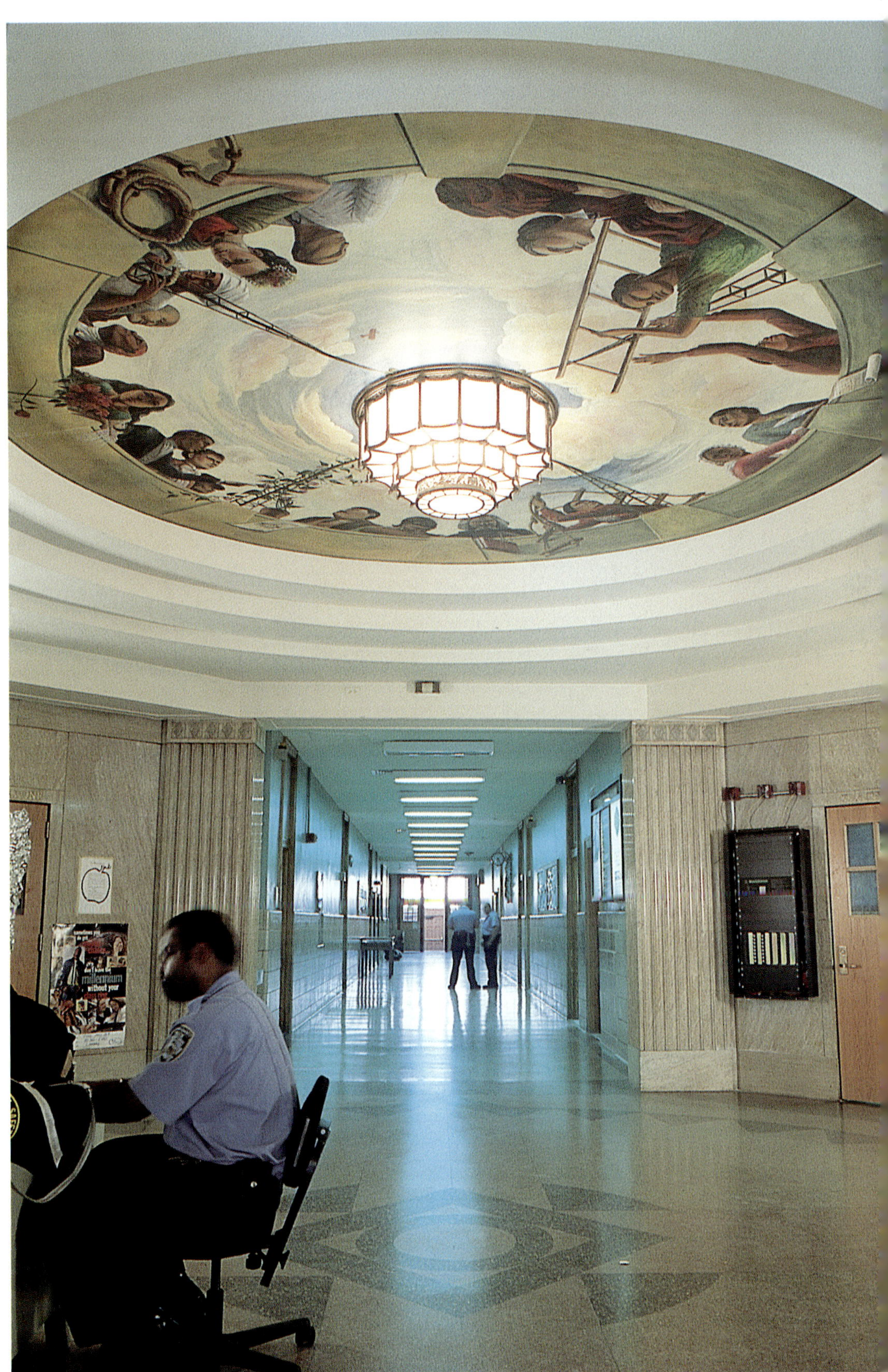

Noah Jemisin

Leaf Over My Shoulder
1998
Acrylic on canvas, watercolor on paper, stainless steel

Davidson Avenue Daycare Center, 1810 Davidson Avenue

ARCHITECT/DESIGN AGENCY
Department of General Services
SPONSOR AGENCY
Agency for Child Development

The four paintings and suspended sculpture that comprise Noah Jemisin's *Leaf Over My Shoulder* were inspired by the artist's years of collecting and studying children's artwork. The pieces, which include images of a carousel, a Ferris wheel, horses, and swimmers, mimic the fantastical elements common in children's artwork. The artist intented that the project would speak to children in their own familiar artistic language and inspire their imagination and creativity. "My hope is that one day a great young Bronx artist will evolve from being inspired by these works," Jemisin has said.

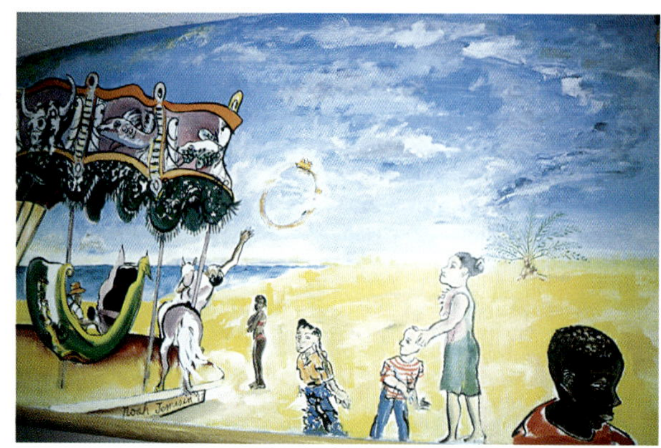

Kristin Jones and Andrew Ginzel

Encyclic
2004
Stainless steel, marble, glass, mixed media

Public School 102, 1827 Archer Street

ARCHITECT/DESIGN AGENCY
School Construction Authority
SPONSOR AGENCY
Board of Education

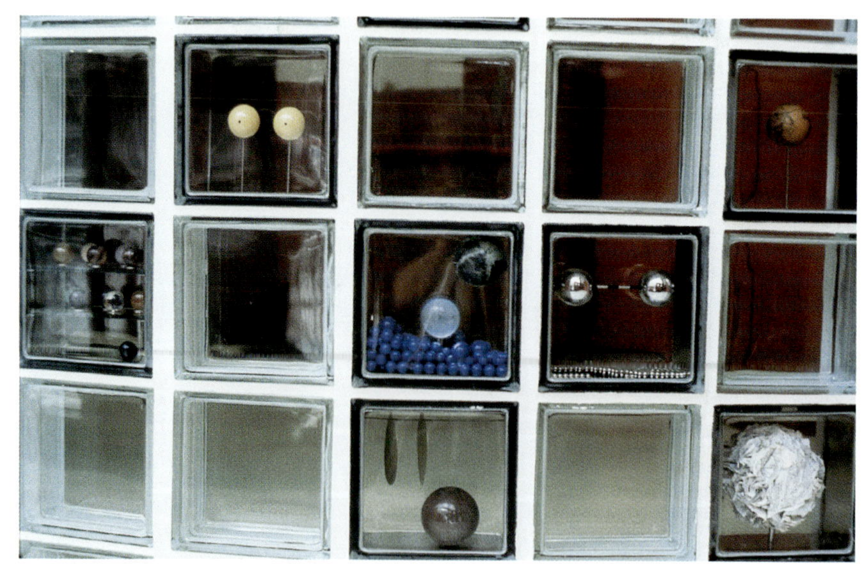

Kristin Jones and Andrew Ginzel created several projects for both the exterior and interior of P.S. 102, which are collectively entitled *Encyclic*. On the Taylor Avenue entrance, the artists inserted a pair of small doors between the exising pair of full-scale doors. They intended this miniaturized entrance-way, which is inset with circular lenses, to serve as a metaphor for innocence and the growth students experience throughout their time in grade school. In addition, the artists etched question marks into glass blocks on the school's façade, highlighting the school's role as a place of questioning and discovery. Inside the school, within a wall made from hollow glass blocks, the artists installed an array of small balls, made of metal, glass, or stone. These balls, collected from around the world, are meant to suggest planetary and geological discovery. Models of planets of various sizes and materials are also mounted on walls throughout the school. Each is inscribed with a single word relating to learning and curiosity, such as "why," "how," "seek," "ask," "question," "explore," "examine," and "look."

Liberty and **Liberty as Justice**
1998
Oil on canvas

Bronx Housing Court,
1118 Grand Concourse

ARCHITECT
Rafael Vinoly Architects
DESIGN AGENCY
Department of Design and Construction
SPONSOR AGENCY
Office of Court Administration

Located in the Bronx Housing Court, Vitaly Komar and Alexander Melamid's two paintings, *Liberty* and *Liberty as Justice*, explore iconoclasm by reinterpreting and conflating classic images of American freedom—the Statue of Liberty and Lady Justice. *Liberty* is a traditional representation of the statue transposed on to a bright red background. *Liberty as Justice* (right) depicts the Statue of Liberty blindfolded and holding the scales of justice.

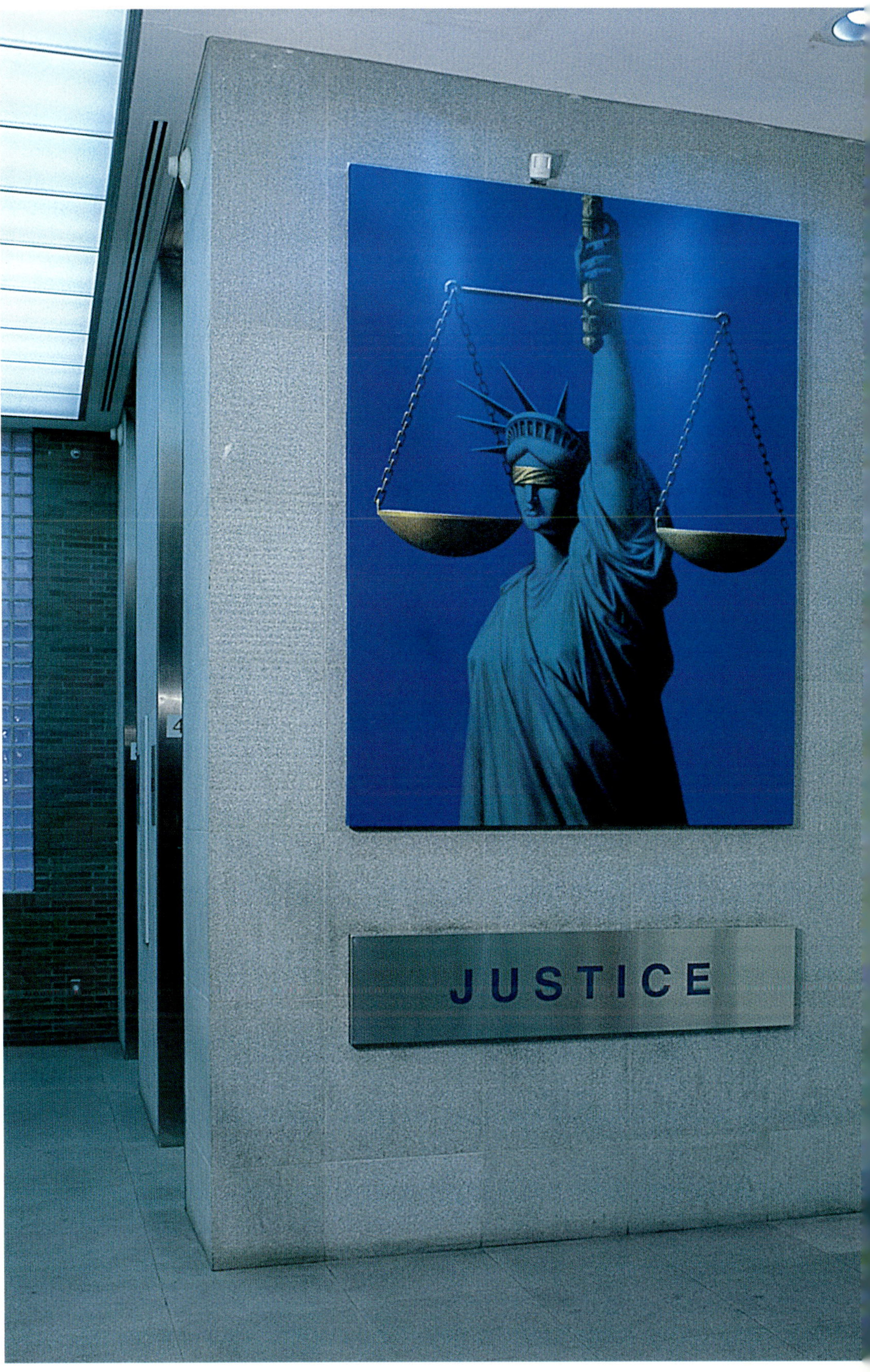

Vitaly Komar and Alexander Melamid

Justen Ladda

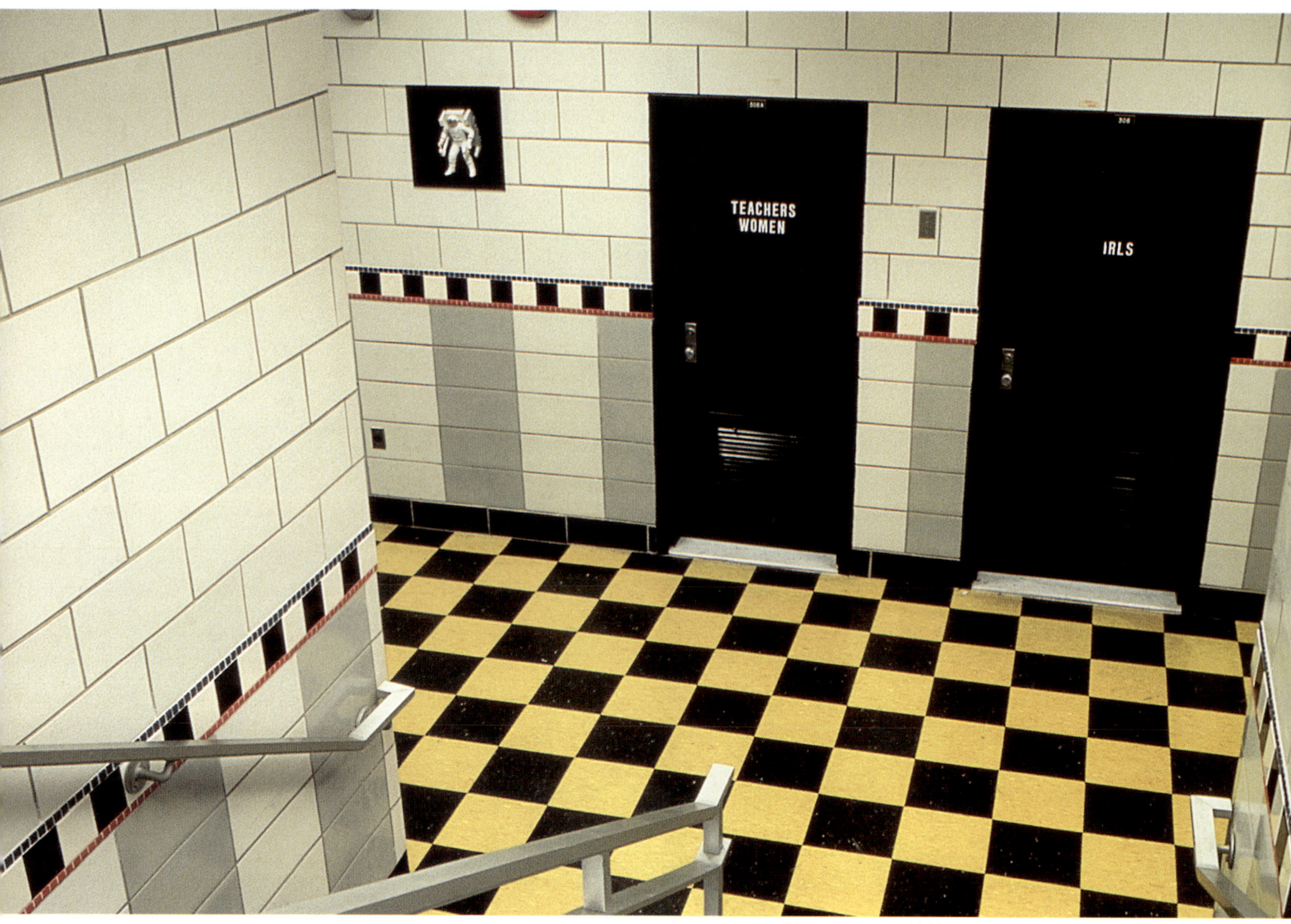

Untitled
1991
Painted bronze, glazed tile, glass mosaic

Public School 7,
3201 Kingsbridge Avenue

ARCHITECT/SPONSOR AGENCY
Board of Education
DESIGN AGENCY
School Construction Authority

Art Commission Award for Excellence in Design 1991

For P.S. 7's new wing, Justen Ladda created colorful floor and wall tiles for the hallways, restrooms, stairwells, and classrooms. The artist also designed mosaic panels, each illustrating a different landscape—waterfalls, mountain ranges, and seascapes. These were fabricated off-site and installed over the drinking fountains.

Water
1995
Glazed tile, mosaic

Public School 72, 2951 Dewey Avenue

ARCHITECT
Fleming Corporation
DESIGN AGENCY
School Construction Authority
SPONSOR AGENCY
Board of Education

Inspired by the water-bound Throg's Neck neighborhood, Ladda created a series of mosaic murals featuring water motifs for P.S. 72. The mosaics are installed throughout the school's hallways and depict a coral reef underwater scene, a seascape, and a surfer on a huge wave. Other mosaics located along a hallway and staircase feature a Greek key ornament.

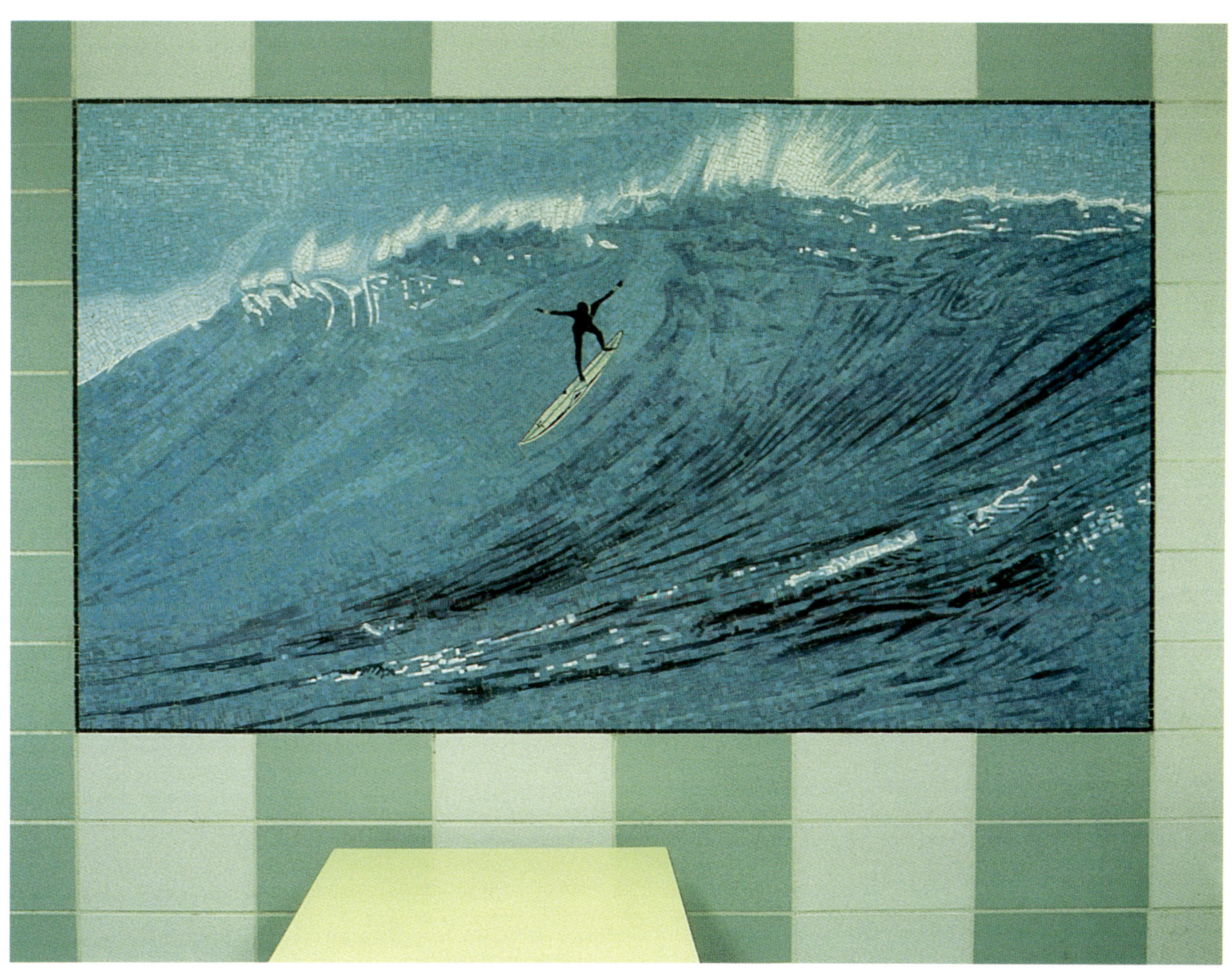

Justen Ladda

Gregg LeFevre

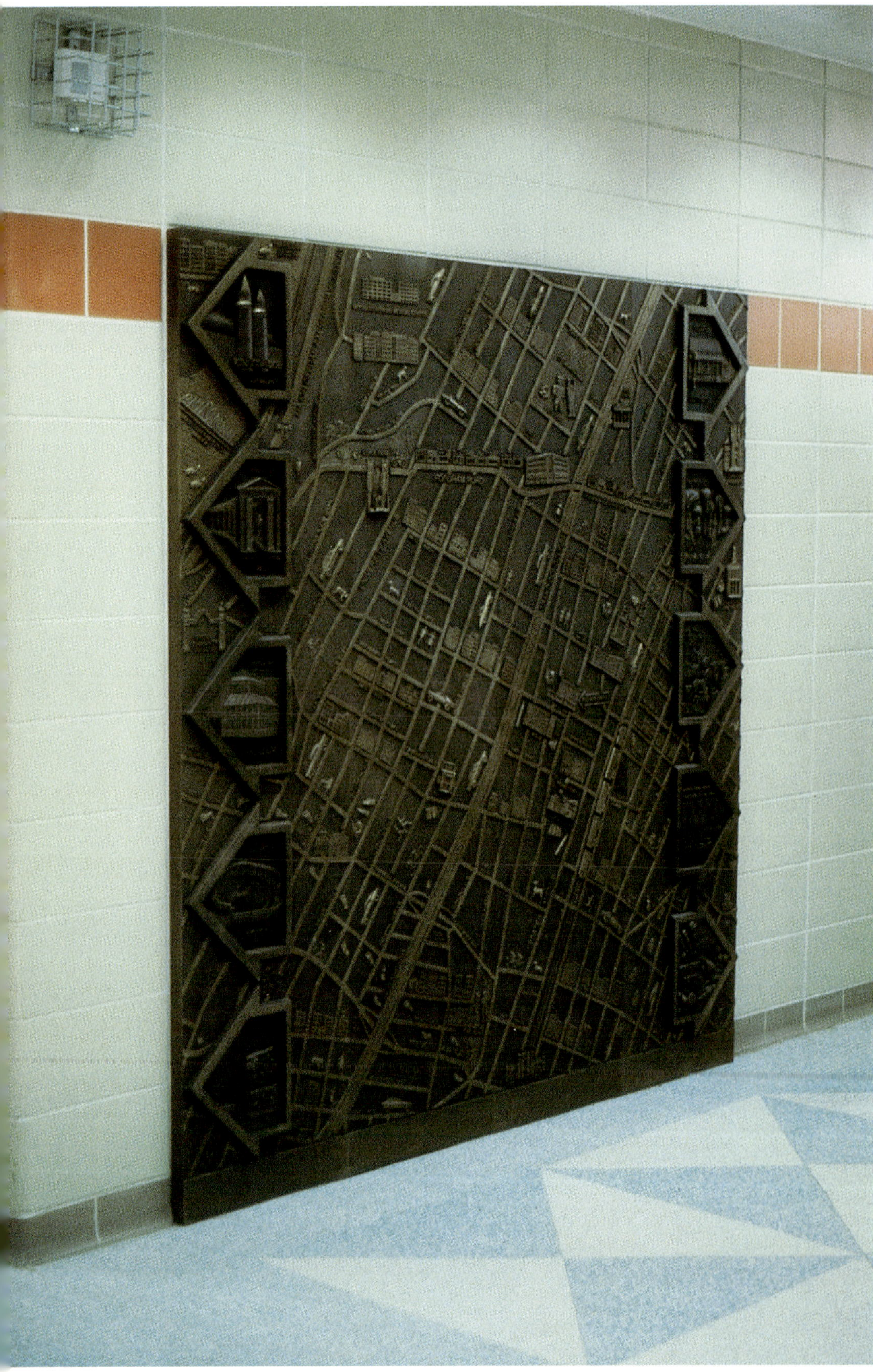

The Bronx
1994
Bronze

Public School 209, 313 East 183rd Street

ARCHITECT/DESIGN AGENCY
School Construction Authority
SPONSOR AGENCY
Board of Education

At P.S. 209, Gregg LeFevre created a large-scale bronze map of the school's environs, illustrated with over two hundred relief carvings designed in collaboration with forty students. The map, entitled simply *The Bronx,* includes dozens of hand-carved details that reveal aspects of the history and character of the borough. The work incorporates ten landmarks from around the borough, visible in arrow-shaped insets on either side of the map.

Steven Mayo

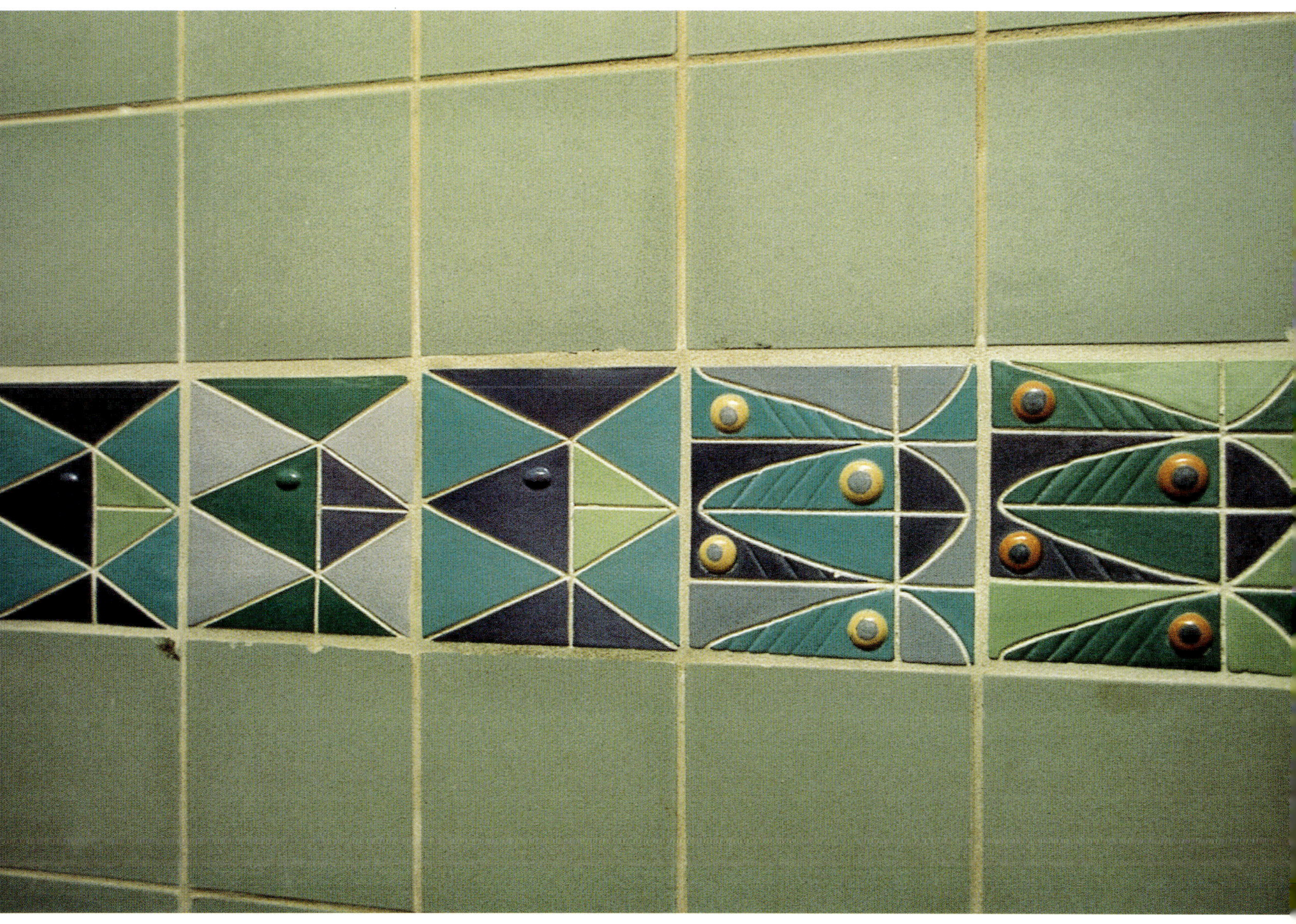

Pets
1996
Ceramic relief

Public School 11 Annex,
1399 Ogden Avenue

ARCHITECT
Castro-Blanco Piscioneri Associates
DESIGN AGENCY
School Construction Authority
SPONSOR AGENCY
Board of Education

For his work at P.S. 11 entitled *Pets*, Steven Mayo designed a series of ceramic tiles showing birds, fish, frogs, and lizards morphing into crocodiles and other reptiles. The artist employed soft pastel, tropical and earth-colored stains with a matte finish. He has said of the project: "I get so much from watching and working with the students. Each interaction is a learning experience where we bounce ideas off each other and meet new horizons."

Matt Mullican

Law, Government and Justice
2003
Oil-stick and paint on canvas, cast-stone relief

High School for Law, Government and Justice, 244 East 163rd Street

ARCHITECT
Hillier Architecture
DESIGN AGENCY
School Construction Authority
SPONSOR AGENCY
Department of Education

Matt Mullican's project at the High School for Law, Government and Justice explores the terms in the school's name. For the exterior of the school, the artist created a large-scale cast-stone relief featuring symbols of justice, such as a courthouse and jurors. For the interior lobby, he created an oil-stick rubbing on painted canvas that pairs these same symbols with images of scales, a star, and the figure of Lady Justice.

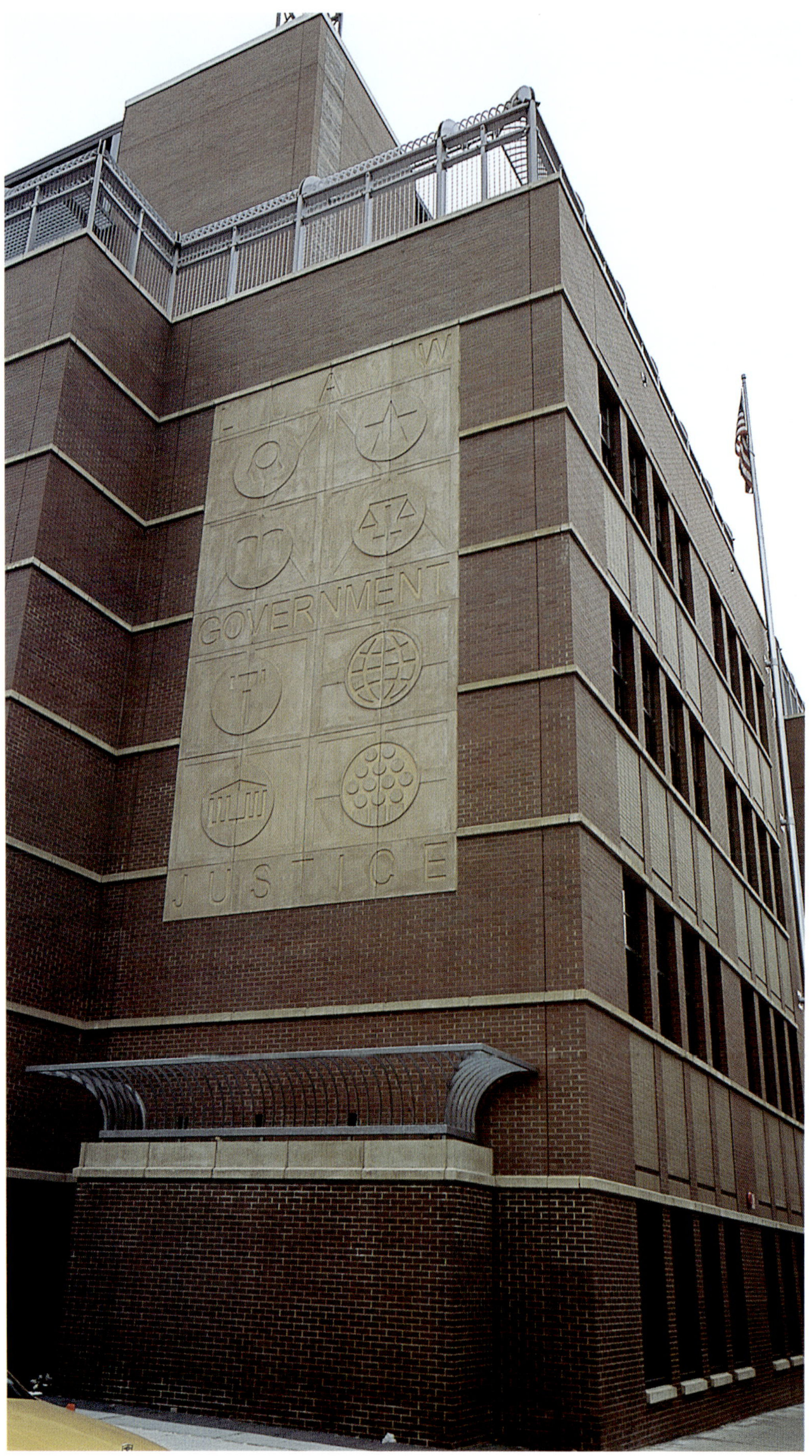

Twelve Sculptures for E.C.C. # 4
1997
Painted bronze

Public School 236 Annex,
1871 Walton Avenue

ARCHITECT
Castro-Blanco Piscioneri Associates
DESIGN AGENCY
School Construction Authority
SPONSOR AGENCY
Board of Education

Tom Nussbaum's installation at the P.S. 236 Annex, formerly known as Early Childhood Center # 4, consists of twelve small, brightly painted cast-bronze sculptures, each of them located in a niche adjacent to a classroom door. The sculptures depict small groups of children, adults, and animals in various relationships to each other. In one sculpture, for instance, a woman holds a little boy in her arms; in another, a bear reads a story to a girl sitting on his lap. Mounted at a child's eye-level, where they can easily and freely be touched, the pieces also serve as location markers for the children when they travel through the school's hallways.

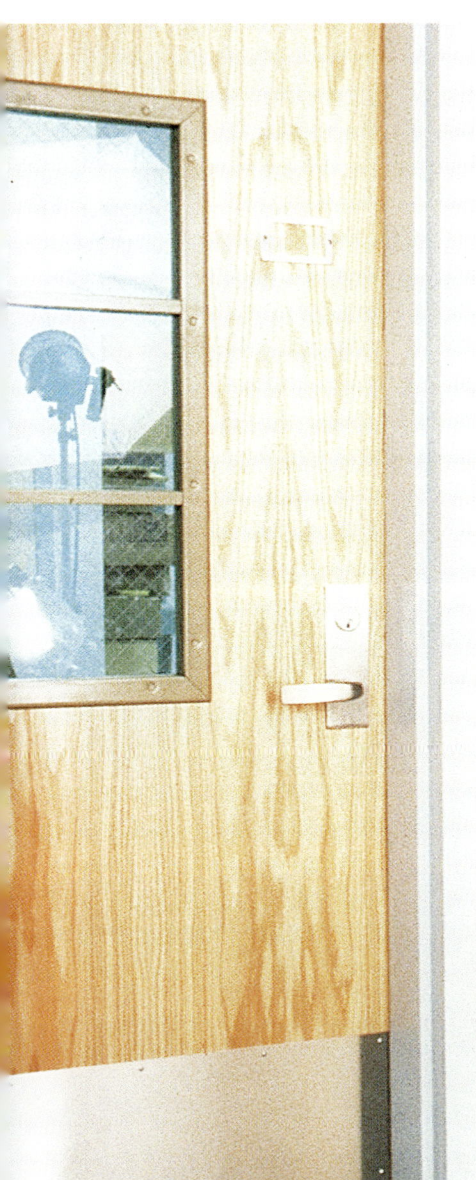

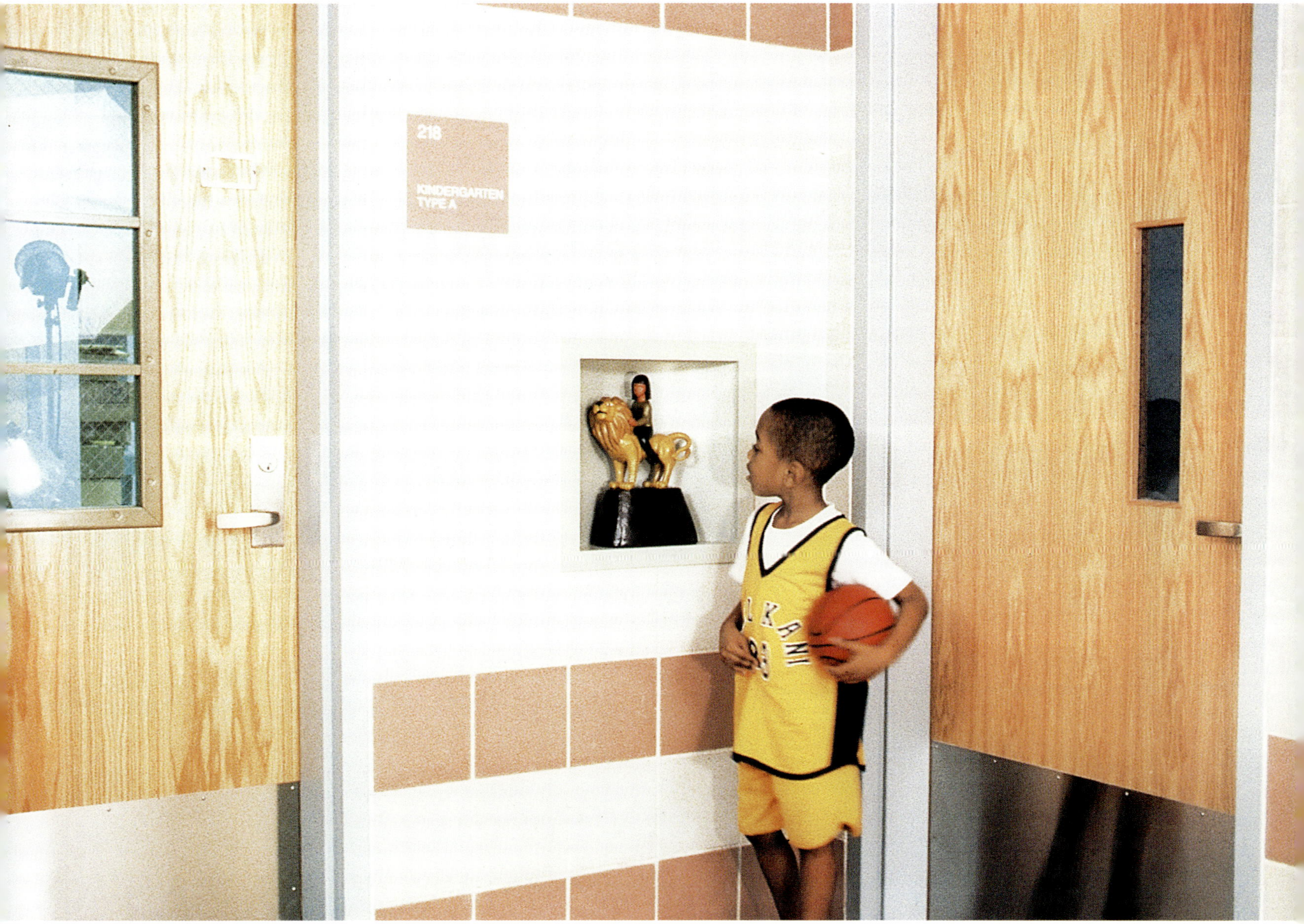

Tom Nussbaum

Open Voyage
1992
Aluminum

Public School 279, 2100 Walton Avenue

ARCHITECT
Perkins & Will
DESIGN AGENCY
School Construction Authority
SPONSOR AGENCY
Board of Education

Bob Rivera's *Open Voyage* is a multi-colored, freestanding aluminum sculpture that arches across the roof of the gymnasium of P.S. 279. The sculpture is constructed of pieces of aluminum bolted together. Through the varied use of open shapes and colors, the sculpture, which measures 19 × 40 feet (5.8 × 12.2 m), was designed to complement the surrounding architecture in the neighborhood.

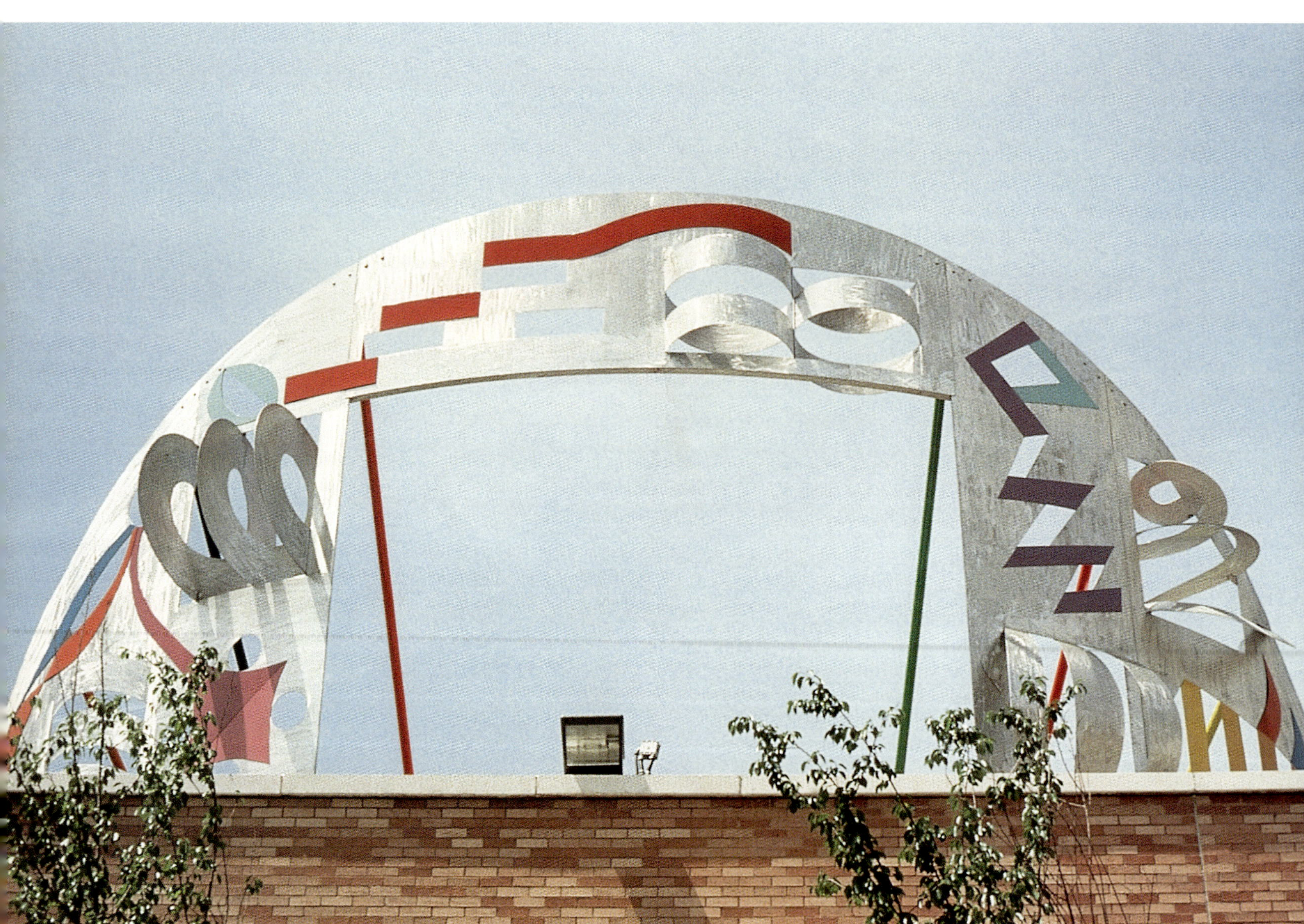

Bob Rivera

Freddy Rodriguez

The Garden
1995
Terra-cotta, granite, bronze

Public School 37, 360 West 230th Street

ARCHITECT
Liebman Melting Partnership
DESIGN AGENCY
School Construction Authority
SPONSOR AGENCY
Board of Education

Freddy Rodriguez's project for the entrance of P.S. 37 features three elliptical terra-cotta columns encircled by vines, flora, and insects. The artist also designed red and blue granite paving in the shape of a guitar. The design is further embellished by six bronze strips representing guitar strings.

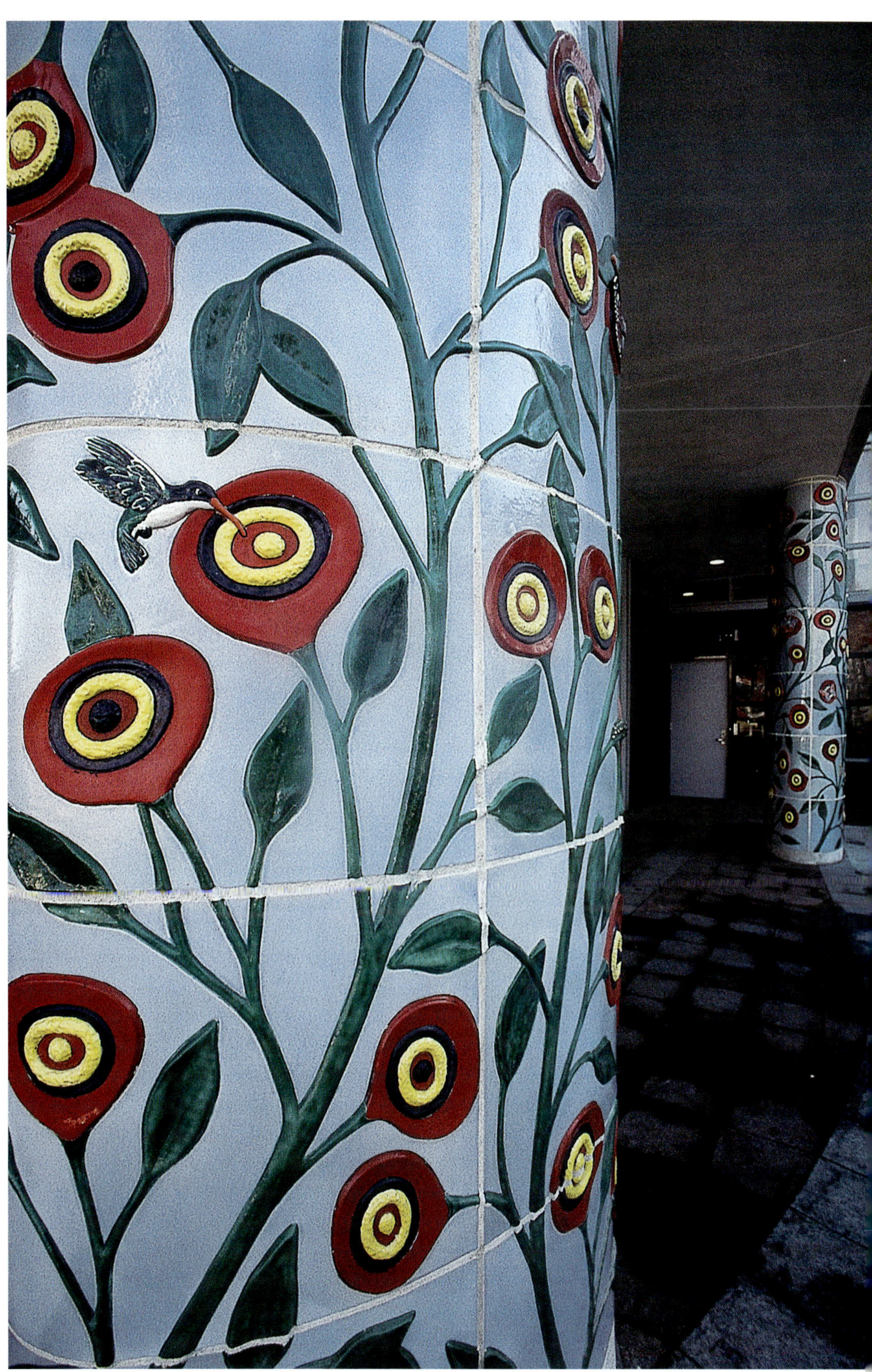

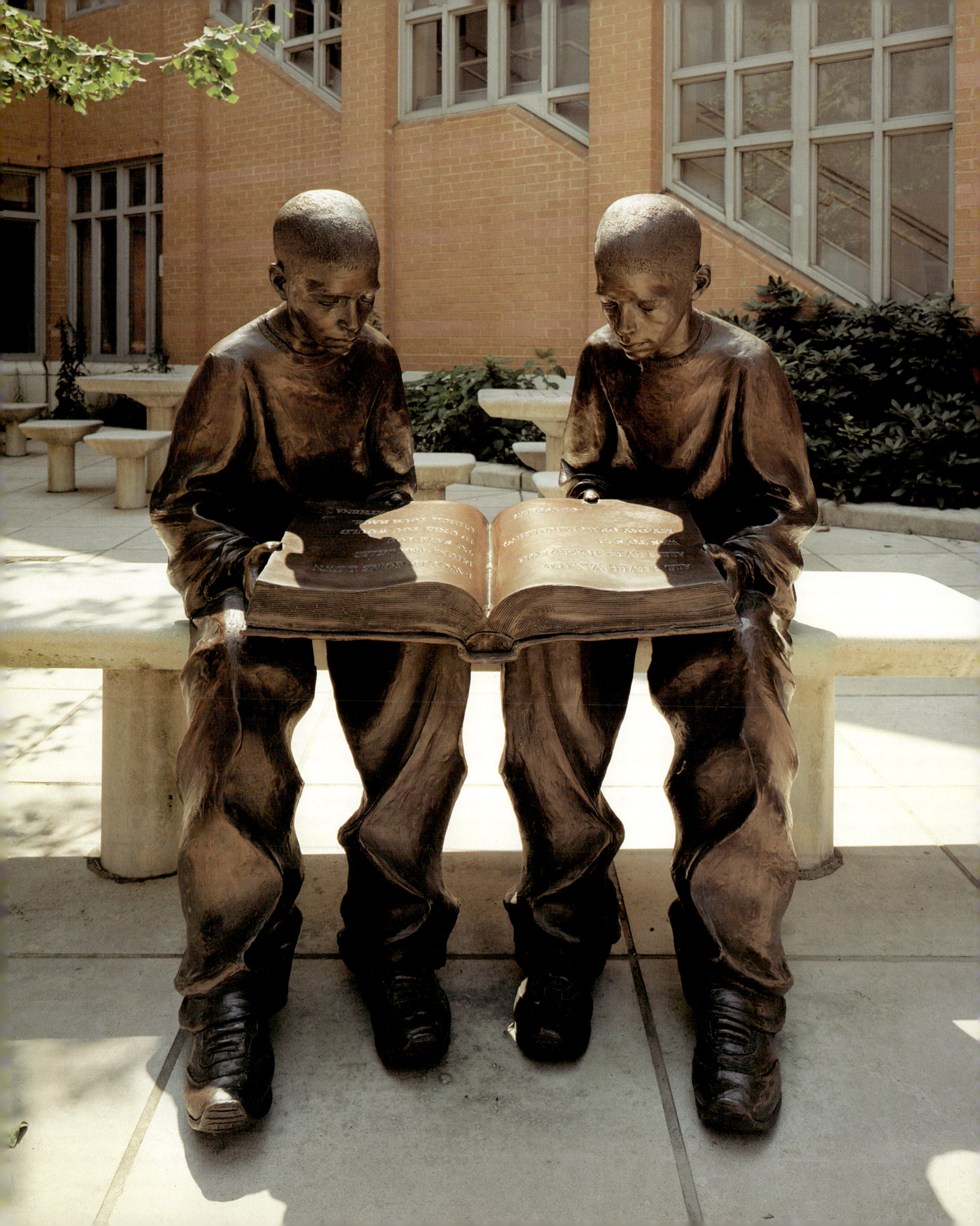

Tim Rollins + KOS

Achilles and Odysseus (opposite)
2001
Bronze, watercolor, oil and acrylic paint, marble, granite

Horizon Juvenile Center,
560 Brook Avenue

ARCHITECT
Kaplan McLaughlin Diaz
DESIGN AGENCY
Department of Design and Construction
SPONSOR AGENCY
Department of Juvenile Justice

Art Commission Award for Excellence in Design 1996

For their work at the Horizon Juvenile Center, Tim Rollins + KOS (Kids of Survival) drew from themes in the Greek epics *The Iliad* and *The Odyssey*. Based on the designs of young residents, the artists created three large paintings depicting Odysseus' arduous journey home. These paintings hang in the center's lobby. Rollins + KOS also composed, enlarged, and painted the residents' designs on to a background of actual book pages torn from copies of *The Odyssey*, and glued them on to stretched linen. In addition, the artists created a sculpture for the inner courtyard depicting two identical figures representing Achilles and Odysseus. The two young men, dressed in contemporary clothes, sit together reading a book. Two quotations are visible on the pages they read: one is the goddess Athena's words to Achilles, the other a self-reflection by Odysseus. The sculpture suggests that Achilles' self-destructive rage and Odysseus' capacity for self-redemption are the two parts of every human personality that benefit from concern, compassion, and love.

Christy Rupp

Time Flies
1997
Bronze, brass, copper, aluminum

Public School 4 Annex,
1717 Fulton Avenue

ARCHITECT
Castro-Bianco Piscioneri Associates
DESIGN AGENCY
School Construction Authority
SPONSOR AGENCY
Board of Education

Christy Rupp's *Time Flies*, located at the P.S. 4 Annex, is a series of sculptures of animals in bronze, brass, copper, and aluminum plate that encircle the two-sided clocks installed throughout the center's hallways. The artist has said that her goal was to "emphasize that even a city made of steel and concrete is a habitat. I'd like to help children to see their relationship to a larger environment, be it natural or man-made."

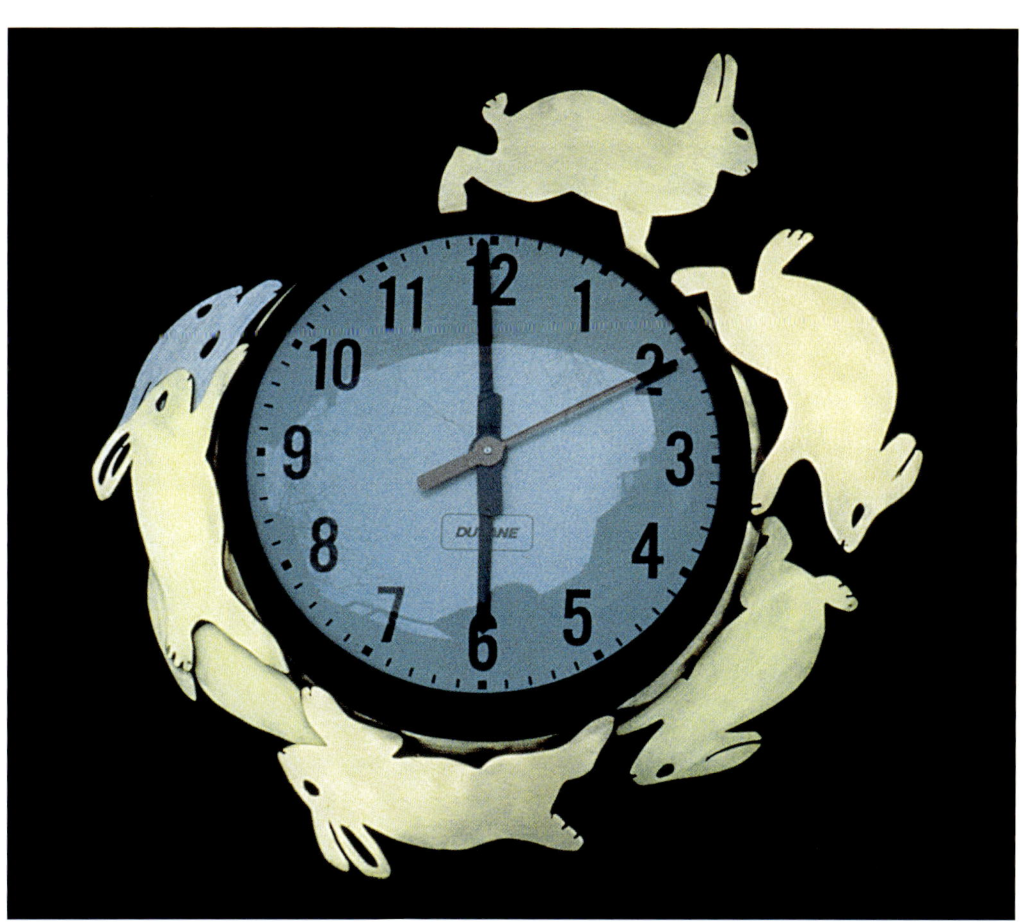

David Saunders

Firehat
1988
Aluminum

Firehouse for Engine Company 71, 720 Melrose Avenue

ARCHITECT
Stephen Kagel and Associates
DESIGN AGENCY
Department of General Services
SPONSOR AGENCY
Fire Department

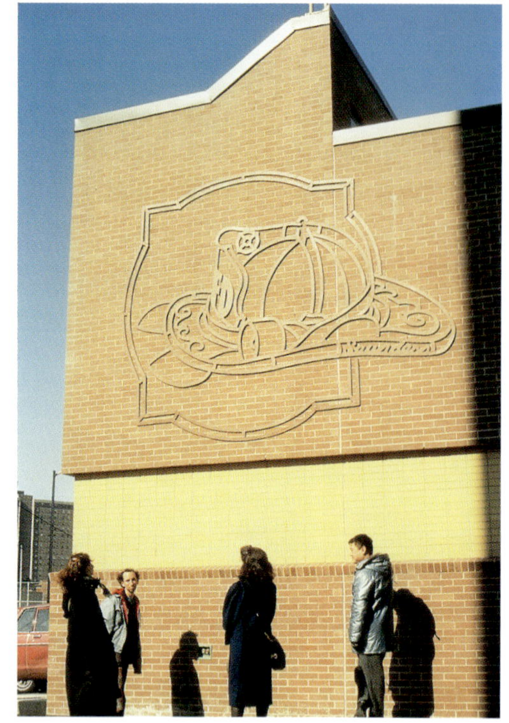

For his work at Engine Company 71—a cast-aluminum sculpture measuring 11 × 13 feet (3.3. × 4 m)—David Saunders drew on the rich details of the Fire Department's traditional leather fire helmet. The artist included the crest and shield, showing the visor in the at-ease position, and tilting the brim forward to reveal the embossed leaf pattern. To individualize this symbol of fire protection, Saunders customized the hat by fixing a flashlight to its brim with a broad strap. He has described *Firehat* as a "homage to the important role of the individual firefighter."

Vicki Scuri

Butterfly Garden
1996
Steel, Lexan polycarbonate resin, cedar planters, steel trellises, landscaping materials

Public School 188, 760 Grote Street

ARCHITECT/DESIGN AGENCY
School Construction Authority
SPONSOR AGENCY
Board of Education

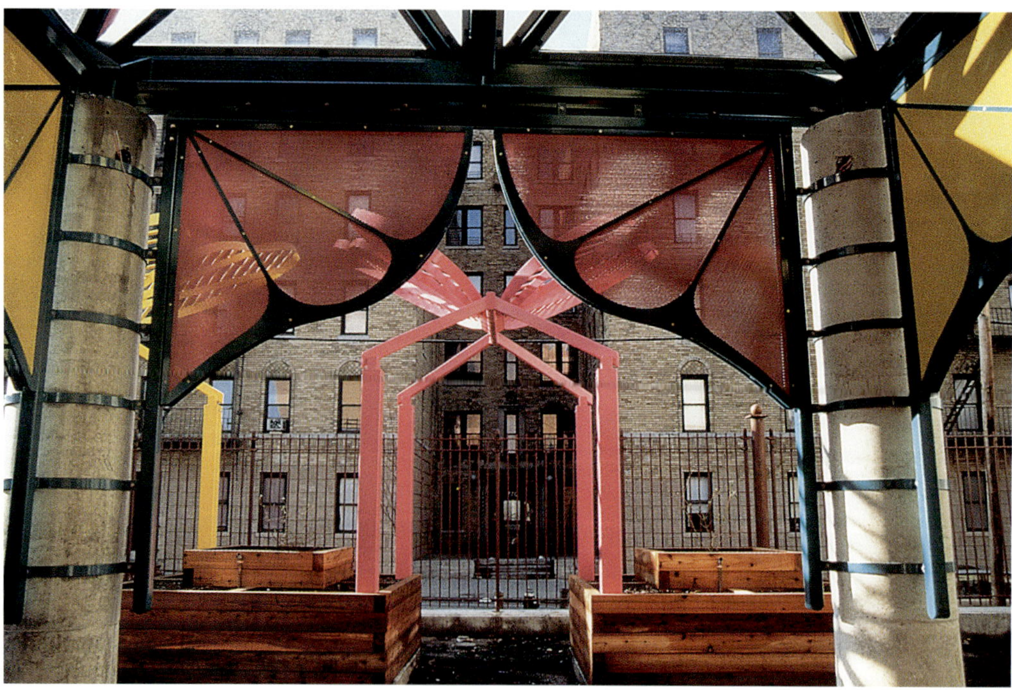

Vicki Scuri's *Butterfly Garden* has transformed the asphalt playground at P.S. 188 (known as P.S. 34 when the piece was commissioned). The garden's central feature is a gazebo, which is framed by colorful "butterfly wings" made from steel and Lexan polycarbonate resin. The gazebo leads the school children to a procession of raised cedar planters and winged butterfly trellises. The garden also contains more than three thousand bulbs and plants, in varieties that tend to attract butterflies.

Thresholds
1999
Painted aluminum

Public School 83,
950 Rhinelander Avenue
Public School 360,
2880 Kingsbridge Terrace

ARCHITECT/DESIGN AGENCY
School Construction Authority
SPONSOR AGENCY
Board of Education

Located at two separate Bronx schools, P.S. 83 and P.S. 360, Alison Sky's *Thresholds* frames the doorway to every classroom in both schools. The project, arranged in a different color scheme on each floor, features colorful panels along the sides of each door that can also be used to frame the children's artwork or class projects. In the transom area over each door is an etched glass panel featuring an inspirational quotation or message associated with learning and discovery.

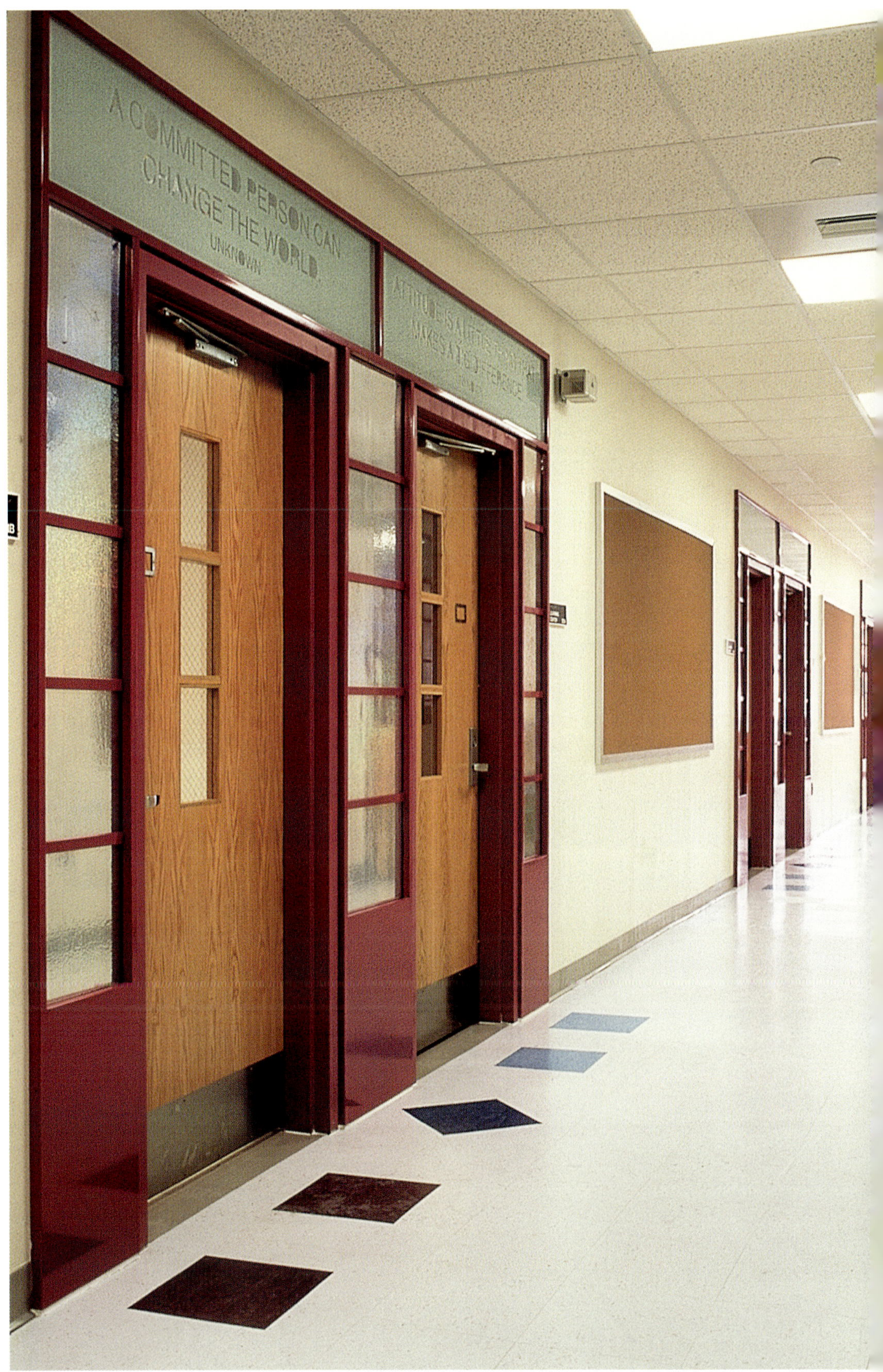

Alison Sky

Therman Statom

Luz
2001
Fiberglass, terrazzo, aluminum, glass

Children's Pride Day Care Center,
800 Concourse Village East

ARCHITECT
Castro-Blanco Piscioneri Associates
DESIGN AGENCY
Department of Design and Construction
SPONSOR AGENCY
Agency for Child Development

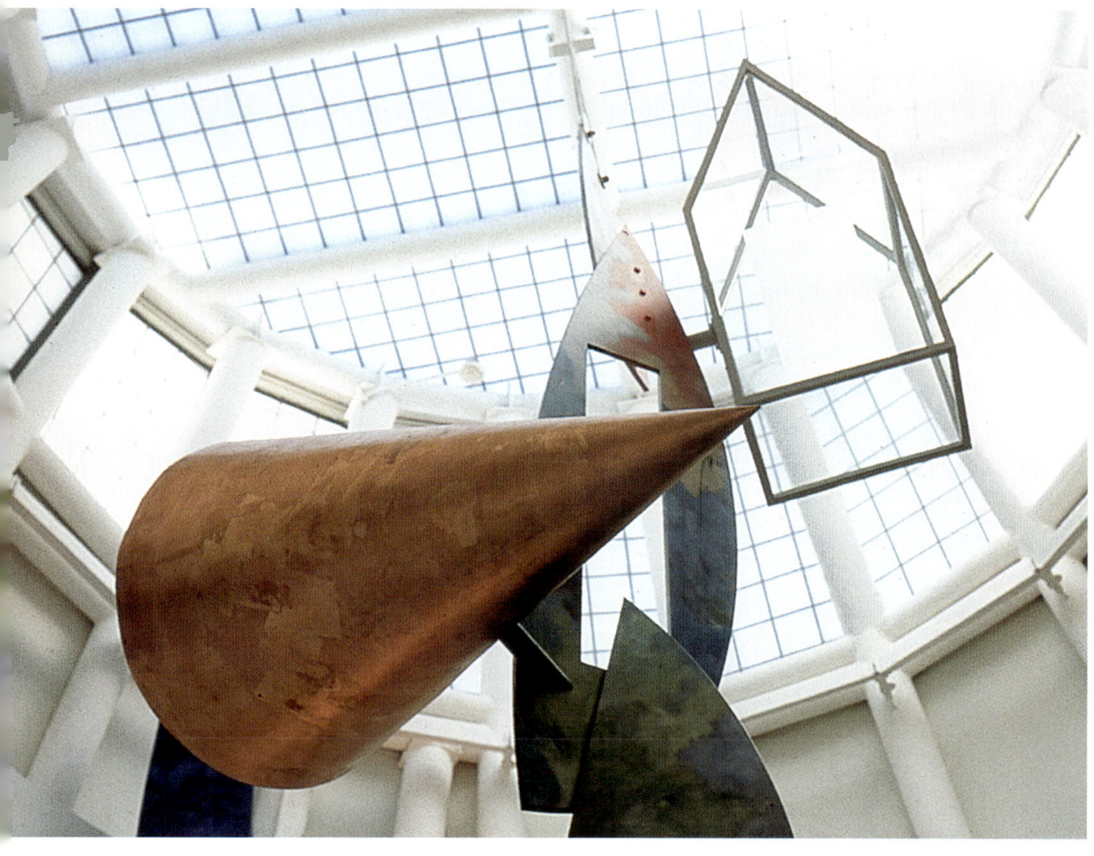

Located in the lobby of the Children's Pride Day Care Center (known as the Concourse Village East Day Care Center when the piece was commissioned), Therman Statom's installation, *Luz,* consists of two parts: an expansive terrazzo floor, and a huge metal and glass sculpture that hangs from the ceiling. The floor is inlaid with green-leaf shapes while the sculpture resembles a large-scale child's mobile, the elements of which include a fiberglass painted moon, a copper cone shape, metal painted leaves, and a clear glass house.

Jorge Tacla

Memories of the Bronx
1998
Mixed media on canvas

Bronx Housing Court,
1118 Grand Concourse

ARCHITECT
Rafael Vinoly Architects
DESIGN AGENCY
Department of Design and Construction
SPONSOR AGENCY
Office of Court Administration

Jorge Tacla's paintings for the Bronx Housing Court, entitled *Memories of the Bronx,* refer to the process of building the courthouse. In one piece, an excavation hole is cut into an unspoiled landscape; in the other, the grid of the topographical street-plan surrounds a pile of the excavated earth. The artist intended for the work to connect the memory of the past to the reality of the present.

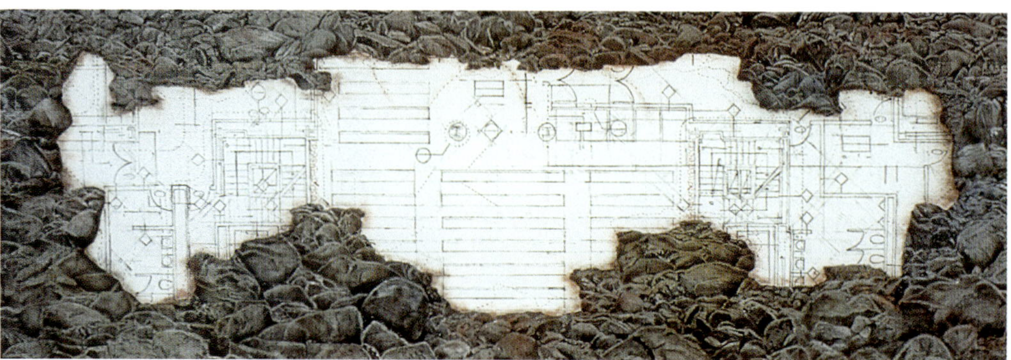

Hall of Fame Gate
1996
Bronze

Public School 15, 2195 Andrews Avenue

ARCHITECT
Ehrenkrantz Eckstut and Kuhn
DESIGN AGENCY
School Construction Authority
SPONSOR AGENCY
Board of Education

For his work at P.S. 15, Brinsley Tyrell drew inspiration from the Hall of Fame for Great Americans, a nearby early twentieth-century Bronx landmark. The artist installed a new and updated *Hall of Fame Gate* on the two main entrance gates of the school. First carved in high relief and then cast in bronze, the gates contain thirty-six portraits that honor outstanding individuals, mostly notable African-Americans such as Harriet Tubman, Marion Anderson, Thurgood Marshall, and Colin Powell.

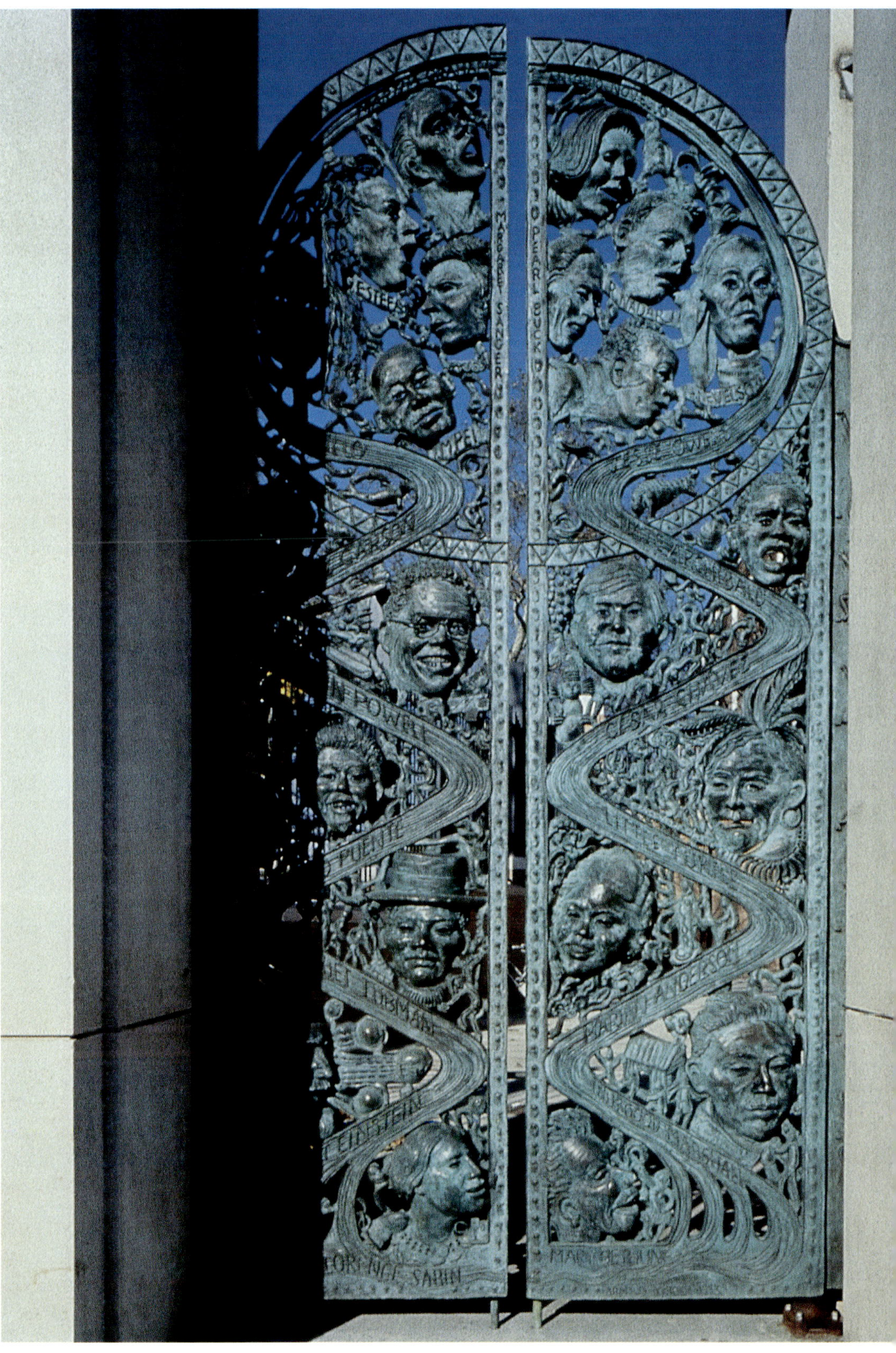

Brinsley Tyrell

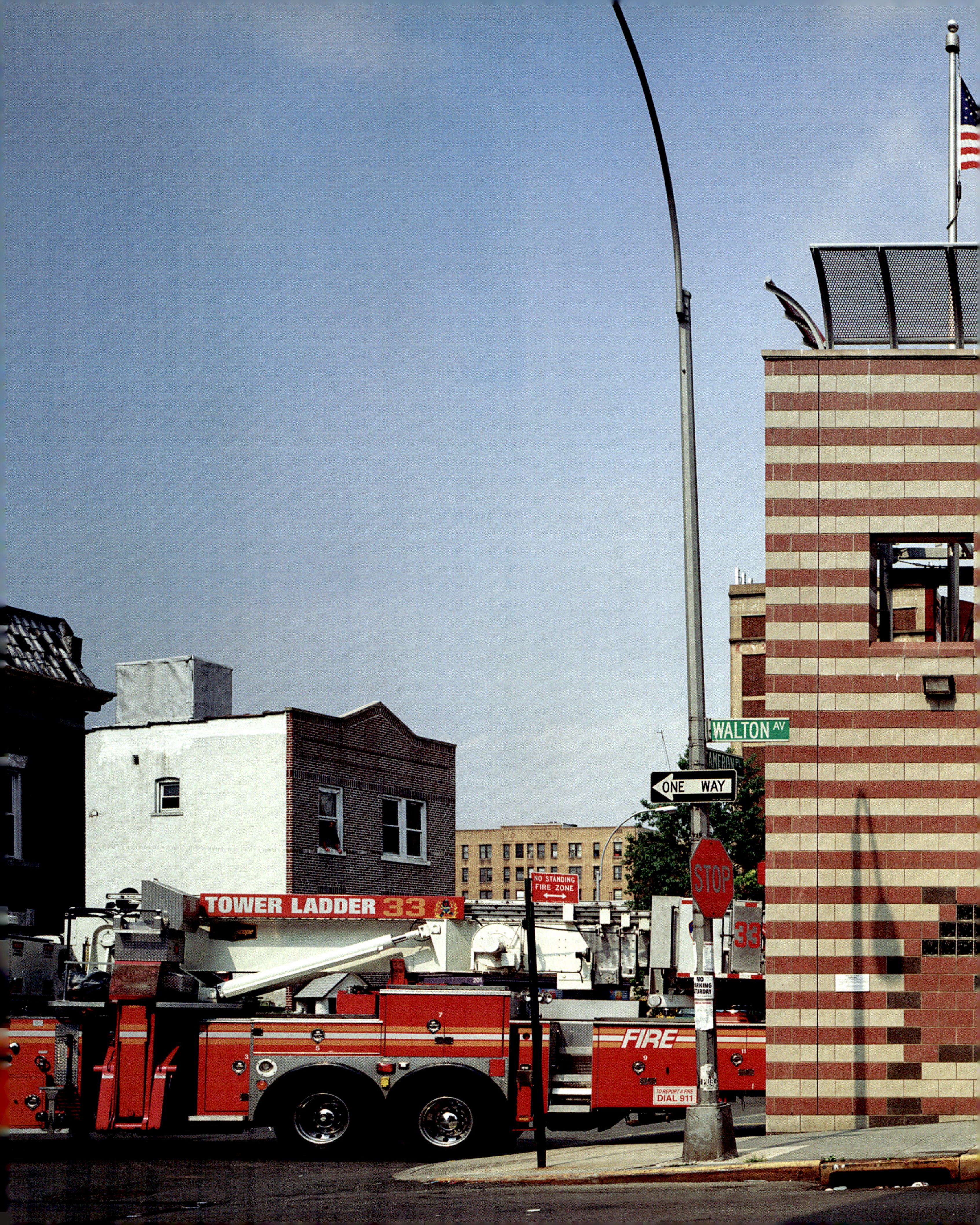
TOWER LADDER 33
WALTON AV
ONE WAY
NO STANDING
FIRE ZONE
STOP
33
FIRE
TO REPORT A FIRE
DIAL 911

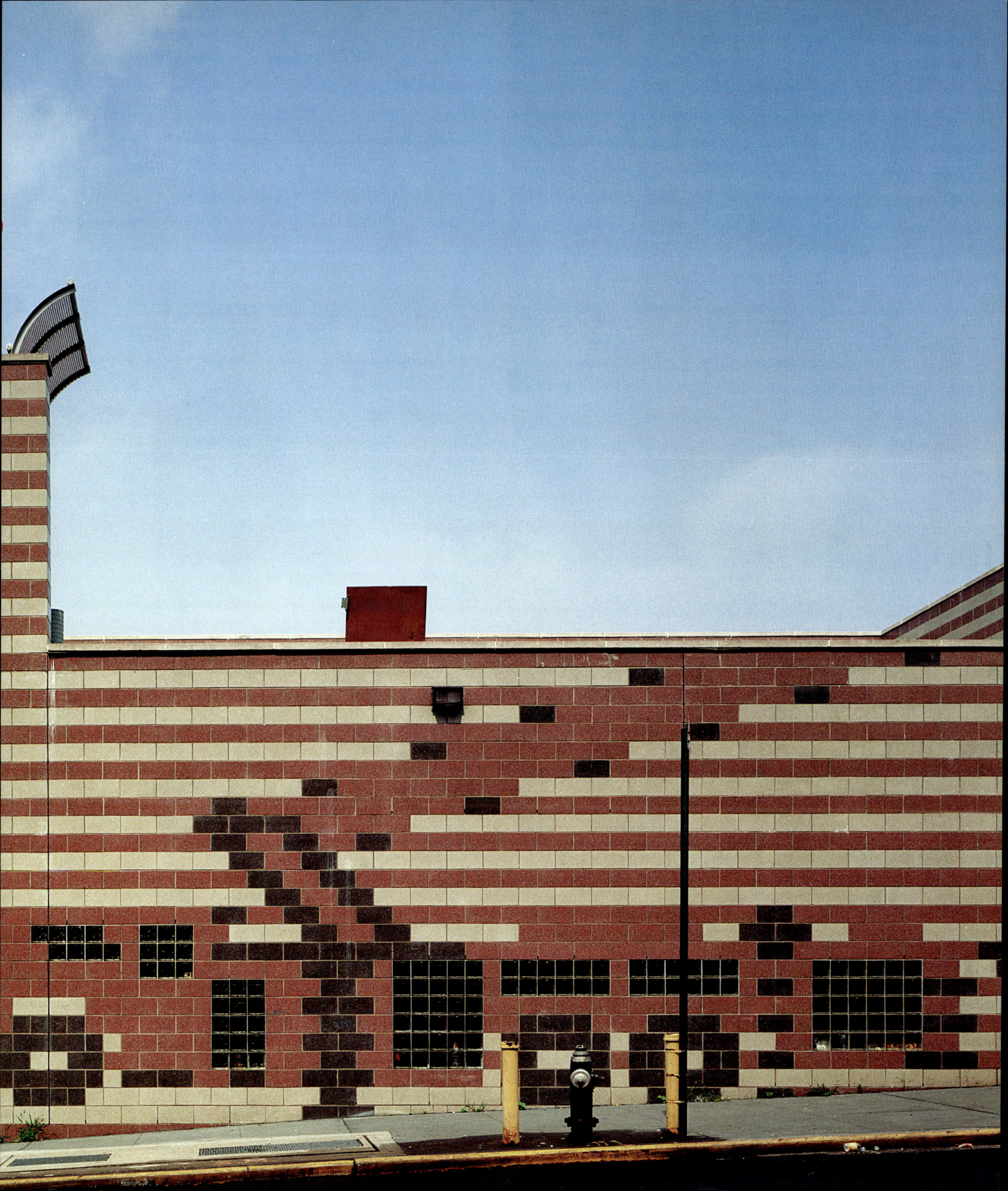

Mierle Laderman Ukeles

Honor 2000 (previous pages)
2000
Concrete masonry units, etched-glass block, cast-glass brick

Engine Company 75 Firehouse,
2175 Walton Avenue

ARCHITECT
Richard Dattner and Partners Architects
DESIGN AGENCY
Department of Design and Construction
SPONSOR AGENCY
Fire Department

Mierle Laderman Ukeles's artwork for Engine Company 75 honors the Bronx firefighters who have died in the line of duty over the last century. *Honor 2000* features a large image of a ladder truck constructed into the façade of the firehouse, as well as a series of embedded glass blocks engraved with the names of the deceased firefighters. The artist also created two carved glass hands in relief, modeled from the hands of a father and his three-year-old daughter who were saved by firefighters of this firehouse. Ukeles has remarked: "Public art can create permeable membranes between the inside and outside of systems, spaces, and even the souls of citizens . . . . I hope the wall between the inside and the outside of the firehouse becomes transparent, that it is melting a bit because of this artwork."

Anton Van Dalen

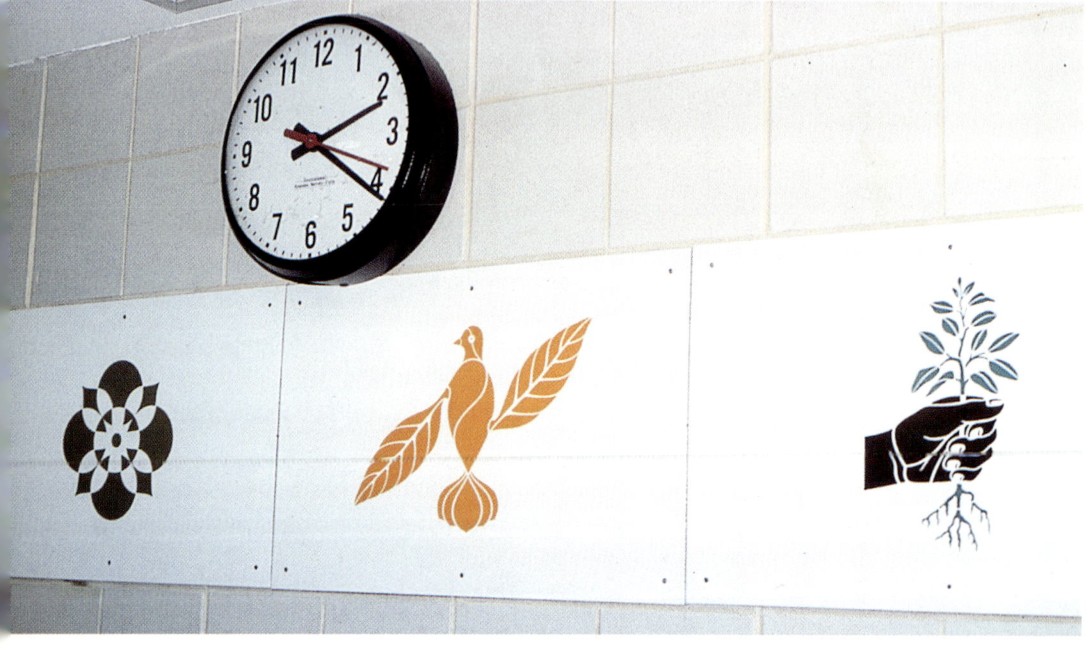

Garden Path, **Garden Wall**, and **The Flying Book**
2000
Terrazzo tiles, porcelain enamel, paint on plywood

Public School/Intermediate School 20,
3020 Webster Avenue
ARCHITECT
Ehrenkrantz Eckstut and Kuhn
DESIGN AGENCY
School Construction Authority
SPONSOR AGENCY
Board of Education

Located in the hallway leading to the lunchroom at P.S./I.S. 20, Van Dalen's frieze, *Garden Path*, features rectangular porcelain enamel tiles, each depicting a white flower atop a brightly colored tile background. For the lunchroom, the artist created a similar frieze, entitled *Garden Wall* (left), which features tiles with colored drawings of birds, leaves, flowers, and hands. In the library, Van Dalen painted a plywood mural, entitled *The Flying Book,* which portrays birds made to look like cars, planes, and clocks.

Mind, Health, Spirit, and Body
1999
Mosaics

Walton High School,
2780 Reservoir Avenue

ARCHITECT
Lev Zetlin Associates
DESIGN AGENCY
School Construction Authority
SPONSOR AGENCY
Board of Education

Each of Carrie Mae Weems's four mosaic panels for Walton High School portrays a young man or woman beneath one of the following words: Mind, Health, Spirit, and Body. The figures are based on photographs the artist took of students at the school. The 10 foot (3 m) tall panels were originally created for the school's swimming pool, which was to have been renovated, but were installed in the school's gymnasium when the pool renovation failed to take place. In addition, Weems created a mosaic-tile plaque emblazoned with the school emblem.

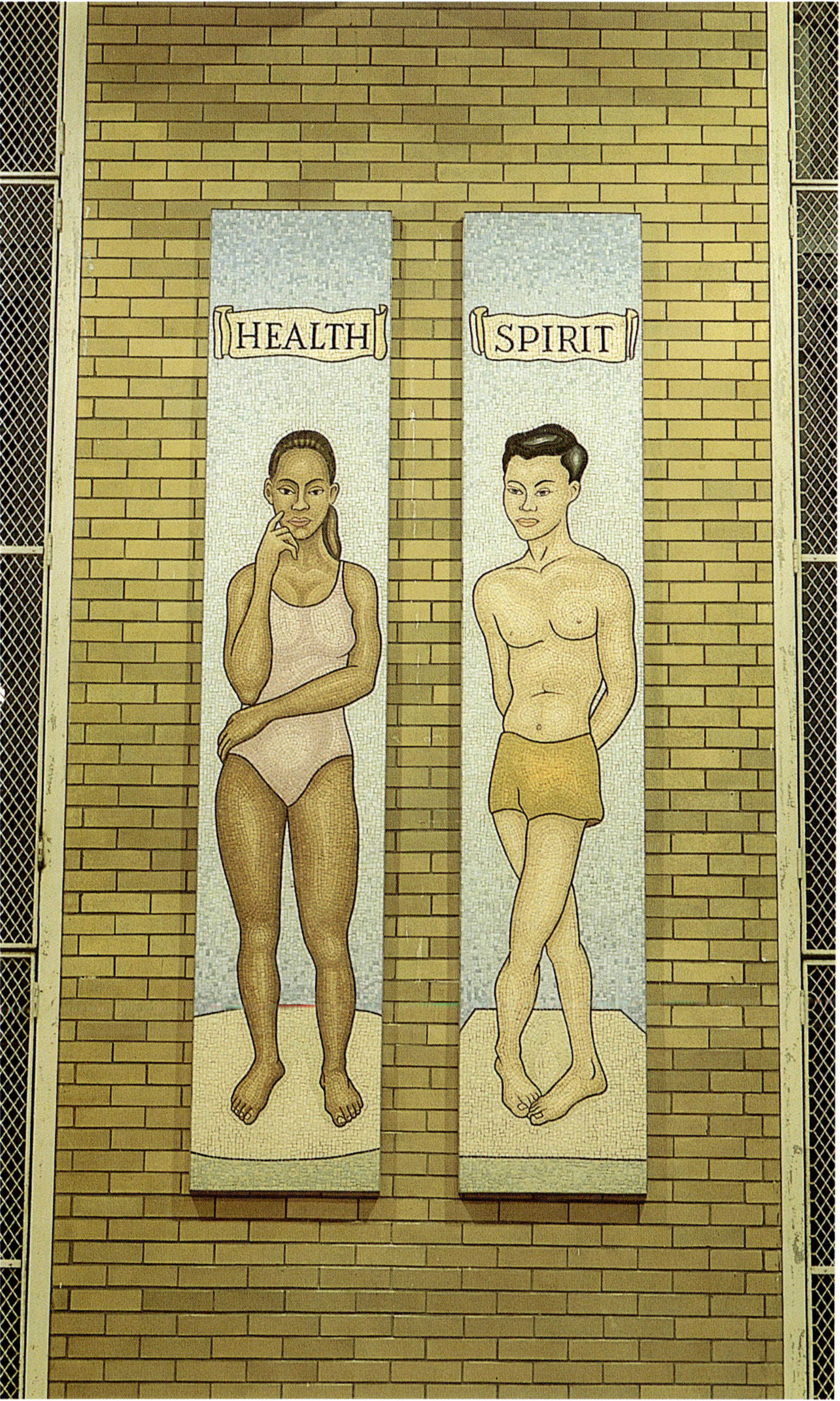

Carrie Mae Weems

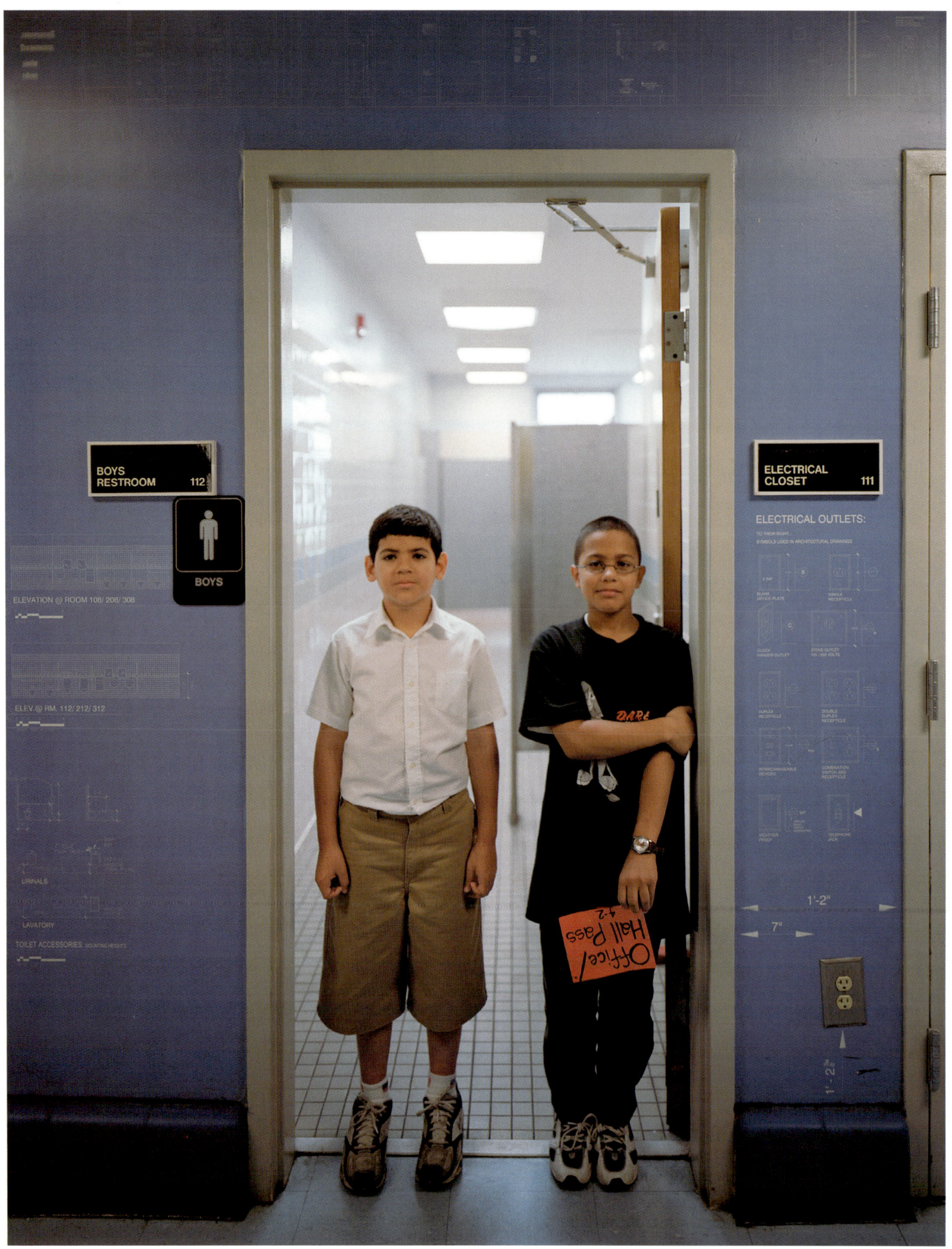
BOYS
RESTROOM 112
BOYS
ELEVATION @ ROOM 108/ 208/ 308
ELEV. @ RM. 112/ 212/ 312
URINALS
LAVATORY
TOILET ACCESSORIES
ELECTRICAL
CLOSET 111
ELECTRICAL OUTLETS:
1'-2"
7"
DARE
Office/
Hall Pass
4-2

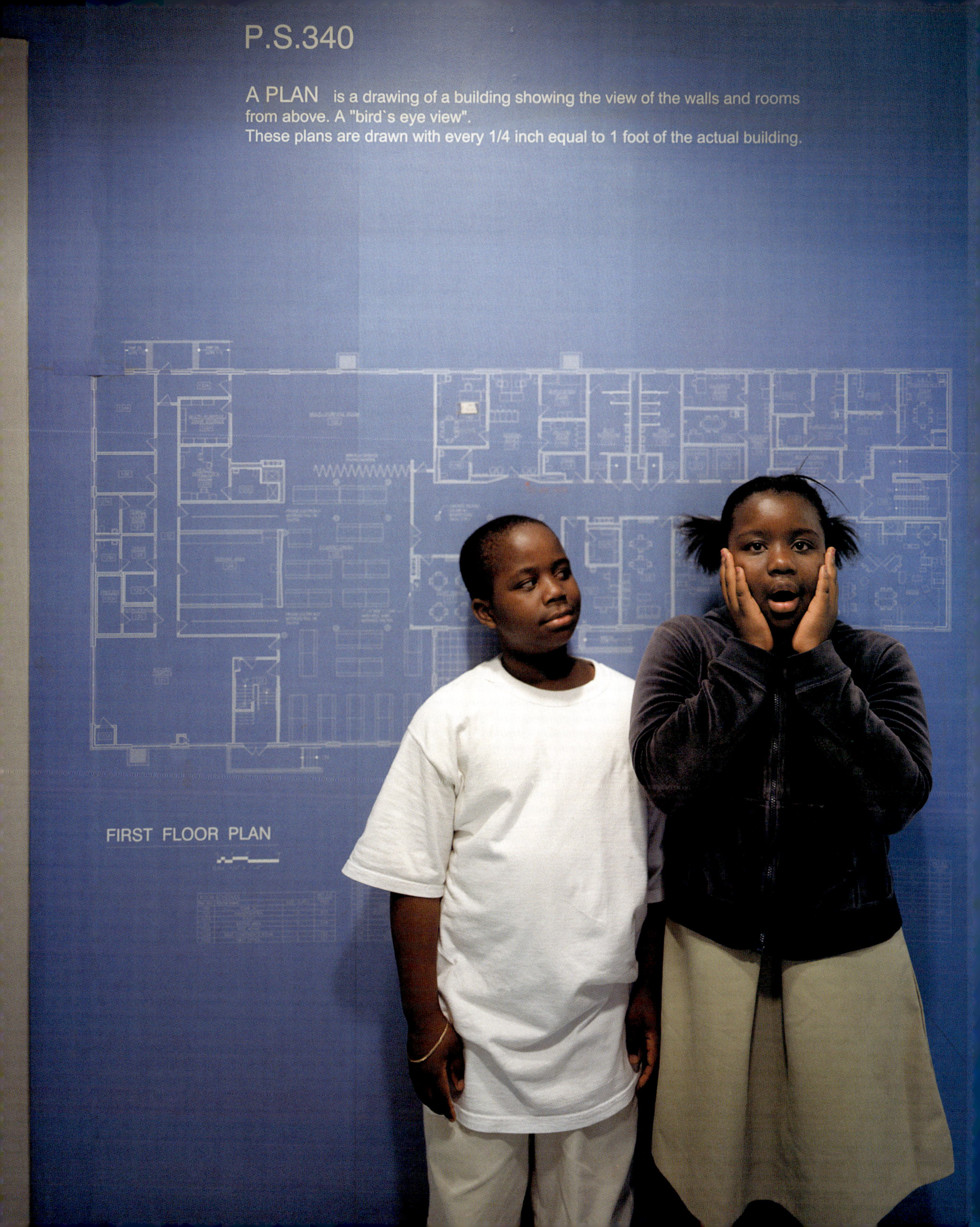

P.S.340

A PLAN is a drawing of a building showing the view of the walls and rooms from above. A "bird`s eye view".
These plans are drawn with every 1/4 inch equal to 1 foot of the actual building.

FIRST FLOOR PLAN

Drawing P.S. 340 (previous pages)
1999
Vinyl
A Coordinate Plane Patio
1999
Concrete, brass, vinyl

Public School 340, 25 West 195th Street

ARCHITECT/DESIGN AGENCY
School Construction Authority
SPONSOR AGENCY
Board of Education

Allan and Ellen Wexler's 112 foot (34 m) long wall mural at P.S. 340 presents various floor plans and detailed construction drawings based on the actual architectural plans for the school. *Drawing P.S. 340* (previous pages) includes the elevation drawings of the hallway and variously scaled maps that situate the school in the community, City, and country. The artists also created a grid for the entry plaza, which students can examine in order to understand how architectural measurements relate to one another. The artwork is intended to provide students with a schematic overview of the new school and an opportunity for architectural study.

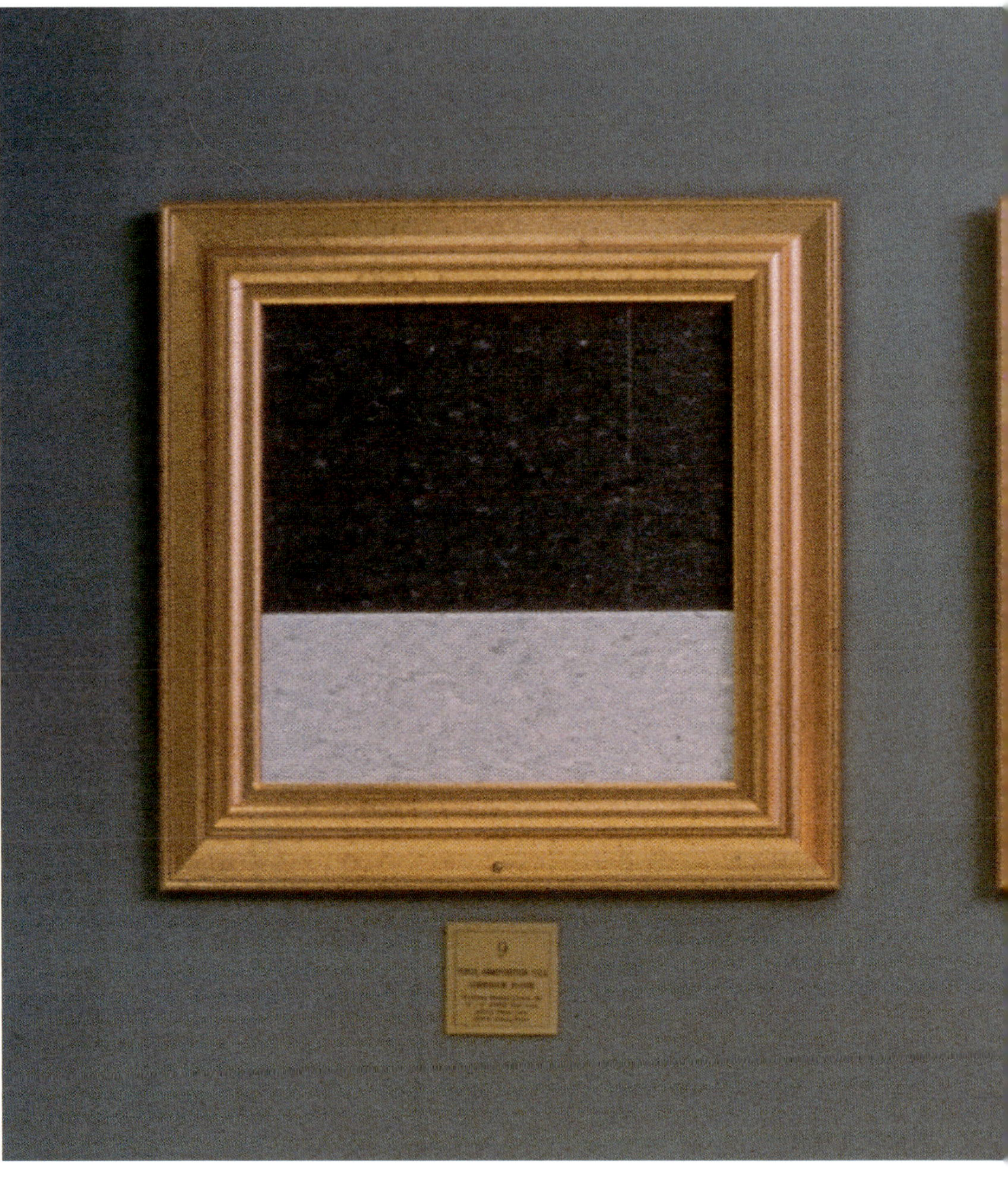

Allan and Ellen Wexler

Allan and Ellen Wexler

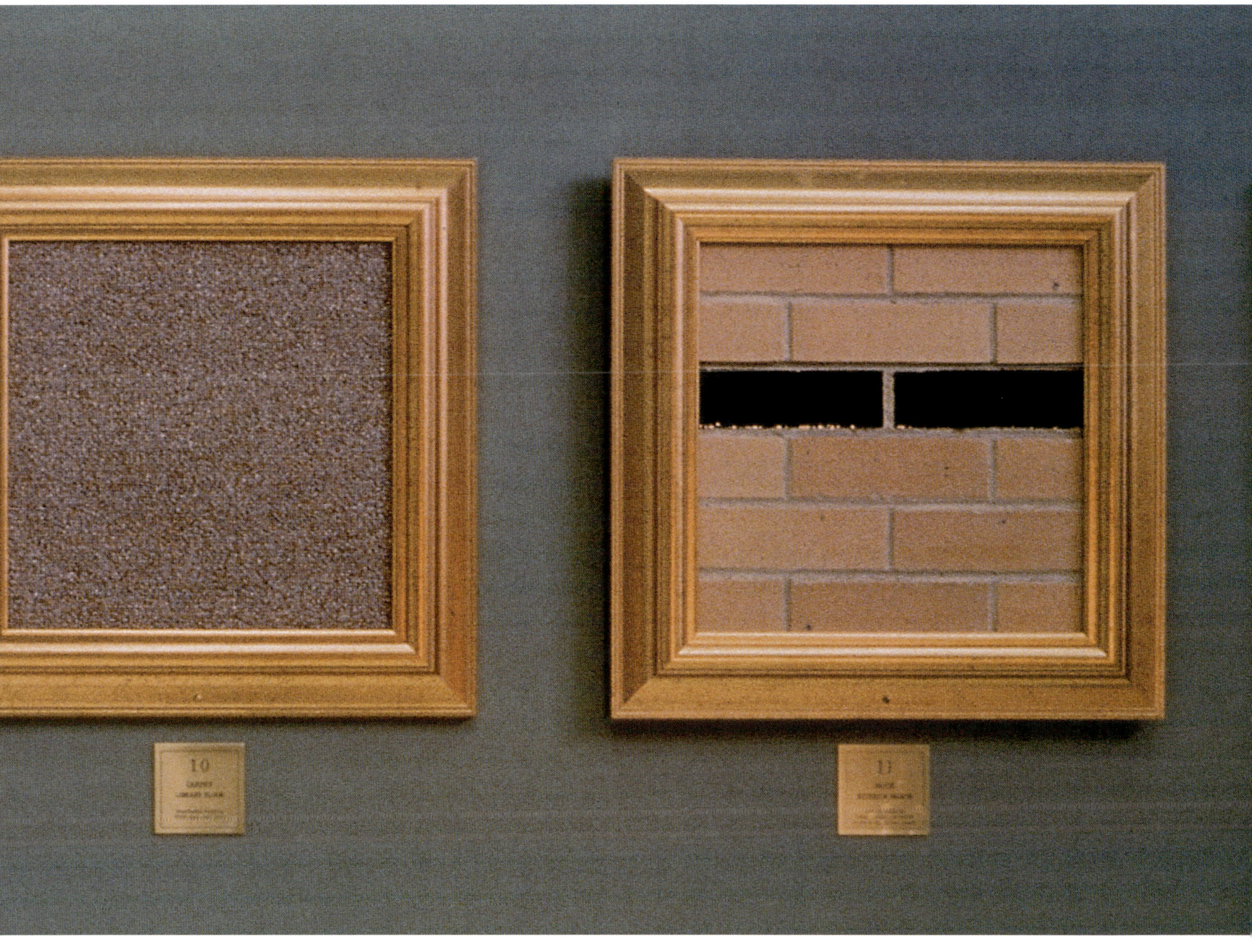

Abstractions I.S. 254
1999
Framed building materials

Public School 254,
2452 Washington Avenue

ARCHITECT/DESIGN AGENCY
School Construction Authority
SPONSOR AGENCY
Board of Education

Located in the lobby of P.S. 254, Allan and Ellen Wexler's artwork features sixteen golden frames containing a variety of surfaces, colors, shapes, and forms taken from the actual surface materials of the school. The artists chose to present these materials in museum-like frames in order to isolate them from their customary context and function. Each piece has a descriptive brass plaque etched with a number. At various locations on the school's first floor, corresponding plaques indicate the location of the materials in use. According to the artists, the project is intended to encourage an awareness of the inherent beauty of building materials and to promote an active engagement with architecture.

Janet Zweig

Your Voices
1997
Bronze

Walton High School,
2780 Reservoir Avenue

ARCHITECT
Lev Zetlin Associates
DESIGN AGENCY
School Construction Authority
SPONSOR AGENCY
Board of Education

Janet Zweig's interactive installation at Walton High School is comprised of twelve bronze letter-boxes mounted on the marble walls in the school's main lobby. Each box is inscribed with one of the following words: "wishes," "fears," "dreams," "secrets," "problems," "opinions," "worries," "suggestions," "fantasies," "complaints," "obsessions," and "ideas." Students are encouraged to respond in writing to the cues and to drop their notes in the appropriate boxes. The artist intended for these notes to be printed and distributed by a student editorial group and compiled annually for a publication kept in the school library.

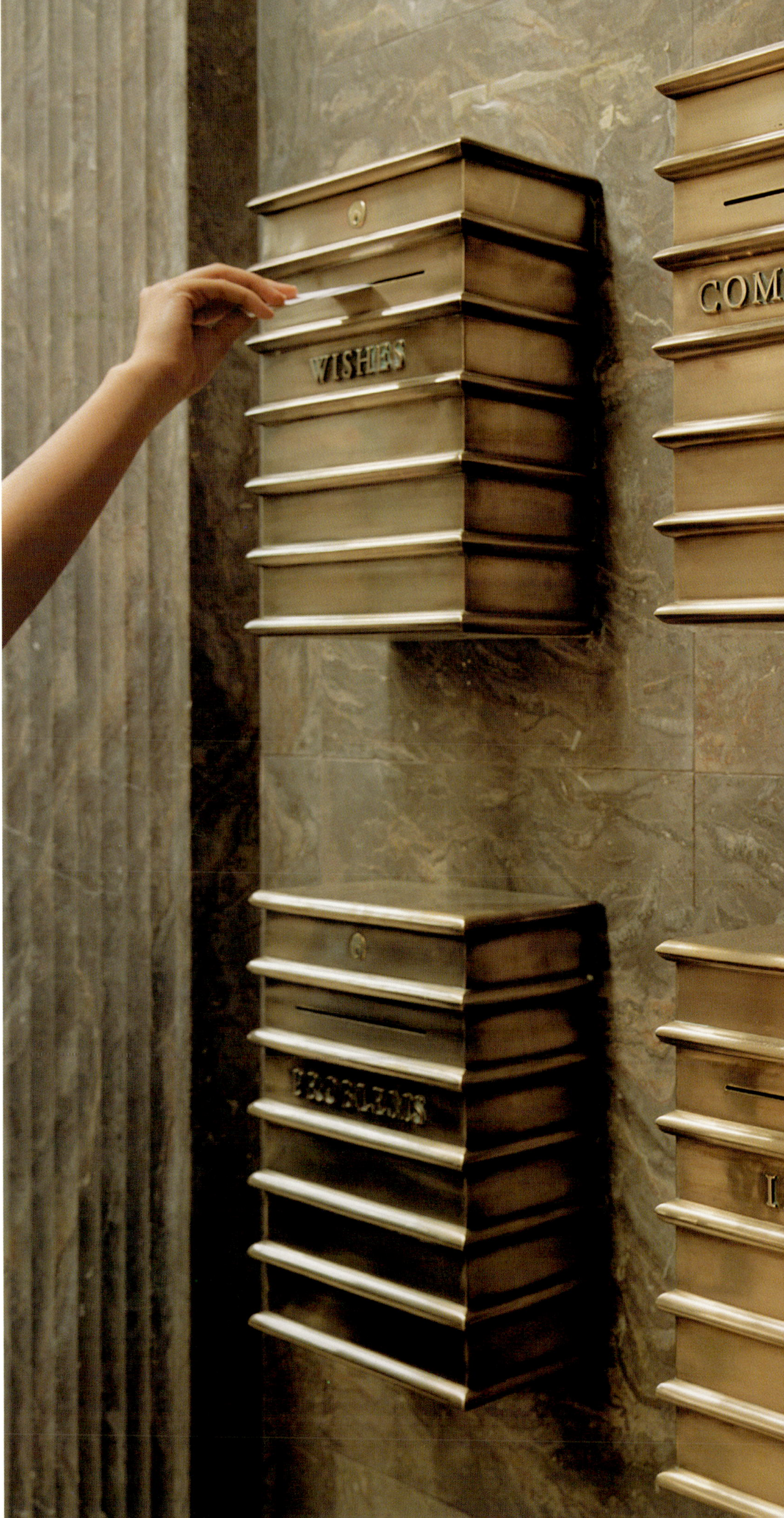

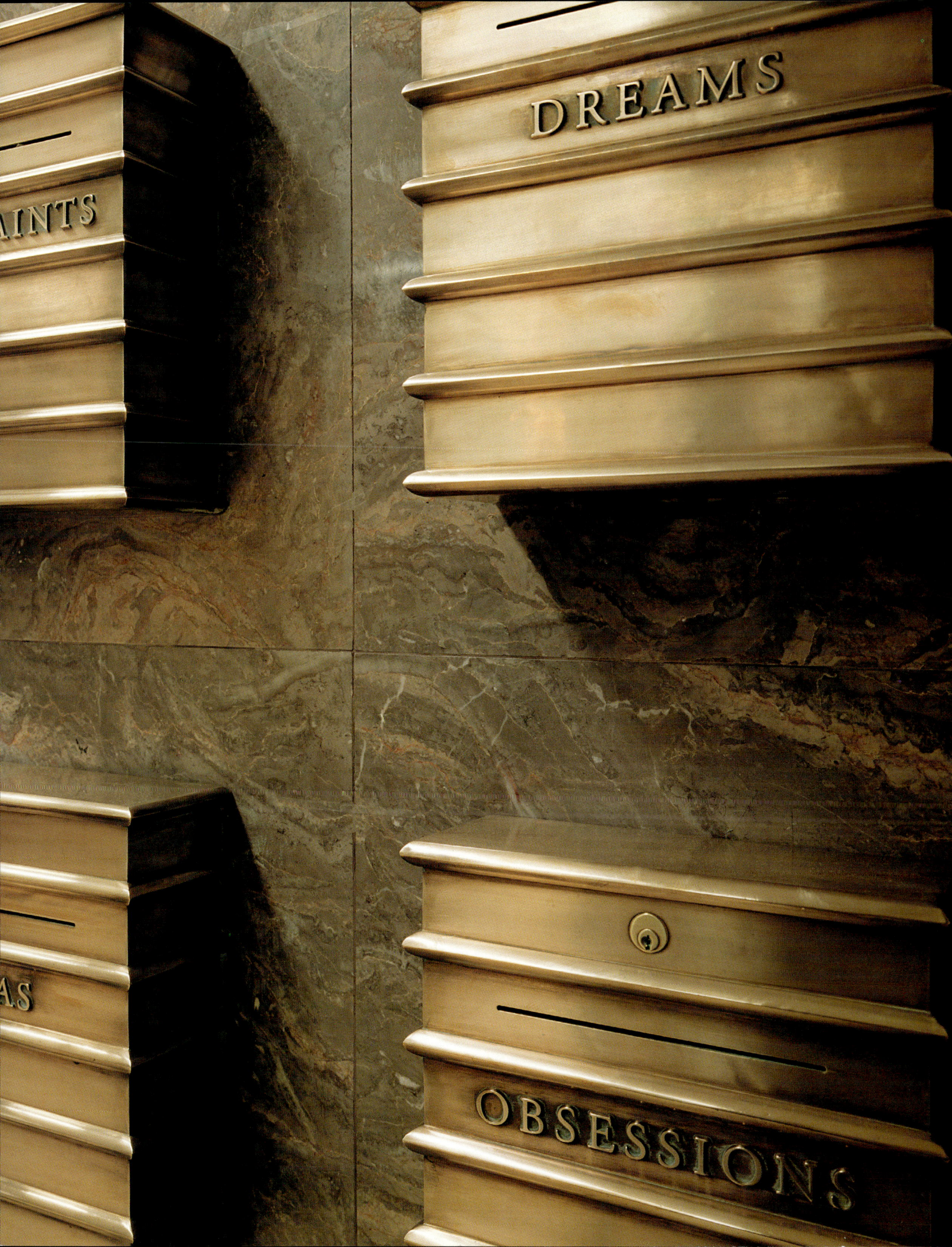
DREAMS
OBSESSIONS

Completed projects ● (see map)

1 **Alice Adams**
2 **Rhoda Andors**
3 **Ron Baron**
4 **Dawoud Bey**
5 **Frank Big Bear**
6 **Willie Birch**
7 **Rolando Briseno**
8 **Lee Brozgold**
9 **Bill and Mary Buchen**
10 **Dina Bursztyn**
11 **Scott Burton**
12 **Carole Byard**
13 **Y. David Chung**
14 **Melvin W. Clark**
15 **Jackie Peters Cully**
16 **Agustin de Andino**
17 **Claudia DeMonte**
18 **Julie Dermansky**
19 **Ogundipe Fayomi**
20 **Susan Gardner**
21 **Peter Gourfain**
22 **Jane Greengold**
23 **Jose Rafael Guzman**
24 **Mags Harries**
25 **Ralph Helmick and Stuart Schechter**
26 **Robin Holder**
27 **Wopo Holup**
28 **Arlan Huang**
29 **Carlton Ingleton**
30 **M.L.J. Johnson**
31 **Roberto Juarez**
32 **George Mason**
33 **Valerie Maynard**
34 **Ed McGowin**
35 **Mike Metz**
36 **Robert Ressler**
37 **Faith Ringgold**
38 **Toshio Sasaki**
39 **Ben Schonzeit**
40 **Charles Searles**
41 **Pedro Silva**
42 **Ned Smyth**
43 **Ned Smyth**
44 **Nitza Tufino**
45 **Emmett Wigglesworth**
46 **Krzysztof Wodiczko**

Projects in progress ▲ (see map)

47 Vito Acconci
Edge of the Plant/Edge of the Neighborhood
Perimeter Treatment
Newtown Creek Water Pollution Control Plant, Greenpoint Avenue and Provost Street
Engineer: Hazen and Sawyer, Greeley and Hansen, Malcolm Pirnie Tri-Venture
Architect/Landscape Architect: Polshek Partnership Architects/Quennell Rothschild Associates
Sponsor Agency: Department of Environmental Protection
Art Commission Award for Excellence in Design 1998

48 Chakaia Booker
Sculpture
Society for the Preservation of Weeksville and Bedford-Stuyvesant History, 1698–1708 Bergen Street
Architect: Caples Jefferson Architects
Design Agency: Department of Design and Construction
Sponsor Agency: Department of Cultural Affairs

49 Jim Conti
Core
Light installation
Hamilton Avenue Bridge
Engineer: Greenman Pederson, Inc.
Sponsor Agency: Department of Transportation

50 Julian Laverdiere
Engine Company 277, 582 Knickerbocker Avenue
Architect: STV
Design Agency: Department of Design and Construction
Sponsor Agency: Fire Department

51 Jody Pinto
Garden design
Third Water Tunnel Shaft Site 21B, Kent Avenue
Sponsor Agency: Department of Environmental Protection

52 Liliana Porter
Untitled with Sitting Rabbit
Wall design, sculptures
LaVaughn Robert Moore Childcare Center, 333 Hinsdale Street
Architect: Michael Fieldman Architects
Design Agency: Department of Design and Construction
Sponsor Agency: Agency for Child Development

53 Michael Rakowitz
Midwood High School, 2839 Bedford Avenue
Architect: HLW
Design Agency: School Construction Authority
Sponsor Agency: Department of Education

54 Moses Ros
La Casita
Powder-coated steel sculpture
Williamsburg Childcare Center, 243 South Second Street
Architect: Beckhard Richlan Associates
Design Agency: Department of Design and Construction
Sponsor Agency: Agency for Child Development

55 Christy Rupp
Tidal filter fence and pier design
Coney Island Water Pollution Control Plant, Knapp Street
Engineer: Pirnie-Baker
Sponsor Agency: Department of Environmental Protection

56 George Trakas
Waterfront nature walk
Newtown Creek Water Pollution Control Plant, Greenpoint Avenue and Provost Street
Engineer: Hazen and Sawyer, Greeley and Hansen, Malcolm Pirnie Tri-Venture
Architect/Landscape Architect: Polshek Partnership Architects/Quennell Rothschild Associates
Sponsor Agency: Department of Environmental Protection

57 Tim Watkins and Carol May
Sundancers
Suspended sculptures
Kensington Library, 4209–4217 18th Avenue
Architect: Sen Architects
Design Agency: Department of Design and Construction
Sponsor Agency: Brooklyn Public Library

58 Meg Webster
Garden for Green Space
Garden design
Fourth Avenue and Sackett Street
Sponsor Agency: Department of Environmental Protection

Conservation projects

Abram Champanier
Alice Flies Over the East River Bridges, 1990
WPA Mural Restoration
Cumberland Neighborhood Family Care Center, 39 Auburn Place
Alan M. Farancz, Conservation Studio, Inc.

Abram Champanier
Alice and Friends at Coney Island Playland, 1990
WPA Mural Restoration
Coney Island Hospital Emergency Room, 2601 Ocean Parkway
Alan M. Farancz, Conservation Studio, Inc.

Thomas Jones
Brooklyn Public Library Grillework, 1941
Conservation, 1995
Grand Army Plaza
Steven A. Tatti, Conservator

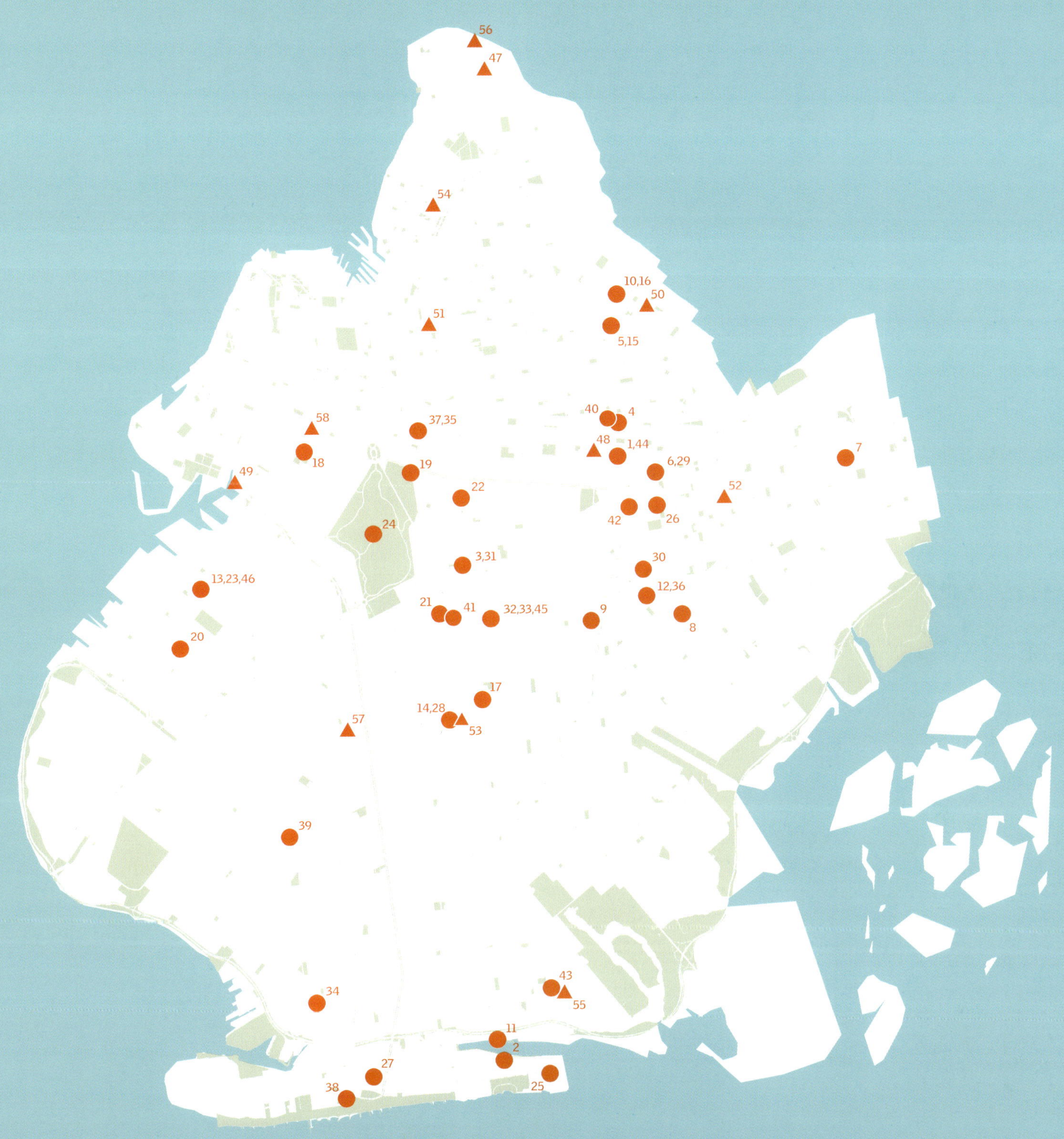
56
47
54
10,16
50
51
5,15
40
4
58
37,35
48
1,44
7
18
19
6,29
49
22
52
42
26
24
3,31
30
13,23,46
12,36
21
41
32,33,45
9
8
20
17
14,28
53
57
39
43
55
34
11
2
27
25
38

Brooklyn

Interview: Meg Webster

I'm doing a community-run, native plant demonstration site on Fourth Avenue and Sackett Street. It's my first public art project. I've done earthworks before, but this project is more like landscape architecture than my work generally is. It will include ponds surrounded by solar panels, many, many plants, a composting area, and a number of permanent little buildings and structures, designed with the help of an architect. The challenge is to try to bring things together: public space and intimacy, natural rawness and a sense of permanence, something "outside" that provides the shelter associated with an interior space.

There will be signage that describes the native plants and their importance—how they feed the birds and insects and create a better environment. I'm hoping that when people wander in, they'll enjoy sitting in a shady, watery glen, as well as learn something. I believe that educational programming should be a big part of this kind of project.

Previous to this commission, I've installed a number of gardens in front of museums. But they've all been temporary, so I could experiment with making things a little more wild. Almost all the institutions appreciated my work but, in the end, they really didn't want their landscape to look that way. It was scary for them to see nature out of control and looking unkempt. This new piece, like some other community gardens in the neighborhood, will look a little wild too.

But what's different here is that the ongoing aspects of this project will be in the hands of the community. People in the neighborhood are forming a not-for-profit organization and the site will eventually be leased to them. We'll keep an eye on the site; one important aspect of this project is that it is an experiment in maintenance. The pond, for example, could become a sand form and the plants would take care of themselves as much as possible. But a bigger issue is invasive plants, so the project will demand hands-on community interaction and monitoring, on an ongoing basis.

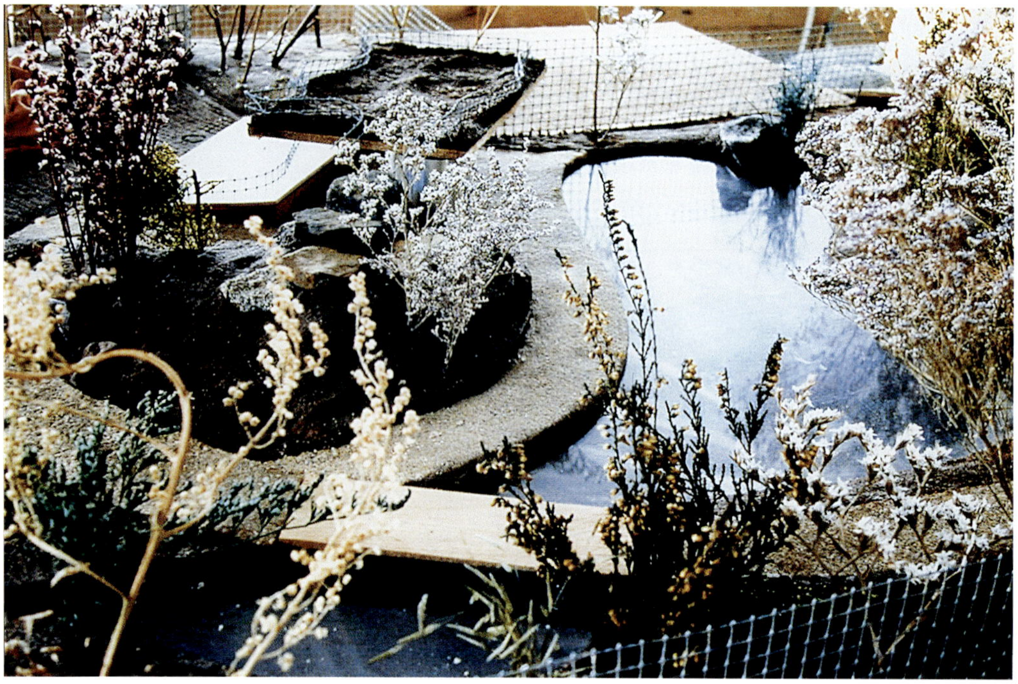

Meg Webster, Proposal for *Garden for Green Space*, 2004.

But the problem with doing public art—from the standpoint of an inexperienced artist—is the timing. The piece takes up a lot of space in my being. So it is hard to turn on and then wait. But overall, the project has been a great experience. I started to do the kind of work I do because I wanted to bring material and forms directly to people. I wanted to create an intimate and direct experience with a native material, and to bring people to an awareness of the sanctity of all beings. I don't know how these goals will play out in the end. There's magic in a project like this, a sense that the forms you make are very immediate. And I think that this creates a different kind of viewing situation and public experience.

Alice Adams

African Garden
1994
Cast iron, steel, wood

Public School 12, 430 Howard Avenue

ARCHITECT
Perkins & Will
DESIGN AGENCY
School Construction Authority
SPONSOR AGENCY
Board of Education

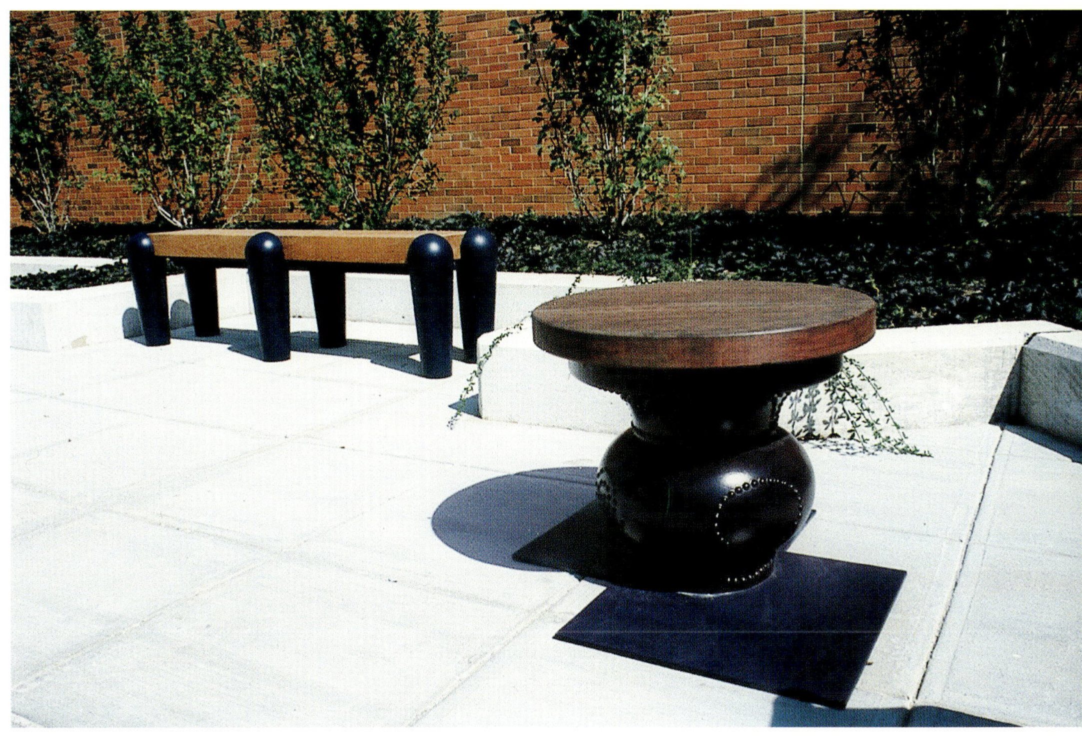

Alice Adams designed a schoolyard garden and seating area between two playgrounds at P.S. 12. Inspired by African design and woodwork, *African Garden* includes fourteen cast-iron fabricated steel and wooden seats surrounded by various plantings flanking a path. The sculptural qualities of the fabricated components emphasize and pay homage to the richness and formal diversity of traditional gardens and garden furniture.

Rhoda Andors

Ecotones
1995
Fresco

Public School 195, 131 Irwin Street

ARCHITECT/DESIGN AGENCY
School Construction Authority
SPONSOR AGENCY
Board of Education

Rhoda Andors's series of circular frescoes reflect the geographic proximity of P.S. 195 to the natural marine world that surrounds Brooklyn's Manhattan Beach. The murals, which are located on a wall in the school's auditorium, incorporate the aquatic, terrestrial, and aerial life of the area, such as a laughing gull giving the "long call," a signal of the coming of spring.

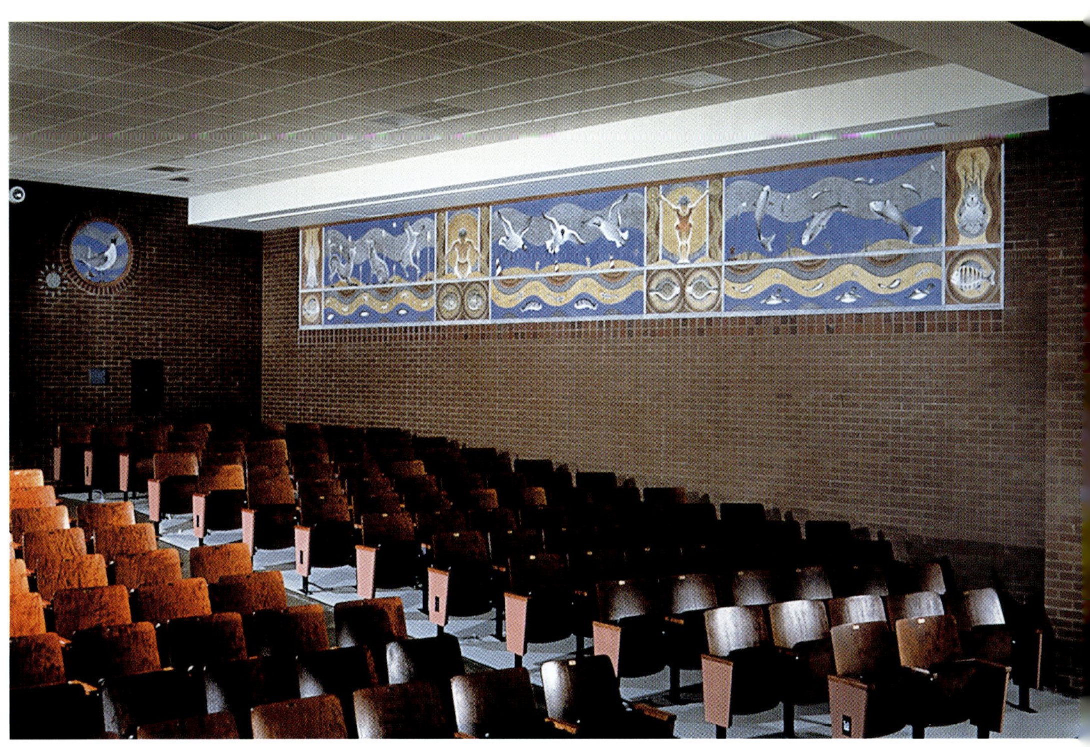

Gates of Knowledge
1995
Painted bronze

Intermediate School 2,
655 Parkside Avenue

ARCHITECT
Richard Dattner and Partners Architects
DESIGN AGENCY
School Construction Authority
SPONSOR AGENCY
Board of Education

Suspended over the gates of I.S. 2, Ron Baron's sculpture features rows of well-worn books held together at each end by playful cherubs. Below the gates and at the students' eye-level are shelves containing large-scale bronze books, baseballs, a baseball cap and glove, apples, and bookends. In conceptualizing his project, Baron's intention was "to create a bridge or continuum between the community and the school, rather than a barrier. I produced sculptures that expressed ideas about the intrinsic value of learning, exploration, and recreation."

Ron Baron

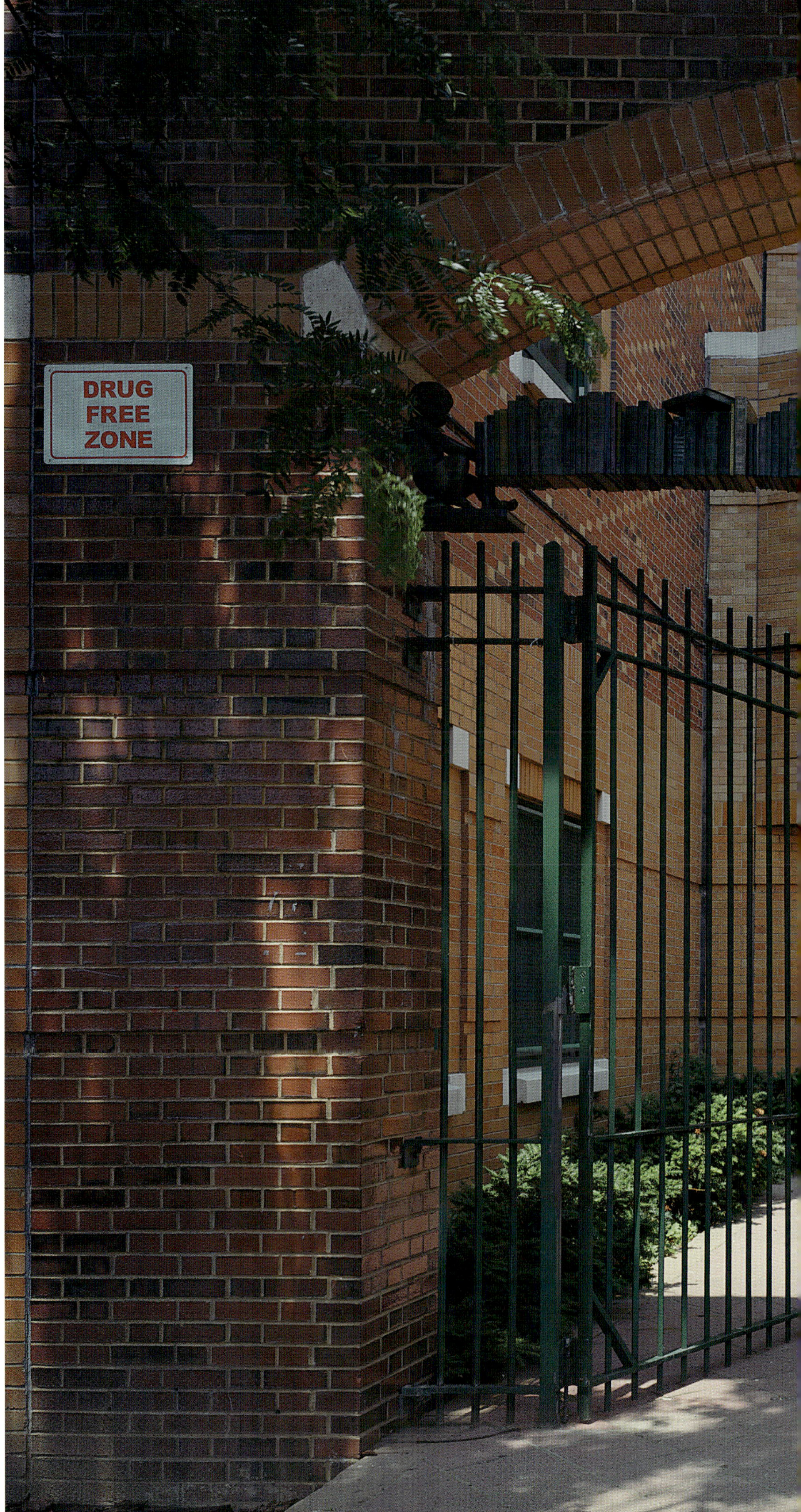

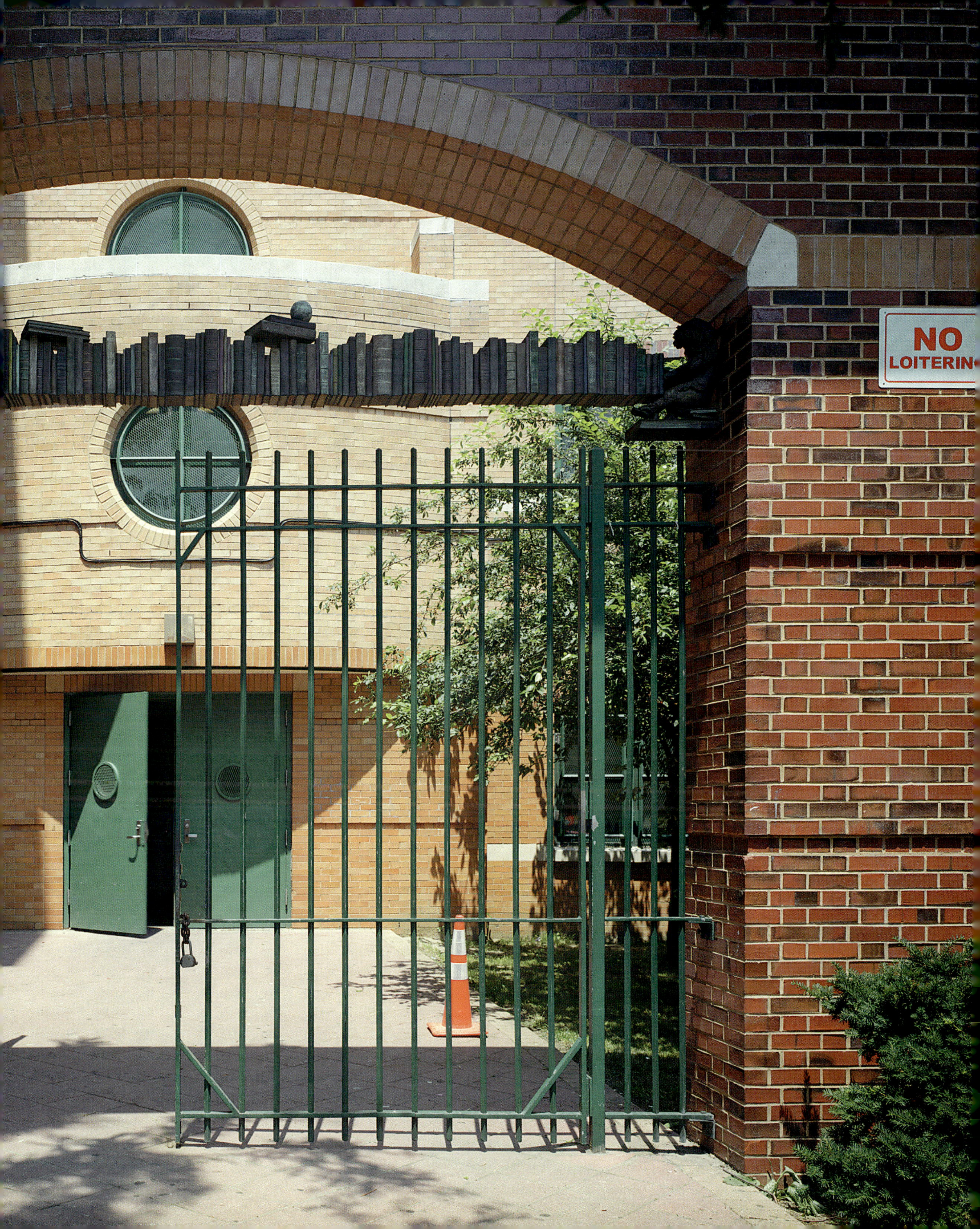
NO
LOITERIN

Dawoud Bey

Community Photography Project
1991
Gelatin silver prints

Bedford-Stuyvesant Multi-Service Center, 1958 Fulton Street

ARCHITECT
George Cooper Rudolph III, Architects
DESIGN AGENCY
Department of General Services
SPONSOR AGENCY
Human Resources Administration

Art Commission Award for Excellence in Design 1989

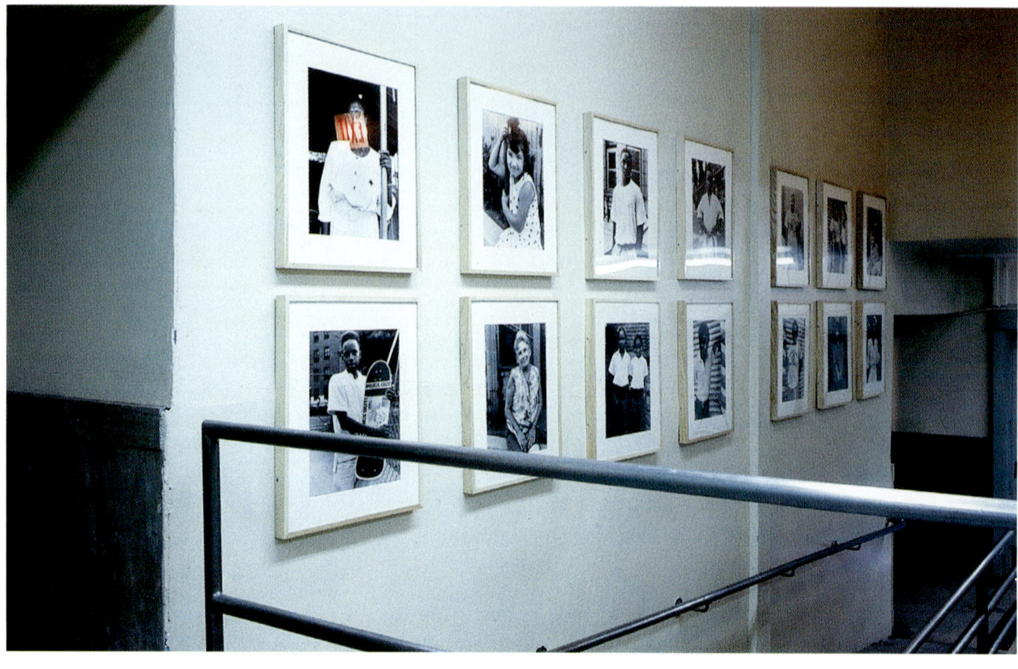

Dawoud Bey's twenty-four large-scale, black-and-white portrait photographs taken of various people in the Bedford-Stuyvesant community reflect the area's ethnic demography. The photographs, which are located throughout the community center, depict images of African-American, Caribbean, and Hispanic neighborhood residents of all age groups. Bey used a 4 × 5 camera and Polaroid material so that he could make instant prints available to his subjects.

Frank Big Bear

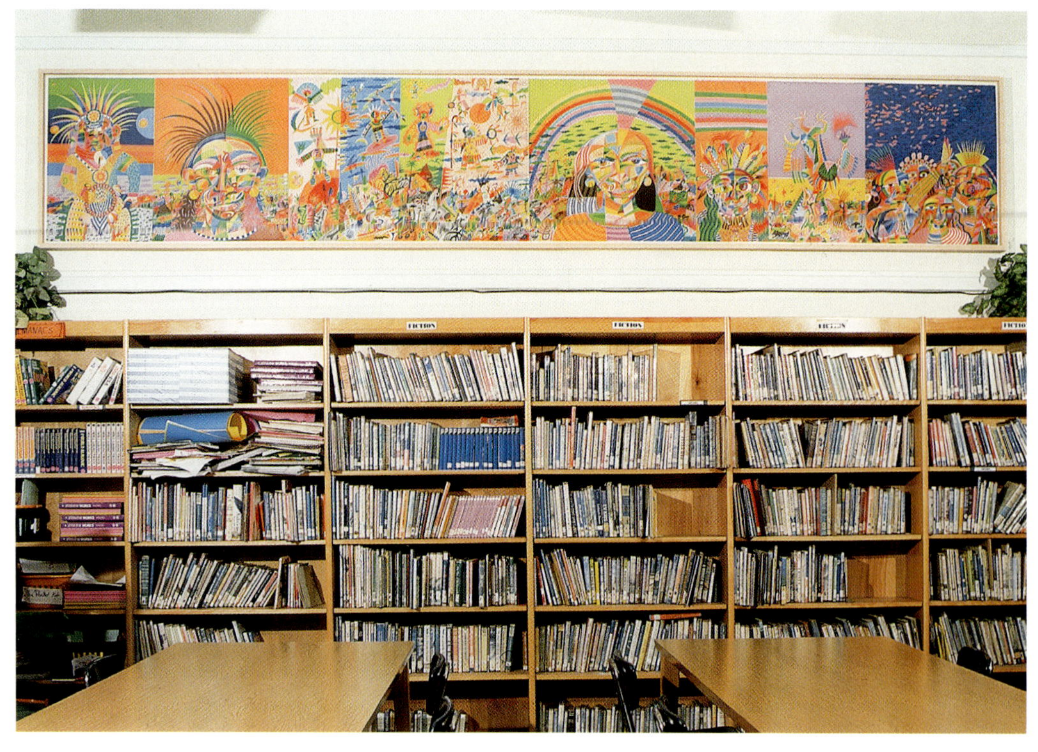

Dream Catcher Love Song
1998
Colored pencil on paper

Public School 75, 95 Grove Street

ARCHITECT
Paul Pearson
DESIGN AGENCY
School Construction Authority
SPONSOR AGENCY
Board of Education

The culmination of three years' work by Frank Big Bear, *Dream Catcher Love Song* is a set of works on paper framed above the bookcases in the library of P.S. 75, also known as the Mayda Cortiella School. The fantastical and colorful depictions of Native American life encompass ideas of history, culture, science, and nature, and are meant to inspire and stimulate the students' imaginations. The drawings "read like a visual Native American epic," wrote the *Public Art Review* in the fall of 1998.

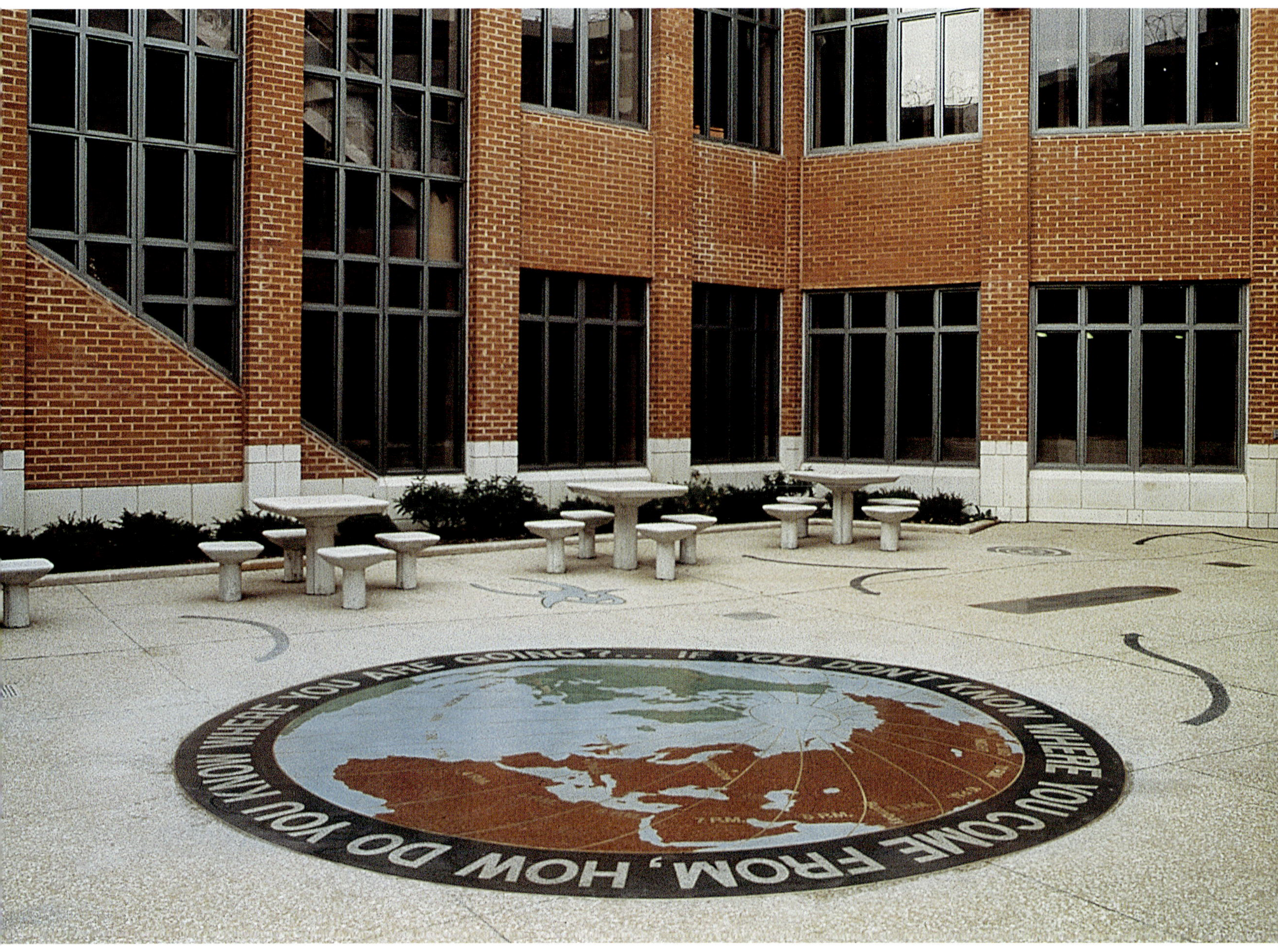

If You Don't Know Where You Come From, How Do You Know Where You Are Going?
1997
Terrazzo

Crossroads Juvenile Center,
17 Bristol Street

ARCHITECT
Kaplan McLaughlin Diaz
DESIGN AGENCY
Department of Design and Construction

SPONSOR AGENCY
Department of Juvenile Justice

The title of Willie Birch's courtyard terrazzo floor for the Crossroads Juvenile Center is derived from a Ghanaian proverb. Birch created a world map with multi-colored terrazzo enclosed in a brass circular shape. According to the artist, the blue in the floor represents the waters of the world; the green represents Europe, Asia, and North and South America; and the yellow, Africa, because of its significance as the birthplace of humankind. The figures and symbols in the outer portion of the circular map area—an Egyptian pyramid, a Mayan temple, a statue of Buddha, a statue of Zeus, a palm tree, and the Statue of Liberty—represent aspects of different cultural heritages that contribute to the contemporary experience of living in the United States. The artist also created five terrazzo tables and benches in the courtyard to add an abstract sculptural contrast to the map's narrative content.

Willie Birch

Family Library Table
1995
Epoxy enamel, painted steel, cast aluminum

Cypress Hills Library,
1197 Sutter Avenue

ARCHITECT
Hellmuth, Obata + Kassabaum, Inc.
DESIGN AGENCY
Department of General Services
SPONSOR AGENCY
Brooklyn Public Library

Rolando Briseno's library gate is the focal point of the overall fence design and, when closed, resembles a bird's-eye view of a library table with a book punctuating the center. Surrounding the book are four figures representing a family, one of which is seated at a computer monitor. The gate's arabesque is modeled on an aerial view of the building, and its form is repeated in the colored tiles that extend around the library.

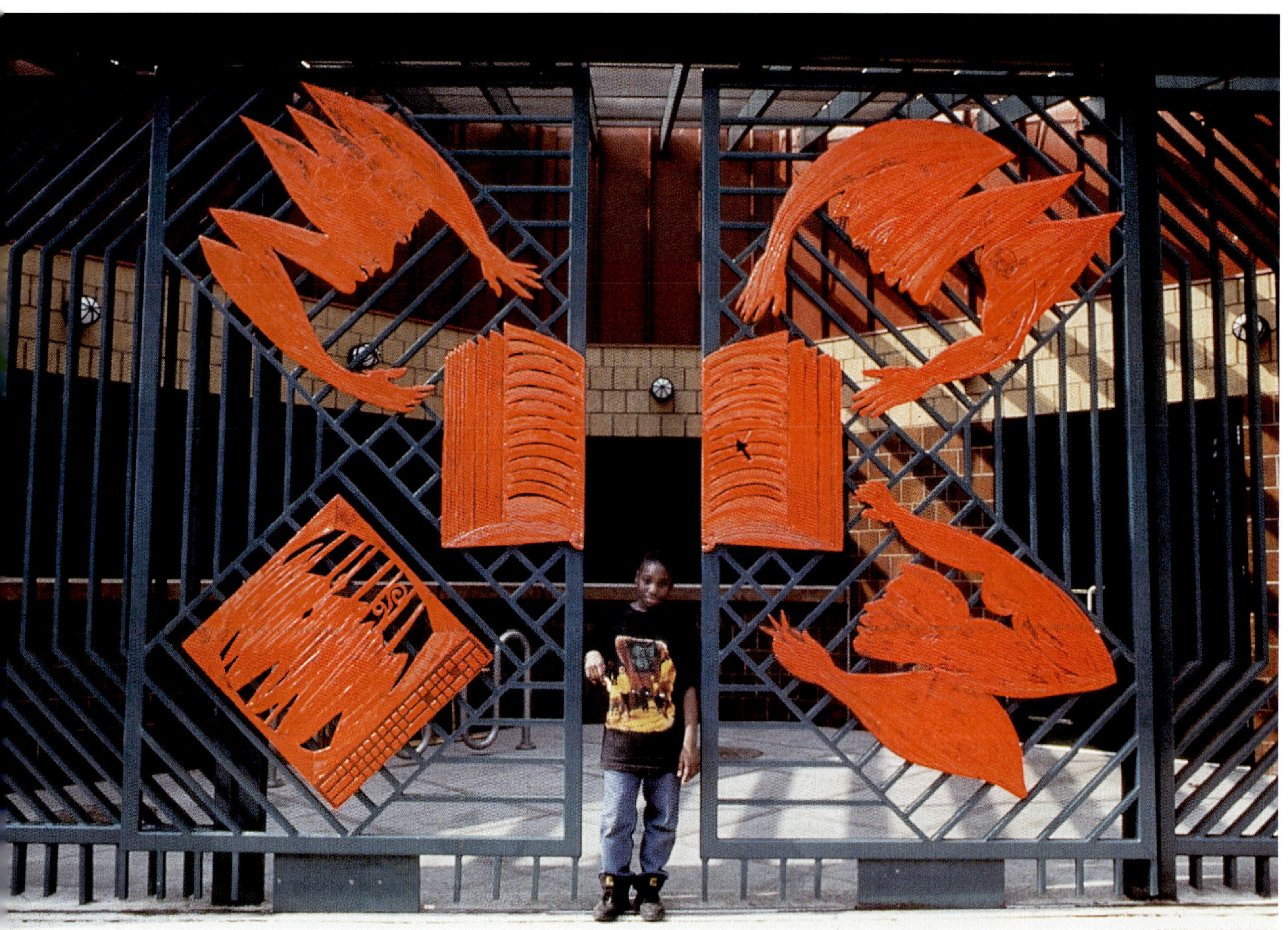

Rolando Briseno

Lee Brozgold

Beacon
2003
Stained glass

Public School 66, 845 East 96th Street

ARCHITECT
Urbahn Associates
DESIGN AGENCY
School Construction Authority
SPONSOR AGENCY
Department of Education

Brozgold's large stained-glass window in P.S. 66 features as its central image a beacon radiating light, the symbol adopted by School District 18 and a reference to the history of this seafaring community. A large, colorful diamond containing scenes of life in Canarsie, the local neighborhood, flanks the beacon, and a sprinkling of panels representing flowers, birds, and fish native to the area breaks the symmetry of this design. Brozgold drew from the cultural demographic of the area, using West African traditions of quilt design in the repeated diamond patterns.

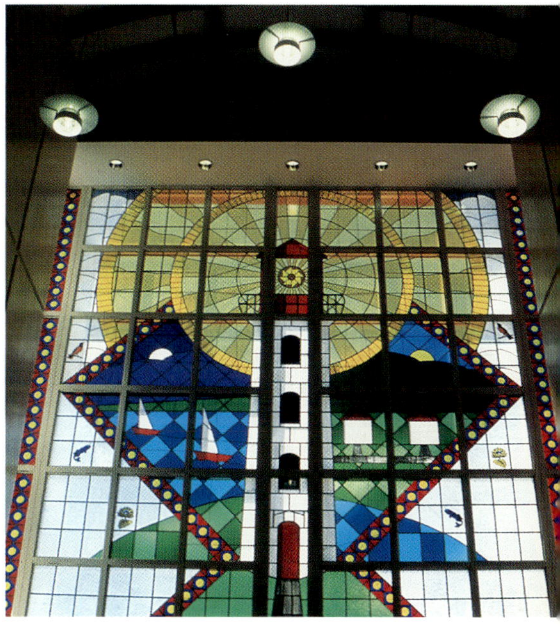

Bill and Mary Buchen

Sound Carnival
1996
Bronze, concrete, steel

Public School 244, 5404 Tilden Avenue

ARCHITECT
Montoya-Rodriguez, P.C.
DESIGN AGENCY
School Construction Authority
SPONSOR AGENCY
Board of Education

Bill and Mary Buchen designed this pair of playgrounds to help students explore music and the physics of acoustics. In an early-childhood play area, children communicate through colorful, steel "telephone tubes" that are interconnected underground. In the play area for older children, groupings of bronze drums serve the dual purpose of engaging children in communal music-making, and acting as seats and tables. Children hear their voices and drum-playing reverberating from the center of the dishes and through grates in the concrete benches. Across the playground, conga-shaped "talking drums" of Afro-Cuban origin are flanked by large parabolic dishes, which amplify voices by channelling sounds to a central point. Also located in the playground for older children is a pair of stainless-steel sculptures of palm trees, which children can play by slapping the ends of the tuned pipes that form the canopy of the tree.

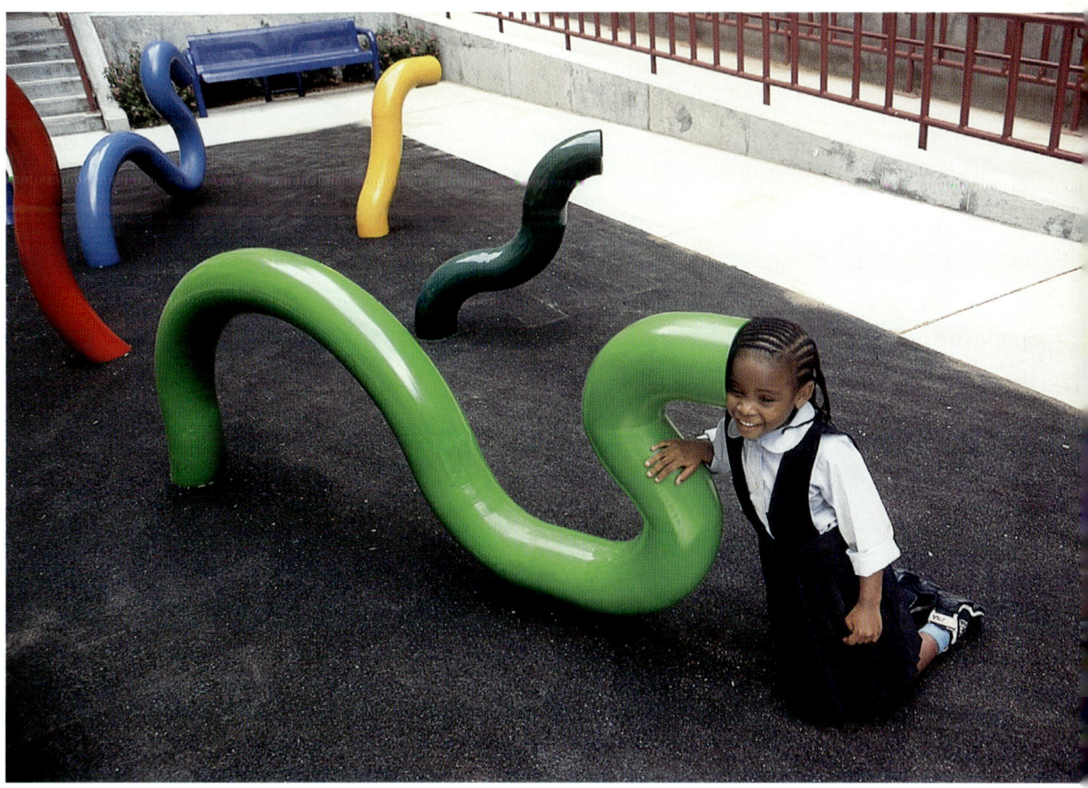

Dina Bursztyn

Paths and Stars
1995
Ceramics

Public School 376A, 194 Harman Street

ARCHITECT/DESIGN AGENCY
School Construction Authority
SPONSOR AGENCY
Board of Education

Installed throughout the school's three floors, Dina Bursztyn's *Paths and Stars* features thirty-four ceramic panels, many with images linking mythology and contemporary life. Each floor's panels have a unifying theme. The panels on the first floor include references to "Turtle Island," as New York was once called by Native Americans, along with images of the City's subway system. The panels on the second floor feature the tree of life along with images of faces and masks. The third-floor panels feature three full moons and constellations as well as the image of a child's hopscotch game.

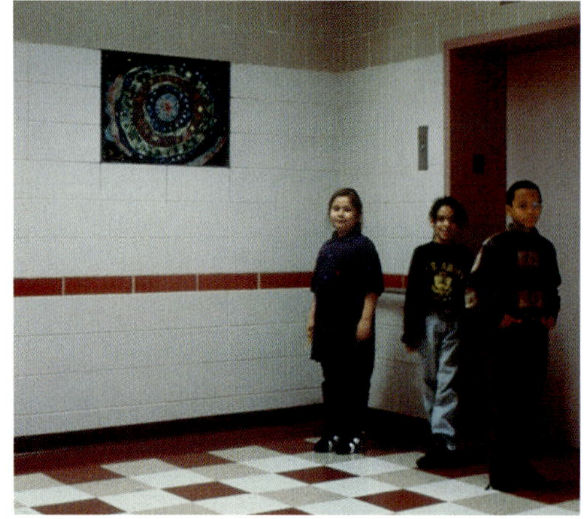

Scott Burton

Design Team Project
1994
Mixed media

Sheepshead Bay fishing piers,
Emmons Avenue

ARCHITECT
Michael J. Koenen
DESIGN/SPONSOR AGENCY
Economic Development Corporation

Art Commission Award for Excellence in Design 1990

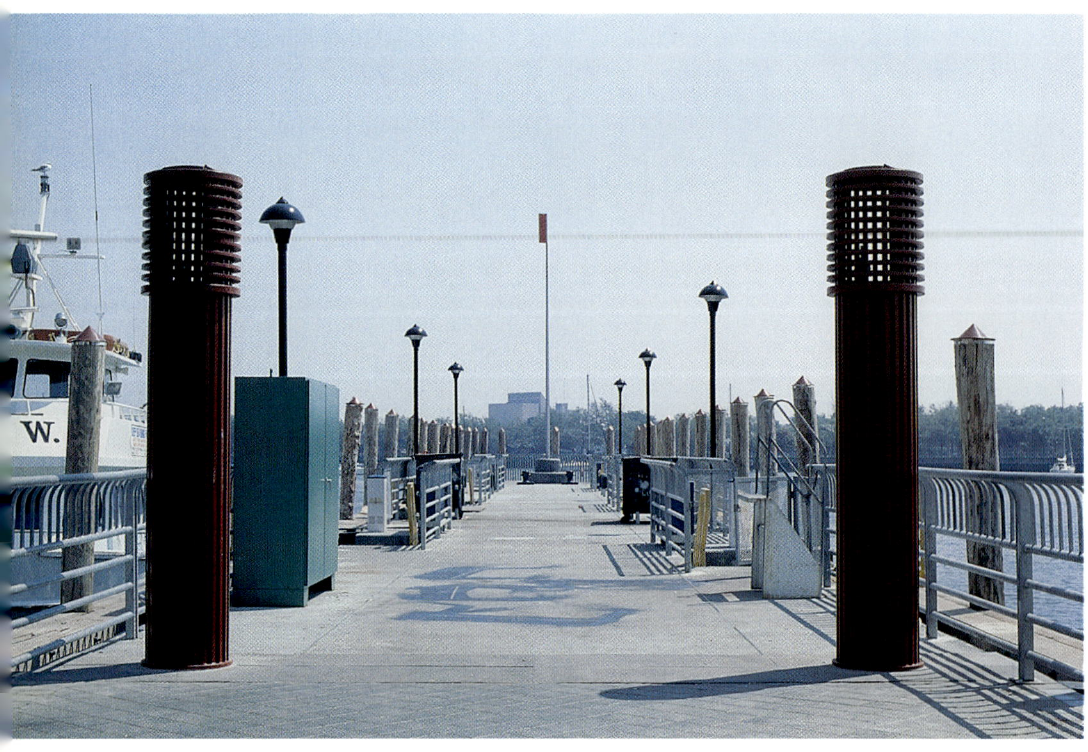

Scott Burton's refurbishment of the Sheepshead Bay fishing piers provides modern amenities while maintaining the historic character of the seventy-year-old piers. Burton framed the entry to each pier with lights and a perforated steel bench. At the end of each pier, the artist constructed a wooden ottoman and a second perforated steel bench to provide a quiet space to enjoy the water traffic and the view. The ottomans also serve as bases for 34 foot (10.4 m) tall poles that fly wind vanes shaped into colorful numbers to identify each pier. The wind vanes are visible from Emmons Avenue and the elevated roadway of the Shore Parkway, three blocks away. Burton has said of his work: "My greatest challenge with [the project] was to discover how my contribution as an artist would fit into this very practical and down-to-earth setting."

First In The Heart Is The Dream
1996
Ceramic tile, terrazzo

Public School 233, 9301 Avenue B

ARCHITECT
Robert Coles Architect
DESIGN AGENCY
School Construction Authority
SPONSOR AGENCY
Board of Education

Located in the main lobby of P.S. 233, also known as the Langston Hughes School, Carole Byard's murals and terrazzo floor feature themes inspired by Langston Hughes's poem "Freedom's Plow" (1943). According to the artist, the brightly colored ceramic tile murals, which depict students engaging in the arts and sciences, are each based on a different theme: creativity, growth, aspirations, and dreams. The terrazzo floor features text from the Hughes poem, surrounded by brass symbols of the sun and moving water.

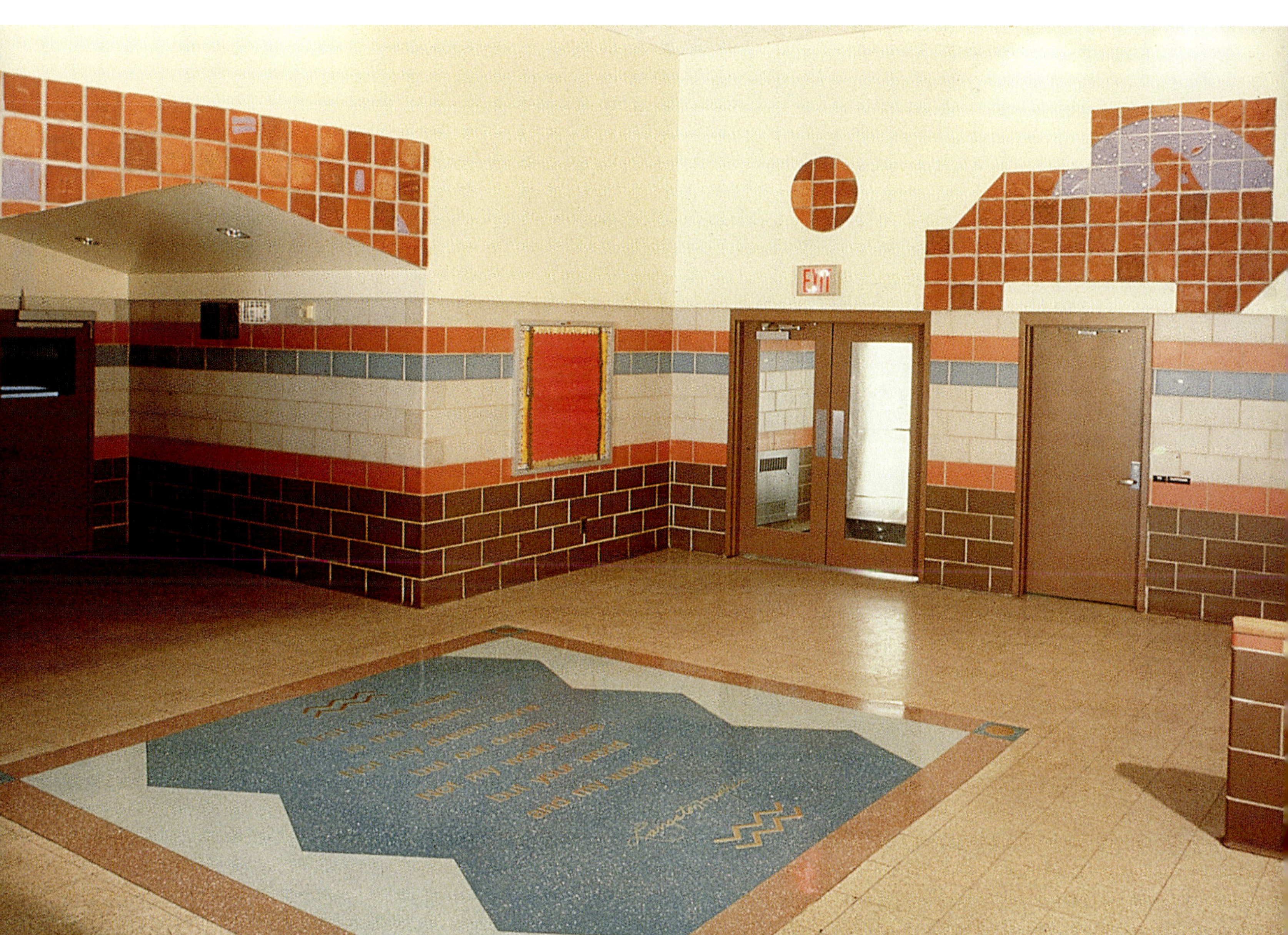

Carole Byard

Sunset Park Synergy
1998
Mosaics

Public School 24, 427 38th Street

ARCHITECT/DESIGN AGENCY
School Construction Authority
SPONSOR AGENCY
Board of Education

David Chung's *Sunset Park Synergy* captures daily life in the Sunset Park neighborhood surrounding P.S. 24. The mosaic tile mural consists of two panels flanking the school's central auditorium doors. One mosaic panel depicts Sunset Park's landmarks and buildings, and scenes of people engaged in their daily activities (below). The adjacent panel portrays five students studying science and math alongside their professional counterparts, doctors and scientists.

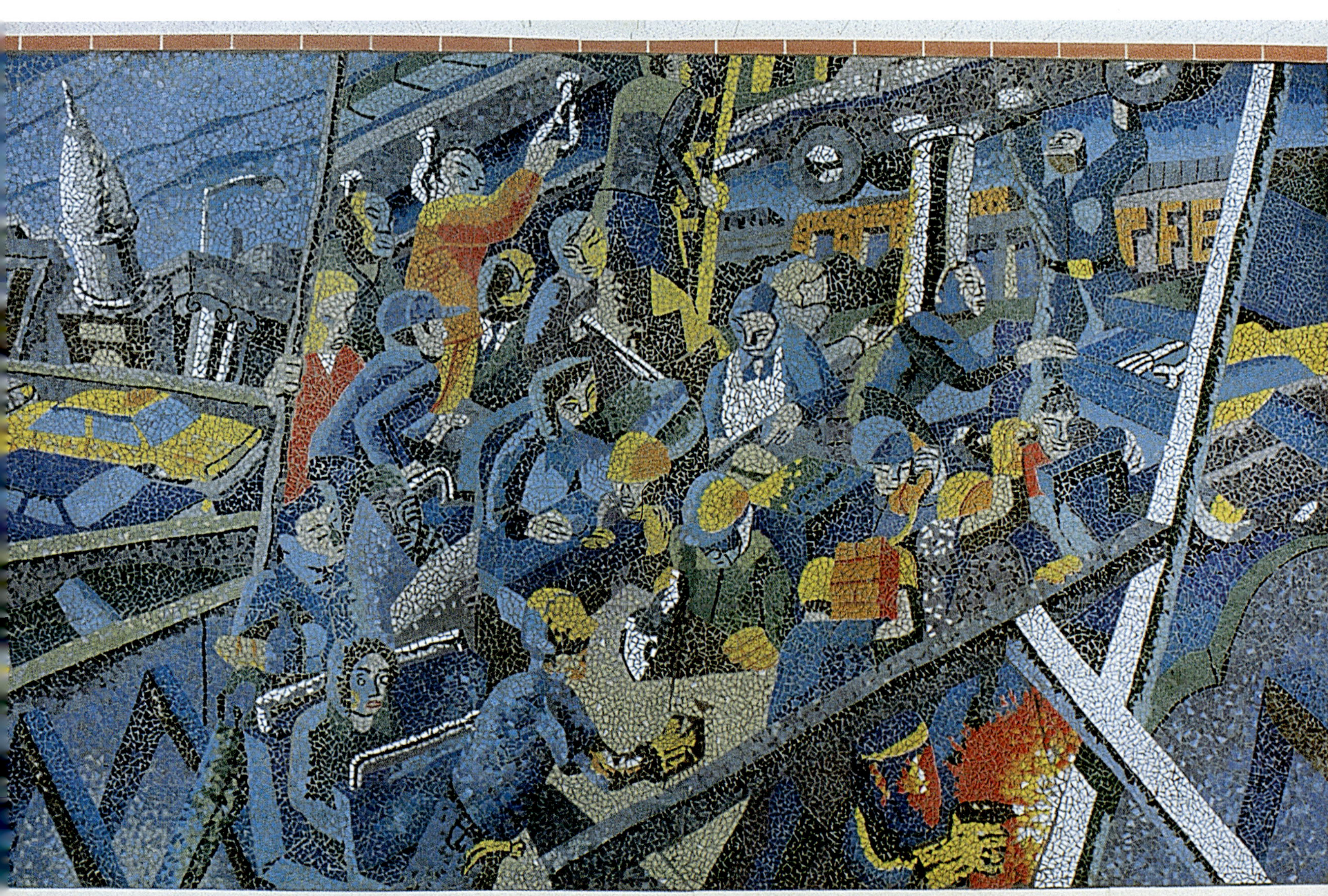

Y. David Chung

Melvin W. Clark

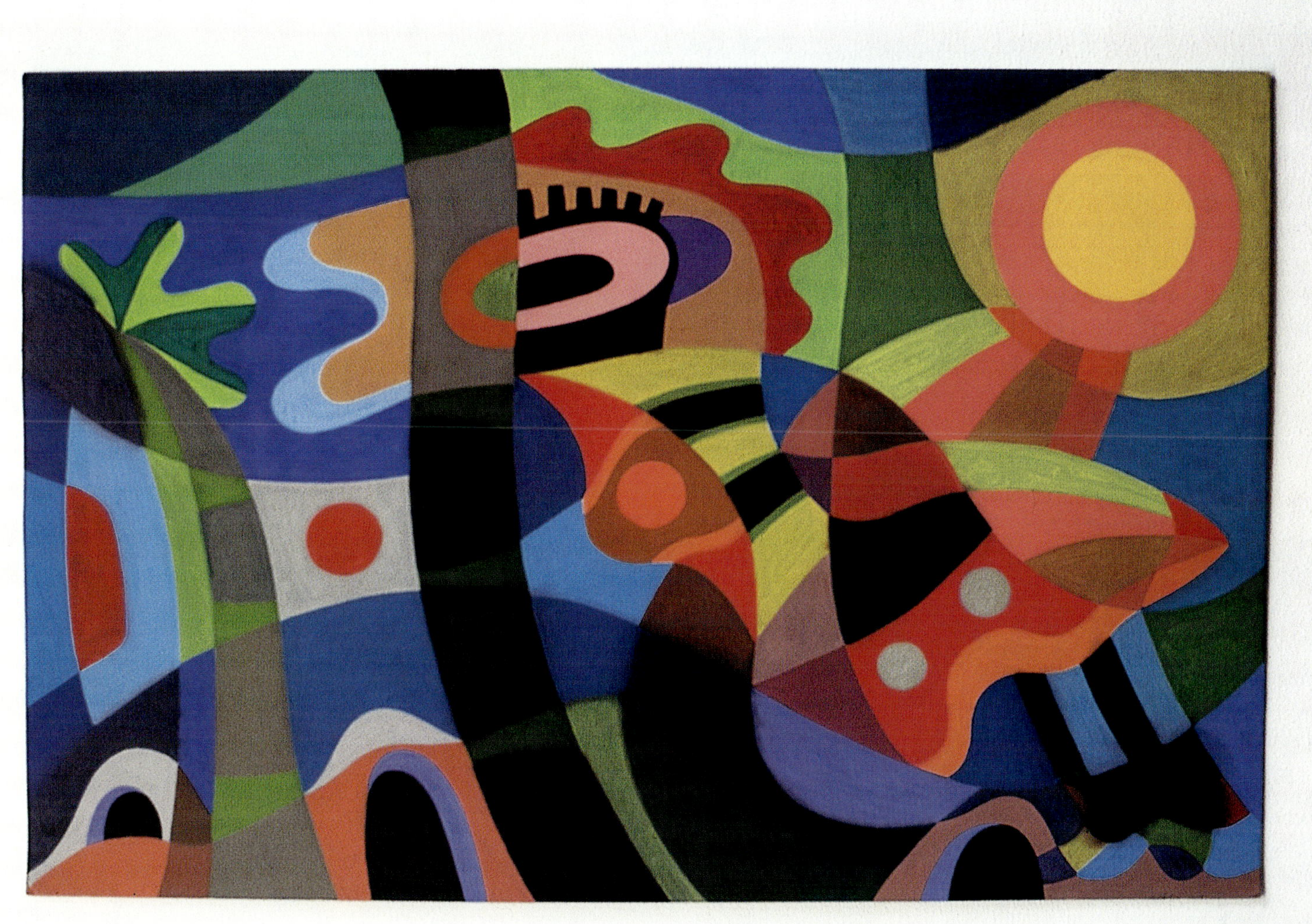

Enchanted Dreams and **Sun Bird**
1996
Ceramics

Public School 152, 725 East 23rd Street

ARCHITECT
Roberta Washington/Robert Trayham
Coles Associated Architects
DESIGN AGENCY
School Construction Authority
SPONSOR AGENCY
Board of Education

Melvin Clark designed two mosaic tile murals for P.S. 152. *Enchanted Dreams* is a surreal composition comprised of semi-abstract dancing animals and musicians playing instruments, while *Sun Bird* (above) depicts a large abstract bird being serenaded by a horn player under a bright sun. The artist intended for the artwork to provide the students at P.S. 152 with an inventive and colorful interpretation of the musical experience.

Jackie Peters Cully

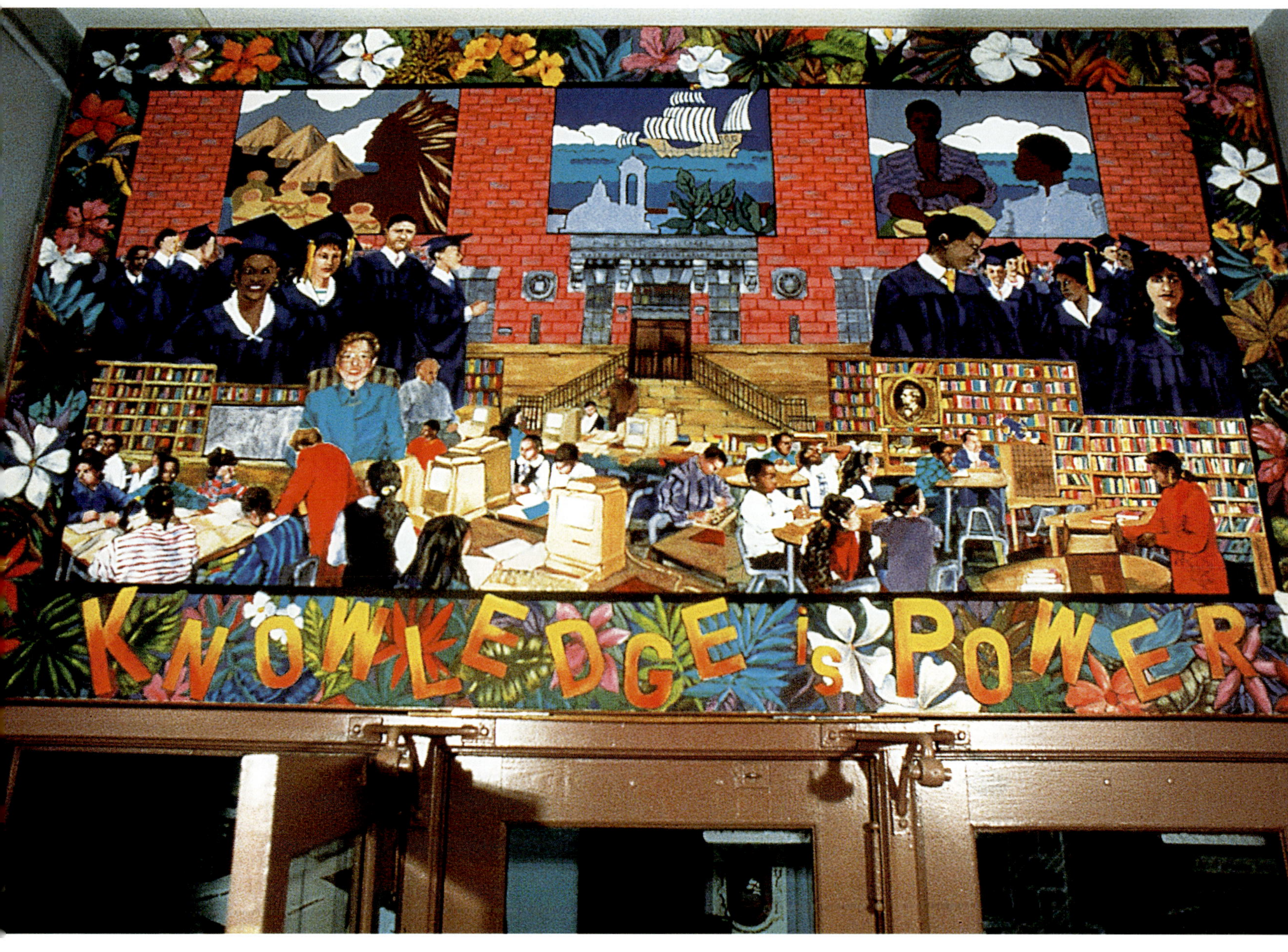

Children of Promise
1996
Painted mural

Public School 75, 95 Grove Street

ARCHITECT
Paul Pearson
DESIGN AGENCY
School Construction Authority
SPONSOR AGENCY
Board of Education

Jackie Peters Cully's mural painting, *Children of Promise,* celebrates Puerto Rican culture and the ethnically diverse neighborhood that surrounds the Brooklyn school. The school's motto, "Knowledge is Power," is featured prominently along the bottom of the mural, which extends around three walls in the school's vestibule. Along the left-hand wall, a quotation from Martin Luther King, Jr.'s "I Have a Dream" speech is printed on golden oak in black vinyl lettering. The right-hand wall bears the names of four great Puerto Rican leaders: the poet Lola Rodriguez de Tio; the political leader Luis Muñoz Rivera; the musician and composer Juan Morell Campos; and the scientist Augustin Stahl.

Transformations of the Earth
1995
Ceramics

Public School 376A, 194 Harman Street

ARCHITECT/DESIGN AGENCY
School Construction Authority
SPONSOR AGENCY
Board of Education

For his ceramic tile relief mural *Transformations of the Earth,* Agustin de Andino has superimposed one landscape on to another, depicting a collage of stars and terrain in hues of sienna and blue-gray layered over plant forms and a mountain and forests. Below the forests lurk symmetrical shadows, suggestive of amber skyscrapers. The artist intended for this piece, which is located on the exterior of P.S. 376A, to convey his concern with the deterioration of the natural environment.

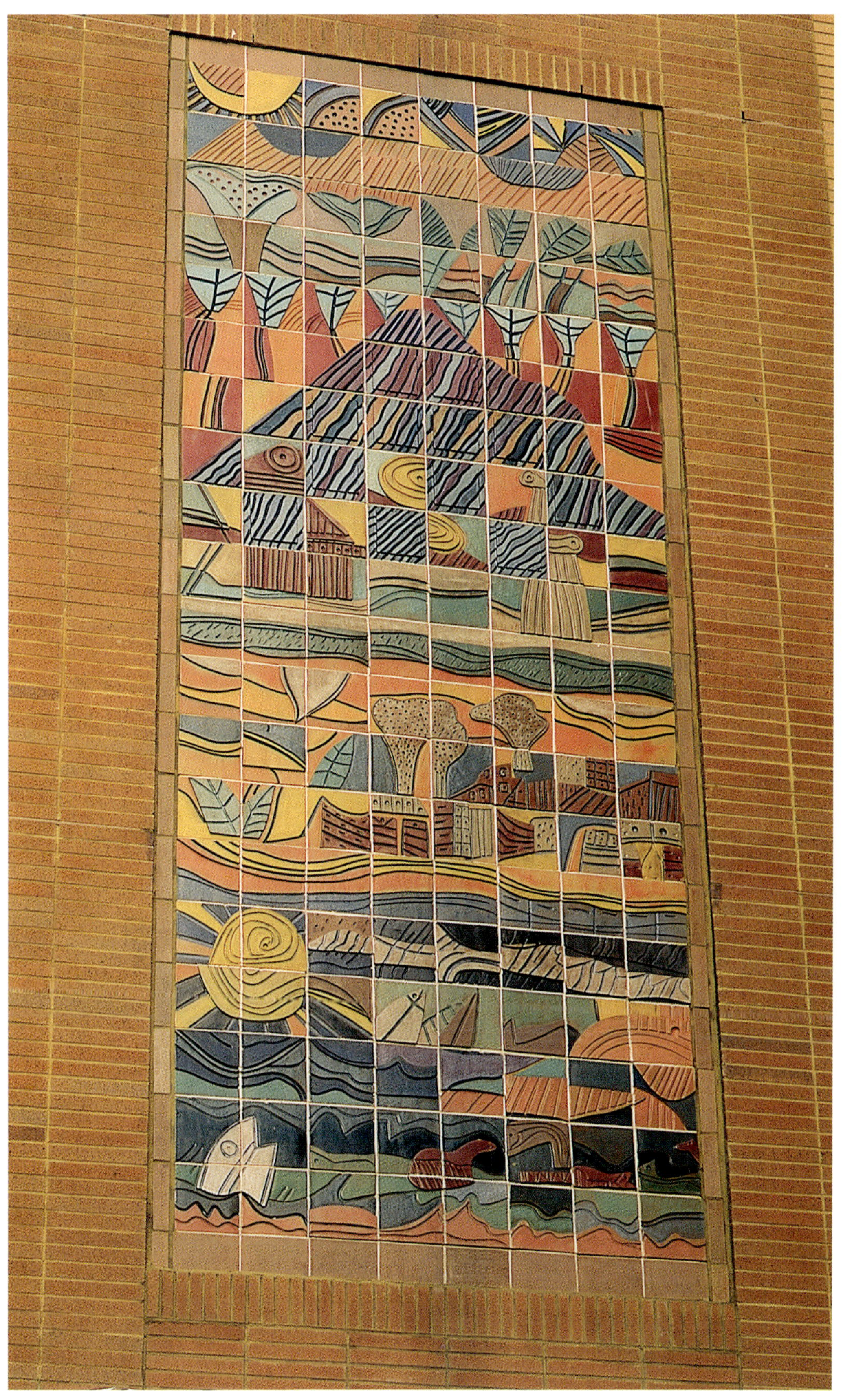

Agustin de Andino

Shrine to Learning
1993
Wood, pulp paper, acrylic paint, clay

Clarendon Library,
2035 Nostrand Avenue

ARCHITECT
Perkins Eastman
DESIGN AGENCY
Department of General Services
SPONSOR AGENCY
Brooklyn Public Library

Claudia DeMonte's bookcase sculpture at the Clarendon Library is a heavily decorated, three-dimensional, functional shelving unit. The top of this "shrine to learning" has a peaked roof and niches for low-relief sculptures relating to major types of subject matter found in the library, such as architecture, art, and history. On the surface of the work, globe and map shapes made of pulp paper and covered with acrylic paint feature countries relevant to the community's ethnically diverse population.

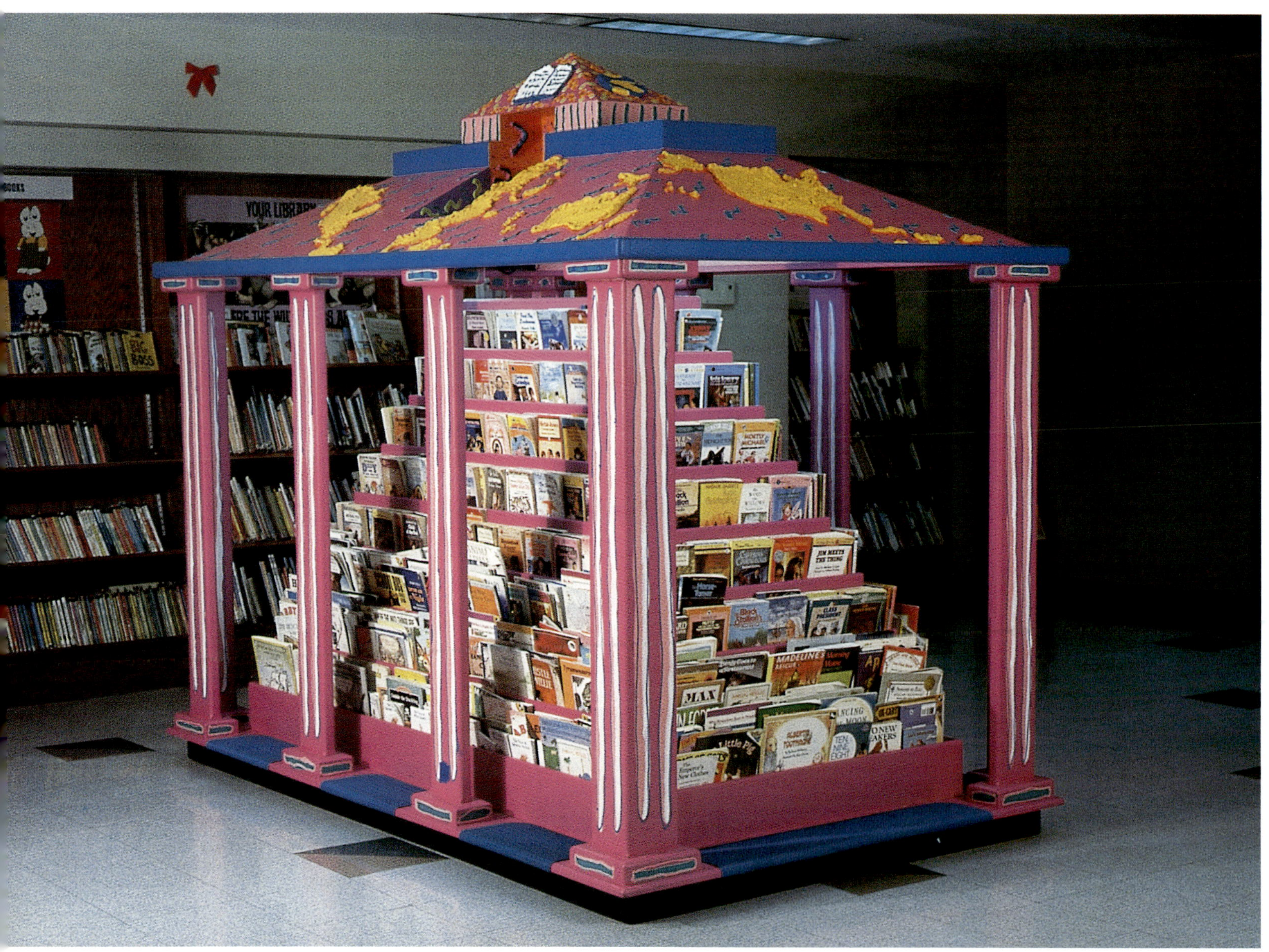

Claudia DeMonte

Julie Dermansky

Yellow Bird Floor
2000
Linoleum, steel

Alonzo Daughtry Day Care Center,
333 Second Street

ARCHITECT
Buttrick, White, and Burtis
DESIGN AGENCY
Department of Design and Construction
SPONSOR AGENCY
Agency for Child Development

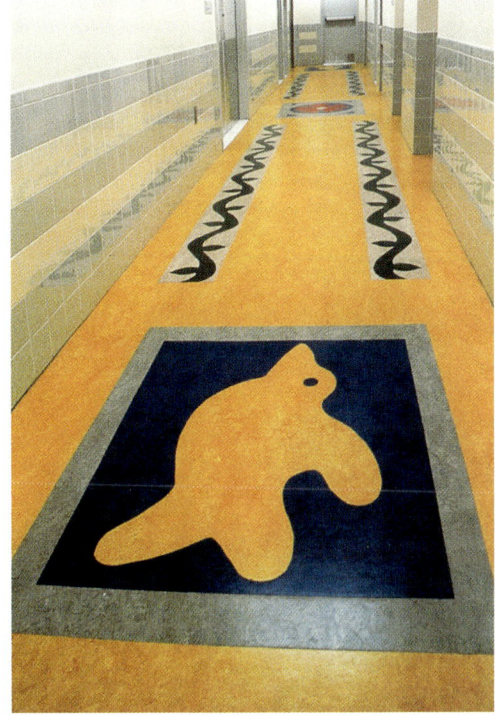

For *Yellow Bird Floor,* Dermansky employed a motif of birds and flowers in primary colors to transform the linoleum that covers the two floors of the Alonzo Daughtry Day Care Center. The installation also includes decorative steel cut-outs of birds, flowers, and turtles that the artist welded into the center's staircase railing. Dermansky has said of her work for this piece: "Creating work for a specific audience to enhance and stimulate their day-to-day experience is very satisfying to me, in ways the work I make in my studio for myself is not."

Ogundipe Fayomi

Ronald McNair Monument
1994
Bronze, granite

Dr. Ronald McNair Park, Eastern
Parkway and Washington Avenue

DESIGN/SPONSOR AGENCY
Department of Parks and Recreation

Ogundipe Fayomi's sculptural tribute to Dr. Ronald Erwin McNair, who died in the explosion of the Space Shuttle Challenger in 1986, consists of two bronze plaques featuring images of McNair's life and achievements and a life-size bust mounted on a pyramidal monument of polished Missouri red granite. The monument, which includes various quotations from McNair carved into the red stone, is situated in the middle of a circle of contrasting granite pavement. The pavement's circumference is the same size as that of the Space Shuttle Challenger. Fayoni has said of his work: "On the whole this monument will give the visual power of the geometric, the realism of the portrait, and relief and inspiration in the quotations."

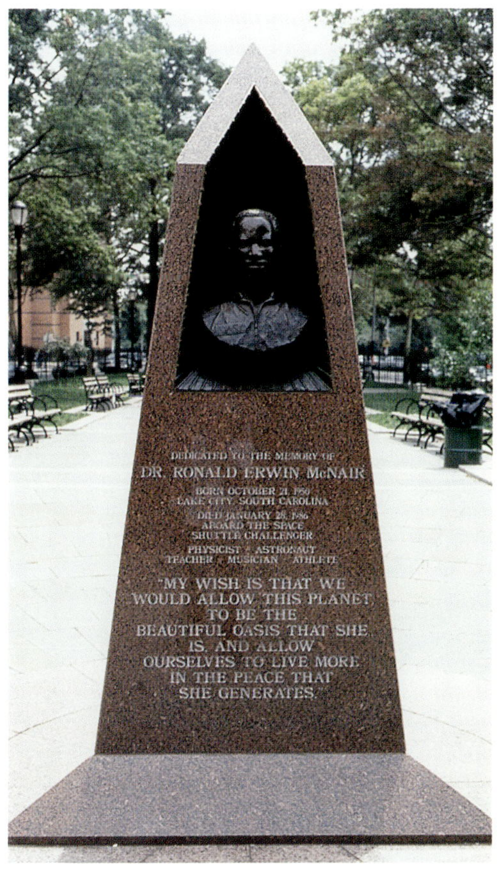

Susan Gardner

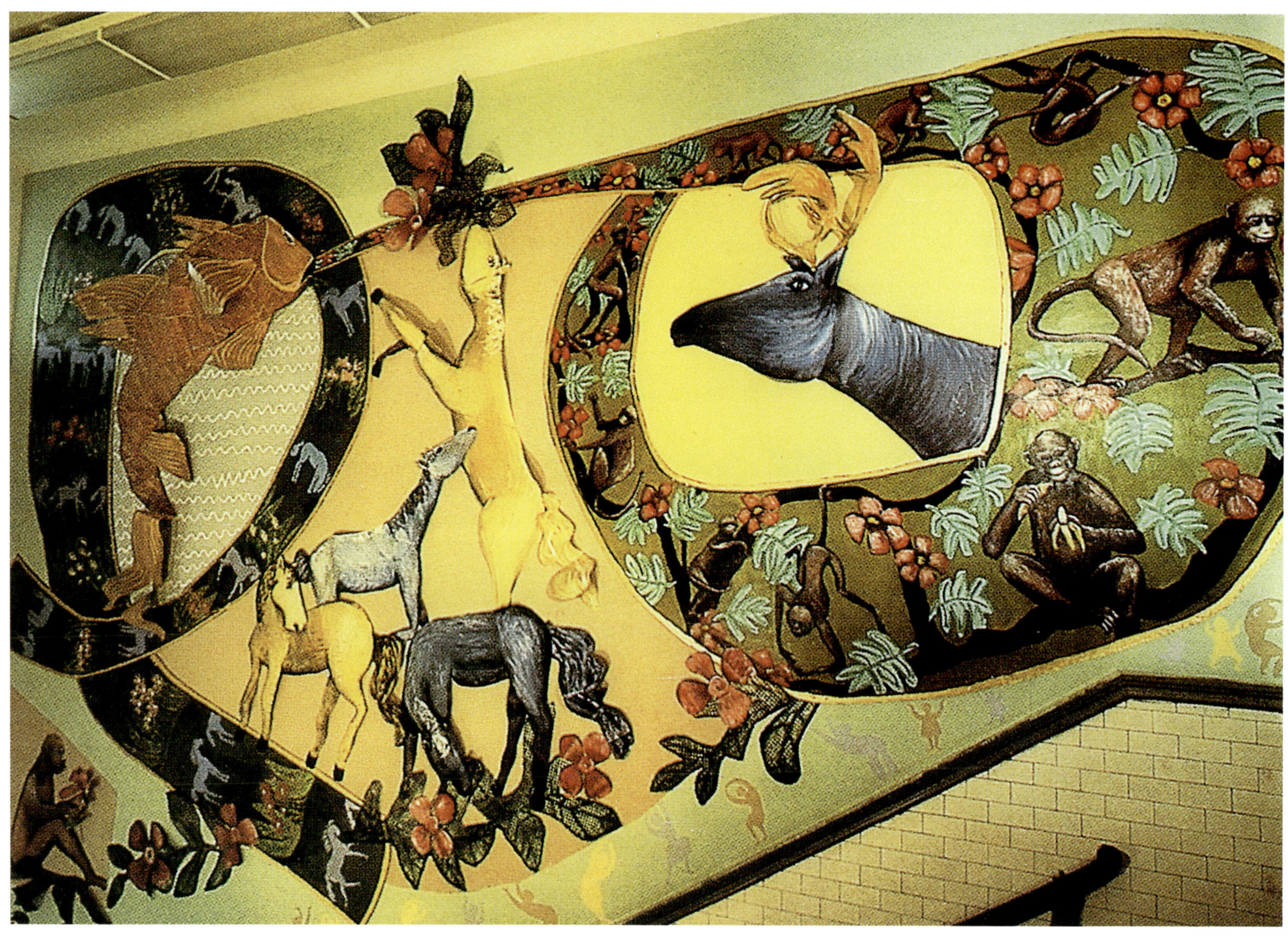

Animal Party
1987
Paint, mixed media

Public School 94, 5010 Sixth Avenue

ARCHITECT
Division of School Buildings, Board of Education
DESIGN/SPONSOR AGENCY
Board of Education

Susan Gardner's two whimsical murals of animals and lush, tropical foliage are installed at P.S. 94 in the Sunset Park neighborhood. A parade of flamingos, a big gorilla, a fish, flowers, and a blue moose preside from opposing walls over the once dark stairwell of the building's main entrance (above). Along the bottom edge of the murals, a line of dancing children, painted in silhouette, observe the animal party. Gardner has said that her intent was "to transform the forbidding, gloomy entrance staircase into a welcoming one that children, especially smaller ones, would be eager to enter and experience."

We Shall Overcome
1994
Bronze
Powerful Days
1994
Bronze

Public School 6, 43 Snyder Avenue

ARCHITECT
Gruzen Samton Steinglass
DESIGN AGENCY
School Construction Authority
SPONSOR AGENCY
Board of Education

Peter Gourfain's *We Shall Overcome* (right) is a large-scale bronze sculpture of an arm and hand that rises from a concrete pedestal in front of P.S. 6. Carved into the sculpture are significant scenes from African-American history, such as Martin Luther King, Jr.'s march on Washington, D.C. Gourfain continued his project in the school library by designing *Powerful Days*, a bronze bas-relief that features the same images as those on the sculpture outside.

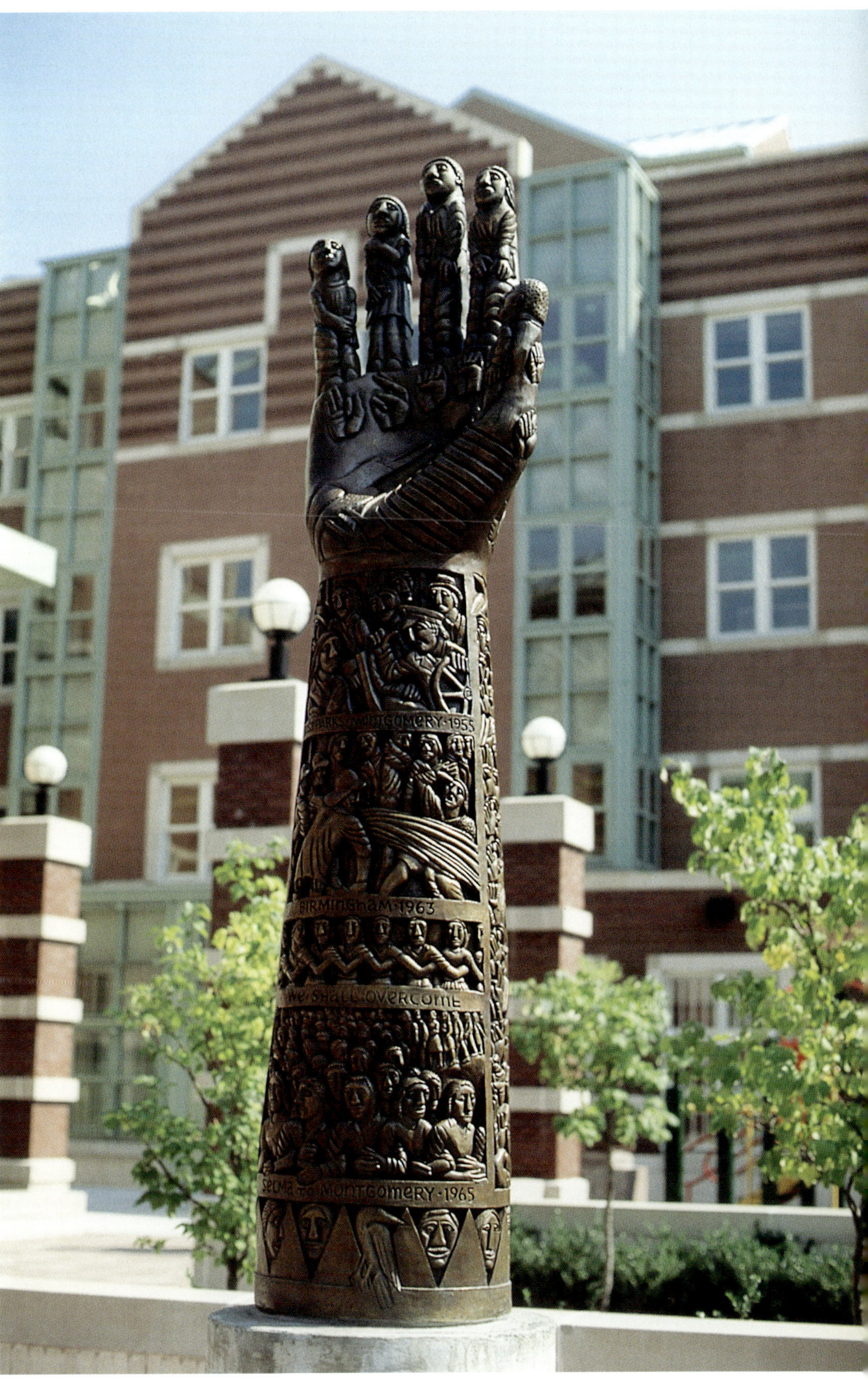

Peter Gourfain

Spirals
2000
Terra-cotta, glass, bronze, mixed media

Middle College High School at Medgar Evers College, 1186 Carroll Street

ARCHITECT
Davis Brody Bond
DESIGN AGENCY
School Construction Authority
SPONSOR AGENCY
Board of Education

Jane Greengold's work at Middle College High School was inspired by her research into chaos theory and contemporary science. *Spirals*, a multi-part installation located on each of the school's five floors, explores the different ways spirals appear in space and nature. The largest of the pieces, a 12½ × 20 foot (3.8 × 6 m) terra-cotta mural of a spiral galaxy based on NASA color-enhanced photographs, is located at the school's entrance. Glass blocks set into the walls of the second and fourth floors feature sandblasted images of natural spirals such as ferns and the centers of sunflowers. Six-million-year-old fossils embedded in Saharan limestone are also installed in the walls on these floors. Four bronze plaques depicting spiral images from the Ashanti, Greek, Irish, and Andean cultures are mounted on the walls of the fifth floor, and a spiral of the mathematical golden rule appears on the school's fence.

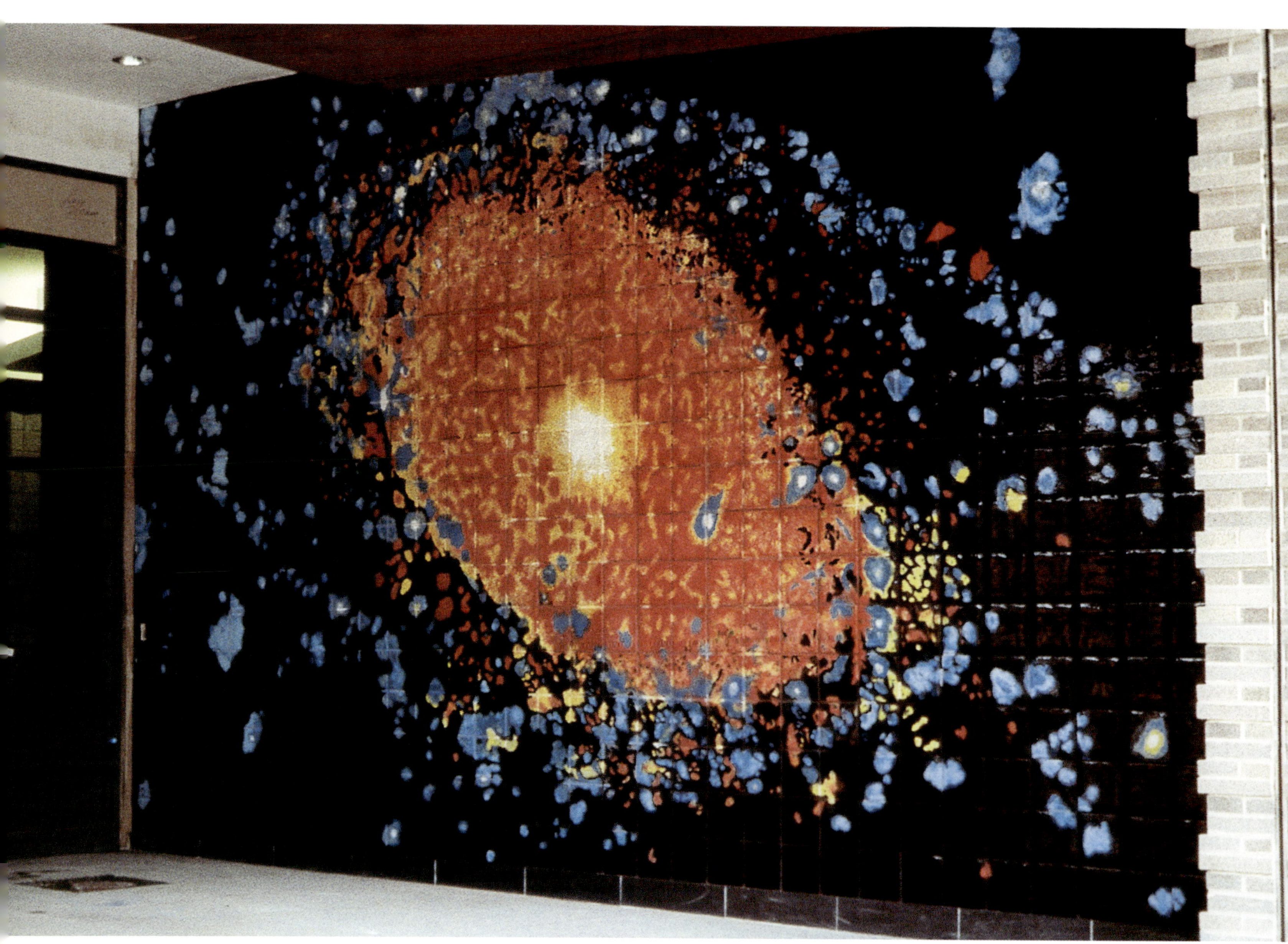

Jane Greengold

Jose Rafael Guzman

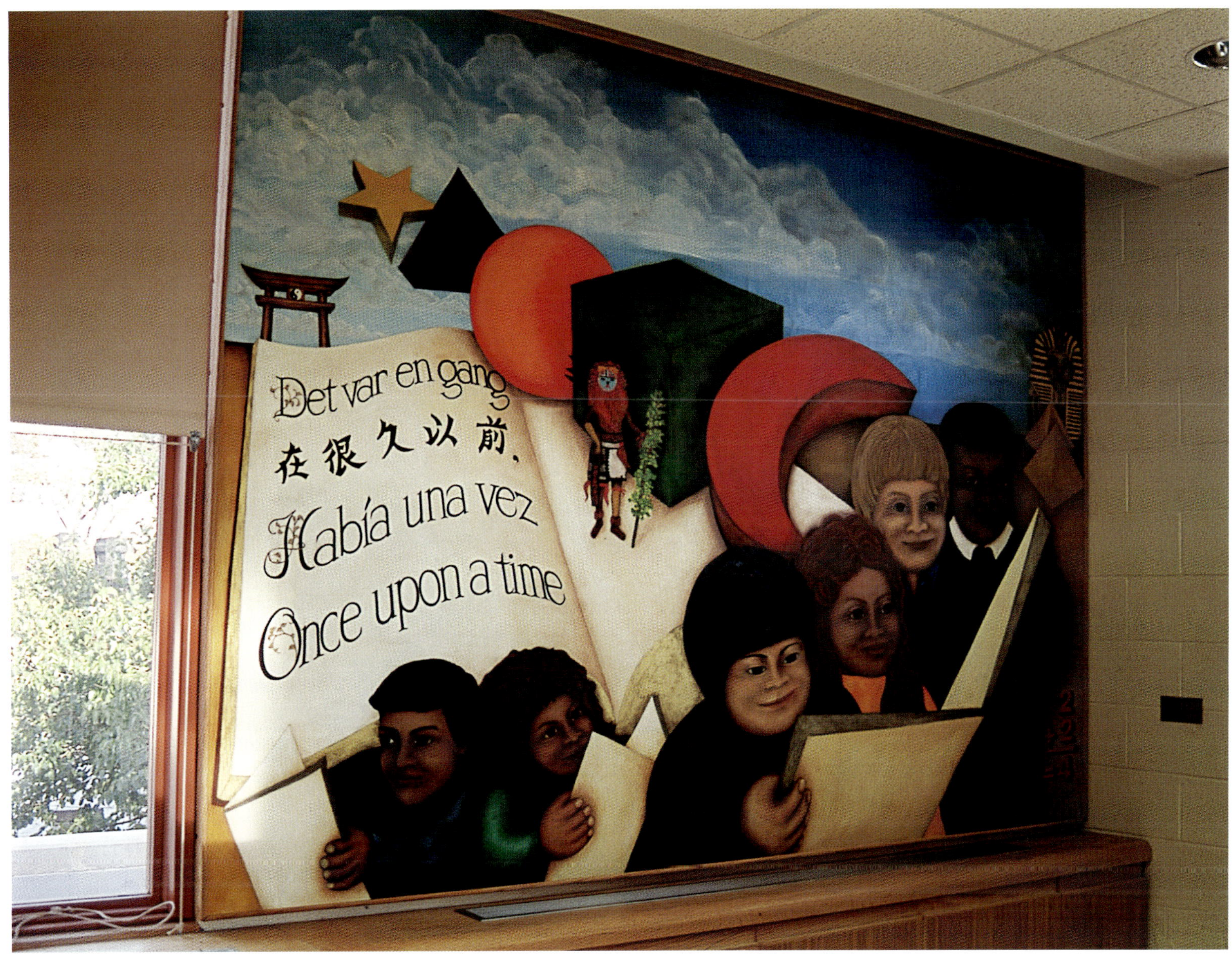

And They Lived
1998
Oil on canvas

Public School 24, 427 38th Street

ARCHITECT/DESIGN AGENCY
School Construction Authority
SPONSOR AGENCY
Board of Education

Located on facing walls in the library of P.S. 24, Jose Rafael Guzman's two murals depict images associated with elementary school education, including adults and children reading books together, building blocks, and basic mathematical equations. The murals each feature a large open book; one is inscribed with the phrase, "Once upon a time . . . ," and the other with "And they lived . . . ," referring to the beginning and the end of a children's story.

Mags Harries

Topiary: A Twenty Year Project
1993
Aluminum frames, topiary

Prospect Park Zoo, 450 Flatbush Avenue

ARCHITECT
Goldstone and Hinz
DESIGN/SPONSOR AGENCY
Department of Parks and Recreation

Mags Harries created nine larger-than-life topiary frames of various creatures for the main court of the Prospect Park Zoo. The color-coated, aluminum-filigree sculptures, which include a Jackson chameleon, an octopus, and five river eels, loom beside or straddle one of the park's main entry paths. At the base of each sculpture is a grouping of Korean boxwoods. As the plants grow, their foliage wraps around and fills the sculptures, bringing the presently hollow sculptural forms to life. "Time plays a major role in this artwork," Harries has written. "The children visiting the zoo will, over time, observe the boxwood gradually filling the forms. They may, in fact, return with their own children and mark the passage of time with the memory of the topiary at its various stages."

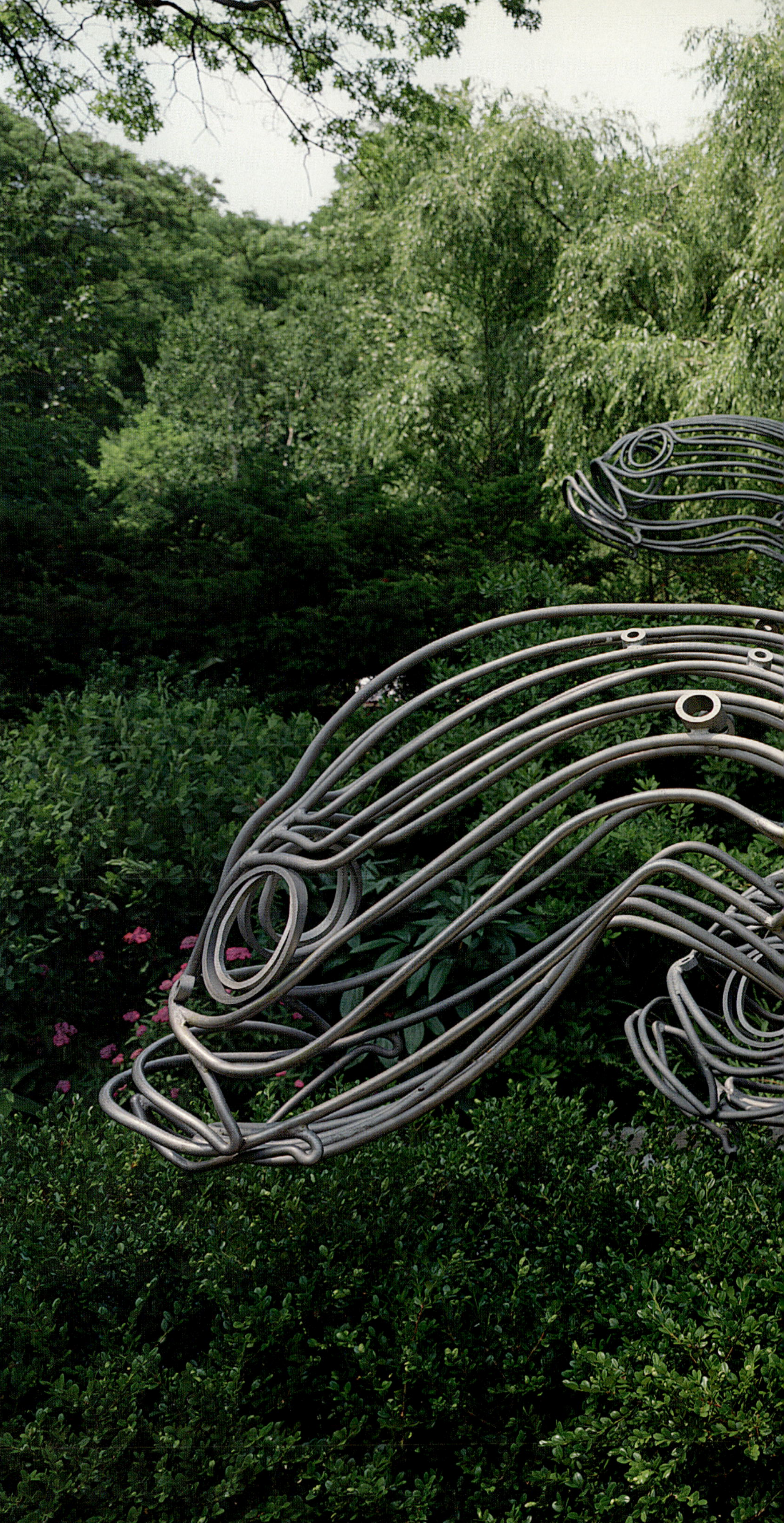

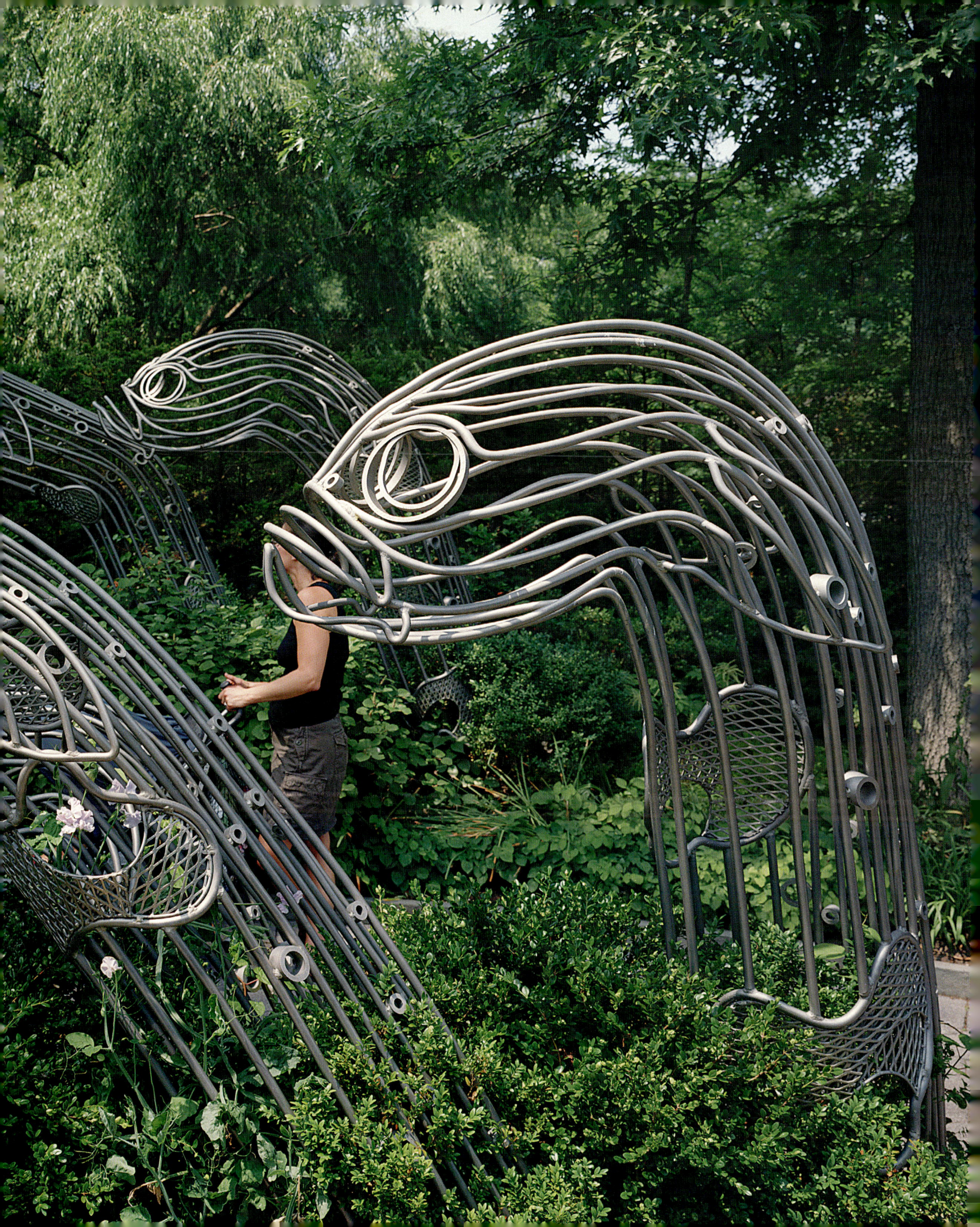

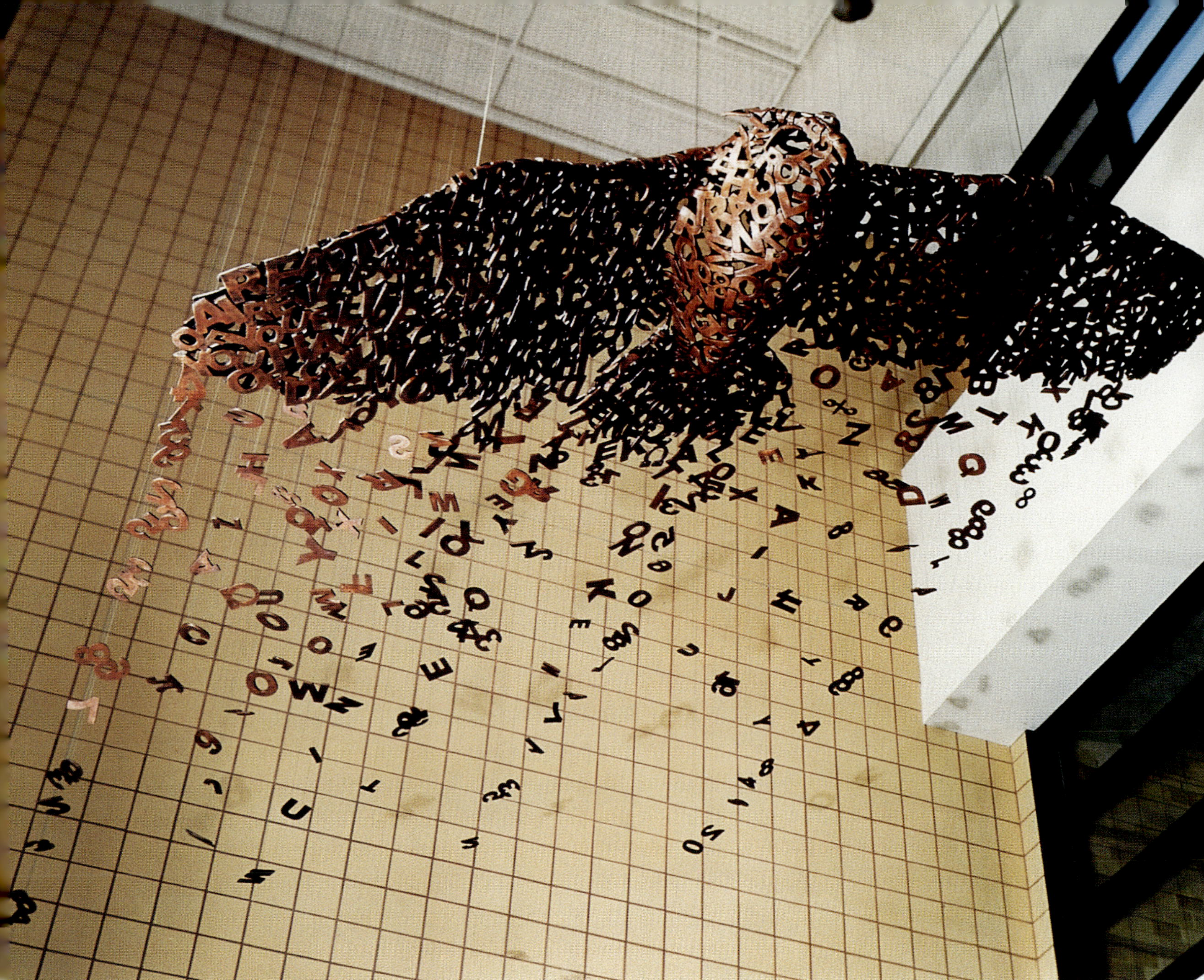

Genius
2002
Bronze, cable-cast bronze, stainless-steel cable

Leon M. Goldstein High School for the Sciences, 2001 Oriental Boulevard

ARCHITECT/DESIGN AGENCY
School Construction Authority
SPONSOR AGENCY
Board of Education

Genius is a bronze sculpture of a great-horned owl in flight, suspended over the main entrance to the Leon M. Goldstein High School for the Sciences. Ralph Helmick and Stuart Schechter created the owl out of hundreds of cast-bronze numerals, symbols, and letterforms culled from language and science, which dissolve into a disparate array behind the owl's tail. Within the sculpture, rows of numbers display the decimal equivalent of pi, and letters spell out the names of major scholars from various fields. Viewers who carefully examine the undersides of the owl's wings can decipher a quotation from Walt Whitman.

Ralph Helmick and Stuart Schechter

Robin Holder

Rites of Passage
1997
Stained glass, wood, paint, ceramics

High School Redirection,
226 Bristol Street

ARCHITECT
Rothzeid Kaiserman Thomson and Bee
DESIGN AGENCY
School Construction Authority
SPONSOR AGENCY
Board of Education

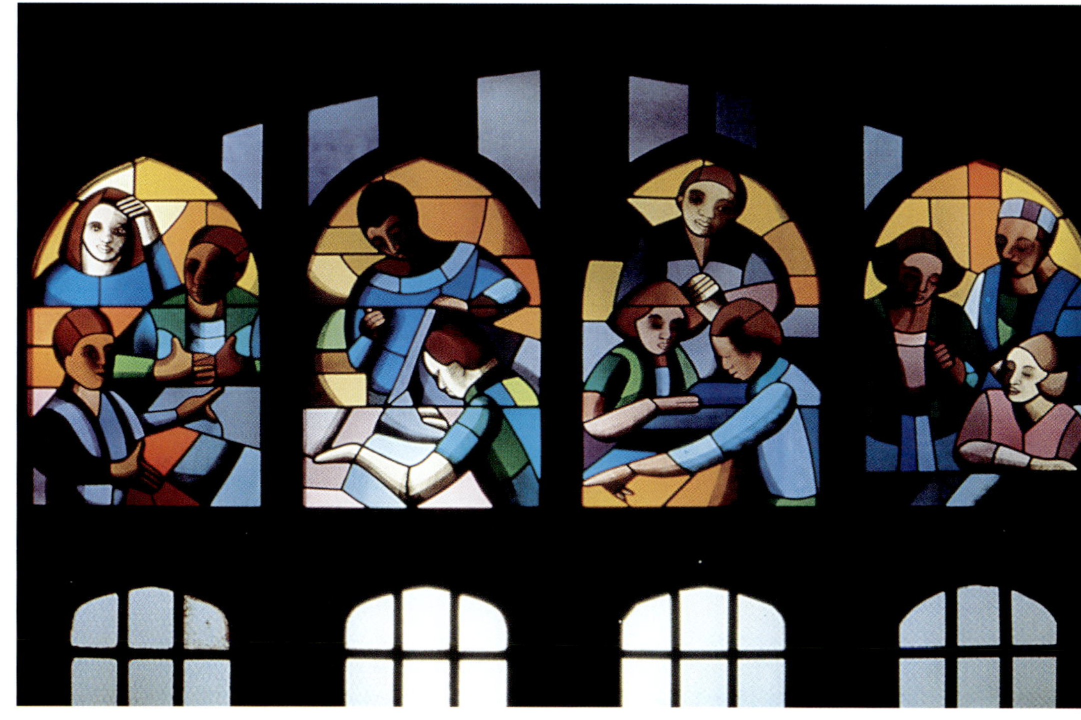

Robin Holder's *Rites of Passage*, at the High School Redirection, includes a series of stained-glass windows and painted wooden reliefs depicting aspects of student life. The windows, which are located in the school's lobby and second-floor conference room, feature students working and studying together. The painted reliefs, which are installed at each end of the school's hallways, are encased in recessed cabinets and surrounded by sky-blue and pale green ceramic tiles.

Wopo Holup

Jim Thorpe Garden Fence
1996
Steel, cast iron, landscaping materials

Public School 370,
3000 West First Street

ARCHITECT
Lee Harris Pomeroy Associates
DESIGN AGENCY
School Construction Authority
SPONSOR AGENCY
Board of Education

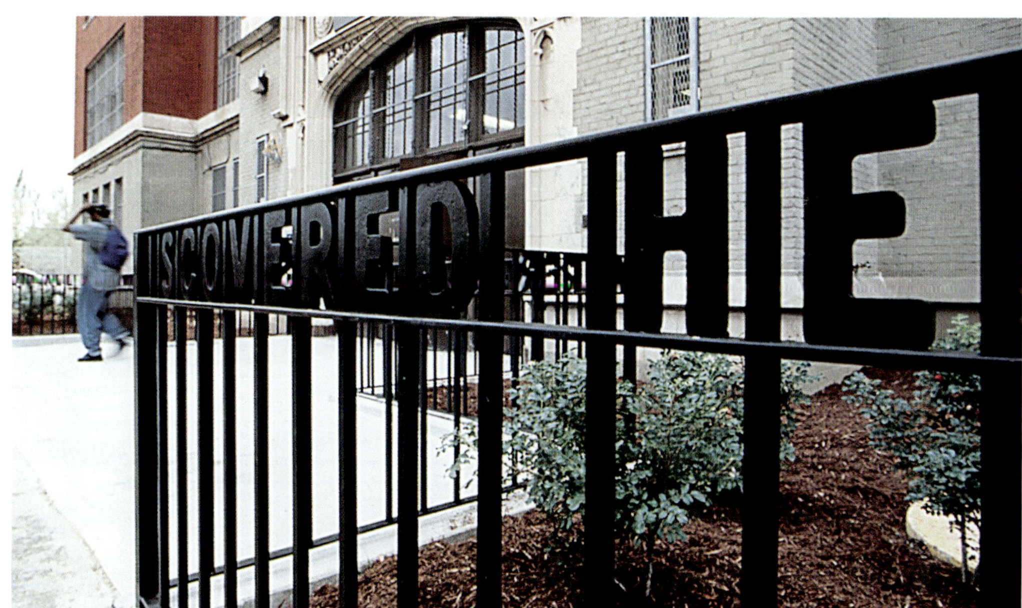

Wopo Holup's 184 foot (56 m) long fence of welded steel and cast iron for P.S. 370 serves as a tribute to the Olympic athlete Jim Thorpe. Incorporated into the fence, which surrounds two small gardens in front of the school, is a short biography of Thorpe's life cast in 6 inch (15 cm) tall iron letters. The text runs the length of the fence, and reads: "Jim Thorpe U.S. athlete recognized the greatest all-around athlete of the 20th century. Born May 22, 1887 Oklahoma Territory Sac and Fox Tribe. Twice named halfback on All-American teams won pentathlon and decathlon 1912 Olympic games. After it was discovered he had played semi-pro baseball summers 1910–11 his medals were taken and Olympic records erased, died 1953. Amateur status and medals restored 1983."

Arlan Huang

American Origins
1996
Glass

Public School 152, 725 East 23rd Street

ARCHITECT
Hirsch/Danois Partnership
DESIGN AGENCY
School Construction Authority
SPONSOR AGENCY
Board of Education

Located in the classrooms at P.S. 152, Arlan Huang's sculptures, collectively entitled *American Origins*, feature 247 glass stones encased in glass blocks, which are etched with information from the school's archives. The text includes a 1908 graduation program cover and a commencement program, a 1910 and 1912 Parents' Day announcement, the school song, and a listing of all the students enrolled in 1908 giving details of their race, religion, ethnicity, and place of birth. The artist included transparent, translucent, and opaque colors in creating the glass stones, some of which are whole, and others cracked or broken.

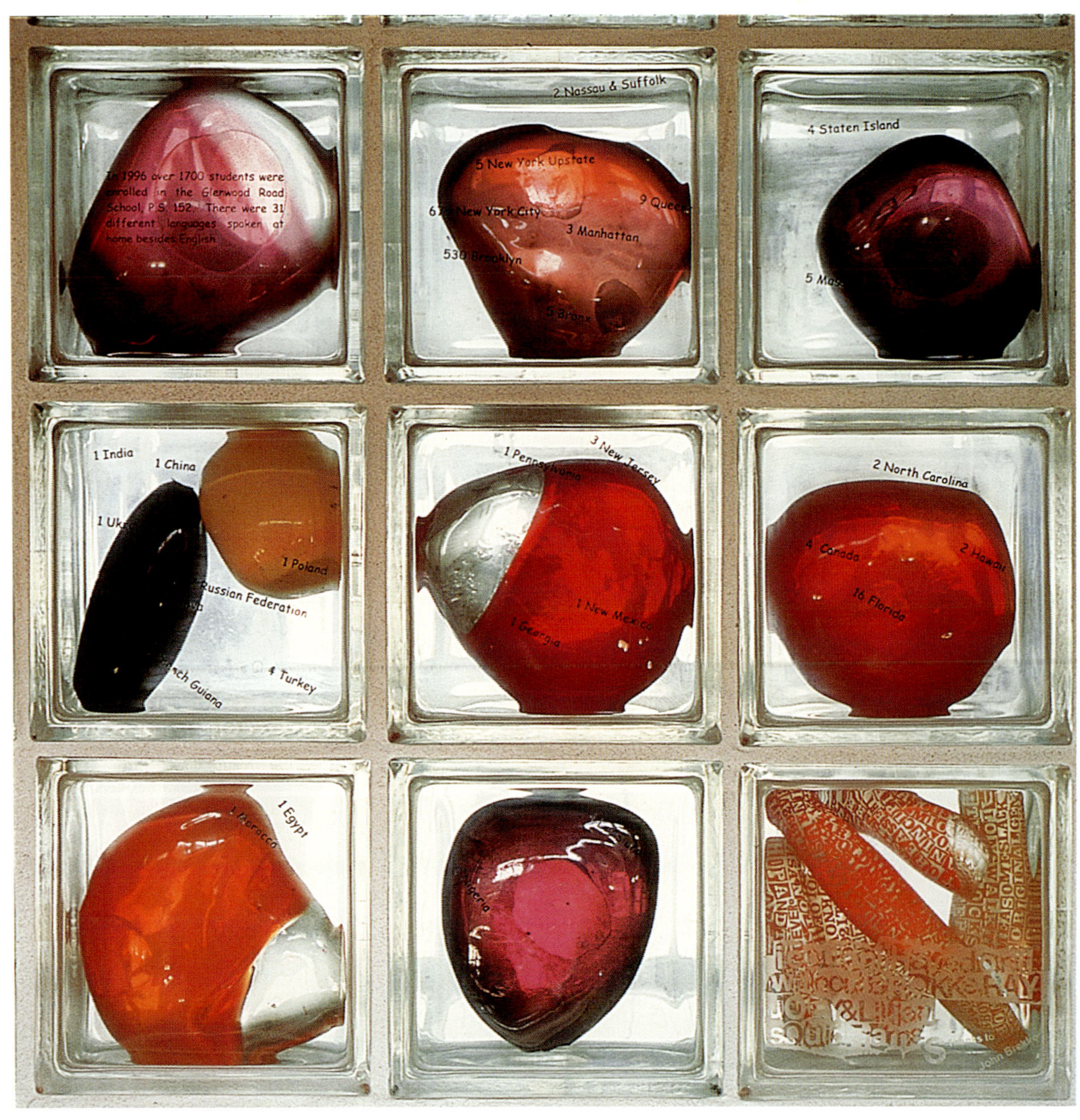

Carlton Ingleton

The Spirit of Love
1997
Wood, mixed media, concrete

Brooklyn Juvenile Detention Center, 17 Bristol Street

ARCHITECT
Kaplan McLaughlin Diaz
DESIGN AGENCY
Department of Design and Construction
SPONSOR AGENCY
Department of Juvenile Justice

Carlton Ingleton's *The Spirit of Love* is an installation of murals and a series of forty medallions for the Brooklyn Juvenile Detention Center. The murals, located in the main lobby, feature representations of artistic, architectural, and scientific achievement, and are linked by a central panel showing embracing figures standing on a stack of books. The cast concrete medallions that are inset on the site's exterior walls depict representations of spiritual affinity and progressive alliances in art and technology.

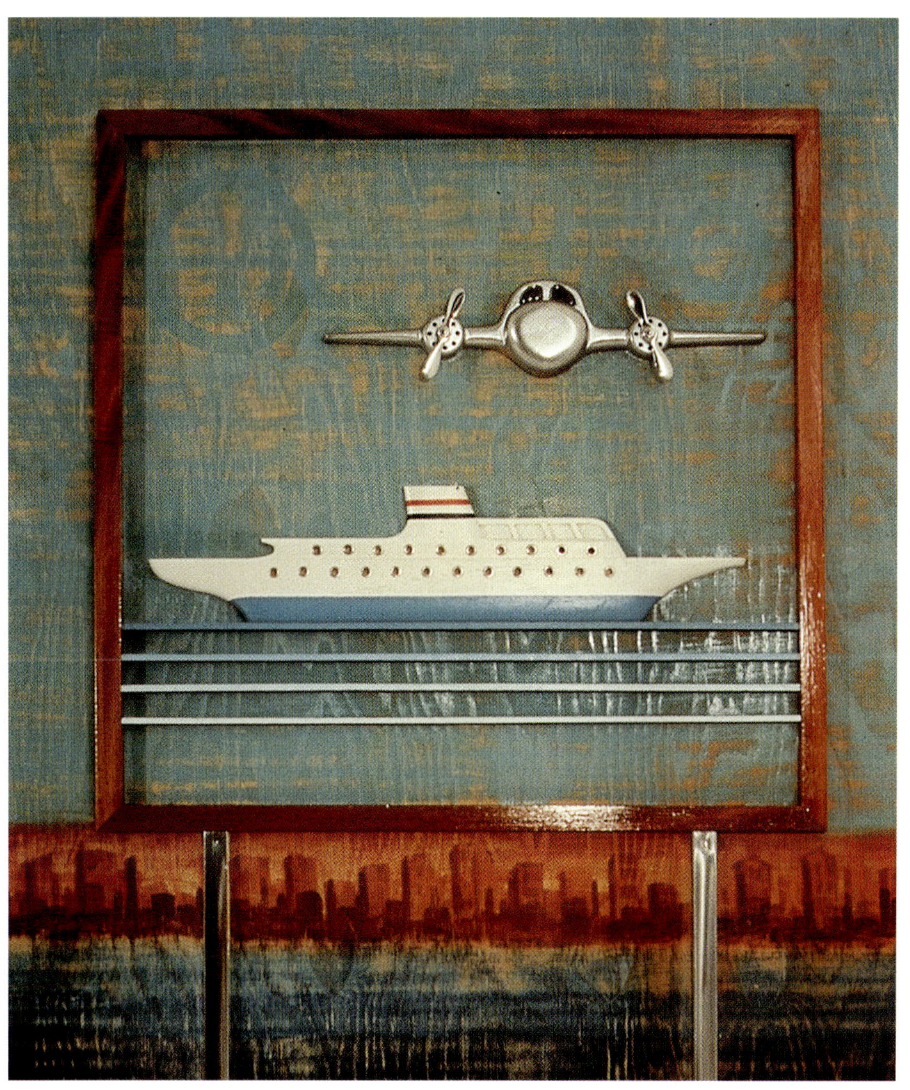

M.L.J. Johnson

I Can Read
1995
Acrylic, wood

East Flatbush Library, 9612 Church Avenue

ARCHITECT
Roger C. Lewis and Associates
DESIGN AGENCY
Department of General Services
SPONSOR AGENCY
Brooklyn Public Library

For his work at the East Flatbush Library, M.L.J. Johnson created a pictogram and wall mural based on the phrase, "I Can Read." Inspired by Native American culture, the pictogram is comprised of twelve totemic structures, each of which features words or phrases that the artist believes are endowed with intrinsic, communicative value. Johnson also painted a freestanding bookshelf, which he topped with a wooden figure of a bird.

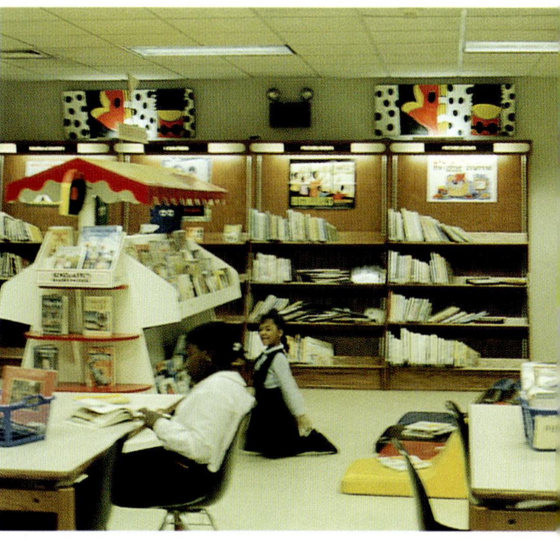

Calendar
1995
Aluminum, paint, Plexiglas, terrazzo

Intermediate School 2,
655 Parkside Avenue

ARCHITECT
Richard Dattner and Partners Architects
DESIGN AGENCY
School Construction Authority
SPONSOR AGENCY
Board of Education

On the ceiling of the main entrance lobby at I.S. 2 is Roberto Juarez's *Calendar*, a 22 foot (6.7 m) wide circular mural made up of four vivid concentric bands of color. Images of plant life are painted over the surface and include a palm tree from the tropics, a flower from an Egyptian wall painting, and a bowl of fruit from a Persian miniature painting. The mural, executed on aluminum using high-load golden acrylic paint textured with Plexiglas shavings, echoes the terrazzo floor below.

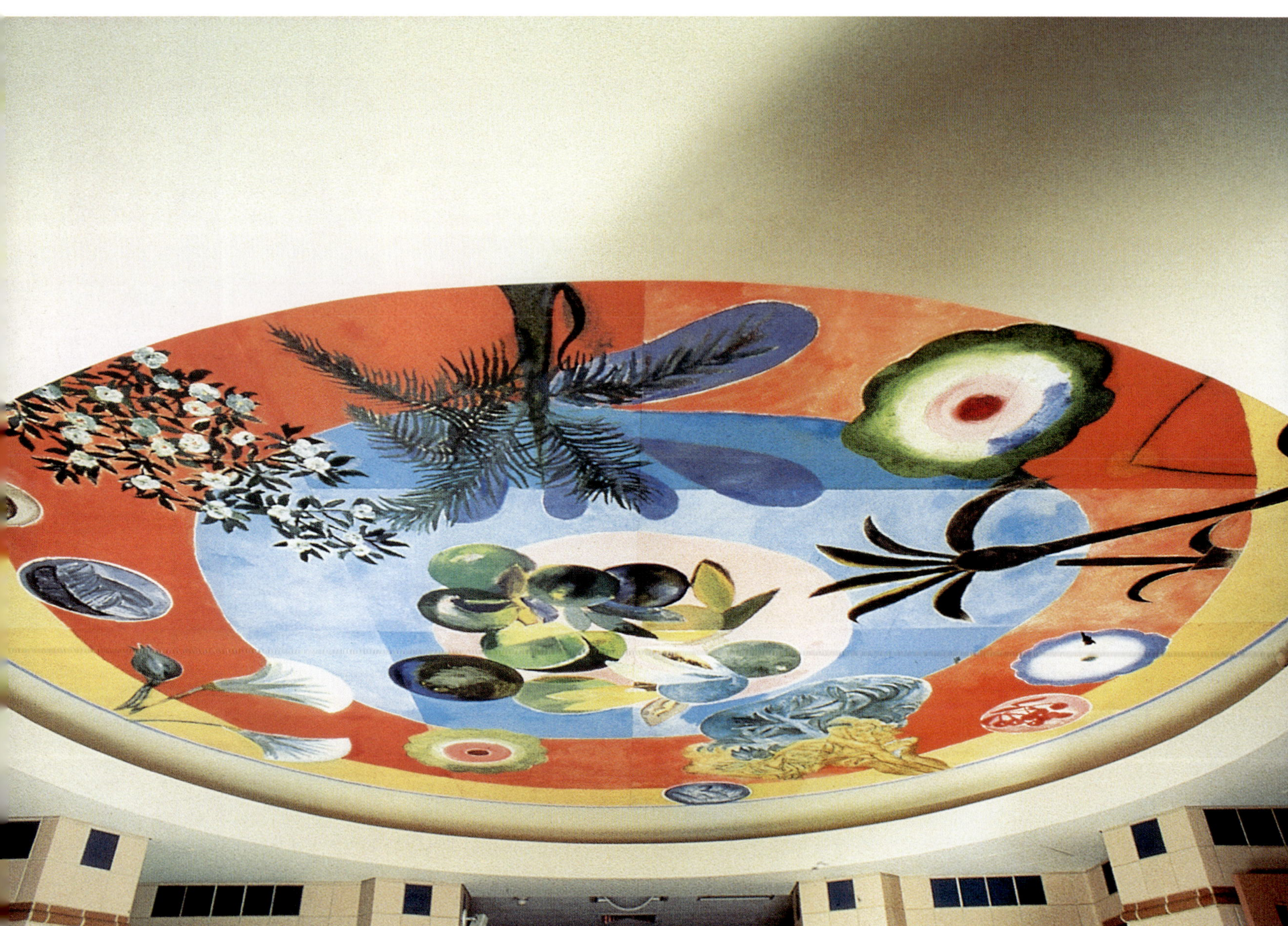

Roberto Juarez

George Mason

Untitled
1995
Hand-carved terra-cotta bas-reliefs

Public School 181,
1023 New York Avenue

ARCHITECT
Swanke Hayden Connell
DESIGN AGENCY
School Construction Authority
SPONSOR AGENCY
Board of Education

George Mason's glazed terra-cotta reliefs, located on the exterior façade of P.S. 181, depict the intricate and fanciful headdresses worn by participants in Brooklyn's annual West Indian Day Parade. The terra-cotta hue of the work complements the surrounding brick façade. The artist also included blue and turquoise in the recessed areas of the reliefs, to reference the blue waters of the Caribbean Sea.

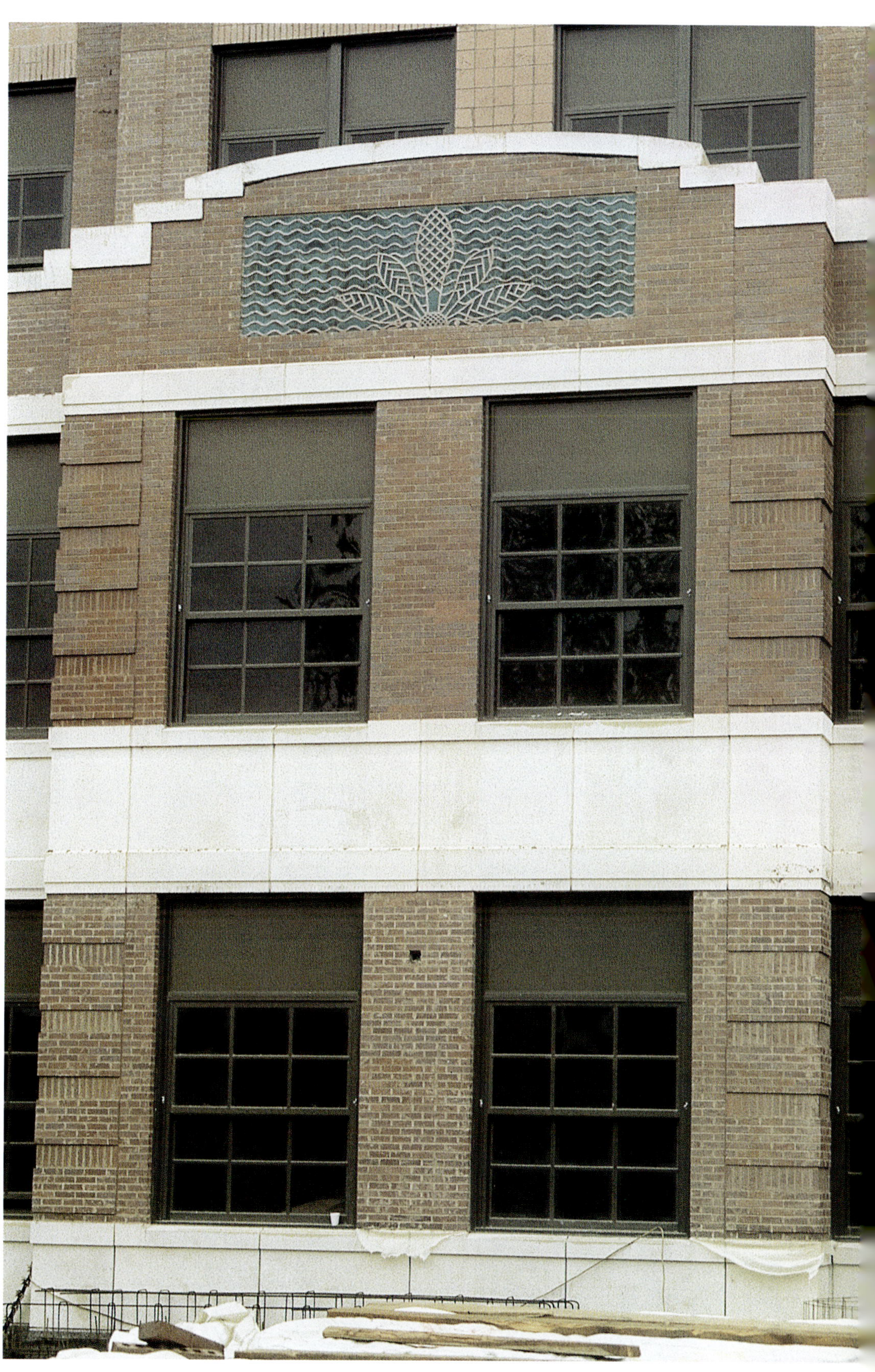

Valerie Maynard

Untitled
2001
Wood, cast concrete

Public School 181,
1023 New York Avenue

ARCHITECT
Swanke Hayden Connell
DESIGN AGENCY
School Construction Agency
SPONSOR AGENCY
Board of Education

Valerie Maynard has created two sets of work at P.S. 181. At the entrance to the school's auditorium are low-relief woodcarvings depicting a mother and child, an image which the artist intended to represent education as a nurturing force. Maynard's second installation at the site is a low-relief cast-concrete work that depicts stylized figures of children playing (below). This work is embedded in the wall that encircles the early-childhood playground.

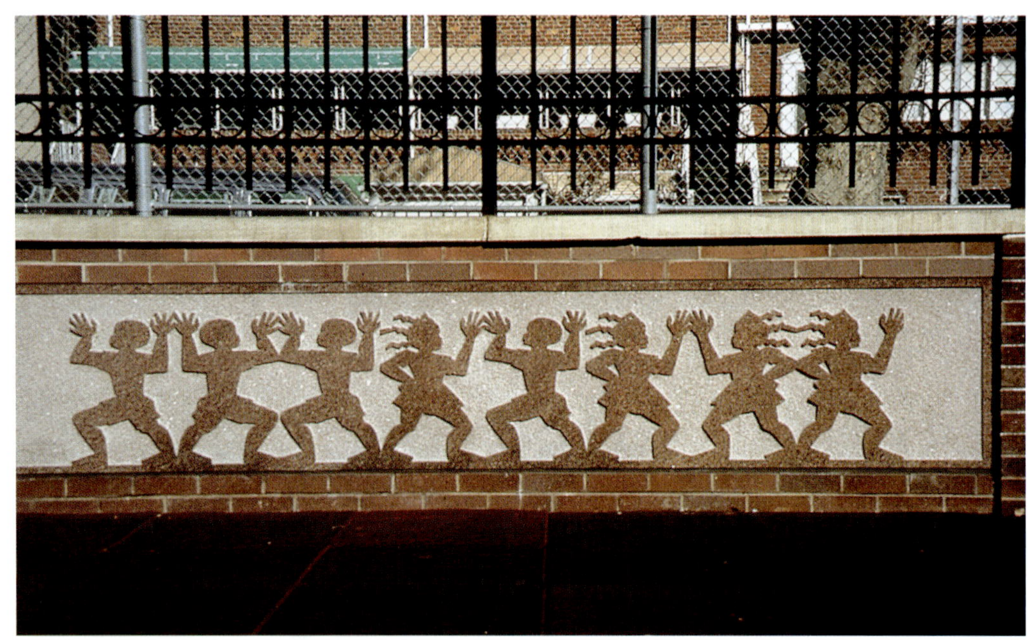

Ed McGowin

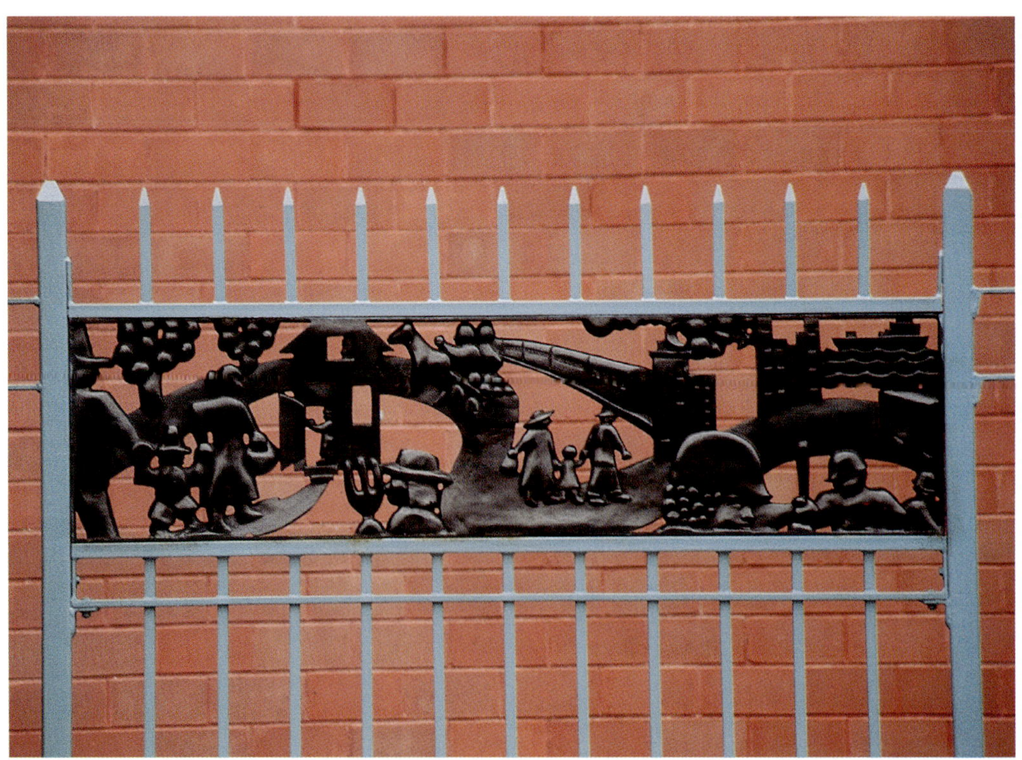

Work History
1997
Bronze

Occupational Training Center 721,
64 Avenue X

ARCHITECT
Castro-Blanco Piscioneri Associates
DESIGN AGENCY
School Construction Authority
SPONSOR AGENCY
Board of Education

For his artwork at Occupational Training Center 721, Ed McGowin used stylized imagery to trace the history of work, from the agrarian age through the industrial age to the information age. *Work History* consists of fifty-four cast-bronze panels, incorporated as a 300 foot (91.4 m) long frieze in the fence surrounding the center. McGowin has said that his aim in this work was to create a narrative piece that was relevant to the site's purpose.

look/act/dream
1996
Aluminum

Public School 22, 443 St. Mark's Avenue

ARCHITECT
Perkins & Will
DESIGN AGENCY
School Construction Authority
SPONSOR AGENCY
Board of Education

Mike Metz's work, *look/act/dream*, consists of twelve cast-aluminum medallions incorporated into the wrought-iron fence on the Classon Street perimeter of P.S. 22. Each medallion features shapes designed by students that can be interpreted in several different ways. One medallion, for example, depicts what could be seen as a group of balloons or potted flowers or even a pair of clippers. The sentence, "Look at the ___ acting like a ___ dreaming of a ___," appears on each medallion, with the intention of encouraging students to add their own text, and thus think creatively about the possible meanings of each image.

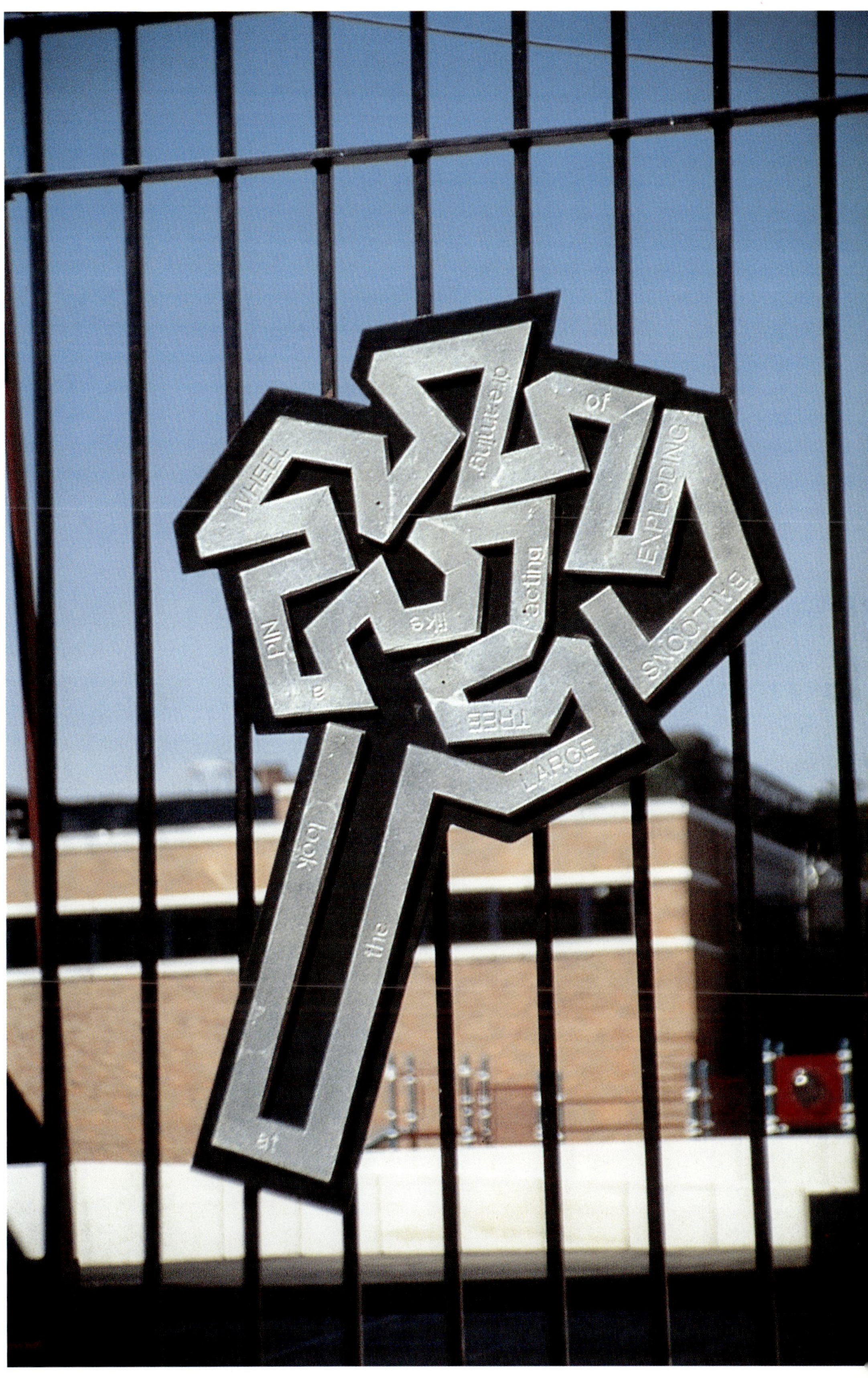

Mike Metz

Rivers
1998
Wood

Public School 233, 9301 Avenue B

ARCHITECT
School Construction Authority
SPONSOR AGENCY
Board of Education

Robert Ressler's artwork for P.S. 233 was inspired by the school children's interpretation of Langston Hughes's poem "The Negro Speaks of Rivers" (1922):

> I've known rivers:
> I've known rivers ancient as the world
> and older than the flow of human
> blood in human veins.
> My soul has grown deep like the rivers.

Ressler designed and fabricated three hard-wood panels using imagery from more than a hundred children's drawings of rivers. The brilliantly colored panels hang in the school's auditorium.

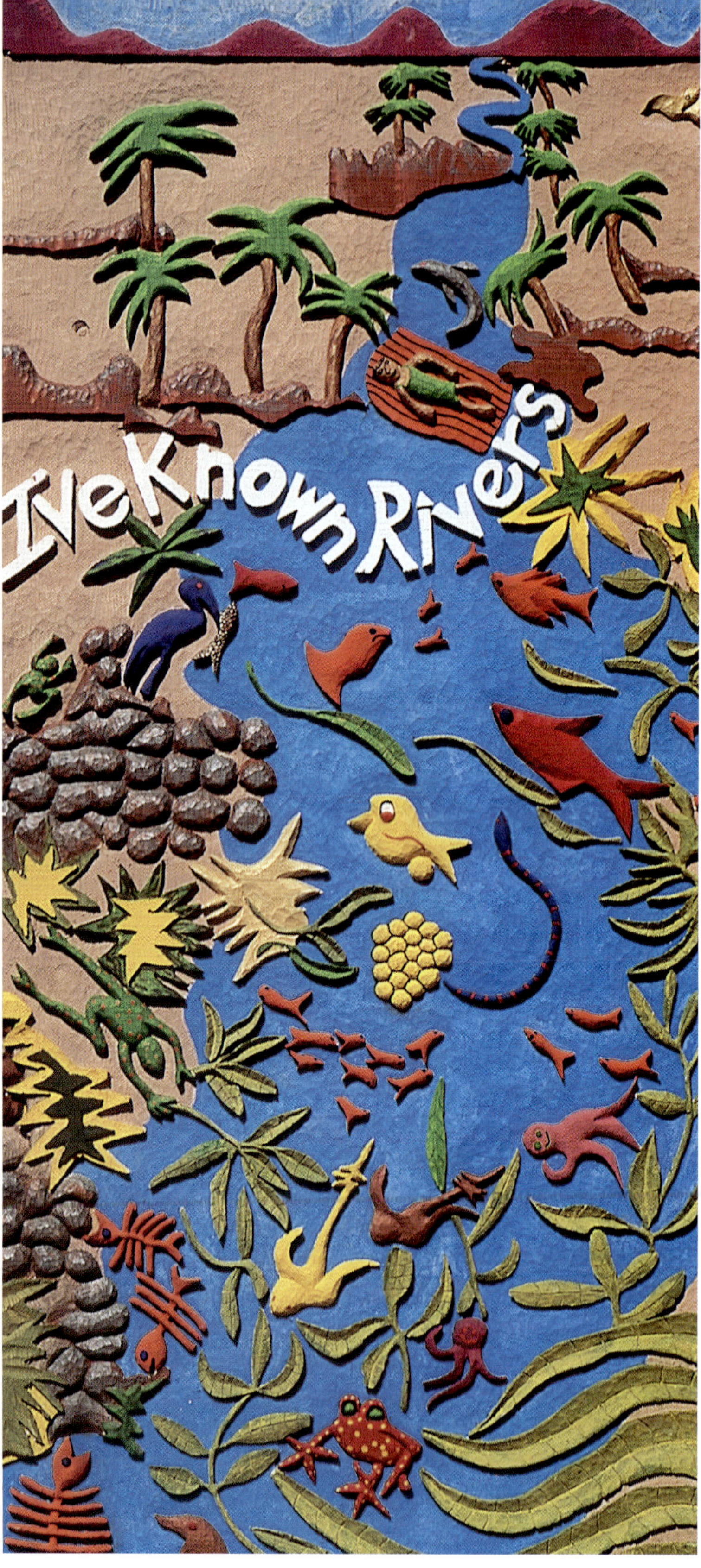

Robert Ressler

Faith Ringgold

The Crown Heights Children's Story Quilt
1996
Painted quilt

Public School 22, 433 St. Mark's Avenue

ARCHITECT
Perkins & Will
DESIGN AGENCY
School Construction Authority
SPONSOR AGENCY
Board of Education

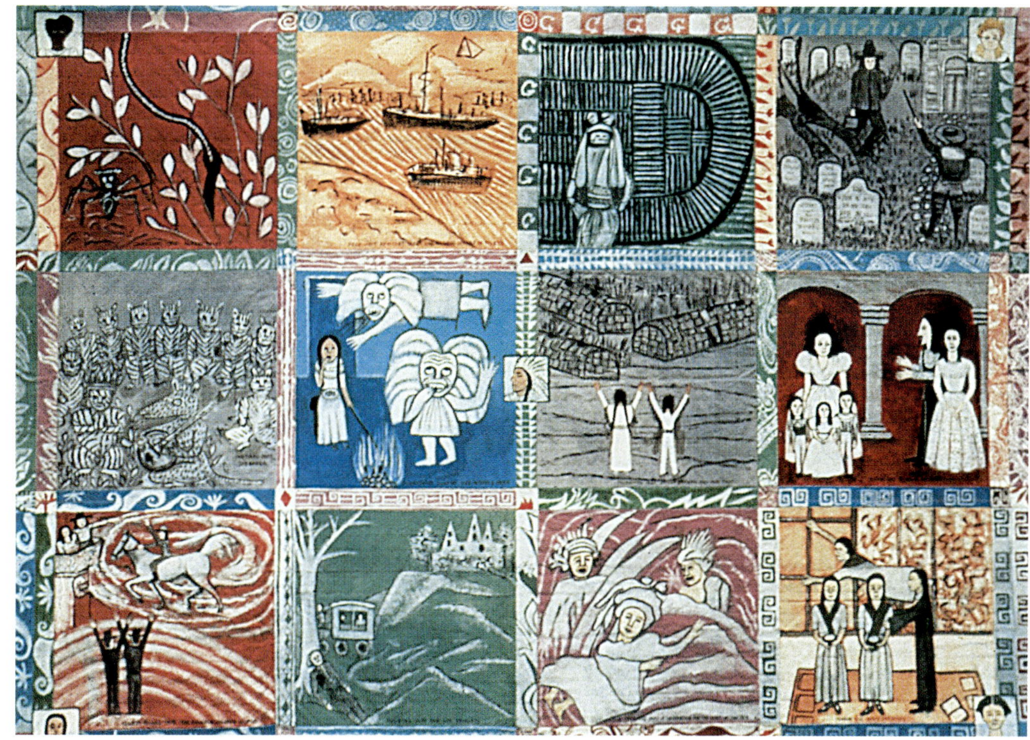

For her painted quilt at P.S. 22 in the Crown Heights section of Brooklyn, Faith Ringgold researched folktales from the various cultures of the surrounding neighborhood, and incorporated scenes from them into the quilt that hangs in the school library. The twelve folktales pictured in the quilt are: *The Negro Speaks of Rivers* (African-American); *Anansi Stories* (Jamaican); *We Wear the Mask* (West African); *The Ghost of Peg Leg Peter* (Dutch); *The Banza* (Haitian); *The Winged Head* (Algonquin); *Bright Morning Runs East* (Mohawk); *Catherine the Wise* (Italian); *The Rainbow-Colored Horse* (Puerto Rican); *Sea and Mountain Spirits* (Vietnamese); *Which is Witch* (Korean); and *The Lost Princess* (Jewish).

Toshio Sasaki

First Symphony of the Sea (following pages)
1992
Concrete, terrazzo, ceramics

The New York Aquarium, Surf Avenue and West Eighth Street

ARCHITECT
Goldstone and Hinz
DESIGN AGENCY
Department of General Services
SPONSOR AGENCY
Department of Cultural Affairs

Art Commission Award for Excellence in Design 1992

For *First Symphony of the Sea,* Toshio Sasaki transformed the 332 foot (101 m) concrete wall facing the boardwalk at Coney Island. Beginning at the Aquarium entrance, the work features familiar fish shapes, in three dimensions, which appear to be swimming within the concrete, gradually becoming more shadowy beneath the broadening wave patterns. As you walk east along the boardwalk, these embedded sculptures become increasingly abstract, depicting geometric shapes such as capsules, zygotes, and inverted cones—a vortex of waves and egg-like forms that recall more basic forms of life in transformation. The concrete relief was cast in twenty-six sections, and terrazzo and ceramic elements were attached to the wall after fabrication.

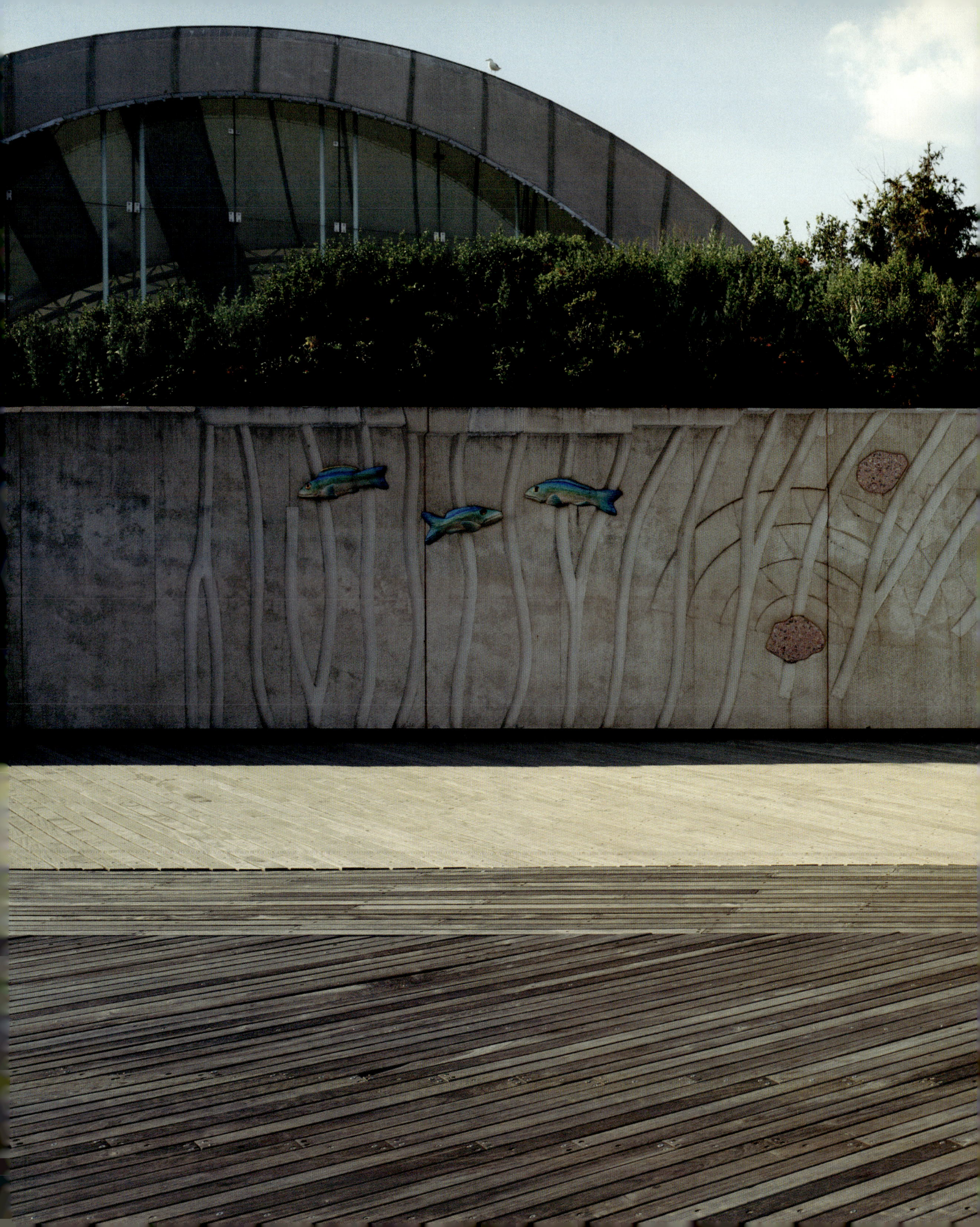

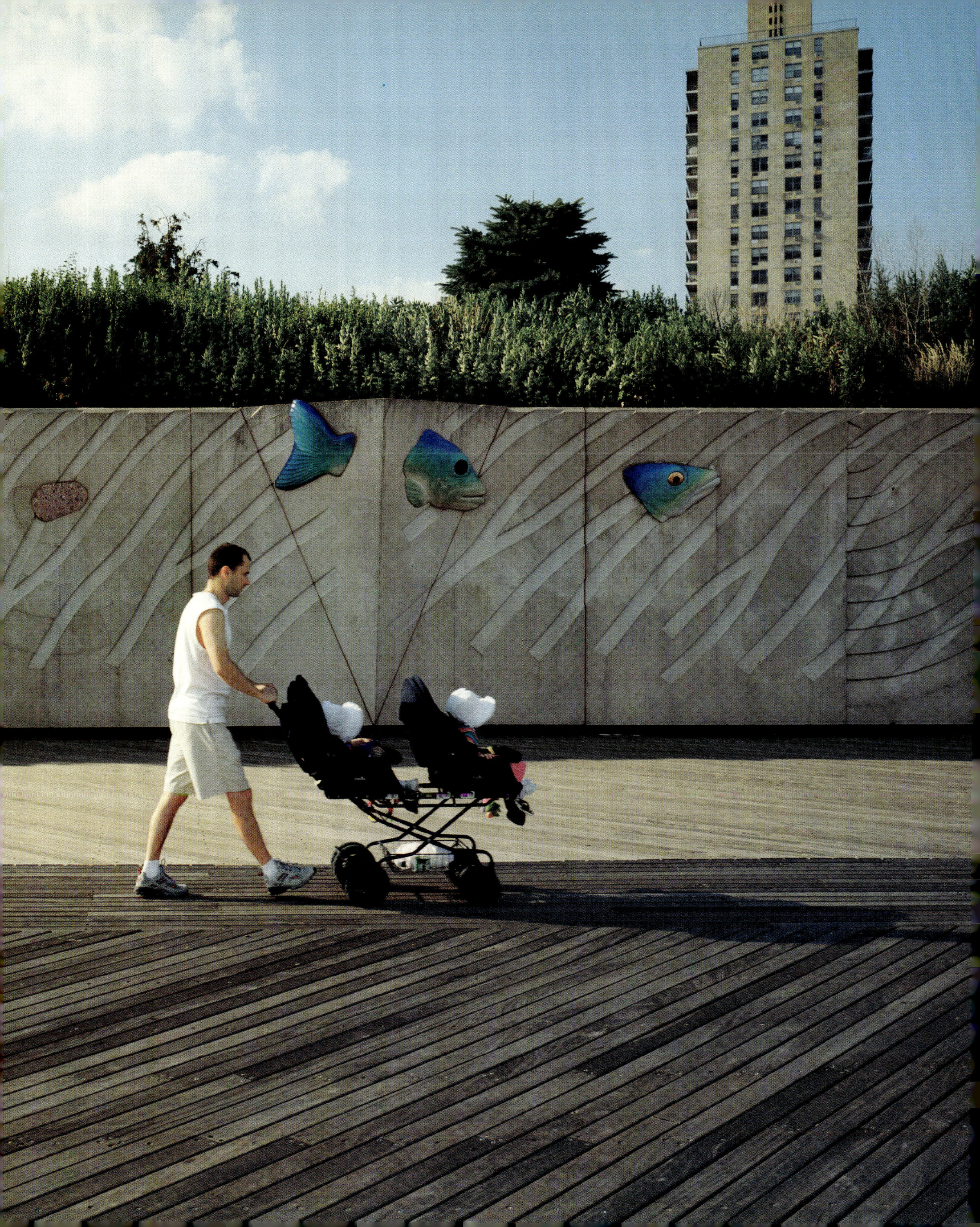

Ben Schonzeit

Common Ground
1996
Oil on canvas

Public School 205, 6701 20th Avenue

ARCHITECT
Rice Partnership
DESIGN AGENCY
School Construction Authority
SPONSOR AGENCY
Board of Education

Located in the main stairway of P.S. 205, Ben Schonzeit's two paintings, collectively entitled *Common Ground*, portray a topographical map of the world that blends into an image of the sky in the Northern Hemisphere. Over the map, Schonzeit painted images relating to the neighborhood, such as a Sicilian marionette made by a local puppeteer and a penguin from the Coney Island Aquarium. He also depicted popular board games such as Monopoly and checkers, and sports such as soccer.

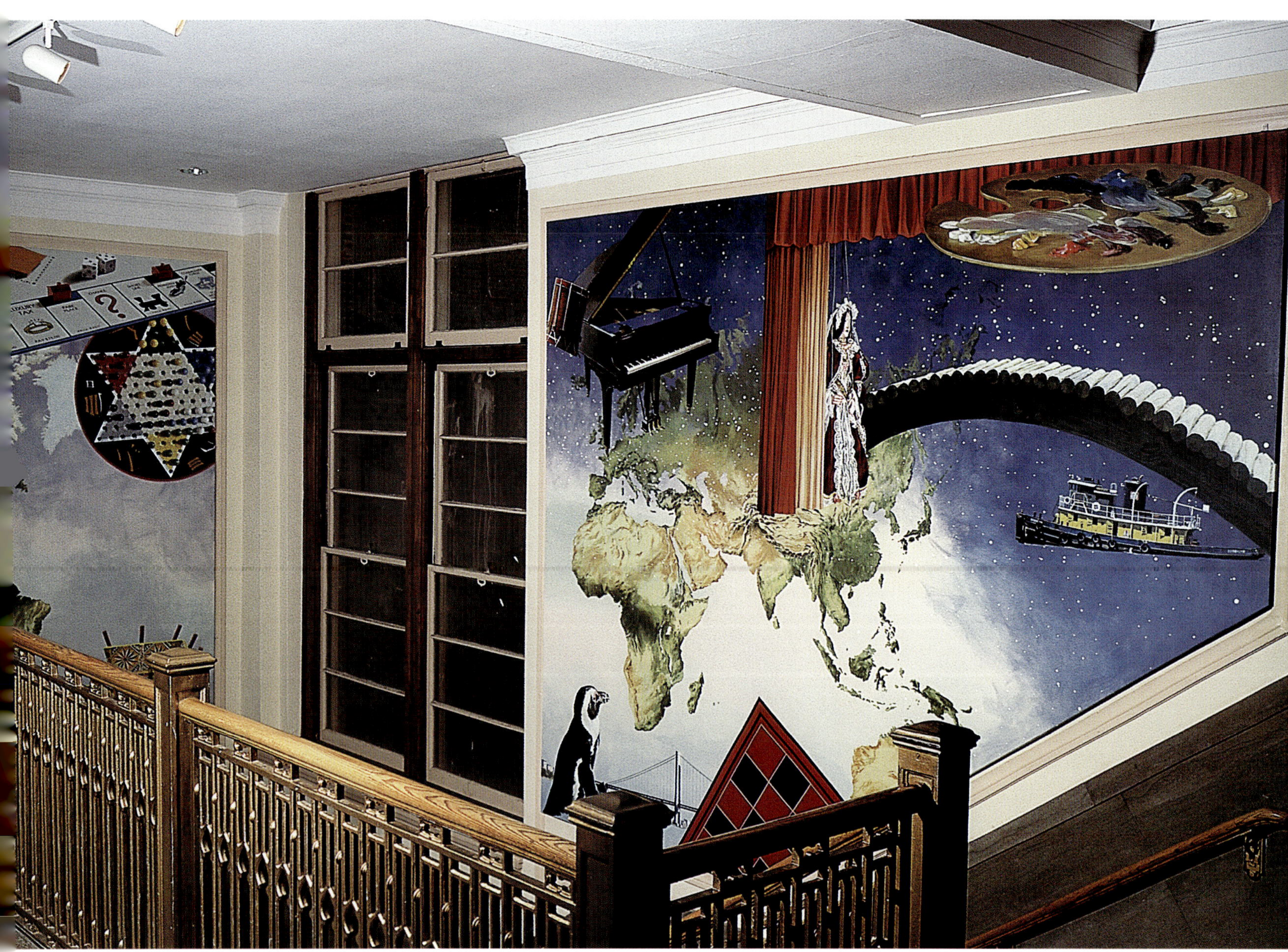

Freedom's Gate
1997
Bronze

Fulton Street Traffic Triangle,
Fulton Street and Ralph Avenue

DESIGN/SPONSOR AGENCY
Department of Transportation

At the center of the Fulton Street Traffic Triangle, Charles Searles created a large-scale bronze sculpture with curvilinear and arched forms deliberately designed to contrast with the surrounding rectangular buildings. The artist intended the work to serve as a conspicuous landmark for this Brooklyn community.

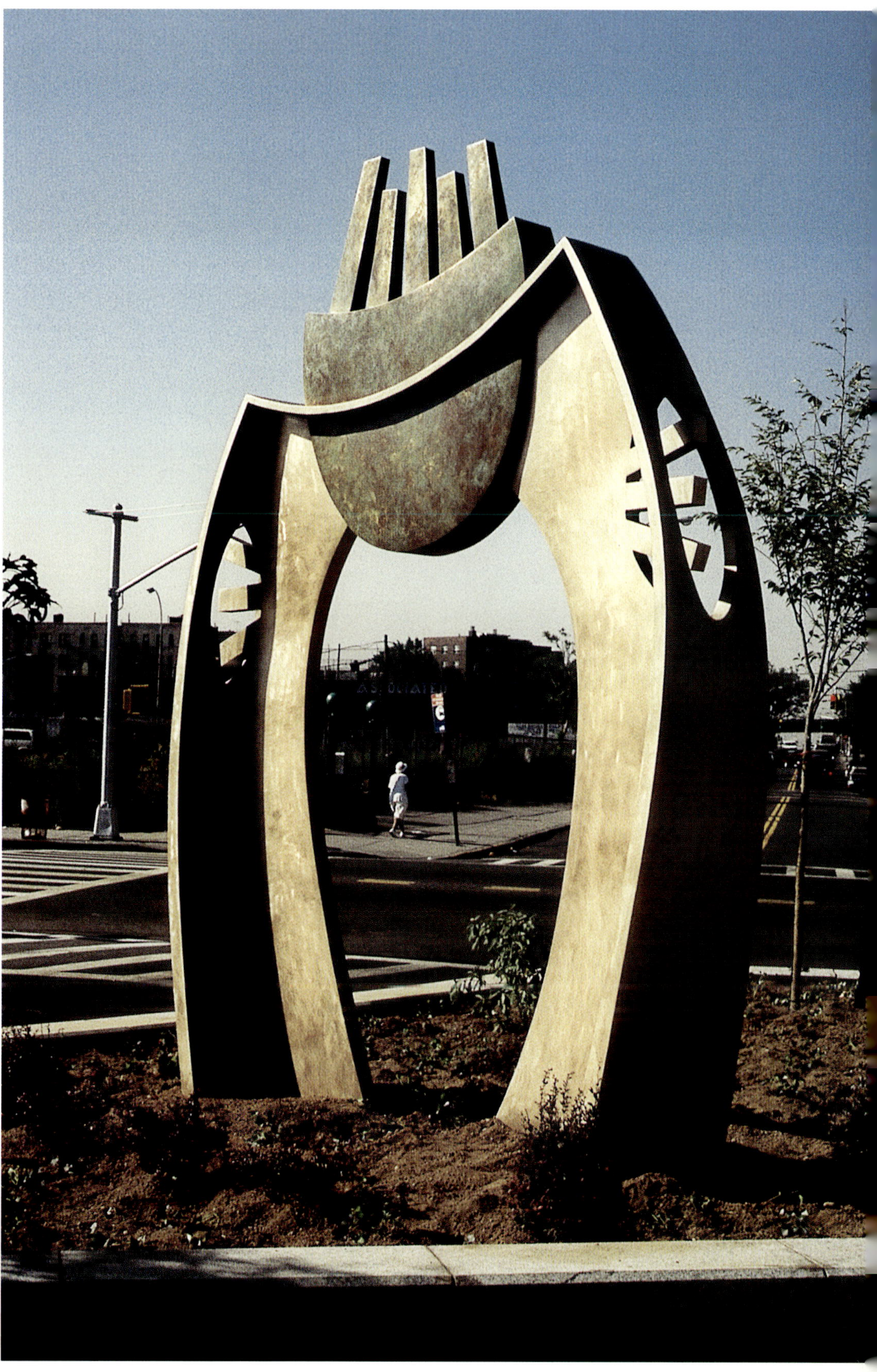

Charles Searles

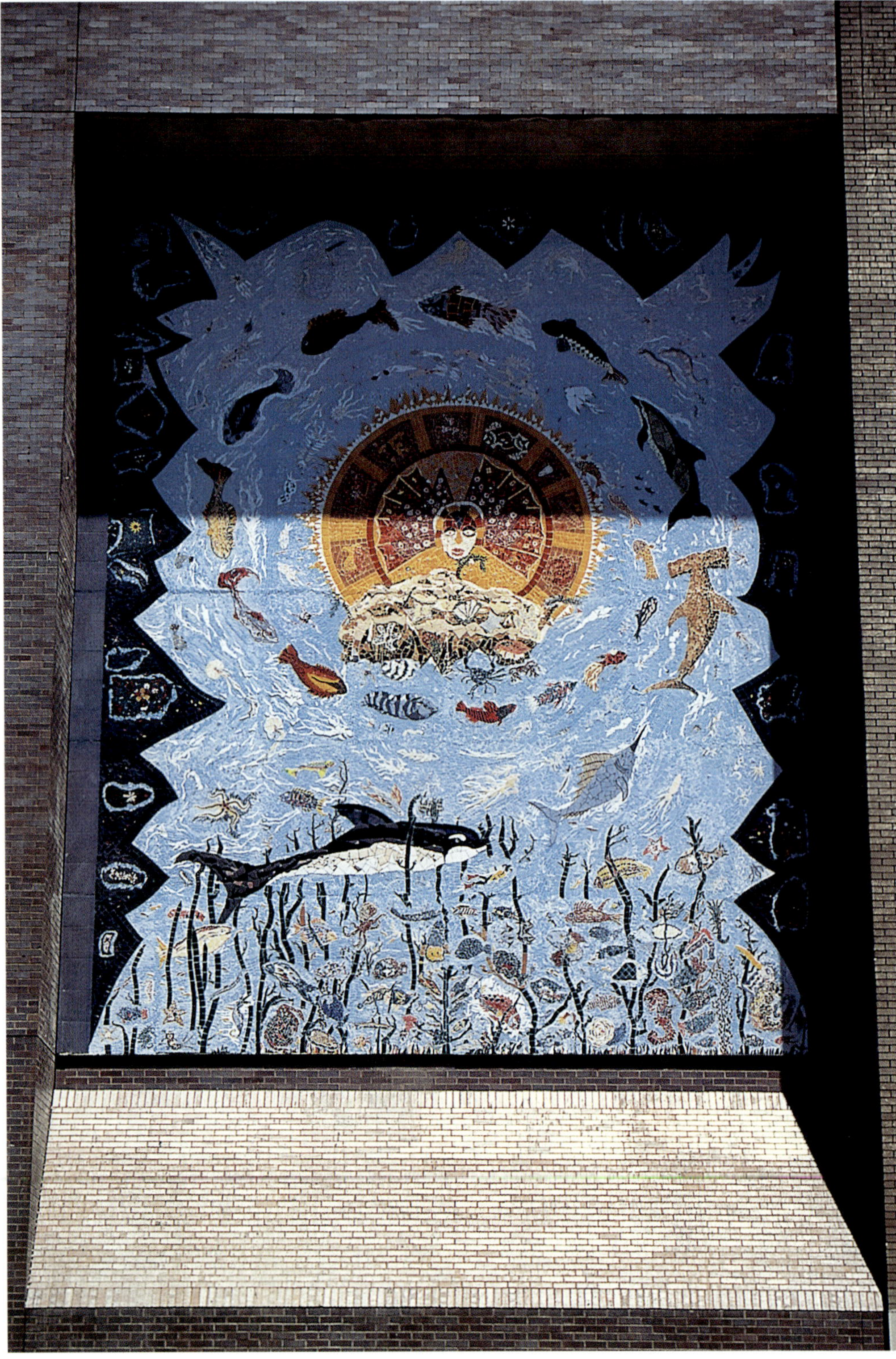

Caribbean Sea
1995
Ceramic mosaic

Intermediate School 246,
72 Veronica Place

ARCHITECT
Montoya-Rodriguez, P.C.
DESIGN AGENCY
School Construction Authority
SPONSOR AGENCY
Board of Education

Pedro Silva's mosaic mural for I.S. 246 features images from, and references to, life in the Caribbean. In the center of the mural is a bright carnival mask of the Sun god, surrounded by marine life, including fish, plants, sand, and coral. A wide border portrays several islands with tropical landscapes. Students collaborated with Silva on the project by cutting and piecing together the tiles that form the mosaic.

Pedro Silva

Ned Smyth

Destination
2002
Glass, marble

Public School 156, 104 Sutter Avenue

ARCHITECT
Mitchell/Giurgola
DESIGN AGENCY
School Construction Authority
SPONSOR AGENCY
Board of Education

Ned Smyth drew on the school's performing arts curriculum for his transparent colored-glass and marble mural, entitled *Destination,* which runs along the main staircase of P.S. 156. The abstract vertical bands of color in the mural allude to the folds of a theater's curtains, and the oval forms suggest the glare of spotlights. Specially designed lighting illuminates the mural and casts students' shadows on to the white marble ovals; as Smyth has said, "the people on the stairs become a living part of the artwork."

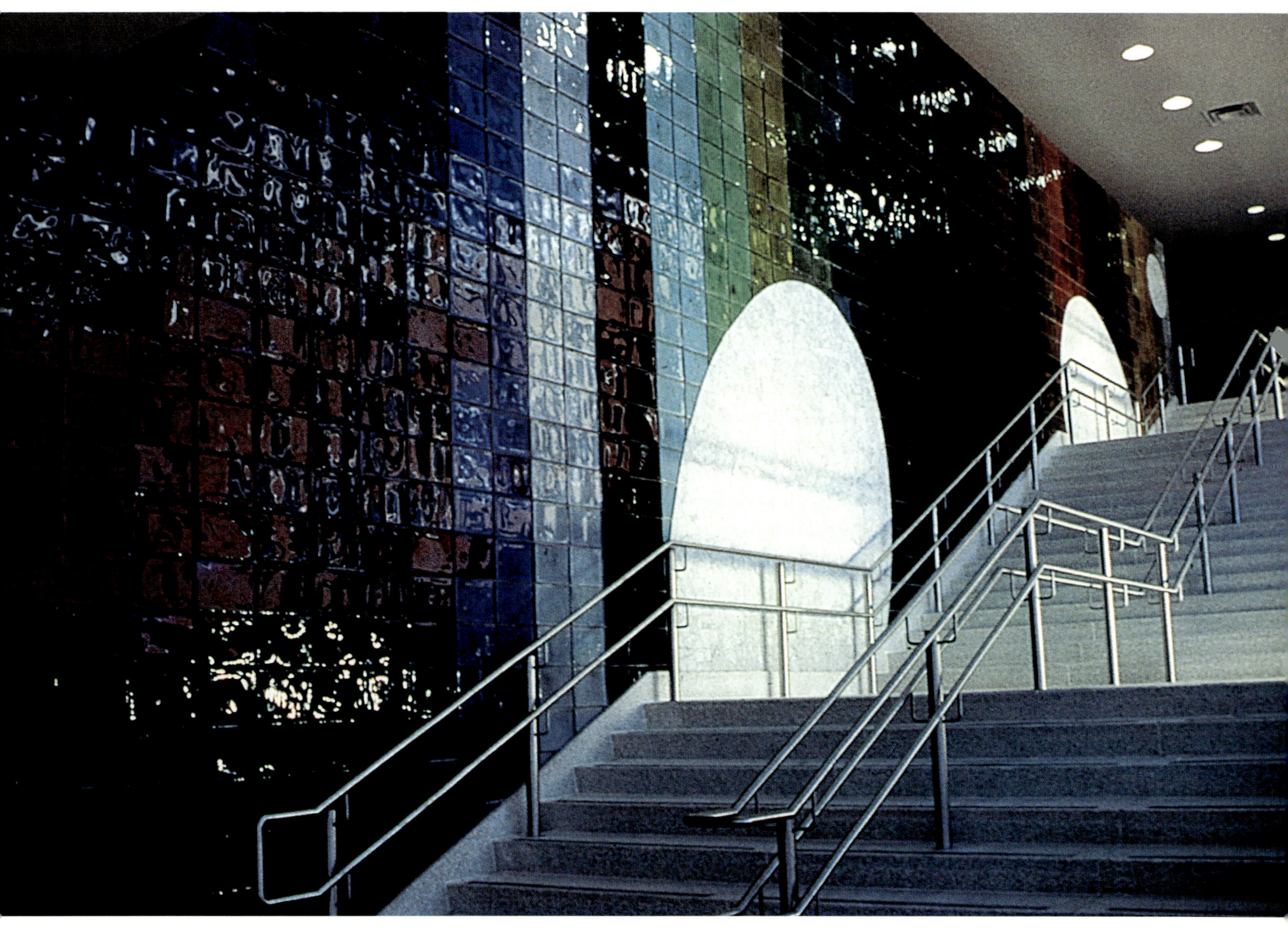

Ned Smyth

Wave Wall in Green (opposite)
1996
Chain-link fencing, landscaping materials

Coney Island Water Pollution Control Plant, 2591 Knapp Street

ARCHITECT
Pirnie-Baker
DESIGN/SPONSOR AGENCY
Department of Environmental Protection

Art Commission Award for Excellence in Design 1989

Ned Smyth's chain-link fence, entitled *Wave Wall in Green*, surrounds the perimeter of the Coney Island Water Pollution Control Plant. Designed both to soften and to secure this environmental complex, which is sited in a residential area, the industrial chain link is disguised with plantings of vines, flowers, grasses, bushes, and trees. Where the fence is visible, it appears like water amid lush green islands. Smyth intended this work to represent the role the plant performs: the cleaning of water and the protection of the environment.

Nitza Tufino

Feather Explosion
1994
Ceramic mural

Public School 12, 430 Howard Avenue

ARCHITECT
Perkins & Will
DESIGN AGENCY
School Construction Authority
SPONSOR AGENCY
Board of Education

Nitza Tufino's ceramic mural for P.S. 12 depicts scenes from Brooklyn's West Indian Day Parade, held annually on Labor Day. Featured prominently are images of the traditional and often fanciful costumes and masks worn by parade participants. The mural is divided into daytime scenes of the parade on the left-hand side, and nighttime scenes on the right-hand side.

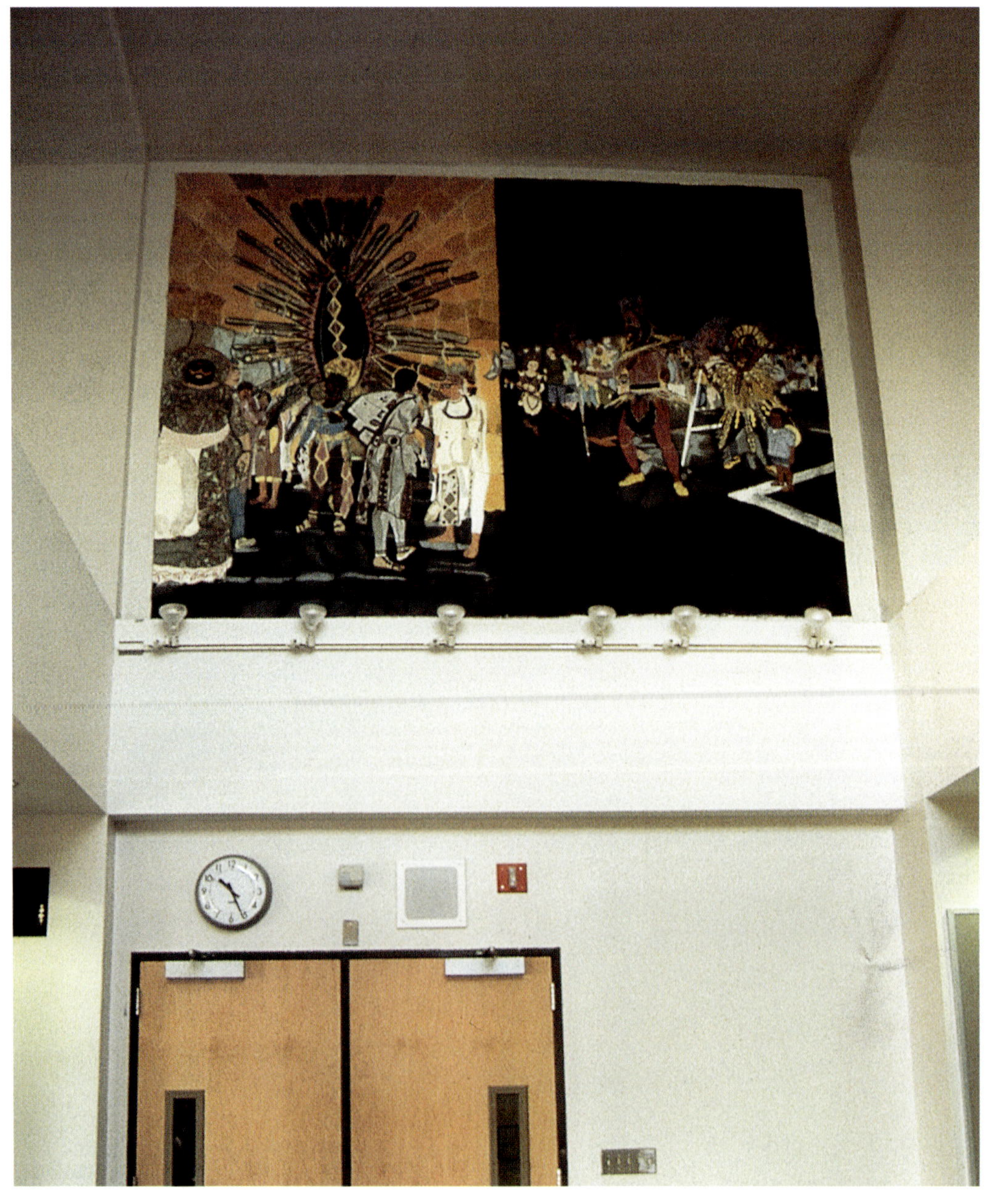

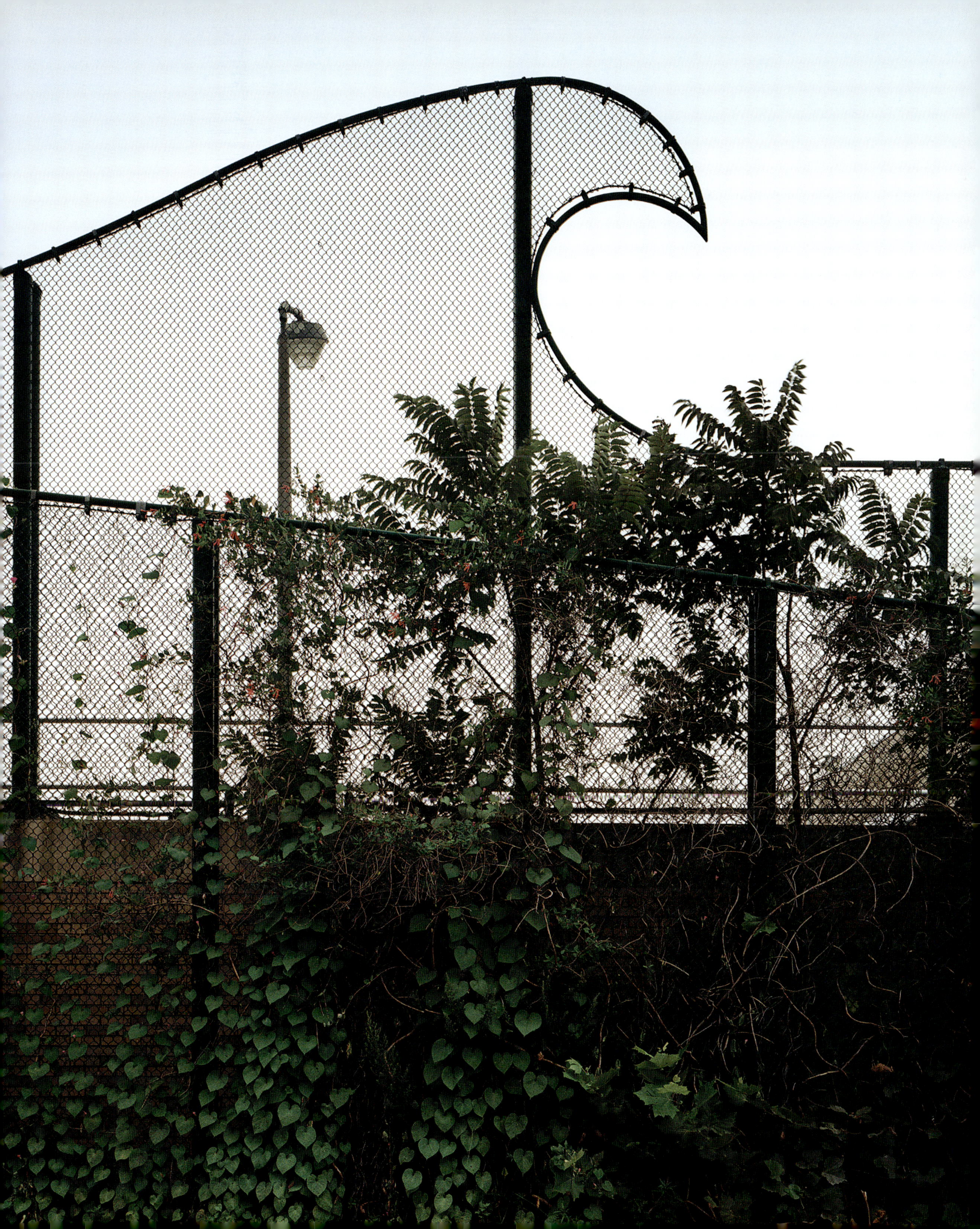

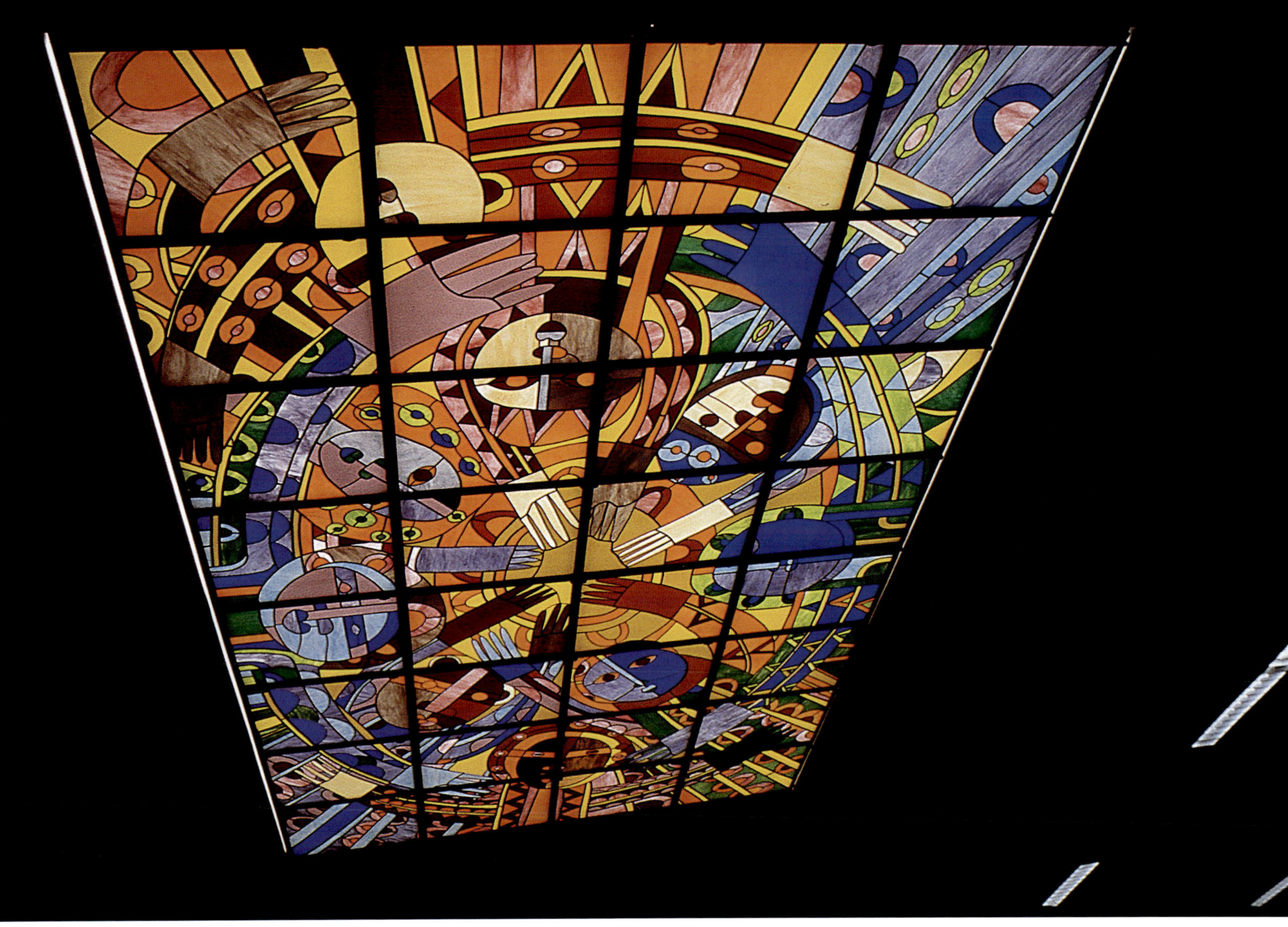

We Are The Children, Elated Elders, and Tune Into Truth
1999
Acrylic on wood, stained glass

Public School 181, 1023 New York Avenue

ARCHITECT
Swanke Hayden Connell
DESIGN AGENCY
School Construction Authority
SPONSOR AGENCY
Board of Education

Emmett Wigglesworth's artificially illuminated stained-glass skylight, *We Are The Children* (above), and pair of painted murals in the auditorium in P.S. 181 provide color and light in an otherwise dimly lit space. Each of the murals features interconnected serpentine forms and jewel-like patterns of color, as well as images of people reaching out to those in the adjacent mural.

Emmett Wigglesworth

Krzysztof Wodiczko

Windows
1998
Photographic lightboxes

Public School 24, 427 38th Street

ARCHITECT/DESIGN AGENCY
School Construction Authority
SPONSOR AGENCY
Board of Education

Krzysztof Wodiczko's lightboxes, installed in P.S. 24's windowless auditorium, were designed to create the illusion of five metal-framed windows with views. The artist based the images in the boxes on photographs of sunsets taken in Sunset Park, the neighborhood in which the school is located. The lightboxes turn on automatically when the auditorium lights are switched off, and darken when the lights are switched back on, maintaining the true character of windows in varying light conditions.

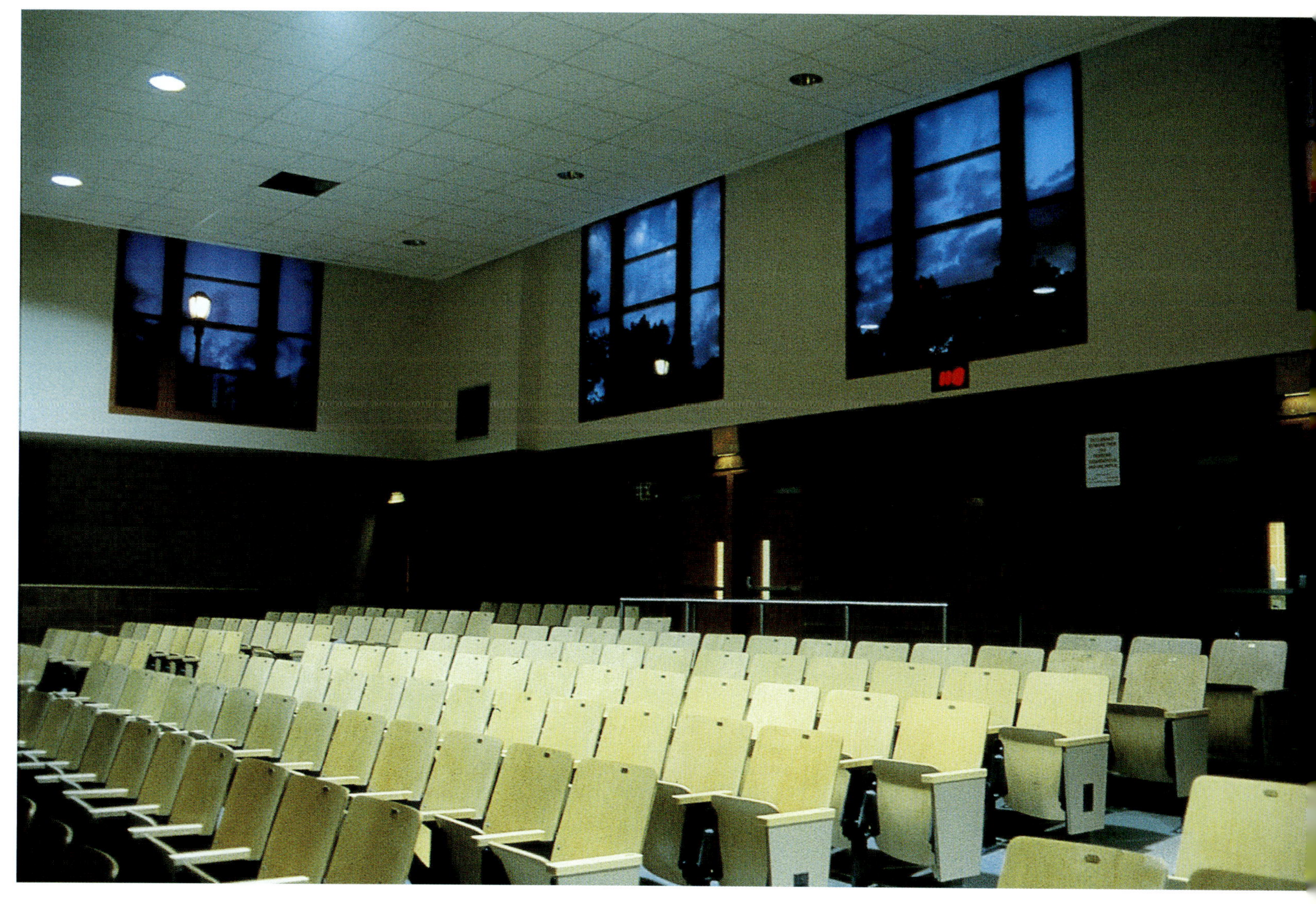

Completed projects ● (see map)

1 Emma Amos
2 Stephen Antonakos
3 Tomie Arai
4 Tomie Arai
5 Camille Billops
6 Andrea Blum
7 Deborah Brown
8 Colin Chase
9 Carl Cheng
10 Houston Conwill, Estella Conwill Majozo, and Joseph DePace
11 Michael Cummings
12 Pablo Delano
13 Donna Dennis
14 Mel Edwards
15 Daniel Galvez
16 Marina Gutierrez
17 Richard Haas
18 Maren Hassinger
19 Maren Hassinger
20 Brower Hatcher
21 Robin Holder
22 Doug Hollis
23 Valerie Jaudon
24 Kristin Jones and Andrew Ginzel
25 Gabriel Koren
26 Joyce Kozloff
27 Ora Lerman
28 Donald Lipski
29 Mike Mandel and Larry Sultan
30 Antonio Martorell
31 Milo Mottola
32 Celia Muñoz
33 Lorenzo Pace
34 Jorge Luis Rodriguez
35 Charles Searles
36 Nobi Shioya
37 Arlene Slavin
38 Vincent D. Smith
39 Kit-Yin Snyder
40 Pat Steir
41 Michelle Stuart
42 Allan and Ellen Wexler
43 Martin Wong

Projects in progress ▲ (see map)

44 Dennis Adams
Slips
Viewing-deck benches, photographic lightboxes
Whitehall Ferry Terminal, Whitehall and South Streets
Architect: Fred Schwartz
Sponsor Agency: Economic Development Corporation

45 John Brekke
Migration
Glass disks
Open Door Senior Center, 240 Centre Street
Architect: Edward I. Mills and Associates
Design Agency: Department of Design and Construction
Sponsor Agency: Department for the Aging

46 Malcolm Cochran
Stateroom in a Bottle
Carbon steel with thermal-sprayed zinc, bronze, mixed media
Hudson River Park, West 54th Street and West Side Highway
Architect: Richard Dattner and Partners Architects
Landscape Architect: Miceli Kulik Williams & Associates
Sponsor Agencies: Hudson River Park Trust, New York City Department of Parks and Recreation, New York State Office of Parks, Recreation and Historic Preservation

47 Ming Fay
Whitehall Crossing
Granite benches
Whitehall Ferry Terminal, Whitehall and South Streets
Architect: Fred Schwartz
Sponsor Agency: Economic Development Corporation

48 Alison Saar
Swing Low
Bronze sculpture
Harriet Tubman Memorial, 122nd Street and Frederick Douglass Boulevard
Landscape Architect: Quennell Rothschild Associates
Design Agency: Department of Design and Construction
Sponsor Agency: Manhattan Borough President/ Department of Transportation

49 Nari Ward
Voice Works
Three stainless-steel sculptures
Barrier Signage
Porcelain enamel
West Harlem Waterfront, 125th Street and 11th Avenue
Landscape Architect: W Architecture
Sponsor Agency: Economic Development Corporation

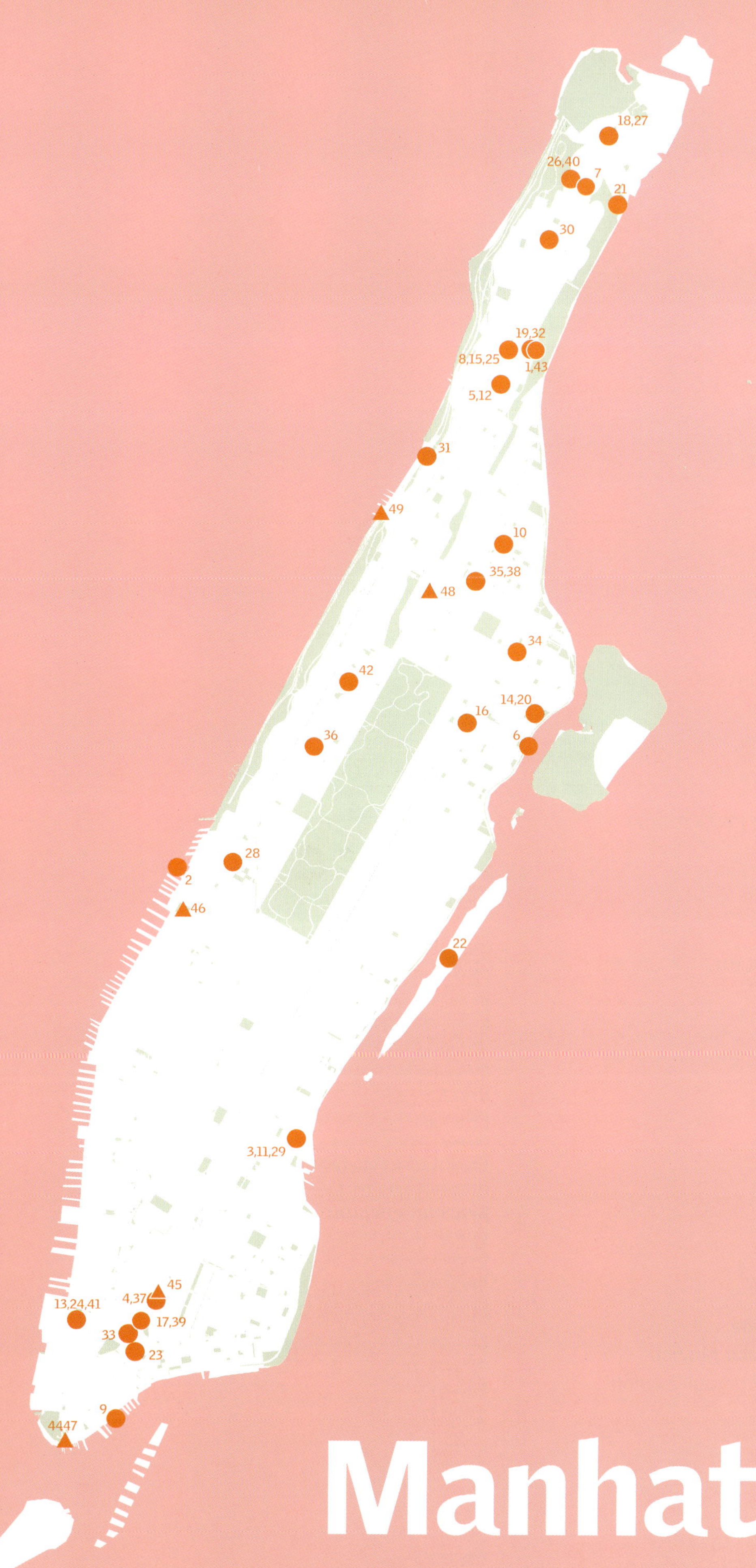
18,27
26,40
7
21
30
19,32
8,15,25
1,43
5,12
31
49
10
35,38
48
34
42
14,20
16
6
36
28
2
46
22
3,11,29
45
4,37
13,24,41
17,39
33
23
9
4447

Manhattan

Interview: Nari Ward

I'm working on two projects for the West Harlem Waterfront Project, and for one of them I wanted to deal with sound. But because Percent for Art pieces have to be permanent, and sound installations are difficult to maintain, I've decided to focus on the ephemeral and subjective qualities of sound, and to explore how sound translates back into memory. To do that, I've been going out and talking to people about the sounds that comfort them—the familiar sounds they hear in their homes and in the neighborhood—and their memories of them.

With the help of the Percent for Art program and the community board, I developed and distributed a questionnaire. I've also spent a lot of time talking with people in places like the Floridita Restaurant on Broadway and 126th Street. I've gotten a range of responses, some quirky, some poetic. And as I sort through them, I'm focusing on the written and verbal responses that most effectively bring to mind sounds and auditory situations. My goal is to take snippets of these evocative descriptions—one woman, for example, chose the phrase "raindrops on the window"—and juxtapose them with details about the neighborhood that also evoke images and memories. A reference to a place such as the old Claremont Hotel, for example, like the descriptions of remembered sound, will evoke a neighborhood landmark that exists vividly, but only in the community's memory.

My plan is to fabricate a dozen sculptures that look like the metal highway barriers you often see along the side of roads. On them, I'll present these evocative texts as white type on a green background, using a porcelain-enamel signage system that will run the length of the barriers. People will encounter these sculptures as they make their way along the new park on the waterfront.

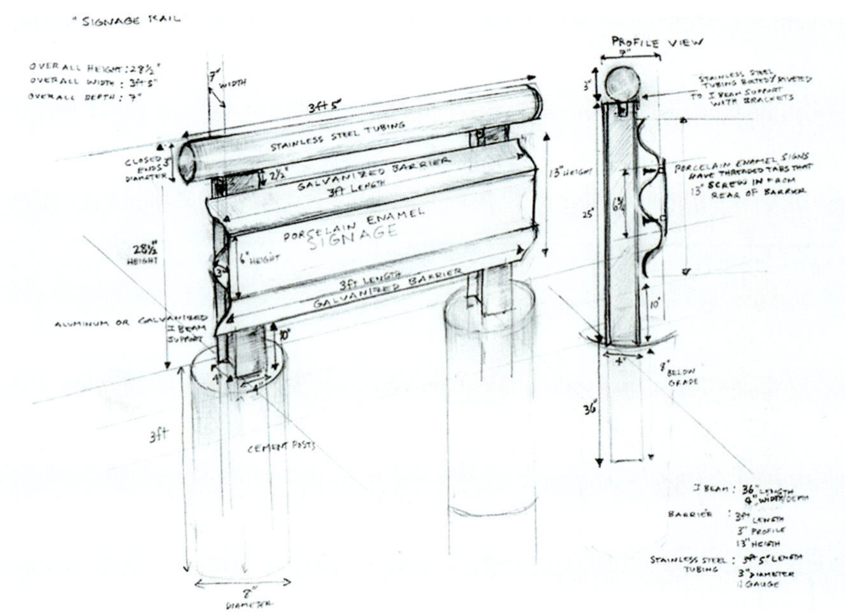

Nari Ward, Proposal for *Barrier Signage*, porcelain enamel, West Harlem Waterfront, 2003.

Public art has always intrigued me. I was born in Jamaica, came to New York, and moved to Harlem. When I went to openings, I always felt as though I was an outsider, and wondered whether this was the audience I wanted to talk to. On some level, the art audience was. But I also thought about the people I saw in my neighborhood, in Harlem, every day. In my earlier work, I often dealt directly with the neighborhood. I rented spaces (which were cheaper then), and did installations, and people in the neighborhood who were curious would come by and become part of a dialogue. That was when I realized that I could straddle two realities—the art world's reality and the reality of the community and everyday folks. As my career developed, and I got opportunities to do projects in more traditional art venues, I didn't have as much time for community projects, and I began to long for those kinds of opportunities. So when this Percent of Art project came around, I thought I'd give it a try.

In order to attract attention in a chaotic urban landscape, I try to work with things that are familiar, but in a way that transforms them or the experience of encountering them. I want people to stop for a moment and ask themselves, "What is that?" And then I'm always looking for ways to hold people for a moment longer, in the hope that their questions will continue. It's not a strategy that's going to work all the time, or with everybody, but I keep trying. Even if people are not conscious of it in those moments, there's a dialogue going on, even if it's unspoken.

The Sky's the Limit
1995
Glass mosaic

Intermediate School 90, 21 Jumel Place

ARCHITECT
Richard Dattner and Partners Architects
DESIGN AGENCY
School Construction Authority
SPONSOR AGENCY
Board of Education

Emma Amos's work, a mixture of Venetian- and Tiffany-style flat-glass mosaics, is installed on the ceiling 10 feet (3 m) above the school's lobby space. The colorful composition includes dancers, athletes, and students of diverse ethnicities, as well as symbols of culture, history, and art. The artist intended that these playful figures, which float on a brilliant blue background, would transform the entry area into a celebration of life, discovery, and learning.

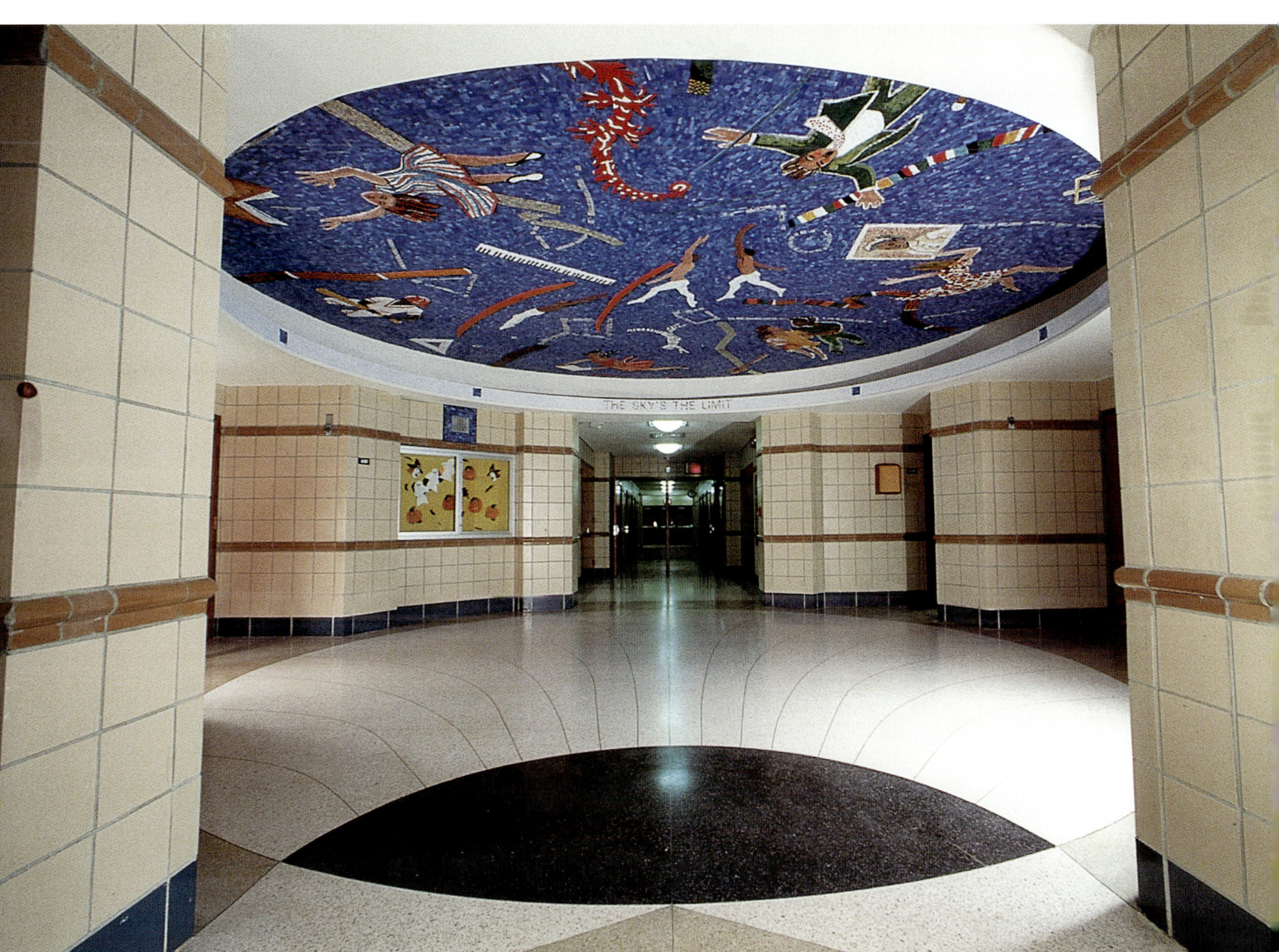

Emma Amos

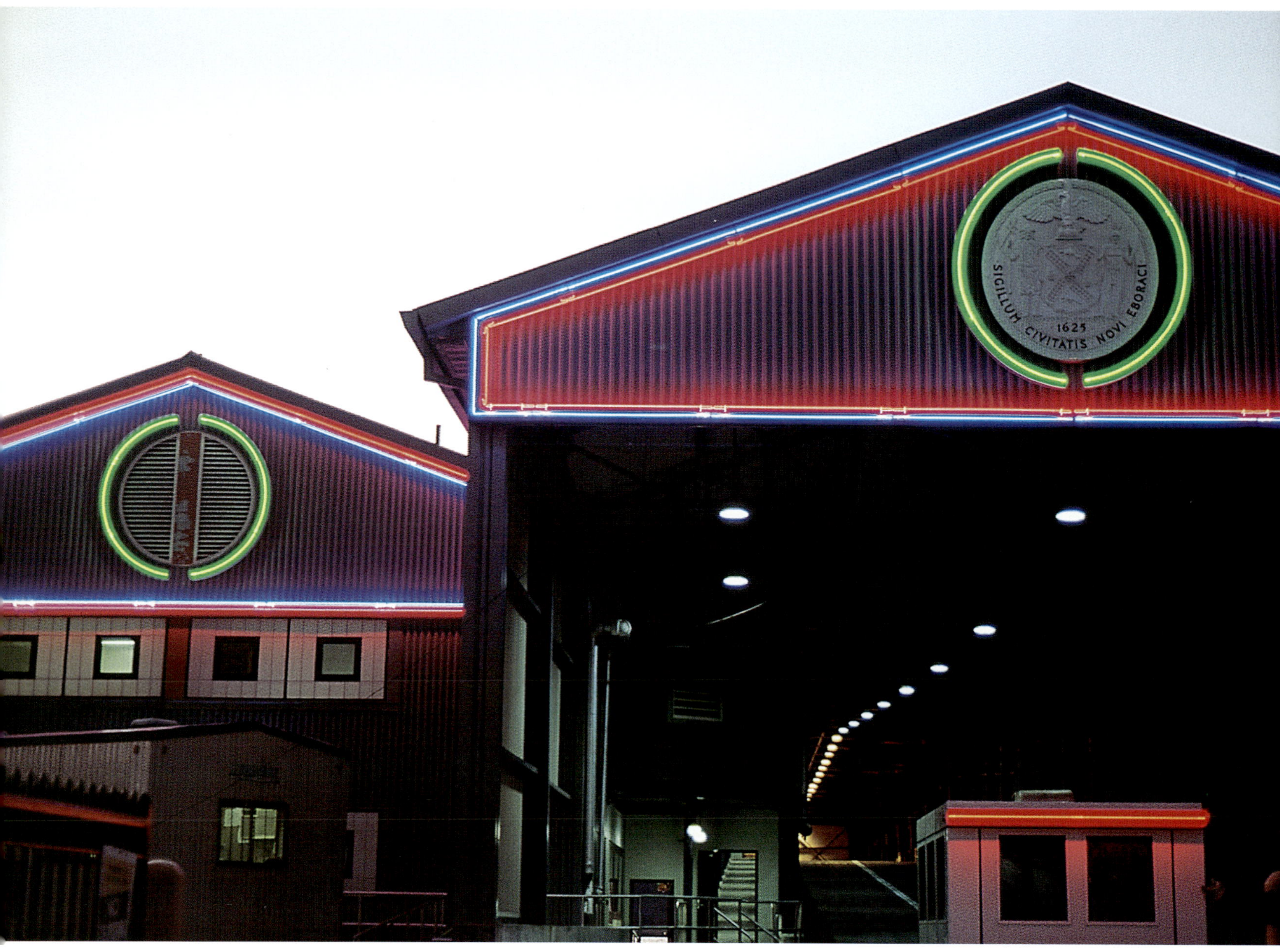

Neon for the 59th Street Marine Transfer Station
1990
Neon

59th Street Marine Transfer Station, 59th Street and 12th Avenue

ARCHITECT
Richard Dattner and Partners Architects
SPONSOR AGENCY
Department of Sanitation

In the tradition of the neon lighting used on New York City's commercial signs, Stephen Antonakos composed an arrangement of colored neon tubes for the renovation of the Marine Transfer Station on the West 59th Street pier. Red neon light frames alternate windows along the north façade of the station, and is visible from the Henry Hudson Parkway. Neon light also accentuates the pediment forms of the west façade, evoking the forms of classical architecture. In an article in *The New Yorker*, it was judged that "the effect is subdued, stately, and somewhat spiritual, like the haloes above votive candles in a dimly lit church."

Stephen Antonakos

Tomie Arai

Song for a Child
2001
Glass and marble mosaic

New Children's Center, 492 First Avenue

ARCHITECT
Richard Dattner and Partners Architects
DESIGN AGENCY
Department of Design and Construction
SPONSOR AGENCY
Administration for Children's Services

Located on a curved wall in the First Avenue lobby of an intake center for foster children, Tomie Arai's *Song for a Child* is a glass and marble mosaic triptych based on a children's lullaby of the same name. In two of the panels, images of swirling leaves, ribbons on a kite, and a young child kicking a ball are arranged like notes on a musical bar. In the central panel (below), four young faces look out at the viewer expectantly. The artist intended that the image of the sun rising over a cityscape, as seen through an open window, would suggest a new day and a brighter future.

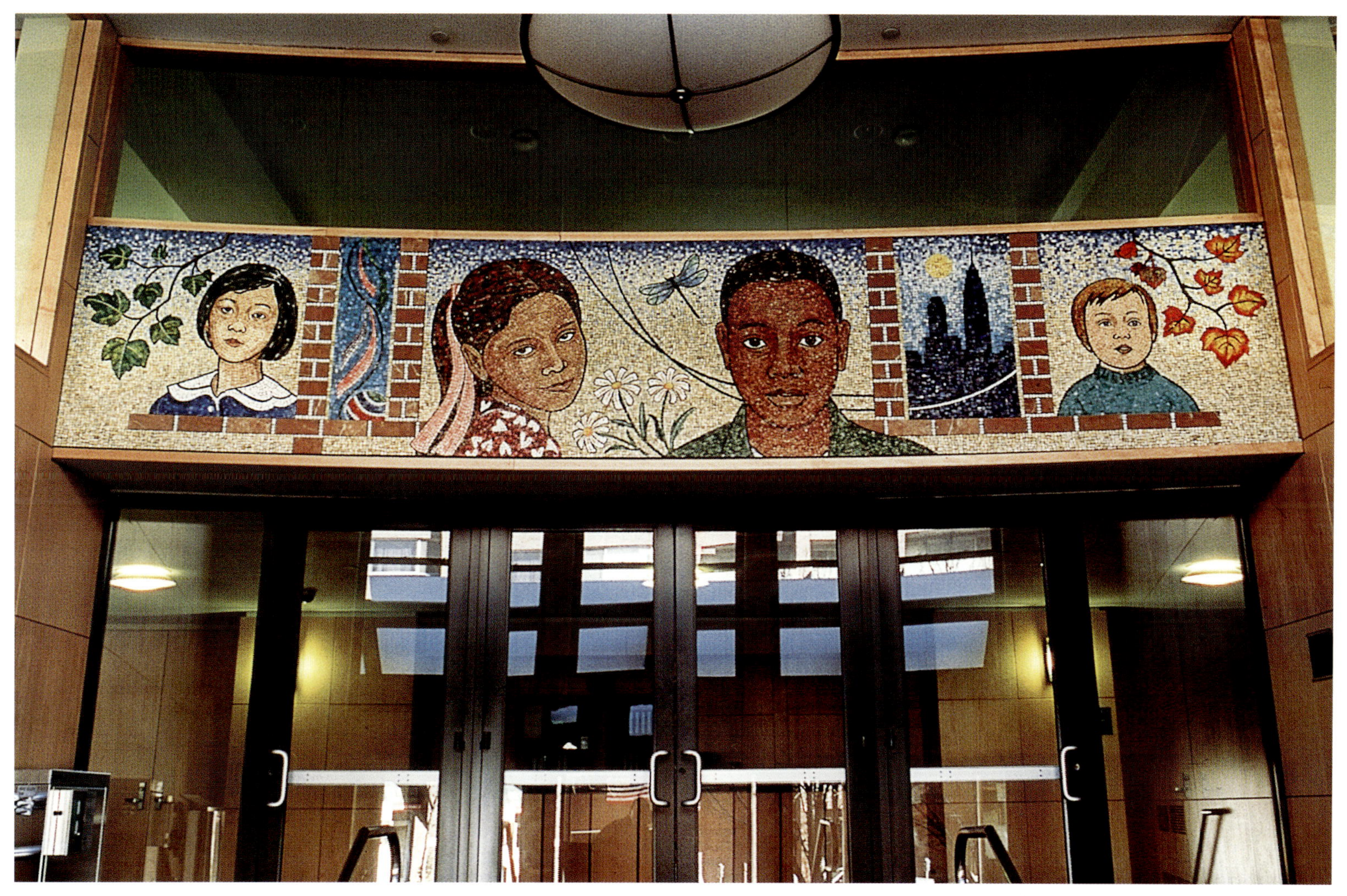

Tomie Arai

Discovery
1996
Terrazzo, brass, glass block

Public School 130, 143 Baxter Street

ARCHITECT
William Nicholas Bodouva + Associates
DESIGN AGENCY
School Construction Authority
SPONSOR AGENCY
Board of Education

Tomie Arai designed a terrazzo floor and glass-block masonry for P.S. 130, one of New York City's oldest schools. Located in a lobby that connects the historic part of the school with its new wing, Arai's artwork resembles a matching game, with the twenty brass images in the floor tiles matching those etched into the glass-block wall. Images of fish, butterflies, and starfish are among those included in the piece. Three brass strips in the shape of a wave also run the length of the lobby floor. Arai has said that she hoped that "arranging the artwork in the form of a game would encourage students to enjoy the process of looking at, and moving through, the newly designed spaces of their school."

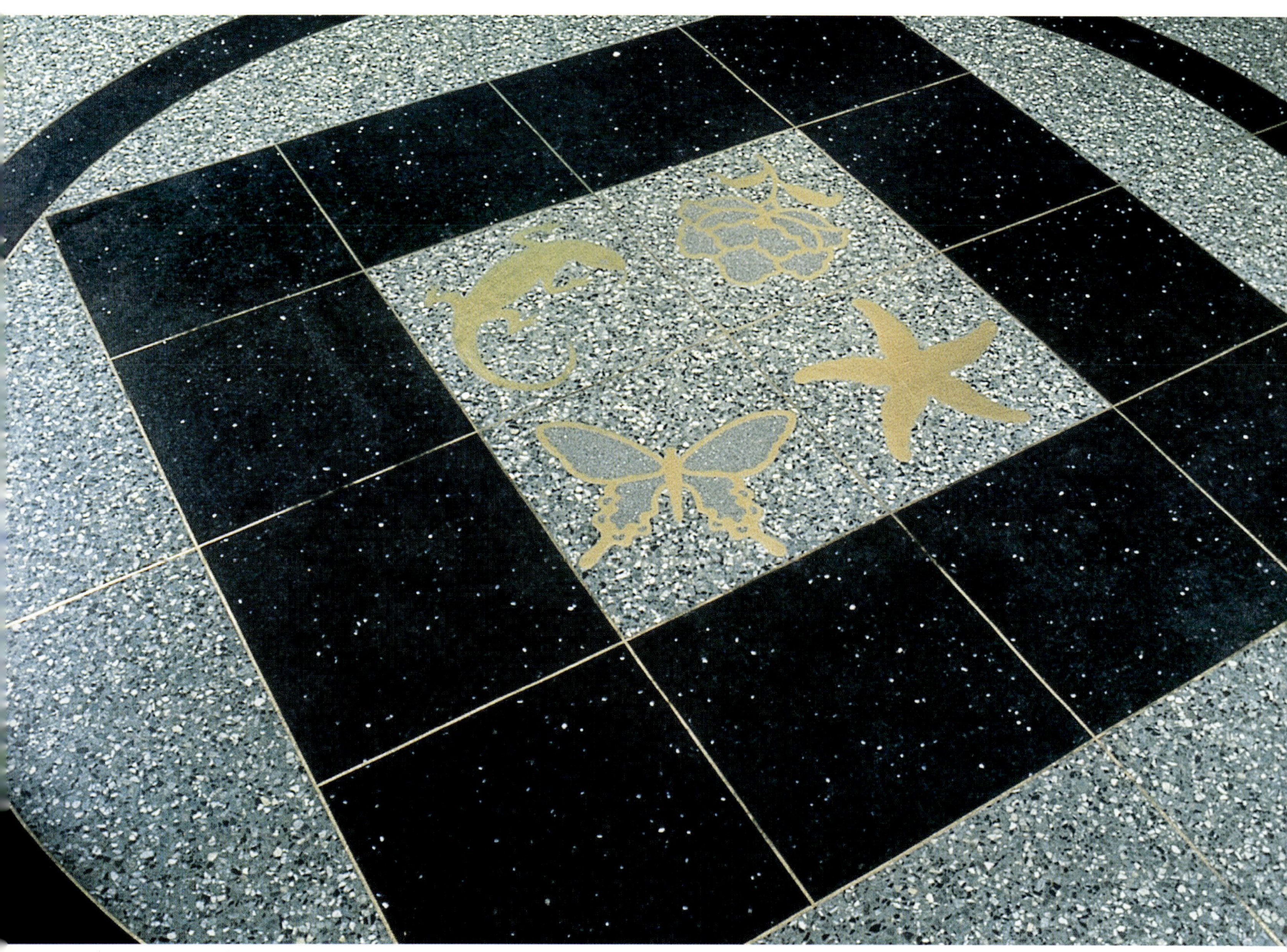

P.S. 4 On Stage (Stage Left) and (Stage Right), The Library, and Good Morning in New York
1996
Ceramics

Public School 4, 500 West 160th Street

ARCHITECT
Gruzen Samton Steinglass
DESIGN AGENCY
School Construction Authority
SPONSOR AGENCY
Board of Education

Camille Billops's four handmade ceramic tile murals, located at P.S. 4, portray students' school-day activities in whimsical scenes that combine images of City life with those taken from Dominican folklore and song. In the diptych *P.S. 4 On Stage (Stage Left) and (Stage Right)*, children are shown painting scenery, filming a scene, wearing costumes, and performing in a play. In *The Library* (right), children and animals, including a snake and an alligator, engage in activities together against the backdrop of the New York skyline. Billops's *Good Morning in New York* illustrates the City's diversity by showing New Yorkers wishing each other "good morning" in dozens of different languages.

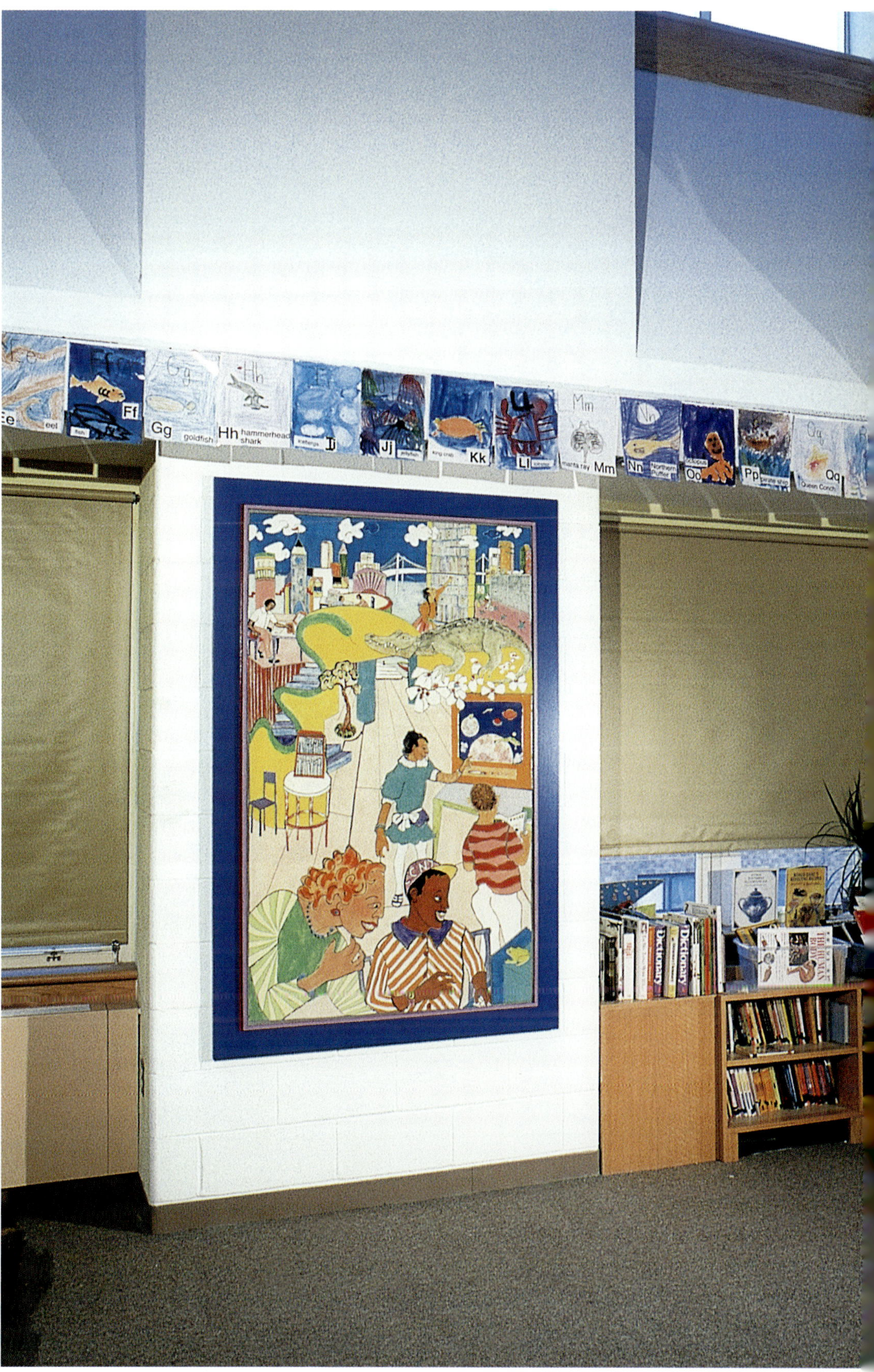

Camille Billops

107th Street Pier
1991
Rustic and polished terrazzo, concrete, exposed aggregate, steel

East 107th Street Recreational Pier, 107th Street and FDR Esplanade

ARCHITECT
Cavaglieri and Sultan
DESIGN AGENCY
Department of Parks and Recreation
SPONSOR AGENCY
Economic Development Corporation

Art Commission Award for Excellence in Design 1991

Andrea Blum's work features a number of elements designed to bring the 107th Street pier to life without undermining the existing structure. Blum created a new paving pattern executed in yellow, black, and white terrazzo and brushed gray concrete, and refurbished the concrete benches that encircle the lower level with yellow and black polished terrazzo. Materials were chosen for their ease of maintenance. Together with the renovated East River Esplanade, the finished pier provides much-needed recreational space for the East Harlem community.

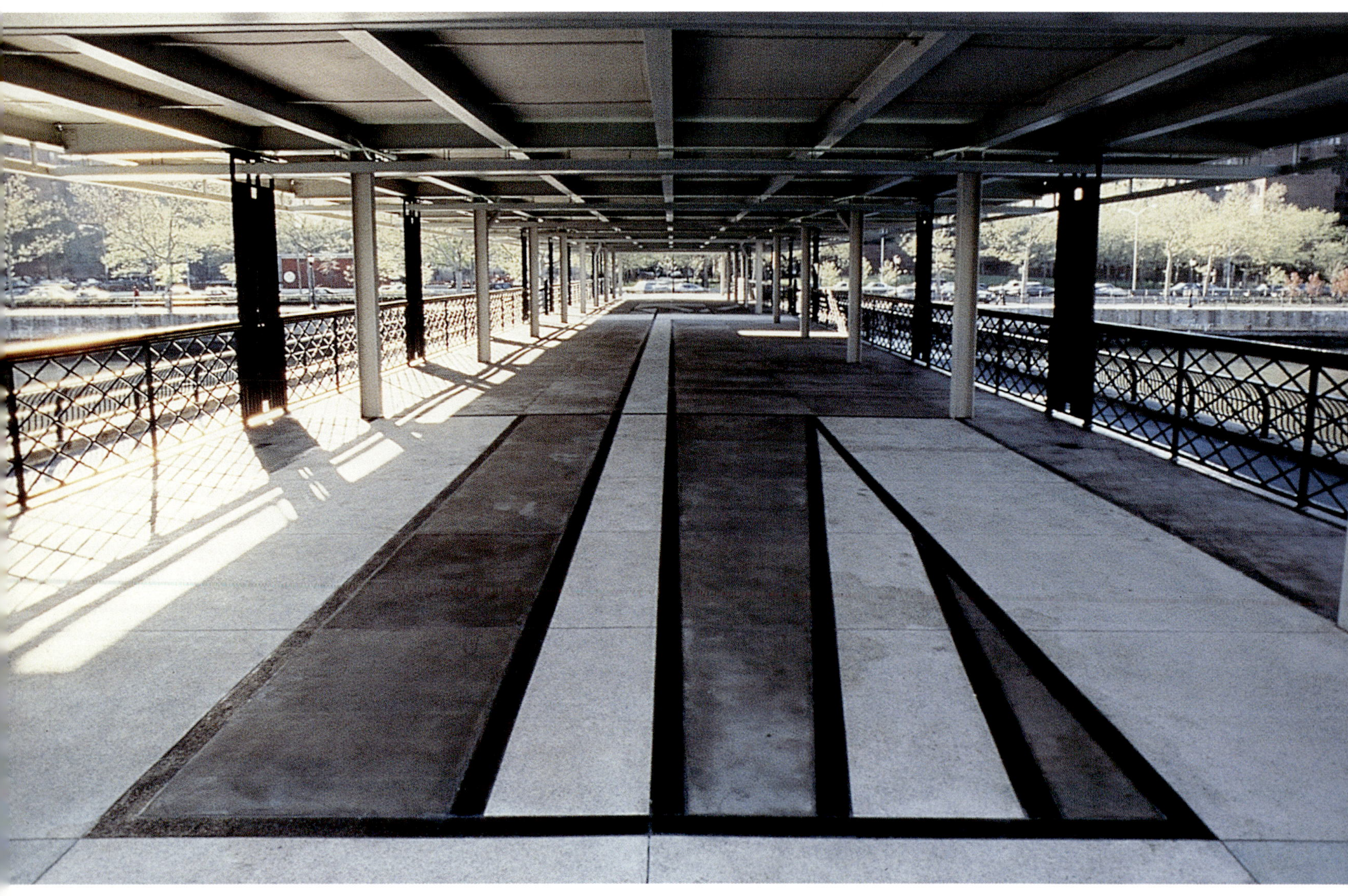

Andrea Blum

Deborah Brown

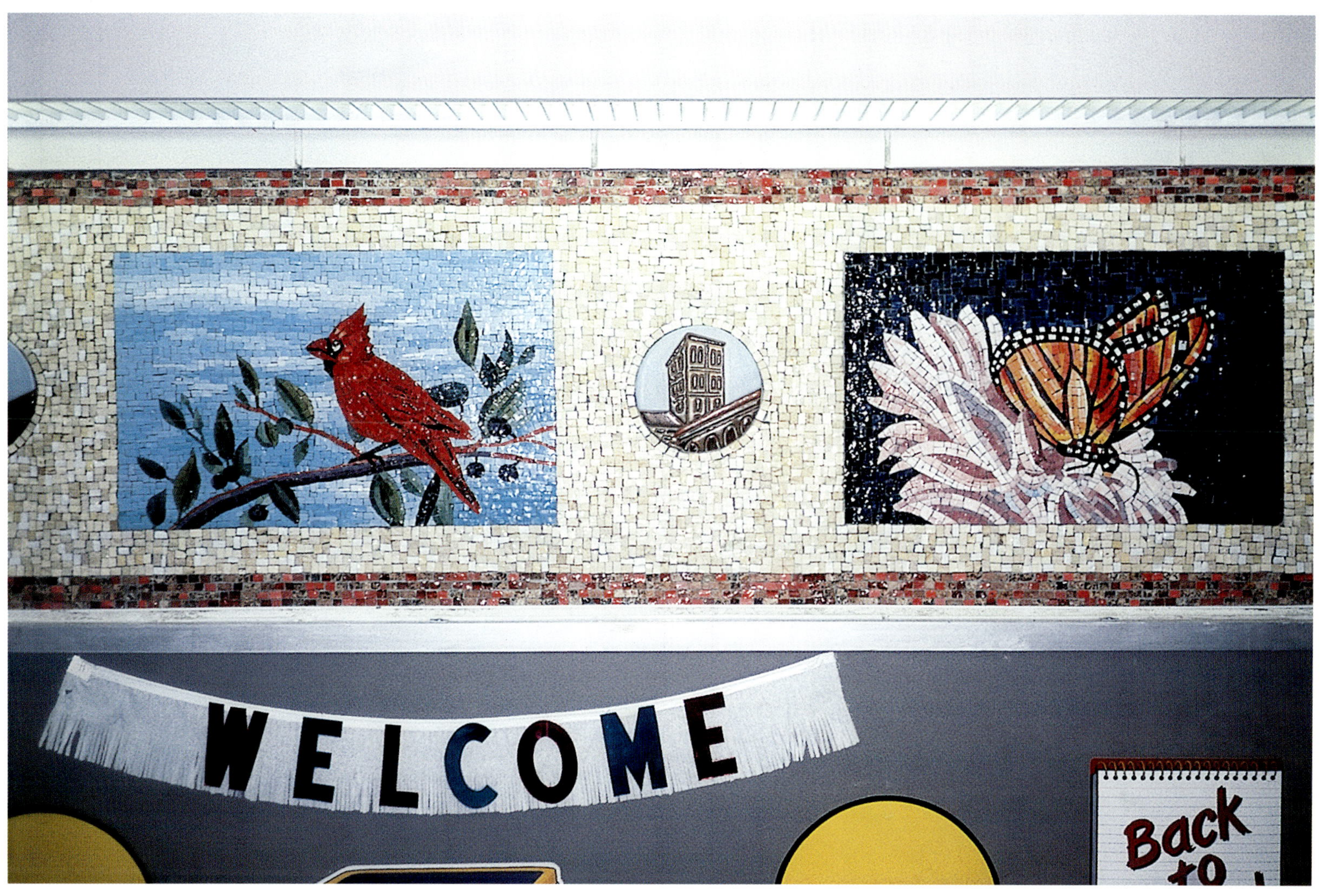

The Seasons: Wildlife and Vistas of Fort Tryon and Inwood Hill Parks
2001
Mosaic

Public School 178, 1218 Elwood Street

ARCHITECT
Kliment & Frances Halsband Architects
DESIGN AGENCY
School Construction Authority
SPONSOR AGENCY
Board of Education

Inspired by the nearby Fort Tryon and Inwood Hill parks, Deborah Brown designed a mosaic of thirty-two rectangular images of animals and landscapes alternating with twenty-nine circular images of The Cloisters, the branch of The Metropolitan Museum of Art devoted to the art and architecture of medieval Europe. The mosaic runs along the top of the school's cafeteria walls. Each of the four walls depicts images from a different season: winter, spring, summer, and fall.

Colin Chase

Elegy for El-Hajj Malik Shabazz
1997
Etched glass, bronze

Audubon Ballroom, 3940 Broadway

ARCHITECT
Davis Brody Bond

DESIGN/SPONSOR AGENCY
Economic Development Corporation

Etched in the glass of the main entrance to the building where Malcolm X was assassinated in 1965, Colin Chase's artwork serves as a subtle tribute to the famed civil rights leader. Chase designed a series of etched-glass windows that relate to the "X" motif: a symbol of inversion, an hourglass, and the mathematical symbol for an unknown factor. In the upper left and right panels the X is combined with concentric circles, while in the two central panels the X is merged with Kufic calligraphy that refers to Islamic prayer.

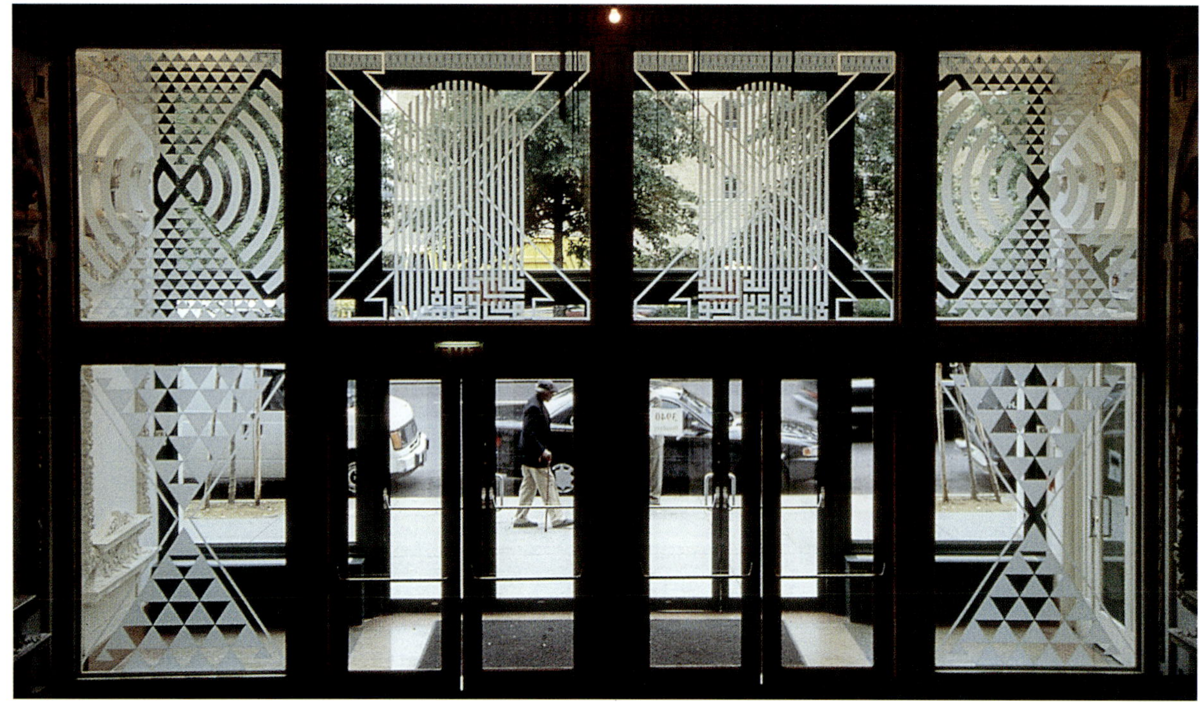

Carl Cheng

Community Island Pond (opposite) and **Shadow Garden**
2001
Steel, wood

Wall Street Esplanade and Pier 11, Maiden Lane and South Street

ARCHITECT
Smith-Miller and Hawkinson Architects and Judith Heintz Landscape Architecture

DESIGN AGENCY
Economic Development Corporation
SPONSOR AGENCY
Department of Transportation

Carl Cheng's *Community Island Pond* (opposite) is located on a ferry pier and approached via a small pedestrian bridge over the East River. The work features cut-out metal silhouettes of anonymous faces of New Yorkers mounted on a steel canopy grid overlooking a pool of water surrounded by a railing and seating. When light shines through the grid, the faces are reflected in and abstracted by the water below. *Shadow Garden*, which is located on the promenade, is a smaller version of *Community Island Pond*.

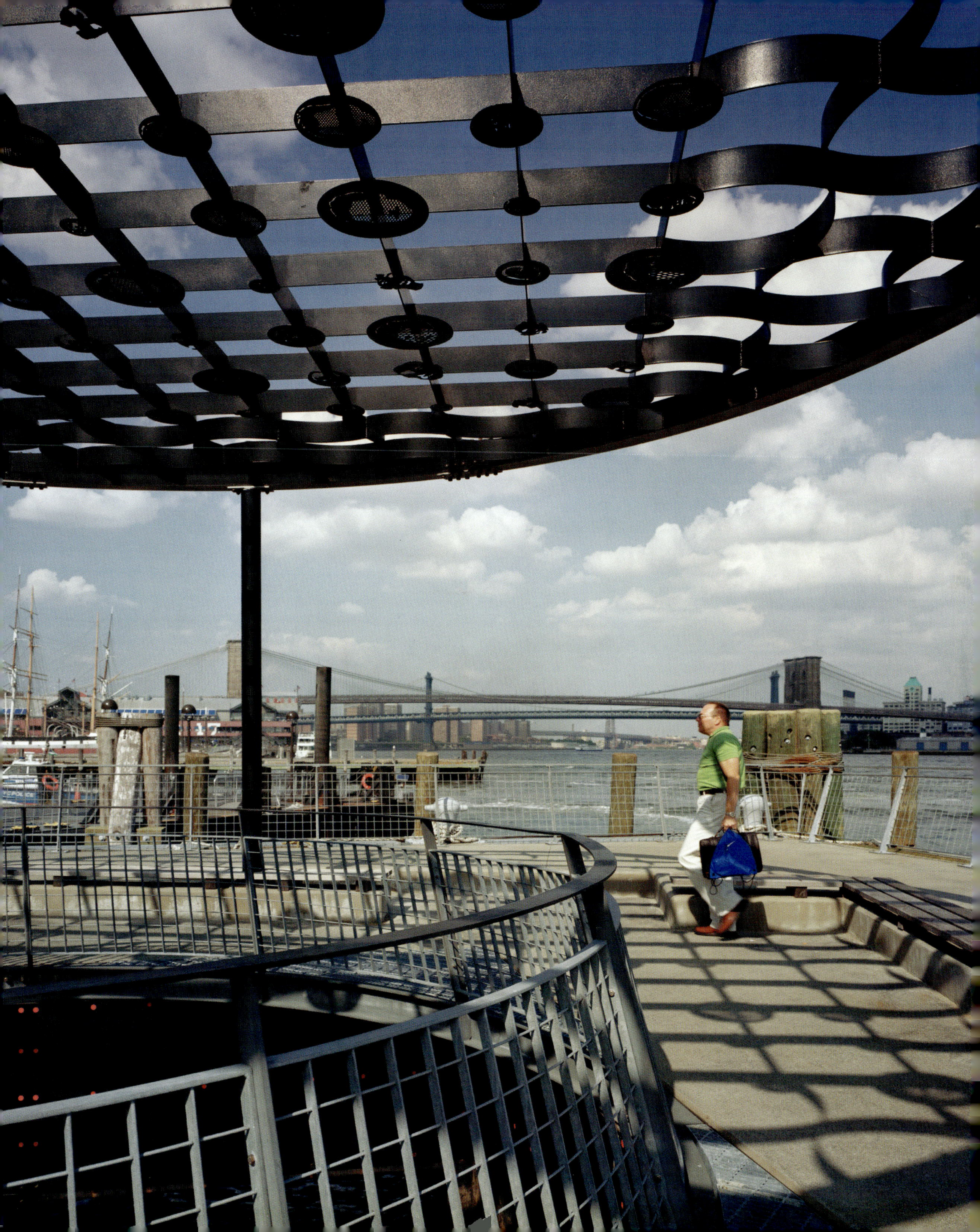

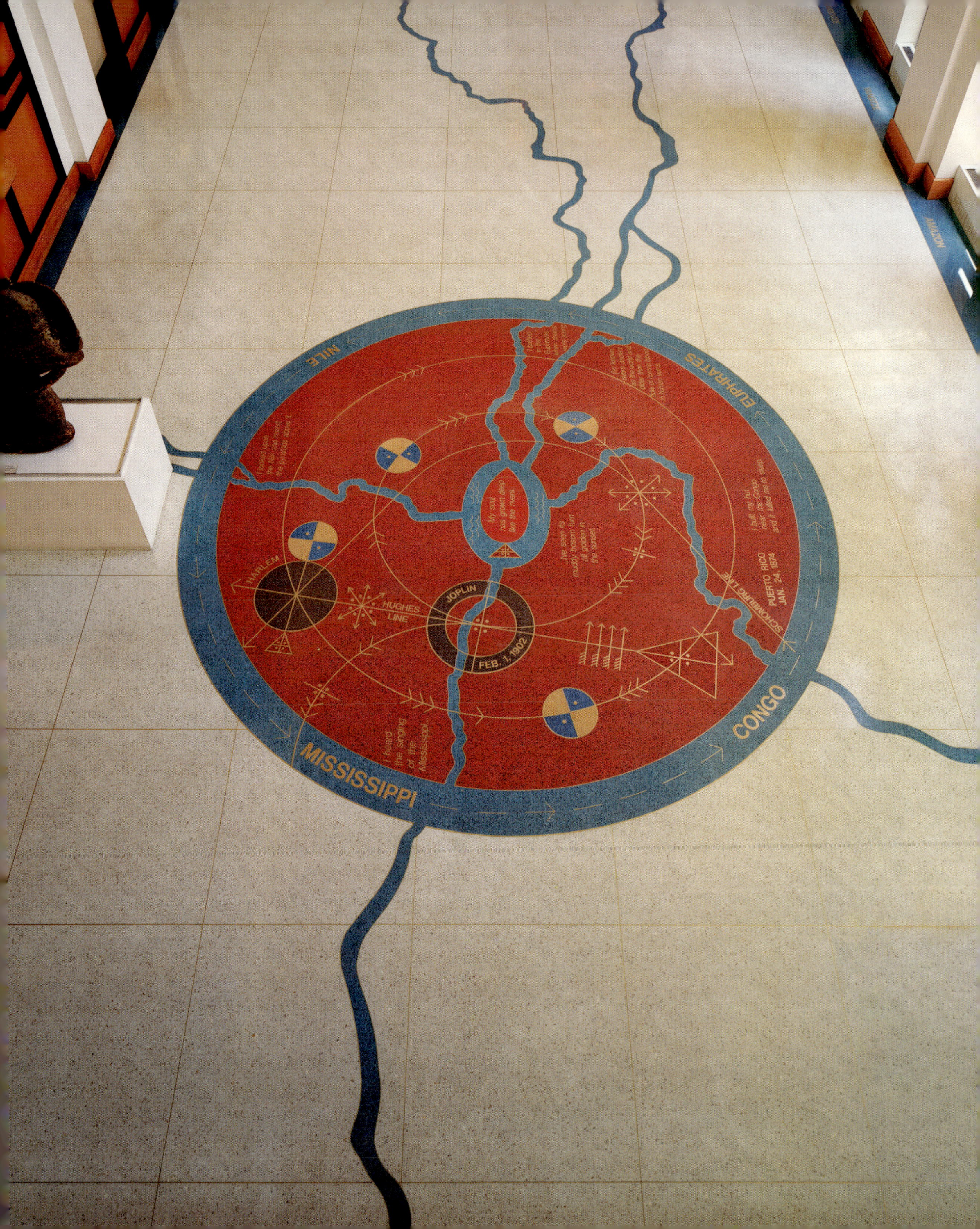
NILE
EUPHRATES
CONGO
MISSISSIPPI
My soul has grown deep like the rivers.
...I've seen its muddy bosom turn all golden in the sunset.
I built my hut near the Congo and it lulled me to sleep.
PUERTO RICO JAN. 24, 1874
SCHOMBURG LINE
HARLEM
HUGHES LINE
JOPLIN
FEB. 1, 1902
I heard the singing of the Mississippi

Houston Conwill, Estella Conwill Majozo, and Joseph DePace

Rivers (opposite)
1991
Terrazzo

Schomburg Center for Research in Black Culture, 515 Malcolm X Boulevard

ARCHITECT
Bono/Ryder Associates
DESIGN AGENCY
Department of General Services
SPONSOR AGENCY
New York Public Library

Art Commission Award for Excellence in Design 1990

The terrazzo floor plan designed by Houston Conwill, Estella Conwill Majozo, and Joseph DePace, entitled *Rivers*, fills the lobby entrance of the Schomburg Center's auditorium. The cosmological diagram pays homage both to the poet Langston Hughes and to the bibliophile Arthur Schomburg, after whom the building is named. The design features a mandala with inset verses from Hughes's poem, "The Negro Speaks of Rivers" (1922), and terrazzo rivers flow outward. The poet's ashes lie beneath the center of the design, which is etched with the concluding line of the poem, "My soul has grown deep like the rivers."

Michael Cummings

Carnival Time, **Kitty with Flowers**, **Coral Reef**, and **Monarch Butterfly**
2000
Quilts

New Children's Center, 492 First Avenue

ARCHITECT
Richard Dattner and Partners Architects
DESIGN AGENCY
Department of Design and Construction
SPONSOR AGENCY
Administration for Children's Services

Art Commission Award for Excellence in Design 2001

Michael Cummings created the four brightly colored quilts that hang in the lobby of the New Children's Center, a processing center for foster-care children. *Carnival Time*, *Kitty with Flowers*, *Coral Reef*, and *Monarch Butterfly* all depict playful and recognizable scenes intended to comfort and visually engage the children staying at the center.

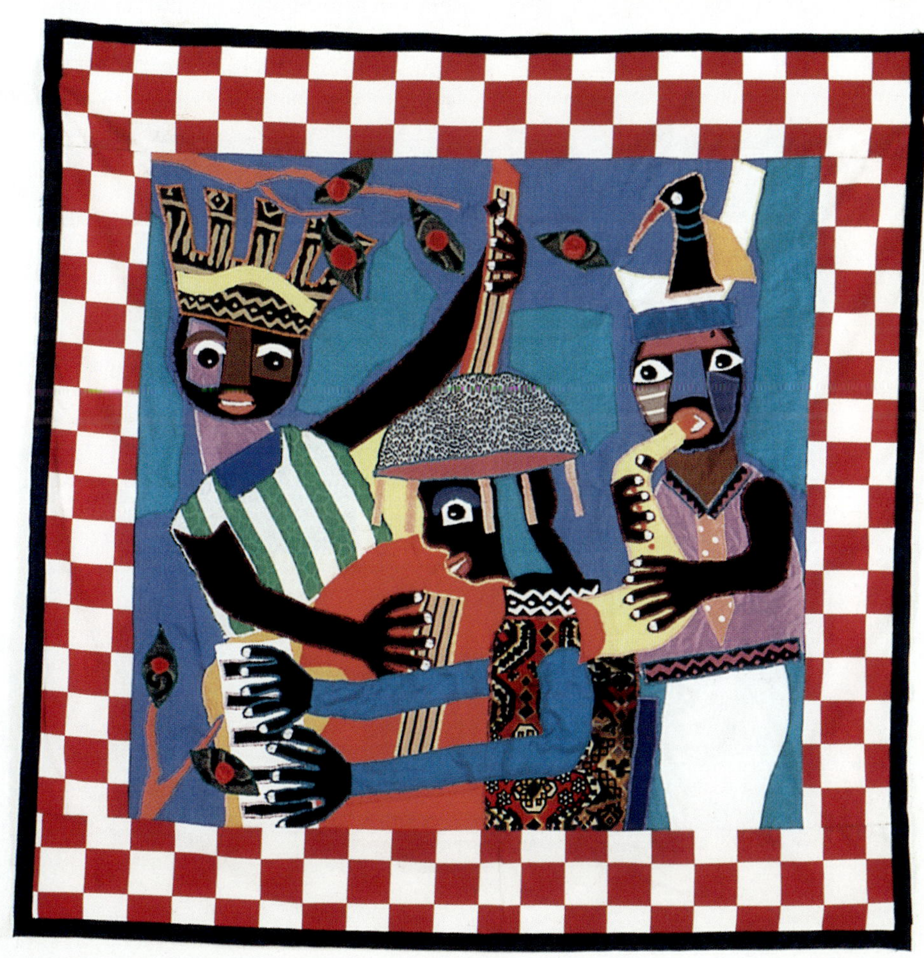

Images of Washington Heights
1995
Gelatin silver prints

Public School 4, 500 West 160th Street

ARCHITECT
Gruzen Samton Steinglass
DESIGN AGENCY
School Construction Authority
SPONSOR AGENCY
Board of Education

Pablo Delano's project for P.S. 4 in Washington Heights consists of fourteen large black-and-white photographs inset in niches in the school's dramatic two-level main corridor. The photographs depict scenes of daily neighborhood life and events celebrating the history, aspirations, and cultural traditions of the community, and the strengths that bind it together.

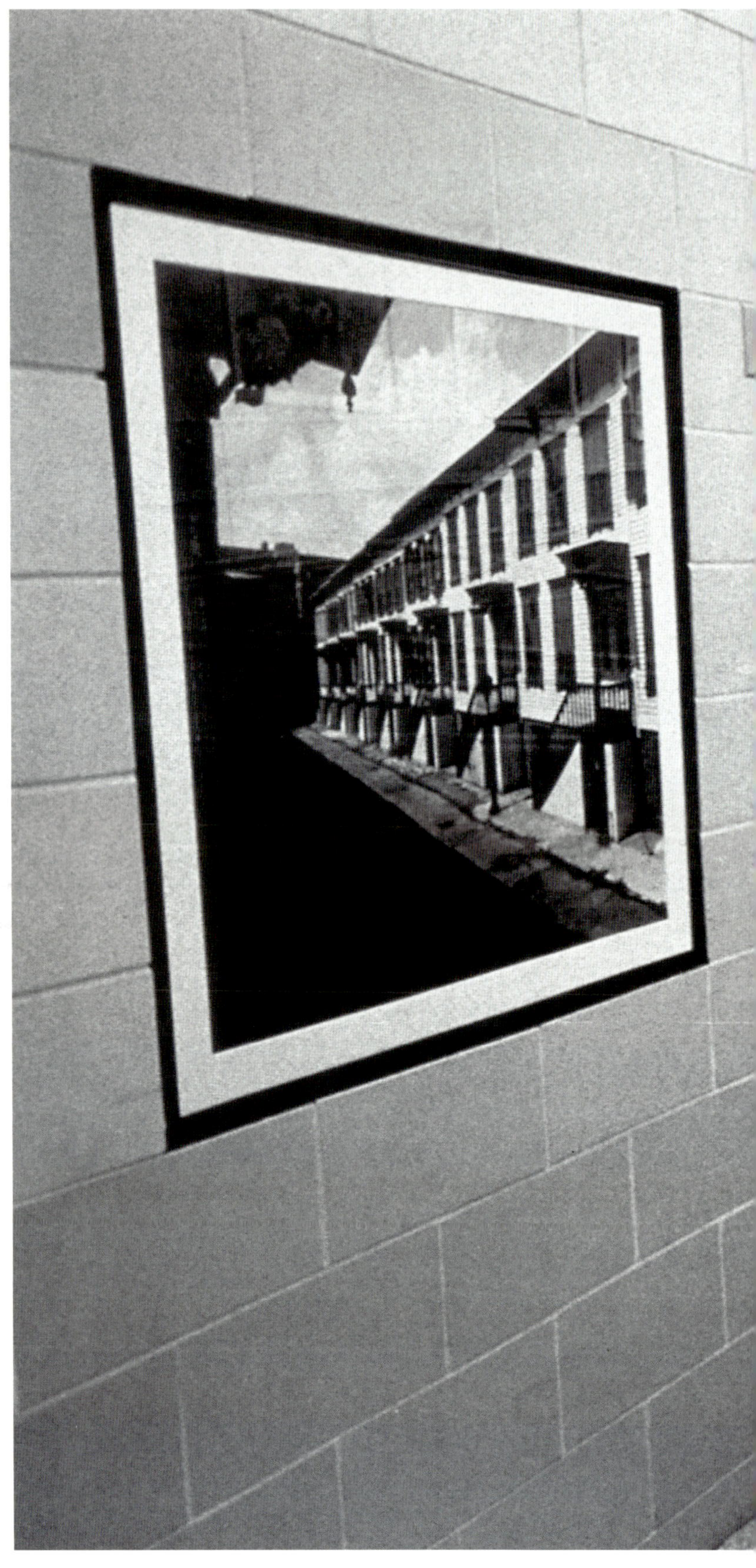

Pablo Delano

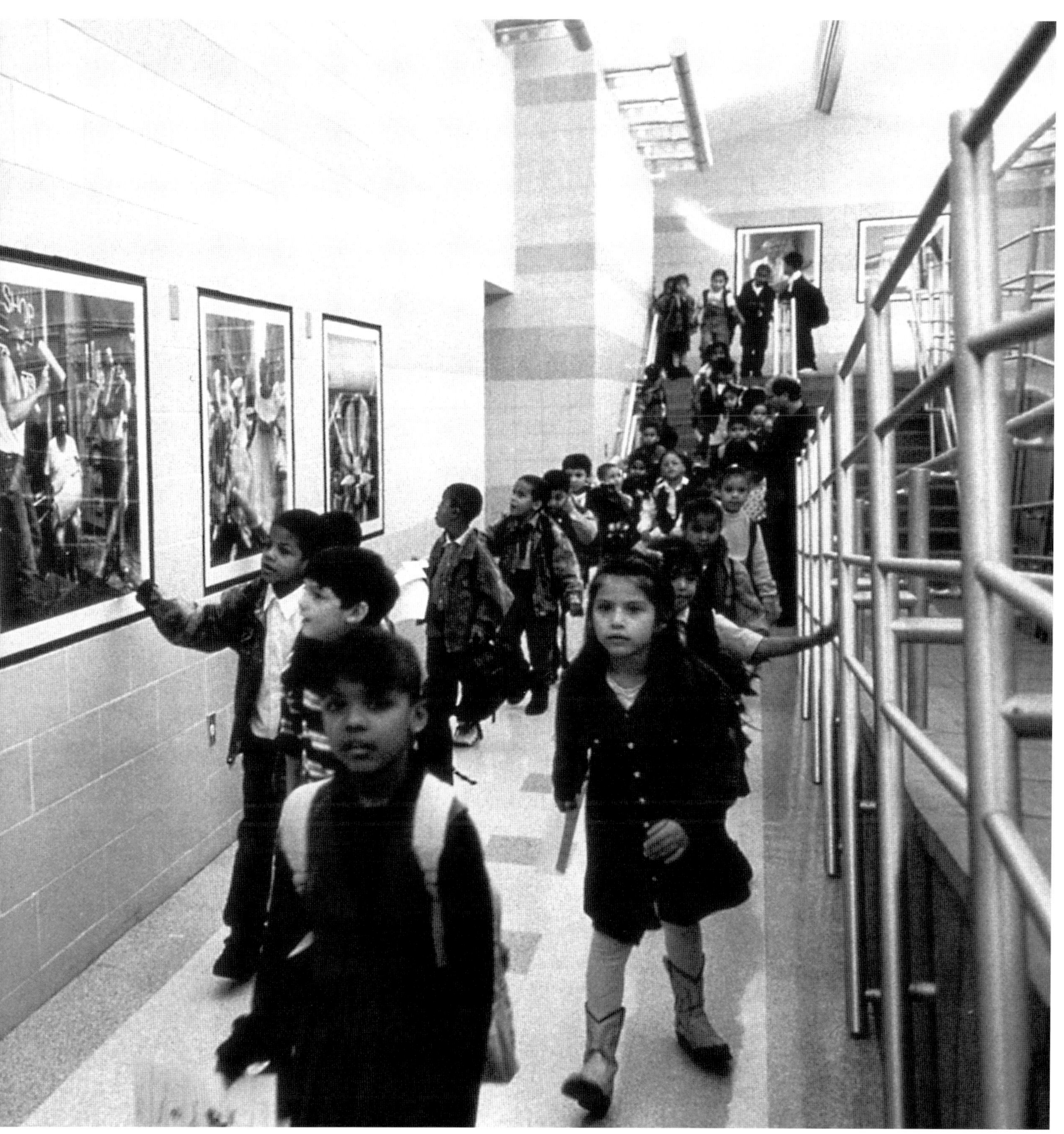

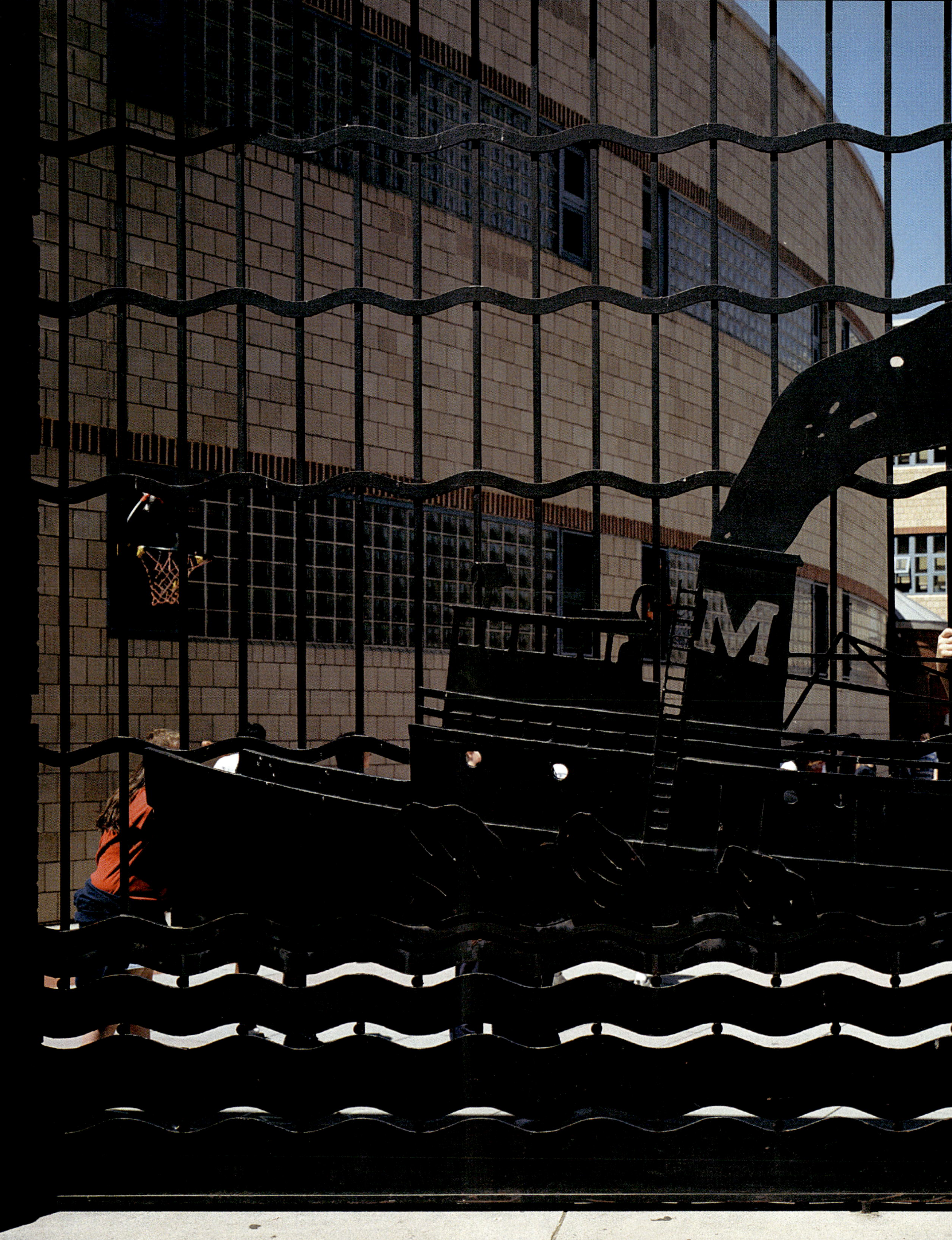

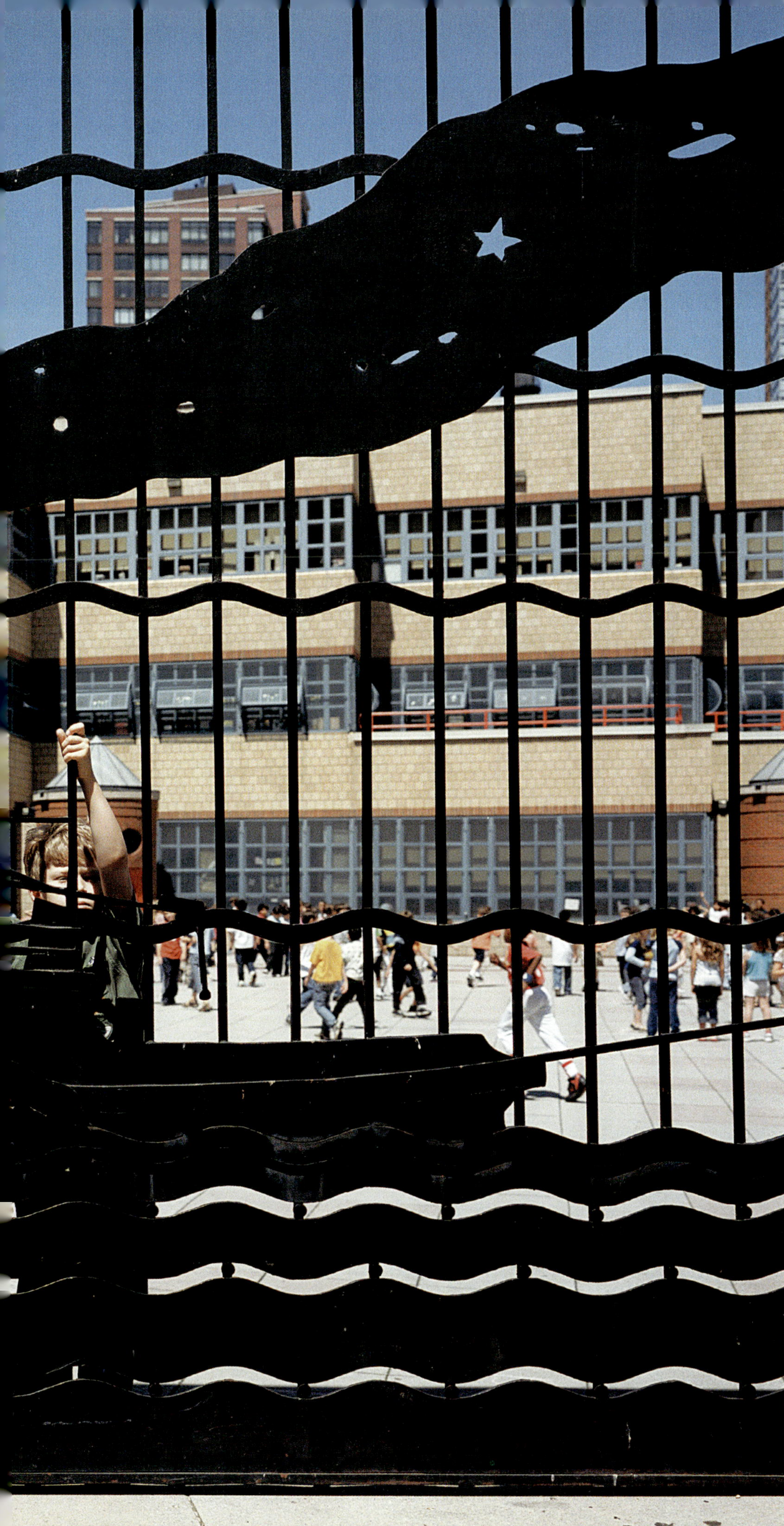

Donna Dennis

Dreaming of Far Away Places: The Ships Come to Washington Market
1998
Steel
Thirteen Ceramic Medallions
1990
Ceramics

Public School 234,
292 Greenwich Street

ARCHITECT
Richard Dattner and Partners Architects
DESIGN AGENCY
School Construction Authority
SPONSOR AGENCY
Board of Education

Art Commission Award for Excellence in Design 1986

Donna Dennis turned to the rich history of New York's harbor and the Washington Market for her fence at P.S. 234 in Tribeca. The steel fence (left), composed of fourteen panels set into arches, portrays a dynamic procession of silhouetted ships gallantly parading around the schoolyard. The ships are based on actual historic vessels that cruised New York's harbor, and the fence captures the vitality of the City's shipping industry. For the building's façade, the artist designed and hand-painted thirteen ceramic medallions representing the historic activity of Washington Market.

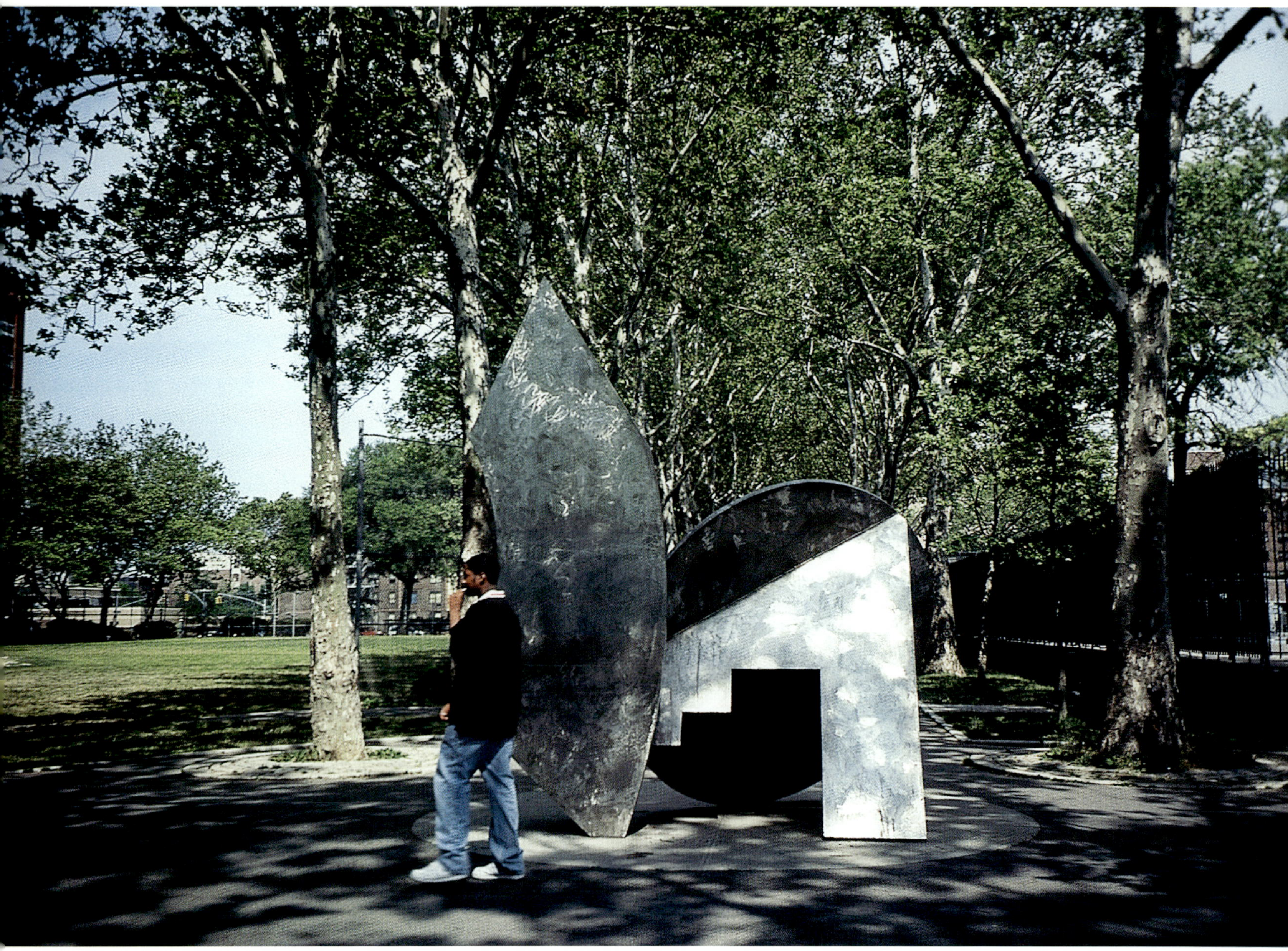

Tomorrow's Wind
1995
Stainless steel

Thomas Jefferson Park and Pool,
2180 First Avenue

ARCHITECT
Miceli Kulik Williams & Associates
DESIGN/SPONSOR AGENCY
Department of Parks and Recreation

Mel Edwards's stainless steel abstract sculpture, entitled *Tomorrow's Wind*, features a large disk tilted upwards to mirror the sun. Adjacent to the disk is a towering vertical form, bisected at its base by a shape reminiscent of a stairway or building block. These three elements balance each other and reflect the shapes of nearby buildings. Edwards has said of this work: "The sculptural forms, site, and creative imagination are combined to give a new experience to the community of viewers."

Mel Edwards

Daniel Galvez

Homage to Malcolm X (following pages)
1997
Oil on canvas

Audubon Ballroom, 3940 Broadway

ARCHITECT
Davis Brody Bond
DESIGN/SPONSOR AGENCY
Economic Development Corporation

Daniel Galvez's mural *Homage to Malcolm X* at the Audubon Ballroom incorporates images from print, film, and television documenting the events in Malcolm X's life and the civil rights movement. In an effort to connect the history of the ballroom to its current surrounding neighborhood, the artist juxtaposed portraits of civil rights leaders with portraits of contemporary Harlem residents, such as a local café owner and a construction worker who helped renovate the ballroom. Galvez employed the technique of under-painting, using black and white in most of the work but overlaying some areas with subtle hues of glazes and color. This technique allows some images to appear to be old while those around them look contemporary, further bridging the distance between past and present.

Marina Gutierrez

Untitled
1996
Painted aluminum

Julia de Burgos Latino Cultural Center, 1689 Lexington Avenue

ARCHITECT
Borrero/Plumey Joint Venture
DESIGN/SPONSOR AGENCY
Economic Development Corporation

Marina Gutierrez's installation for the renovation of the Julia de Burgos Latino Cultural Center features suspended mobile structures of silhouetted aluminum cut-outs and painted images inspired by the work of the Puerto Rican poet Julia de Burgos. Twelve silhouettes are suspended from seven points in the atrium, which are visible from both the lobby and the second-floor balcony. Air currents cause the double-sided images to move and reconfigure themselves, resembling a kinetic, visual poem.

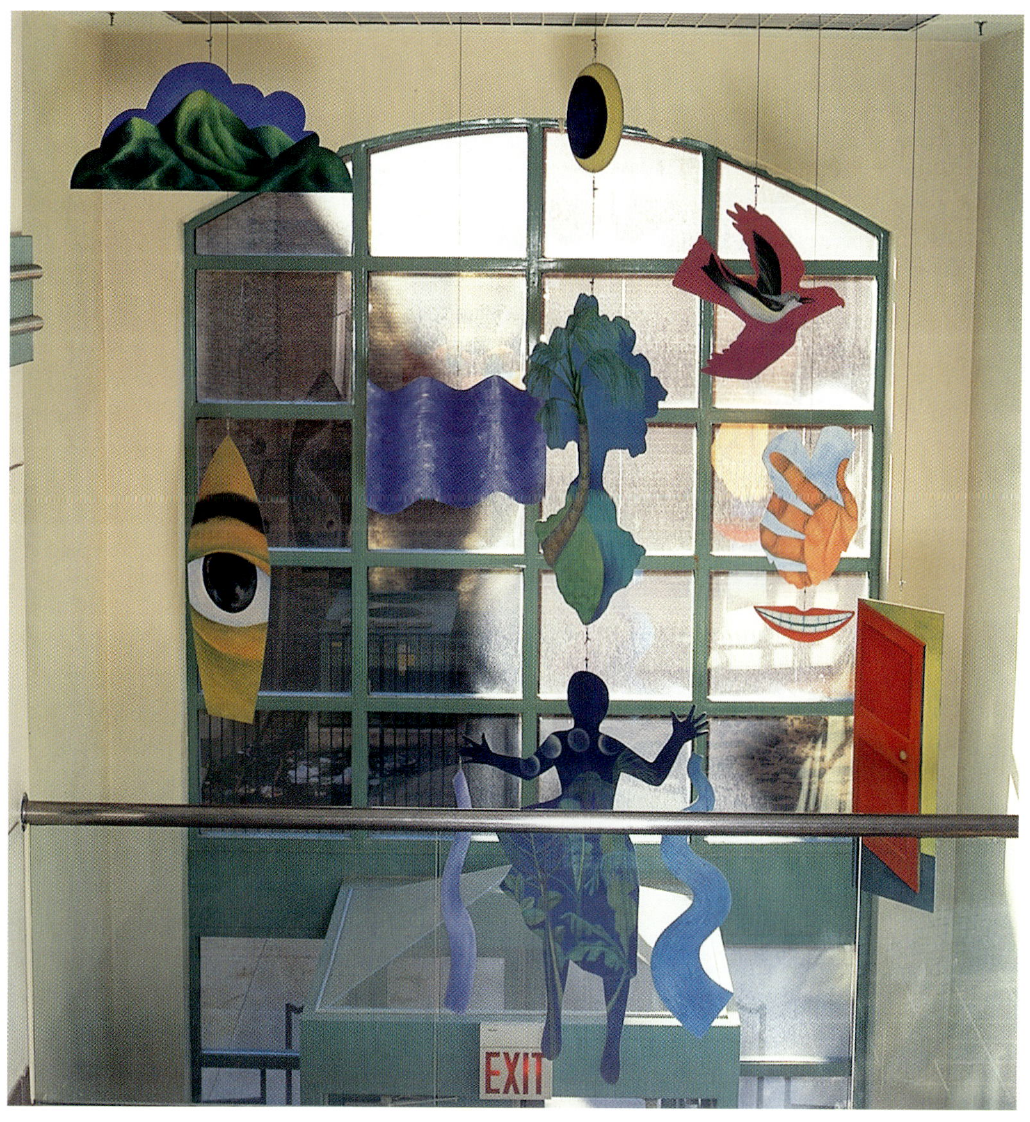

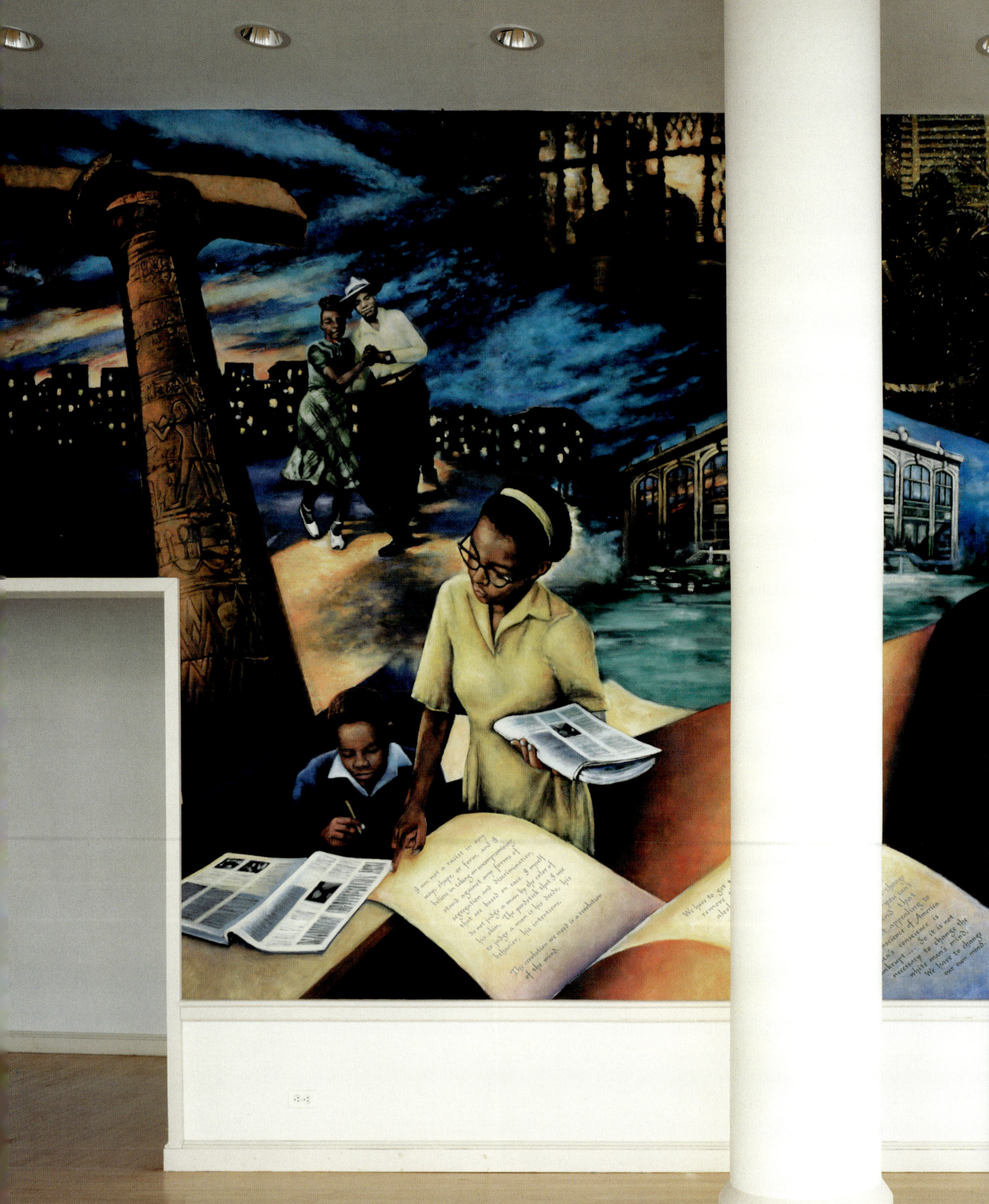
I am not a racist in any
way, shape, or form, and I
believe in taking an uncompromising
stand against any forms of
segregation and discrimination
that are based on race. I myself
do not judge a man by the color of
his skin. The yardstick that I use
to judge a man is his deeds, his
behavior, his intentions.
The revolution we need is a revolution
of the mind.
necessary to change the
white man's mind.
We have to change
our own mind.

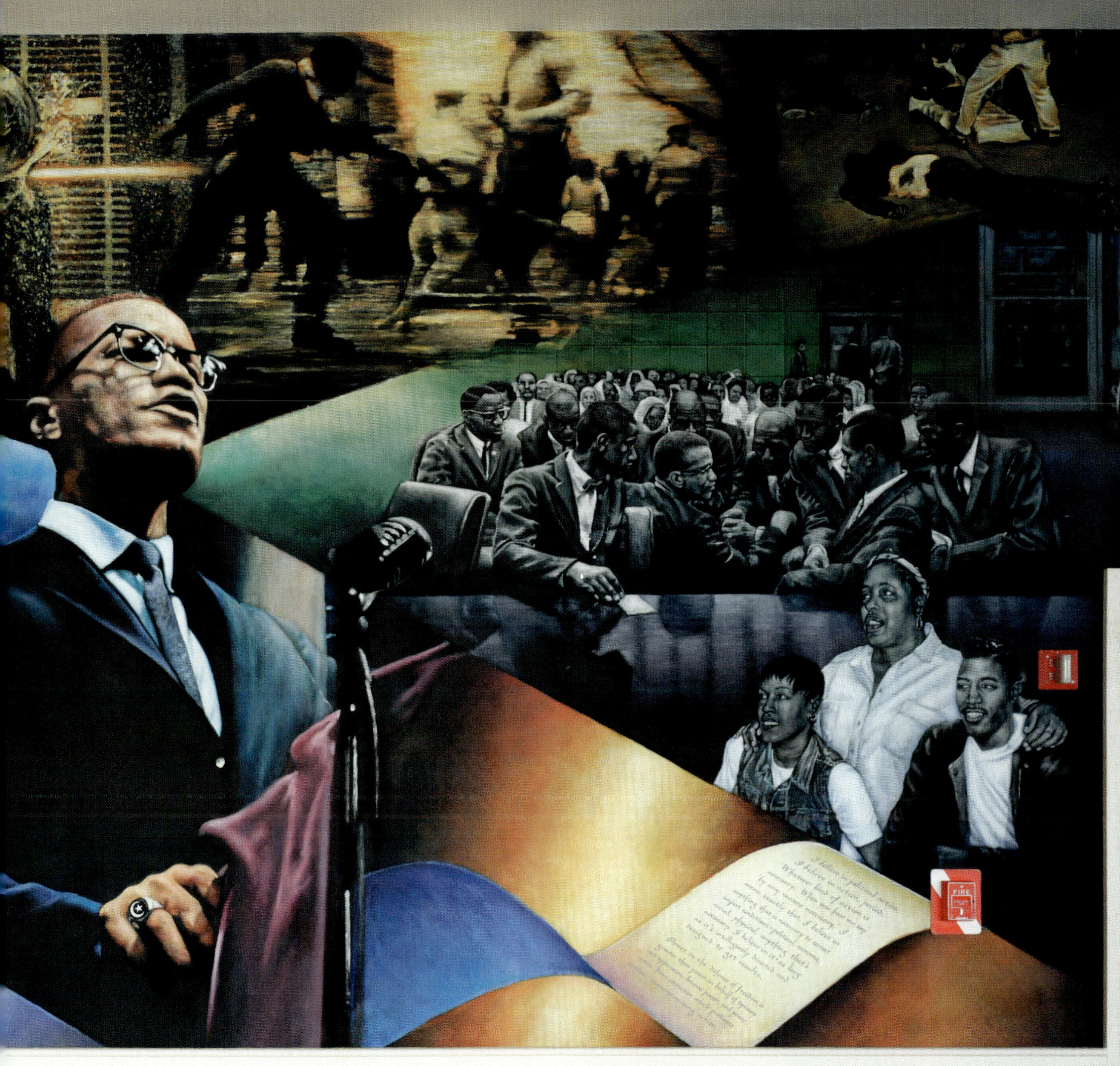
I believe in political action.
I believe in action, period.
Whatever kind of action is
necessary. When you hear me say
'by any means necessary,' I
mean exactly that. I believe in
anything that is necessary to correct
unjust conditions–political, economic,
social, physical, anything that's
necessary. I believe in it–as long
as it's intelligently directed and
designed to get results.
Power in the defense of freedom is
greater than power in behalf of tyranny

Richard Haas

The Judgment of Solomon and
The Judgment of Pao Kung
1988
Sculptural cast apoxy, cement
Immigration on the Lower East Side
1988
Painted mural

Bernard B. Kerik Complex,
125 White Street

ARCHITECT
Urbahn Associates
DESIGN AGENCY
Department of General Services
SPONSOR AGENCY
Department of Corrections

Art Commission Award for Excellence in Design 1988

Richard Haas's artwork at the Bernard B. Kerik Complex includes two sculptural friezes and a seven-paneled mural. The friezes, located on a bridge that connects Baxter and Centre Street, illustrate King Solomon and Pao Kung, a Sung Dynasty Chinese judge. Haas's mural, depicting the history of immigration on the Lower East Side (right, detail of panel entitled "Immigrant Arrival"), is painted in broad caricature style and is located on the Baxter Street façade of the building.

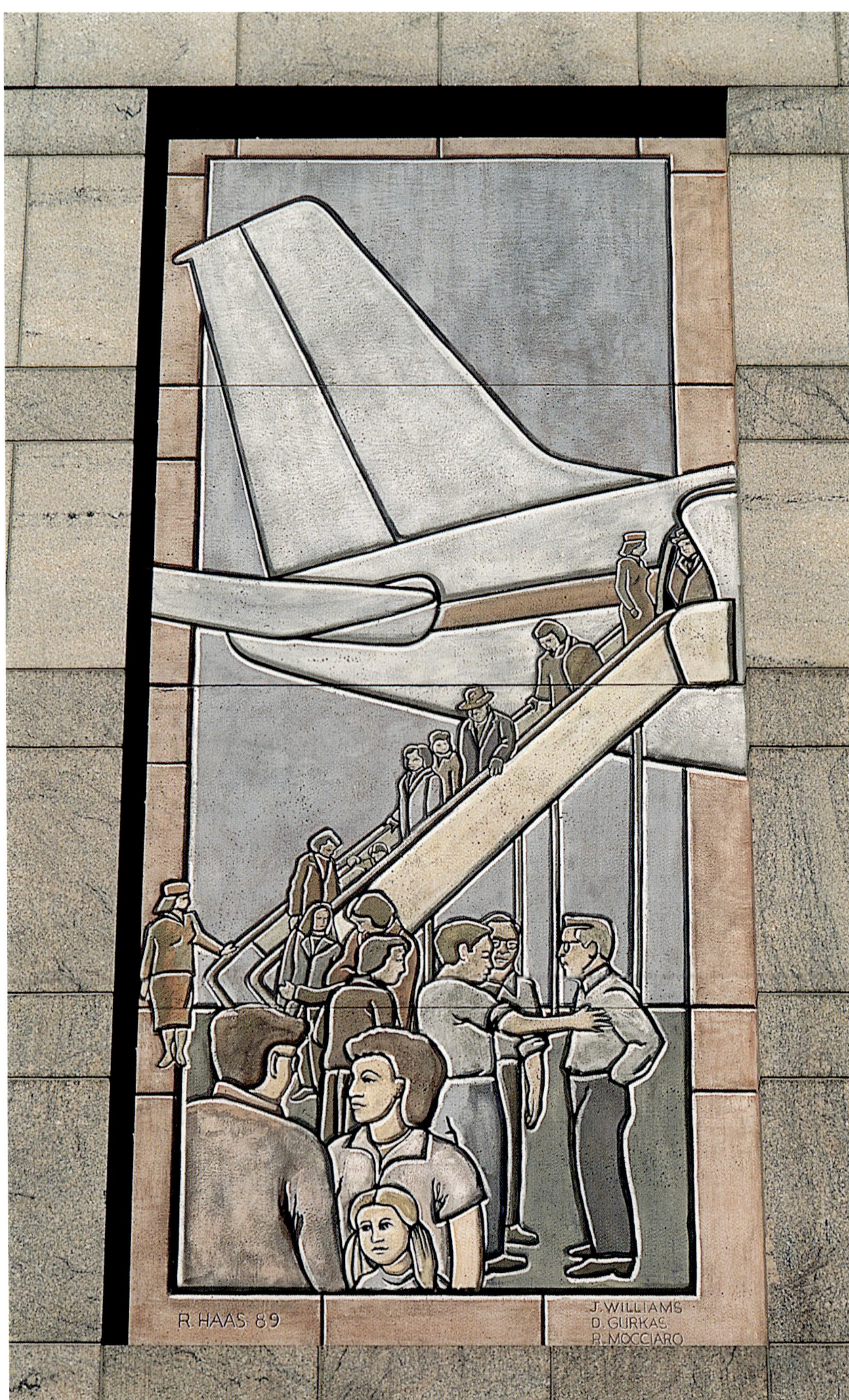

Ancestor Walk
1996
Concrete, embedded artifacts

Public School 311, 4862 Broadway

ARCHITECT
Gruzen Samton Steinglass
DESIGN AGENCY
School Construction Authority
SPONSOR AGENCY
Board of Education

Inspired by Native American dwelling sites that have been found near P.S. 311 (formerly P.S. 176), Maren Hassinger created *Ancestor Walk,* a sloping wall that begins at the top of the school gate and descends to ground level at the playground. Hassinger designed objects that refer to prehistoric Native American culture, including vessels, tools, and arrowheads, and mounted them along the top of the wall or embossed them along the sides. The artist explains that the work is "a memory piece that binds us to our past."

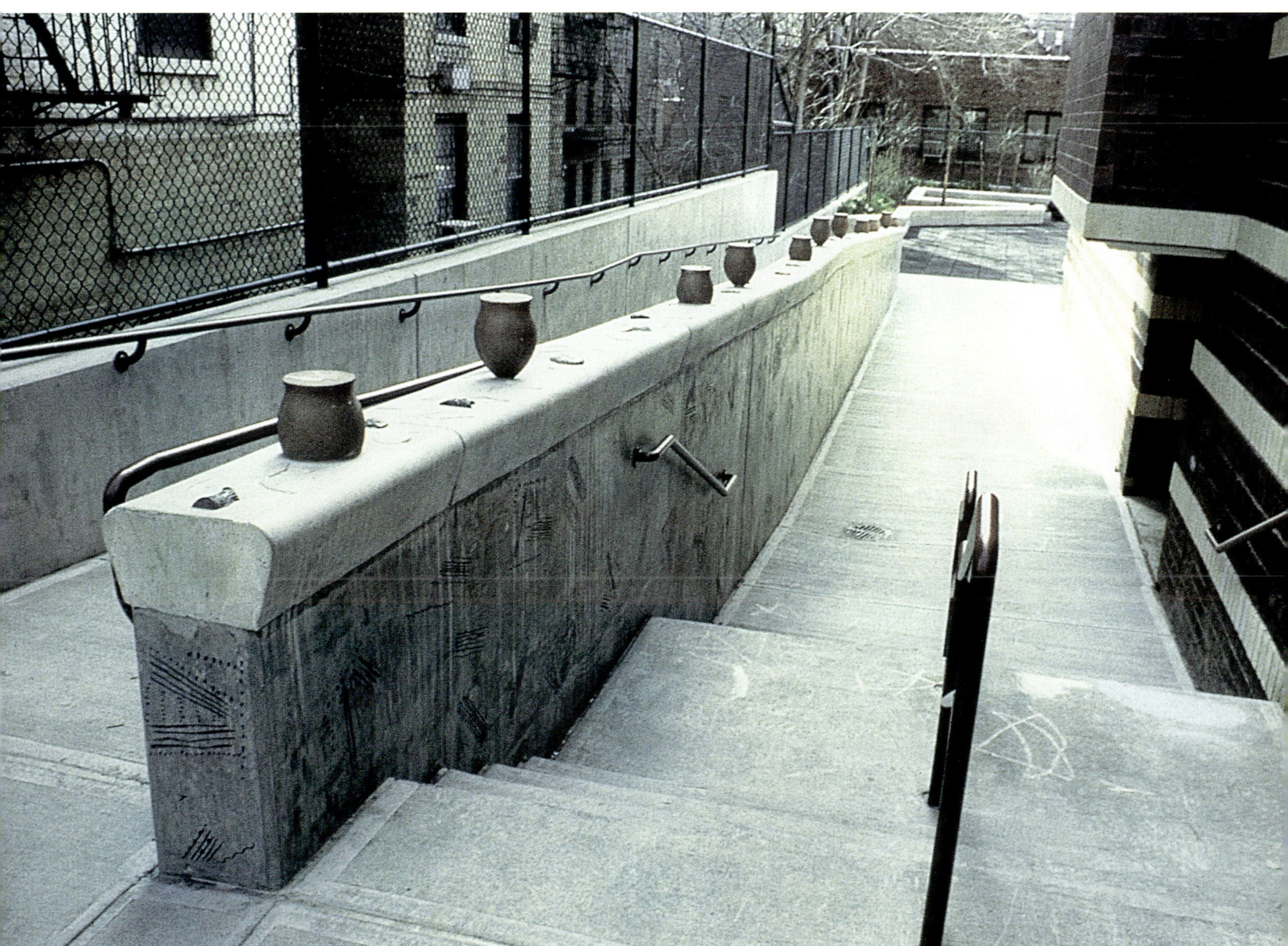

Maren Hassinger

Fence of Leaves
1995
Painted steel

Public School 8, 465 West 167th Street

ARCHITECT
Gruzen Samton Steinglass
DESIGN AGENCY
School Construction Authority
SPONSOR AGENCY
Board of Education

Maren Hassinger's painted steel fence and gate at P.S. 8 feature a tropical motif of leaves and trees. Mangrove, palm, ohia, and papaya trees, as well as leaves from philodendrons, Swiss cheese plants, and passionflowers twist and turn along the length of the fence, surrounding the school children with tropical foliage.

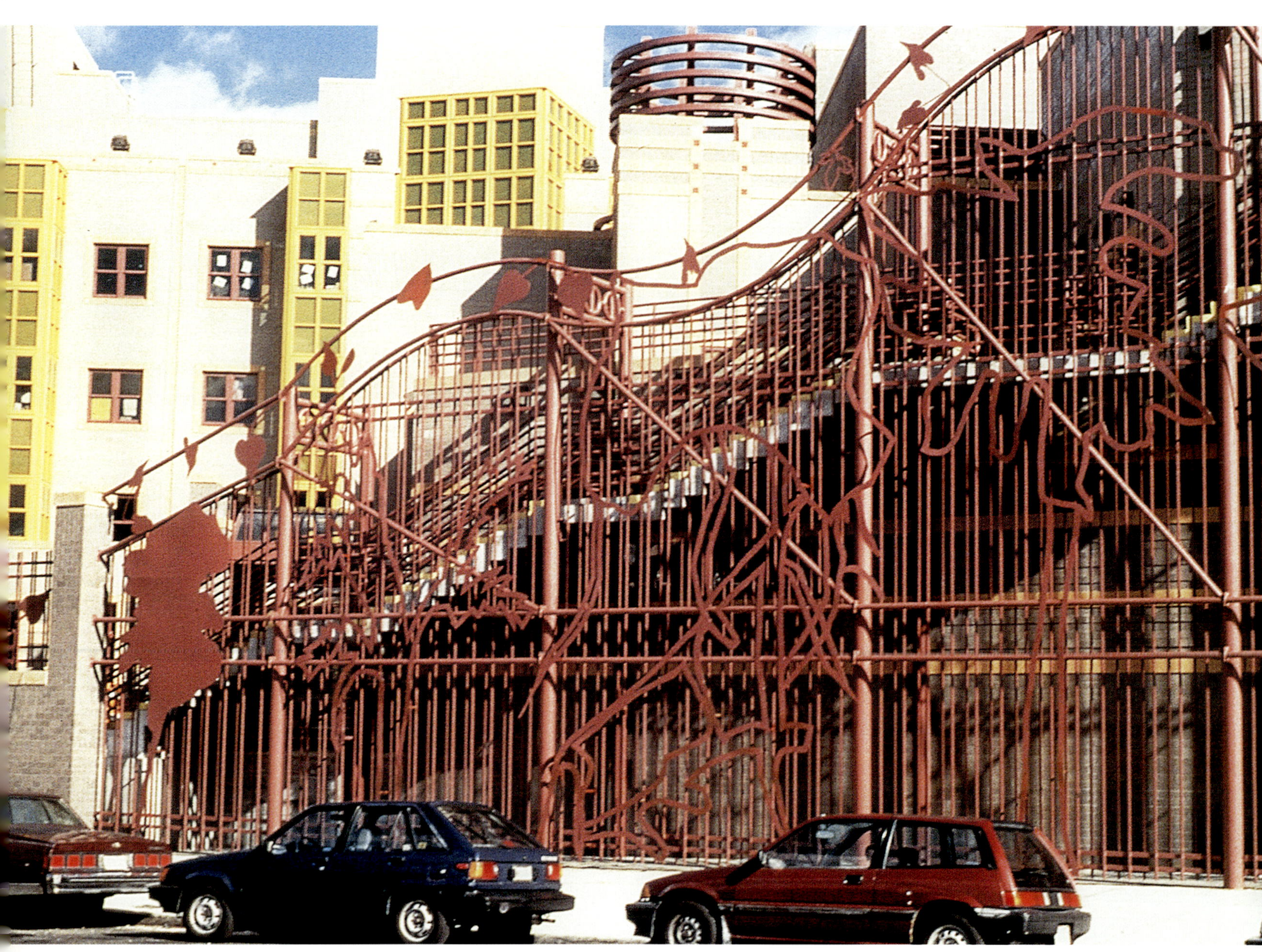

Maren Hassinger

Brower Hatcher

El Arbol de Esperanza
1995
Stainless steel, nickel-plated brass, bronze

Thomas Jefferson Park,
2180 First Avenue

ARCHITECT
Miceli Kulik Williams & Associates
DESIGN/SPONSOR AGENCY
Department of Parks and Recreation

Brower Hatcher's 18 foot (5.4 m) tall sculpture of a tree is sited among the real trees that line the paths of Thomas Jefferson Park. The polished stainless-steel trunk supports a globe constructed from a translucent matrix of color-coated stainless-steel rods connected by nickel-plated brass fittings. With the guidance of the artist, students from River East School and the Thomas Jefferson Park Recreational Center created small bronze figures, which are now displayed on the tree's branches. These objects, which include pizza slices, dogs, worms, and a bird in its nest, represent what the students recognize as common sights in the park.

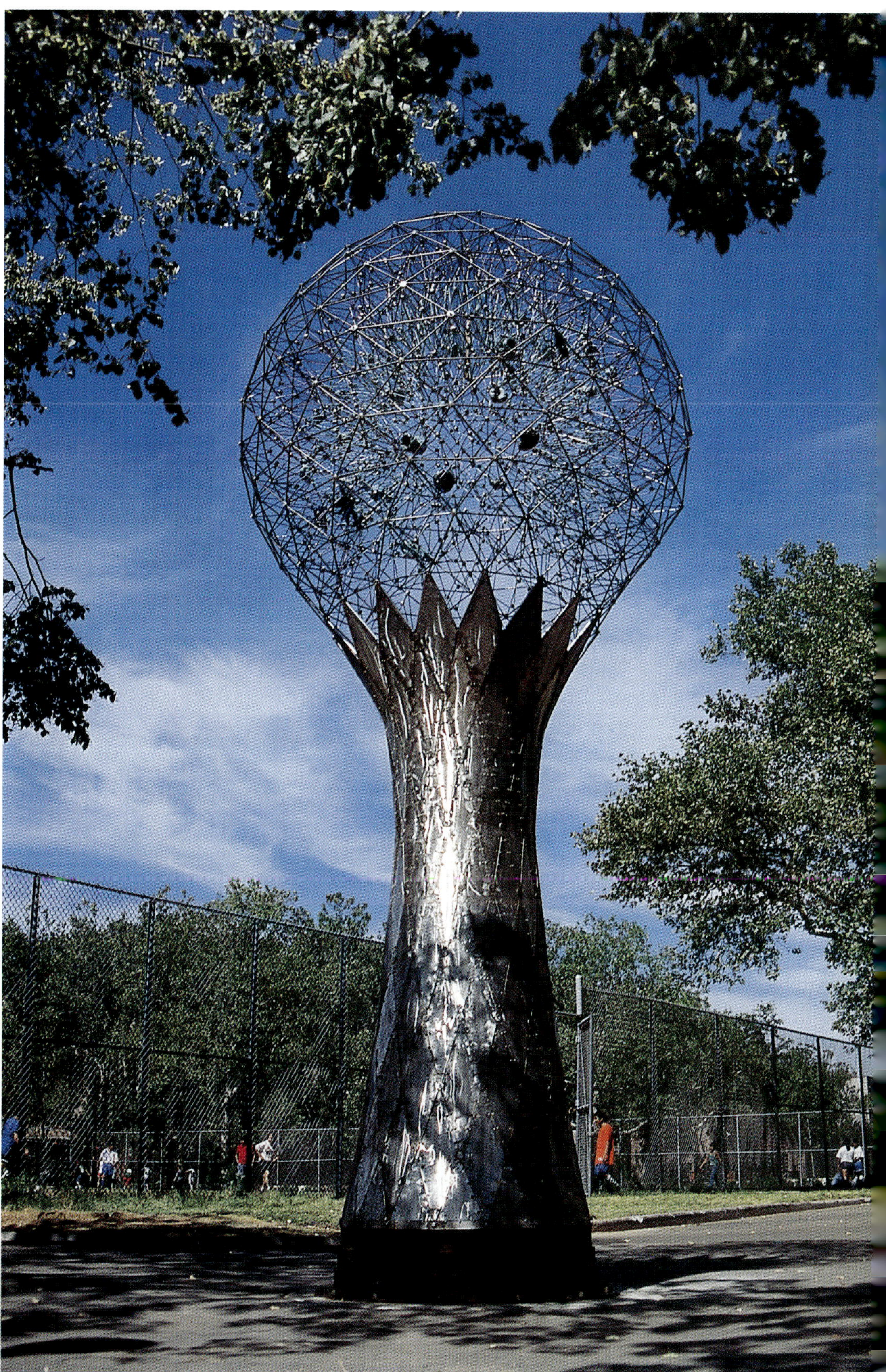

Camino des Animales
1992
Cement

Public School 5, 3703 Tenth Avenue

ARCHITECT
Gruzen Samton Steinglass
DESIGN AGENCY
School Construction Authority
SPONSOR AGENCY
Board of Education

Robin Holder's cement paving design for the entry plaza of P.S. 5 features large, colorful animal shapes, including bears, butterflies, fish, cats, and birds, carved into the paths leading to the school. The artwork's deep red paving, framed by a brilliant turquoise border, forms a geometric design that echoes the architecture of the school building.

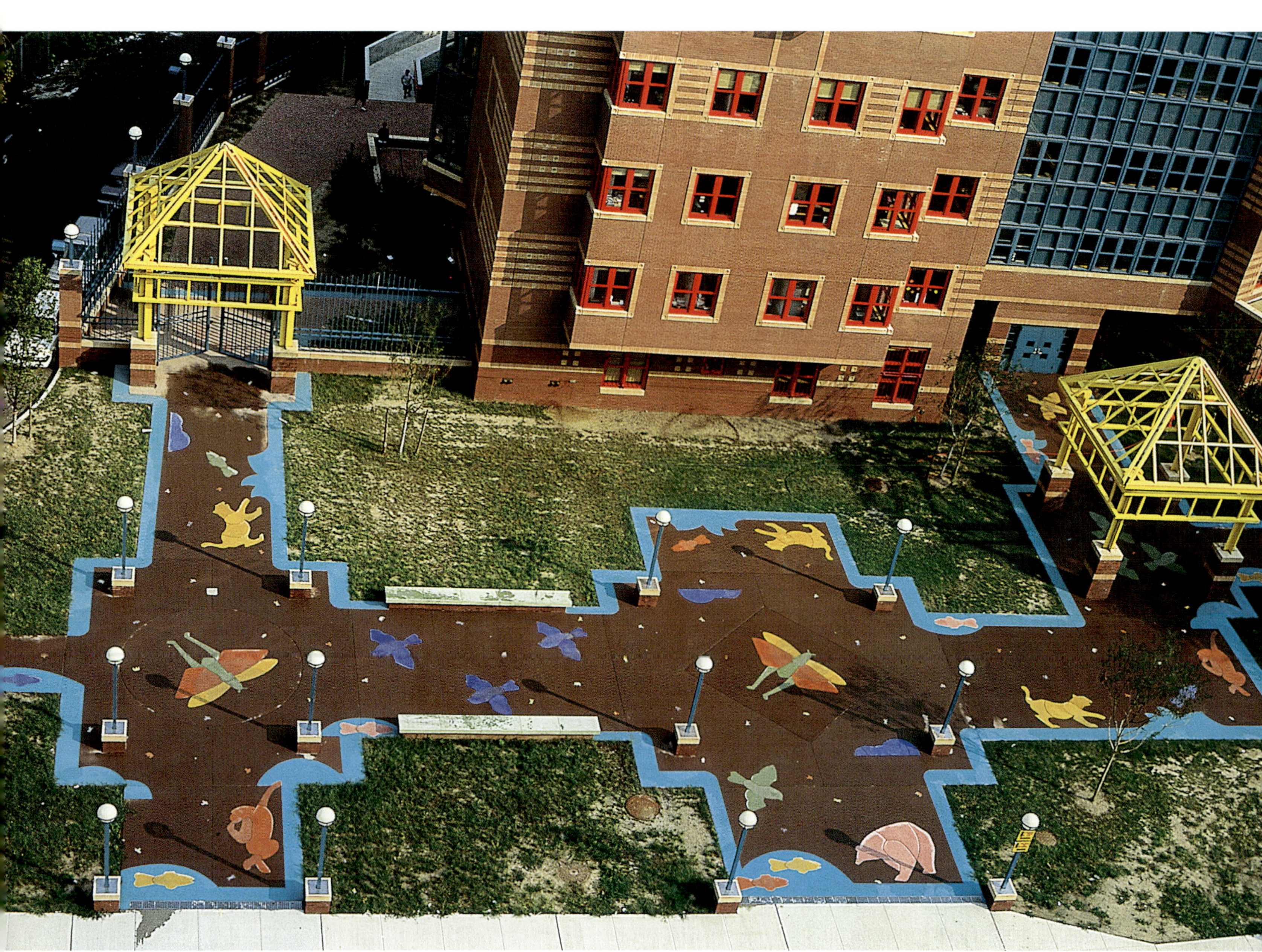

Robin Holder

Doug Hollis

Weather Pavilion
1994
Stainless steel, stone, weather instruments

Public/Intermediate School 217,
645 Main Street, Roosevelt Island

ARCHITECT
Michael Fieldman Architects
DESIGN AGENCY
School Construction Authority
SPONSOR AGENCY
Board of Education

Doug Hollis's work at P.S./I.S. 217 on Roosevelt Island features a stainless-steel, gazebo-like structure with four columns supporting weather-reading instruments, including an anemometer, a barometer, a thermometer, and a rain gauge. *Weather Pavilion* also features instruments such as a central wind organ, a compass, and a wind-zither, which respond sonically to the changing wind. Hollis placed a circular seating area of stone benches within the pavilion, to serve as a gathering place for students or as an outdoor classroom.

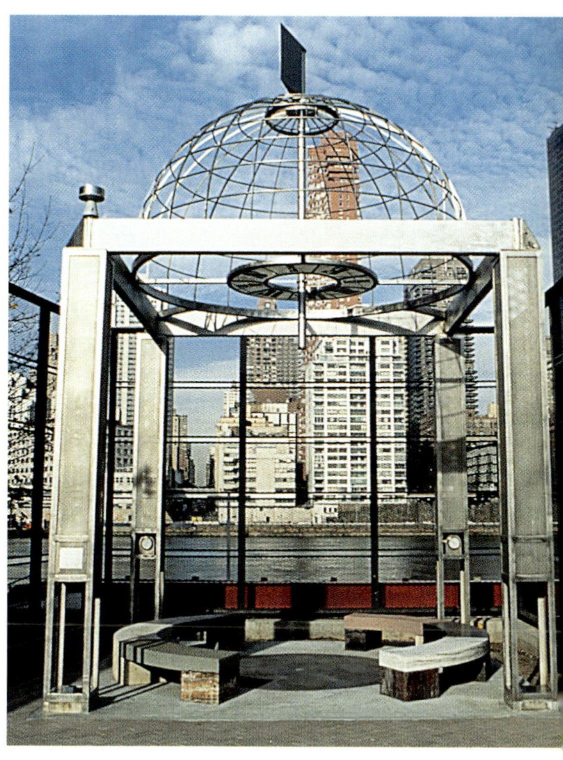

Valerie Jaudon

Reunion
1989
Brick, granite

One Police Plaza, Civic Center

ARCHITECT
Iffland, Kavanagh, Waterbury
Landscape Architect: James Balsley
DESIGN AGENCY
Department of General Services
SPONSOR AGENCY
Police Department

Art Commission Award for Excellence in Design 1987

Valerie Jaudon designed a new paving scheme, entitled *Reunion*, for the surface of the 3 acre (1.2 ha) brick walkway that connects Police Headquarters with the Municipal Building in Lower Manhattan. Drawing on the plan for the Municipal Building's original 1910 inner courtyard, Jaudon designed traditional brick patterns of herringbone and basket-weave fields in brick and granite. The red-brick sidewalk serves as a frame for inlaid-granite fractured diagonals and overlapping circles 34 feet (10.4 m) in diameter. The artist intended to make the pedestrian traffic passage more human in scale, while preserving the monumental character of the plaza.

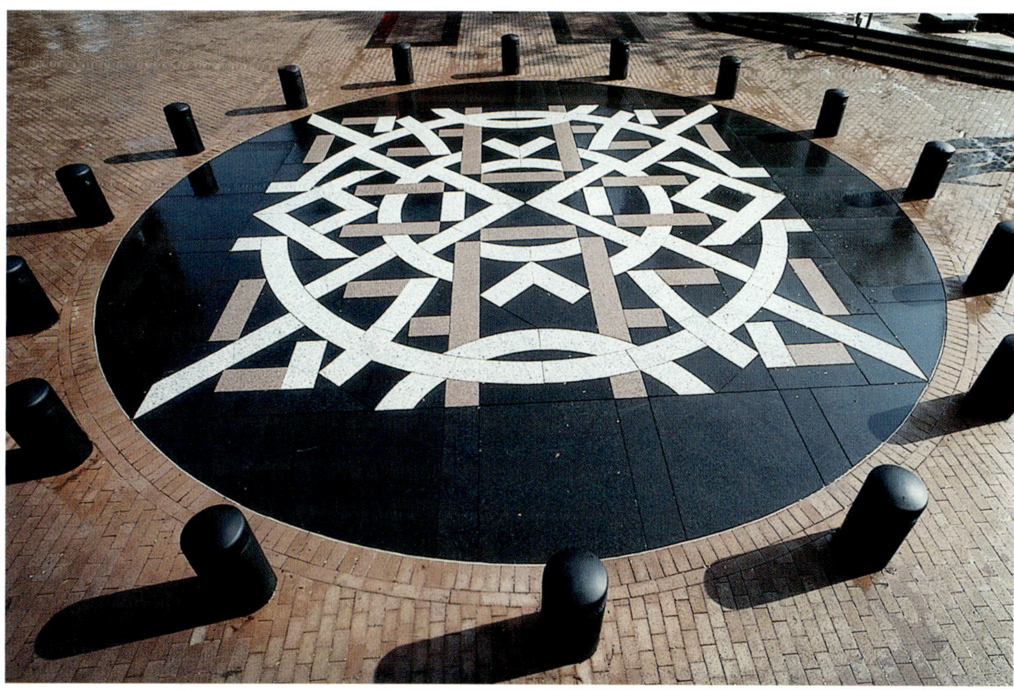

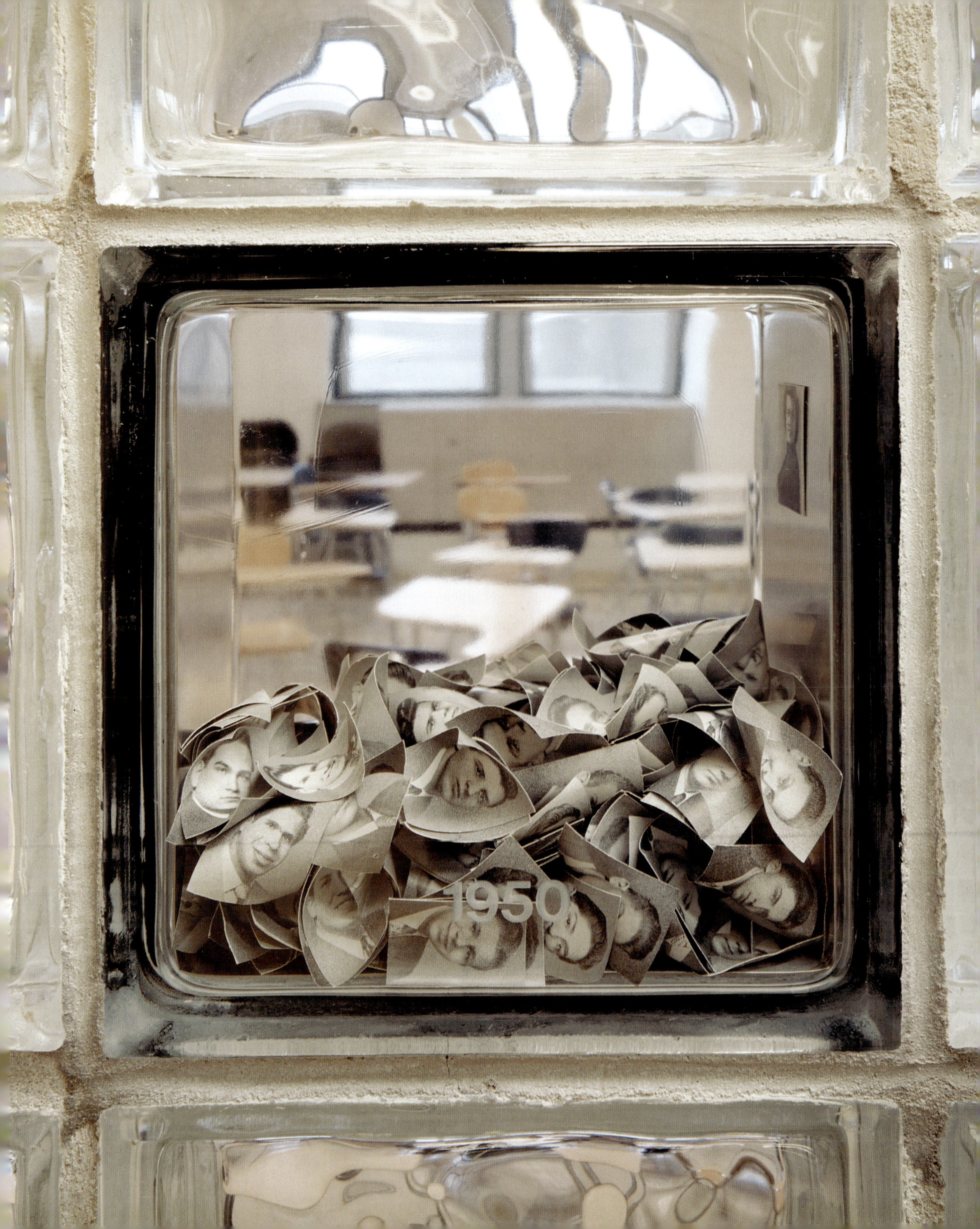
1950

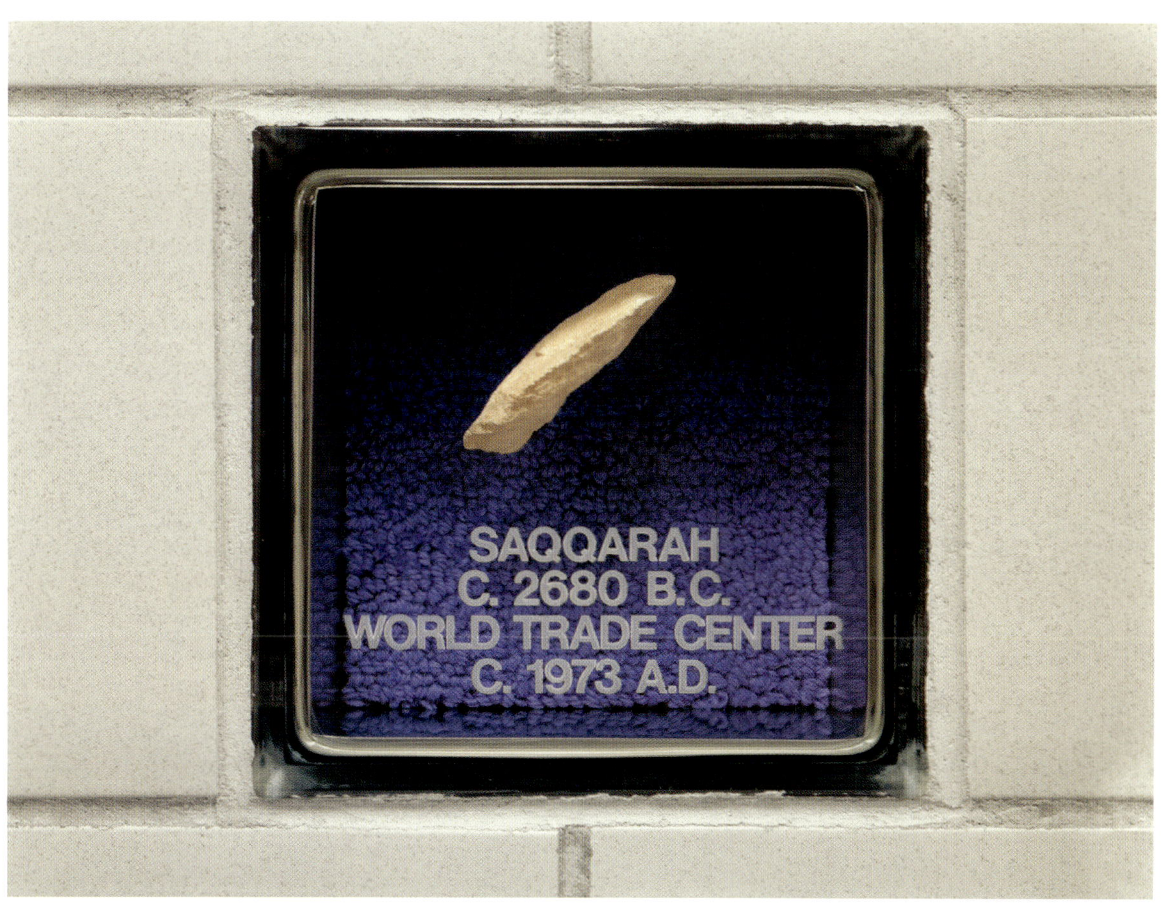
SAQQARAH
C. 2680 B.C.
WORLD TRADE CENTER
C. 1973 A.D.

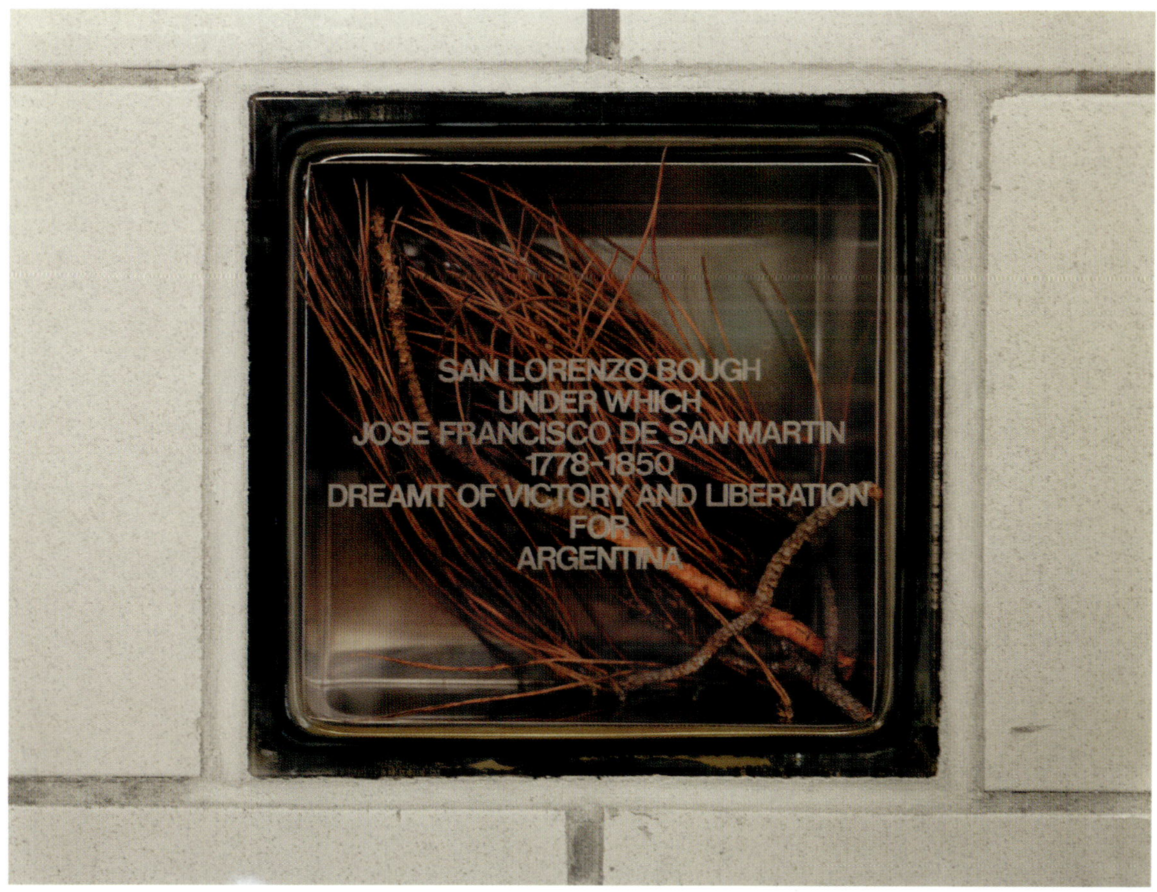
SAN LORENZO BOUGH
UNDER WHICH
JOSE FRANCISCO DE SAN MARTIN
1778-1850
DREAMT OF VICTORY AND LIBERATION
FOR
ARGENTINA

Kristin Jones and Andrew Ginzel

Mnemonics (previous pages)
1992
Glass blocks, cultural artifacts, ephemera

Stuyvesant High School,
345 Chambers Street

ARCHITECT
Cooper, Robertson and Partners
ASSOCIATE ARCHITECT
Gruzen Samton Steinglass

DESIGN AGENCY
School Construction Authority
SPONSOR AGENCY
Board of Education

Art Commission Award for Excellence in Design 1989

Mnemonics, by Kristin Jones and Andrew Ginzel, is an installation of more than four hundred hollow glass blocks containing artifacts from around the world. The blocks are embedded in the walls throughout the ten-story Stuyvesant High School in Lower Manhattan. The majority of blocks contain a diverse range of historic artifacts, including water from the Nile and the Ganges rivers, a flask of melted snow from Mount Fuji, and a fragment of the Great Wall of China. Eighty-eight blocks commemorate the school's history and, in addition, a further eighty-eight blocks are currently empty, awaiting artifacts to be chosen by future graduating classes. A chunk of rubble from the first bombing of the nearby World Trade Center was chosen by the 2003 graduating class.

Gabriel Koren

El-Hajj Malik Shabazz, Malcolm X
1997
Bronze

Audubon Ballroom, 3940 Broadway

ARCHITECT
Davis Brody Bond
DESIGN/SPONSOR AGENCY
Economic Development Corporation

Art Commission Award for Excellence in Design 1996

Gabriel Koren's *El-Hajj Malik Shabazz, Malcolm X* at the Audubon Ballroom in Harlem, the site of Malcolm X's assassination, is the first public sculpture of the famed civil rights leader in New York City. Koren positioned this life-size bronze sculpture of Malcolm X in such a way that he appears to speak to the people who visit the ballroom. As the artist has explained: "I felt the responsibility to bring him back to the Audubon Ballroom, as if he never left."

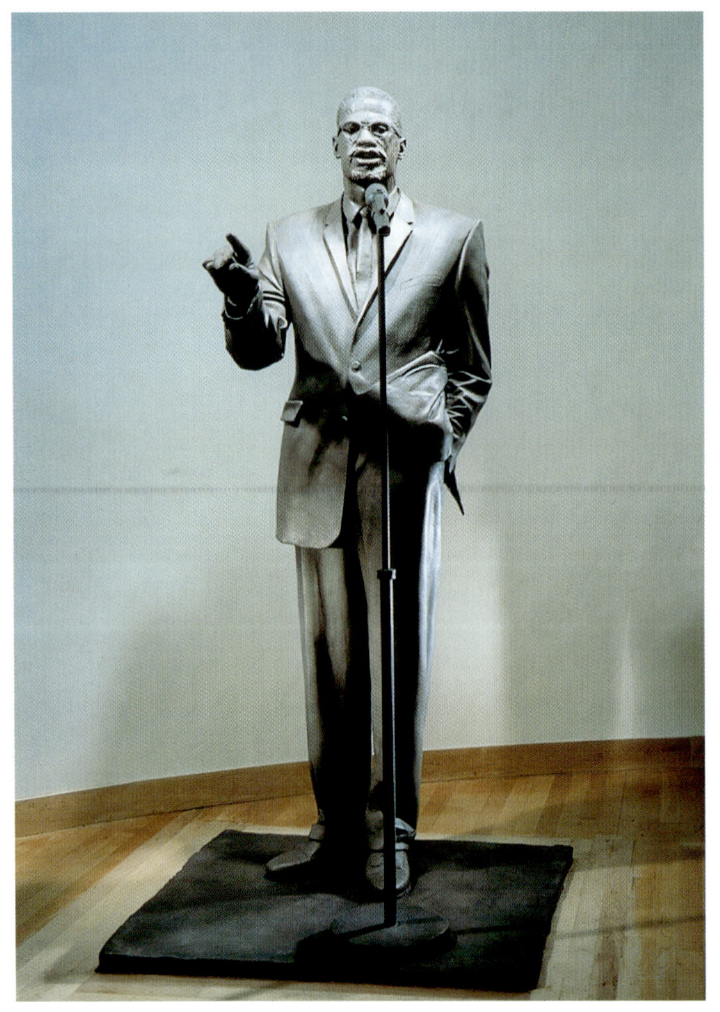

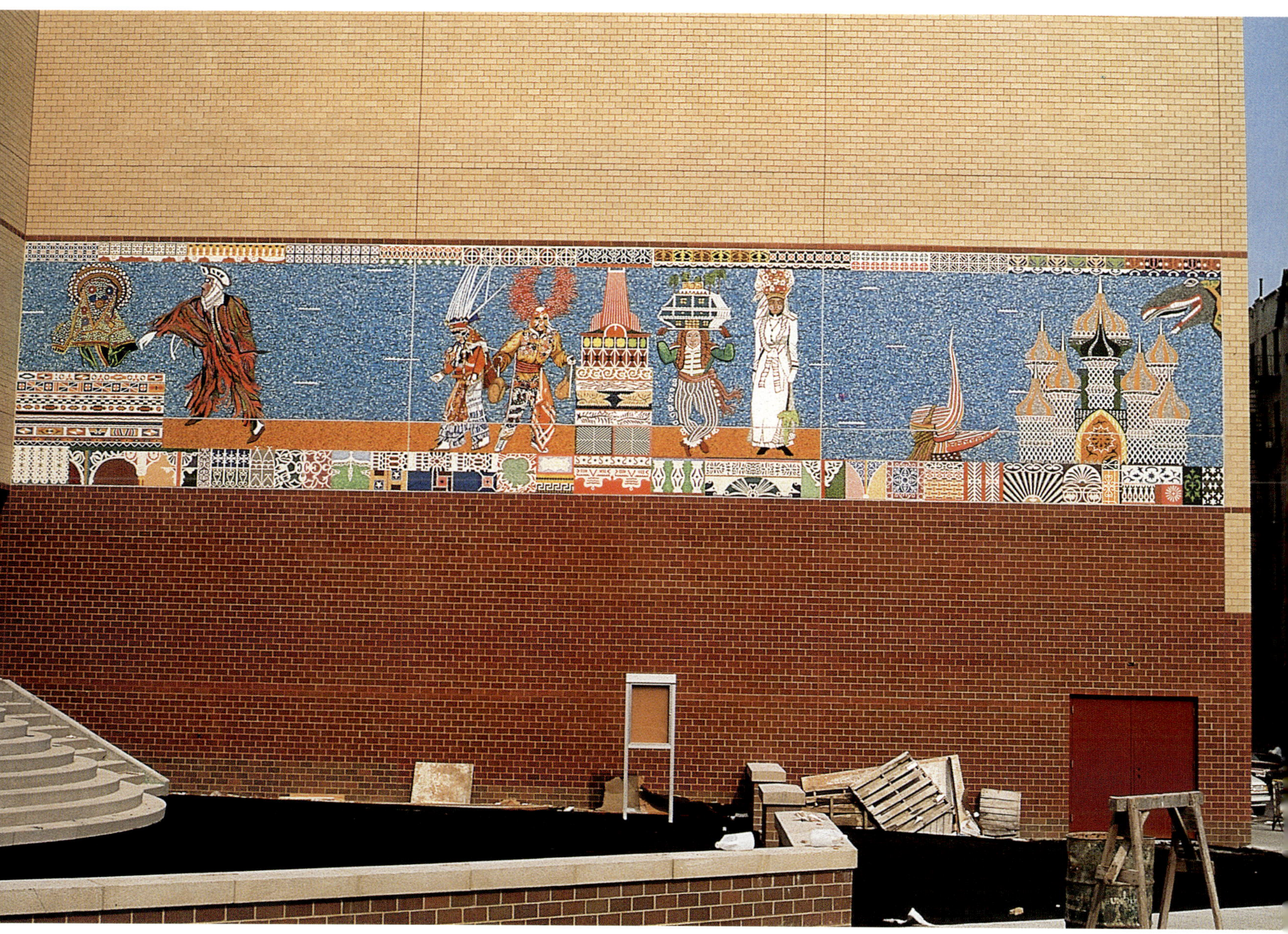

Untitled
1991
Glass mosaics

Intermediate School 218,
4600 Broadway

ARCHITECT
Richard Dattner and Partners Architects
DESIGN AGENCY
School Construction Authority
SPONSOR AGENCY
Board of Education

Joyce Kozloff chose to reflect the student body's predominantly Caribbean origins at I.S. 218 in Upper Manhattan by including architectural and festival imagery from that culture in her glass-mosaic frieze. The large central area of the mural is saturated with turquoise, and the prominent costumed figures are drawn from the traditional Jonkonnu street bands. In the center of the piece, Kozloff depicts elements of architecture commonly found in Haiti, including lattices, windows, gates, and shutters with peaked roofs.

Joyce Kozloff

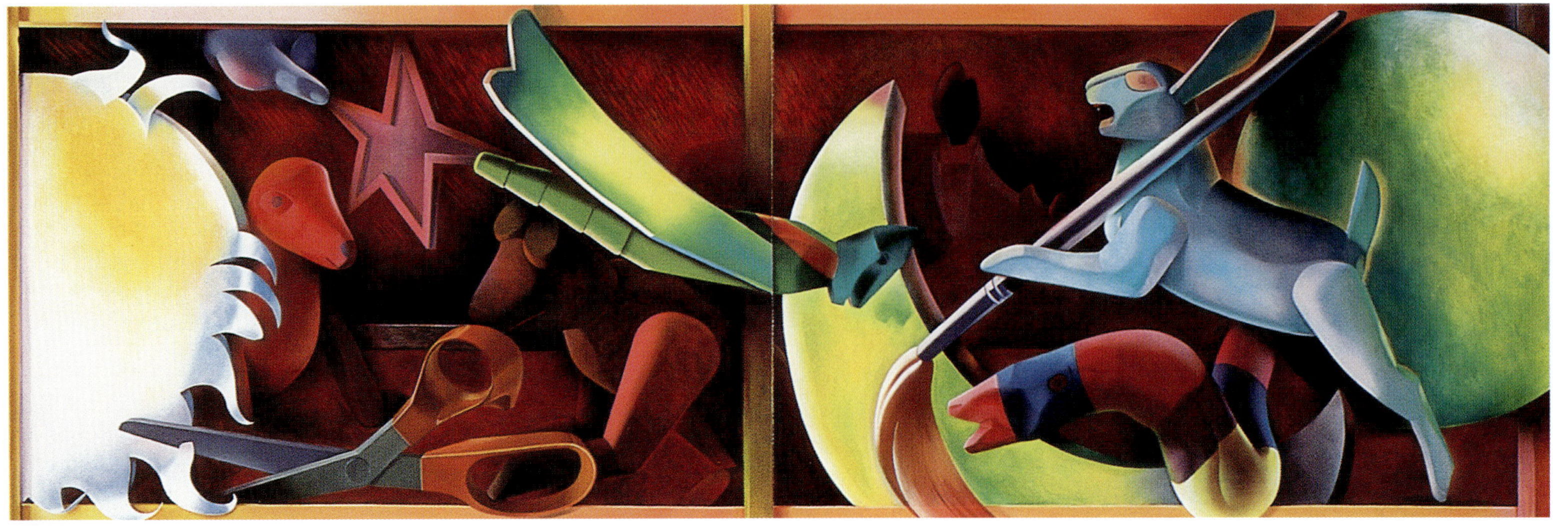

Inside the Ark
1997
Oil on canvas, Hydrocal

Public School 311, 4862 Broadway

ARCHITECT
Gruzen Samton Architects
DESIGN AGENCY
School Construction Authority
SPONSOR AGENCY
Board of Education

Based on the story of Noah's Ark, Ora Lerman's *Inside the Ark* is a narrative mural of ten oil-on-canvas panels that run continuously along the sides of the peaked cathedral ceiling in the library of P.S. 311 (formerly P.S. 176). The cavernous space helps to emphasize the mural's illusion that the viewers below are inside the ark as it returns to the port of New York after the Flood. In Lerman's narrative mural cycle, her brush itself becomes a character in the story, and a symbol of transformation. The animals depicted use the brush to re-create the elements in the world that have been destroyed by the Flood. Another brush, seen laid down at the edge of the frame, suggests the end of work, and the return of calm and order.

Ora Lerman

Donald Lipski

The LaGuardia Suite
1998
Mixed media

LaGuardia High School,
100 Amsterdam Avenue

SPONSOR AGENCY
Board of Education

For his project at LaGuardia High School, a school for the performing arts, Donald Lipski transformed real objects associated with the performing arts, such as musical instruments, music stands, microphones, tutus, and dance shoes, into works of visual art. The sculptures hang on the walls flanking the entrance to the school's theater.

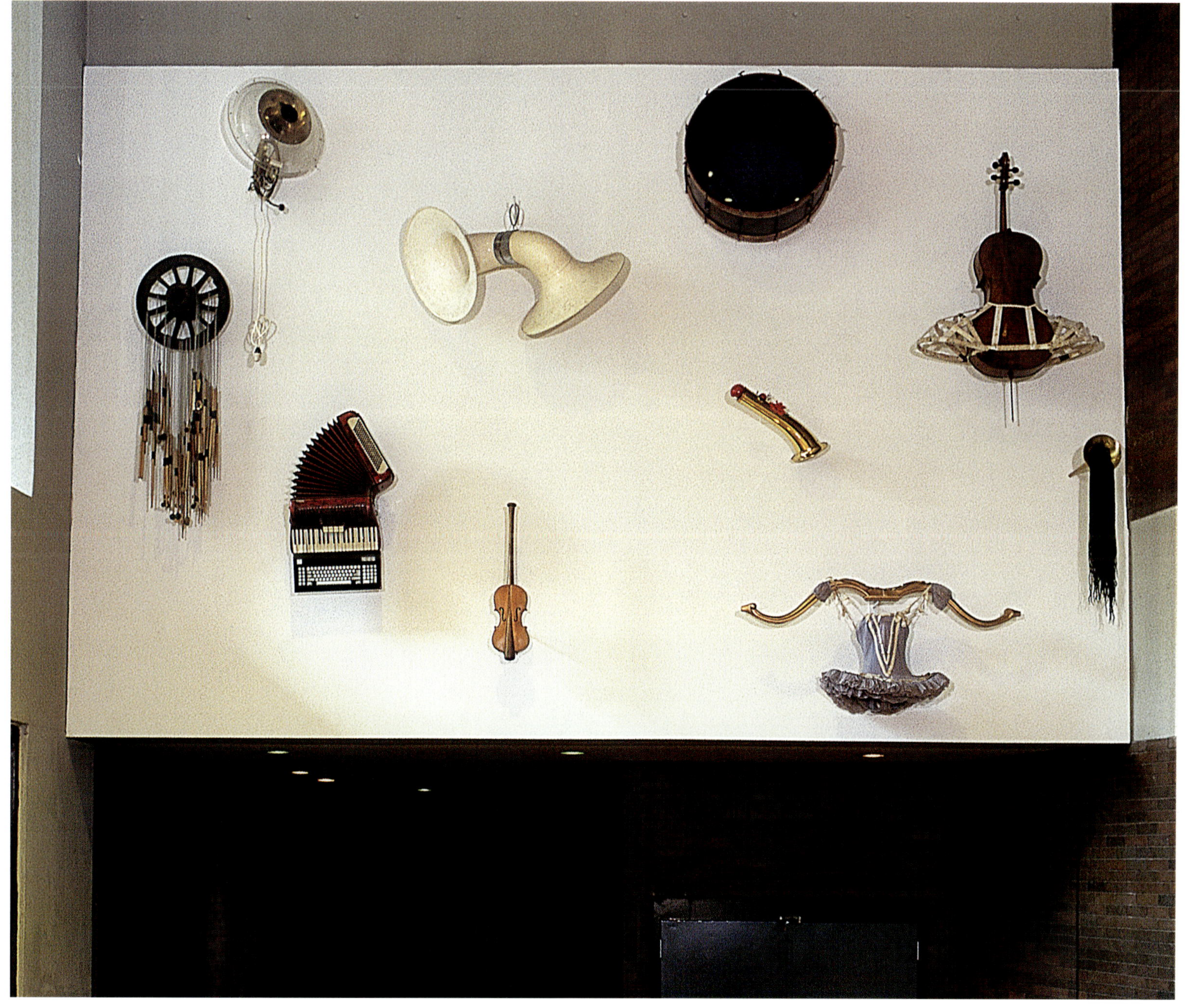

Bulletin Board
2000
Mosaics

New Children's Center, 492 First Avenue

ARCHITECT
Richard Dattner and Partners Architects
DESIGN AGENCY
Department of Design and Construction
SPONSOR AGENCY
Administration for Children's Services

Based on a child's bulletin board, Mike Mandel and Larry Sultan's mosaic work for the New Children's Center features both drawings made by children and photographs of children. The artists designed *Bulletin Board* to include images that would be familiar and comforting to children entering the center, a foster-care placement facility. The work features a drawing of a colorful house and a photo-booth strip of pictures showing children having fun and making funny faces. The mural is fabricated with half-inch (1.3 cm) square porcelain tiles, allowing its images to maintain a photographic quality.

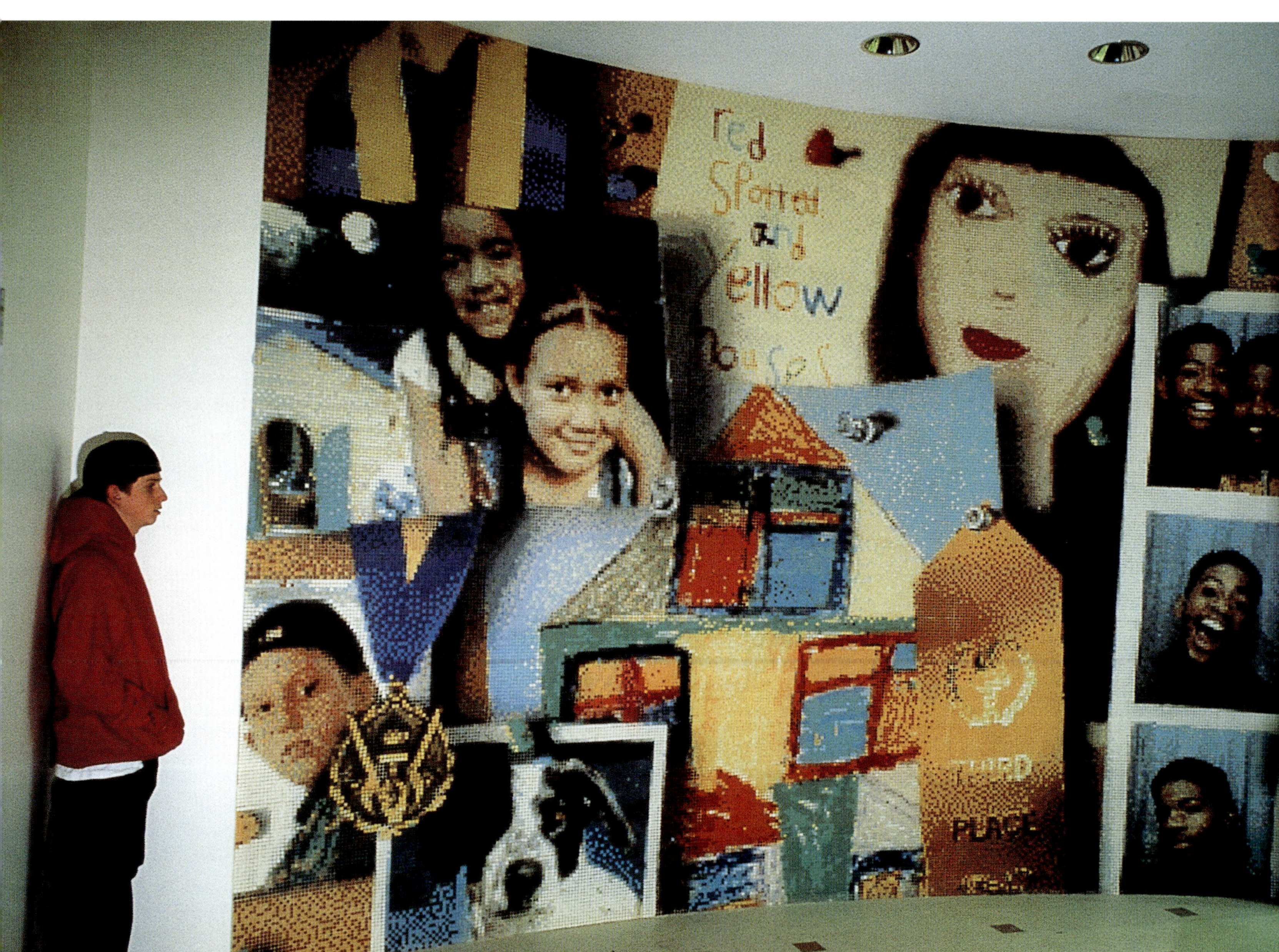

Mike Mandel and Larry Sultan

Antonio Martorell

Children's ABC
1995
Woodcut mural on fabric

Public School 48, 4360 Broadway

ARCHITECT/DESIGN AGENCY
School Construction Authority
SPONSOR AGENCY
Board of Education

For his project at P.S. 48, Antonio Martorell photographed children in gym classes posing as letters of the alphabet. From the photographs, the artist created twenty-six colored woodcuts that he then printed on a variety of textured and colored fabrics. The fabric letters are framed and hung in the school auditorium alongside the initial carved wood blocks. On the two flanking walls, the blocks and letters spell out a quotation from Eugenio Maria de Hostos, an early twentieth-century educator of Dominican and Puerto Rican heritage. Written in both English and Spanish, the quotation reads: "Ignorance is the worst enemy of civilization."

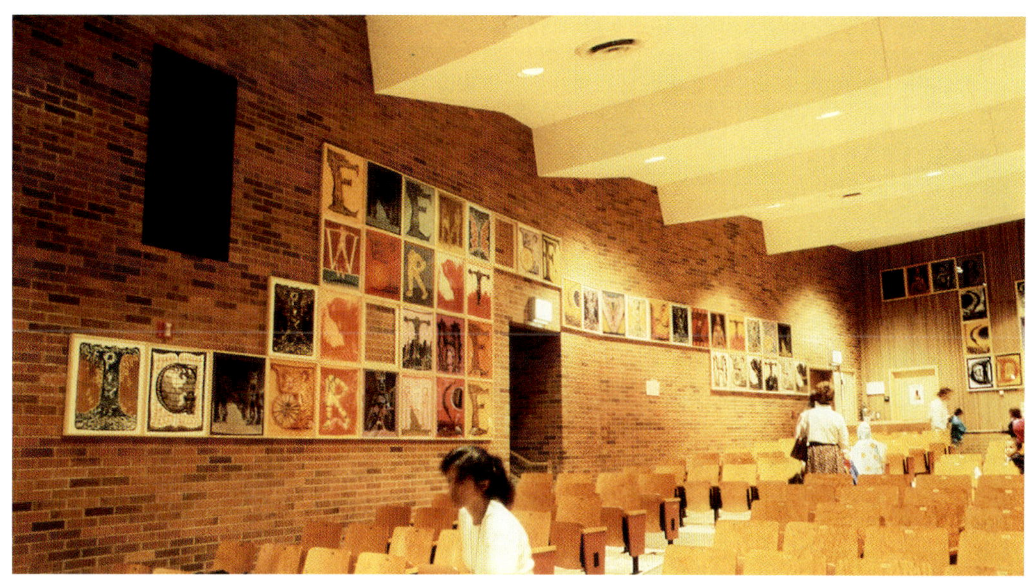

Milo Mottola

Totally Kid Carousel (pages 24–25)
1998
Painted fiberglass on a wood, metal, and foam armature

Riverbank State Park/North River Sewage Treatment Plant, 679 Riverside Drive

ARCHITECT
Richard Dattner and Partners Architects
SPONSOR AGENCY
Department of Environmental Protection
OPERATING AGENCY
New York State Parks

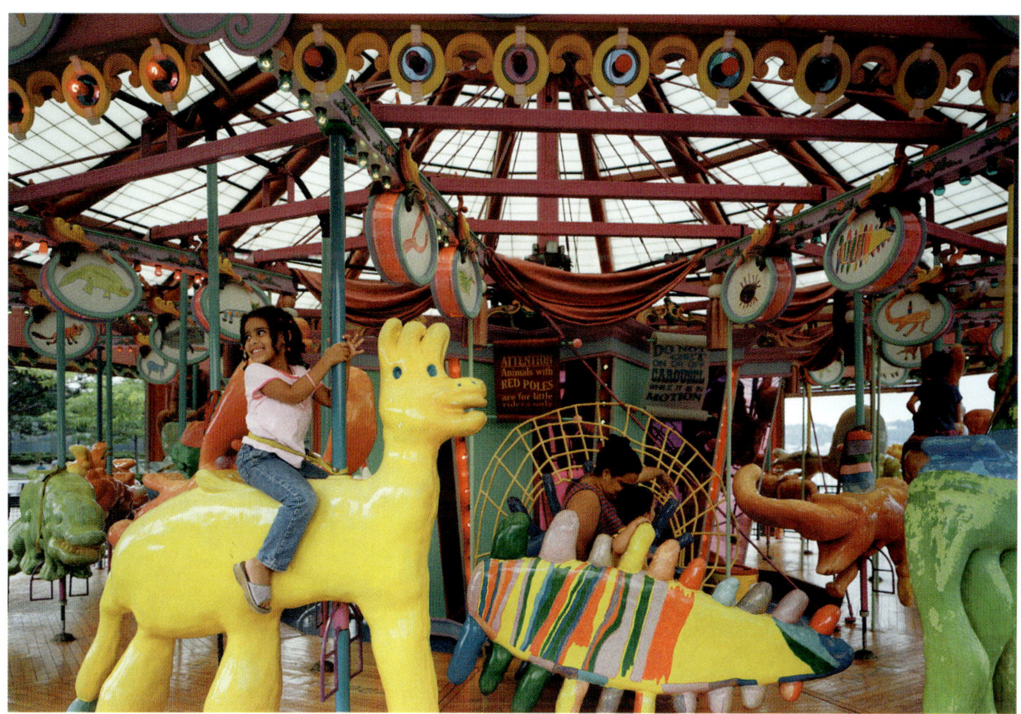

Milo Mottola created a working carousel near the Hudson River waterfront at Riverbank State Park. *Totally Kid Carousel* features thirty-six colorful fiberglass sculptures that the artist designed, based on school children's drawings of their favorite animals. These large and whimsical animal forms serve as the seats on the carousel. Above each seat hangs the child's original drawing. The artist also commissioned local musicians to compose the accompanying music.

Celia Muñoz

Mind Games
1995
Etched glass

Public School 8, 465 West 167th Street

ARCHITECT
Gruzen Samton Steinglass
DESIGN AGENCY
School Construction Authority
SPONSOR AGENCY
Board of Education

Celia Muñoz's work for P.S. 8, entitled *Mind Games*, features glass blocks etched with different symbols, including representations of the five senses, architecture, and urban design. The project is installed in several areas of the school: murals on the first- and second-floor lobby walls, a mural in the administrative office window, single blocks in the first-floor reading area, and single blocks in individual classroom windows. The largest of the murals, located in the school's first-floor lobby, is shaped like an open book.

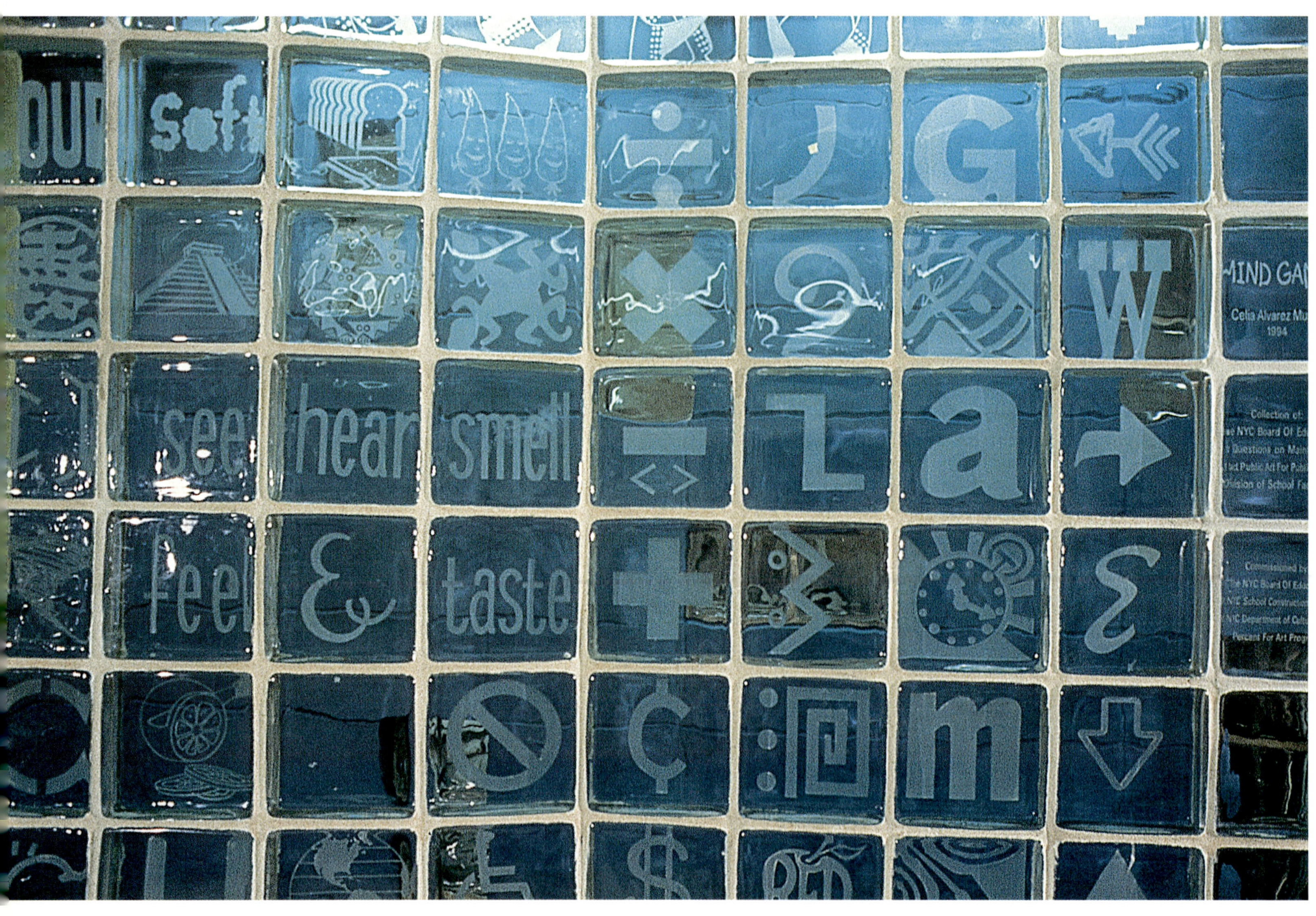

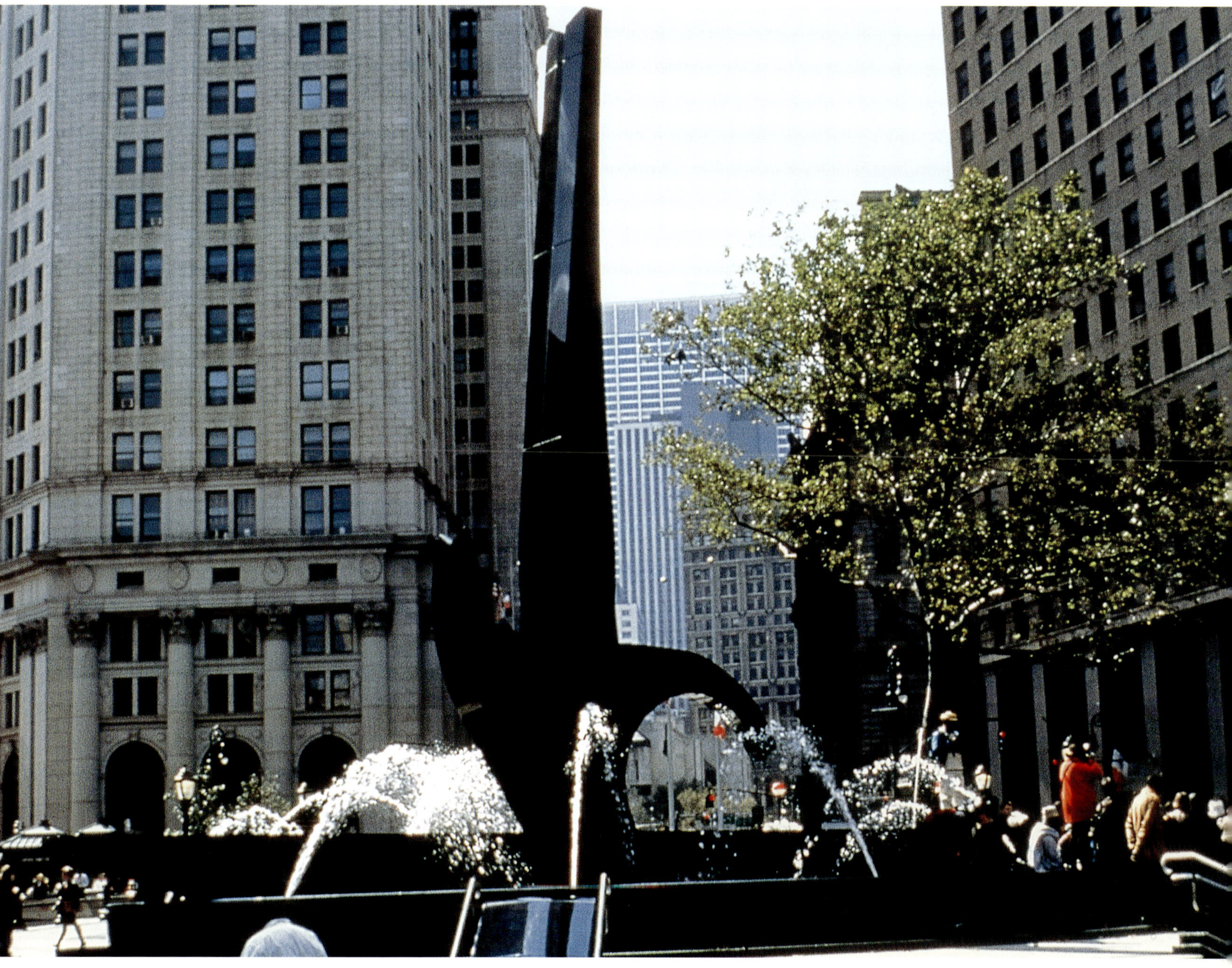

Triumph of the Human Spirit
2000
Granite

Foley Square

ARCHITECT
Coe Lee Robinson Roesch
DESIGN/SPONSOR AGENCY
Department of Parks and Recreation

Lorenzo Pace built *Triumph of the Human Spirit* on a rediscovered African burial ground in Manhattan's Foley Square near City Hall. Over 60 feet (18.3 m) tall, and weighing more than 300 tons (305 tonnes), the massive black granite sculpture depicts an abstract female antelope form mounted on a boat-shaped base. The artist has stated that the piece was inspired by *chi waras*, the traditional carved antelope effigy figures from West Africa that symbolize the way in which generations of men and women have work effectively together to ensure successful harvests. The sculpture serves as a monument to honor African men and women brought to America as slaves.

Lorenzo Pace

Growth
1985
Painted steel

East Harlem Artpark, Sylvan Place and East 120th Street

ARCHITECT
Housing Preservation and Development Open Spaces Program
DESIGN/SPONSOR AGENCY
Department of Parks and Recreation

Jorge Luis Rodriguez's abstract sculpture for the East Harlem Artpark was the first project completed by the Percent for Art program. *Growth* rises directly from the cobblestones of a rejuvenated park that sits between the landmark Harlem Courthouse and a housing project for senior citizens. The sculpture's flowing shapes, reminiscent of plants, birds, and insects, reinforce the theme of renewal that is central to the redevelopment of this once neglected park.

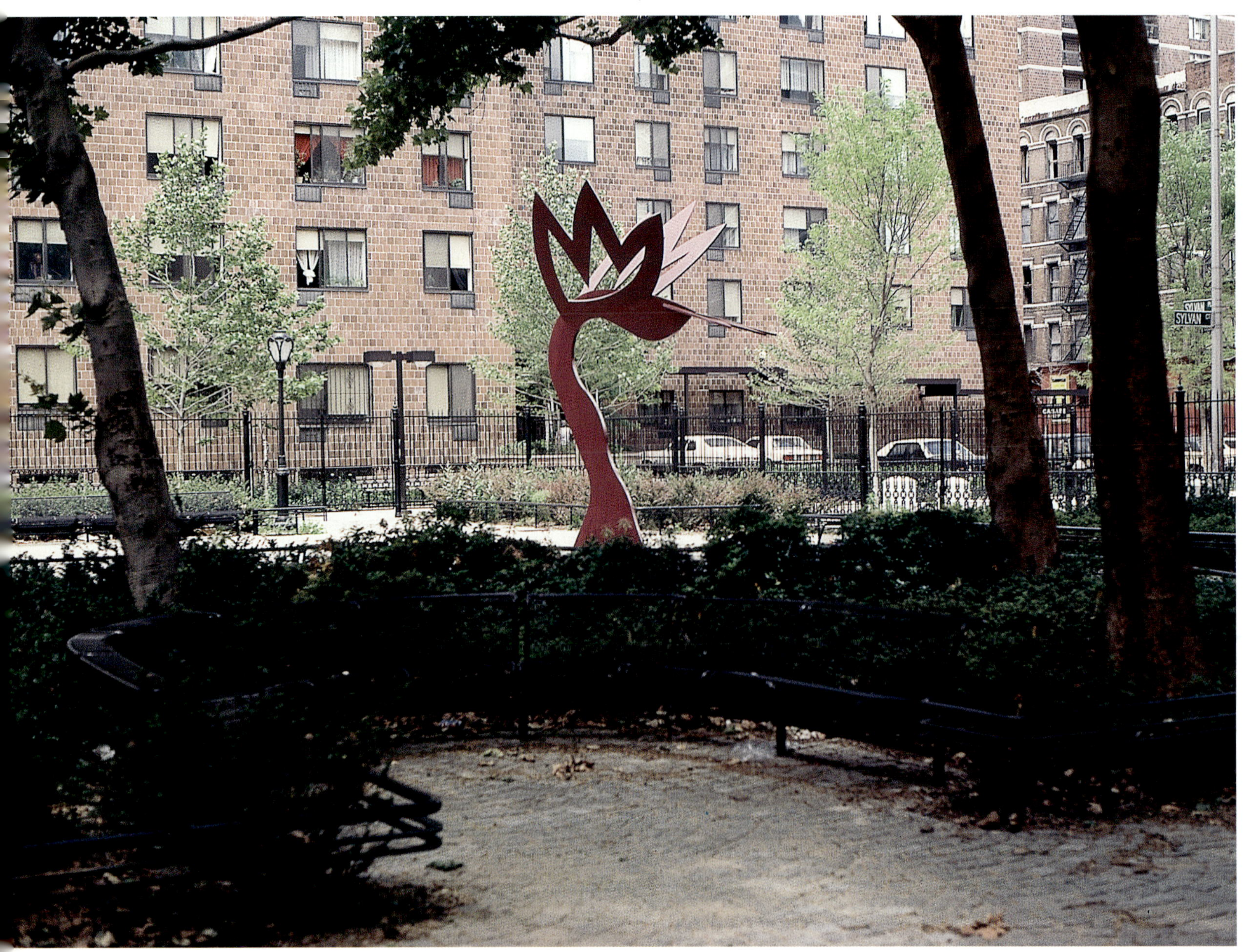

Jorge Luis Rodriguez

Charles Searles

Cultural Harmony
1990
Mixed media

Oberia D. Dempsey Multi-Service Center of Central Harlem, 127 West 127th Street

DESIGN AGENCY
Department of General Services
SPONSOR AGENCY
Human Resources Administration

Cultural Harmony consists of four relief sculptures—abstract amalgams of straight lines, bows, and voids—mounted on the walls of the center's auditorium. According to Charles Searles, these richly colored sculptures are inspired by the artwork of many cultures, including African, Native American, Asian, and Caribbean. Searles has said of his work: "Knowing that the artwork would touch many people, I wanted to represent many cultural backgrounds as well as project a positive feeling of living energy that would hopefully leave the audience with a good feeling."

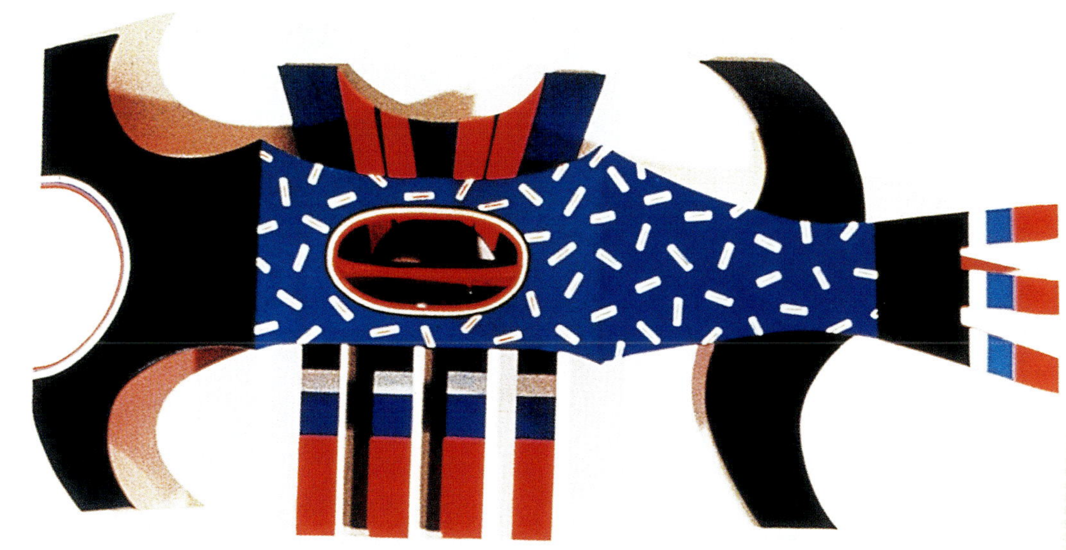

Nobi Shioya

Las Meninas
1998
Bronze

Public School 166, 132 West 89th Street

ARCHITECT
Fox & Fowle
DESIGN AGENCY
School Construction Authority
SPONSOR AGENCY
Board of Education

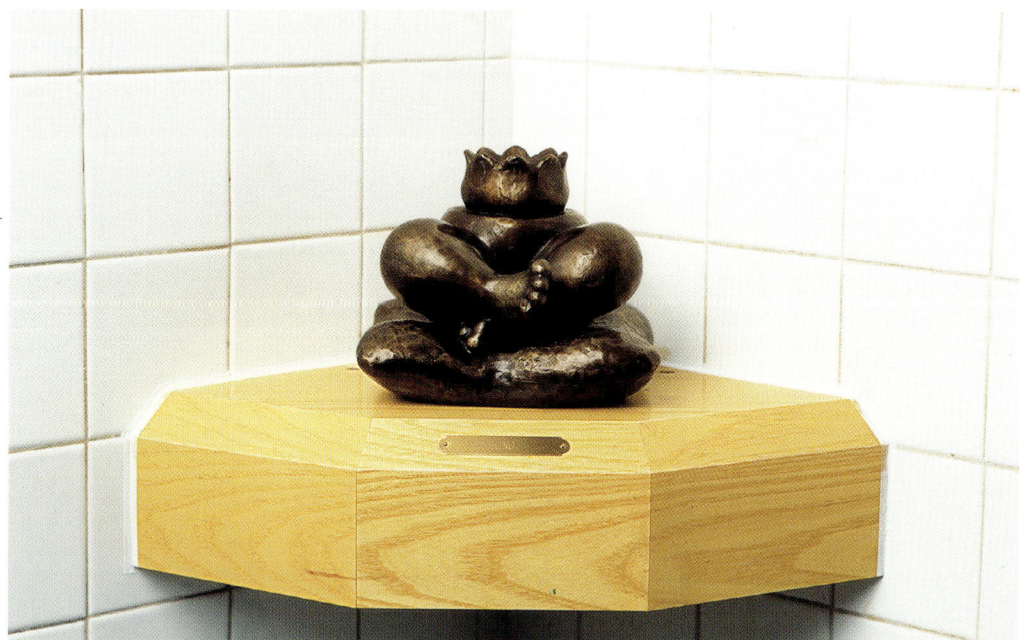

Nobi Shioya's nineteen small bronze sculptures of different animals and shapes are situated throughout the hallways of P.S. 166. The title of the piece, *Las Meninas*, was inspired by the Diego Velázquez painting (1656) of the same name. Shioya intended students to touch and interact with the sculptures, which range in size from a 2 inch (5 cm) snail to a 36 inch (91 cm) high dog. Also featured are a bison, a gorilla, a salamander, a fish, an elephant, and a bird, as well as various geometric shapes.

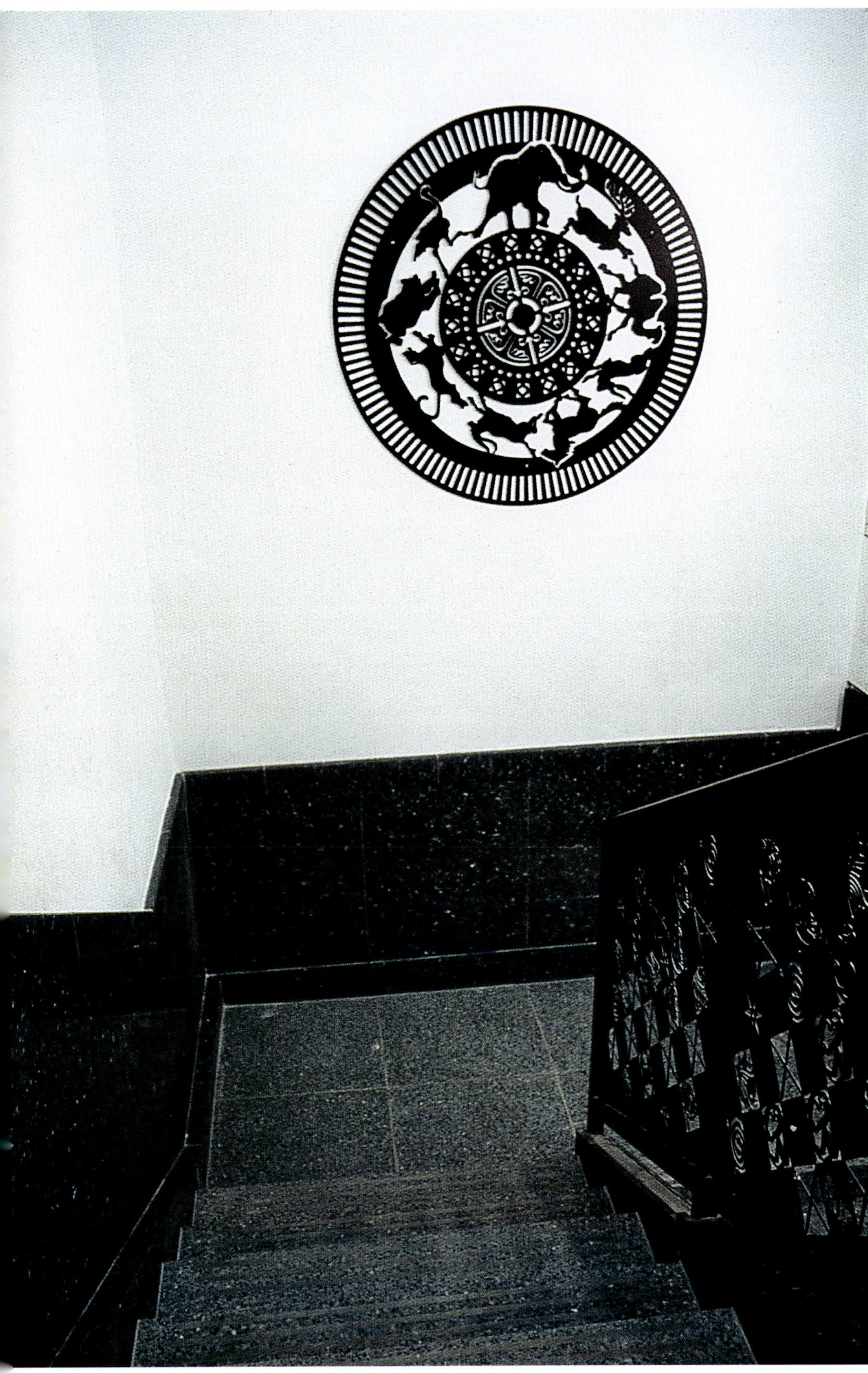

Hopscotch
1996
Steel
Running Wild
1996
Steel

Public School 130, 143 Baxter Street

ARCHITECT
William Nicholas Bodouva + Associates
DESIGN AGENCY
School Construction Authority
SPONSOR AGENCY
Board of Education

Arlene Slavin's *Hopscotch,* located at P.S. 130 in the heart of Chinatown, consists of nine laser-cut steel stair rails on the school's main staircase. The work features a series of motifs that figure prominently in Chinese culture, such as rabbits, dogs, and monkeys, along with designs of stars, flowers, and sea shells. The animals seen in *Hopscotch* are also featured in *Running Wild* (left), a plate disk sculpture attached to the wall of the stairwell.

Arlene Slavin

Vincent D. Smith

Jonkonnu Festival Wid the Frizzly Rooster Band
1991
Oil on canvas, collage elements

Oberia D. Dempsey Multi-Service Center of Central Harlem, 127 West 127th Street

DESIGN AGENCY
Department of General Services
SPONSOR AGENCY
Human Resources Administration

Vincent Smith's murals for the Oberia D. Dempsey Multi-Service Center of Central Harlem depict scenes from a major West Indian celebration, the Jonkonnu festival, a Christmas carnival involving bands and masquerades. Within the series, the largest mural shows a parade or block party with costumed people on stage, dancing to music. The smaller paintings display crowds of people lining the sidewalk, with buildings and stores in the background.

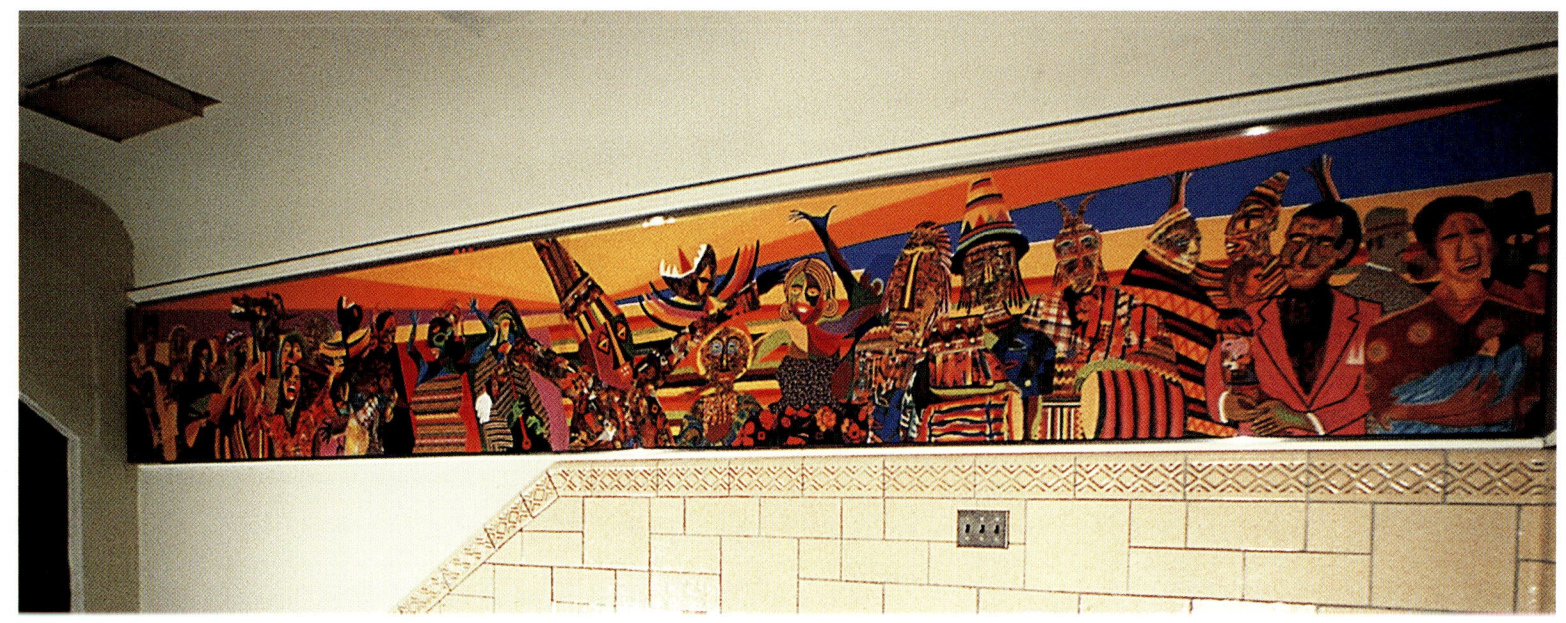

Kit-Yin Snyder

Judgment (following pages)
1992
Stainless steel, wire mesh, granite, trees, pavers

Bernard B. Kerik Complex, 125 White Street

ARCHITECT
Urbahn Associates

DESIGN AGENCY
Department of General Services
SPONSOR AGENCY
Department of Corrections

Art Commission Award for Excellence in Design 1988

Located outside the Bernard B. Kerik Complex, Kit-Yin Snyder's work features two back-to-back, stainless-steel wire-mesh thrones representing the Old Testament Judge Solomon's throne, and seven 16 foot (4.8 m) tall wire-mesh columns representing the Seven Pillars of the Temple of Wisdom of Solomon. The thrones are situated on the bridge over the plaza of the Detention Center and the columns are placed on White Street. In the pavement of the plaza, the artist also embedded colored pavers depicting two Chinese characters signifying righteousness, and apple trees, the fruit of which signifies knowledge.

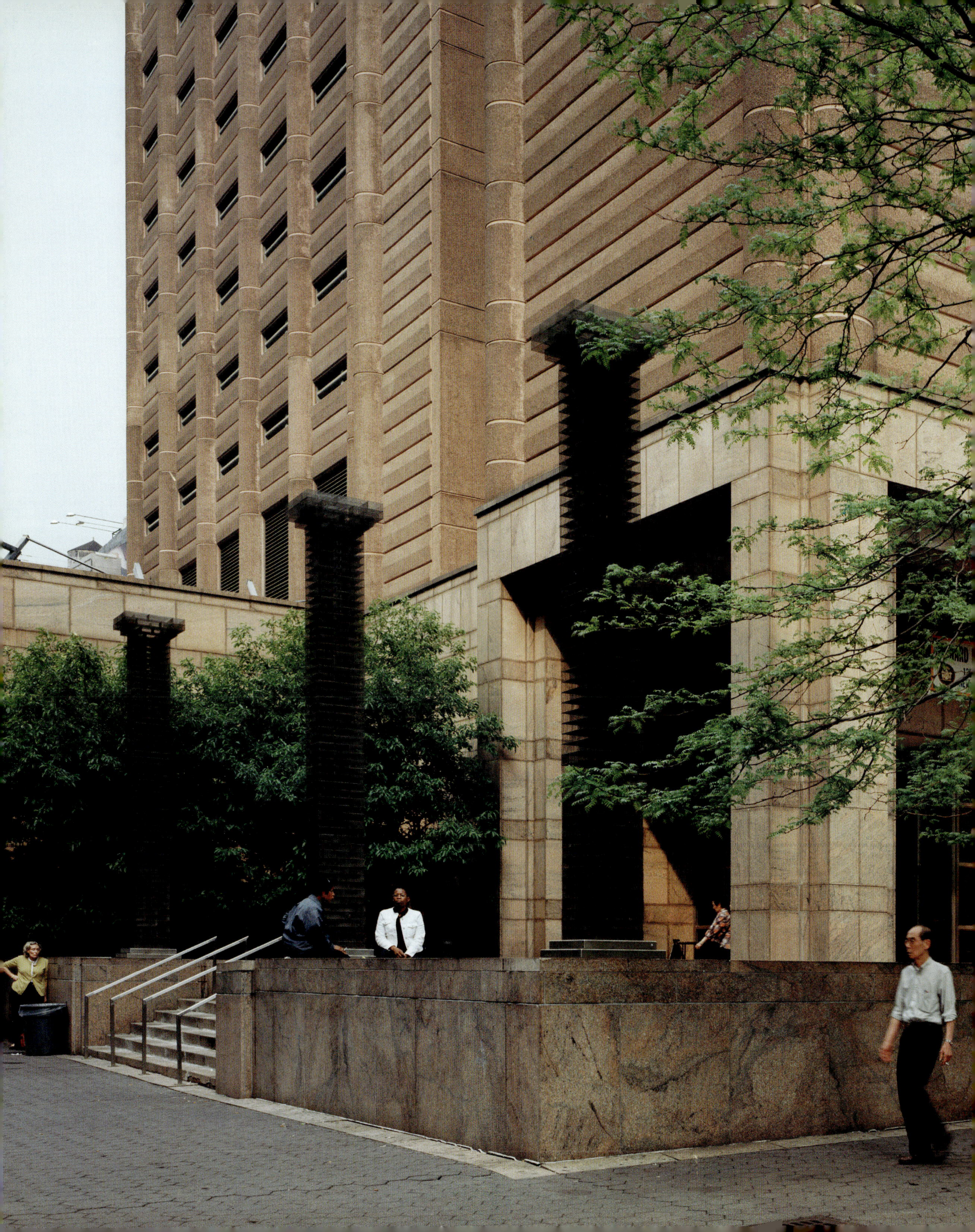

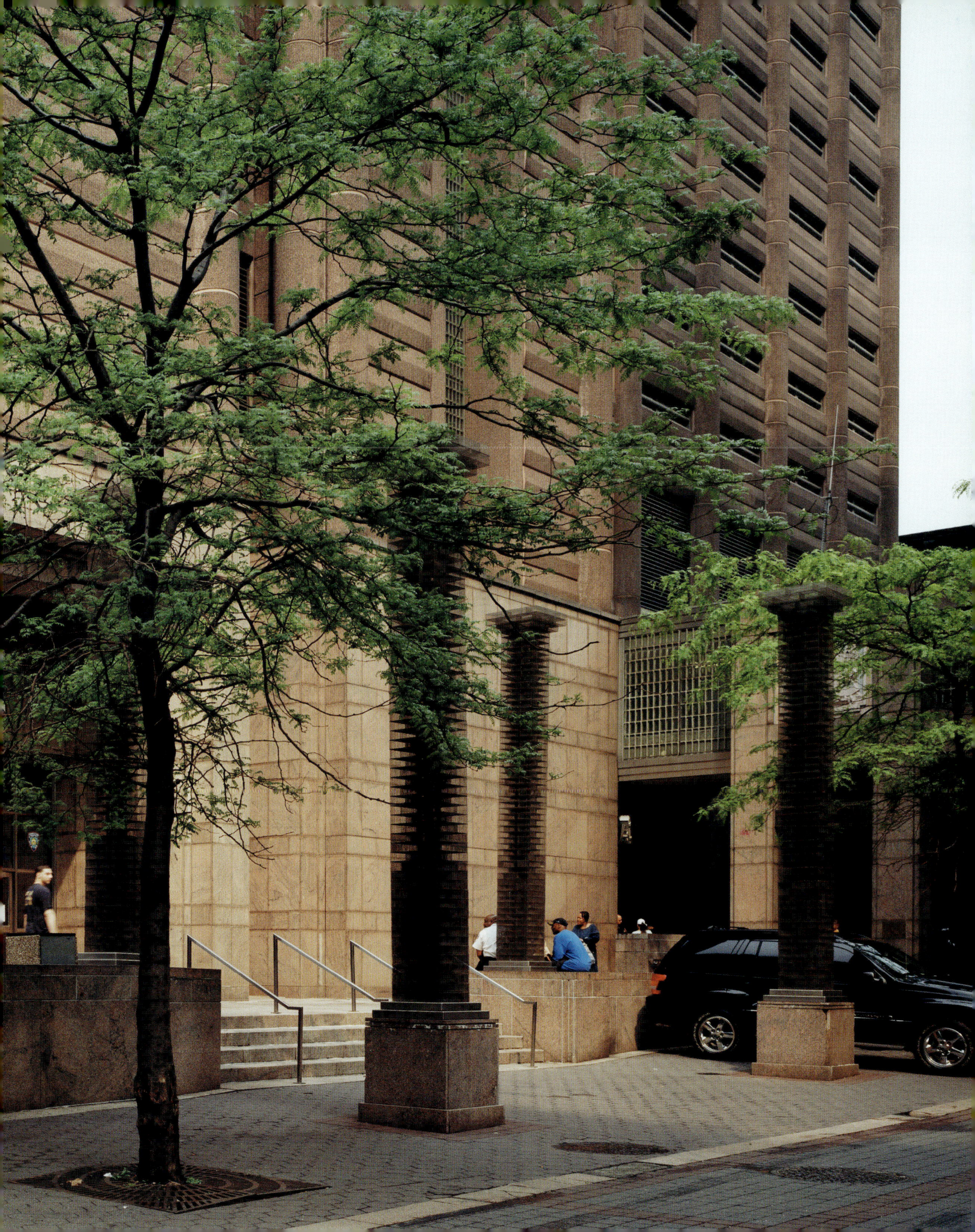

Pat Steir

Looking Lesson
1992
Porcelain enamel

Intermediate School 218,
4600 Broadway

ARCHITECT
Richard Dattner and Partners Architects
DESIGN AGENCY
School Construction Authority
SPONSOR AGENCY
Board of Education

For *Looking Lesson,* Pat Steir created a frieze of 137 porcelain enamel tiles for the cafeteria walls in I.S. 218. Each diamond-shaped tile features an individual shape or line, which represents one of the building-blocks of visual art. When viewed as a collection, the series is a lesson in the fundamentals of art.

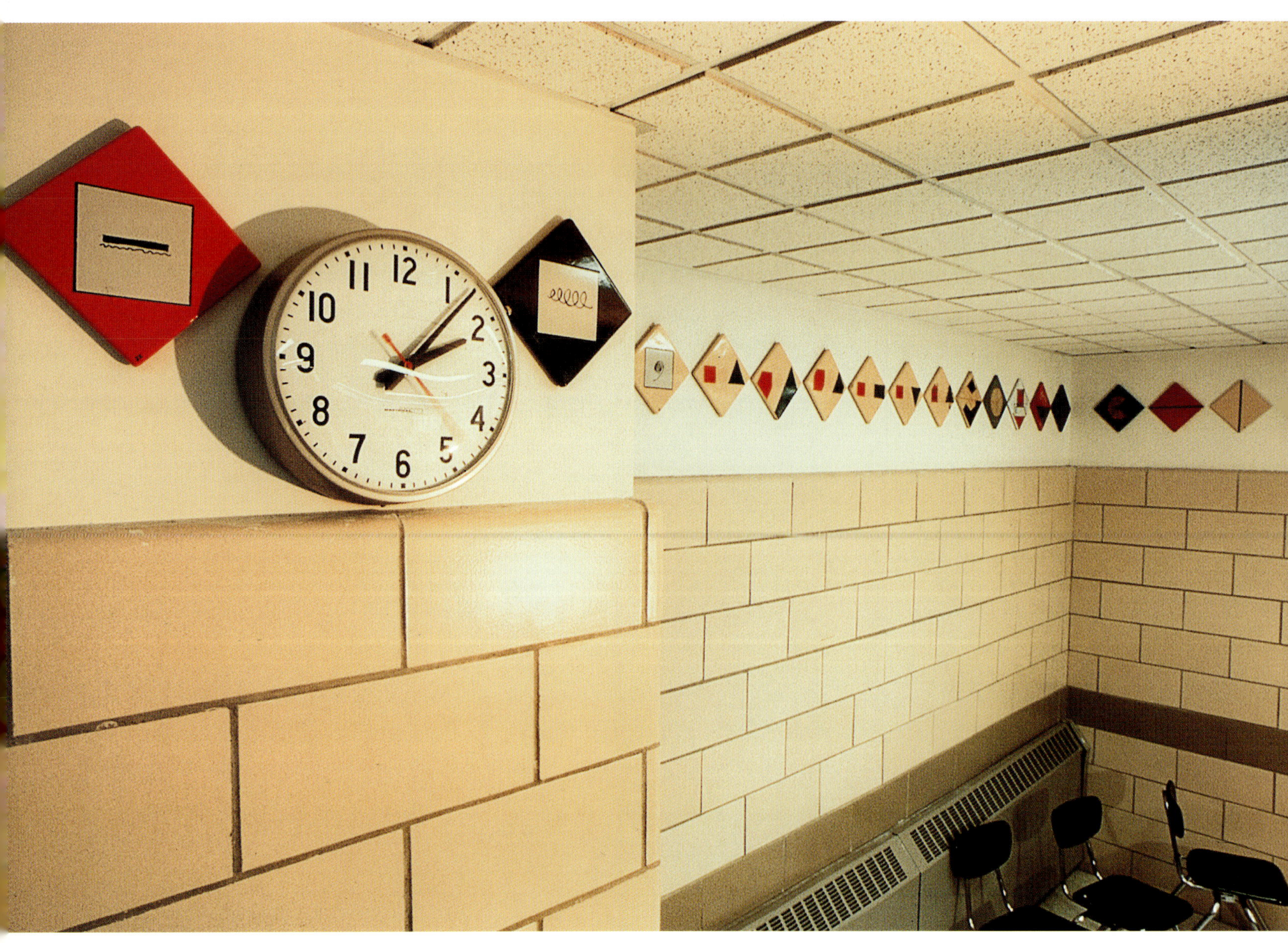

Tabula
1992
Marble

Stuyvesant High School,
345 Chambers Street

ARCHITECT
Cooper, Robertson and Partners
ASSOCIATE ARCHITECT
Gruzen Samton Steinglass
DESIGN AGENCY
School Construction Authority
SPONSOR AGENCY
Board of Education

Art Commission Award for Excellence in Design 1989

Michelle Stuart's *Tabula*, located in the entrance lobby of Stuyvesant High School, consists of thirty inlaid "paintings" of differently colored and stratified pieces of etched marble. Below the grand staircase, six marble panels—three installed on each side—are etched with drawings that refer to different systems of knowledge, including botany, astronomy, mathematics, language, and exploration. The artist used marble from quarries in Brazil, India, Spain, Africa, Italy, and the United States.

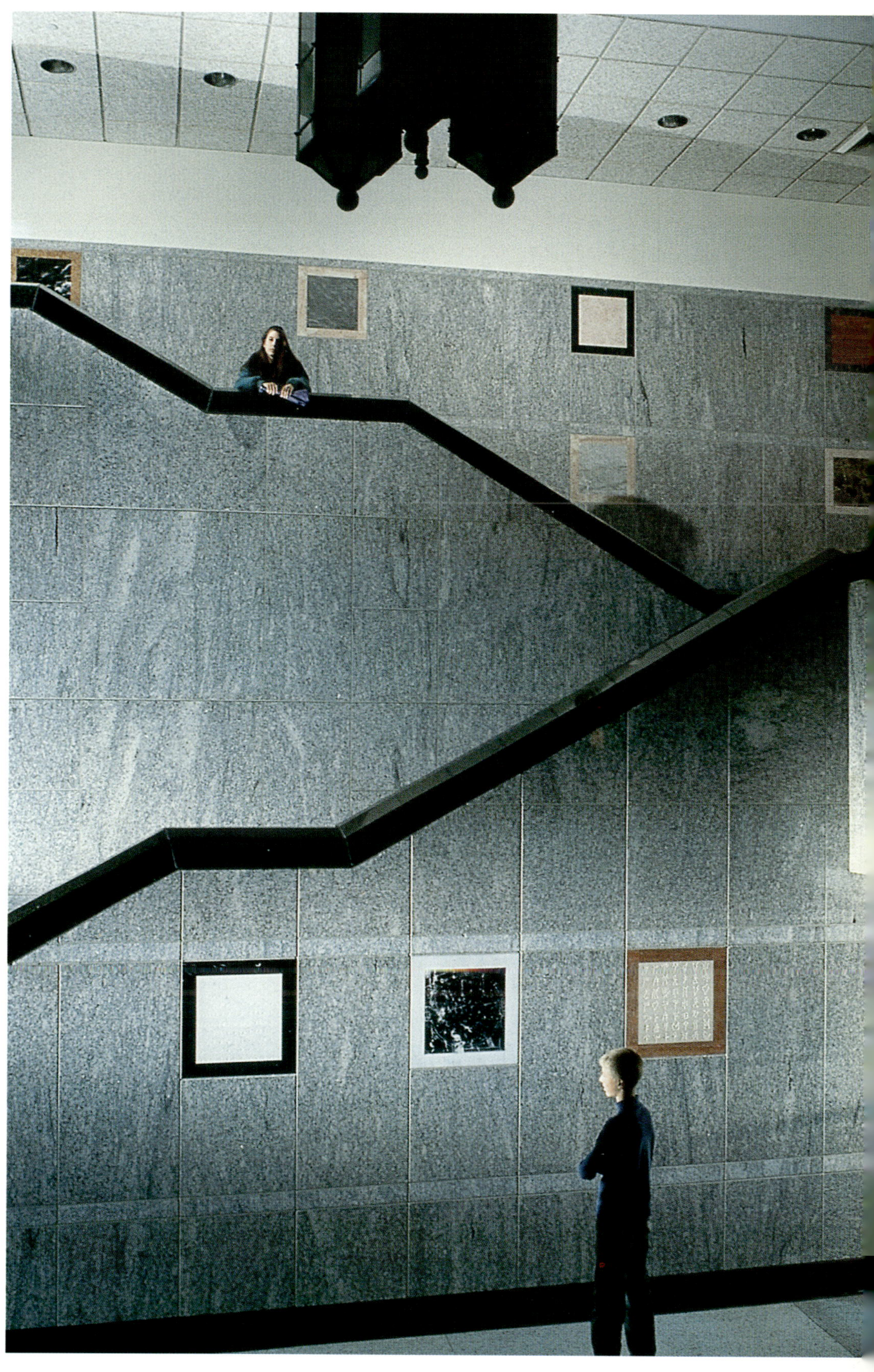

Michelle Stuart

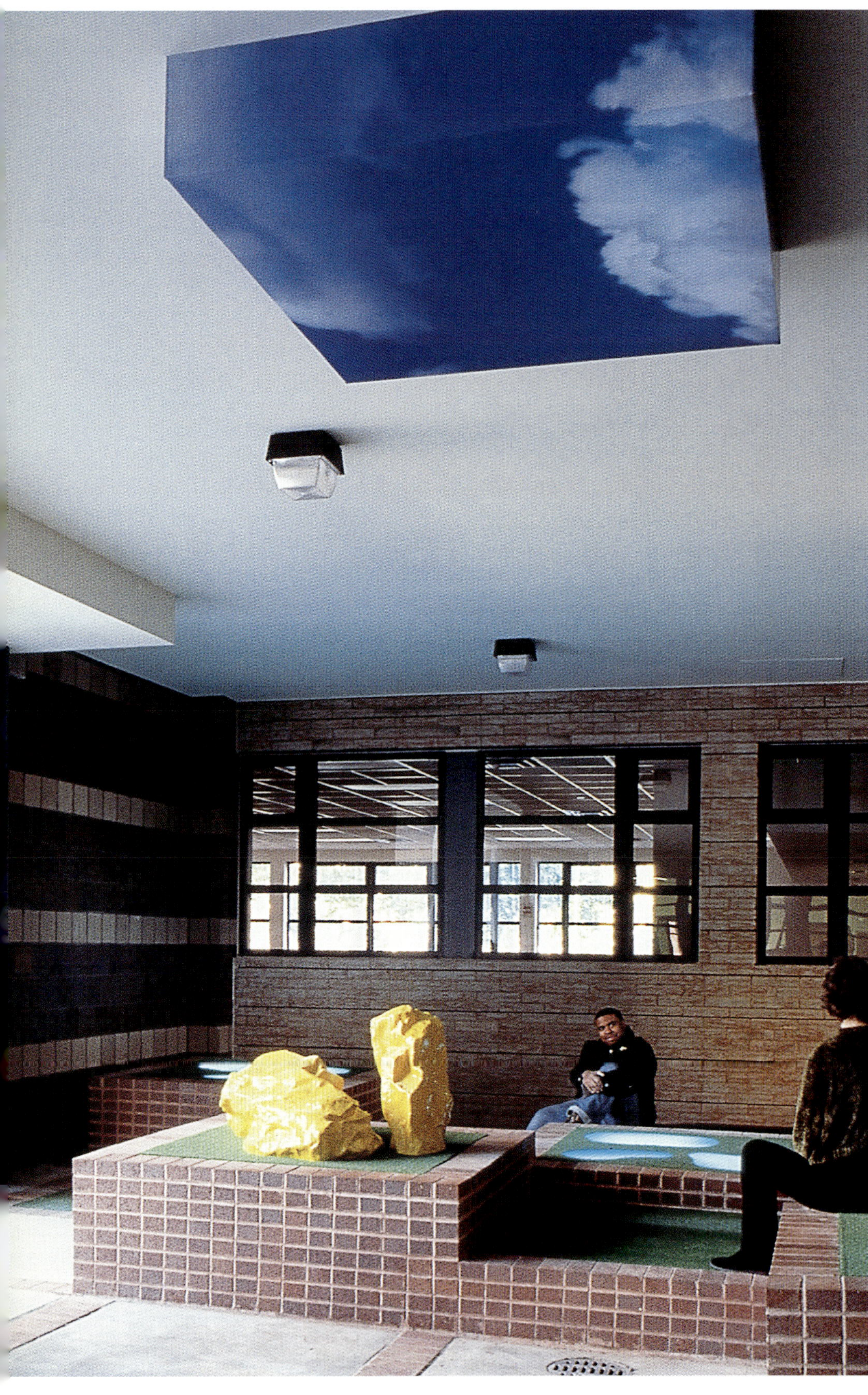

West Side High School Park
1999
Brick, artificial turf, Plexiglas, fiberglass, paint

West Side High School,
140 West 102nd Street

ARCHITECT
John Ciardullo Associates
DESIGN AGENCY
School Construction Authority
SPONSOR AGENCY
Board of Education

Allan and Ellen Wexler created an artificial park for the front entrance to West Side High School. The artists raised sections of the brick and cement floor to create an urban landscape that incorporates man-made nature into its mathematical grid. Taxicab-yellow boulders, lush green Astroturf, and blue opaque Lucite water, lit from below, provide not a real park but an interpretation of nature with apparent artificiality. As Ellen Wexler has written: "Integrating art into schools is a challenge and opportunity to open up eyes and awaken curiosities . . . . The students have a new school and we want them to really see it. We want to enhance their relationship to their school, by giving them the eyes of an artist."

Allan and Ellen Wexler

Martin Wong

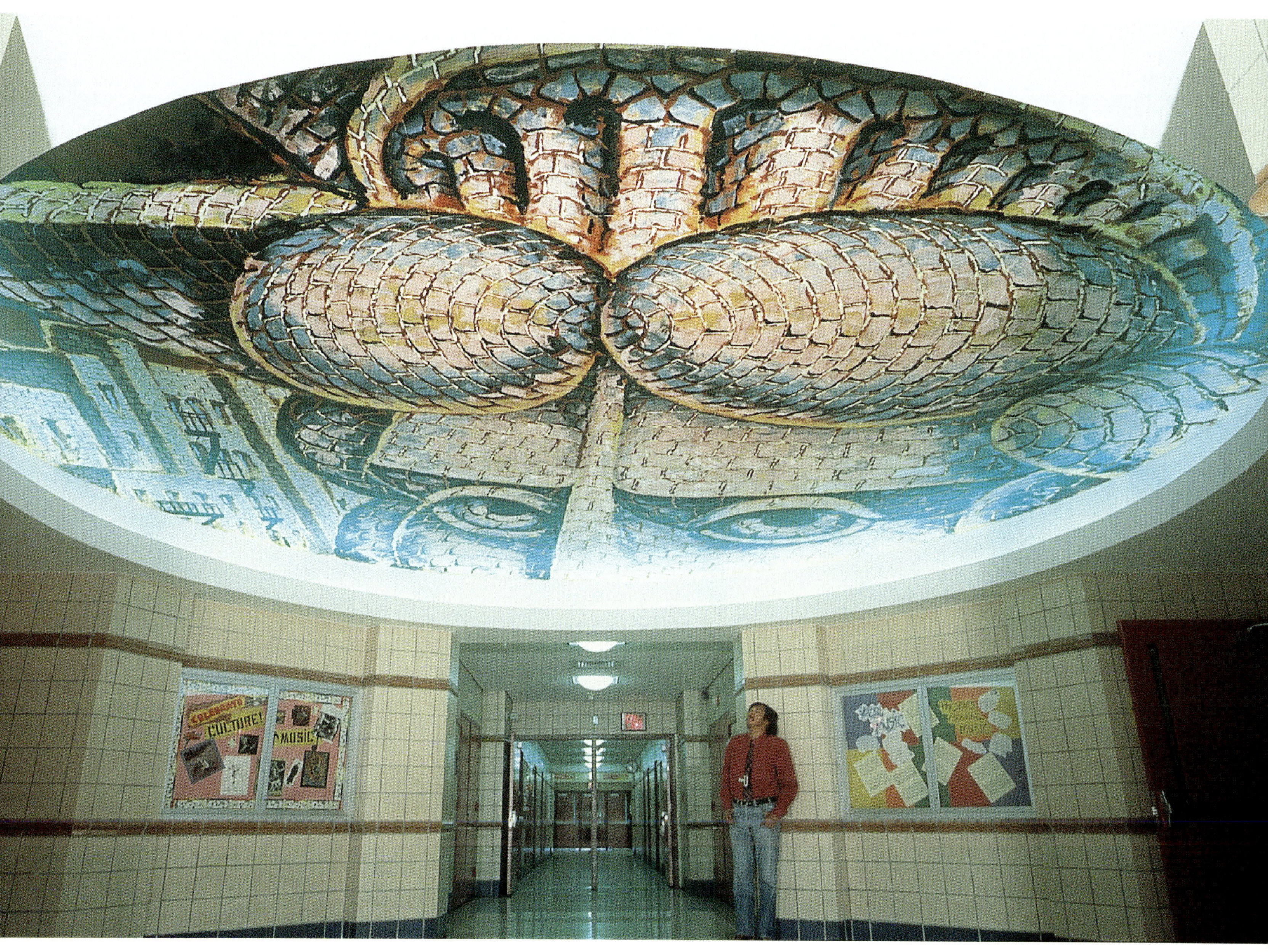

Miss Liberty Face
1995
Acrylic, plywood

Intermediate School 90, 21 Jumel Place

ARCHITECT
Richard Dattner and Partners Architects
DESIGN AGENCY
School Construction Authority
SPONSOR AGENCY
Board of Education

Martin Wong's mural, *Miss Liberty Face*, watches over the students of I.S. 90 from the circular ceiling of the school's third-floor lobby. Wong's interpretation of the eyes and crown of the Statue of Liberty is modeled to replicate the brick of the buildings surrounding the school. Wong has said of the artwork: "My intention was to show the illusion that the mural was a hole in the ceiling with a brick Statue of Liberty face staring down at you."

Completed projects ● (see map)

1 **Dennis Adams**
2 **Mac Adams**
3 **Ann Agee**
4 **Alice Aycock**
5 **Mo Bahc**
6 **Meg Belichick**
7 **Ed Carpenter**
8 **Alfredo Ceibal**
9 **Jackie Chang**
10 **Colin Chase**
11 **Amy Cheng**
12 **Mel Chin**
13 **Sung-Ho Choi**
14 **Nancy Chunn**
15 **Willie Cole**
16 **Noel Copeland**
17 **Sheila Levrant de Bretteville**
18 **Claudia DeMonte**
19 **Donna Dennis**
20 **Julie Dermansky**
21 **Chris Doyle**
22 **Ming Fay**
23 **Jackie Ferrara**
24 **Phillip Galgiani**
25 **Cadence Giersbach**
26 **Ann Gillen**
27 **Elizabeth Grajales**
28 **Elizabeth Grajales**
29 **Ousmane Gueye**
30 **Mags Harries with Lajos Heder**
31 **Skowmon Hastanan**
32 **Barry Holden and Nina Yankowitz**
33 **Wopo Holup**
34 **Ik-Joong Kang**
35 **Bing Lee**
36 **Robyn Love**
37 **Clyde Lynds**
38 **Howard McCalebb**
39 **Ed McGowin and Claudia DeMonte**
40 **Yong Soon Min**
41 **Matt Mullican**
42 **Anna Valentina Murch**
43 **Kazuma Oshita**
44 **Eung Ho Park**
45 **Kathleen H. Ruíz**
46 **Maura Sheehan**
47 **Susumu Shingu**
48 **Kathleen Spicer**
49 **Carol Sun**
50 **Fred Tomaselli**
51 **Susan Tunick**
52 **Lane Twitchell**
53 **Ursula von Rydingsvard**
54 **Michael Kelly Williams**
55 **Philemona Williamson**
56 **Fred Wilson**
57 **Steve Wood**
58 **Andy Yoder**

Projects in progress ▲ (see map)

59 **Luca Buvoli**
The Big Wave—Not-a-Superhero in the Ocean of Language
Polycarbonate sheets, fiberglass polyester resin
Public School 253, 1307 Central Avenue
Architect: Urbahn Associates
Design Agency: School Construction Authority
Sponsor Agency: Department of Education

60 **James Carpenter**
Moire Light Wall
Glass and light installation
New York Hall of Science, Flushing Meadows Corona Park, 47-01 111th Street
Architect: Polshek Partnership Architects
Design Agency: Department of Design and Construction
Sponsor Agency: Department of Cultural Affairs
Art Commission Award for Excellence in Design 2000

61 **James Casebere**
Photographs
High School for Architecture and Urban Planning, 94-06 104th Street
Architect: STV Group
Design Agency: School Construction Authority
Sponsor Agency: Department of Education

62 **Barbara Ellman**
Paintings
Cambria Heights Library, 218-13 Linden Boulevard
Architect: Schaardt & Fallan, de Silva/Beatty, Harvey & Associates
Design Agency: Department of Design and Construction
Sponsor Agency: Queens Borough Public Library

63 **Jane Greengold**
Best on the Beach
Fence design
Far Rockaway Firehouse, 4806 Rockaway Beach Boulevard
Architect: Beyhan Karahan Associates
Design Agency: Department of Design and Construction
Sponsor Agency: Fire Department

64 **Samm Kunce**
Glass, brick
Sunrise Yards Maintenance Facility, 88-02 Pitkin Avenue
Architect: Gruzen Samton Architects
Design Agency: Department of Design and Construction
Sponsor Agency: Department of Transportation

65 **Martha Madigan**
Oak Seasons
Glass wall
Public/Intermediate School 499, 148-20 Reeves Avenue
Architect: Michael Fieldman Architects
Design Agency: School Construction Authority
Sponsor Agency: Department of Education

66 **Paul Henry Ramirez**
Going Up, Up, Up
Enamel paint, laser-cut aluminum
Public School 254, 84-40 101st Steet
Architect: SBLM Architects
Design Agency: School Construction Authority
Sponsor Agency: Department of Education

67 **Toshio Sasaki**
Diagonal Sonata/Asymmetric Inversion
Cast concrete wall design
Long Island City Library, 38th Avenue and 21st Street
Architect: Helpern Architects/Raymond Gomez and Associates
Design Agency: Department of Design and Construction
Sponsor Agency: Queens Borough Public Library

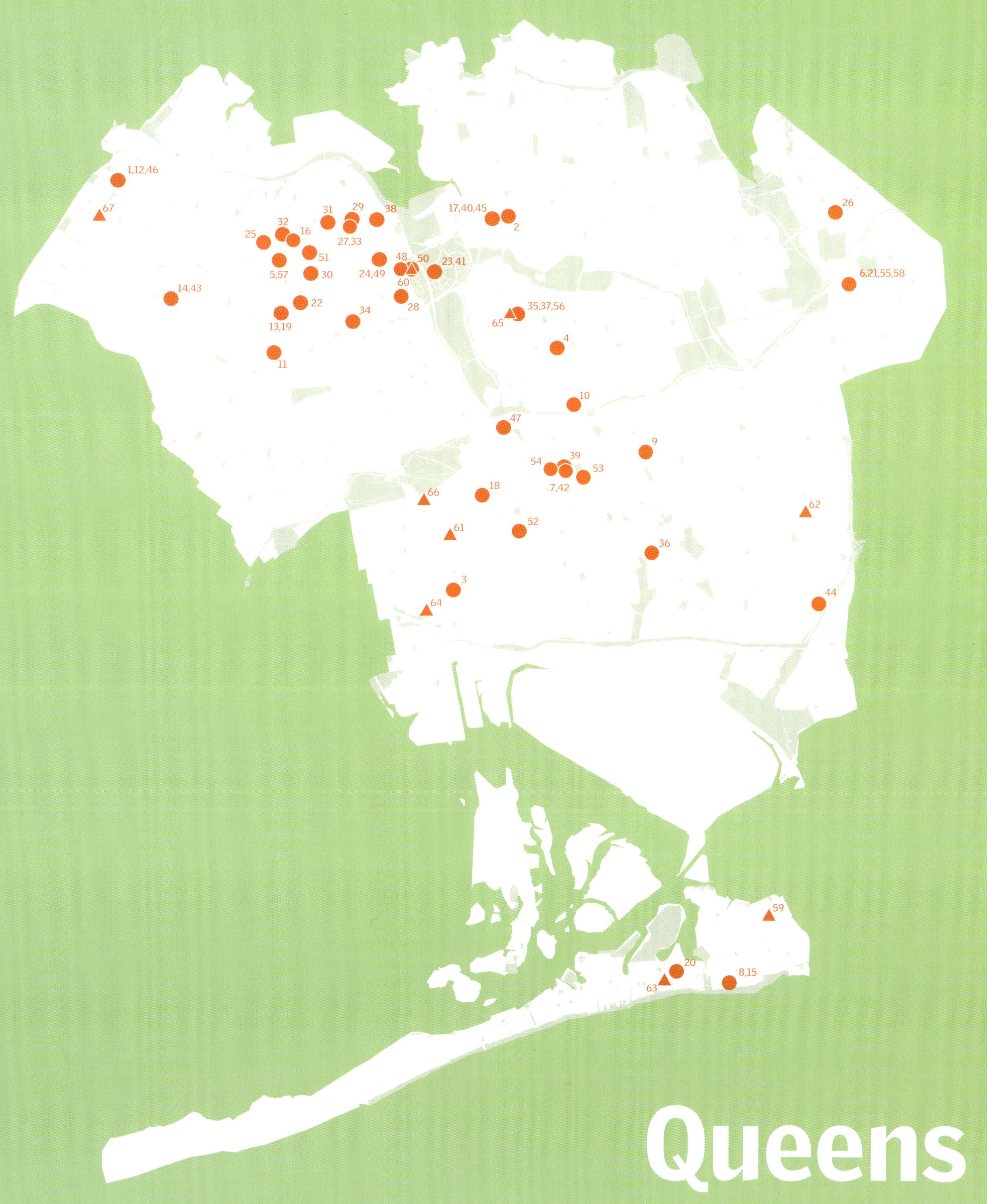
1,12,46
67
31
29
38
17,40,45
2
26
32
16
25
27,33
51
48
50
23,41
24,49
5,57
30
60
6,21,55,58
14,43
22
28
35,37,56
34
65
13,19
4
11
10
47
9
39
54
53
7,42
18
66
62
61
52
36
3
64
44
59
20
8,15
63
Queens

Tributaries
1995
Photographic lightboxes

Long Island City High School,
14-30 Broadway

ARCHITECT
Gruzen Samton Steinglass
DESIGN AGENCY
School Construction Authority
SPONSOR AGENCY
Board of Education

Dennis Adams's *Tributaries* features a series of back-illuminated photographs installed above twelve drinking fountains throughout the school's corridors. The artist selected the photographic images to evoke seminal moments in the American civil rights movement, and included accompanying phrases associated with the era. The text is written at an angle that is readable as students drink from the fountains. Adams explains that the title of the work has dual meanings: "It references a branch of water that flows away from the main stream [and] suggests a line of dissent, a rupture in the dominant movement of society. In another sense, it references a tribute, suggesting a site of commemoration." See also the interview with Dennis Adams, page 168.

Dennis Adams

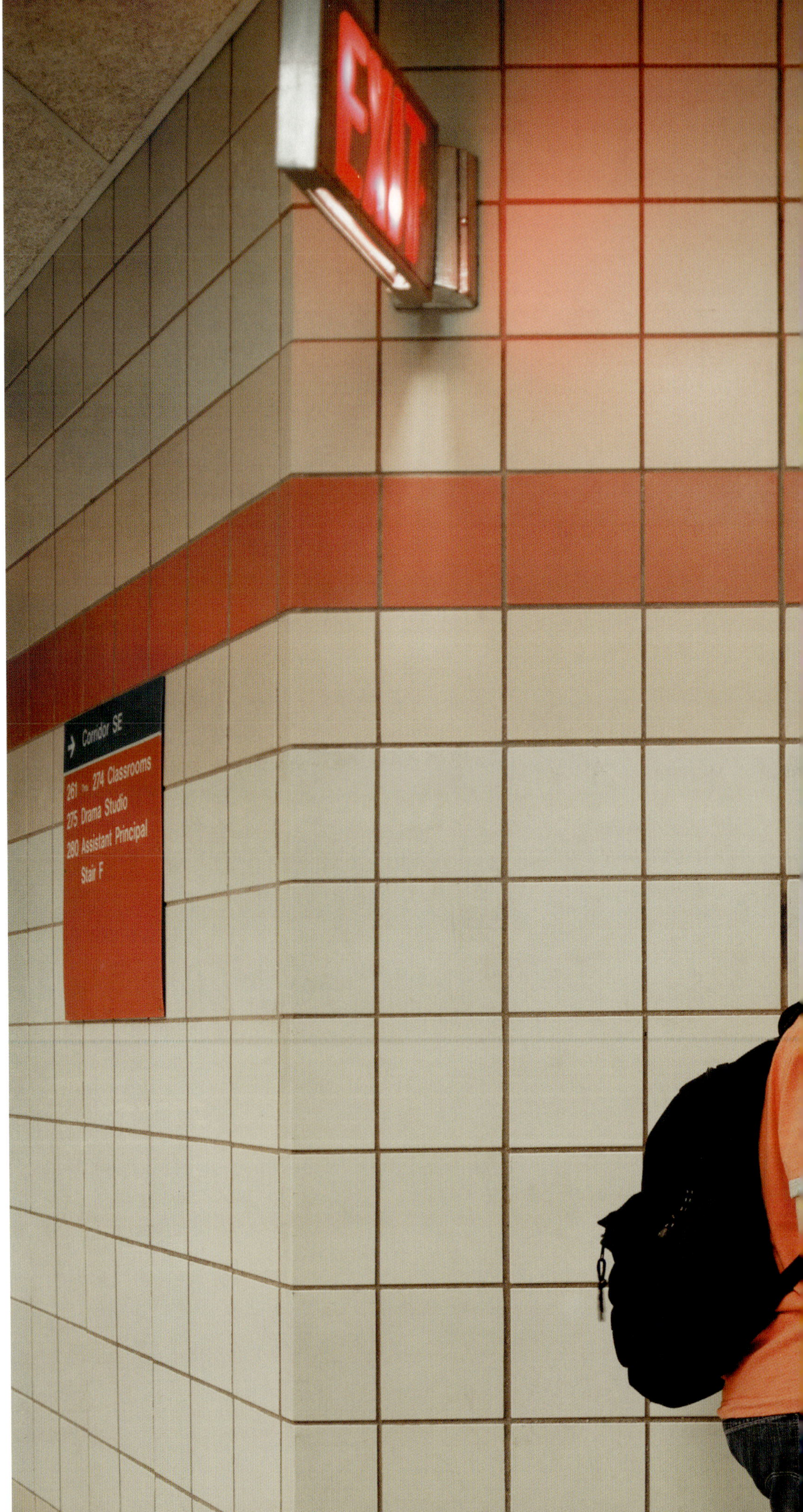

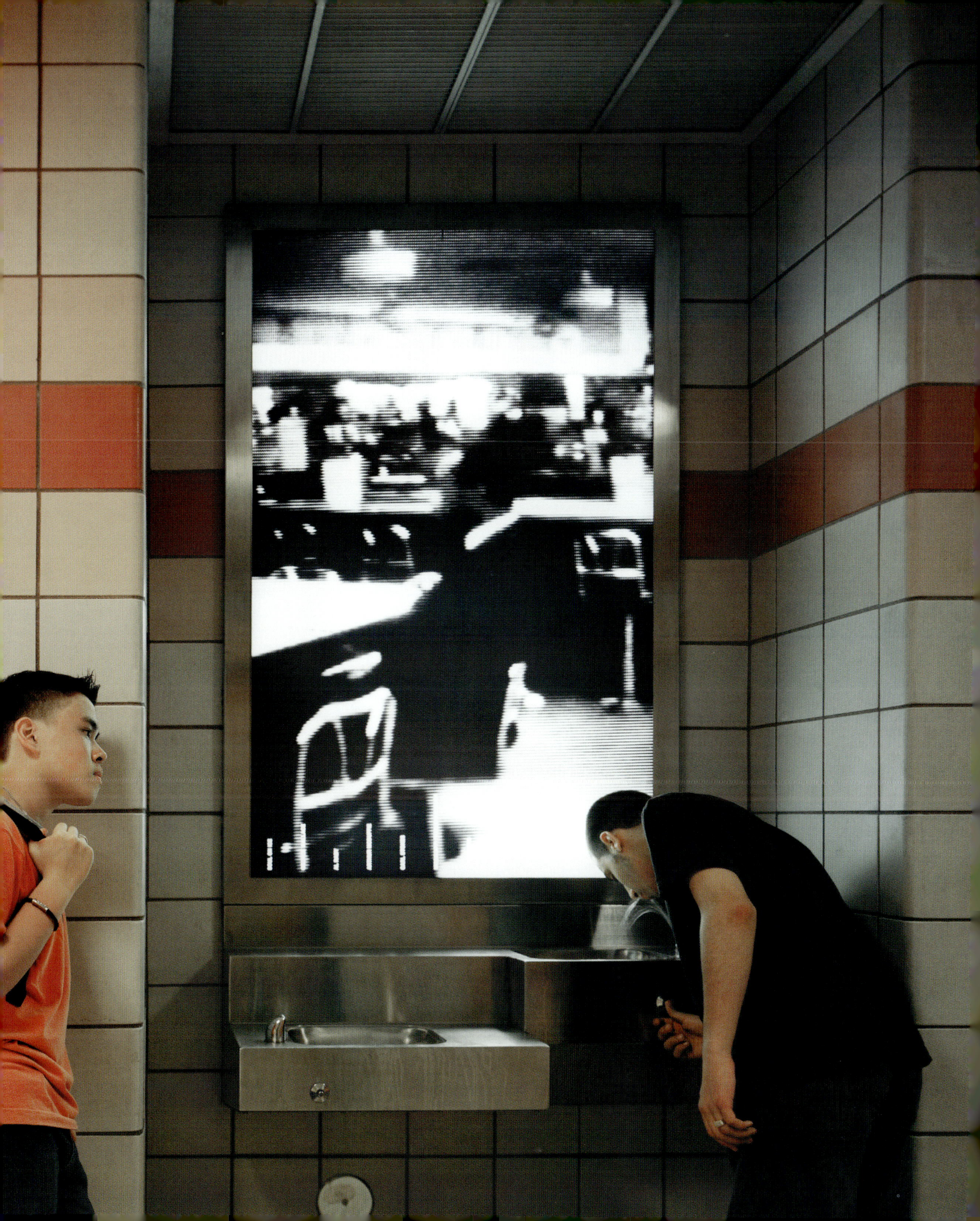

Interview: Dennis Adams

I was hesitant at first to take on a project in a high school. For the most part, I have resisted working in institutions with a specific audience. Also, I hated my own high-school experience, which I felt was very uncreative and too authoritarian. So I proceeded with caution, but also with a desire to improve or open up what for me had been a very restrictive and unproductive situation.

I knew, from the beginning, that I did not want to decorate the building or create a new place within it. I like to work with the given architecture or functional aspects of a place. I was drawn to the drinking fountains because they were already mapped throughout the building. They are stations between classes and programs, sites of transition and free moments where students might exchange a piece of information, gossip, dissent, or perform other social interactions outside the more restricted areas. These sites are also places where people pause for a moment and take on a humble body posture, places where their rhythm is broken. I thought of taking advantage of this moment for its potential to enlighten, in the way ideas can come to us in the small broken rhythms of everyday life. It was only after I chose the site that the idea for creating a work about the civil rights movement came to me. I started thinking very obviously about those double drinking fountains for blacks and whites that were central to images of American racism. I graduated from high school in 1966. For me, the civil rights movement was the defining moment of my generation. Even though I am not African-American and was too young at the time to understand its full implications, it was, nevertheless, the catalyst for my first political speculations and questions. So, in a way, this work was directly related to my own high-school years.

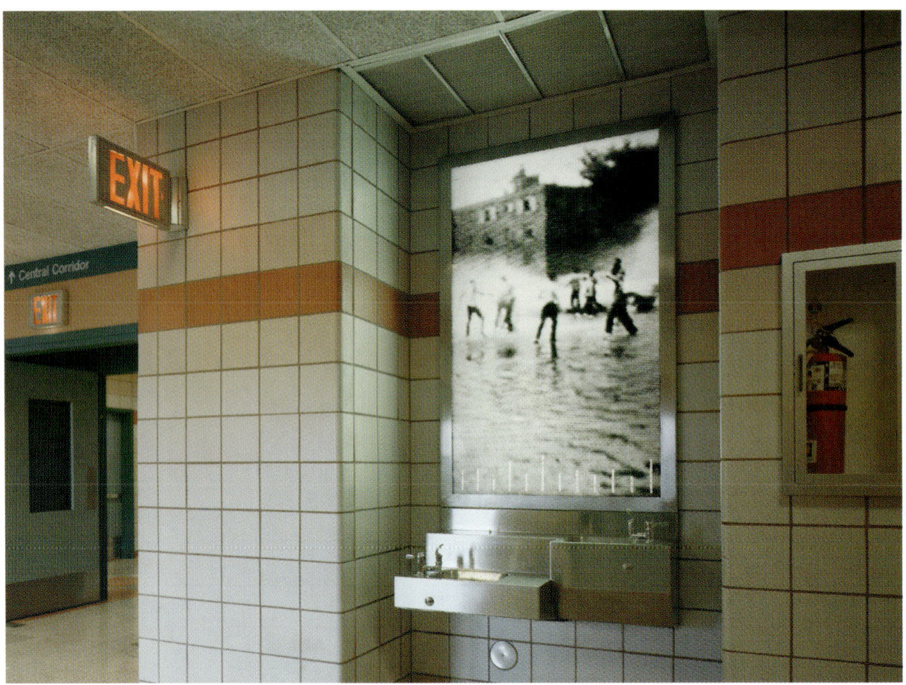

Dennis Adams, *Tributaries*, 1995,
Long Island City High School (pages 166–67).

The list of names, places, and events that overlay each photographic image do not directly describe it, nor are they specifically connected to each other outside of their shared subject. I have nothing new to say about the civil rights movement and I do not want to put forward any kind of declaration. The work is as disjunctive and open-ended as its subject. I want the audience to be stimulated to think for themselves, ask questions, and invest in their own research. In this sense, I see the work as a kind of first question, hesitant, unformed, and hopefully, beautifully naïve. I love first questions; for me this is where artistic investigation and audience come together. Anything more becomes too sure of itself.

When I first presented the idea to the school community, I was shocked to find that there were a couple of teachers who were very resistant. They felt that the civil rights movement was too limited a subject and did not address the diversity of their students. I can't imagine a subject more appropriate to every student. From these most fundamental questions about human rights develop just about every other line of thinking from the Enlightenment to the present. The civil rights movement is not a subject for a specific audience; its messages, in fact, resist ownership of any kind.

On the other hand, I remember how well the project was received by the students. They were the ones that made me want to do it.

World Patterns and Fables
1996
Ceramic tiles, mosaic murals

Public School 20, 142-30 Barclay Avenue

ARCHITECT
Eliseo Bostwick and Purcell
DESIGN AGENCY
School Construction Authority
SPONSOR AGENCY
Board of Education

Mac Adams's *World Patterns and Fables* consists of four large-scale ceramic and mosaic murals, two located in the hallways of P.S. 20 and two in the school's enclosed play area. The artist researched fables and textile prints from countries that represent the multi-ethnic community in which the school is located. Within each mural are mosaic disks that depict silhouettes of the animal characters from the fables. Each of the mosaic disks is surrounded by samples of textile prints.

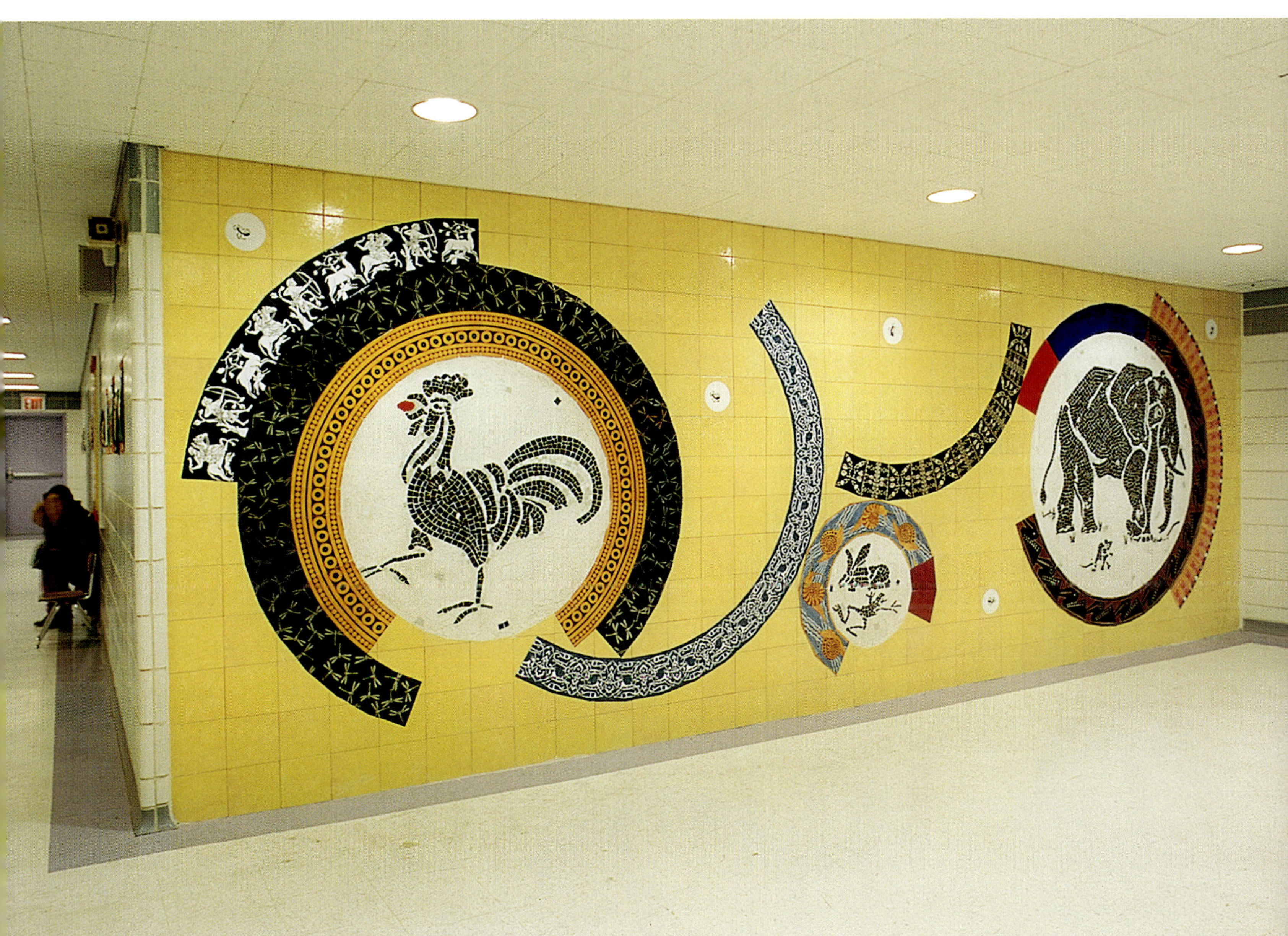

Mac Adams

World's Fair 2003
2003
Porcelain, ceramics

Intermediate School 137,
109-15 98th Street

ARCHITECT/DESIGN AGENCY
School Construction Authority
SPONSOR AGENCY
Board of Education

Ann Agee's tiled wall and built-in display case are located in the lobby of I.S. 137. The wall tiles, painted with ceramic glazes and enamels, feature floating circles of various sizes and colors. Within each is an image of junior high-school students in the midst of creative work against backdrops of decorative landscapes. Ornamental details around the circular painted frames are drawn from Dutch, Mexican, Islamic, and Chinese art. The display case is filled with porcelain figurines of junior high-school students. Agee has explained that her idea was "to design something that would respond in contrast to the institutional materials that the school is made of. I wanted the lobby to be full of warmth and happiness. Essential to me were several things: that the tiles be handmade, that the figurines be small and hand-built . . . and that everything be hand-painted."

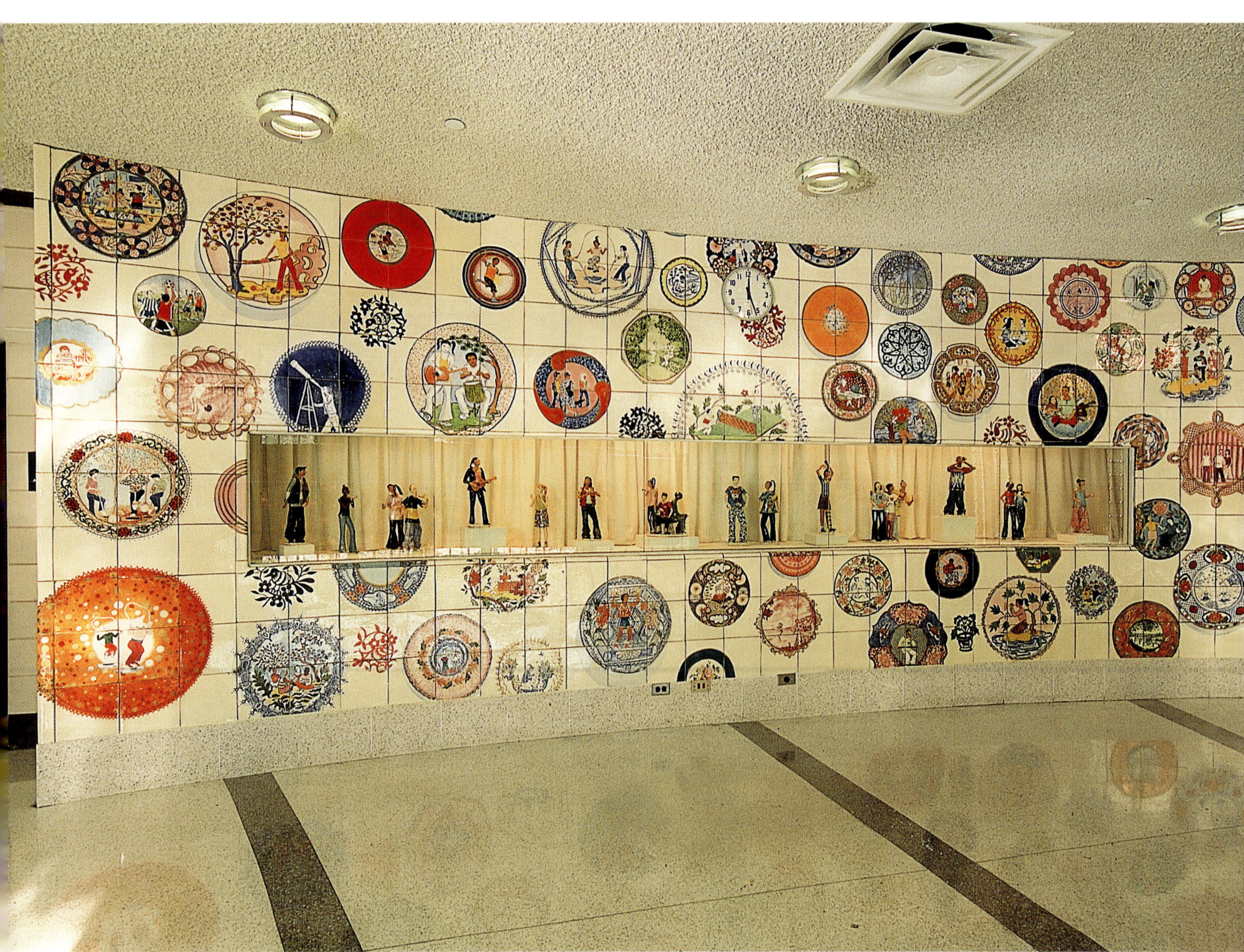

Ann Agee

Alice Aycock

Project for the 107th Police Precinct, Queens, New York (following pages)
1992
Painted steel

107th Precinct and Borough Command Center, 71-01 Parsons Boulevard

ARCHITECT
Perkins Eastman

DESIGN AGENCY
Department of General Services
SPONSOR AGENCY
Police Department

Located on the rooftop of a police precinct, Alice Aycock's large-scale sculpture consists of various pieces of painted gray steel and a large disk, inspired by a medieval astrolabe. Arranged around the disk are fragments of doors, steps, wheels, and a vessel-like form from which light emanates at night. The composition of the artwork serves as a visual counterpoint to the building's compact, angled, horizontal design. The work can be viewed from the streets below and from surrounding buildings.

Mo Bahc

Junction
1995
Mosaic and etched stone

Public School 69, 77-02 37th Street

ARCHITECT
Urbahn Associates
DESIGN AGENCY
School Construction Authority
SPONSOR AGENCY
Board of Education

Mo Bahc's mosaic in the lobby of P.S. 69 features diverse cultural symbols combined with images found in nature. The vertical mosaic sections of the mural borrow motifs from traditional and folk art from different parts of the world, including Spain, India, China, Persia, Africa, and the United States. The granite section in the center of the mural is drawn from Korean folk art and depicts a mountain range and body of water. On the top and bottom of the stone panels are images of the twelve Western and twelve Eastern zodiac signs.

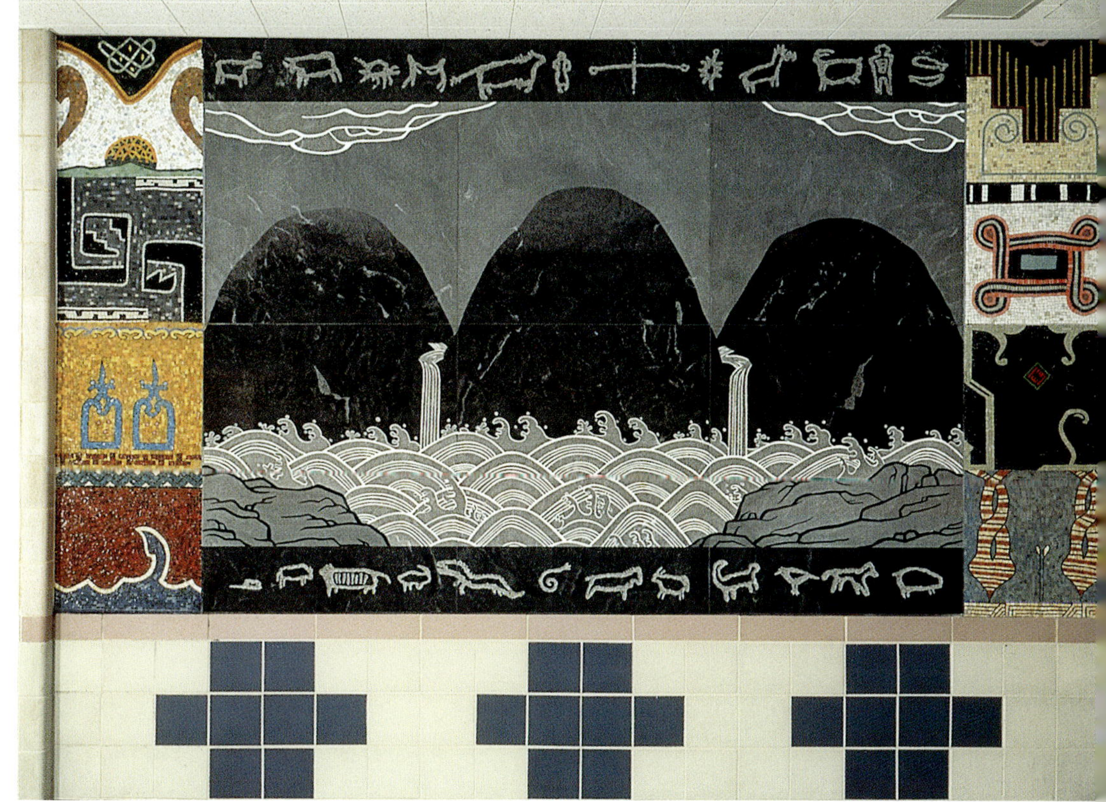

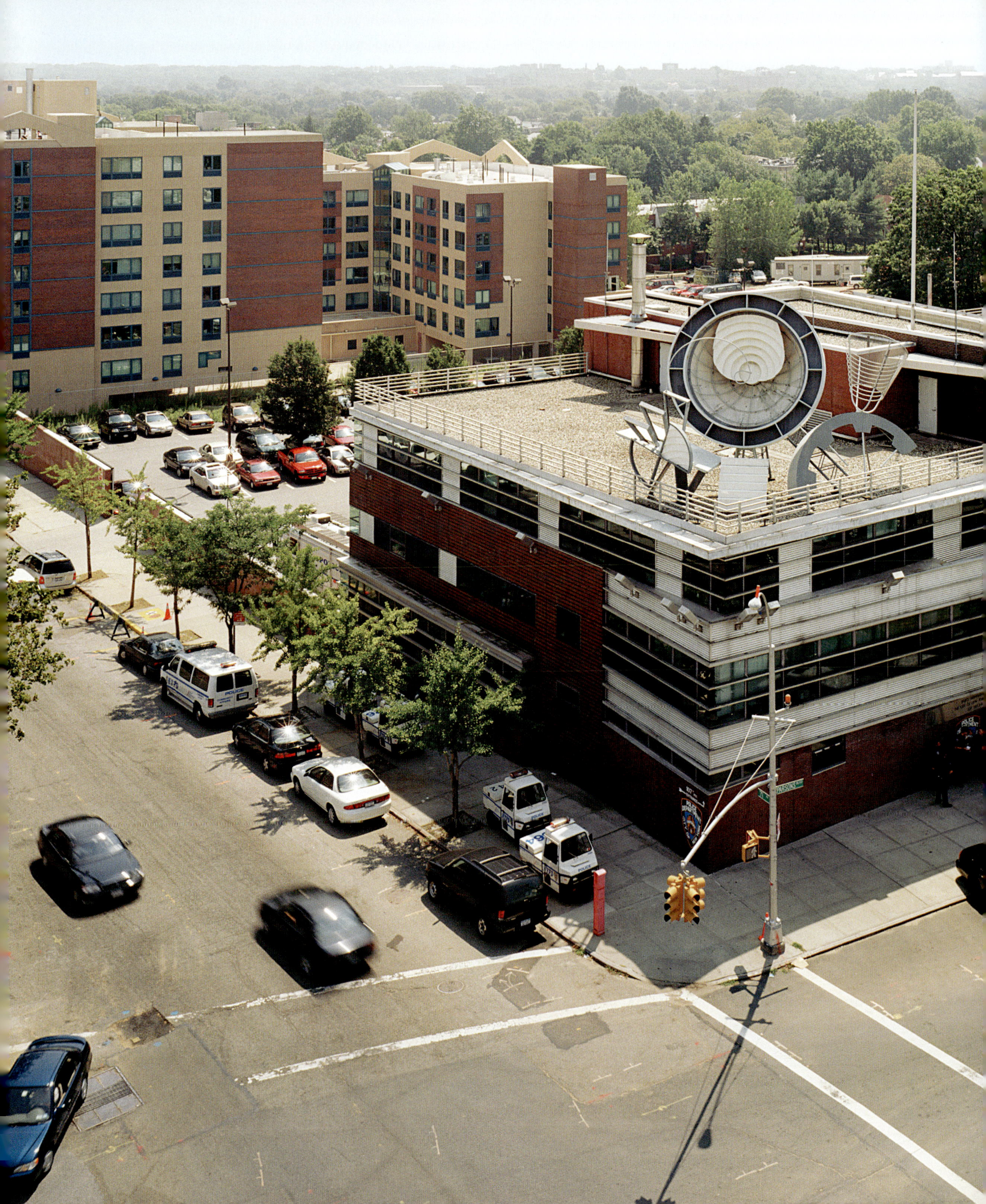

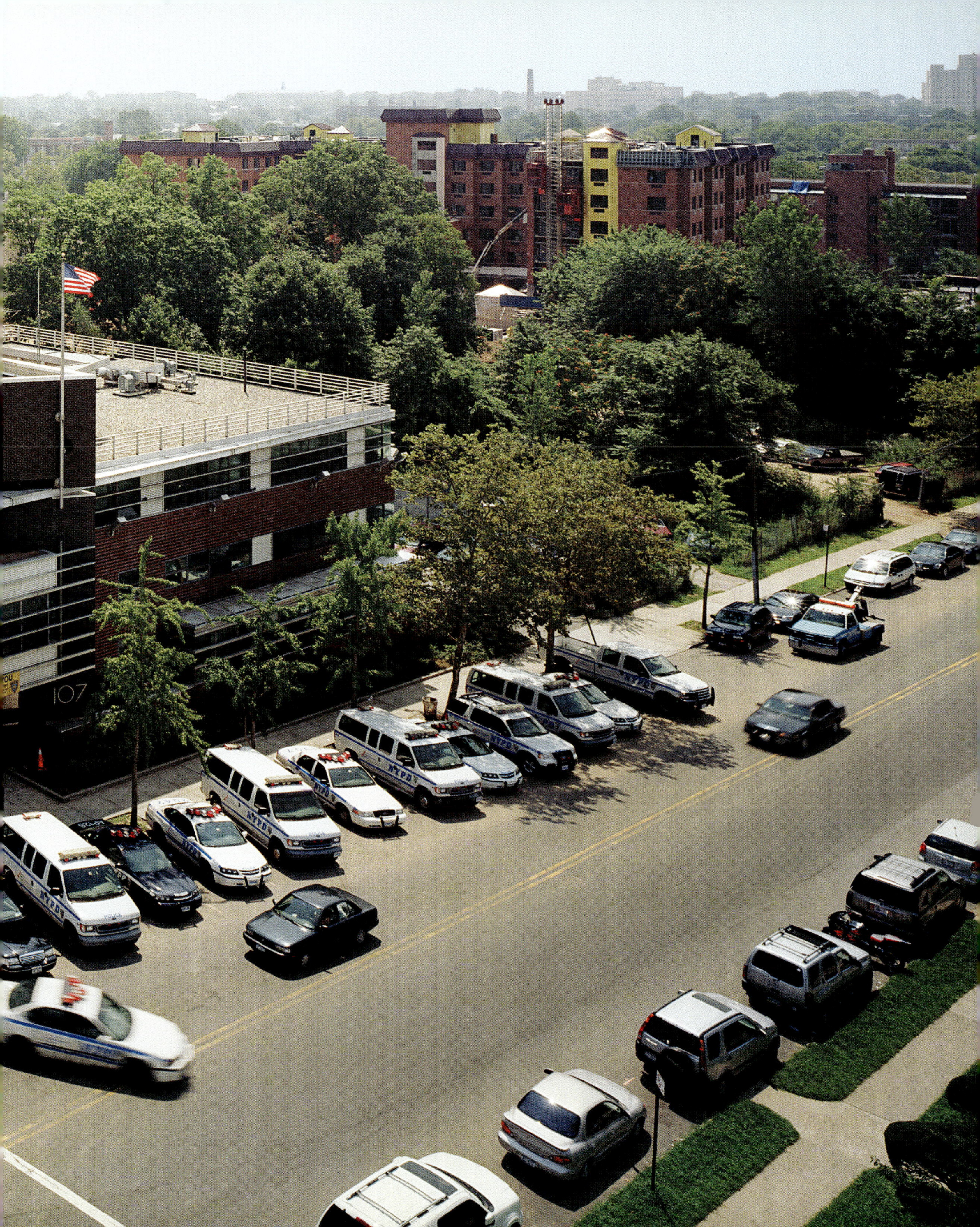
107
NYPD

All the Colors, dedicated to poet and educator Kenneth Koch
2003
Aluminum, stainless steel

Public/Intermediate School 266,
74-10 Commonwealth Boulevard

ARCHITECT
SBLM Architects
DESIGN AGENCY
School Construction Authority
SPONSOR AGENCY
Department of Education

Meg Belichick's sculptural artwork spans 20 feet (6.1 m) between two brick columns, and hovers 7 feet (2.1 m) above the plaza in front of P.S./I.S. 266. Inspired by writing workshops that the artist led in several public schools in Queens, *All the Colors* features text from a student's poem: "I remember all the colors like this/ orange green blue red pink purple silver gold/ I don't remember when I didn't close the crayon box." The name of each color is carved out of aluminum and woven with stainless-steel wire.

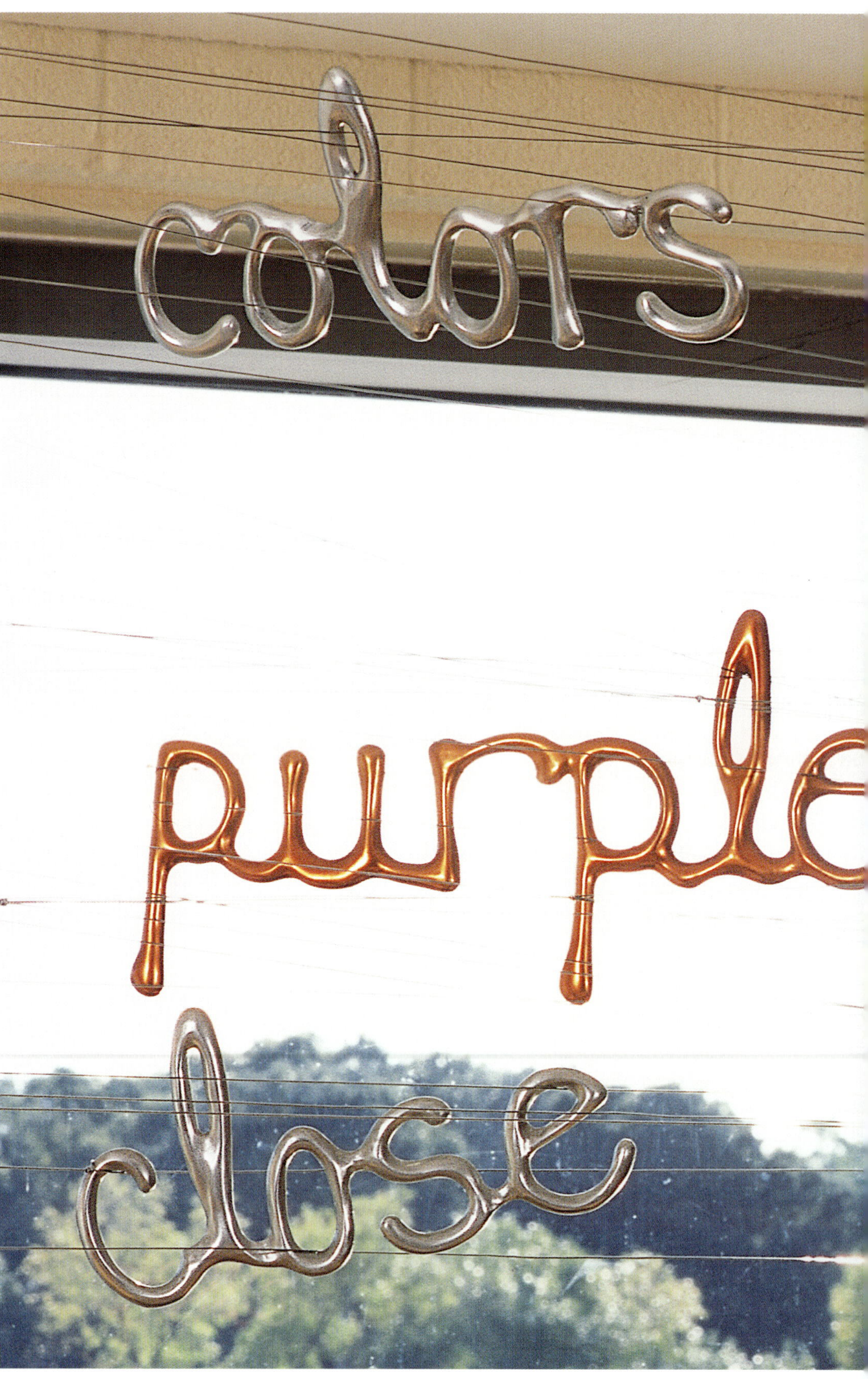

Meg Belichick

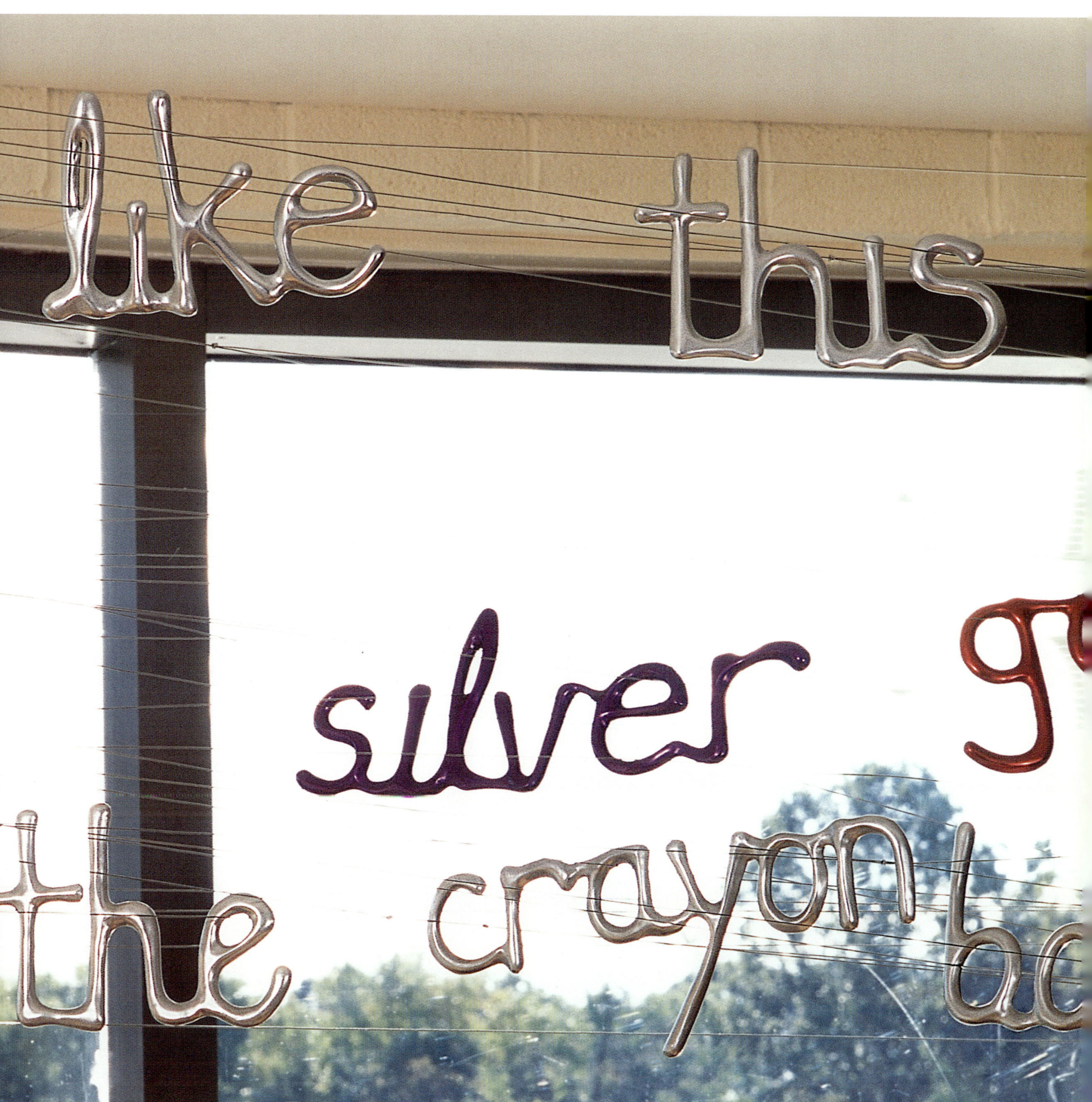
like thus
silver
the crayon

Ed Carpenter

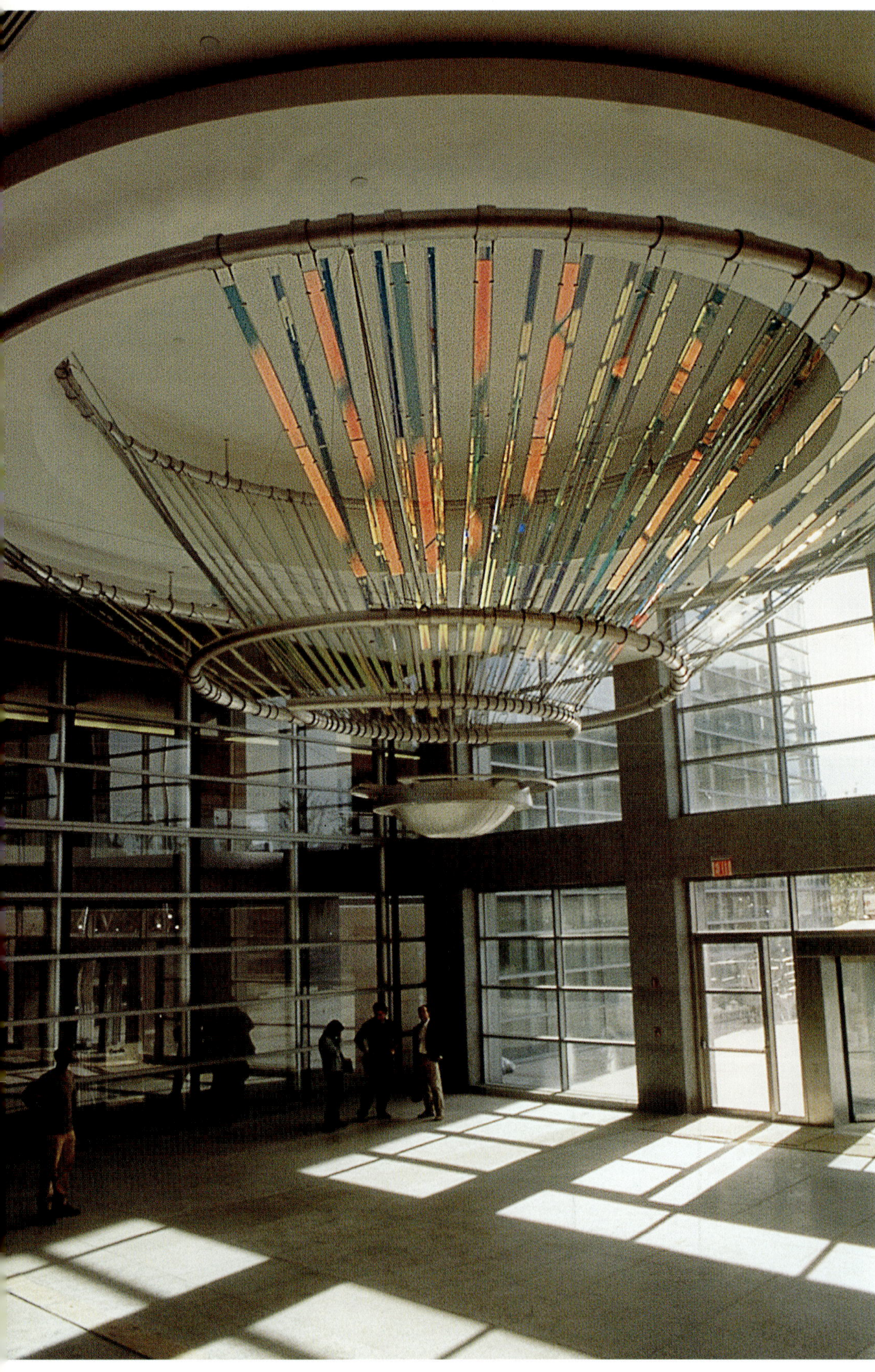

Ojo
1997
Glass

Queens Civil Court,
89-17 Sutphin Boulevard

ARCHITECT
Perkins Eastman
DESIGN AGENCY
Dormitory Authority of the State of New York
SPONSOR AGENCY
Office of Court Administration

Ed Carpenter's sculpture in the lobby of the Queens Civil Court building is titled *Ojo,* the Spanish word for "eye." The suspended sculpture, manufactured from dichromatic glass, changes color with the varying degrees of light that filter into the space throughout the day. "My intention," Carpenter has written, "was to create a luminous architectural organism, growing out of the structure of the building but distinct from it; simultaneously guarding and crowning the lobby; grand in scale but delicate and transparent; technical and organic; vigilant but welcoming. Like the law itself, it is layered and faceted, mercurial as Truth."

The Flying Imagination
1996
Painted mural on canvas

Public School 43, 160 Beach 29th Street

ARCHITECT
Ehrenkrantz Eckstut and Kuhn

DESIGN AGENCY
School Construction Authority
SPONSOR AGENCY
Board of Education

Alfredo Ceibal's brightly painted mural in P.S. 43 serves as a visual narrative of the history of aviation. The mural includes images of birds flying outside an open window and a toy airplane attached to a fan by a string, to illustrate how air currents and speed make an object fly. Also shown is a young boy throwing a paper plane, which gradually transforms into a parade of airplanes from different periods in history and ends with a space shuttle entering the solar system.

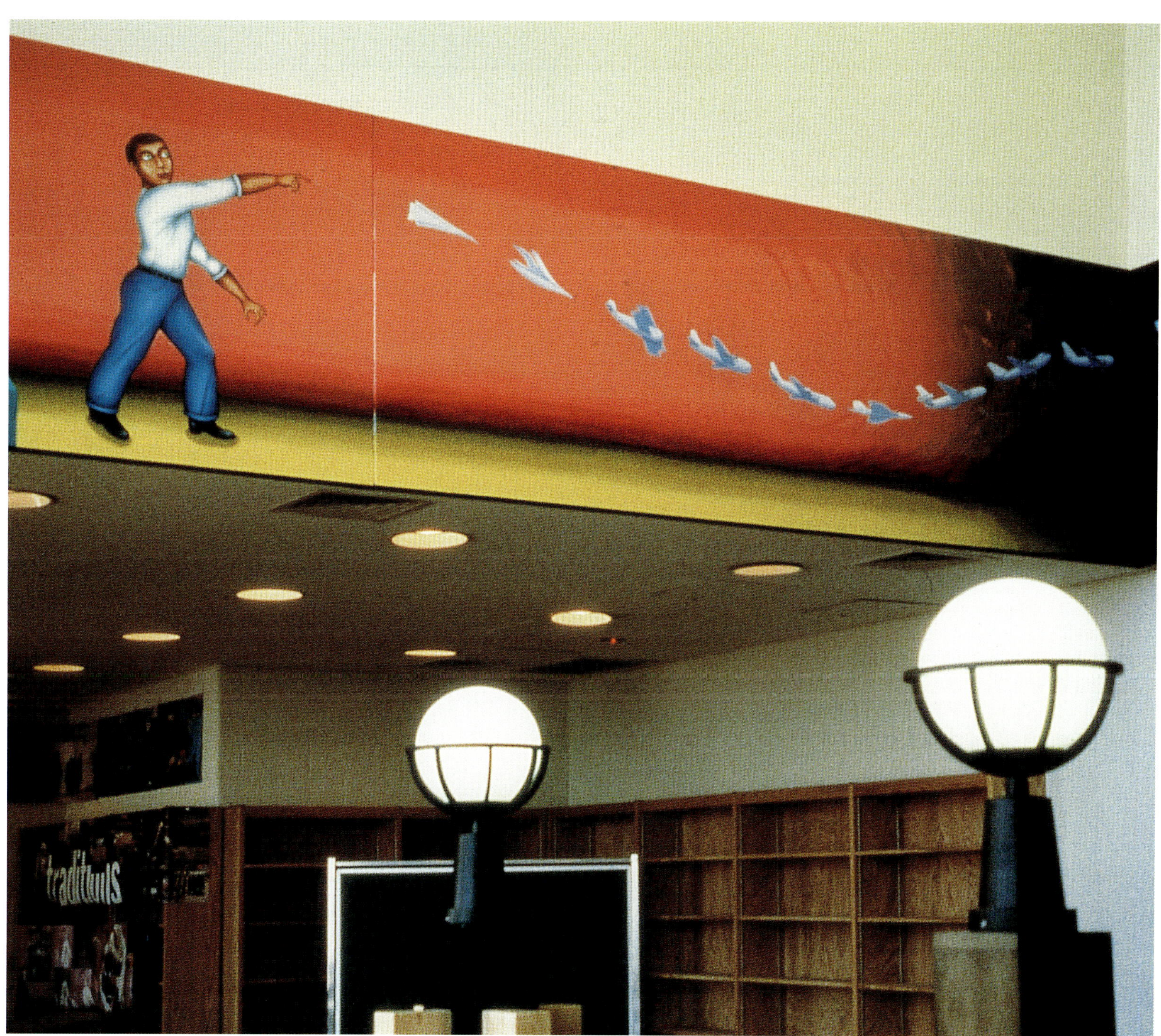

Alfredo Ceibal

In Other Words
2003
Glass-mosaic tiles, inlaid marble

Public School 268, 92-07 175th Street

ARCHITECT
John Ciardullo Associates, P.C.
DESIGN AGENCY
School Construction Authority
SPONSOR AGENCY
Department of Education

Installed in the school's main lobby, main staircase, and auditorium lobby, Jackie Chang's three large-scale murals, collectively entitled *In Other Words,* feature various words associated with education alongside images of galaxies, nebulas, celestial charts, and the planet Earth. Within a featured word, some letters forming other words are highlighted or made larger than the root word, offering students a different perspective on language construction. The artist has written: "For the project, I was inspired by the words that shape and define our education, and the infinite possibilities of what we can learn and discover."

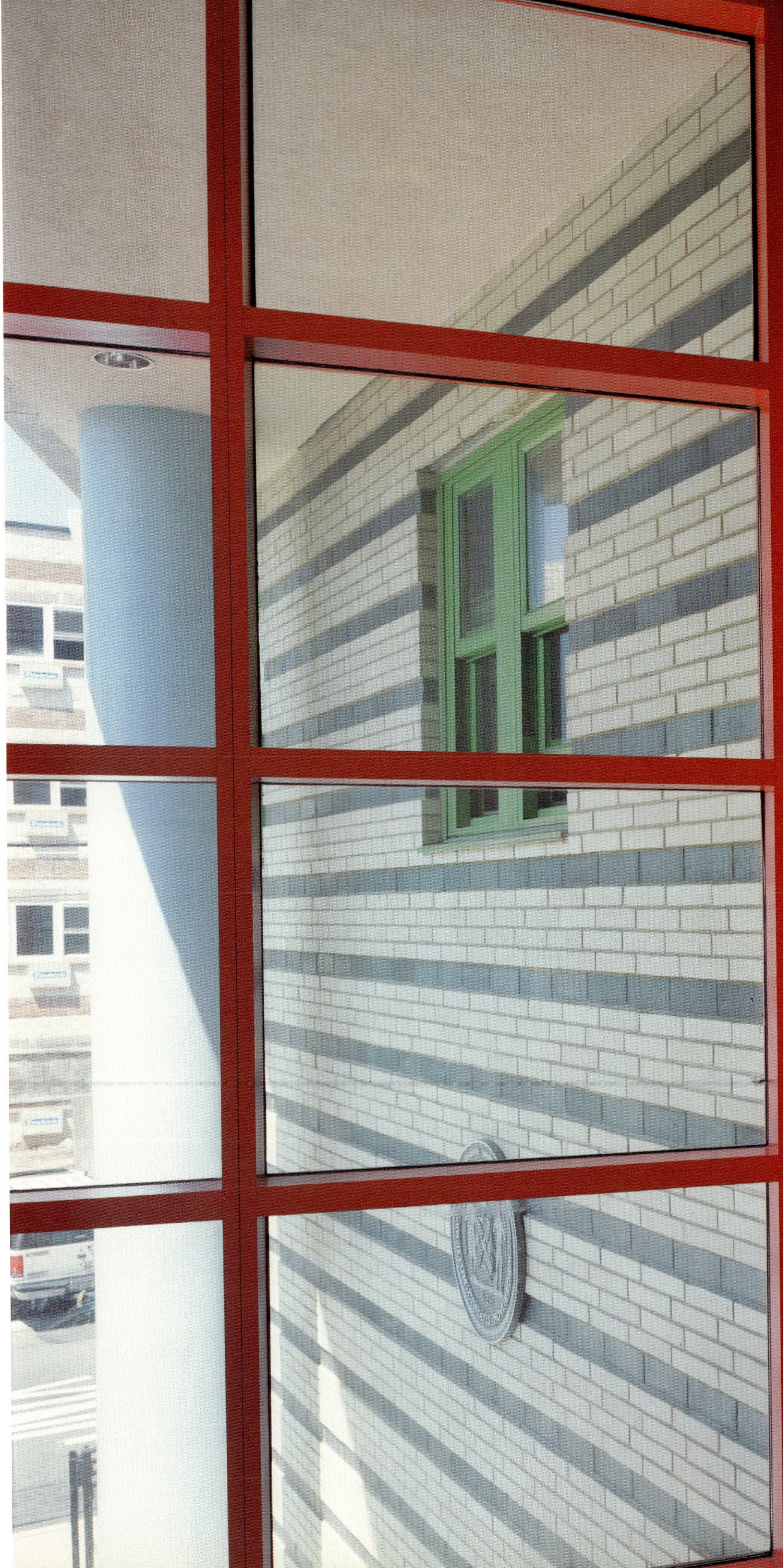

Jackie Chang

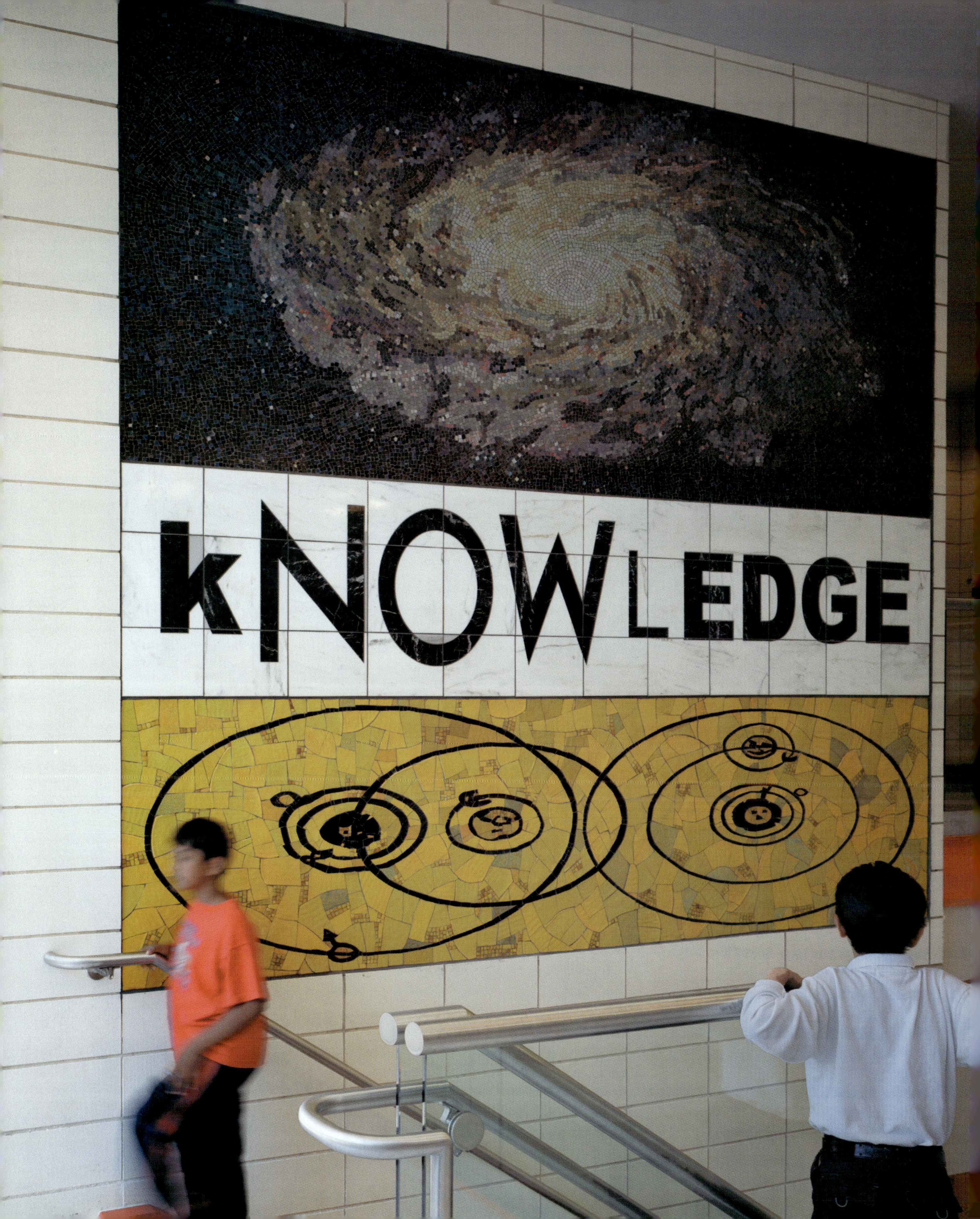
kNOWLEDGE

Colin Chase

Breath and **Mandala** (pages 182–83)
2002
Etched glass, serigraphy

Queens Hospital Center, 82-70 164th Street

ARCHITECT
Davis Brody Bond/Perkins & Will

DESIGN AGENCY
Dormitory Authority of the State of New York
SPONSOR AGENCY
Health and Hospitals Corporation

Colin Chase's *Breath* and *Mandala* are executed on clear glass and mirrors using serigraphs and a combination of lightly etched and deeply carved sandblasting. Located in multiple spaces throughout the hospital complex, the work features a series of bird and nature motifs on glass and mirrored panels (pages 182–83) as well as geometric designs symbolic of the universe, known as mandalas, to create a nurturing and therapeutic environment.

Amy Cheng

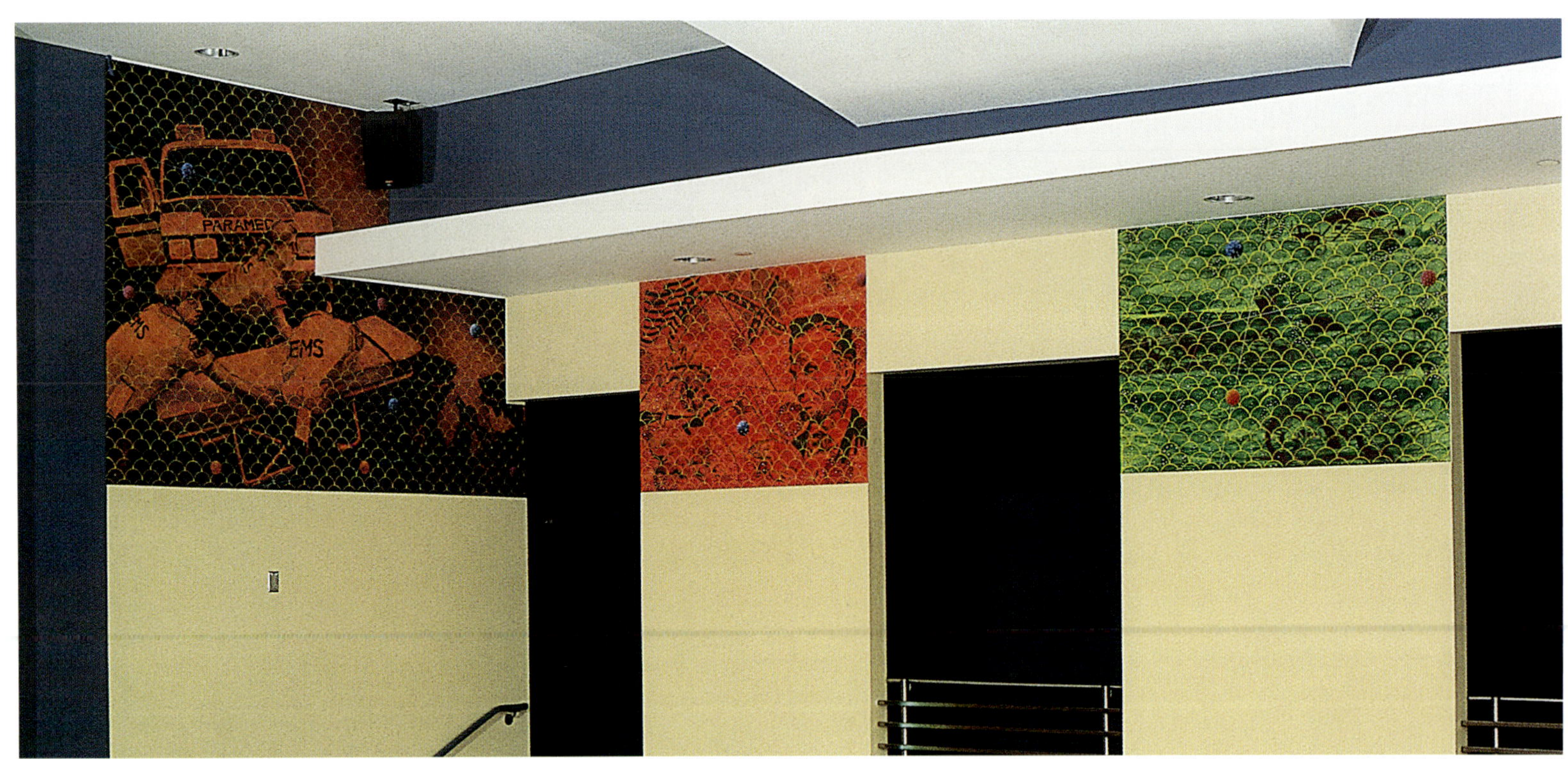

Seen Through the Layers of Time
2002
Painted mural

Public School 58, 72-50 Grand Avenue

ARCHITECT
Perkins Eastman
DESIGN AGENCY
School Construction Authority

SPONSOR AGENCY
Department of Education

Amy Cheng's painted murals bracket the auditorium stage at P.S. 58, also known as the "School of Heroes" in dedication to the neighborhood men and women who died serving the Fire and Police Departments and Emergency Medical Services on September 11, 2001. Mural panels depict scenes of rescues performed by these public servants and incorporate them into a narrative timeline of American history, with images of the Mayflower Pilgrims, the American Revolution, the Civil War, World War II, and the civil rights movement. Cheng has written of the work: "As the students grow up and learn American history they will begin to recognize the imagery and understand the references made in the panels."

Landmind
1995
Metal and glass

Long Island City High School,
14-30 Broadway

ARCHITECT
Gruzen Samton Steinglass
DESIGN AGENCY
School Construction Authority
SPONSOR AGENCY
Board of Education

For his project entitled *Landmind* at Long Island City High School, Mel Chin etched the altitudes of famous mountain ranges, such as the Andes and the Himalayas, into the risers of the stairs in the lobby's main stairway. These etchings are complemented by topographical illustrations of the altitudes set atop the railing's posts. The glass below the railing is etched with cultural symbols from the regions in which the ranges are located. A large chart at the foot of the stairs further explains the altitudes and provides a world map highlighting their locations. According to the artist, the artwork incorporates various graphic icons that link ideas about geographic, scientific, and cultural invention.

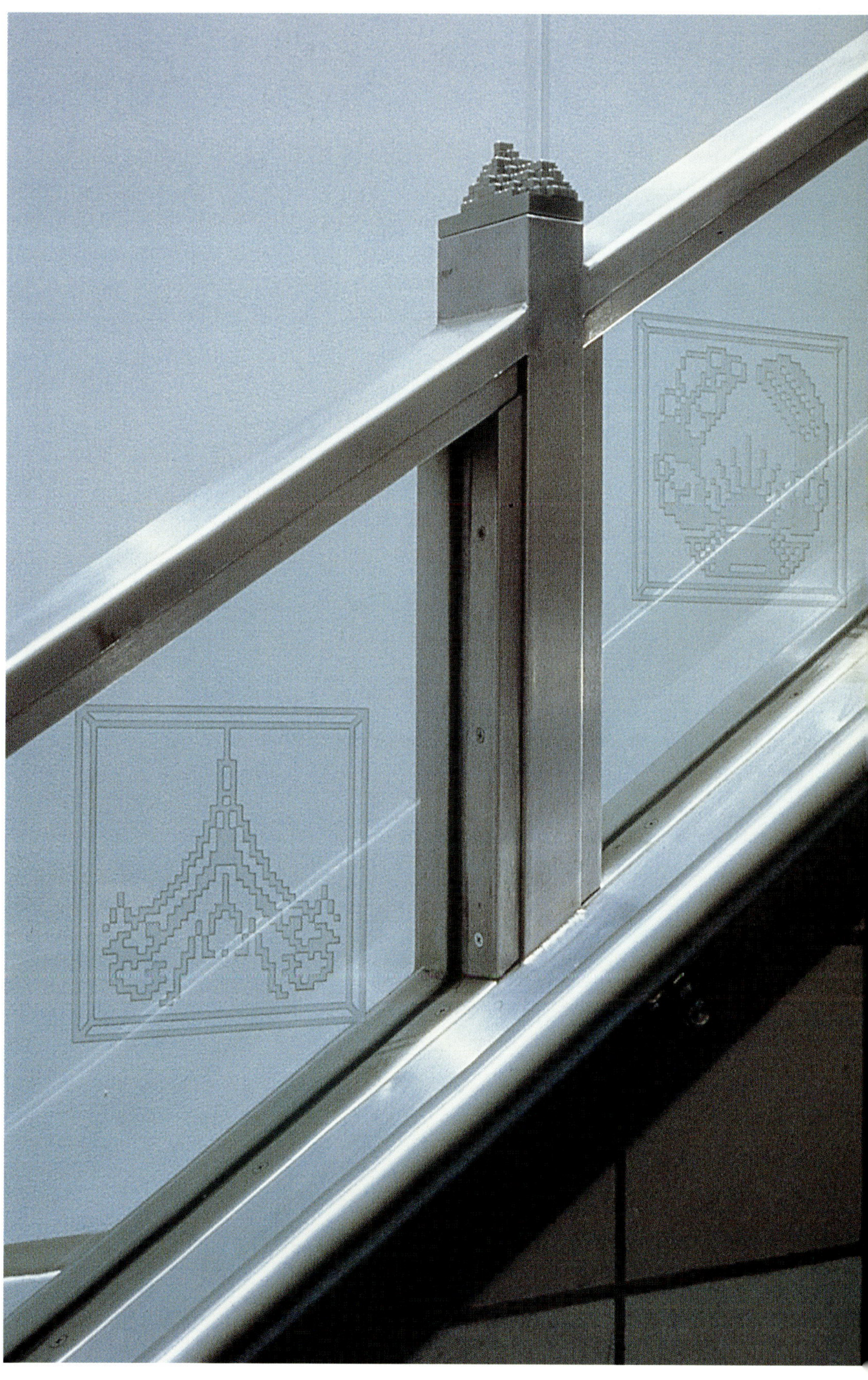

Mel Chin

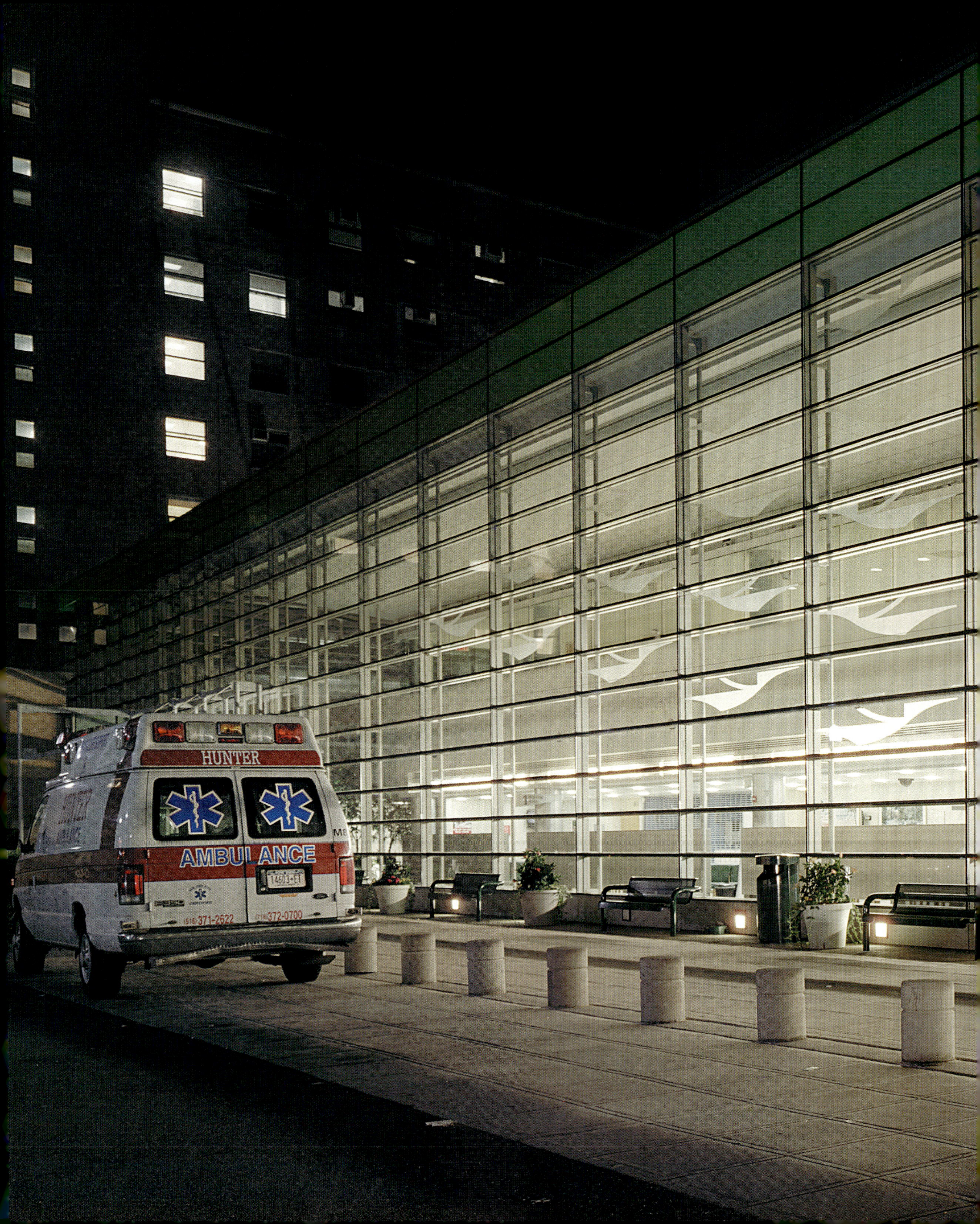
HUNTER
AMBULANCE
(516) 371-2622
(718) 372-0700

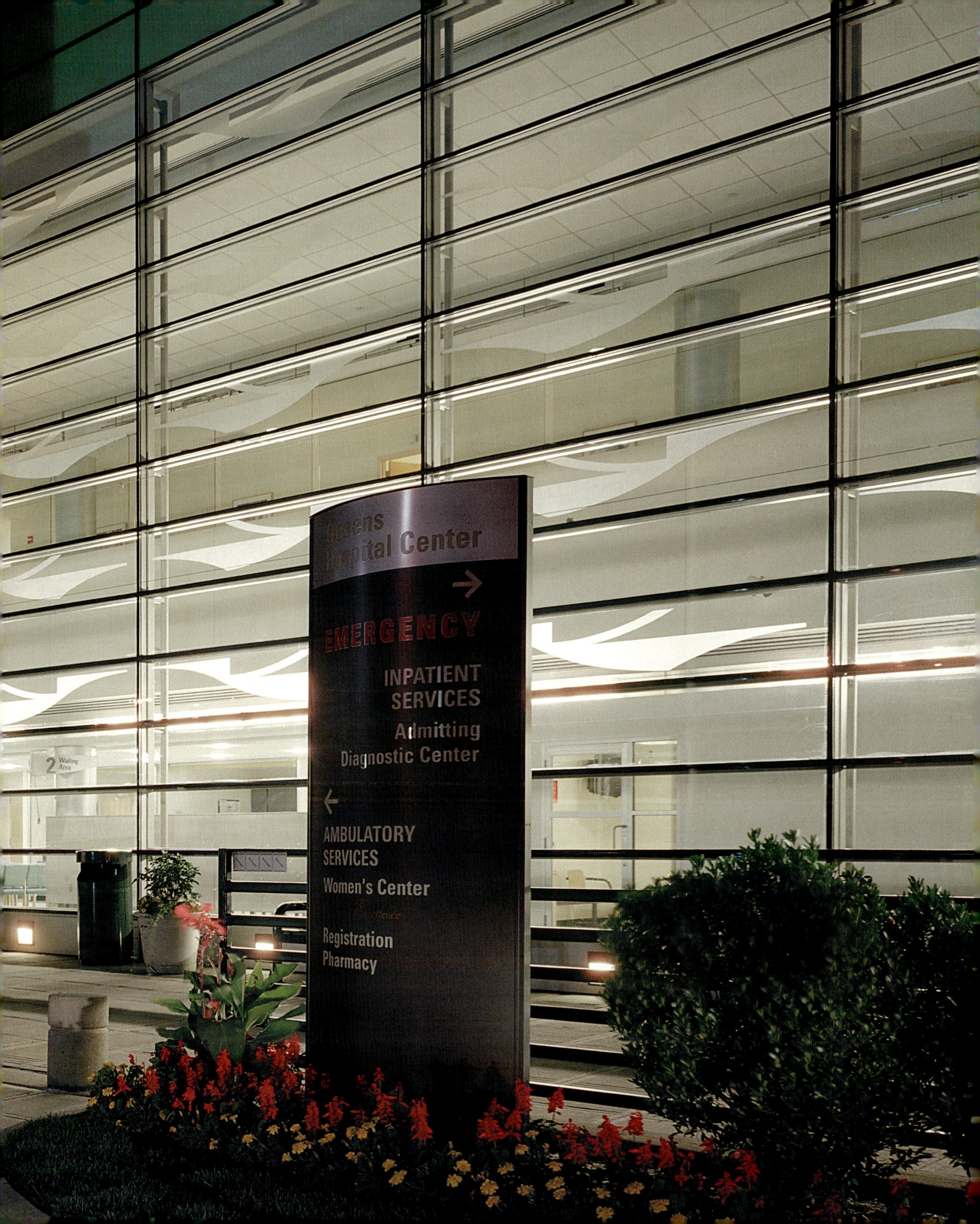
Queens
Hospital Center
EMERGENCY
INPATIENT
SERVICES
Admitting
Diagnostic Center
AMBULATORY
SERVICES
Women's Center
Registration
Pharmacy

Sung-Ho Choi

My America
1996
Ceramic tile
American Pie
1996
Silkscreen

Intermediate School 5,
50-40 Jacobus Street

ARCHITECT
Richard Dattner and Partners Architects
DESIGN AGENCY
School Construction Authority
SPONSOR AGENCY
Board of Education

Sung-Ho Choi's murals at I.S. 5 depict aspects of twentieth-century American history that have shaped the country's experience and identity. *My America* (below), located on the rear wall of the auditorium lobby, is a map of the United States comprised of sixty-five jigsaw-shaped tiles, each containing media images of major events, including Martin Luther King, Jr. marching in the streets and children visiting the Vietnam War Memorial in Washington, D.C. *American Pie* is a representation of the American flag silk-screened with images appropriated from community newspapers in many different languages.

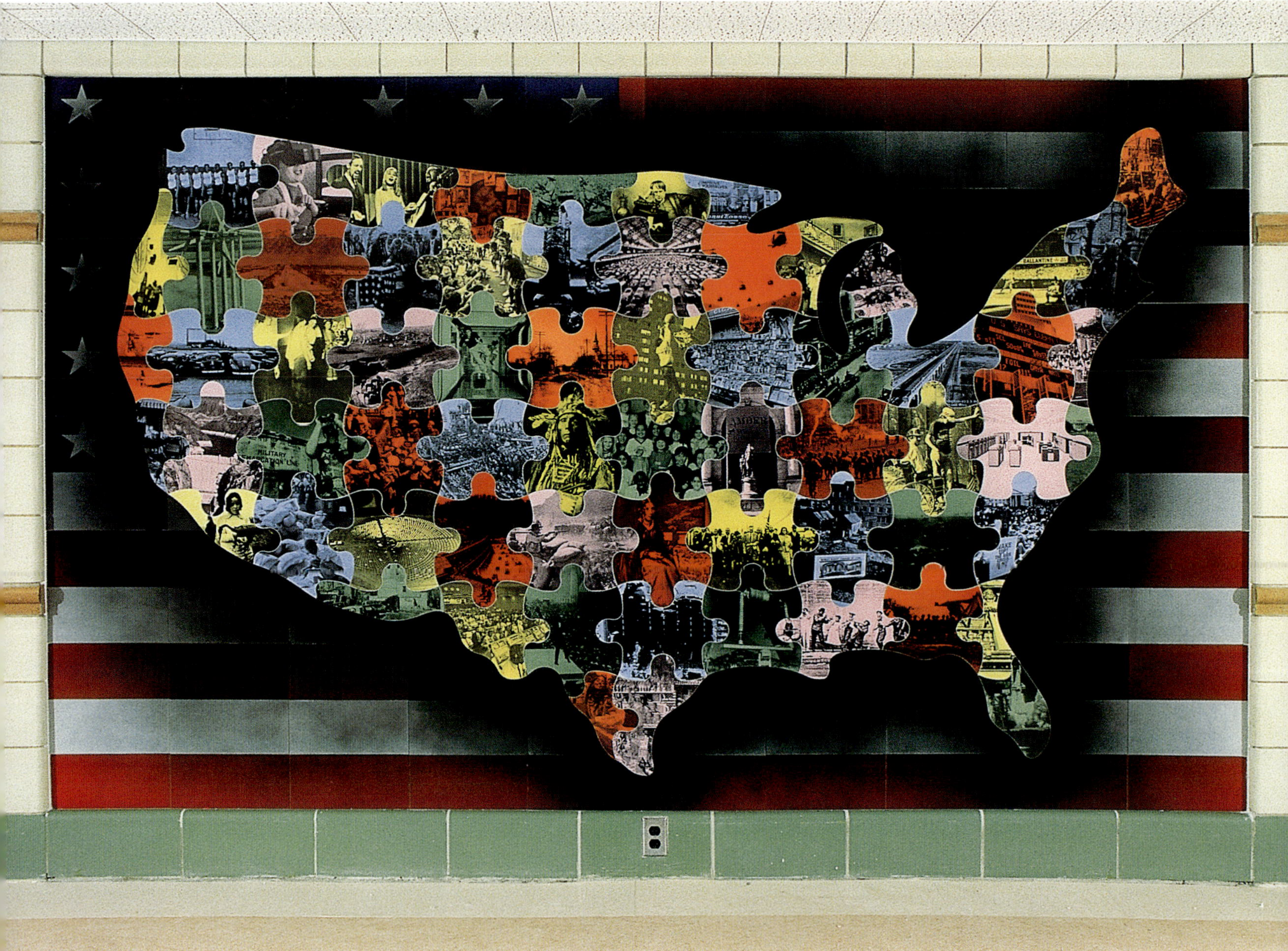

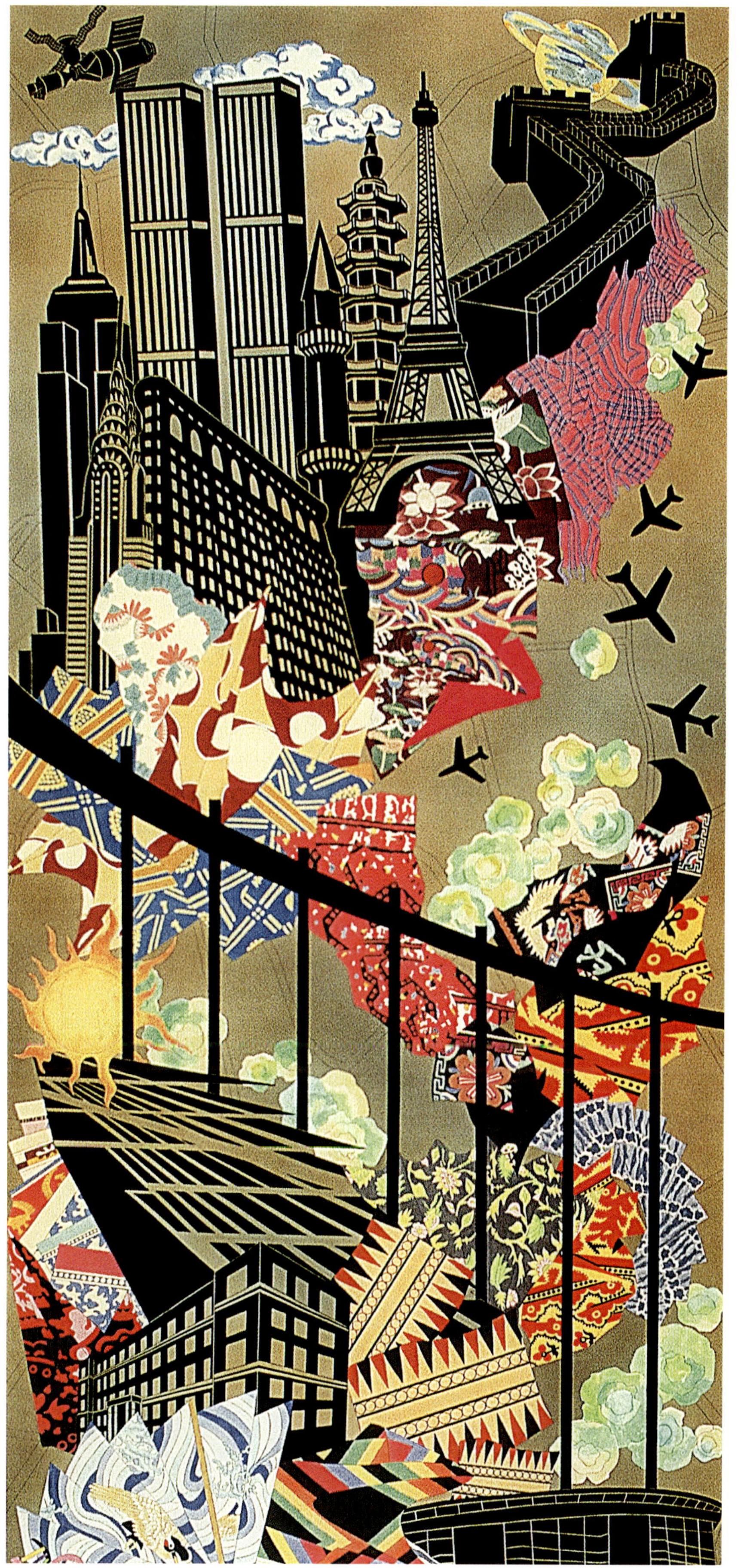

Mapping Queens
1997
Acrylic ink and oil on canvas

Intermediate School 125,
46-02 47th Avenue

ARCHITECT
A. Epstein and Sons
DESIGN AGENCY
School Construction Authority
SPONSOR AGENCY
Board of Education

Located at I.S. 125, Nancy Chunn's colorful two-paneled painted mural, entitled *Mapping Queens*, features familiar images associated with Queens. In one panel (left), the artist has symbolically connected Queens to the world through images of airplaines and international landmarks. Surrounding both panels, Chunn painted fabric patterns from different parts of world.

Nancy Chunn

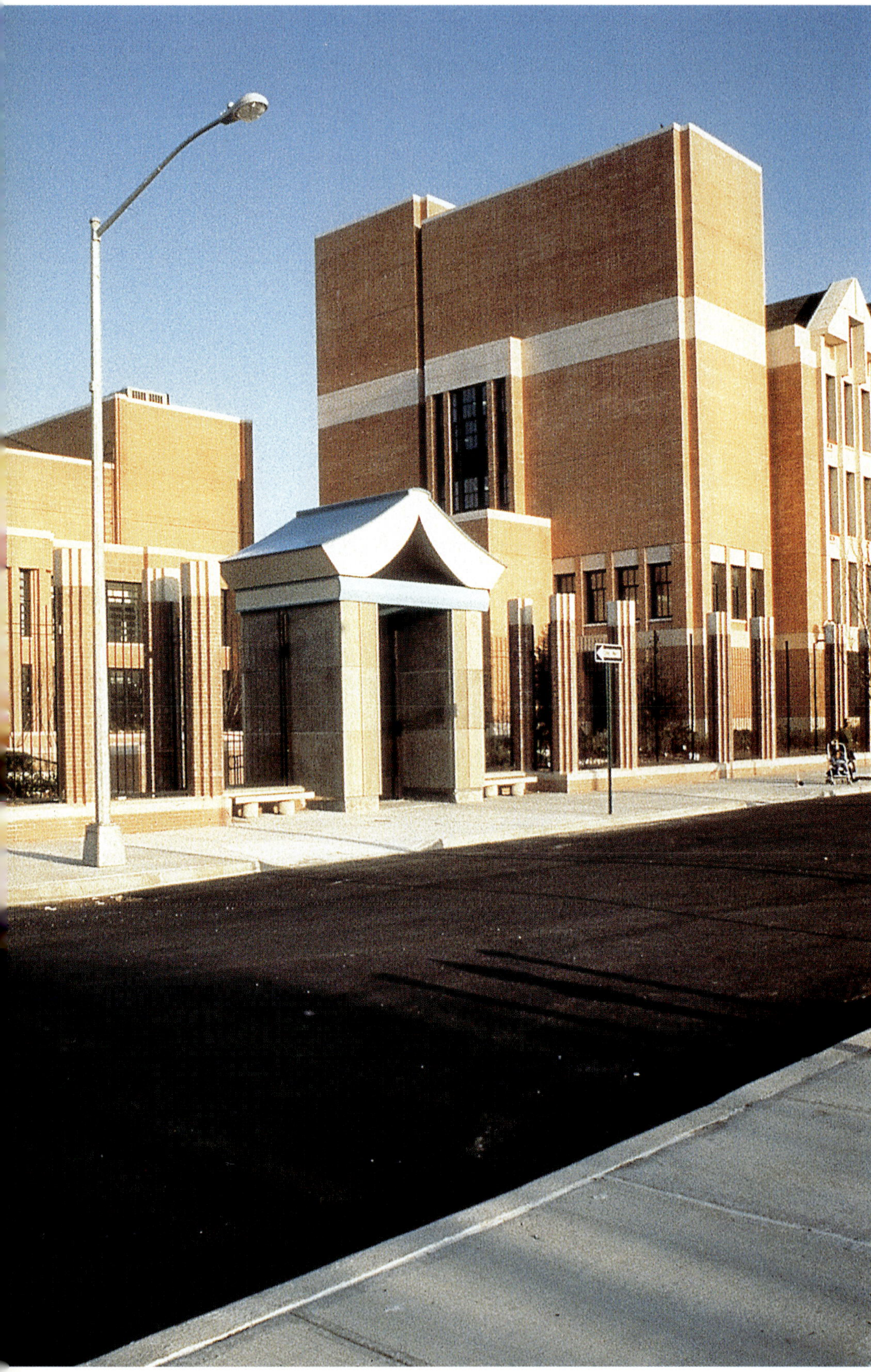

Gatehouse to Knowledge
1996
Fiberglass, concrete

Public School 43, 160 Beach 29th Street

ARCHITECT
Ehrenkrantz Eckstut and Kuhn
DESIGN AGENCY
School Construction Authority
SPONSOR AGENCY
Board of Education

Willie Cole created an entrance for P.S. 43 that integrates elements of architecture with one of the most iconic symbols of school and knowledge: the book. In *Gatehouse to Knowledge*, fabricated from fiberglass and concrete, book spines serve as pillars that support a large open book, which forms the arch of the gatehouse. Cole has said of his artwork: "To a small child this sculpture is a gateway to fantasies, dreams, adventures, and new ideas . . . just like the school itself."

Willie Cole

Noel Copeland

Myth Animals
2000
Ceramics

Public School 212, 34-25 82nd Street

ARCHITECT
Anderson LaRocca Anderson
DESIGN AGENCY
School Construction Authority
SPONSOR AGENCY
Board of Education

For his work in the corridor walls at P.S. 212, Noel Copeland created large ceramic-tile murals, collectively entitled *Myth Animals*, which he designed to resemble the building façades in the surrounding Jackson Heights neighborhood. At the center of each mural, Copeland incorporated colorful images of animal forms. The artist completed ten different designs for a total of forty tiles spread throughout the building's five floors.

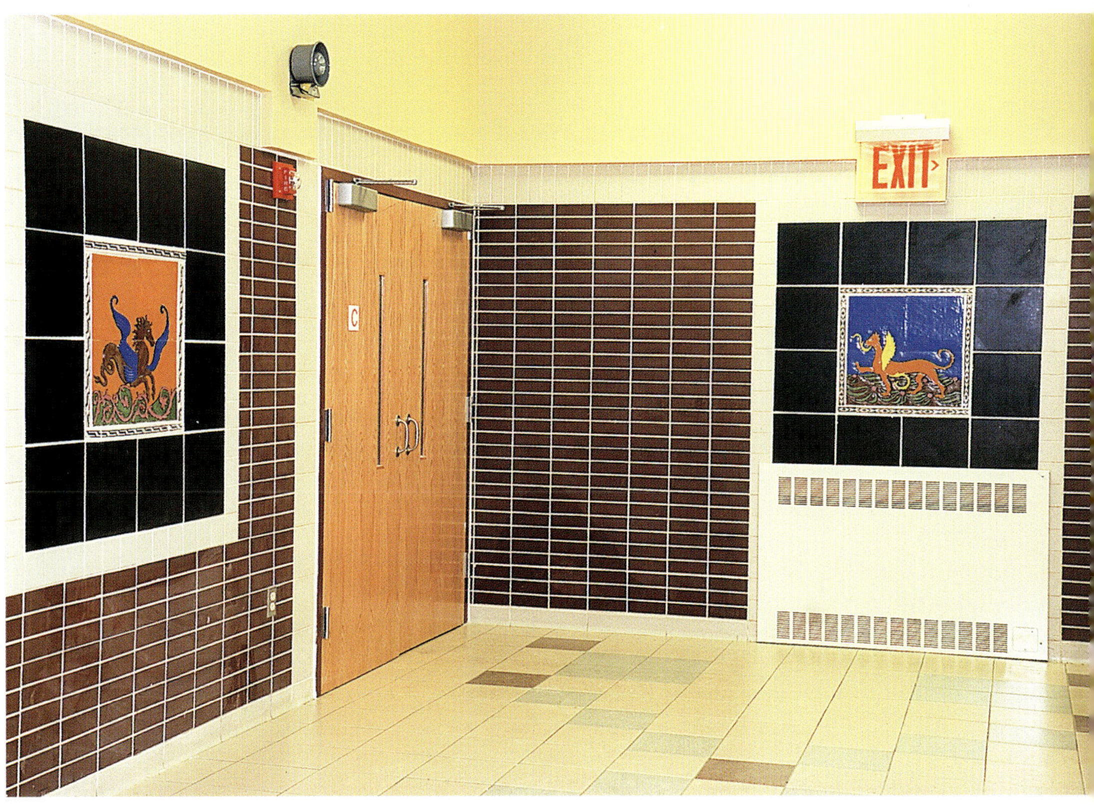

Sheila Levrant de Bretteville

Search: Literature (following pages)
1998
Etched granite

Flushing Regional Branch Library,
41-17 Main Street

ARCHITECT
Polshek Partnership Architects
DESIGN AGENCY
Department of Design and Construction
SPONSOR AGENCY
Queens Borough Public Library

For her project, entitled *Search: Literature*, at the Flushing Regional Branch Library, Sheila Levrant de Bretteville researched tales of literal and symbolic journeys from around the world, and sandblasted a selection of titles in their original languages and in English on the granite steps leading up to the library's entrance. The artist selected the traditional tales and familiar titles from countries represented in Flushing's diverse immigrant community. De Bretteville has said of the work: "I wanted a metaphor that would combine the aspect of searching for something at the library with the Flushing area, which has historically been a place where immigrants come in search of freedom and a better life."

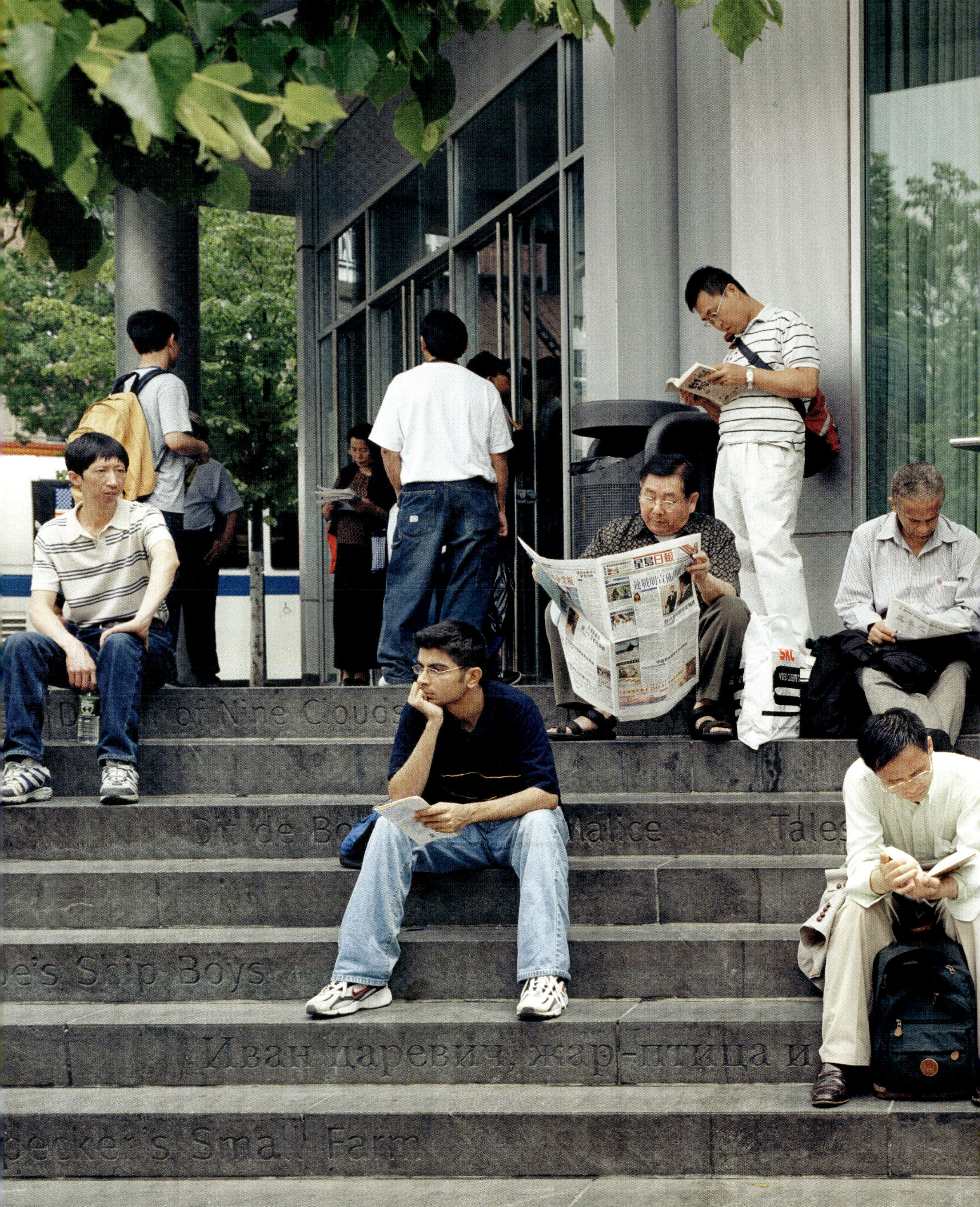
of Nine Clouds
Dit de
Malice
Tales
Ship Boys
Иван царевич, жар-птица и
Small Farm
星島日報

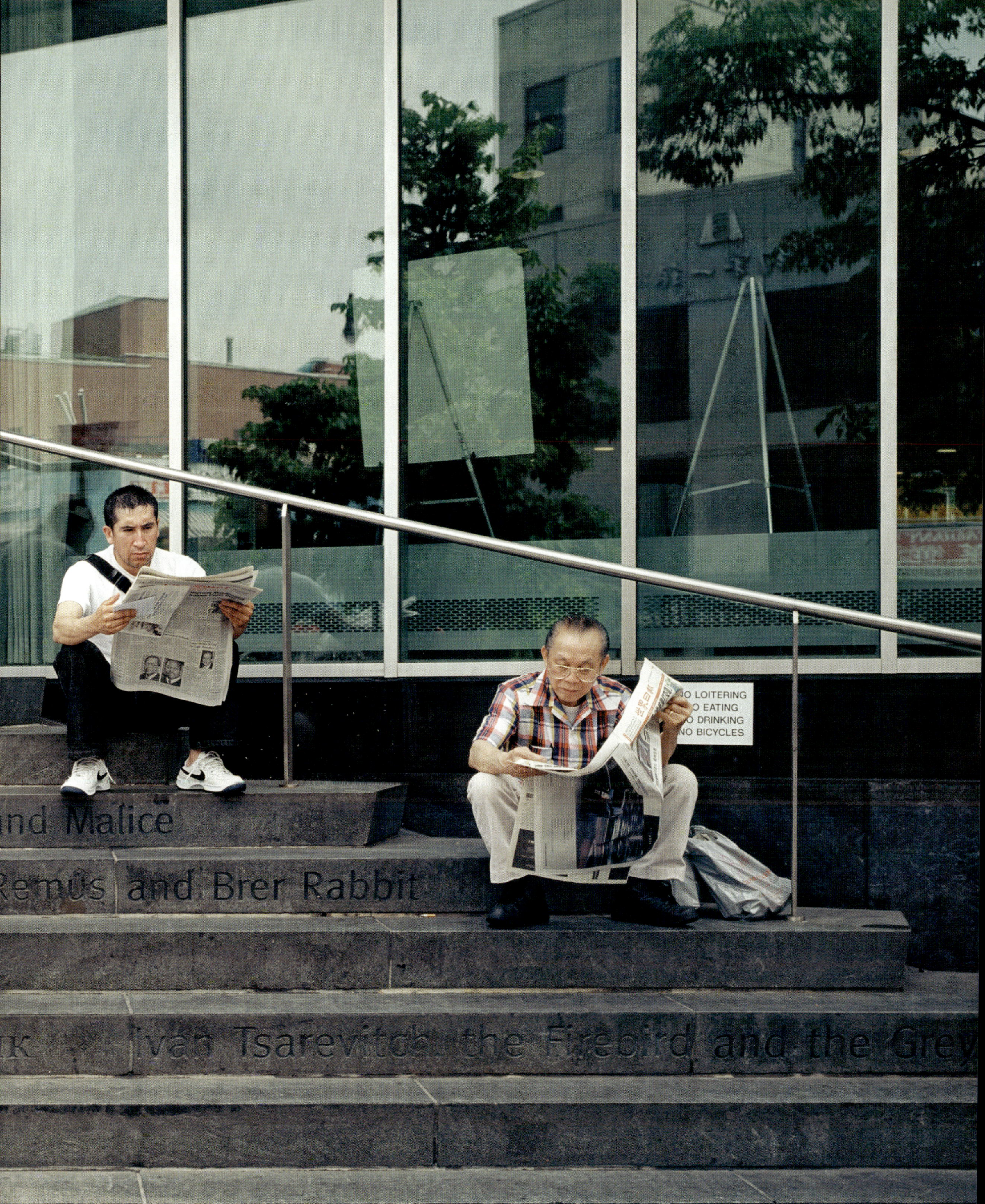

O LOITERING
O EATING
O DRINKING
NO BICYCLES
nd Malice
Remus and Brer Rabbit
Ivan Tsarevitch the Firebird and the Grey

Animal Count
1995
Ceramics

Public School 51, 87-45 117th Street

ARCHITECT/DESIGN AGENCY
School Construction Authority
SPONSOR AGENCY
Board of Education

Animal Count, Claudia DeMonte's 30 foot (9.1 m) long ceramic-tile mural in the lobby entrance of P.S. 51, draws from the lush color and dense imagery of children's art. Animals, the alphabet, and numbers are incorporated into her design, as well as references to the Richmond Hill neighborhood's history.

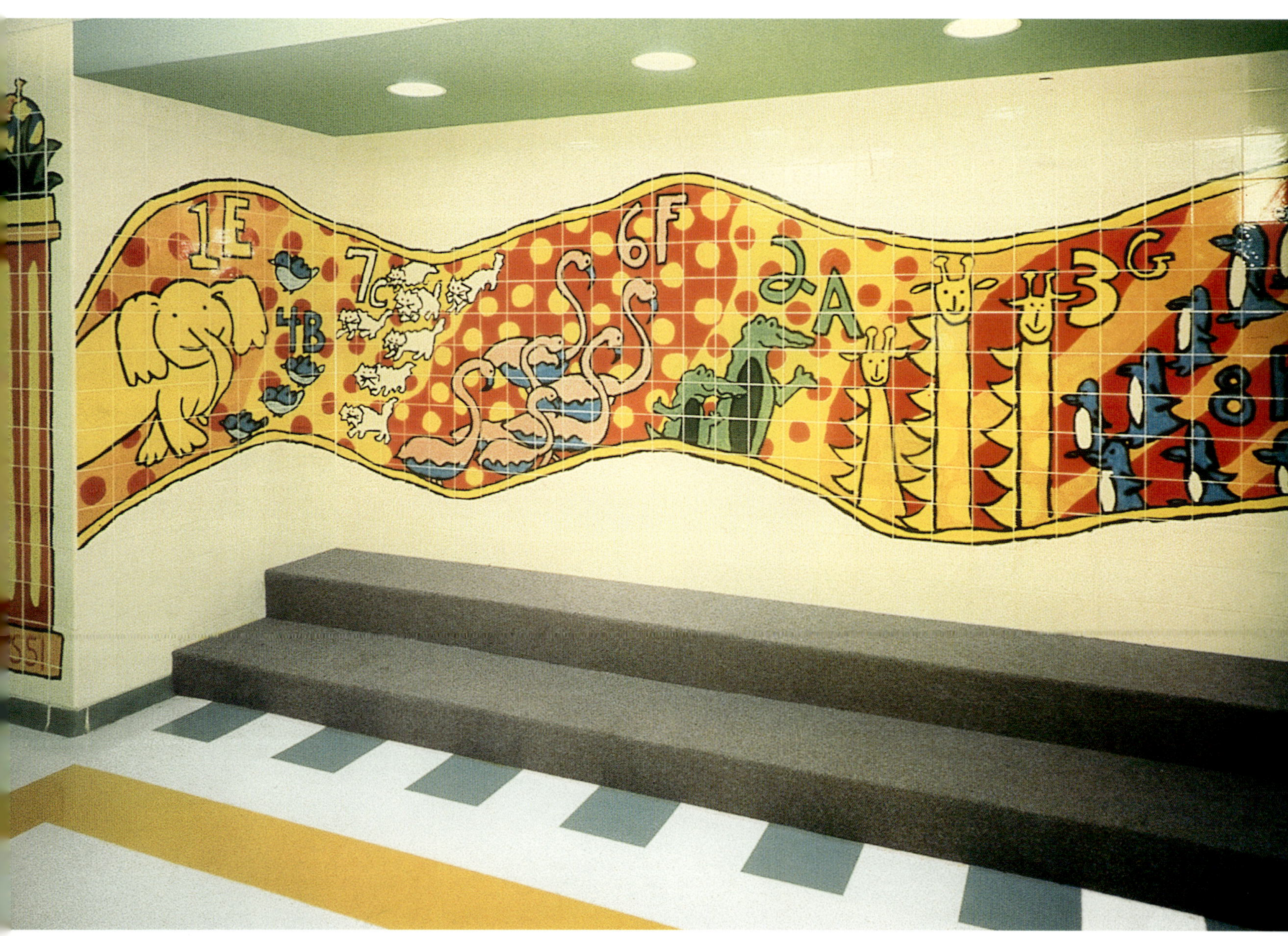

Claudia DeMonte

Donna Dennis

Daedalus Bedazzled
1996
Steel

Intermediate School 5,
50-40 Jacobus Street

ARCHITECT
Richard Dattner and Partners Architects
DESIGN AGENCY
School Construction Authority
SPONSOR AGENCY
Board of Education

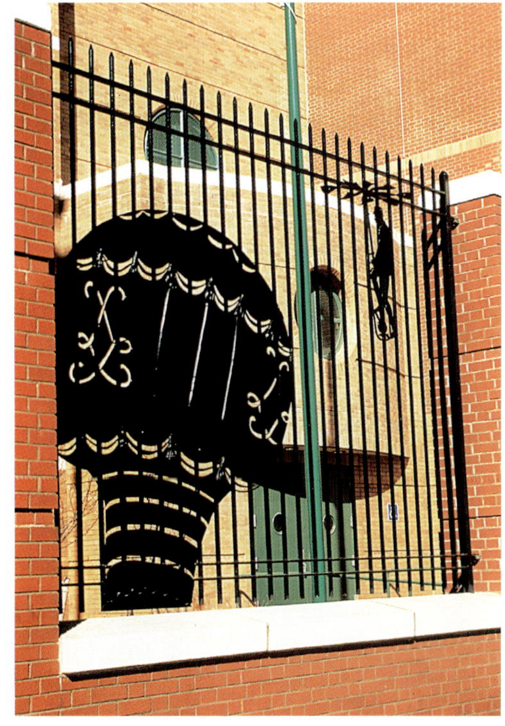

Donna Dennis's design for the fence surrounding I.S. 5 explores the topic of early experiments in flight as testament to the human imagination. On the Jacobus Street entrance, the artist designed panels and a gate depicting three such experiments. In one, Daedalus's son Icarus from the Greek myth, clad in feathers, is portrayed in mid-flight over the gate. For the 51st Street fencing, quotations from early aviators Antoine de Saint-Exupéry and Beryl Markham are displayed to remind passers-by of the wonder of a bird's-eye view of the world.

Julie Dermansky

Ocean Fence and **Ocean Floor**
2000
Steel, linoleum

Beach Channel Drive Day Care Center,
44-22 Beach Channel Drive

ARCHITECT
The Edelman Partnership/Architects
DESIGN AGENCY
Department of Design and Construction
SPONSOR AGENCY
Agency for Child Development

For *Ocean Fence* and *Ocean Floor,* located at the Beach Channel Drive Day Care Center, Julie Dermansky drew inspiration from the familiar landscape of the surrounding beach community. For *Ocean Fence* (right), the artist welded into the fence steel cut-outs of 144 different sea creatures, and added individually cut lengths of wave shapes along the top, giving the artwork a sense of movement. The artist transformed the linoleum floor inside the center to create *Ocean Floor*, employing an ocean motif with images of waves and sea life.

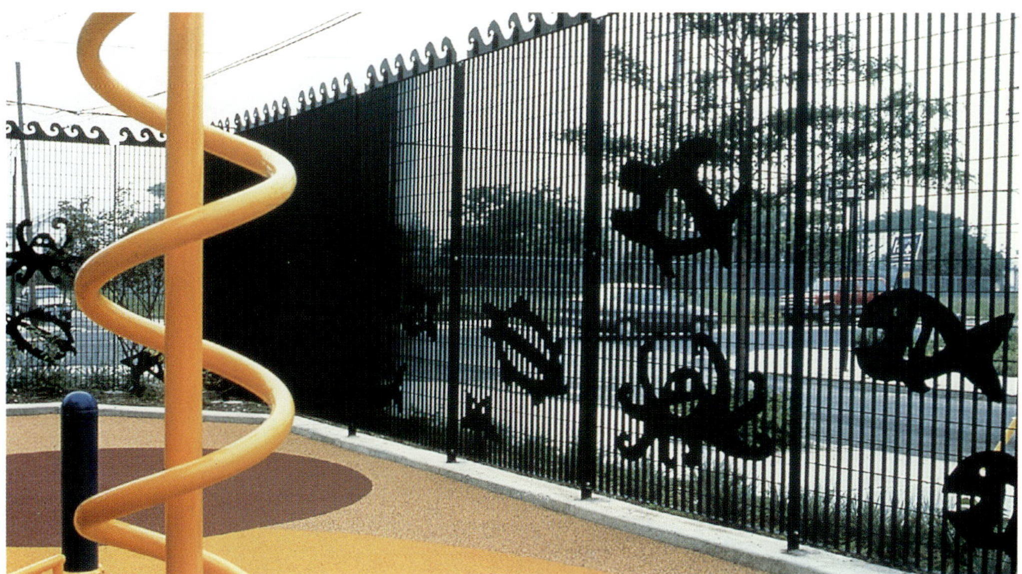

Chris Doyle

Field Trips
2003
Hand-painted ceramic tiles

High School of Teaching, Liberal Arts and Sciences,
74-20 Commonwealth Boulevard

ARCHITECT
SBLM Architects
DESIGN AGENCY
School Construction Authority
SPONSOR AGENCY
Department of Education

For *Field Trips*, Chris Doyle translated his travels around the borough of Queens on to the walls of a Queens high school. Two hundred and fifty tiles were hand-painted with familiar scenes of the borough, rendering a walk through the hallways a symbolic walk through Queens. Featured on the tiles are architectural achievements such as the TWA terminal at John F. Kennedy International Airport and the New York Hall of Science, as well as typical Queens houses and other buildings and sites. The tiles are spread throughout the building, so that students, teachers, and visitors come across new pieces of *Field Trips* gradually over their time at the school. The tiles are also displayed in a mural sited outside the school's cafeteria.

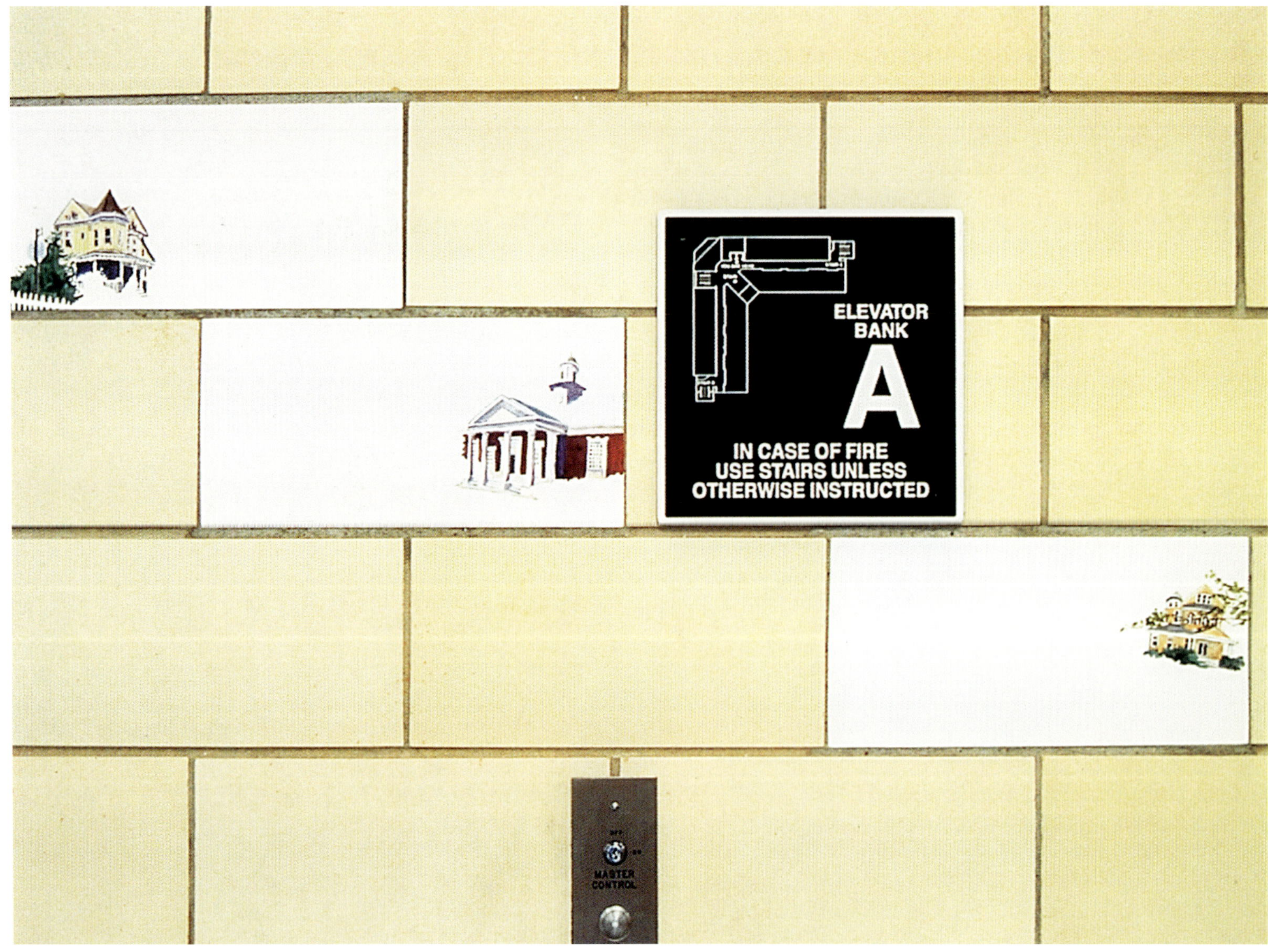

Leaf Gate, **Keys in Flight**, **Seed of Elm**, **The Spirit of the Elm**, and **Elm in Bloom Sprouting Buds**
1995
Bronze

Public School 7, 80-55 Cornish Avenue

ARCHITECT
Ehrenkrantz Eckstut and Kuhn
DESIGN AGENCY
School Construction Authority
SPONSOR AGENCY
Board of Education

Ming Fay's giant bronze sculptures of plant life are scattered over seven locations at P.S. 7. Juxtaposed with the real foliage surrounding the school, the 20 foot (6 m) high leaves and 14 foot (4.3 m) seed pods are meant to provide new perspectives on the beauty and wonder of natural forms, giving students, teachers, and visitors to the school a new appreciation of the ordinary.

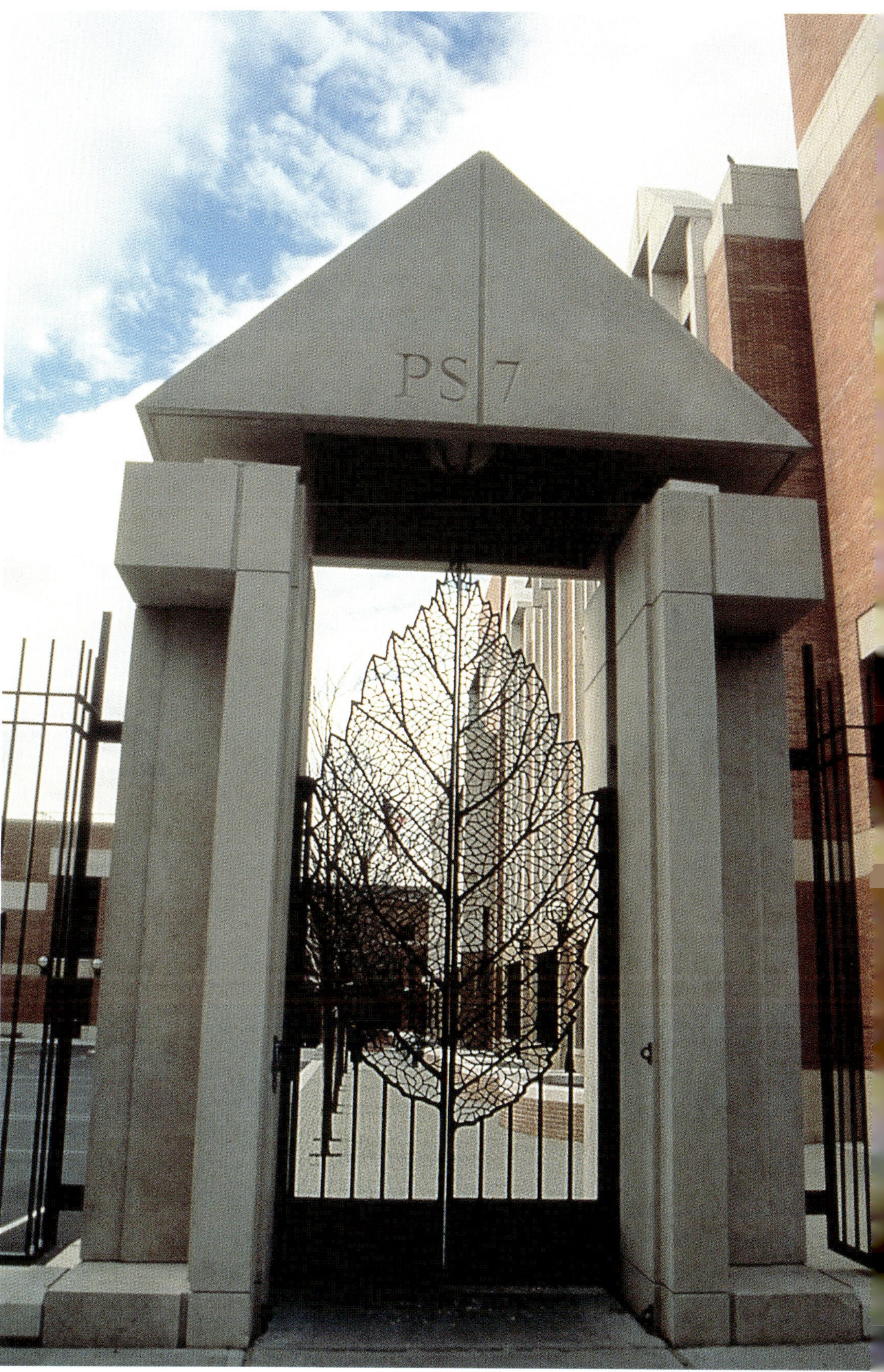

Ming Fay

Flushing Bay Promenade
2001
Brick, granite

Flushing Bay Promenade, Flushing Meadows Corona Park

ARCHITECT
Miceli Kulik Williams & Associates
SPONSOR AGENCY
Department of Parks and Recreation

Jackie Ferrara's pavement design for the Flushing Bay Promenade complements two existing structures in the same location, designed by architect Felix Candela for New York's 1964–65 World's Fair. Using black, red, and buff-colored brick, Ferrara's design links the floors beneath Candela's canopies to the long linear path that connects them. Red granite benches, rectangular along the path and crescent-shaped under the canopies, accent the area. The two circular floor spaces beneath the arches of Candela's structures, combined with the curved and rectangular benches, offset the geometric patterns of the brick paving. The installation pays homage to the World's Fair while reflecting the topography, function, and history of the park.

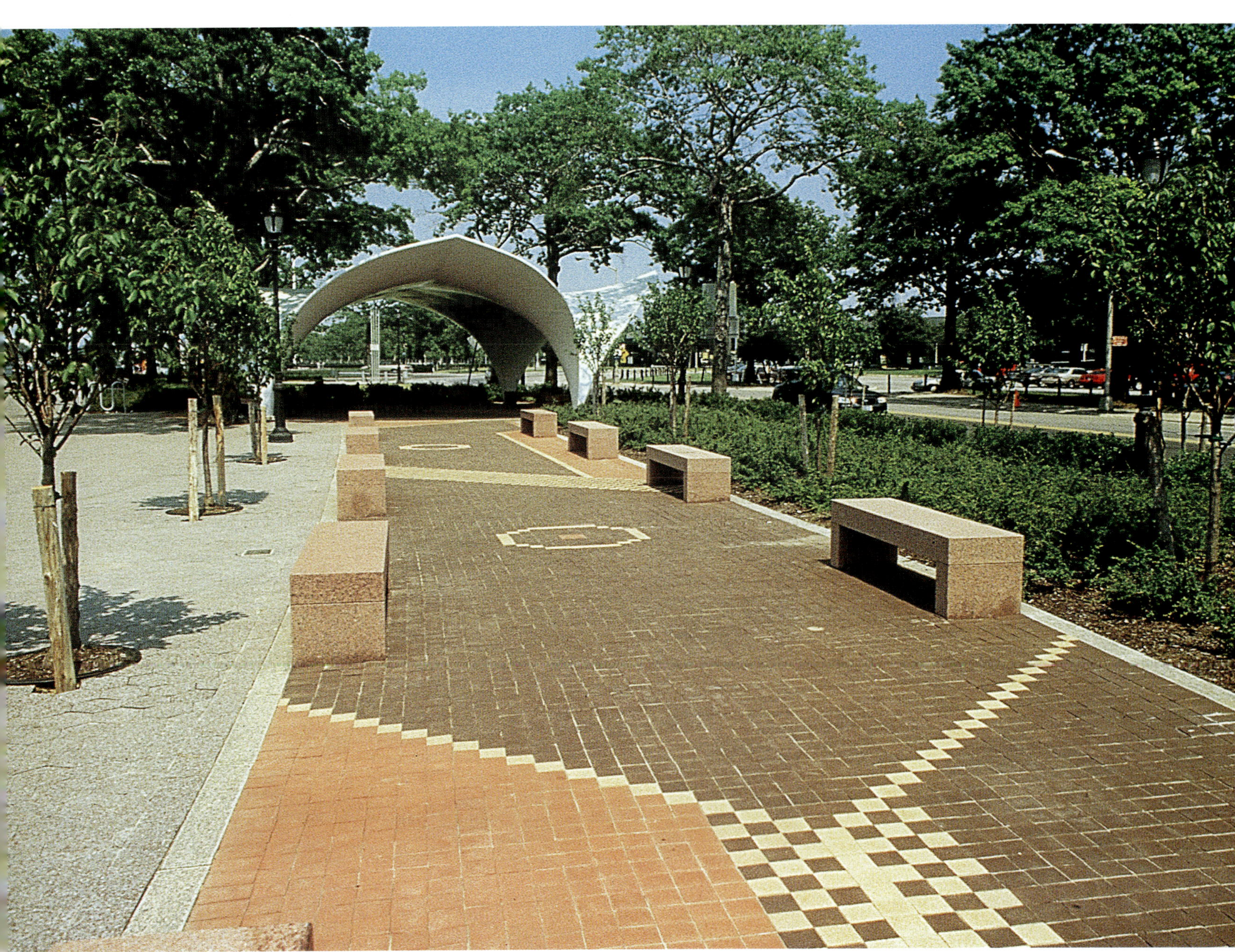

Jackie Ferrara

Phillip Galgiani

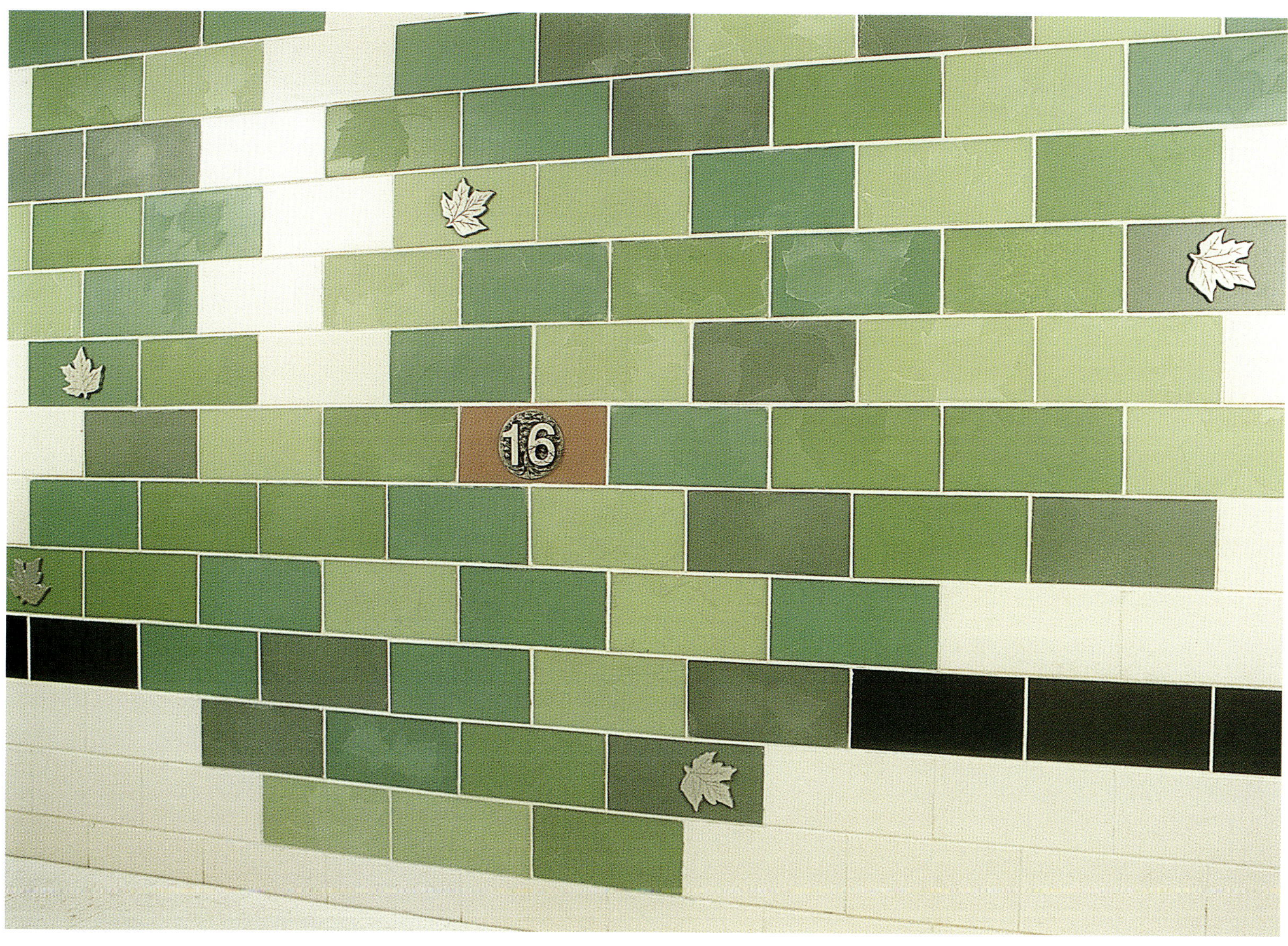

Four Seasons
2001
Sandblasted glazed cement blocks, cast aluminum

Public School 16, 41-15 104th Street

ARCHITECT
Montoya-Rodriguez, P.C.
DESIGN AGENCY
School Construction Authority
SPONSOR AGENCY
Board of Education

Located at P.S. 16, Phillip Galgiani's wall installation, *Four Seasons,* is comprised of thirteen clusters of glazed tile blocks placed throughout the building's hallways. Circular medallions featuring the school's emblem—the number sixteen within the boughs of a tree—link one tile group to the next. The changing color palette of glazes and the embedded sand-cast aluminum leaves in each installation reflect the changes in trees during the cycle of the seasons.

Cadence Giersbach

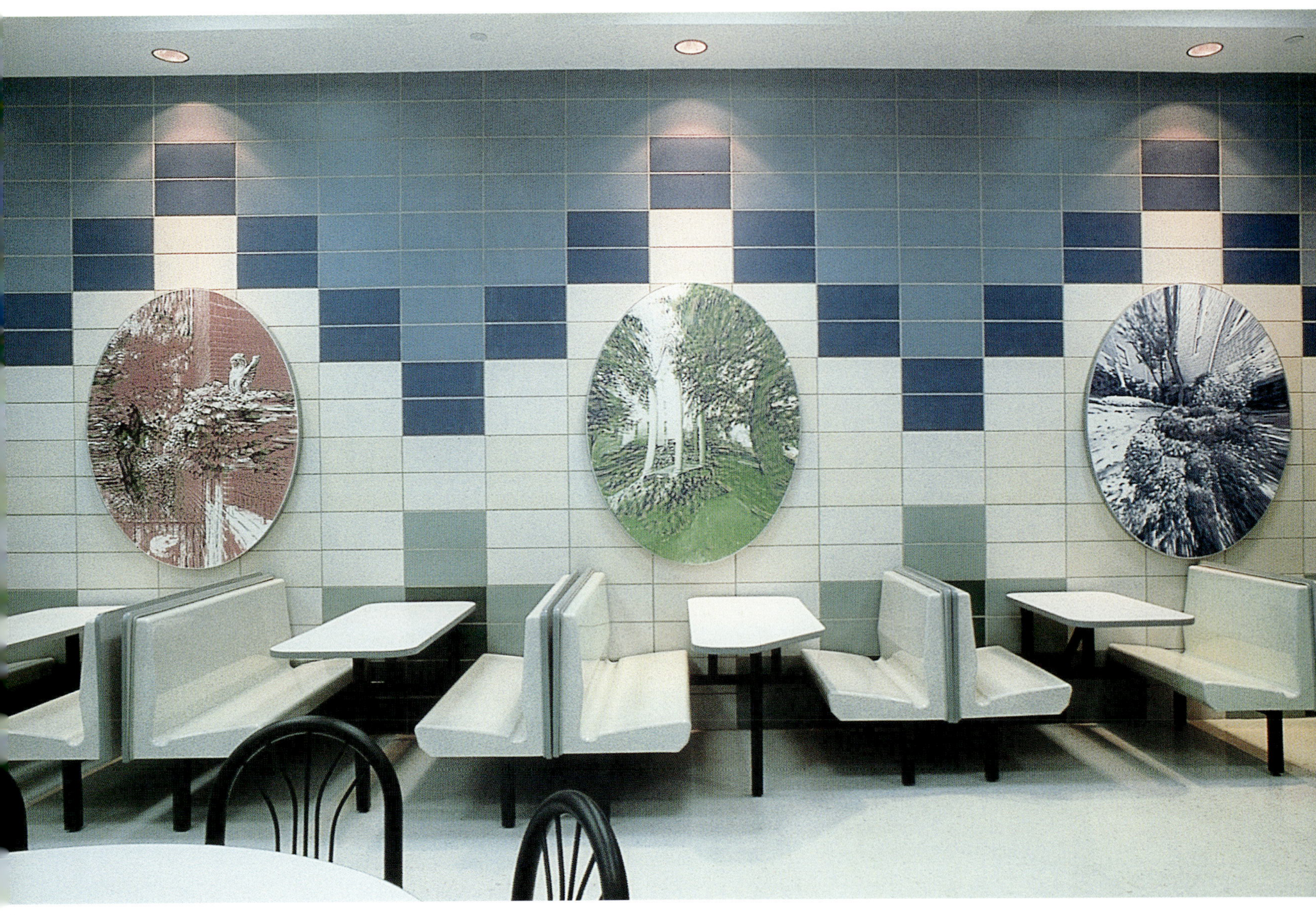

Garden in a School: Impressions of Jackson Heights
2000
Photographic mezzotint, line art silk-screened on to porcelain enamel, aluminum, glazed brick

Intermediate School 230,
73-10 34th Avenue

ARCHITECT
Boswick Purcell Architects
DESIGN AGENCY
School Construction Authority
SPONSOR AGENCY
Board of Education

Cadence Giersbach's wall installation in the windowless cafeteria at I.S. 230 offers students a colorful glimpse into the natural world. Fourteen porcelain-enamel medallions depicting the neighborhood's private gardens encircle the cafeteria. The surrounding glazed brick, in shades of blue and green, creates a decorative framework for the artwork.

Medb's Crown
1987
Aluminum, paint

North Hills Branch Library,
57-04 Marathon Parkway

ARCHITECT
Abraham Geller and Associates
DESIGN AGENCY
Department of General Services
SPONSOR AGENCY
New York Public Library

Named after the mythological Celtic queen Medb, Ann Gillen's sculptural relief forms a crown over the circular information booth in the center of the North Hills Branch Library. Forty-four feet (13.4 m) in circumference, the relief is composed of anodized yellow aluminum shapes riveted on to a deep-blue background, complementing the library's color scheme.

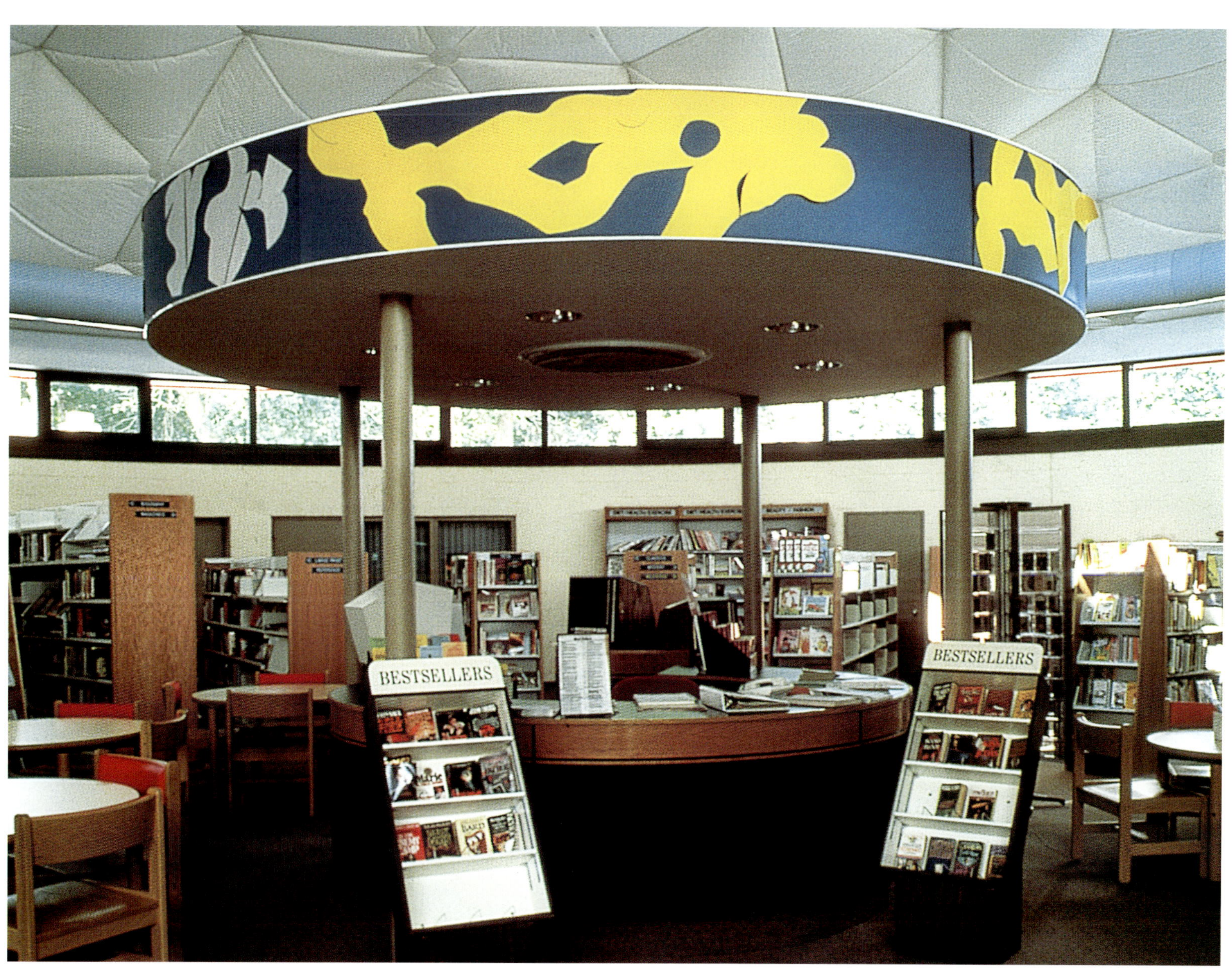

Ann Gillen

Elizabeth Grajales

Who Else Shares Our World?
1992
Ceramics

Public School 92, 99-01 34th Avenue

ARCHITECT
Perkins & Will
DESIGN AGENCY
School Construction Authority
SPONSOR AGENCY
Board of Education

Elizabeth Grajales's work, entitled *Who Else Shares Our World?*, features an installation of more than two hundred ceramic relief tiles depicting various kinds of animal life. Located on columns in the school's corridors and above classroom entrances on each of the building's four floors, the tiles feature many endangered species, such as the African elephant, the black rhino, the manatee, the lemur, and the American bald eagle, as well as animals familiar to City children, such as pigeons and crows.

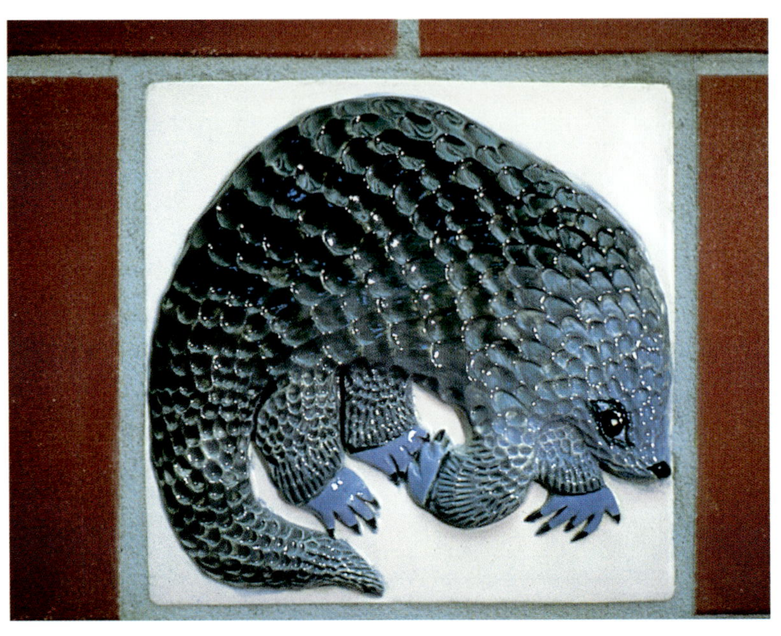

Elizabeth Grajales

What a Wonderful World
1995
Ceramics, concrete

Public School 14, 107-01 Otis Avenue

ARCHITECT
Gran Sultan Associates
DESIGN AGENCY
School Construction Authority
SPONSOR AGENCY
Board of Education

What a Wonderful World, installed throughout the corridors at P.S. 14, includes large-scale ceramic relief tiles that depict images from different continents: a hummingbird (right), a Mayan musician with a rainforest jaguar, kangaroos in the Australian outback, the Arizona desert, a city of high-rise buildings, and an Antarctic seal. Elizabeth Grajales also created exterior wall tiles with images of different species of birds, and a limestone bench at the entrance to the building. In the floor surrounding the bench, Grajales carved individual bricks with symbols of everyday images such as umbrellas, musical instruments, children, helicopters, and dogs.

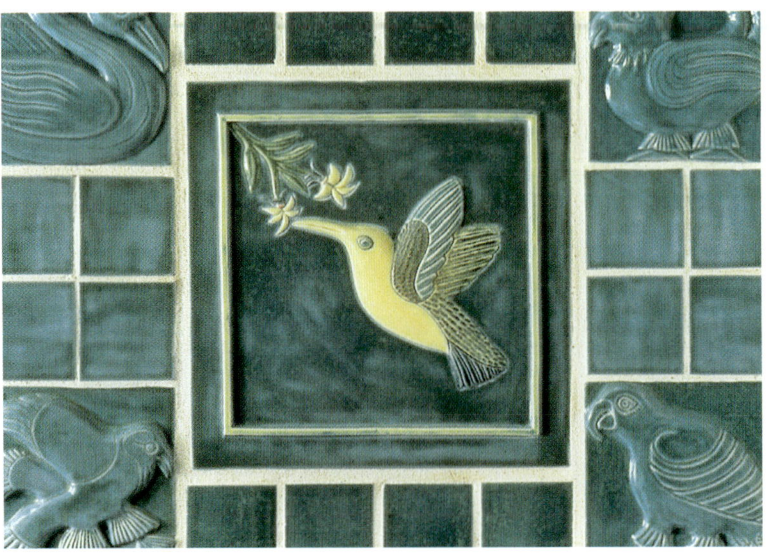

Traveling Books and Secret Pages
1999
Painted oak

Langston Hughes Community Library and Cultural Center, 100-01 Northern Boulevard

ARCHITECT
Garrison McNeil & Associates/ Davis Brody Bond
DESIGN AGENCY
Department of Design and Construction
SPONSOR AGENCY
Queens Borough Public Library

Ousmane Gueye's tribute to the poet Langston Hughes, entitled *Traveling Books and Secret Pages*, features two large sculptures made of oak that has been carved and painted with images of faces and the pages of books. Located at the Langston Hughes Community Library in Queens, the sculptures were inspired by a quotation from Hughes: "Knowledge is the key to life. We all contain it. As individuals with individual minds and universal experiences, the information we can provide one another with is endless."

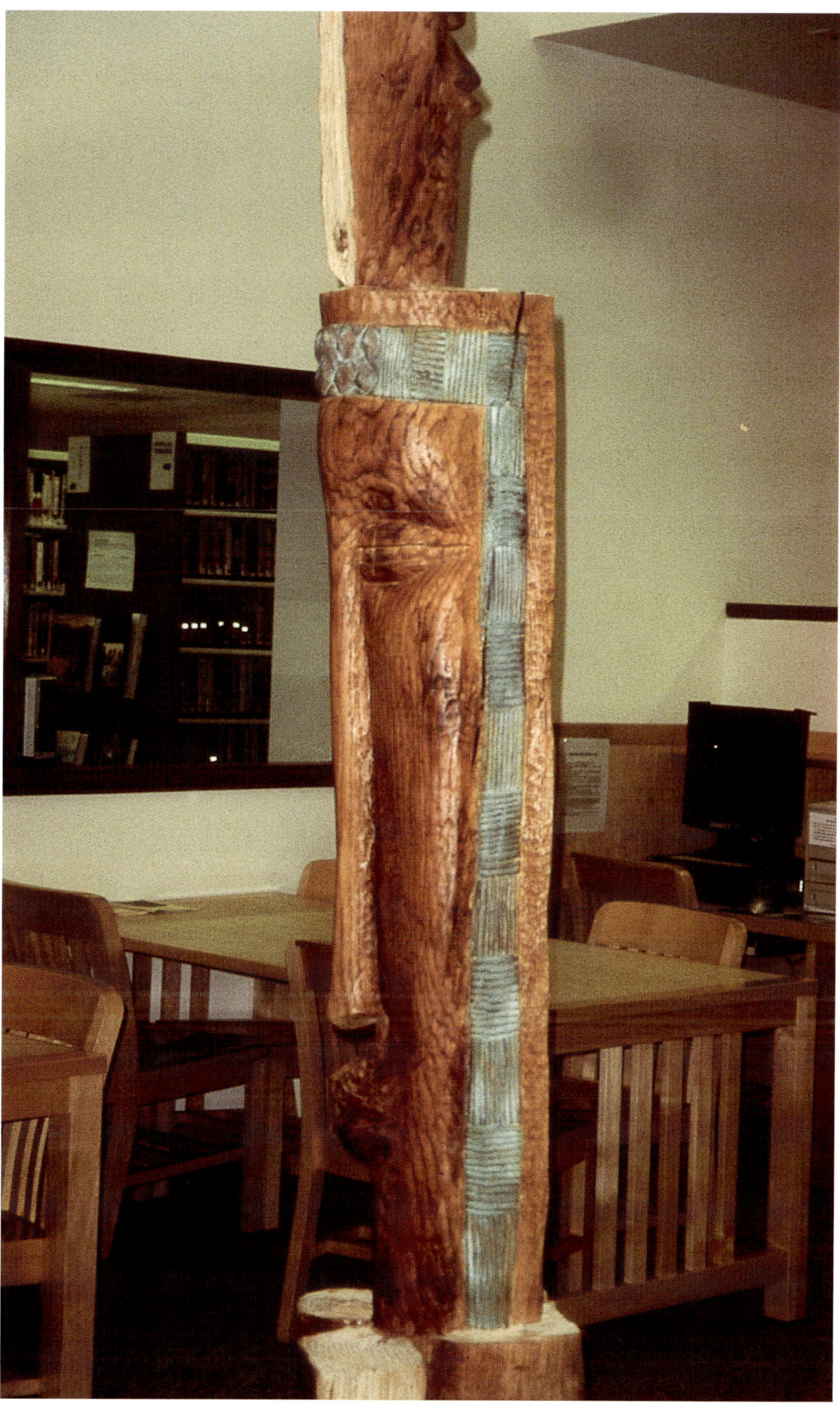

Ousmane Gueye

Terullian Mantle
1995
Tile floor, textiles (flags), sculpted terra-cotta, display case with steel frame and glass

Public School 89, 85-28 Britton Avenue

ARCHITECT
William Tabler
DESIGN AGENCY
School Construction Authority
SPONSOR AGENCY
Board of Education

Mags Harries's and Lajos Heder's project for P.S. 89 celebrates International Day, the school's annual multicultural festival. The artists created a ceremonial cloak sewn from international flags in a wagon-wheel pattern derived from early American quilts. The garment, worn by the school's principal during the International Day Parade, is displayed throughout the year in the lobby behind glass surrounded by a terra-cotta relief. The annual removal of the cloak reveals the painted image of a turtle, one of the Earth's oldest living creatures. Turtle myths and stories have been collected from different cultures and are now part of the school curriculum.

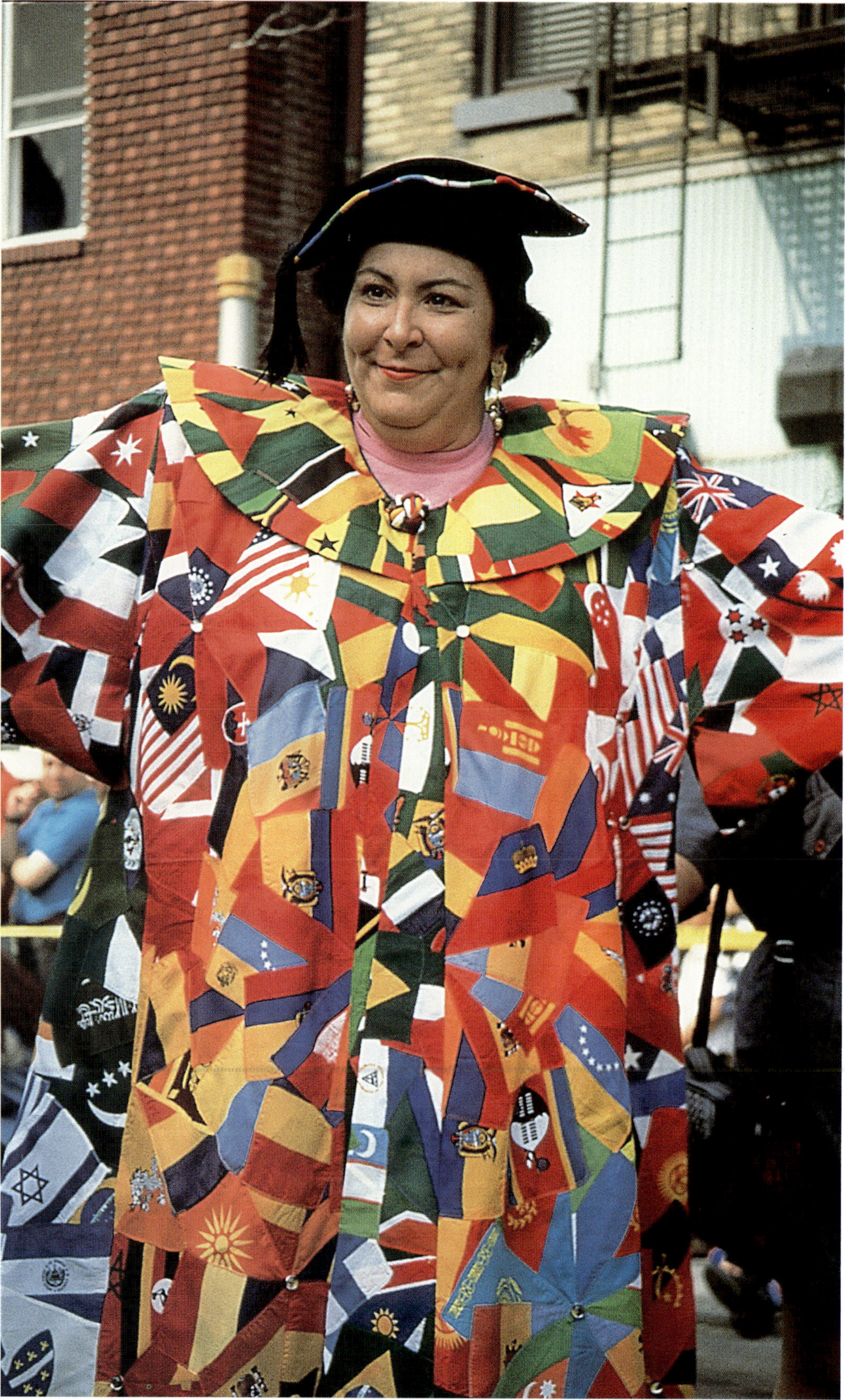

Mags Harries with Lajos Heder

Skowmon Hastanan

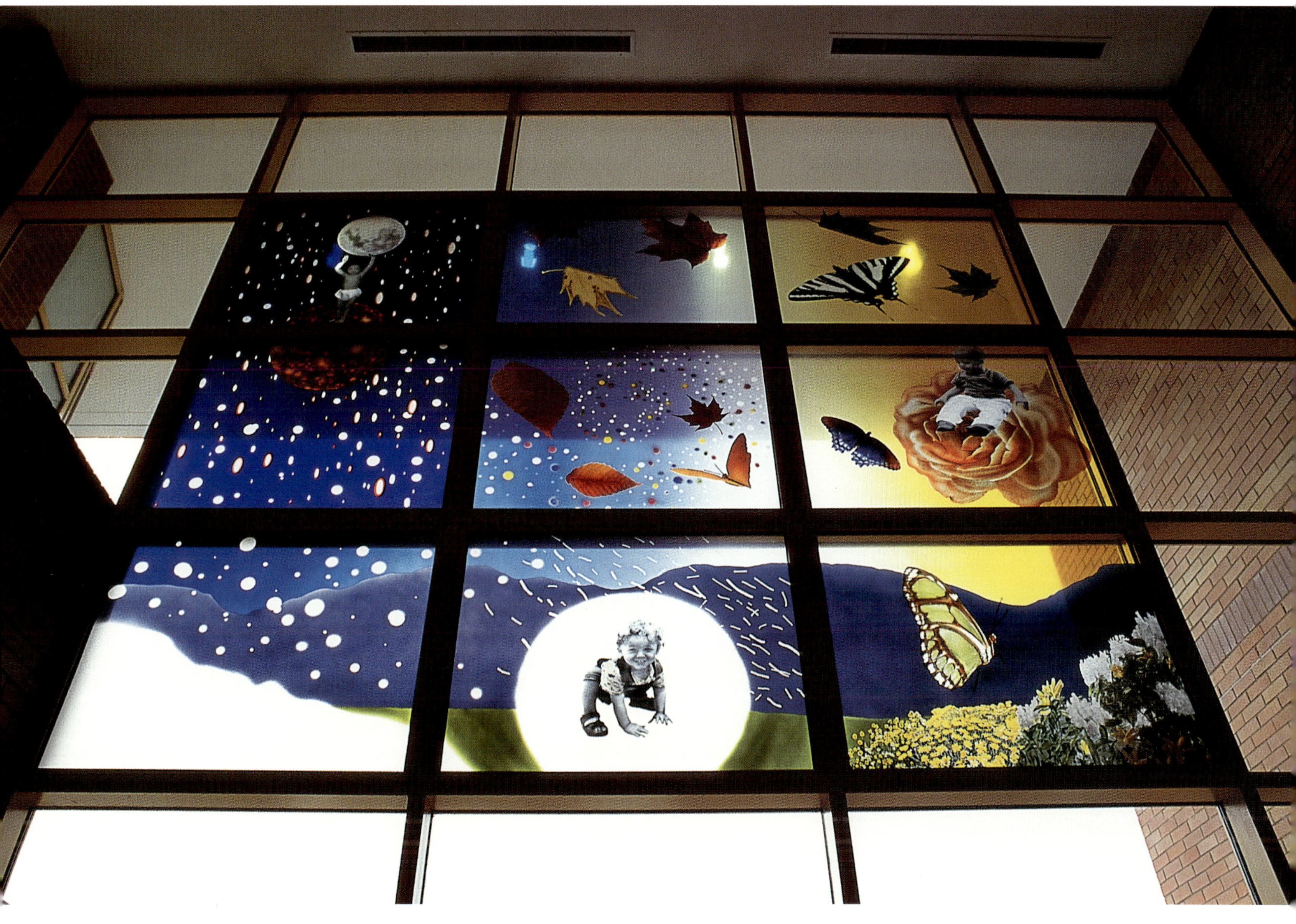

Orbis Venustas
2001
Float-glass painting

Early Childhood Center/Public School 228,
32-80 93rd Street

ARCHITECT
Richard Dattner and Partners Architects
DESIGN AGENCY
School Construction Authority
SPONSOR AGENCY
Board of Education

Skowmon Hastanan's *Orbis Venustas* is a vibrantly colored nine-panel work located in the entrance of the Early Childhood Center at P.S. 228. The artist worked with float-glass painting, a relatively new technique that involves sandblasting, acid etching, slumping, silk-screen printing, spraying, hand-painting, and computer design. The paintings' panels depict fanciful images of children in the midst of the changing seasons. The four seasons converge in the central panel, which features a circular spiraling galaxy, a symbol of eternity.

Barry Holden and Nina Yankowitz

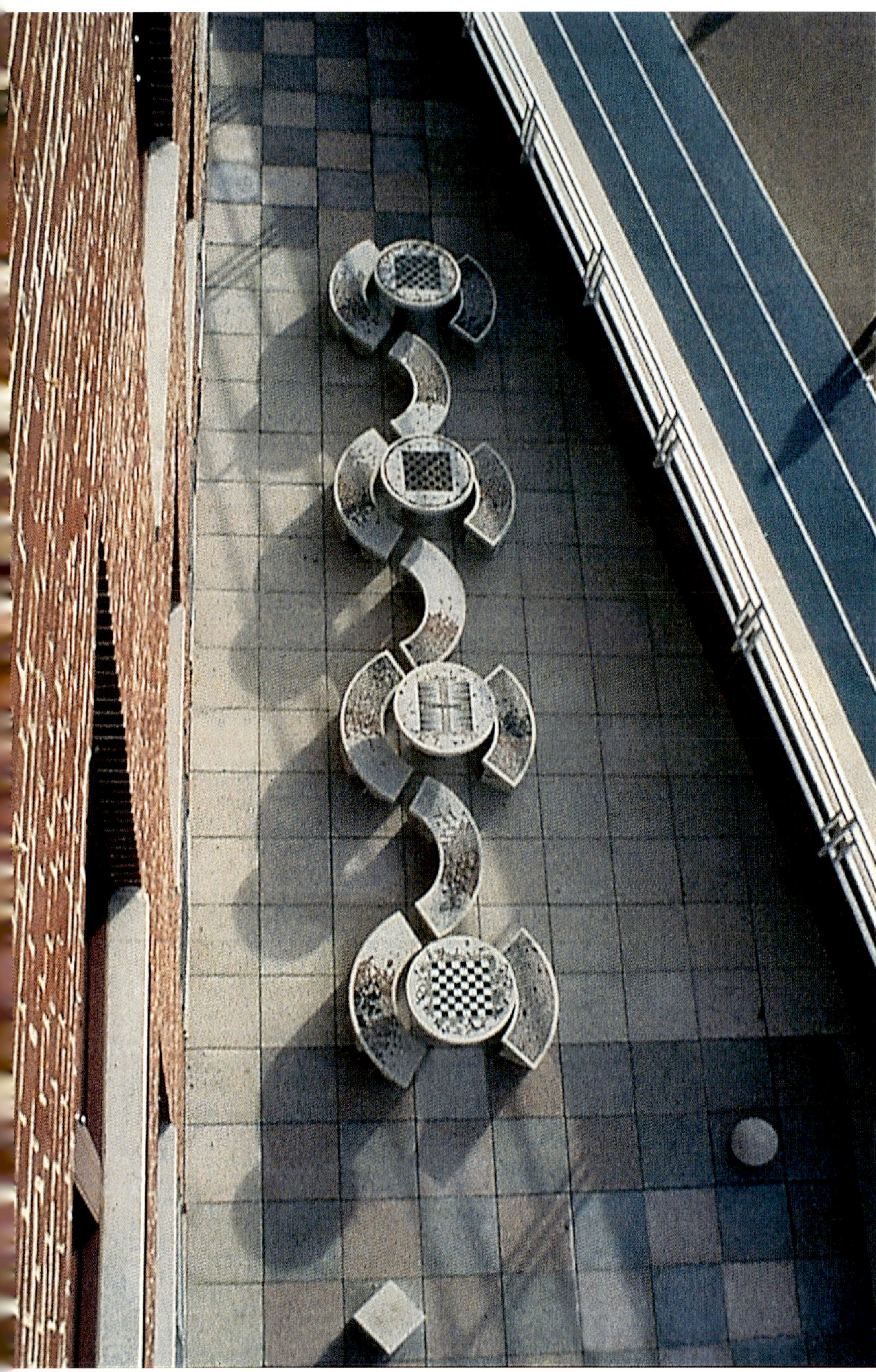

The Garden of Games, The Garden of Scientific Ideas, Gate, and Clock Tower
1997
Granite, concrete, neon, stainless steel

Intermediate School 145,
33-44 80th Street

ARCHITECT/DESIGN AGENCY
School Construction Authority
SPONSOR AGENCY
Board of Education

For *The Garden of Games* (left), sited on the rooftop of I.S. 145, Barry Holden and Nina Yankowitz created an interactive environment that features games, such as chess and backgammon, constructed of granite mosaics and inlaid on to four tables and twenty benches made of cast concrete. The floor of the plaza is fashioned from different-colored squares of concrete, creating the illusion that even the plaza itself is a game board. Similarly, *The Garden of Scientific Ideas* features a game-like learning environment. Sited on a terrace, four interactive bronze sculptures sit on stacked concrete bases and educate students in the basic principles of science, including sound, motion, gravity, and light. The artists also created *Gate*, a decorative wrought-iron gate design with roses, and *Clock Tower*, which stands prominently in the schoolyard.

Runaway Rainbow
1992
Cement

Public School 92, 99-01 34th Avenue

ARCHITECT
Gruzen Samton Steinglass
DESIGN AGENCY
School Construction Authority
SPONSOR AGENCY
Board of Education

Wopo Holup's *Runaway Rainbow* at P.S. 92, a cast-cement mural of a garden bordered by a rainbow, begins in the school lobby and runs through its halls into the cafeteria. The garden features images of potatoes, carrots, tulips, pumpkins, black rabbits, and mice, all of which were selected by the school's fourth- and fifth-grade students. The 71 foot (21.6 m) long rainbow crosses the garden and enters the cafeteria where it zigzags up a wall and "escapes" through a skylight.

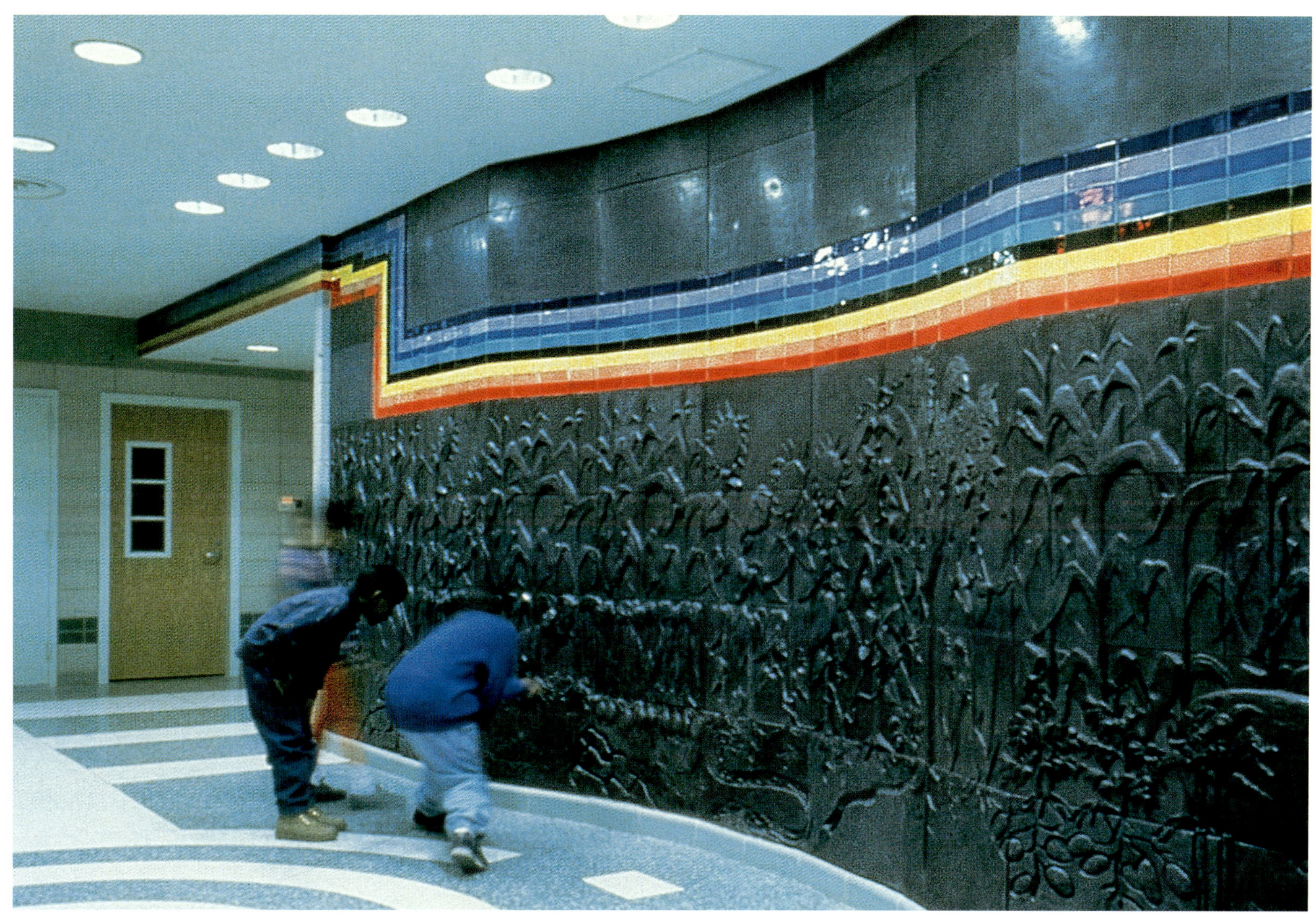

Wopo Holup

Ik-Joong Kang

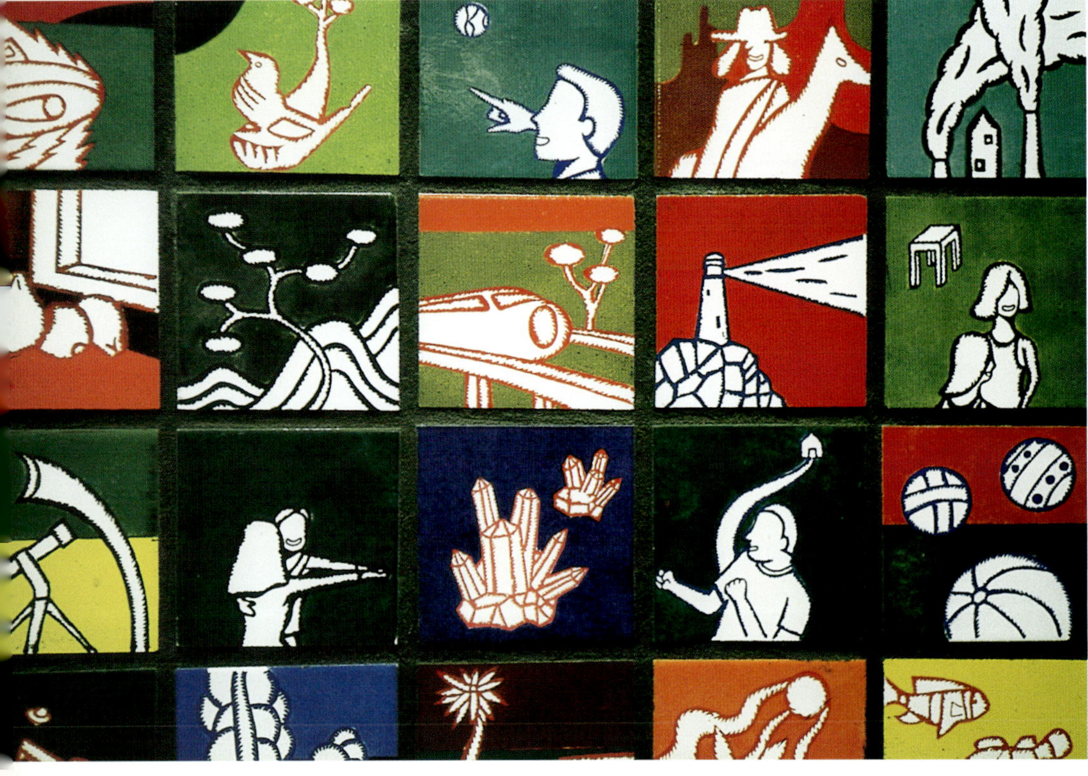

Happy Days
1997
Ceramics

Occupational Training Center,
57-12 94th Street

ARCHITECT
Castro-Blanco Piscioneri Associates
DESIGN AGENCY
School Construction Authority
SPONSOR AGENCY
Board of Education

Located throughout the Occupational Training Center, Ik-Joong Kang's *Happy Days* consists of six colorful murals comprising 3172 individual tiles, each measuring 3 inches (7.6 cm) square. Kang silk-screened each ceramic tile with tiny whimsical images of people, animals, and objects. Together these six bright murals are intended to add cheerfulness to the otherwise stark space.

Bing Lee

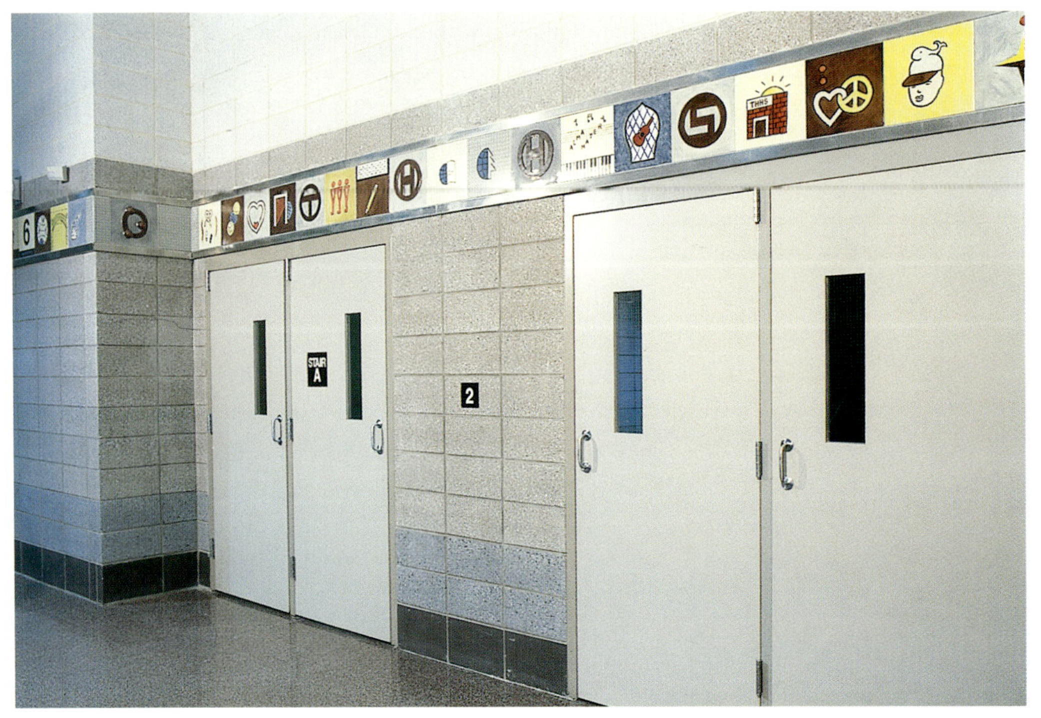

One Line
1995
Ceramics

Townsend Harris High School,
149-11 Melbourne Avenue

ARCHITECT
Hellmuth, Obata + Kassaubaum, Inc.
DESIGN AGENCY
School Construction Authority
SPONSOR AGENCY
Board of Education

Bing Lee's mural for Townsend Harris High School celebrates multiculturalism and racial harmony. The mural, consisting of a single band of flat tiles that runs along each side of the hallway, is composed of approximately six hundred standard 1 foot (30 cm) square tiles and a hundred low-relief tiles. Each tile depicts an individual pictograph of images, icons, or symbols of the artist's invention.

Everyday Courage
2003
Steel boxes, found objects

High School of Law Enforcement and Public Safety, 116-25 Guy Brewer Boulevard

ARCHITECT
Polshek Partnership Architects
DESIGN AGENCY
School Construction Authority
SPONSOR AGENCY
Department of Education

Robyn Love's installation, *Everyday Courage*, at the High School of Law Enforcement and Public Safety celebrates courage in public service. Inspired by the Buddhist tradition of the Wall of 1000 Buddhas, the artist filled three hundred steel boxes with memorabilia and photographs relating to major historical leaders such as Nelson Mandela and Martin Luther King, Jr., as well as to local New York heroes. Love devoted seventy boxes to the September 11th, 2001 tragedy. Objects for the wall were contributed by members of the Federal Bureau of Investigation (FBI), the Police Department (NYPD), the Fire Department (FDNY), and the Metropolitan Transit Authority Police. Students and faculty can view the items through glass panels located in the lobby areas of the school's five floors.

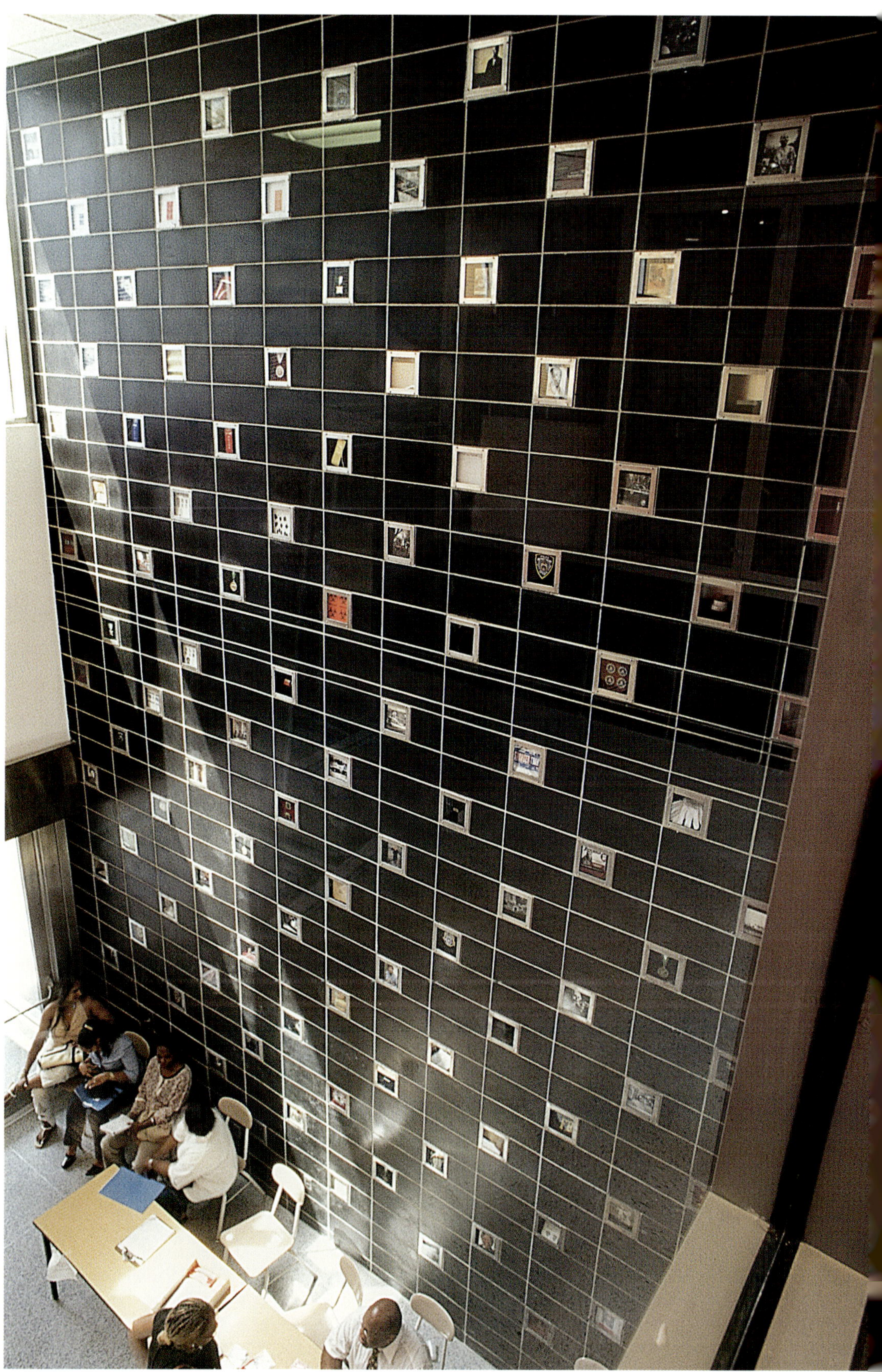

Robyn Love

Ad Astra Per Aspera
1995
Fiber optics, concrete

Townsend Harris High School,
149-11 Melbourne Avenue

ARCHITECT
Hellmuth, Obata + Kassabaum, Inc.
DESIGN AGENCY
School Construction Authority
SPONSOR AGENCY
Board of Education

Clyde Lynds's *Ad Astra Per Aspera* is a digital installation for the entrance to the library at Townsend Harris High School. The artist cast fiber optics in a large concrete lintel and designed digital programs that create continuously changing displays of light, which appear to come from within the stone. Inspired by the school's emphasis on classical texts and curricula, Lynds created patterns that appear on the lintel and then morph into the words of the Latin epigram "*ad astra per aspera*" (through difficulty to the stars). That phrase transforms into a square grid, then a circle, and then disperses into configurations of constellations that re-create the locations of stars in the Western night sky of June 22, 367 BC, as the Greek philosopher and scientist Aristotle would have seen them when he was seventeen years old.

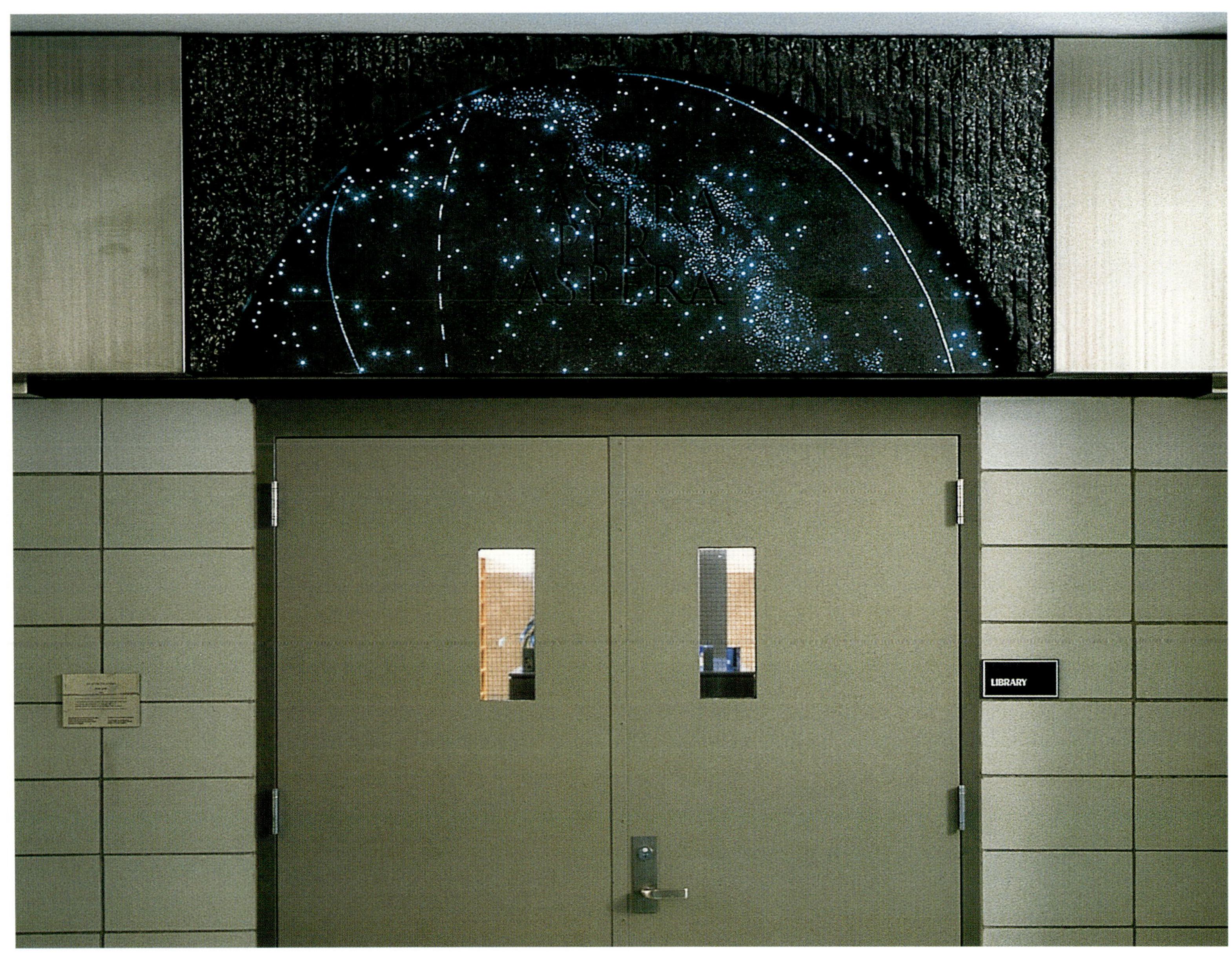

Clyde Lynds

Howard McCalebb

Little Dances
1998
Enamel paint on iron and steel

Louis Armstrong Memorial
Multi-Service Center,
107-20 Northern Boulevard

ARCHITECT
Richard Dattner and Partners Architects
DESIGN AGENCY
Department of General Services
SPONSOR AGENCY
Human Resources Administration
OPERATING AGENCY
Department of Parks and Recreation

For his project at the Louis Armstrong Memorial Multi-Service Center, located near the trumpeter and singer's former home, Howard McCalebb fashioned a freestanding sculpture from iron and steel components. In raised letters on the base, the artist transcribed the following quotation from Louis Armstrong's description of his childhood: "When I was about four or five still wearing dresses, I lived with Mother in a place called Brick Row—a lot of cement, rented rooms sort of like a motel. And right in the middle of that on Perdido Street was the Funky Butt Hall, old, beat up. Big cracks in the wall. On Saturday nights, Mama couldn't find us because we wanted to hear that music. Before the dance the band would play out front about a half-hour. And us little kids would all do little dances."

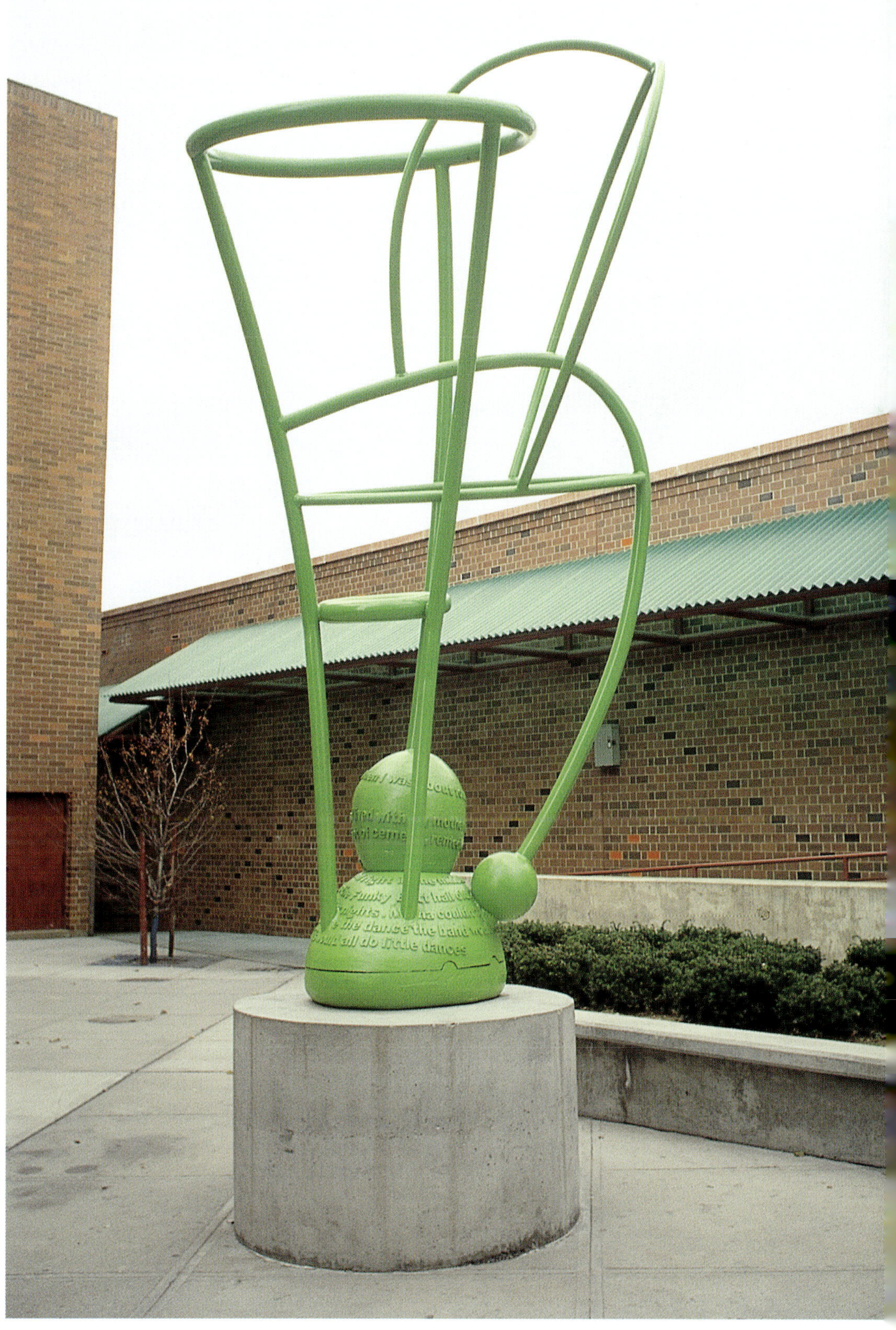

Ed McGowin and Claudia DeMonte

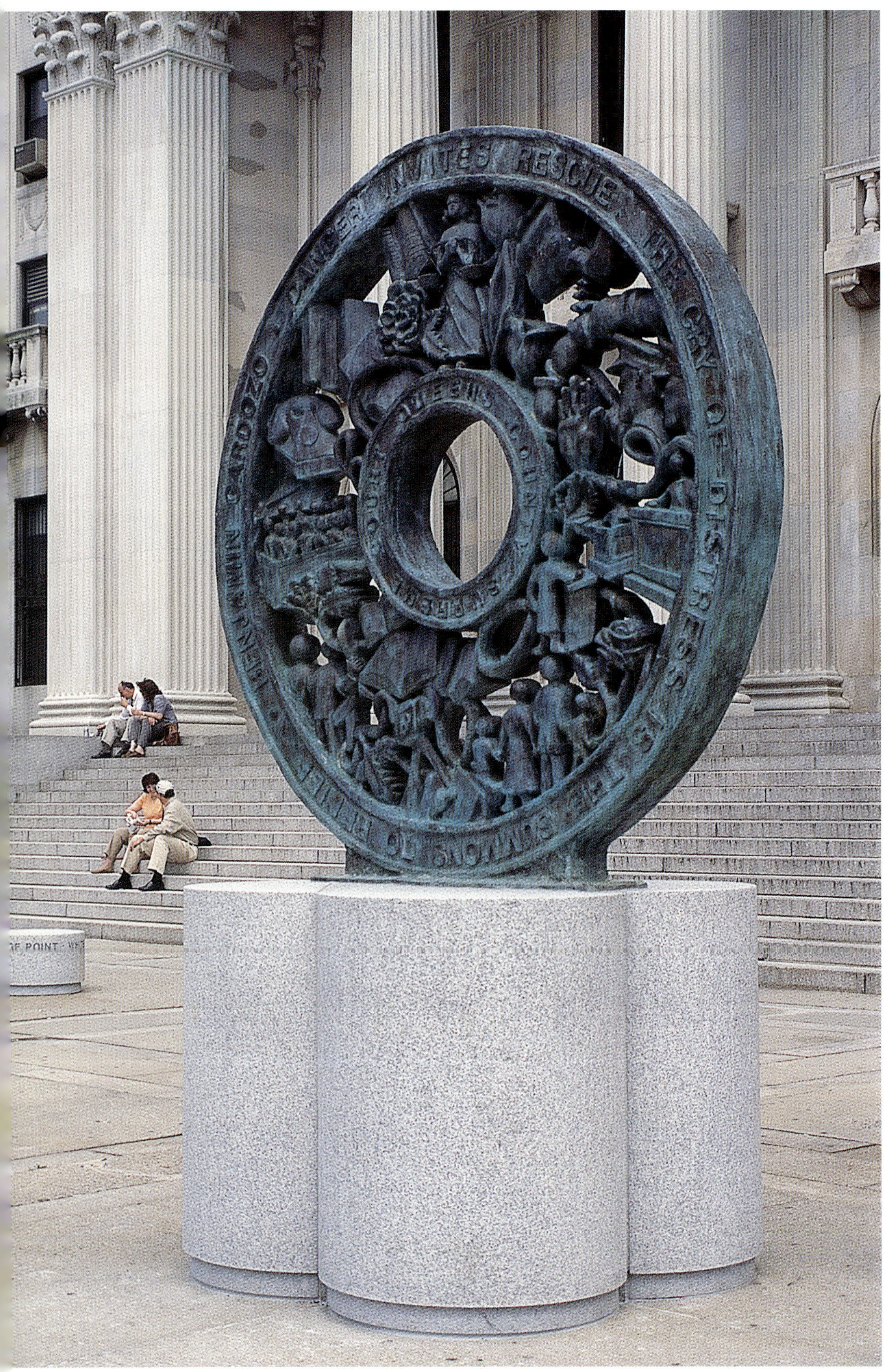

The Wheel of Justice
1998
Bronze, granite

Queens Supreme Court,
88-11 Sutphin Boulevard

DESIGN AGENCY
Department of Citywide Administrative Services
SPONSORS
City Council Members Karen Koslowitz, Archie Spigner, Thomas White, Jr., and the Queens Judicial Advisory Council

Art Commission Award for Excellence in Design 1998

This project, located in front of the Queens Supreme Court, consists of a 12 foot (3.6 m) tall cast bronze and stone sculpture and eighteen engraved stone benches. Narrative images on the 1500 pound (680 kg) bronze sculpture illustrate aspects of the court process, such as juror notification, and symbolic images such as the tulip and rose design taken from the Queens County flag. The stone benches are engraved with the names of all the towns that make up the borough of Queens, such as Jamaica, Flushing, and Astoria.

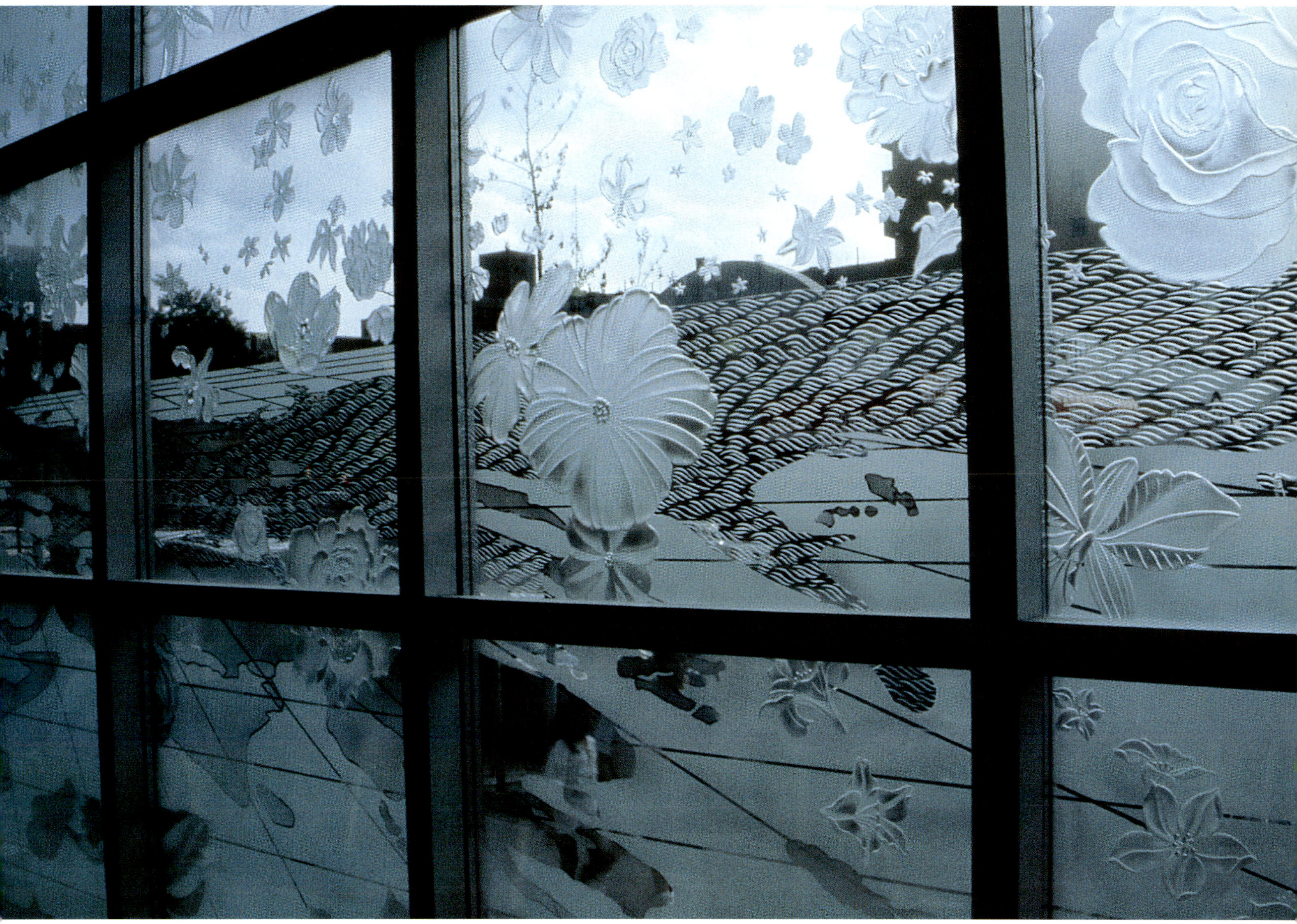

World of Flowers
1998
Etched glass

Flushing Regional Library,
41-17 Main Street

ARCHITECT
Polshek Partnership Architects
DESIGN AGENCY
Department of Design and Construction
SPONSOR AGENCY
Queens Borough Public Library

For her project at the Flushing Regional Library, Yong Soon Min sandblasted a map of the world on to twenty-four glass panels, which she then overlaid with a map of New York City that places Queens in its center. Cascading above these maps are representations of the national flowers of the different countries from which neighborhood residents originate—roses, lilies, orchids, tulips, lotus, and jasmine. The glass panels are located in the children's reading room in the library.

Yong Soon Min

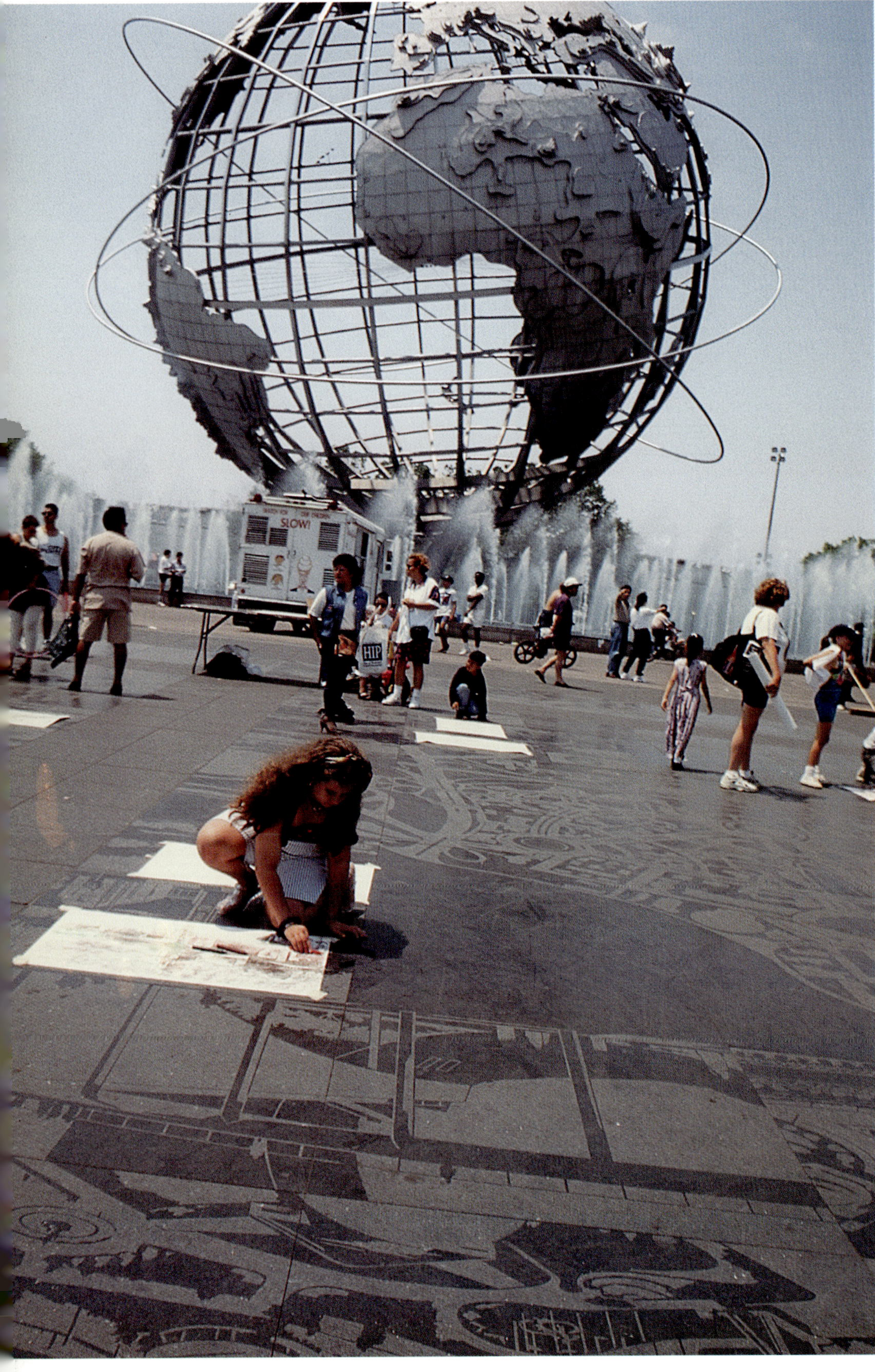

Untitled
1995
Etched granite

Core Area, Flushing Meadows
Corona Park

ARCHITECT
Miceli Kulik Williams & Associates
SPONSOR AGENCY
Department of Parks and Recreation

Located at the site of the 1964–65 World's Fair in the heart of Flushing Meadows Corona Park, Matt Mullican's black granite pavement etching rekindles the spirit of the 1939–40 and 1964–65 World's Fairs. This 3000 square foot (836 sq. m) installation, composed of 464 unique blocks, creates a hieroglyphic documentation of the events, buildings, inventions, and technical achievements advanced by World's Fairs.

Matt Mullican

Anna Valentina Murch

Cycles
1997
Stainless steel, water, granite, aluminum, lacquer, bronze, limestone

Queens Civil Court,
89-17 Sutphin Boulevard

ARCHITECT
Perkins Eastman
DESIGN AGENCY
Dormitory Authority of the State of New York
SPONSOR AGENCY
Office of Court Administration

Anna Valentina Murch's abstract sculpture, located in a courtyard at the Queens Civil Court, features four components: "the Top," a large reflecting stainless-steel disk; "the Wheel," which is rotated clockwise by the wind; "the Doors," which are etched with concentric grooved rings; and "the Vessels," (not pictured) which are stone bowls filled with water. The artist intended for the courtyard to be a sanctuary for contemplation, saying of her piece: "You cannot see the courtyard and the stairway inclusively from one point. As you pace from one corner to another, or climb the stairs to another level, your perception changes as a series of related forms engage with each other and activate the space."

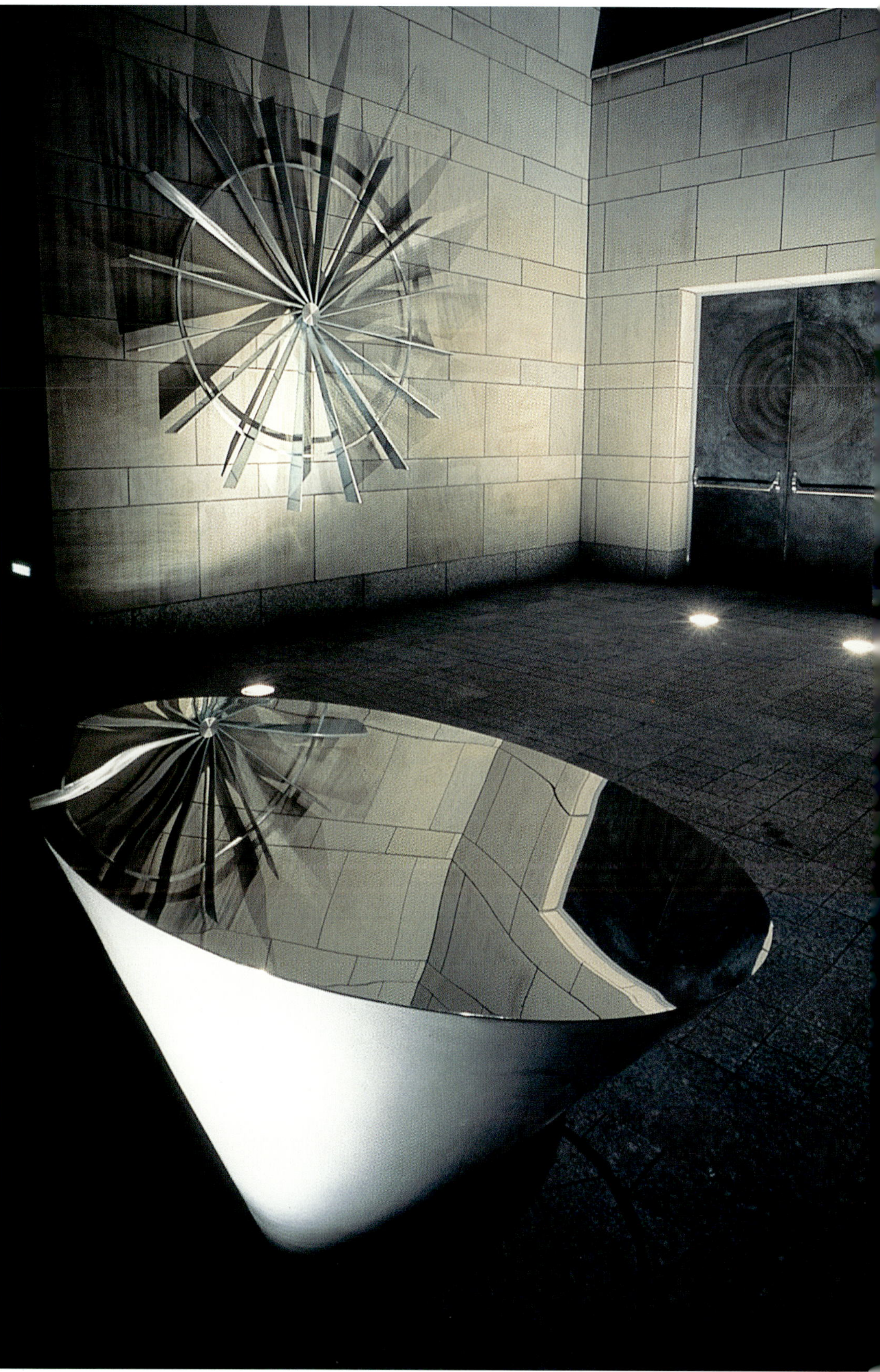

Kazuma Oshita

Woodside Story and **The Opening**
1999
Fiberglas, brass, steel, wood

Intermediate School 125,
46-02 47th Avenue

ARCHITECT
A. Epstein and Sons
DESIGN AGENCY
School Construction Authority
SPONSOR AGENCY
Board of Education

Kazuma Oshita's work at I.S. 125 consists of two hammered brass dioramas. *Woodside Story* (below), installed above the doors to the auditorium, depicts the history of the school's Woodside neighborhood, beginning with the discovery of the New World. *The Opening* is a low relief that depicts various images associated with education.

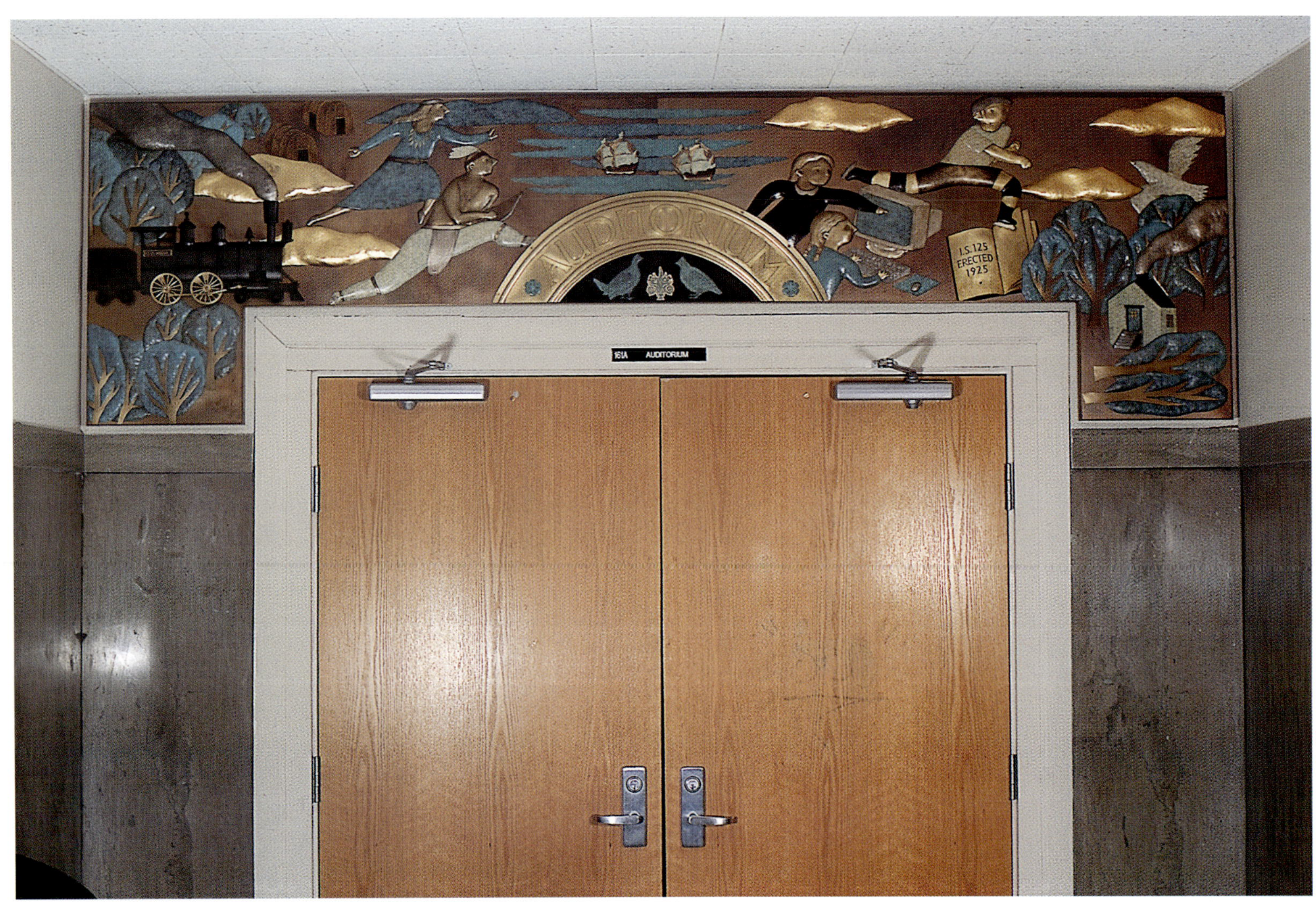

Bowling Ball Curtain
2003
Bowling balls, stainless steel

Public School 270,
233-15 Merrick Boulevard

ARCHITECT
Gruzen Samton Architects
DESIGN AGENCY
School Construction Authority
SPONSOR AGENCY
Department of Education

Suspended from the ceiling of P.S. 270, Eung Ho Park's *Bowling Ball Curtain* is comprised of fourteen hanging chains, each made up of nine steel balls that descend 16 feet (4.9 m) from the ceiling through the lobby's open railing. The balls are all uniformly sized, but range in hue to create a dazzling multi-colored scrim. The sculpture, reminiscent of a beaded curtain, presents a playful spectacle for the school children.

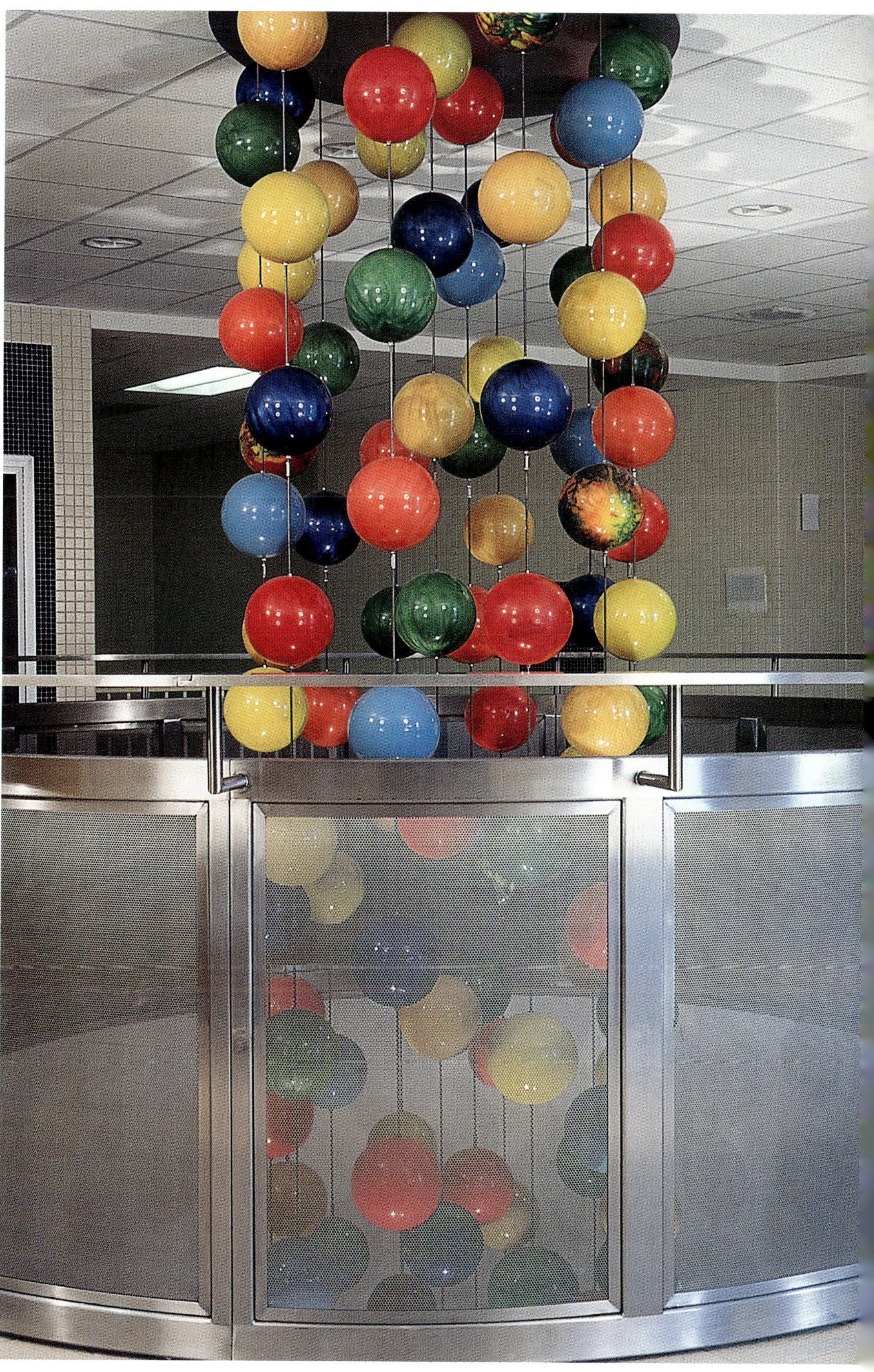

Eung Ho Park

Sequence
1997
Etched granite

Flushing Regional Library,
41-17 Main Street

ARCHITECT
Polshek Partnership Architects
DESIGN AGENCY
Department of Design and Construction
SPONSOR AGENCY
Queens Borough Public Library

Kathleen H. Ruíz's work, *Sequence,* for the Flushing Regional Library, consists of eight granite blocks, each deeply etched with line drawings that depict the early stages of cell growth and the process of one cell dividing into two, and highlighted with gold and silver leaf. The piece is installed on the building's exterior. The artist intended the work to serve as a metaphor for an individual's metamorphosis and a search for information.

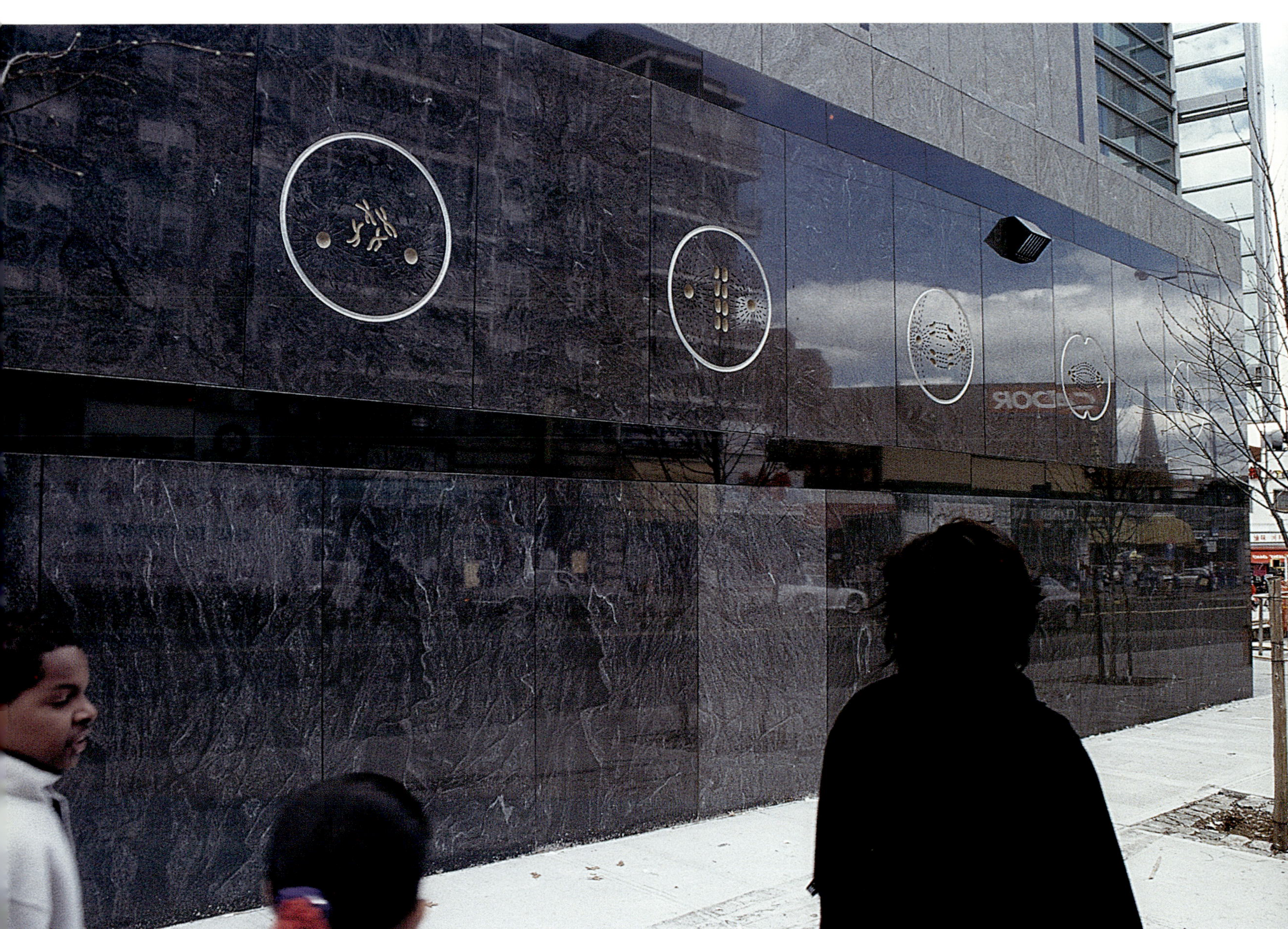

Kathleen H. Ruíz

Maura Sheehan

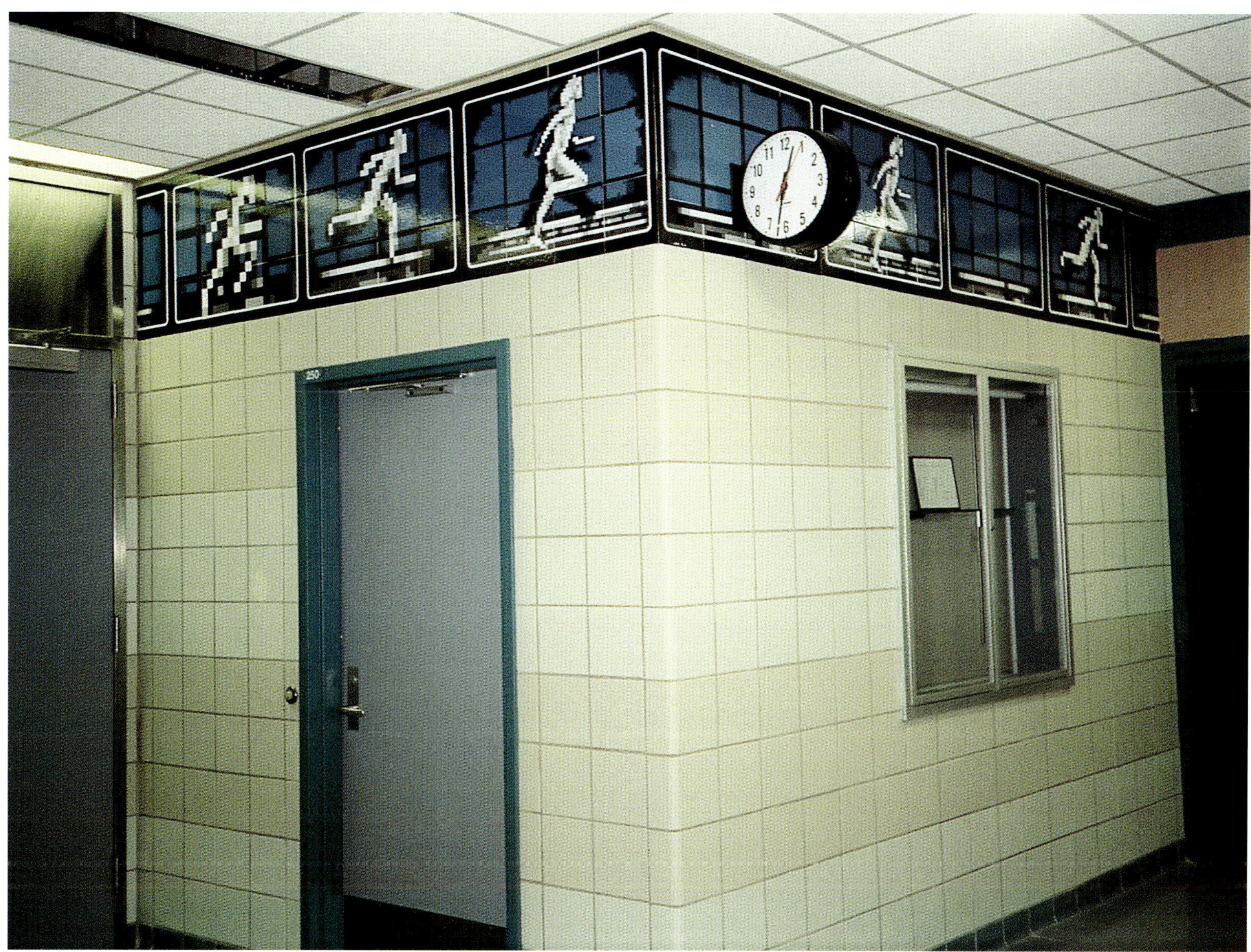

Frieze Frame
1995
Ceramics

Long Island City High School,
14-30 Broadway

ARCHITECT
Gruzen Samton Steinglass
DESIGN AGENCY
School Construction Authority
SPONSOR AGENCY
Board of Education

Designed to resemble an unwinding spool of film, Maura Sheehan's frieze of ceramic tiles runs for 500 feet (152 m) along the top of the lobby walls at Long Island City High School. The work features a series of digitized images of people running, and is arranged to give the effect of continuous motion. The artist has stated that she was inspired by the work of the early photographer Eadweard Muybridge, whose experiments in stop-motion photography in the late nineteenth century were instrumental in the development of motion pictures.

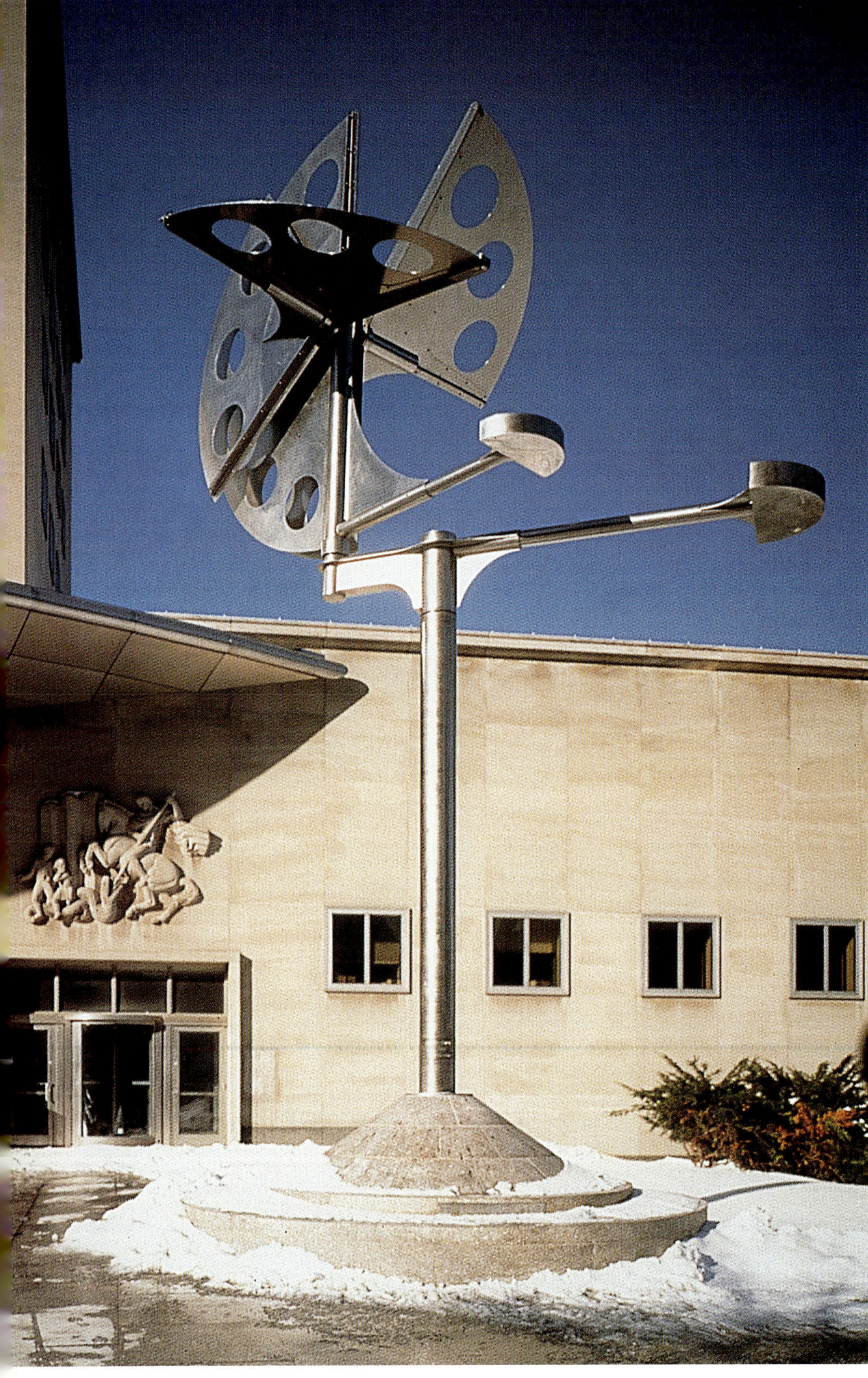

Dialogue with the Sun
1995
Stainless steel

Queens Criminal Court Addition,
125-01 Queens Boulevard

ARCHITECT
Ehrenkrantz Eckstut and Kuhn
DESIGN AGENCY
Department of General Services
SPONSOR AGENCY
Office of Court Administration

Located at the entrance to the Queens Criminal Court Addition, Susumu Shingu's *Dialogue with the Sun* was designed to respond to atmospheric changes. The 30 foot (9.1 m) tall sculpture contains "wings" composed of a half-disk and four quarter-disks that rotate vertically and horizontally, adjusting to changes in the direction and velocity of the wind. The highly polished surfaces mirror the sky and surrounding landscape with every motion. As Shingu has explained: "The sculpture will be at all times alive with motion. It will keep conveying the delicate and various rhythms of the wind to those who come to see it. It will bring a feeling of friendliness and warmth which will serve to ameliorate the solemn and dignified impression of the courthouse."

Susumu Shingu

Kathleen Spicer

Natural Implements
2002
Painted aluminum, terrazzo

Public School 28, 109-10 47th Avenue

ARCHITECT/DESIGN AGENCY
School Construction Authority
SPONSOR AGENCY
Board of Education

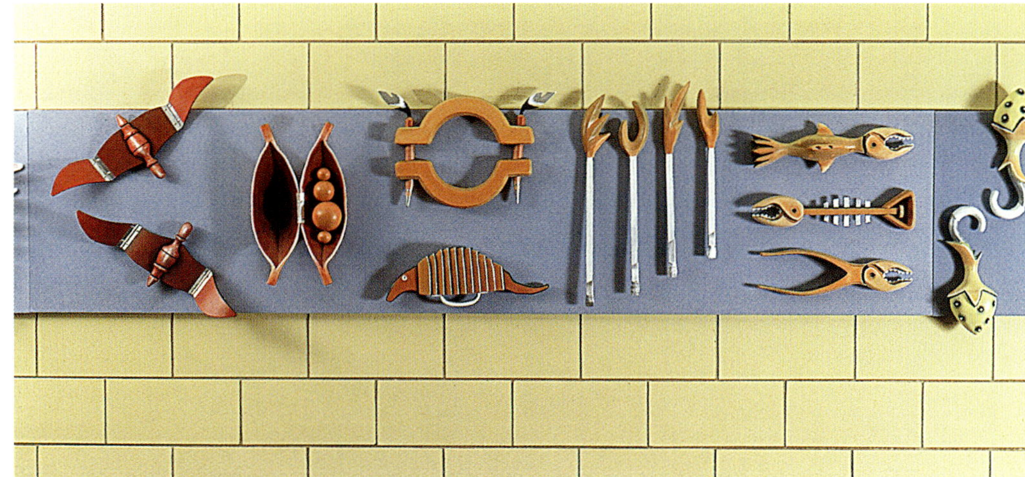

Kathleen Spicer created a series of more than a hundred aluminum sculptures mounted on a large wall at P.S. 28, as well as terrazzo flooring for the school's main lobby. Collectively entitled *Natural Implements*, the sculptures combine common tools with elements from nature: a hammer has the wings of a dragonfly, a plane is transformed into a whale spouting water, propellers turn into geese, and C-clamps become sea horses. The terrazzo flooring features similar images, such as a pair of pliers and a fish, along with a series of overlapping circles.

Carol Sun

P.S. 16: The Tree of Knowledge
1998
Glass and marble mosaic, inlaid vinyl floor

Public School 16, 41-15 104th Street

ARCHITECT
Montoya-Rodriguez, P.C.
DESIGN AGENCY
School Construction Authority
SPONSOR AGENCY
Board of Education

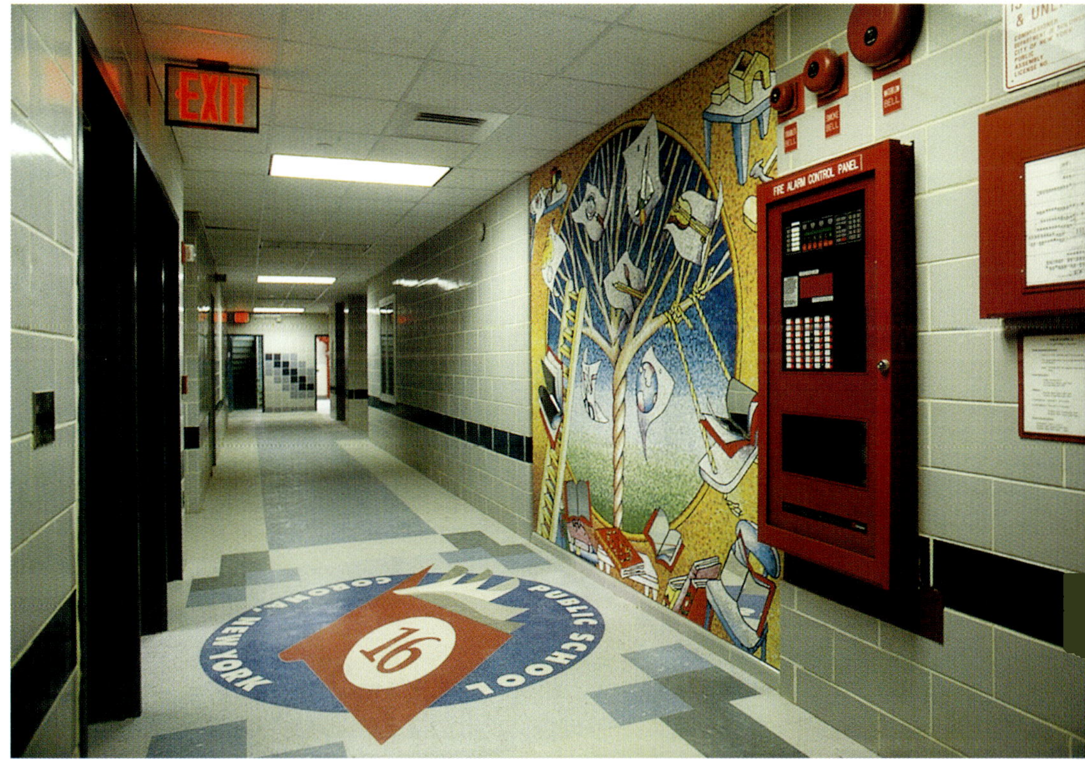

Carol Sun's glass and marble mosaic mural, located in the main entrance of P.S. 16, features a "learning tree" framed in a circular window. The tree is surrounded by objects associated with school life, such as chairs, books, and desks. Looking into the mirrored pages of the mural's books, students can see themselves and become part of the artwork.

Ten-Kilometer Radius (see pages 2–3)
1996
Wood, brass, cibachrome transparencies, lenses, Plexiglas

New York Hall of Science,
47-01 111th Street, Flushing Meadows Corona Park

ARCHITECT
Beyer Blinder Belle
DESIGN AGENCY
Department of Design and Construction
SPONSOR AGENCY
Department of Cultural Affairs

Art Commission Award for Excellence in Design 1992

Located in the rotunda at the New York Hall of Science, Fred Tomaselli's *Ten-Kilometer Radius* features seventy-two small circular color transparencies of different locations in New York that have been embedded into a large circular handrail. The artist based the project on a map he drew of New York City in 1993, on which the Hall of Science is positioned at the center. Radiating from this center point are 72 lines, each extending the equivalent of 10 km (6.2 miles). Tomaselli then traveled to and photographed each of the 72 sites at the 10-km mark. These photographs, of urban and suburban neighborhoods, parkland, rivers, bays, and industrial locations, now represent a time capsule of urban views from 1993. They are presented here as cibachrome transparencies; each transparency is sandwiched between a magnifying film and a circle of white translucent Plexiglas, and embedded in the handrail. Flush-mounted into the handrail above the transparencies are brass signs identifying the precise locations being viewed.

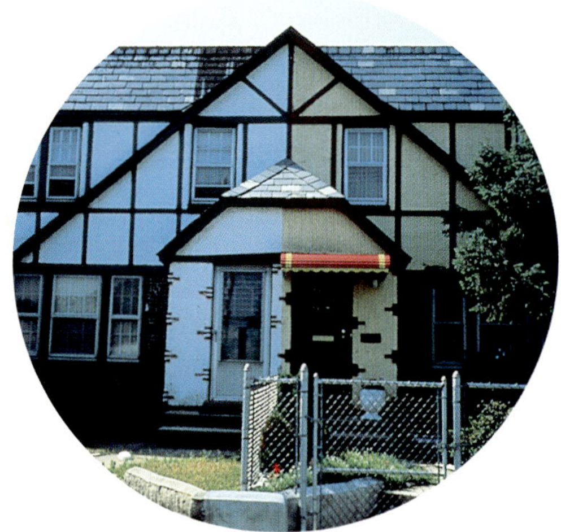

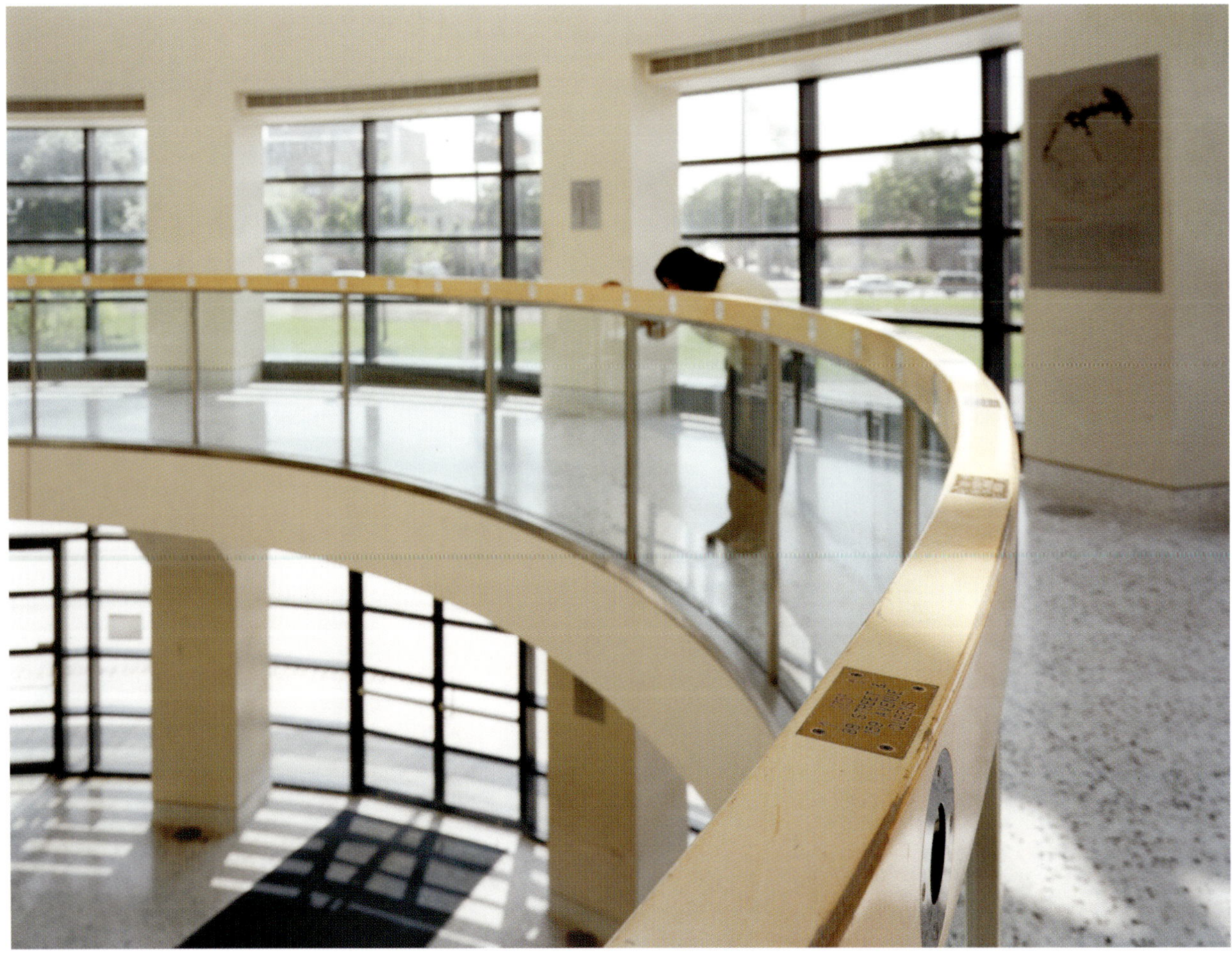

Fred Tomaselli

Susan Tunick

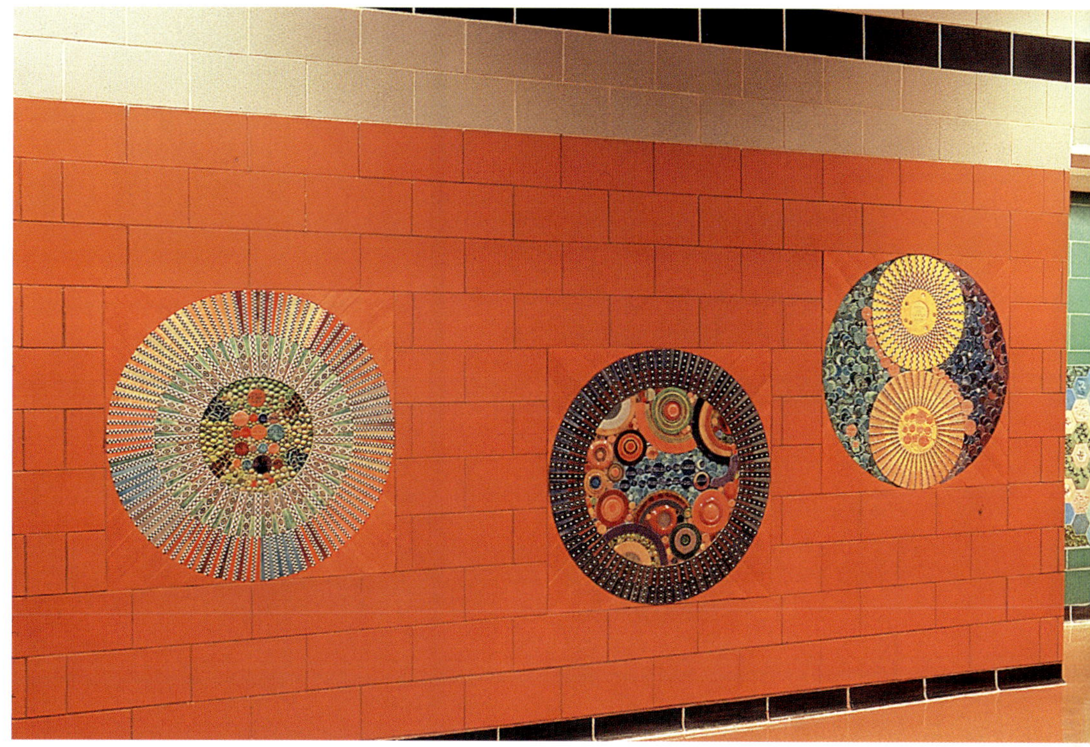

Three Times Three
2002
Ceramics

Public School 222, 86-15 37th Avenue

ARCHITECT/DESIGN AGENCY
School Construction Authority
SPONSOR AGENCY
Board of Education

Susan Tunick's ceramic artwork, entitled *Three Times Three,* for the cafeteria at P.S. 222, includes a patterned floor design, mosaic inserts, and handmade wall tiles. The mosaics are broken up into three distinct parts to correspond to the three separate sections of the wall. A blue background is the setting for triangles, which feature images of water, waves, sea creatures, and shells, while a green color field relates hexagonal forms to beehives, bees, and flowers. On the orange section of the wall, the artist created circles with small mirror inlays that encourage the children to interact with the artwork. Tunick also included the poem "Now We Are Six," by A.A. Milne.

Lane Twitchell

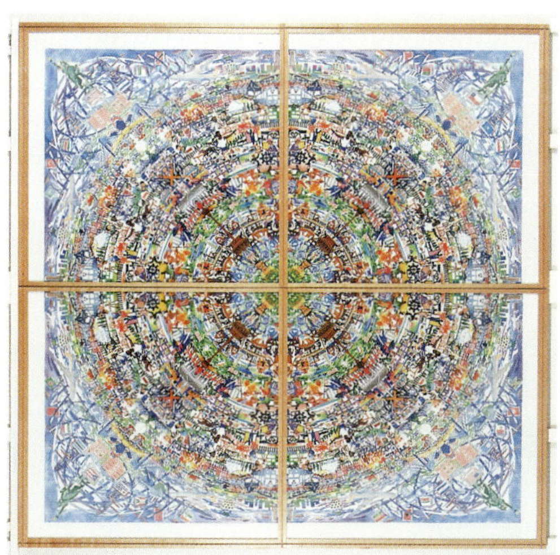

Here Is New York
2000
Cut paper

Public School 161, 101-33 124th Street

ARCHITECT
Richard Dattner and Partners Architects
DESIGN AGENCY
School Construction Authority
SPONSOR AGENCY
Board of Education

For *Here Is New York,* located at P.S. 161, Lane Twitchell created framed images out of cut and folded paper, measuring 8 feet (2.4 m) square, to recount the history of New York City and State. In the center of the composition, New York is depicted as a home to Native Americans living in the abundant natural world. The chronological narrative radiates outward and includes images of the first Europeans arriving by ship and the attendant slave trade, the Revolutionary War, the building of the Erie Canal, the Draft Riots, the emancipation of slaves, the creation of the subway system, the women's suffrage movement, and the emergence of our complex modern metropolis. Twitchell paid particular attention to the borough of Queens and the neighborhood of Richmond Hill, with images of native son and nineteenth-century photographer Jacob Riis, the Queensborough Bridge, the 1939–40 World's Fair, LaGuardia International Airport, and P.S. 161.

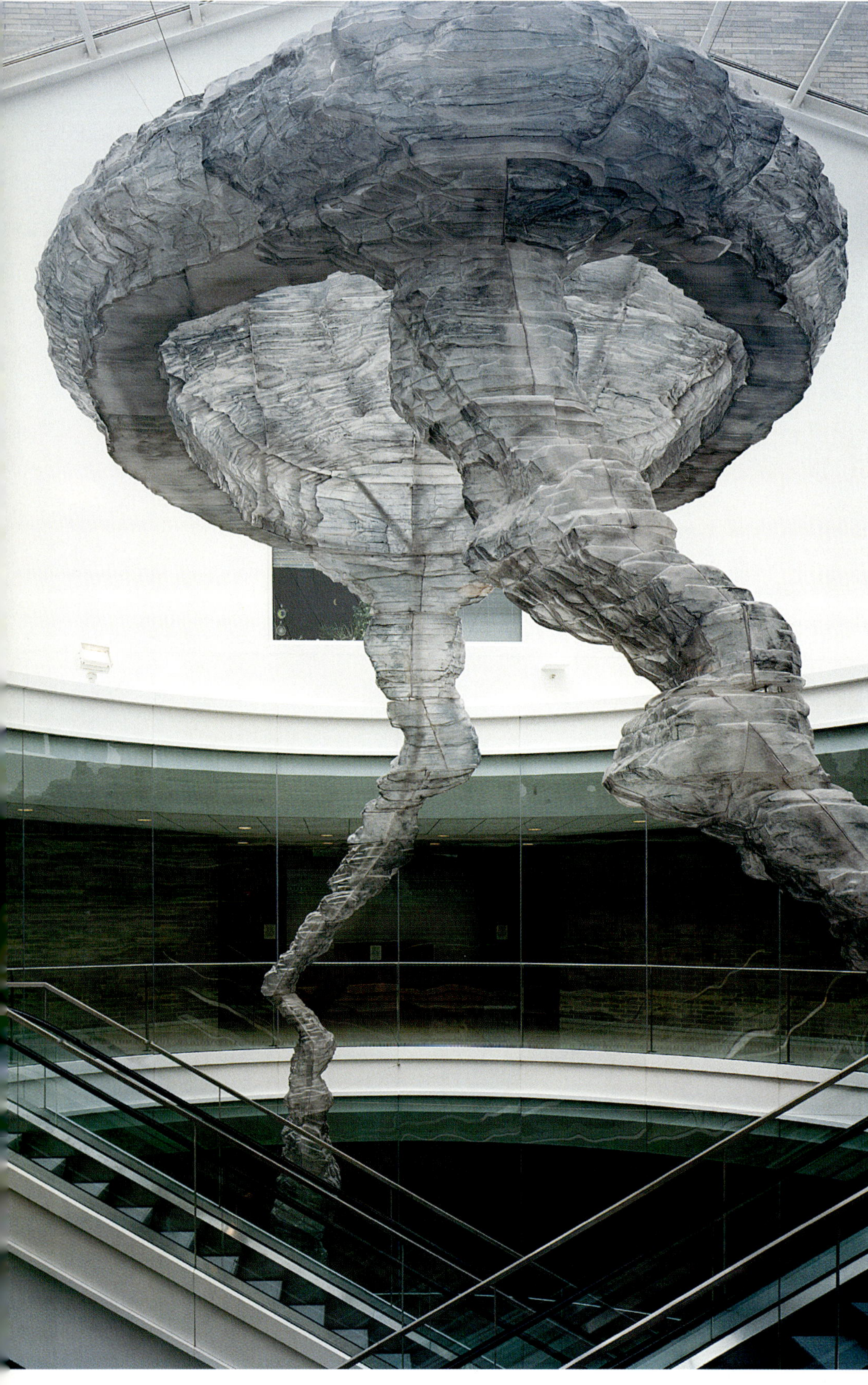

katul katul
2003
Polyester, aluminum

Queens Family Courthouse,
151-20 Jamaica Avenue

ARCHITECTS
Pei Cobb Freed & Partners/
Gruzen Samton Architects
DESIGN AGENCY
Dormitory Authority of the State of
New York
SPONSOR AGENCY
Office of Court Administration

Ursula von Rydingsvard's *katul katul* is an abstract sculpture suspended five floors above the 40 × 40 foot (12.2 × 12.2 m) atrium at the Queens Family Courthouse. Two massive tendrils extend from a 22 foot (6.7 m) wide dome; they are composed of more than two hundred individual sections created out of cedar and then cast in polyester plastic and aluminum with an opaque finish. The title of the work is derived from a Polish children's game that mimics how dough is rhythmically kneaded.

Ursula von Rydingsvard

Michael Kelly Williams

Reach for a Star
1995
Mosaics

Public School 82, 88-02 144th Street

ARCHITECT
L.E. Tuckett
DESIGN AGENCY
School Construction Authority
SPONSOR AGENCY
Board of Education

Located outside the cafeteria and on each floor of P.S. 82's two-story addition, Michael Kelly Williams's celestial-themed glass-mosaic murals feature a field of abstract stars intertwined with floating human figures. The largest mosaic spans a 28 foot (8.5 m) long wall and depicts images of human figures reaching out and growing toward the stars. Many of the stars in the murals were based on designs by the school's third-grade students.

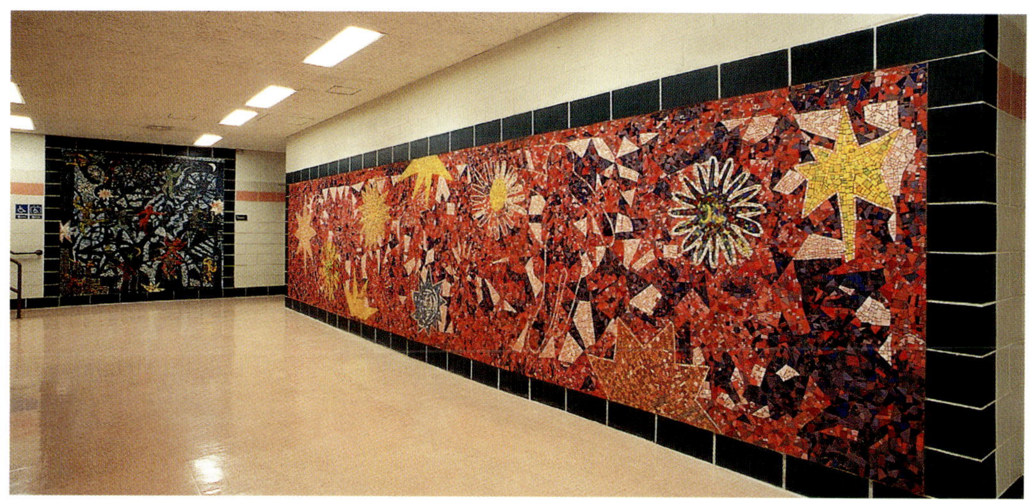

Philemona Williamson

Mosaic Folktales
2003
Glass mosaics

Public/Intermediate School 208,
74-30 Commonwealth Boulevard

ARCHITECT
SBLM Architects
DESIGN AGENCY
School Construction Authority
SPONSOR AGENCY
Department of Education

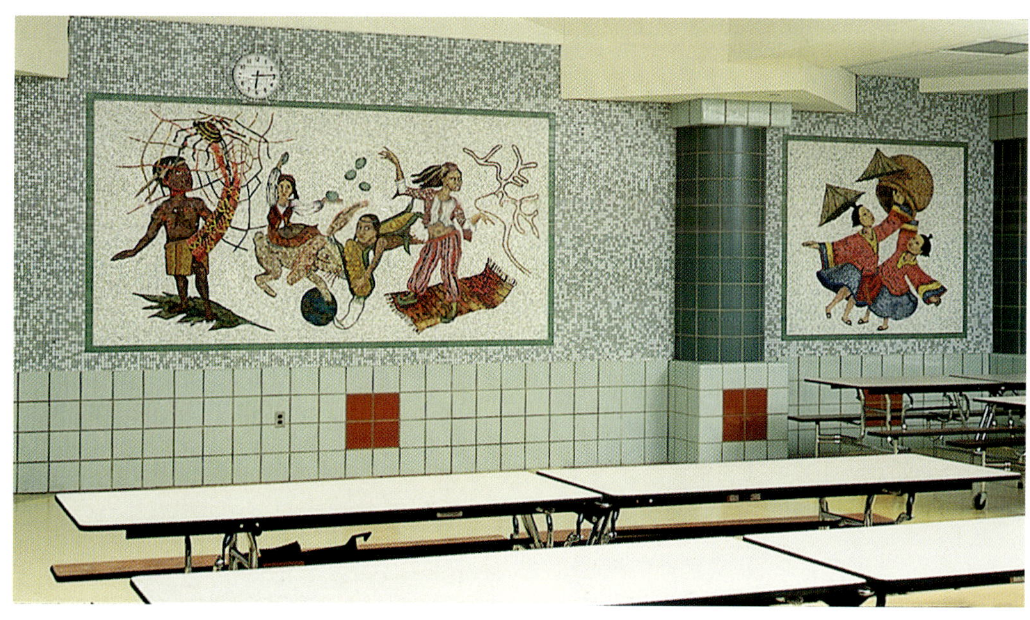

The glass mosaics that comprise Philemona Williamson's *Mosaic Folktales*, located at P.S/I.S. 208 on the Glen Oaks campus in Queens, feature images drawn from Korean, Chinese, Indian, Mexican, and African-American traditional folk and fairy tales. Williamson has said of her work: "These images drawn from literature and oral traditions speak to children of diverse cultural backgrounds of the heroism, poignancy, courage, and sweetness of coming of age in twenty-first-century America."

Fred Wilson

Pangaea
1995
Painted steel

Townsend Harris High School,
149-11 Melbourne Avenue

ARCHITECT
Hellmuth, Obata + Kassaubaum, Inc.
DESIGN AGENCY
School Construction Authority
SPONSOR AGENCY
Board of Education

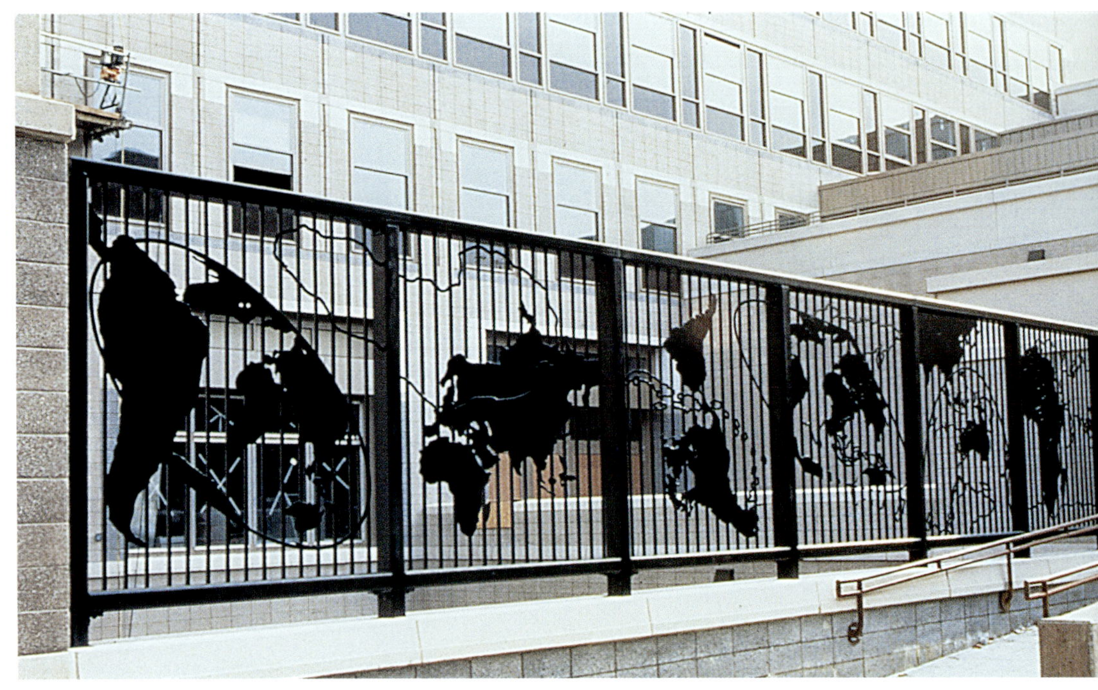

Fred Wilson's painted steel fence and gate surrounding Townsend Harris High School feature a map of the world as envisioned by the artist. Rather than using a cartographer's map as the basis for *Pangaea*, Wilson determined the size and scale of the continents according to his own view of their importance on the international stage. Continents are silhouetted in black, with spokes representing their latitudes. The name of the piece is derived from the theory that hundreds of millions of years ago the Earth consisted of only one landmass, a supercontinent named Pangaea.

Steve Wood

East of the Sun, West of the Moon
1994
Terra-cotta

Public School 69, 77-02 37th Avenue

ARCHITECT
Urban Lichfield Grosfeld
DESIGN AGENCY
School Construction Authority
SPONSOR AGENCY
Board of Education

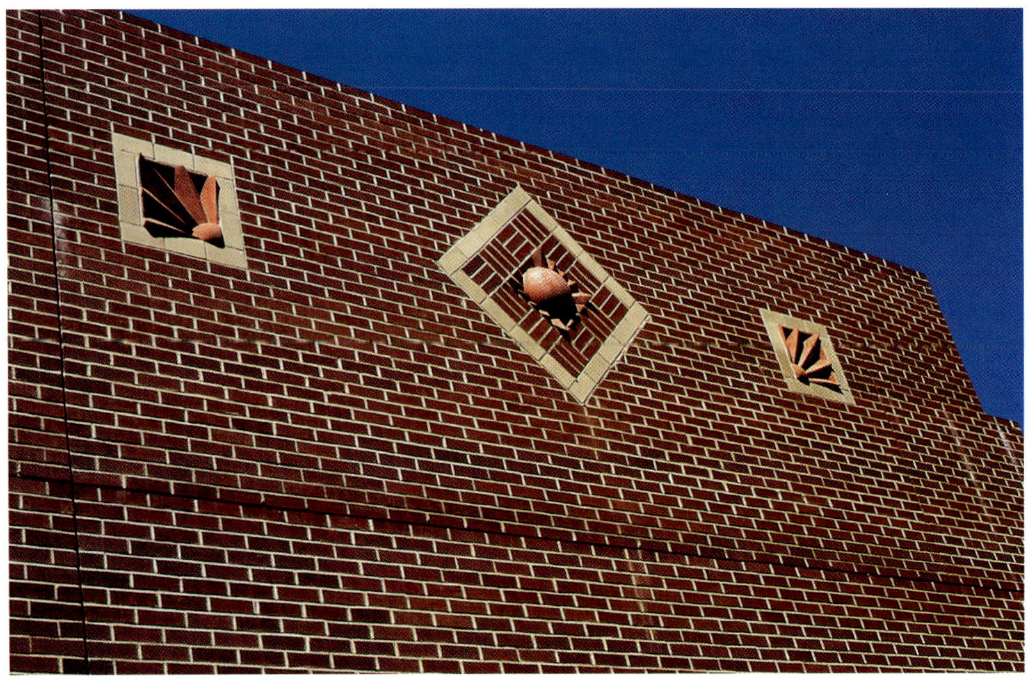

Located on the exterior of P.S. 69, Steve Wood's terra-cotta medallions depict the cycles of the sun and moon as the backdrop for a variety of New York landmarks. *East of the Sun, West of the Moon* illustrates how the rising and setting sun and moon cast different shadows on such landmarks as the Unisphere at Flushing Meadows Corona Park, the Elephant House at the Bronx Zoo, Kennedy International Airport, the face of the Statue of Liberty, Shea Stadium, and the front façade of P.S. 69.

The Three B's
2003
Aluminum, enamel

Glen Oaks Campus,
74-30 Commonwealth Boulevard

ARCHITECT
SBLM Architects
DESIGN AGENCY
School Construction Authority
SPONSOR AGENCY
Department of Education

Andy Yoder's sculptural installation, which adorns the busy thoroughfare of School District 26's Glen Oaks Campus, features representations of three objects associated with school activities—a paintbrush, a beaker, and a barbell—repeated ten times along the roadway. The sculptures were designed to provide protective bollards around the school.

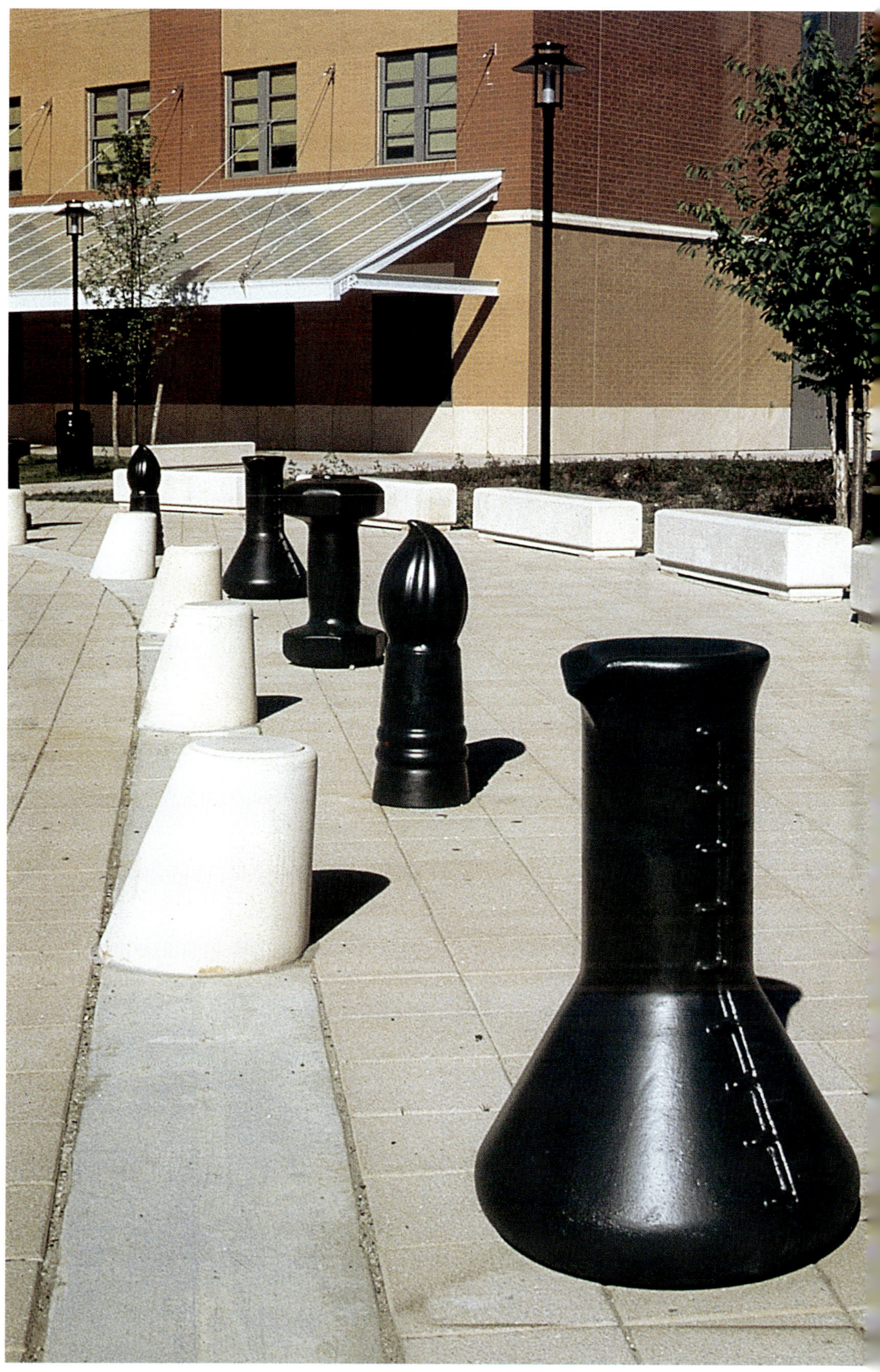

Andy Yoder

Completed projects ● (see map)

1 **Robert Adzema**
2 **Siah Armajani**
3 **Béatrice Coron**
4 **Nancy Dwyer**
5 **Amanda Jaffe**
6 **Elizabeth Turk**
7 **David Wilson**

Projects in progress ▲ (see map)

8 Mike Falco
Photographic lightbox mural
St. George Ferry Terminal, Richmond Terrace
Architect: Hellmuth, Obata + Kassabaum, Inc.
Sponsor Agency: Economic Development Corporation

9 Steve Foust
Bronze sculpture
Staten Island Zoo, 614 Broadway
Architect: Gruzen Samton Architects
Design Agency: Department of Design and Construction
Sponsor Agency: Department of Cultural Affairs

10 Werner Klotz and John Roloff
The Middle of the World
Installation
Staten Island Ferry Boats, St. George Ferry Terminal, Richmond Terrace
Architect: George G. Sharp, Inc.
Design/Sponsor Agency: Department of Transportation
Art Commission Award for Excellence in Design 2002

11 Mierle Laderman Ukeles
Fresh Kills Landfill, Richmond and Yukon Avenues
Master Plan Lead: Field Operations
Sponsor Agencies: Department of Sanitation and Department of City Planning

Conservation project

J.W. Fiske, Co.
Neptune Fountain, 1995
Bronze recasting of 1892 zinc sculpture
Snug Harbor Cultural Center, 1000 Richmond Terrace
Recasting by Modern Art Foundry

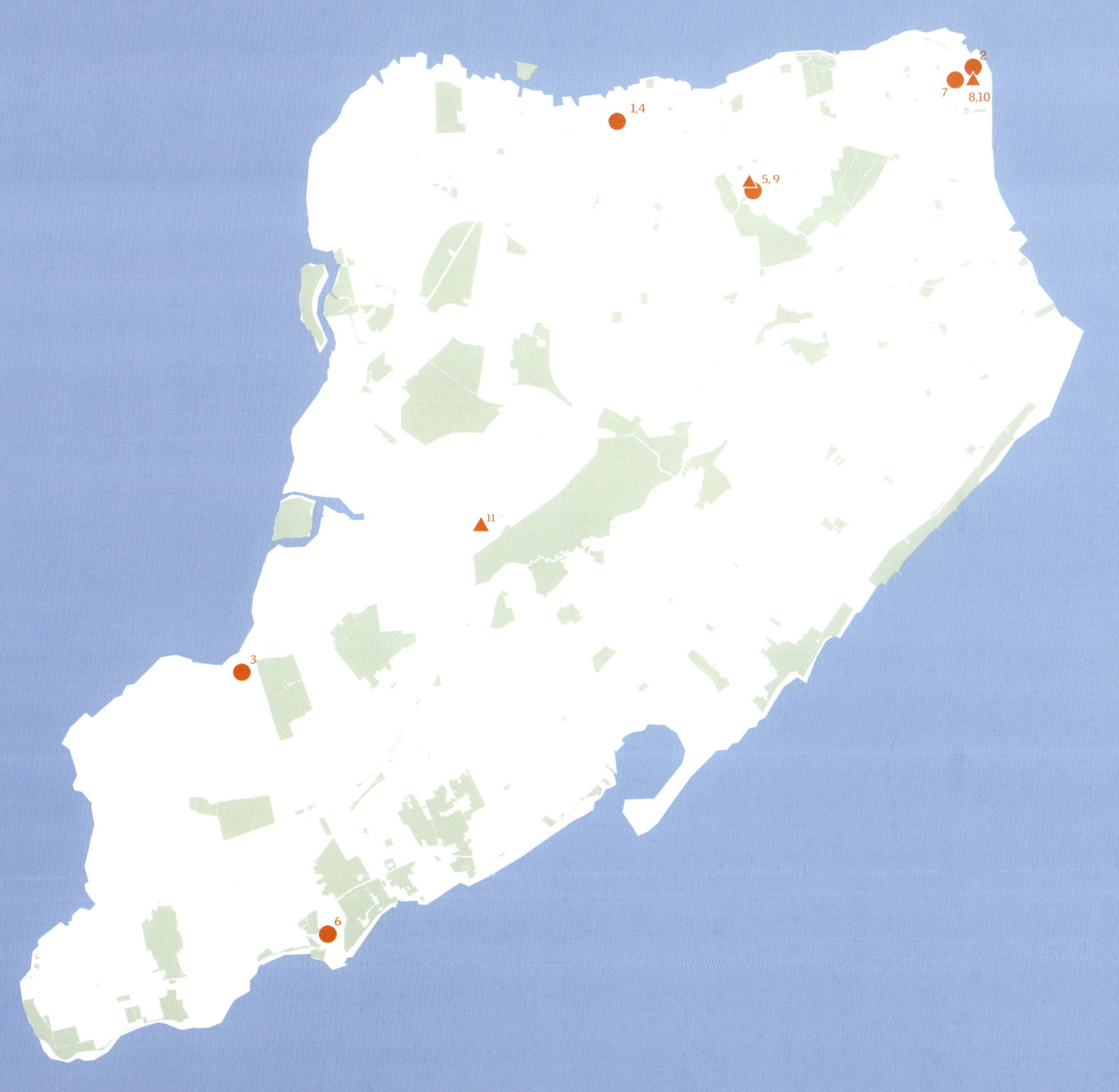

Staten Island

Interview: Mierle Laderman Ukeles

My involvement in the Fresh Kills Landfill project has two distinct scopes. The first, like conventional Percent for Art projects, is to build something. The second is more unusual and ambitious; I'm working with the Department of Sanitation on an ongoing basis, contributing to long-term aspects of the landfill reclamation and transformation project defined by the master plan for the site, which will take decades to implement.

The site is massive. When it's finished, Fresh Kills will be unbelievable—a park two-and-a-half times the size of Central Park. It was opened as a landfill site, fifty years ago, by Robert Moses. Since the 1980s, after New York's other landfills were labeled as hazardous waste sites, all New York City's garbage has been sent here. I have a longstanding interest in landfill projects; in 1978, I got a National Endowment for the Arts grant to create urban earthworks on landfill. I've always wondered why, if you wanted to see an earthwork like *Spiral Jetty* [Robert Smithson, Great Salt Lake, Utah, 1970], you had to get on an airplane. I'm interested in doing earthworks closer to home.

My project involves personal interaction with the Department of Sanitation on an almost daily basis. And the only reason that's possible is because I've worked with them in the past on other art projects. They're comfortable with me and, on this project, I'm part of the mix, there to ask weird, unexpected questions, to bring new perspectives to this monumental project, and particularly to help inform people about, and involve them in, the Fresh Kills project.

It is a breathtaking site, even before aspects of the design master plan go into effect. It's a wildlife refuge, with rolling hills and creeks. But it's also surrounded by dense areas of housing, and by people who are not happy about living across the street from what is still a landfill. I go to the mall, learn about what people know and don't know about the site, and listen to what they'd like to see happen to it. I'm interested in inviting the public in at the very beginning of this mammoth transformation process, and to make a place that's safe for them. My first project was a video that allowed community members to see and learn about the site. Next, I'll help create overlooks at the edge of landfill areas, so people can watch the activity on the site now, and in years to come.

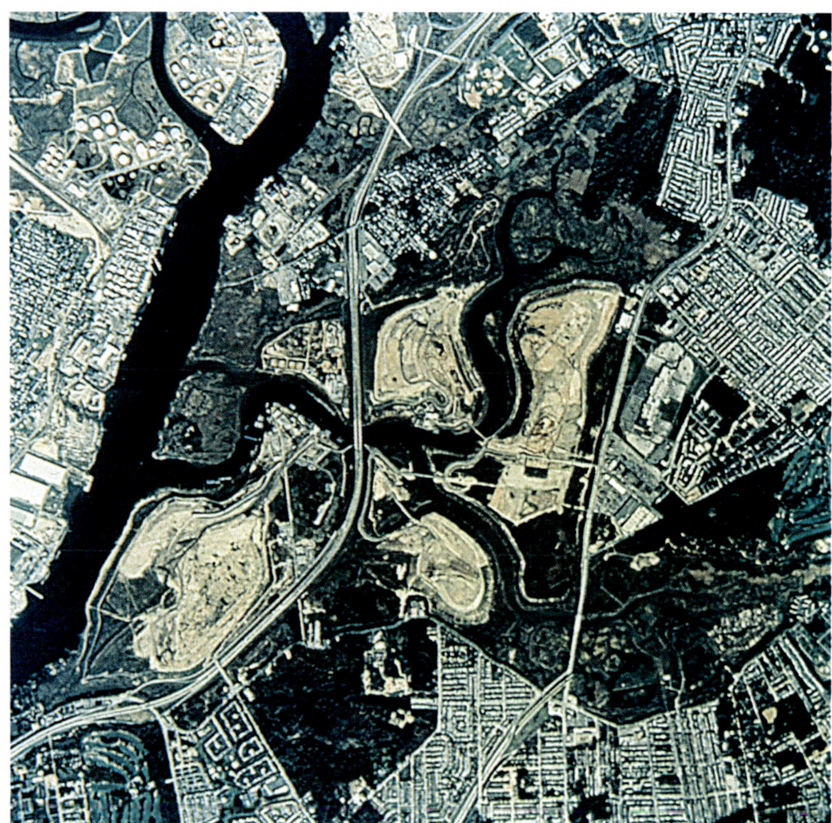

Mierle Laderman Ukeles, Aerial view of Fresh Kills Landfill, *c.* 1990.

I'd also like to create a "sanitation legacy project," to present Fresh Kills as a social sculpture that exists because we've all played a role in making it what it is. Fresh Kills was formed by what people threw away, the garbage of the 100,000,000 who've lived or passed through New York in the last fifty years. The place can't be completed without our personal attempts to help *redeem* it. So, I would like to get a million people from all over the City to participate in this, and to offer something of personal value back to the site. That sounds a bit difficult, but I know it can work, for the following reasons. While most people think of Sanitation as the Department of Garbage and Recycling, I see it as an enormous information system. The Department of Sanitation knows where *everyone* in New York is. Out of their vast knowledge base, they can help collect things, give out computerized receipts, and deliver people's "public offerings" to the landfill to the site, which they'll then be able to locate and visit, when they visit the big, beautiful park in Fresh Kills, sometime in the future.

Sundial
1994
Painted steel, brass paving inserts

Port Richmond High School,
85 St. Joseph's Avenue

ARCHITECT
Shuman Lichtenstein Claman Efron
DESIGN AGENCY
School Construction Authority
SPONSOR AGENCY
Board of Education

Robert Adzema constructed this large, freestanding sundial sculpture from steel and painted it a brilliant yellow hue so that shadows would be made visible. Located on the grounds in front of Port Richmond High School, *Sundial* emphasizes the north–south axis of the site. An aperture near the top of the sundial casts a beam of light on the ground that marks high noon in solar time as it crosses the north–south line.

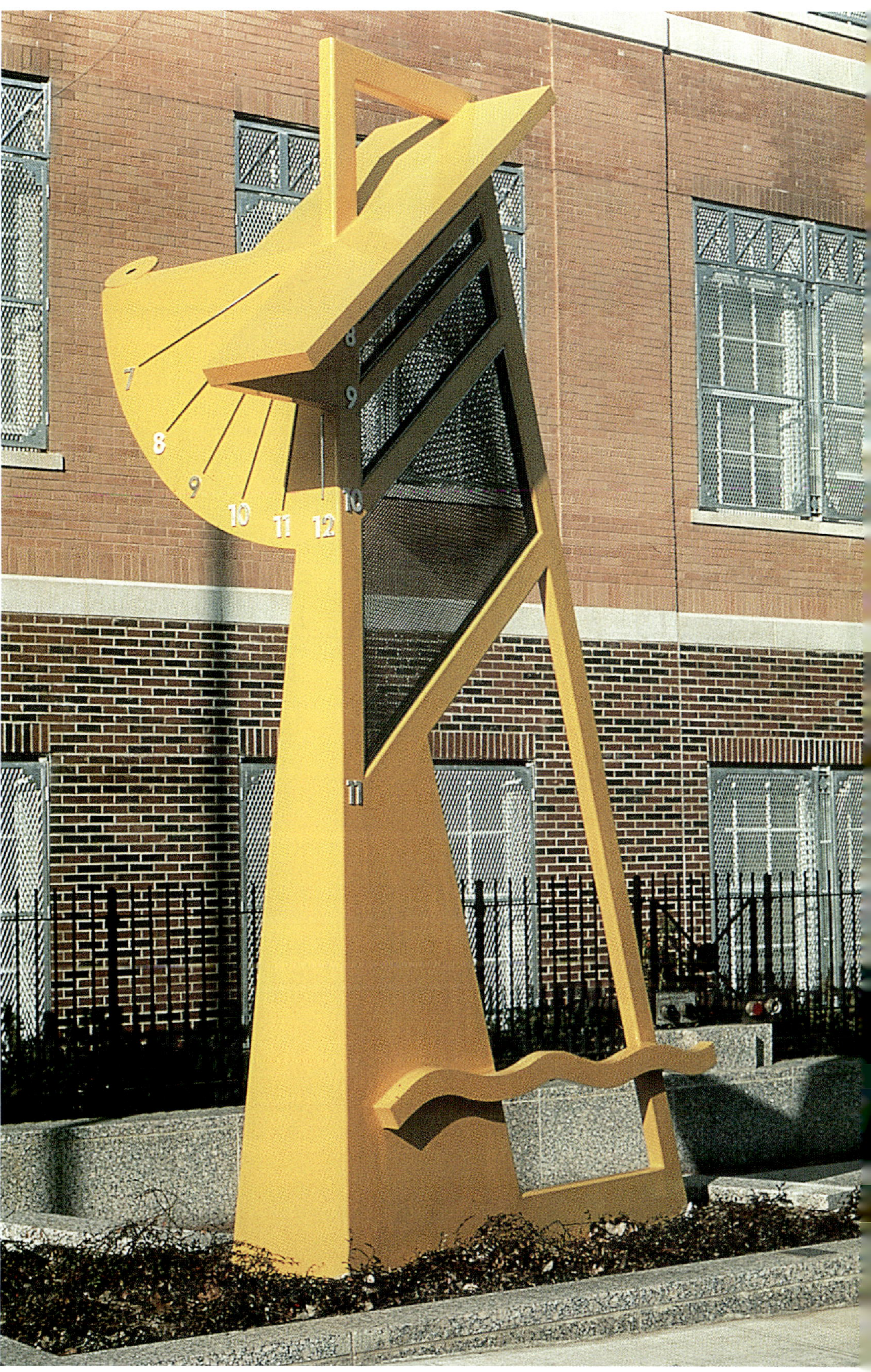

Robert Adzema

Lighthouse and Bridge on Staten Island
1996
Steel, stained glass, wood

North Shore Esplanade at St. George Ferry Terminal

ARCHITECT
Johannson & Walcavage
DESIGN/SPONSOR AGENCY
Economic Development Corporation and Department of Transportation

Located within a public plaza near the St. George Ferry Terminal, *Lighthouse and Bridge* serves as a pedestrian bridge and tower. The artwork, constructed from steel, stained glass, and wood, skillfully connects the utilitarian ferry terminal with its surrounding historic neighborhood and serves as a tribute to the lighthouse that stood there from the 1860s to the 1970s. The poetry of Wallace Stevens is featured along the side of the bridge, illuminating the poet's vision of "a bridge along the bright and blue water."

Siah Armajani

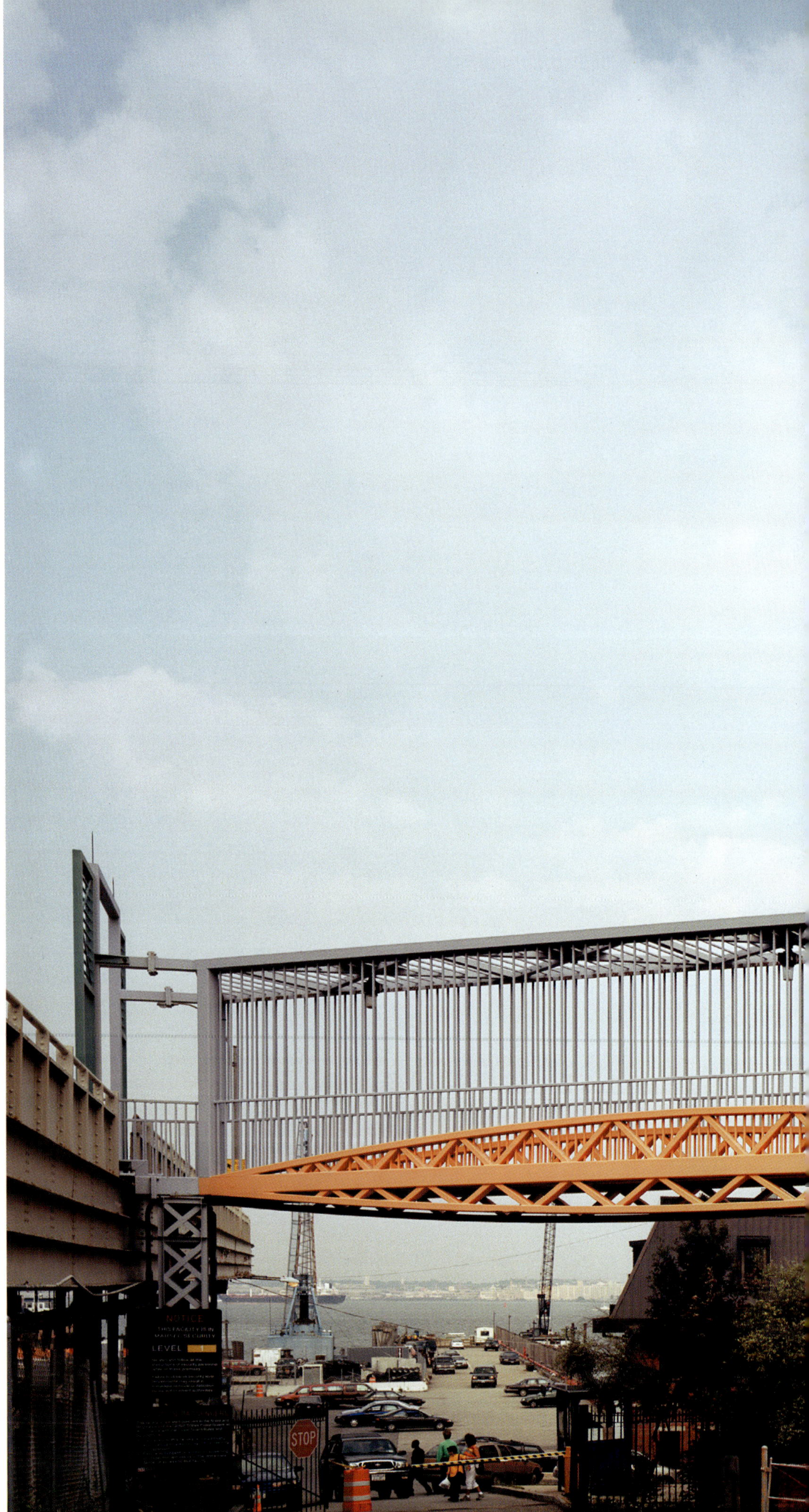

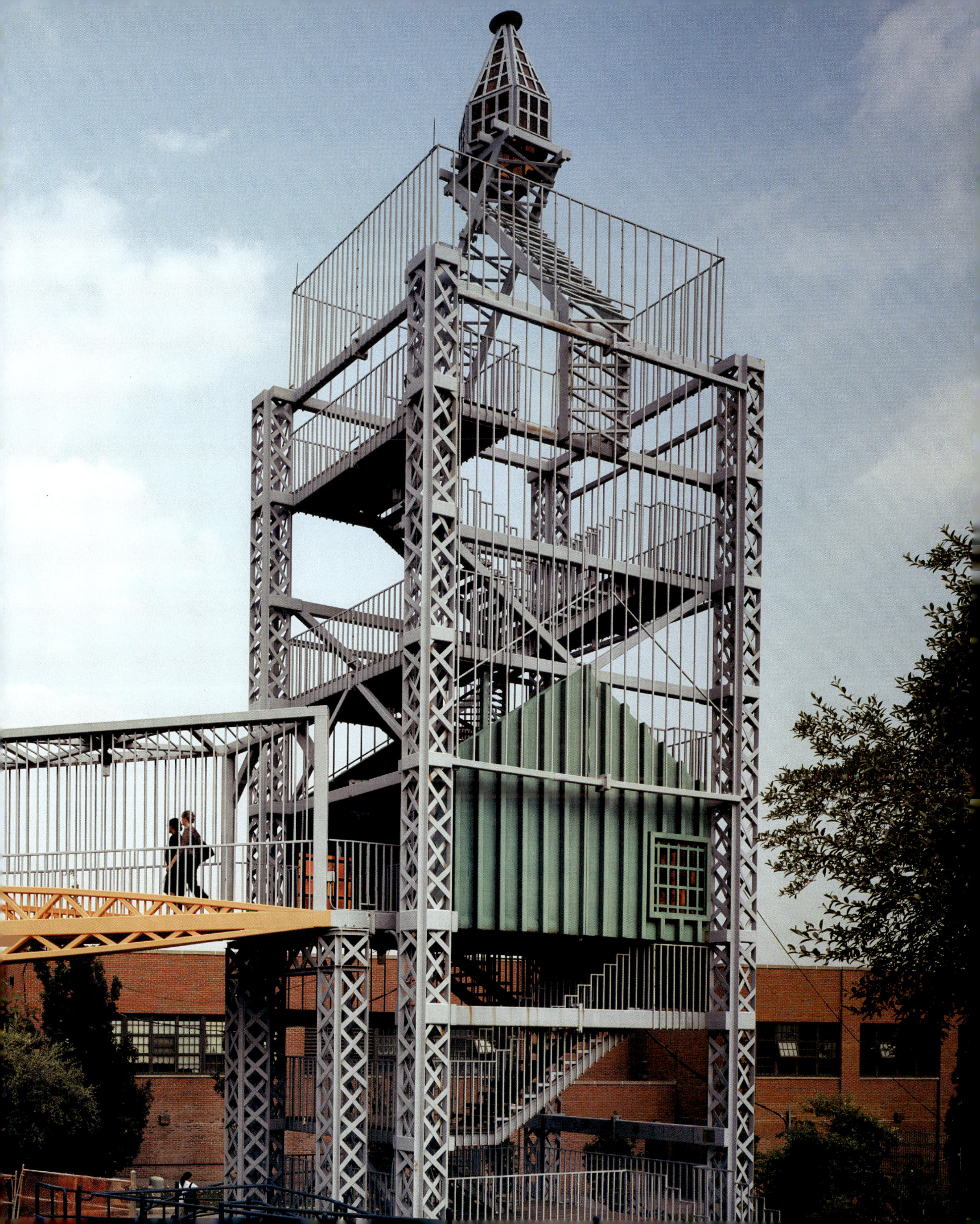

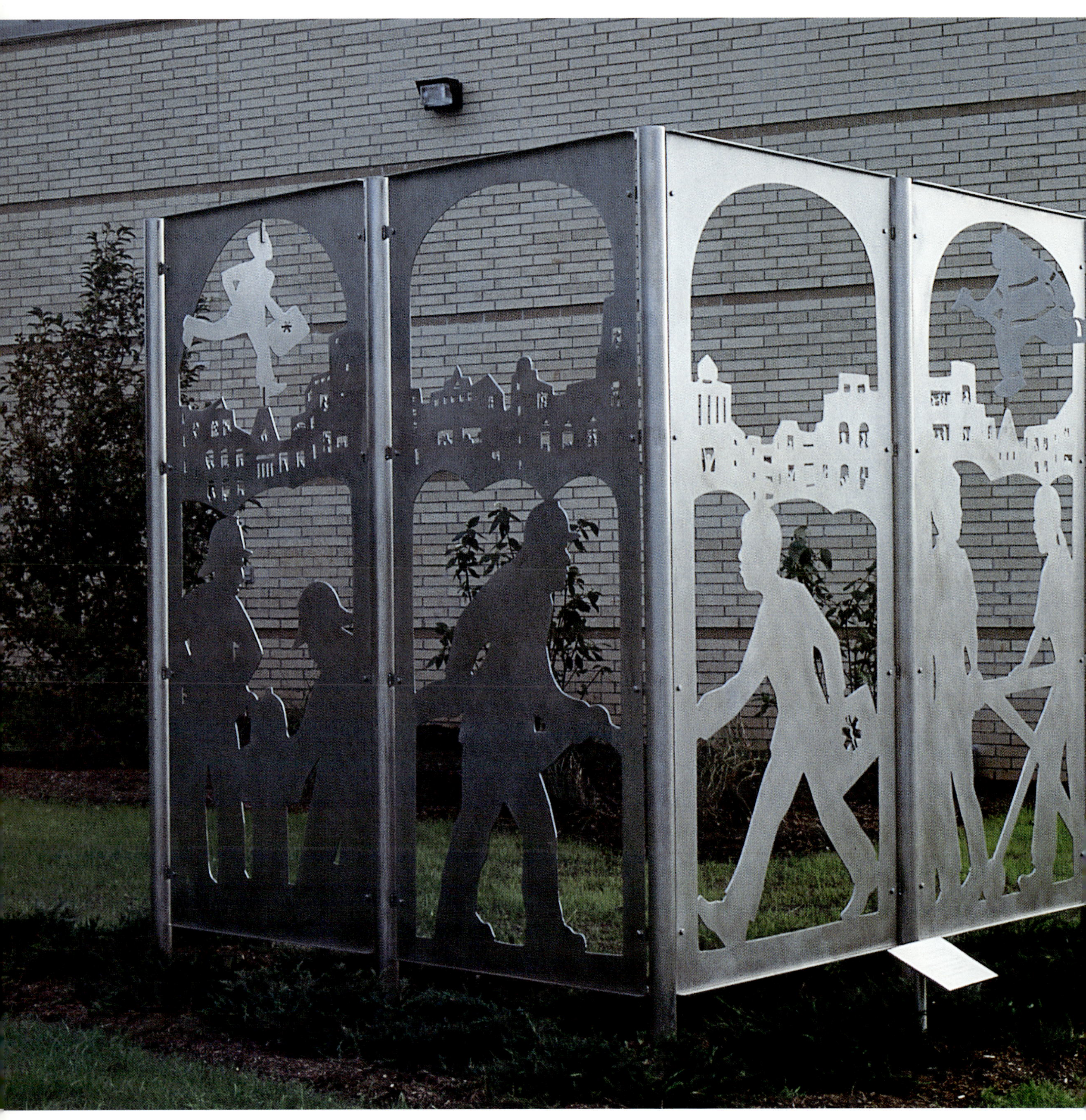

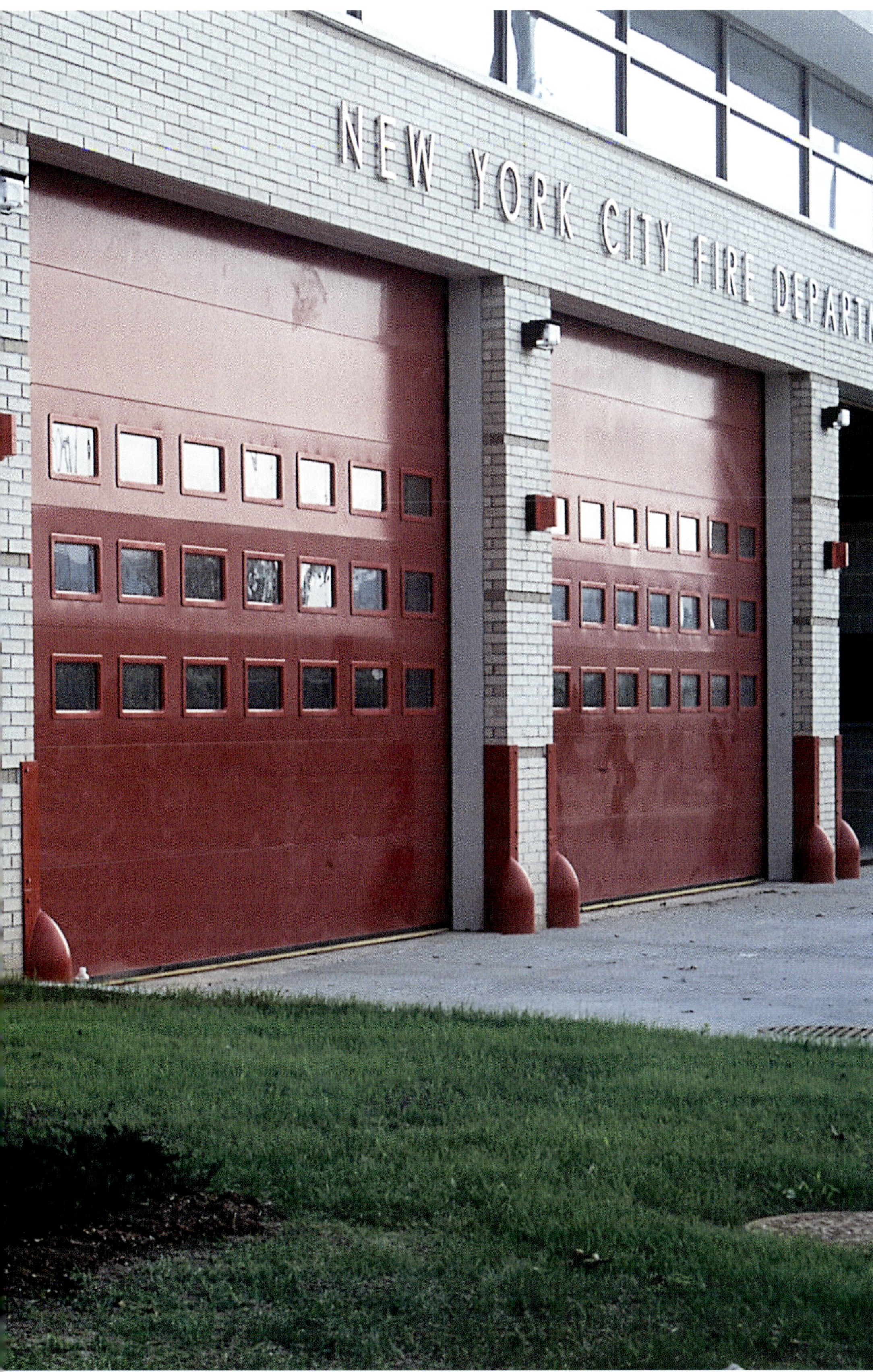

Working in the Same Direction
2003
Stainless steel

Fire and Emergency Station,
1100 Rossville Avenue

ARCHITECT
Ohlhausen DuBois Architects
DESIGN AGENCY
Department of Design and Construction
SPONSOR AGENCY
Fire Department

Béatrice Coron's 9 foot (2.7 m) high book-shaped sculpture celebrates the historic merger in 1995 of the Fire Department and the Emergency Medical Services (EMS) of the City of New York. Located on the grassy lawn in front of the Fire and Emergency Station, the sculpture features stainless-steel cut-outs that illustrate the tasks and tales of both EMS workers and firefighters. Placed above the sculpture are two weathervanes in the shape of a firefighter and an emergency worker, turning in the same direction to respond to an emergency. The sculpture's unique cut-out design creates a dynamic play of shadow and light.

Béatrice Coron

Nancy Dwyer

Hallway Highways (opposite)
1995
Inlaid linoleum
Multiple Choice, Benches
1993
Enamel-coated aluminum

Port Richmond High School,
85 St. Joseph's Avenue

ARCHITECT
Shuman Lichtenstein Claman Efron
DESIGN AGENCY
School Construction Authority
SPONSOR AGENCY
Board of Education

Located at Port Richmond High School, Nancy Dwyer's *Hallway Highways* transforms the hallways of this large high school into metaphorical highways, with solid and dotted yellow traffic lines and white words embedded in the black vinyl floors. Dwyer created the traffic lines out of expressions culled from a student survey, using phrases such as "Ring ring ring/ Five minutes of freedom" and "Don't you dare/ Make me/ Stop not thinking like that." The continuous line of words covers more than 1300 feet (396 m) of hallway floors. *Multiple Choice* is located in an enclosed courtyard behind the school. Five benches of enamel-coated aluminum in the forms of three-dimensional letters spell out the words "always," "often," "sometimes," "seldom," and "never." Each letter is 18 inches (45 cm) tall, and between 15 and 30 inches (38–76 cm) wide, and the words are configured around the courtyard in subtle curves. Students can view these word benches from the classrooms above.

Amanda Jaffe

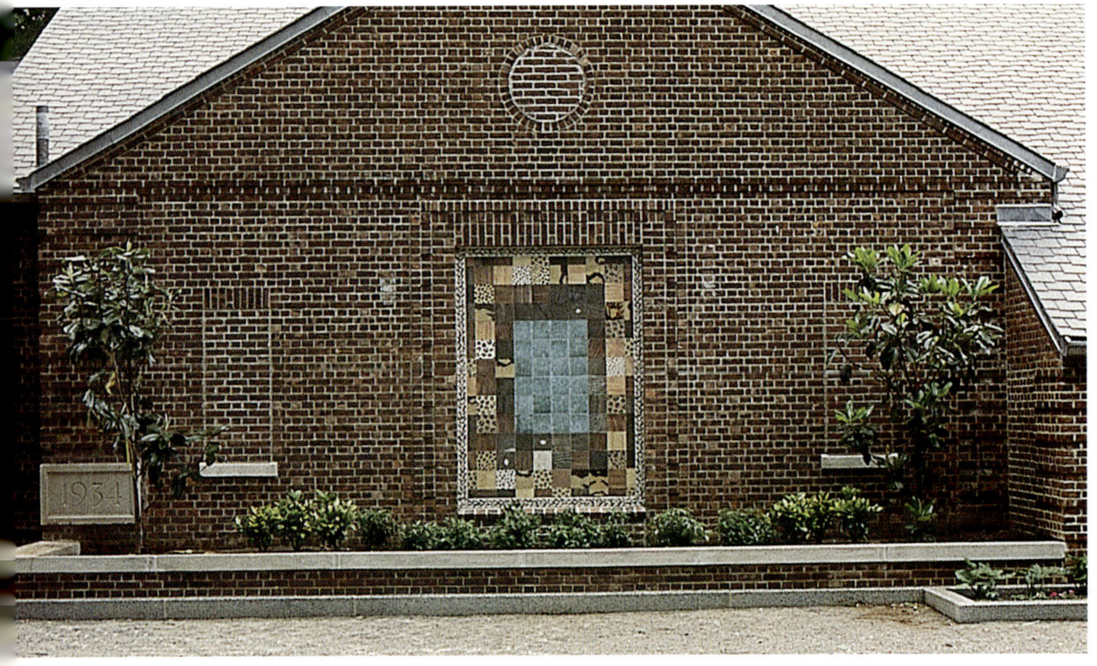

African Savanna and **South American Tropical Forest**
1996
Ceramics

Staten Island Zoo, 614 Broadway
ARCHITECT
Janiga, Coe, and Lee
DESIGN AGENCY
Department of General Services
SPONSOR AGENCY
Department of Cultural Affairs
Art Commission Award for Excellence in Design 1987

For her ceramic murals at the Staten Island Zoo, Amanda Jaffe drew inspiration from the animals of the zoo's African Savanna and Tropical Rainforest exhibits. Both murals feature patterns of the coats of different animals, including tigers and leopards. The animal tiles in *African Savanna* (left) surround a large area of blue tiles representing the water, while the animal tiles in *South American Tropical Forest* surround patterned tiles representing the tropical rainforest.

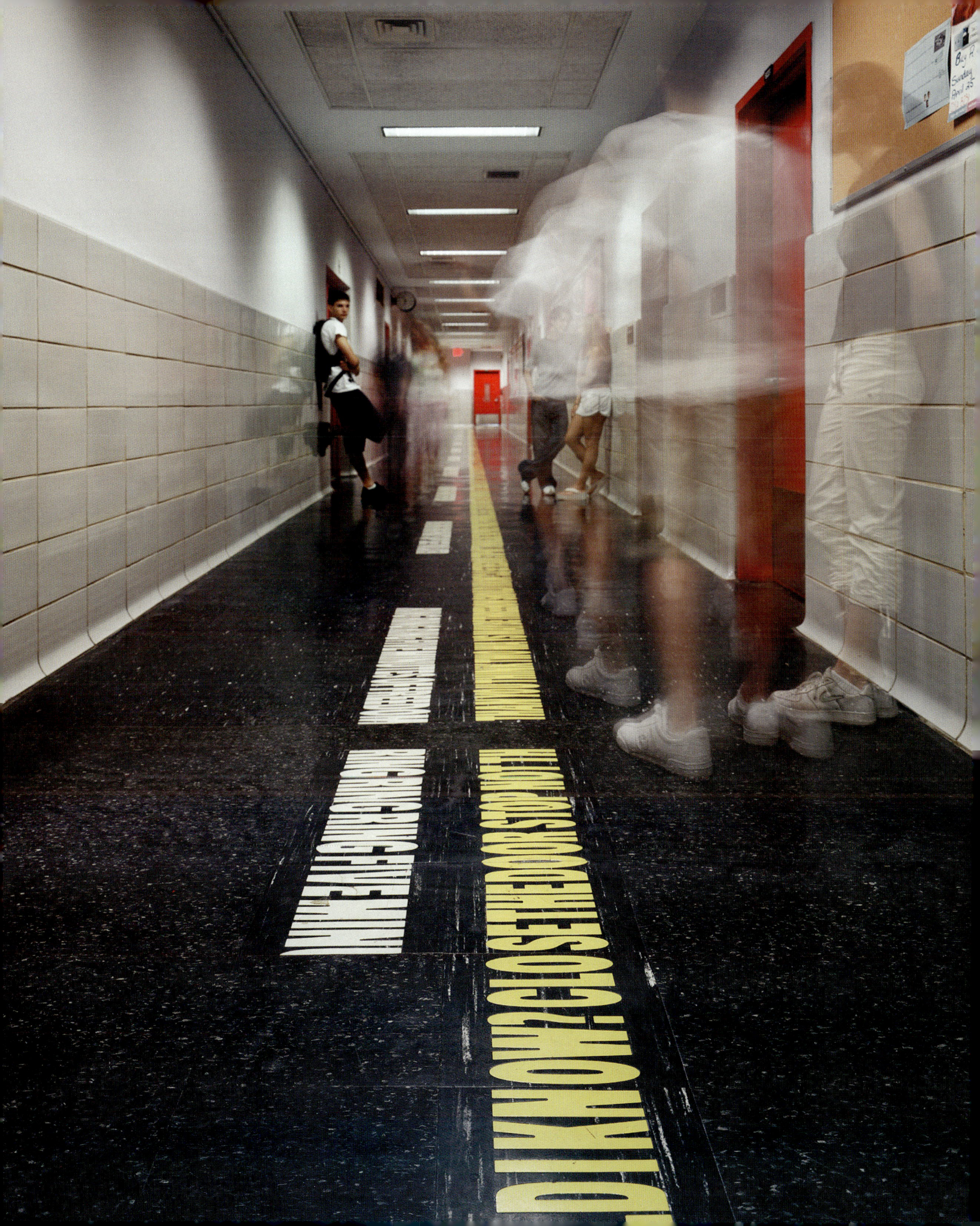

Elizabeth Turk

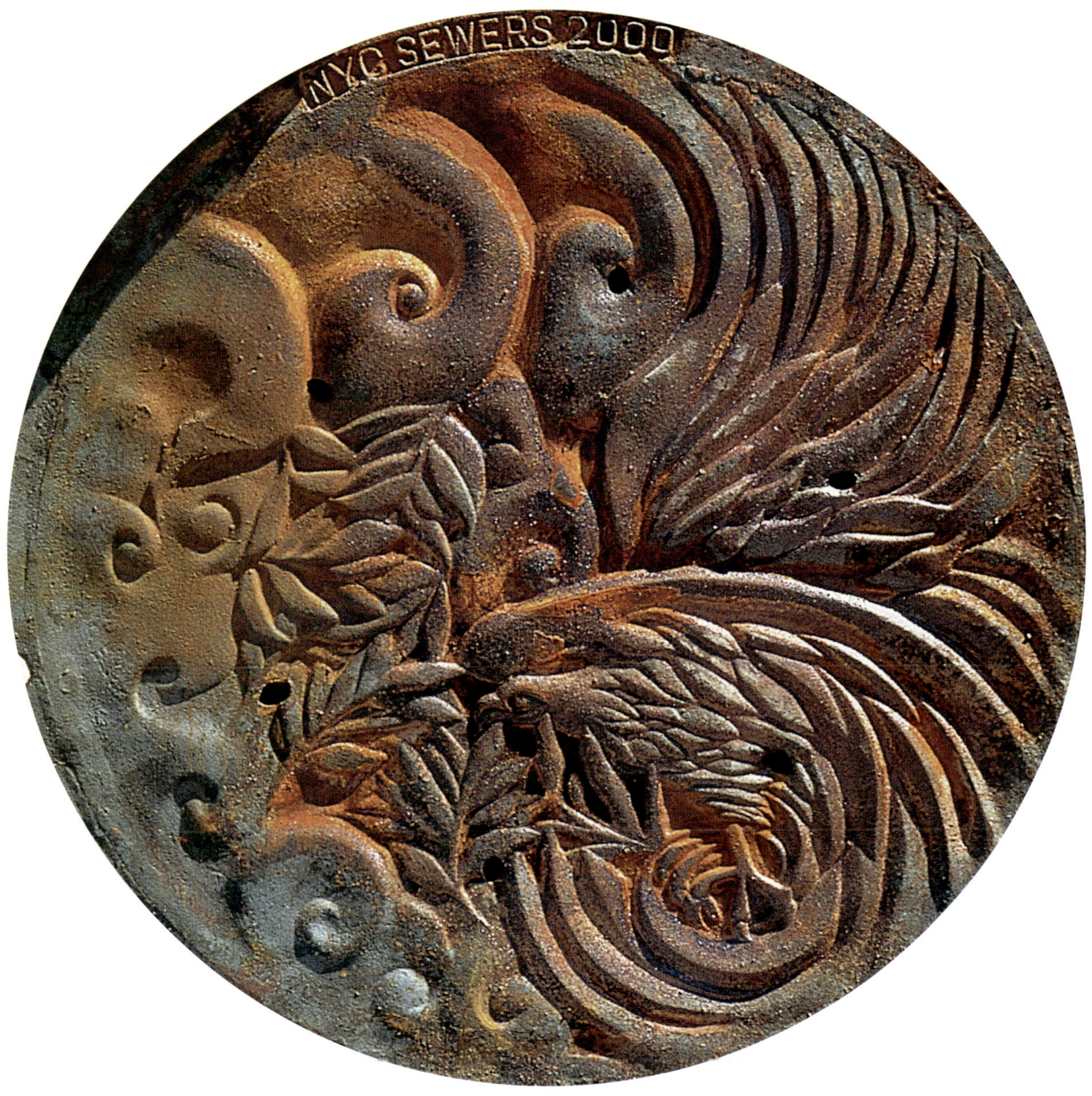

New York City Sewer Covers
2000
Cast iron

Seguine Avenue

DESIGN AGENCY
Department of Design and Construction
SPONSOR AGENCY
Department of Environmental Protection

Art Commission Award for Excellence in Design 2000

Recalling the beautiful imagery and workmanship that characterized New York City's early decorative ironwork, Elizabeth Turk designed eighty-seven cast-iron manhole covers, which are located along Seguine Avenue. Her design combines the imagery of the bird and plant life on Staten Island, and refers to the Staten Island Bluebelt, a natural wetland area that environmentalists are struggling to protect.

Untitled
1989
Leaded glass

St. George Library Center,
5 Central Avenue

ARCHITECT
Helpern Architects
DESIGN AGENCY
Department of General Services
SPONSOR AGENCY
New York Public Library

Art Commission Award for Excellence in Design 1986

David Wilson redesigned the three central Palladian-arched windows of the main reading room at the St. George Library Center. His artwork features an abstract arrangement of transparent, translucent, and opaque leaded glass in muted blues and earth tones, bordered by a red frame. The portion of the windows below the abstract design was left transparent to preserve the room's panoramic view of New York harbor.

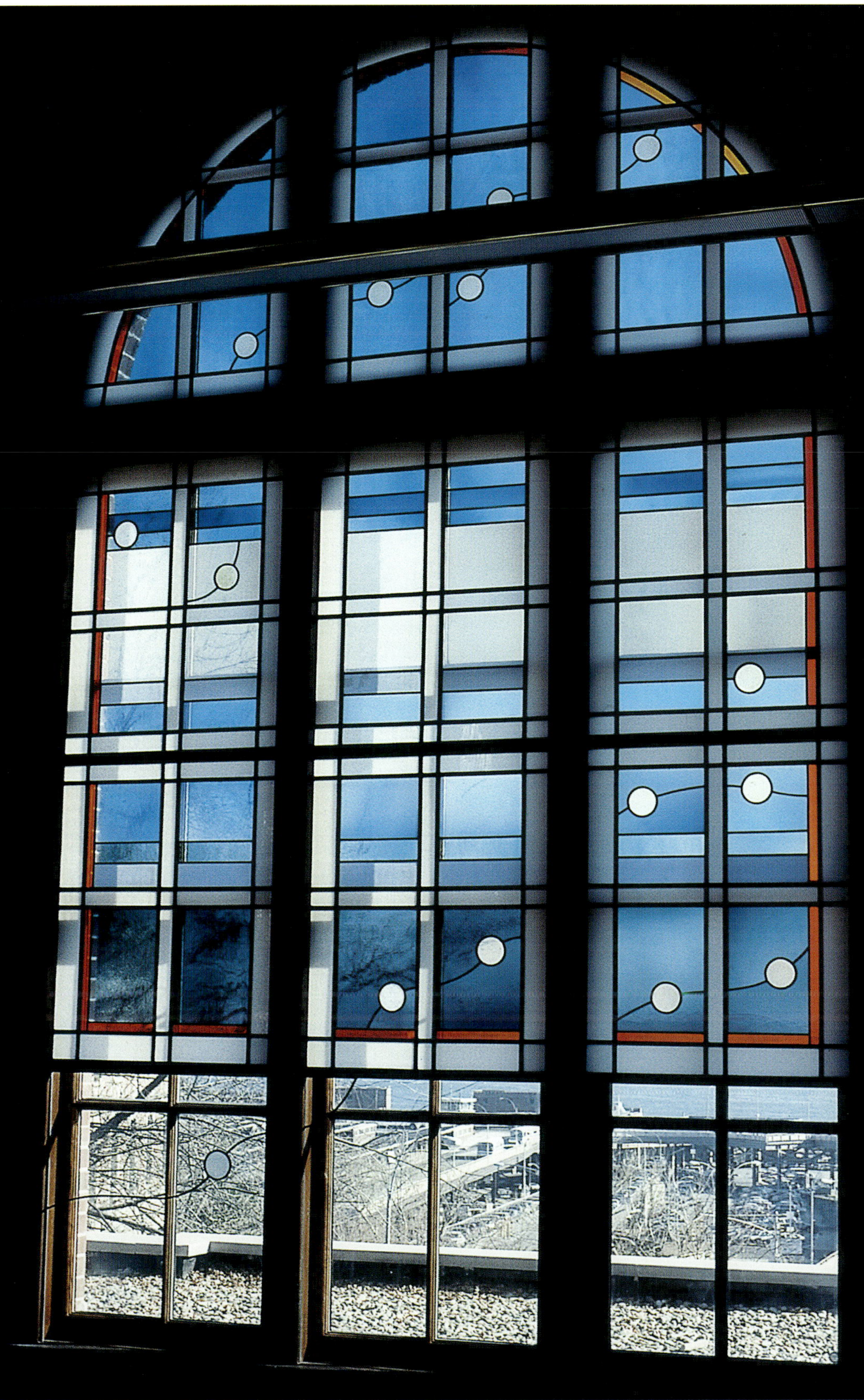

David Wilson

Timeline of Percent for Art Program, New York City

1965 Mayor Robert Wagner issues an executive order supporting the inclusion of artwork in City buildings. Few agencies take advantage of this opportunity.

1971–75 Doris C. Freedman (1928–1981), founder of the Public Art Fund and Director of the Office of Cultural Affairs within the Department of Parks, Recreation and Culture, drafts Percent for Art legislation and begins to lobby the City Council. The City becomes immersed in a fiscal crisis and the legislation lies dormant.

1976 The Office of Cultural Affairs becomes a separate agency: The Department of Cultural Affairs (DCA).

1978 Edward I. Koch is elected Mayor of New York City.

1981 As the City emerges from fiscal crisis, the administration and City Council begin to contemplate Percent for Art legislation. Deputy Mayor Ronay Menschel and Chief of Staff Diane Coffey are key advocates.

1982 City Council passes Percent for Art legislation; Mayor Koch signs it into law. Percent for Art Law requires that one percent of the budget for eligible City-funded construction be dedicated to creating public artworks.

1983 The Percent for Art Law is enacted. Overseen by DCA Commissioner Henry Geldzahler and Deputy Commissioner Randall Bourscheidt, the program is initially administered by the Public Art Fund (Director, Jenny Dixon). Jennifer McGregor is the program's Administrator.
Following the example of the City's Percent for Art legislation, the Metropolitan Transit Authority (MTA) establishes a similar program for its capital construction projects. During the early years of its existence, the MTA's art selection panels are chaired and coordinated by DCA's commissioner.

1984 First artist selection panels meet.

1985 First Percent for Art commission is completed: Jorge Rodriguez's *Growth* at East Harlem Artpark.
The MTA establishes the Arts for Transit Office to oversee the Authority's public art operations.

1986 DCA assumes full administrative responsibility for Percent for Art. Jennifer McGregor continues to direct the program.

1987 First school project completed: *Animal Party* by Susan Gardner at P.S. 94 in Brooklyn. First library project is also completed: *Medb's Crown* by Ann Gillen at the North Hills Branch Library. Twenty-four new works are initiated.

1988 *Projects and Proposals: New York City's Percent for Art Program* exhibition celebrating the program's fifth anniversary is on display at DCA's gallery at 2 Columbus Circle.
First firehouse project is completed: *Firehat* by David Saunders at Engine Company 71, Bronx.

1989 The Board of Education establishes the Public Art for Public Schools program as a way to partner with DCA on Percent for Art projects and to conserve and exhibit the Board's vast collection of art.
First project for the Police Department is completed: *Reunion* by Valerie Jaudon at Police Plaza in Manhattan.

1990 The School Construction Authority (SCA) is established to oversee the construction of new public schools and manage the repair and renovation of capital projects in existing schools. The SCA administers a five-year capital plan that leads to the commissioning of more than a hundred artists for Percent for Art projects.
Tom Finkelpearl becomes the Director of Percent for Art.
First project for the Department of Sanitation is completed: *Neon for the 59th Street Marine Transfer Station* by Stephen Antonakos in Manhattan.

1992 First detention center project is completed: *Judgment* by Kit-Yin Snyder for the Manhattan House of Detention (now named the Bernard B. Kerik Complex).

1995 First courthouse project is completed: *Dialogue with the Sun* by Susumu Shingu for the Queens Criminal Court addition.

1996 Charlotte Cohen becomes the Director of Percent for Art.

1997 First project for the Department of Transportation is completed: *Freedom's Gate* by Charles Searles at the Fulton Street Traffic Triangle in Brooklyn.
First project at an early childhood center is completed: *Time Flies* by Christy Rupp for Public School 4 Annex in the Bronx.
Since the program's inception, 154 Percent for Art projects have been completed.

2003 Mayor Michael Bloomberg hosts the twentieth anniversary celebration of Percent for Art. Former Mayor Koch is awarded the Doris C. Freedman Award, established in 1982 to honor excellence in public design. The ceremony is held at P.S. 234, site of Donna Dennis's *Dreaming of Far Away Places: The Ships Come to Washington Market* (1988).

2004 Since the program's inception, 189 Percent for Art projects have been completed, as well as four conservation projects. An additional thirty-nine projects are underway.

Mags Harries, *Topiary: A Twenty Year Project,* 1993, Prospect Park Zoo, Brooklyn (pages 94–95).

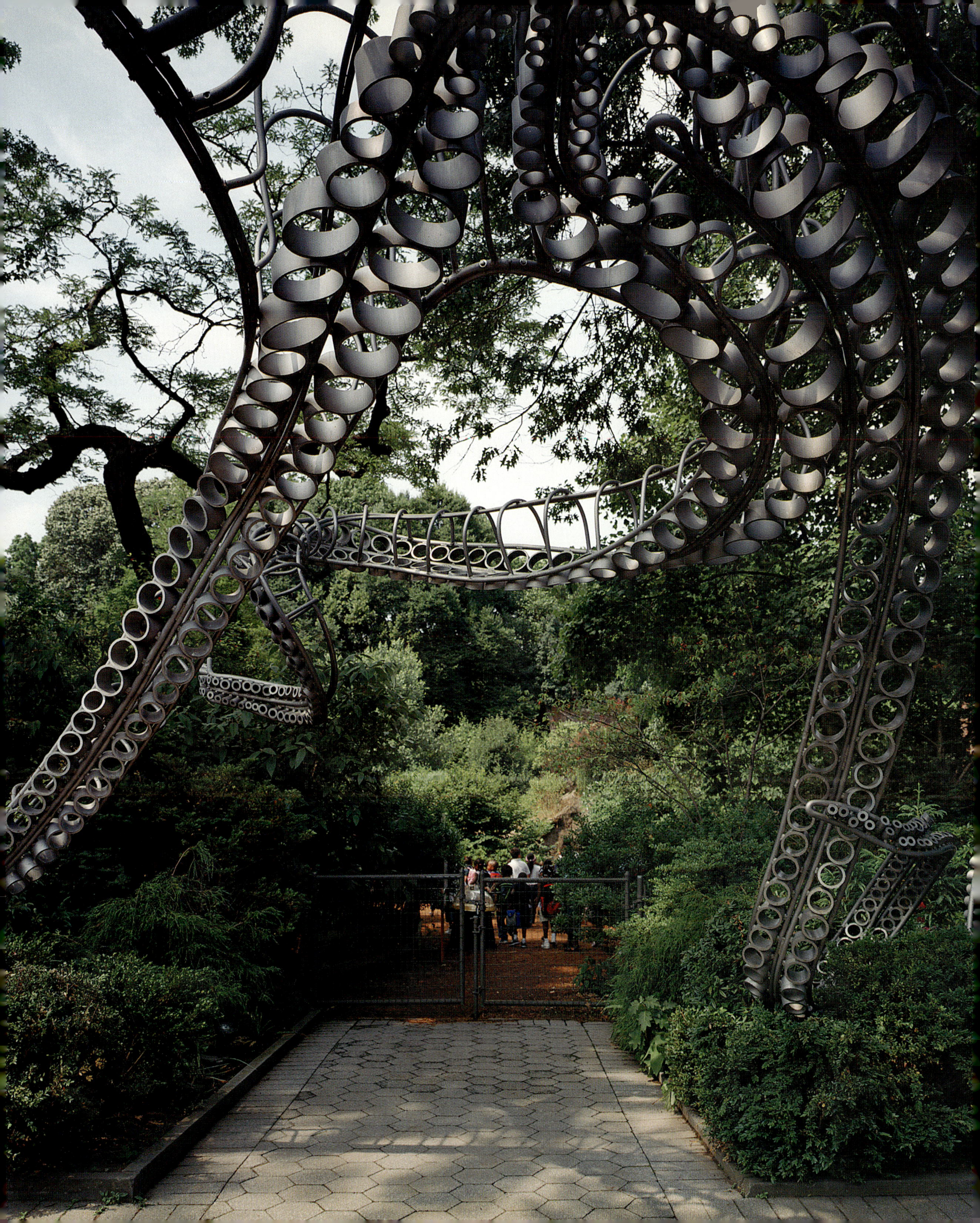

Acknowledgments

This book would not have been possible without Mayor Michael R. Bloomberg and his extraordinary commitment to the creative life of New York City. In addition, Deputy Mayor Patricia Harris has inspired and guided this project from start to finish. Over the years, Patti has been a trailblazer in encouraging New Yorkers to enjoy the depth, breadth, and excellence of the City's art collection.

City Art is the outcome of the exceptional efforts of Marvin Heiferman, the book's editor as well as a gifted curator and writer on art and visual culture. Marvin worked closely with Sara Rutkowski, Director of Public Affairs at the New York City Department of Cultural Affairs (DCA), and Caitlin Nish, the agency's BP Fellow for Public Affairs, to produce editorial content as well as research and organize the documentation of these artworks.

The Department of Cultural Affairs is above all indebted to the Joy of Giving Something Inc. (JGS), which provided generous funding for the editorial development, new photography, and design costs of the project. We are very grateful to JGS for considering this endeavor a meaningful contribution to the public life of New York City.

This book was also made possible by the dedication and involvement of Percent for Art's Director, Charlotte Cohen, and Deputy Director, Catherine Behrend, who, throughout their tenure, have extended the program's capacity for reinventing what public art can be.

A number of dedicated individuals helped guide the project from the beginning. I want especially to thank Diane Coffey for being one of the moving forces behind *City Art*. She was joined early on by Ronay Menschel, Susan Freedman, Phillip Block, Agnes Gund, George Russell, and Alix Colow. Past directors of the program, Jenny Dixon, Jennifer McGregor, and Tom Finkelpearl, have also made important contributions to the project. And we salute former Percent for Art staff: Danielle Biber, Anne Riker Purcell, Kendal Henry, Karen Hwa, Liza Lenas, Daniela Montana, Elizabeth Nesbitt, Renee Piechocki, Mary Prevo, Rondi Silva, and Nadia Tscherney.

And special thanks to Deputy Mayor Harris's Chief of Staff, Nanette Smith, and Senior Advisor, Allison Jaffin, as well as the Executive Director of the City's Art Commission, Jackie Snyder, for all of their support and advice.

In addition, DCA is grateful to the many individuals who offered us insight, expertise and technical assistance throughout the process of producing this book, among them, Jamie Bennett, Maurice Berger, Harvey Blumm, Joan Brookbank, Deidre Burke, Harold Chapnick, Susan Chin, Elaine Cohen, Michele Cohen, Ron Day, Michael De Marco, Xenia Diente, Amy Douthett, Tom Eccles, Jonathan Ells, Gregory Frux, Phillip Gleason, Patricia A. Glunt, Michael Kampouris, William Kazlowski, James Kenny, Jonathan Leiter, Faisal Rusho, Bridget Stoyko, Scott Trent, and Charles Young. Parks Commissioner Adrian Benepe and his wonderful staff provided invaluable assistance.

Percent for Art offers DCA the unique opportunity to provide support for individual artists, who contribute immeasurably to the City's dynamism and identity. The program has been fortunate to work with an incredible range of talented and committed artists, each of whom we thank for enriching public spaces and buildings in New York City. Percent for Art is also indebted to the members of our selection panels, the architects, arts professionals, engineers, construction teams, and community board members, who each play an invaluable role in the process of creating public art.

And finally, our gratitude goes to all those who have found themselves provoked, moved and inspired by Percent for Art projects throughout the City's five boroughs.

Kate D. Levin
Commissioner, New York City Department of Cultural Affairs

Index

First published 2005 by Merrell Publishers Limited

Head office
42 Southwark Street
London SE1 1UN

New York office
49 West 24th Street, 8th floor
New York, NY 10010

www.merrellpublishers.com

In association with

City of New York Department of Cultural Affairs,
330 West 42nd Street, New York, NY 10036
212-643-7770
www.nyc.gov/culture

A catalog record for this book is available from the Library of Congress.

British Library Cataloguing-in-Publication Data:
Heartney, Eleanor, 1954–
City art : New York's Percent for Art Program
1.Percent for Art Program (New York, N.Y.) 2.Art, American – New York (State) – New York 3.Art, Modern – 20th century 4.Art, modern – 21st century 5.Art patronage – New York (State) – New York
I.Title
709.7'471'09048

ISBN 1 85894 290 X

Produced by Merrell Publishers
Designed by Tim Harvey
Copy edited by Mary Scott
Proof-read by Christine Davis
Indexed by Hilary Bird

Printed and bound in China

Front cover image
Ursula von Rydingsvard, *katul katul*, 2003 (page 220)

Back cover images (top to bottom)
**Janet Zweig, *Your Voices*, 1997 (pages 70–71);
Mags Harries, *Topiary: A Twenty Year Project*, 1993 (pages 94–95);
Milo Mottola, *Totally Kid Carousel*, 1998 (pages 24–25, 151);
Dennis Adams, *Tributaries*, 1995 (pages 166–67);
Siah Armajani, *Lighthouse and Bridge on Staten Island*, 1996 (pages 228–29)**

Front inside flap image
Mierle Laderman Ukeles, *Honor 2000*, 2000 (pages 62–64)

Pages 2–3
Fred Tomaselli, *Ten-Kilometer Radius*, 1996 (page 218)

Photographic credits

Acconci Studio: p. 37. David Allee: pp. 2, 3, 11, 12, 24, 25, 27, 40, 41, 56, 62, 63, 66, 67, 70, 71, 76, 77, 94, 95, 106, 107, 113, 127, 128, 132, 133, 136, 137, 144, 145, 151 (bottom), 158, 159, 166, 167, 168, 172, 173, 178, 179, 182, 183, 188, 189, 218 (bottom), 220, 228, 229, 233, 237. Stephen Antonakos: p. 120. Courtesy of the Art Commission: pp. 17, 18, 20, 22 (left), 29, 31, 58 (top), 60 (bottom), 78 (top), 82 (bottom), 89 (bottom), 135, 141, 153, 154, 157 (top), 199, 208, 209, 210, 216, 218 (top), 234. John Back: pp. 124, (courtesy of Ronald Feldman Fine Arts, New York) 185. Bernstein associates, photographers ©: p. 79. Karen Bell: p. 129. Rolando Briséno: p. 80. Bill and Mary Buchen: p. 81 (bottom). Ed Carpenter: p. 176. Jui-Yuan Cheng: p. 93. Clements/Howcroft Photography, Boston: p. 96. Willie Cole: p. 186. Leland A Cook (courtesy of the Art Commission): p. 235. Dennis Cowley: pp. 143 (top), 174, 175, 221 (bottom). Tim Dalal: pp. 89 (top), 191 (bottom). D. James Dee: pp. 47, 99 (top), 160, 184, 195, 203, 204 (bottom). Pablo Delano: pp. 33, 130, 131. Carin Drechsler-Marx: p. 197. Chris Doyle: p. 192. Mel Edwards (courtesy of the Art Commission): p. 134. T Charles Erickson: p. 161. Ming Fay: p. 193. Hermann Feldhaus: p. 180. Courtesy of Ronald Feldman Fine Arts, New York: pp. 21, 226. Jackie Ferrara: p. 194. Tom Finkelpearl: p. 38. Jennifer Gerardi (courtesy of the School Construction Authority): p. 43. Andrew Ginzel: pp. 13, 46 (bottom). Bill Gordy: p. 75 (top). Arlene Gottfried: p. 114. Lydia Gould (courtesy of the School Construction Authority): pp. 59, 68, 69, 162. Jane Greengold: p. 92. Steven Gross: p. 170. Fred Gutzeit (courtesy of the Art Commission): pp. 109, 155 (top). Richard Haas: p. 138. Marvin Heiferman: p. 8. Thomas Hinton (courtesy of the School Construction Authority): p. 52. Noah Jemisin (courtesy of the School Construction Authority): p. 46 (top). MLJ Johnson: p. 99 (bottom). Michael Kambler (courtesy of the School Construction Authority): p. 221 (top). Werner Klotz (courtesy of the Art Commission): p. 23. Gabriel Koren, Sculptor: p. 146. Justen Ladda (courtesy of the School Construction Authority): pp. 48, 49. Amy Lampel (courtesy of the School Construction Authority: p. 97 (top). Timothy K. Lee: p. 142. Peter Lee: p. 78 (bottom). Gregg LeFevre: p. 50. Sarah S Lewis: p. 81 (top). Becket Logan: pp. 75 (bottom), 82 (top), 119, 205, 217 (bottom). David Lubarsky ©: p. 121. Clyde Lynds: p. 206. Gary J. Mamay ©: p. 42. Mike Mandel ©: p. 150. Jason Mandella (courtesy of the School Construction Authority): p. 219 (bottom). Iñigo Manglano-Ovalle (courtesy of the Art Commission): p. 36. Ari Marcopoulos: p. 22 (right). Bard Martin (courtesy of the School Construction Authority): p. 97 (bottom). George Mason: p. 101. Peter Mauss/Esto ©: pp. 191 (top), 219 (top). Courtesy of the Mayor's Office: p. 28. Howard McCalebb: p. 207. Ed McGowin: p. 102 (bottom). Courtesy of the Metropolitan Transportation Authority: p. 30. Mike Metz: p. 103. Daniel Mirer Photography: p. 122. Michael Moran ©: p. 98. Kevin Noble: p. 147. Michael Paras (courtesy of the School Construction Authority): p. 90. Edward Peterson: p. 123. François Portmann: p. 187. Adam Reich: pp. 45, 125, 163. Earl Ripling: p. 232. Bob Rivera: p. 54. Ray Robbennolt (courtesy of the School Construction Authority): p. 196. Burt Roberts: p. 10. Kathleen Ruiz: p. 214; Christy Rupp: p. 57. Manu Sassoonian: (courtesy of the Art Commission) p. 126, (courtesy of the School Construction Authority) p. 217 (top). Ben Schonzeit: p. 108. Courtesy of the School Construction Authority: pp. 14, 19, 26, 39 (top), 44, 51, 53, 55, 60 (top), 61, 65, 83, 84, 85, 86, 87, 102 (top), 104, 105 (top), 111, 112, 139, 140, 148, 151 (top), 152, 171, 177, 181, 198 (top), 198 (bottom), 200, 201, 204 (top), 212, 215, 222 (top), 222 (bottom), 227. Vicki Scuri Siteworks (courtesy of the School Construction Authority): p. 58 (bottom). Carol Shadford: p. 213. Ken Showell: (courtesy of Claudia DeMonte) pp. 88, 190, (courtesy of the School Construction Authority) pp. 91, 156. Pedro P. Silva: p. 110. David Sonberg (courtesy of Mac Adams): p. 169. Jerry Spagnoli: p. 211. Mark Tambella: p. 100. Anton van Dalen: p. 64. Patty Wallace: p. 143 (bottom). Nari Ward (courtesy of the Art Commission): p. 118. Hajime Watanabe: p. 155 (bottom). Meg Webster (courtesy of the Art Commission): p. 74. Larry Wheelock: p. 39 (bottom). Janis Wilkins: pp. 230, 231. Krzysztof Wodiczko © (courtesy Galerie Lelong, New York): p. 115. Martin Wong (courtesy of the Art Commission): p. 18. Yankowitz and Holden ©: p. 202. Andy Yoder: p. 223. Dorothy Zeidman: p. 149